Handwriting Identification: Facts and Fundamentals

Handwriting Identification: Facts and Fundamentals

by

ROY A. HUBER, B.Sc.,
Assistant Commissioner, RCMP (Ret.)

in collaboration with

A. M. HEADRICK, B.Sc.,
Assistant Commissioner, RCMP (Ret.)

Examiners of questioned documents

"Forensic document examination is the study of physical evidence and physical evidence cannot lie. Only its interpretation can err. Only the failure to find it, or to hear its true testimony can deprive it of its value."

Roy A. Huber

CRC Press
Boca Raton   New York

Contact Editor:	Becky McEldowney
Project Editor:	Ibrey Woodall
Marketing Managers:	Barbara Glunn, Jane Lewis, Arline Massey, Jane Stark
Cover design:	Dawn Boyd

Library of Congress Cataloging-in-Publication Data

Huber, Roy A.
     Handwriting identification : facts and fundamentals / Roy A.
    Huber, in collaboration with A.M. Headrick.
        p. cm.
    Includes bibliographical references and index.
    ISBN 0-8493-1285-X (alk. paper)
     1. Writing--Identification.   I. Headrick, A. M. II. Title.
    HV8074.H77   1999
    363.25′.65--dc21   98-50666
                                                                           CIP

Dedication

To my family,

Phyllis, Jim, Heather, and Kevin,

who knew it only as my excuse

for avoiding other things

Foreword

Much that this book contains is not new. It has been available for reading and digestion for as long as 30 years. Even the title *Facts and Fundamentals* was employed by the author to caption a potpourri of comments expressed in August 1982. The fact that many of these comments have received little attention over this period of time is a measure of the past reluctance of document examiners to revise practises and to ameliorate patterns of thinking.

I would presume that every author has a reason for writing a book and these reasons may vary substantially from one author to another. In my estimation the reason for writing a technical or quasi-technical textbook of this kind is not likely to be monetary. It is more liable to be a continuance of its author's long-standing aspiration and oft-stated resolve to educate, consolidate, stimulate, and/or substantiate the precepts on which the proper performance of handwriting examination and study should be conducted and understood.

You and I are free to make our individual assessments as to whether such a goal has been achieved and/or to what extent. Without further comment, may I be so presumptuous as to describe this contribution as the Foreword to the First Edition of a progeny that will be followed by many succeeding and constantly improving revisions.

A. M. (Tom) Headrick,
Assistant Commissioner, RCMP (Ret.)

Preface

Unlike other disciplines, questioned document examination is not an area of forensic science which has witnessed the proliferation of new books articulating new philosophies and describing new techniques. Yet, document examination is not without such needs. Social change and progress in business practises have altered the role, the nature of the document, and the approach to the study of it. Furthermore, the field has been repeatedly challenged to initiate some form of review or program to develop a more objective methodology. This program would improve the field's accuracy and move it under the umbrella of science.

The qualification of handwriting identification as a science is a prominent current topic of discussion. This book attempts to shed some light on it. I still vividly recall writing nearly 35 years ago that "science's fundamental distinction from common sense rests in a single word — *system*." Accordingly, this dissertation is an attempt to develop and present the knowledge respecting handwriting identification in a systematic fashion, providing a basis from which the discipline may evolve and be desirably accepted as a science.

The book has two primary objectives. First, it is an endeavour to present, in a general manner, a new approach to the study of document examination and to handwriting identification in particular. It records a review and consolidation of much of the worthwhile material that has been written on handwriting identification in the English language in the last 100 years. In this consolidation, an attempt has been made to extract valid principles, to dispute, if warranted, previously alleged principles, and to present some new thoughts that put the discipline into a proper perspective for current times. In this respect, it may be the first, if not the foremost, endeavour of its kind. Although it is not offered as a paradigm, it is hoped that the organization of the book will facilitate the addition of new material by readers or writers as it becomes available. It will require such contributions if it is to evolve into a recognized textbook that this discipline so desperately needs.

Second, it is an endeavour to make the information understandable and usable by the legal profession. Concern for this aspect of the matter has prompted the use of a question and answer format. This format, hopefully, will assist in the phrasing of questions to, and the understanding of, responses to be expected from expert witnesses, and/or those who profess to be qualified writing examiners. If, in the process, it serves to distinguish the competent from the incompetent, the discipline will be better for it.

Perhaps a third reason underlying this publication lies in the truism that writing renders ideas tangible and purifies concepts. Call it a catharsis, if you will. Regrettably, age will not permit this author to benefit fully from it, but I often wish that I had pursued this undertaking as a part of my initial training.

I am indebted to Nerine Waldron of the RCMP Scientific Information Centre, who greatly assisted in securing material that I did not have, and to Dr. Brian Baird of the RCMP Central Forensic Laboratory through whose good offices this was arranged. I am also indebted to a long-time friend, William R. Picton, of Edmonton, Alberta, who advised respecting the material on alcohol and intoxication. I am grateful, too, to Jennifer Nuss, a summer student in our office of years ago and now a practising document examiner in western Canada, who produced much of the material included in the Glossary. I am also indebted to Dr. Don Ostaff of Fredericton, New Brunswick, for editorial suggestions.

If asked to describe this work as briefly as possible, one might resort to the rhetoric the reader will find on one of its pages: "It is a didactic dissertation of a quasi-technical nature." Most readers will have other words for it, I am sure.

It may not be an overly scholarly presentation. There are topics that I have touched on because I think they are important to the discipline that I don't fully understand myself. But I wanted to make a beginning. I'd rather attempt to do something — and fail, than attempt to do nothing — and succeed. Would that I had the talent of others to express myself more eloquently, perhaps then, what I have written would be less of a bore and more of an inspiration.

Roy A. Huber
Ottawa, Canada 1999

The Thinker, Rodin, Auguste (1840-1917)
The Metropolitan Museum of Art
Gift of Thomas F. Ryan, 1910. (11.173.9)

The Authors

Roy A. Huber, was trained in the examination of questioned documents in the Crime Detection Laboratories of the Royal Canadian Mounted Police from 1949 to 1951. He has testified as an expert witness in six provinces of Canada, and in the United States. He has authored, or coauthored with Mr. Headrick, 16 published articles and 11 unpublished articles on the subject of questioned document examination, expert evidence, and on science as applied to document examination.

He graduated from Carleton University in 1959 with a Bachelor of Science degree, majoring in chemistry, statistics, and psychology, 10 years after he entered the field of questioned documents. He served for 35 years (1940 to 1975) as a uniformed member of the RCMP, the last 26 years of which were spent in the Crime Detection Laboratories. He retired from the RCMP in 1975, with the rank of assistant commissioner, as director of the laboratories and identification services.

Mr. Huber served as special advisor on security in printing to the Canadian Bank Note Company, printers of currency, stocks, bonds, passports, licences, and negotiable instruments, from 1975 to 1986.

He conducted a private practise in the examination of questioned documents from 1976 to 1996, most of which was shared with Mr. Headrick.

Mr. Huber was editor of the Canadian Society of Forensic Science Journal from 1976 to 1981. He is a past president of the Canadian Society of Forensic Science (1967 to 1968), a fellow of the American Academy of Forensic Sciences, a diplomate of the American Board of Forensic Document Examiners and a former board director (1978 to 1983). He is a past president of the American Society of Questioned Document Examiners (1996 to 1998).

In 1958, Mr. Huber established and organized the Central Bureau for Counterfeits under the RCMP.

In 1960, at the invitation of the Canada Council, Mr. Huber lectured at the Stratford Festival Theatre on Shakespeare's handwriting, at the first Shakespeare Seminar held under the auspices of the universities of Canada.

In 1961, Mr. Huber was appointed as the RCMP representative on the Bank of Canada special committee to redesign Canadian currency.

Alfred M. Headrick attended primary and secondary schools in Brooks, Alberta, receiving the Governor General's Medal for academic achievement. He received a B.Sc. (cum laude) with a major in physics from Mount Allison University in Sackville, N.B.

Prior to entering private practise as an examiner of questioned documents in 1985, he served 35 years in the RCMP, 32 of which were spent in the field of Document Examination and in the administration of the Crime Detection Laboratories. In 1984, he retired from the position of director of laboratories, holding the rank of assistant commissioner.

During the time as a document examiner, 1954 to 1967, he testified as an expert witness in courts in all provinces east of Manitoba and in the state of New York.

Mr. Headrick has held the positions of auditor, editor, and president of the Canadian Society of Forensic Science. He held the position of vice chairman of the Operations Research Committee of the Canadian Association of Chiefs of Police and is currently a life member of that association. He is a former member of the American Society of Questioned Document Examiners.

Table of Contents

7   Special Problems in the Discrimination and Identification of Writing   143

8   The Extrinsical Factors Influencing Handwriting   175

Introduction

The World of Documents

Whatever else we may make of ourselves or of the world about us, and however fast may be our progress in other respects, we are continuously creating a world of documents upon which we are increasingly dependent. Progress has provided both volume and variation in the means by which documents are produced and inscribed.

Inks, pens, pencils, typewriters, printers, and reproduction processes have added new members to their respective families, not all of which will survive in the highly competitive atmosphere. Some have already succumbed, and none, we now know, will be the last innovation of their kind on the consumer market. In many cases, magnetic tapes, disks, and diskettes have become the substrate and electronic fields have become the writing instrument in a family of inscriptions that are so prolific that they challenge the reputation of the rabbit. Notwithstanding the changes in the method of creating the record, the result is a document nonetheless.

Documents are evidence of our compliance with society's requirements, and of the terms and conditions of our interaction with our clients, customers, and neighbours. They are the record of past actions and future intentions, the message bearers of our civilization, and as personifying as a fingerprint or as anonymous as a grain of sand.

As grows our dependence upon documents, so grows our reliance upon their integrity. As documents acquire new values and serve new purposes, it is understandable that they are becoming, more frequently, the instruments of fraudulent manipulation, the targets of counterfeiting, or the means of concealing incriminating truths. This change in the world of documents has had its ramifications upon the field of questioned document examination, placing new demands upon skill and new taxes on knowledge.

Time has had its effects upon handwriting as well, upon its status in the school curriculum, and its role in business and social intercourse. Machines have usurped much of the function of handwriting in the business world. Day by day they continue to invade the personal world. Penmanship is no longer assiduously taught nor extolled as a principal goal for the aspiring student. The old triumvirate has become "reading, recording, and keyboard operation." Handwriting is taught with less aesthetic and more functional consideration. Consequently, it receives greater latitude in method and yields wider variation in the end product. Accordingly, the approach to handwriting identification must be modified.

Handwriting identification is now a sufficiently aged and universally engaged practise. A certain consistency in the methodology, language, demeanour, and thinking of those who pursue it should be expected. The same question should elicit the same response. The same terminology should describe the same subject. The same examination should consider the same evidence. In fact, they don't. The results should be evaluated in the same manner. In fact, they aren't. Clearly, there is need for an explicit restatement of some basic principles that will substitute congruity for inconsistency, sensibility for puerility.

From within the morass, a somewhat solitary appeal is being made to chart a course for the discipline that begins from the perspective:

"Forensic document examination deals with physical evidence and physical evidence cannot lie. Only its interpretation can err. Only the failure to find it or the disinclination to hear its testimony can deprive it of its value."

Our objective is threefold:

- To focus on the significant
- To father valid interpretations
- To foster assessments that the evidence deserves

It may be equally appropriate to say that, in writing this book, we are

• In Quest of Perspicacity •

If, in the process, the discipline gains intellectual growth, we will be content.

History of Questioned Document Examination — in Brief

1

1. Handwriting Identification and the Judicial Process

The examination of disputed handwriting may well be the progenitor of forensic science. Certainly it is one of those rare disciplines to have been born as a forensic necessity, rather than as a discipline established first in its own right for other reasons, and later harnessed for forensic tasks. Historical references indicate that the practise of forgery and related frauds involving documents evolved almost as early as the development of writing. In the days of the Roman Empire, the law provided for the acceptance of expert testimony respecting documents. It was not until centuries later that such testimony was admitted in English-speaking courts.

A. Documents and the Rules of Evidence

The relevancy of documents in civil and criminal litigation is largely dependent on their authorship or origin. Numerous ways have evolved to attest to the truthfulness of a writing. Before the origin of the signature, the application of a wax seal served to authenticate the document. The wax seal bonded the ends of a ribbon of fabric which fed through a slit in the paper and was embossed with a personal motif. Later, signatures served the purpose, but additionally, the legal process has tended to require the signatures of witnesses to the signing.

There have always been situations in which unsigned or anonymous writings on documents were potentially important, e.g., personal notebooks in which relative or incriminating information was recorded. Thus, the provision of proof respecting the authorship of such documents has long been an issue.

Until this century, circumstantial evidence was the vehicle by which authorship was established for many cases. This was used in the absence of witnesses to the act of writing. For many years, courts debated as to what evidence was acceptable. Certainly, the inclination was to seek proof that was independent of the document's circumstances. But, as Wigmore observed, as late as the early 19th century, "the idea of expertise in handwriting was ... a novel one."[1]

In the course of developing an acceptable standard of proof, many related issues surfaced. Should triers of fact (judge or jury) be permitted to compare writings for themselves? If so, what writings could be used as standards? The answer to the first question became affirmative, provided some kind of corroborative evidence was supplied. Corroboration was then sought through the testimony of a *recognition witness* — someone acquainted with the alleged writer's handwriting. Recognition witnesses then became the means by which writing standards were authenticated and tendered as evidence. The extent of the acquaintance with a person's writing and the manner in which it was acquired were without precise boundaries and the evidence provided proved most unreliable.

Thus, any person having observed another person write, even once and even years before, was permitted to testify respecting the authenticity of a writing. Despite the inherent weaknesses in this evidence, shreds of the policy continue to prevail regarding the proof of writing standards. Requirements were then placed upon the standards. They must have some relevance to the matter in dispute and could not simply represent a given person's writing practises.

The case of *Goodtitle d. Revett v. Braham*[2] in 1792 is said to be the first in English-speaking courts in which specially-qualified witnesses were proffered. These witnesses would testify solely from direct comparison between standards and disputed writing rather than from recognition. Their special qualifications were acquired from their experience as inspectors of franks. They checked the authenticity of the signatures of M.P.s and others on mail that was dispatched pursuant to the franking privilege. On that occasion, Lord Kenyon admitted the testimony of two inspectors, on the authority of *Folkes v. Chadd*,[3] in which Lord Mansfield admitted the expert testimony of an engineer.

But the beginning of this kind of testimony was wobbly. The next year the same evidence was refused by the same judge, Lord Kenyon. Not until Massachusetts admitted testimony[4] respecting the comparison of disputed documents with writing standards in 1836, and England passed the *Common Law Procedure Act*[5] in 1854, did the practise become reasonably consistent.

B.   Prior to 1900

By the year 1672, Europeans such as Jacques Raveneau[6] had written on the subject of handwriting identification. In the 1800s, the La Ronciere case, the Dreyfuss letters, and the La Boussiniere will all testified to the endeavour to resolve major issues on the strength of writing examination in that part of the world.

On this continent, Albert S. Osborn is credited with launching handwriting identification as a distinct discipline at the turn of this century. Furthermore, he broadened its scope to include typewriting, ink, and paper examinations under the wider umbrella of document examination. Others of his era, such as Hagan, Frazer, Ames, Lee, and Abbey made their contributions in published form. Osborn's books, however, are still deemed to be the accepted texts of the speciality, although they were not written expressly for that purpose.

While Osborn's success in gaining acceptance for handwriting identification was achieved largely through his writings, lectures, and testimony, there is no doubt that he derived much assistance from his friendship and association with John H. Wigmore, the eminent authority on American evidence law. Wigmore held a great personal interest in forensic science and recognized its potential in the court's search for truth. The claim for document examination as a forensic science can be traced to the oracles of Wigmore, some of which were expressed or quoted in the writings of Osborn just after the turn of the century.

We do not know precisely when the evidence of the handwriting examiner was first admitted in Canadian courts. We do know that provision was made for it in the *Common Law Procedure Act* of 1854 of England and that those authorities were broadened under the *British Criminal Procedure Act* of 1865. Remarkably, the Act applied only to civil proceedings. We know, too, that some courts expressed a preference for expert testimony over lay witness identification of handwriting as early as 1867.[7]

In Canada, the *Common Law Procedure Act* and the *Criminal Procedure Act* were superseded by the *Canada Evidence Act* of 1868,[8] that with some modification, has continued to provide for the admission of expert testimony respecting handwriting — but respecting handwriting only — for the last 130 years. Authority for the presentation of evidence by the document examiner in areas of his work, other than handwriting, must be sought in case and common law. This is the practise insofar as any other discipline within the broad field of forensic science.

The reason for giving handwriting evidence special attention in the *Canada Evidence Act* of 1868 is open to some speculation at this time. There are those document examiners who maintain that it simply bespeaks the fact that handwriting experts were probably the first of the forensic experts to make their contribution to the judicial system. In the absence of precedents, special provision had to be made for their admission. Certainly, the *Canada Evidence Act* of 1868, one of the many early statutes passed after confederation in 1867 when Canada became independent of British rule, merely adopted the provisions of a similar statute on the law books of England from 1856. That being the case, the real reason why writing evidence is segregated under the law from other forms of forensic expertise must lie in the history of British law. We understand that legal history runs remarkably parallel to this in the United States.

C.   The 20th Century — The First 40 Years

Notwithstanding the legislation governing its admission into the courts and into a growing volume of judicial decisions, not all members of the legal profession readily accepted the testimony of the expert witness at the turn of this century. The disparaging manner in which older law literature has referred to their contributions suggests that the vanguard of the profession of forensic scientists left something to be desired in qualification, motivation, or attitude.

> "Skilled witnesses come with such bias on their minds to support the cause in which they are embarked that hardly any weight should be given to their evidence."[9] "... Expert witnesses become so warped in their judgment ... that, even when conscientiously disposed, they are incapable of expressing a candid opinion."[10]

Others, more liberal, said, "Experts are, as a class, shrewd and cunning,"[11] while, occasionally, the pages of law books dripped with sarcasm from such statements as, "He swears scientifically does the expert,"[12] and as one that borders on being a literary classic: "You will be amazed at the elaboration of the system for finding out nothing, which has been invented by science."[13]

Insofar as writing identification, such scepticism, indeed hostility, is alleged to have stemmed from the often disputed rationale that underlay the admissibility of handwriting expert testimony. Undoubtedly, admission was granted simply on the grounds that experts could not be worse than recognition witnesses.[14]

Thus, while legislation resolved the question of admissibility, opponents continued to argue against handwriting identification on the grounds of weight.

"All doubts respecting the competency of the opinion of experts in handwriting based upon mere comparison, as evidence, have been removed by statute, but it still must be esteemed proof of low degree."[15]

A reasonably complete account of the legal history of handwriting identification, as developed and recorded in case law in the United States, may be found in parts II, III, and IV of a seven-part article by Risinger, Denbeaux, and Saks.[16] Although the article has been criticized for its language, its objective, and for a number of errors and omissions, these three parts present one of a very few dissertations in which an endeavour has been made to compile such a record.

Remarkably, the number of persons in Canada offering services to the courts as handwriting examiners during the first 40 years of this century was almost as great as it is at the present time. They were widely distributed across 5,000 miles of sparsely-populated terrain from coast to coast. For the most part, the early examiners of the United States and Canada were sincere, well-intentioned individuals. Despite little training, they had one thing in common: a small collection of the books of Osborn and his contemporaries, Hagan, Brewster, Quirke, Ames, Frazer, and Mitchell.

They came from many walks of life: bankers, lithographers, engravers, court clerks, and police officers. The greatest number of them were teachers of penmanship and business college instructors. Obviously, it was felt that those who taught penmanship and the preparation of written records were better qualified to discriminate between the writing of different persons. This was because, at a time of strict adherence to copybook styles, there was great similarity in the writing of many people. Furthermore, teachers were able to appreciate the capabilities of the average individual in altering or modifying writing habits.

A second and smaller group included bankers, court clerks, and police officials that developed an interest in document examination, probably as a result of their exposure to or involvement in criminal cases. The need for the talents of the document examiner was evident and the availability of such experts was limited.

All were self-taught. None had studied science and few were called upon more than a few times a year. Certainly, document examination offered few opportunities for full-time employment in Canada or the United States until the opening of the federal, state, and provincial police laboratories in 1937 and later.

If and when the successful solution of a civil or criminal case demanded it, more than one document examiner would be engaged to examine the evidence. Often, the second examiner would be Albert S. Osborn. Such were the circumstances in the trial of Bruno Richard Hauptmann for the kidnapping and murder of the son of Charles Lindberg, the famous aviator, in 1934. Osborn and seven other examiners testified respecting the handwriting on a number of ransom notes, and in so doing, established the legitimacy of writing identification in the eyes of the public. On such occasions, examiners would share experiences, learn from one another, and develop their competence. Osborn was a teacher, a stimulus, and an encouragement to those who were less practised. Out of these raw, unorganized beginnings, the profession of the document examiner slowly emerged.

Undoubtedly, the growth and development of the profession over the first 40 years of this century was not too different in Canada from that of the United States. Police or government forensic laboratories established standards for the work, formalized their own training curriculum, and pursued limited programs of research to assemble much needed knowledge. However, these institutions were few in number in both countries and all had very modest resources.

D. 1940 to 1975 — The Next 35 Years

The development of the manual typewriter, the advent of the ball point pen, the introduction of the electric typewriter, and the evolution of the electronic age has grossly affected document examination. They have profoundly changed the means by which society communicates and records its information. The profession of teachers of handwriting is near extinction on this continent. Few are employed in the schools. Penmanship was at one time tenaciously taught and diligently practised. It is, however, no longer extolled as an important student achievement. Writing enjoys greater latitude in learning methods and wider variation in the end product. Whereas the objective in years past was to ensure legibility for the benefit of others, the goal now seems to be to provide a convenient process for note taking, readable chiefly by the writer. Communications and records are matters for machines. Thus, the approach to writing identification has had to be modified significantly.

The forensic science services that have developed since 1940 have established document examination laboratories in most of the major cities across the land. All are administered by the government authorities responsible, directly or indirectly, for law enforcement in the area. For the most part, the services have been available free of charge to law enforcement agencies at all levels.

E. The Last 20 Years

Unfortunately, as yet there is no program of reputable courses offered or training available in Canada or the United States to private persons who wish to enter the discipline. As a result, the few qualified private practising examiners are, frequently, former employees of government forensic laboratories whose personal facilities for performing the work may be inadequate and may vary substantially. For this reason their work is often limited to handwriting studies.

Usually, examiners within the government laboratories are prohibited from participation in civil matters. Policy requires publicly-funded laboratory services to be applied to matters of public interest, (e.g., criminal cases) rather than to the interests of private persons or private enterprise. Understandably, lawyers have, almost in desperation, engaged the services of graphoanalysts, a title coined for themselves by a school of graphologists located in the United States.

The teaching methods, the quality of instruction offered, and the principles propounded in graphoanalysis have been the subject of much controversy over the years. Suffice it to say that the standard of work performed by graphoanalysts, in respect of document examination, has been distressingly poor, and legitimate questions arise as to the number of injustices that have occurred to which they have contributed. In consequence, the profession of document examination has suffered with the victims of these injustices. Furthermore, perhaps because the less competent are more easily influenced, in the minds of some legal authorities, examiners can still be bought to serve the interests of the employer.

No one can say for sure how many pioneering spirits in document examination there may have been in past years in different parts of this vast land. Few have achieved recognition on a national scale. However, the groping efforts of pioneers are yielding to the proven routines of science. Nevertheless, there remain some areas in which we are still pioneers and still groping.

There are concerns in some minds as to whether the services of the document examiner are being utilized as frequently as possible. For others, the greater concerns continue to be, not a question of how often they were there, but how much they could say and how closely it corresponded to the truth.

2.   What Is Document Examination?

Document examination is the discipline that seeks to determine the history of a document by technical or scientific processes.

From the viewpoint of its application to civil and criminal litigation, its forensic function, we wrote years ago, as quoted on this book's cover:

> "Forensic document examination is the study of physical evidence, and physical evidence cannot lie. Only its interpretation can err. Only the failure to find it, or to hear its true testimony can deprive it of its value."

It may entail the study of a complete instrument of communication, or of some element of it: the writing, lettering or printing, the ink, the graphite, the paper, or its surface contour. It may entail, as well, the study of the dimensions of any of its attributes. Furthermore, every examination must be approached with the expectation that it will. Document examination may seek information respecting the origin of the document or evidence of the chronology of the events that subsequently occurred. Notwithstanding the many elements of the document that testify to its history, the handwriting it bears is the element most frequently in dispute.

Questioned handwriting and handlettering, however, may be inscribed on walls or woodwork or on any other physical object of any size, perhaps using paint instead of ink, and broad markers, brushes, or spray cans, instead of the customary writing instruments. The message may be threatening, offensive, obscene, libelous, annoying, or incriminating, and the identity of the author may be essential to the fixing of liability or culpability. Understandably, the document examiner will be called upon to apply his/her skills to identify the author of the inscription, although the medium (e.g., a lavatory wall or a concrete bridge) does not fall within the common definition of a document. While these occasions are infrequent, document examination and, in particular, handwriting identification, should be thought of in this broader context.

The American Society for Testing and Material (ASTM), in their designation E.444-79, has provided a standard description of the scope of the work related to forensic document examination. This scope tends to deal with a document in the more limited sense. The standard description also makes reference to the qualifications of practitioners, although few specifics are provided except by inference. It does, however, clearly segregate forensic handwriting examination from calligraphy, engrossing, and graphology.

3.   Why Is Document Examination Conducted?

The examination of a document is conducted to determine:

- its origin, i.e., where did the document come from?
- its production source, i.e., what person or machine produced it?
- its production process, i.e., how was it made?
- its inscription, i.e., what has faded or been obliterated?
- its chastity, i.e., what changes, if any, have been made to it?
- its integrity, i.e., is it genuine or false?
- its legitimacy, i.e., is it an original or a reproduction, and if so, what generation?

The reason for seeking this information through a technical process is to shed light on events in the history of the document that have occurred prior to its arrival in court. This will enable the court to confirm assumptions that may otherwise be made. It will also allow the court to review the correspondence between the technical testimony of the document itself and the oral testimony of witnesses.

Notwithstanding the breadth of scope of questioned document examination, in practise, most examiners find that 70 percent of their work or more deals with the study of handwriting or of handwritten signatures. If some areas of criminal work tend to provide a somewhat different variety of tasks, certainly the private examiner finds that he or she is more constantly engrossed with handwriting. For these reasons, handwriting is deserving of our most comprehensive attention.

References

1. Wigmore, J., Proof by Comparison of Handwriting; Its History. *Am. L. Rev.* 1896; 481: 494.

2. *Goodtitle d. Revett v. Braham*, 4 (Term. Rep. 497, 1792.)

3. *Folkes v. Chadd*, 3 Doug. 157, 99 Eng. Rep. 589, (K. B. 1782).

4. *Moody v. Rowell*, 34 Mass., 17 Pick. 490, (1836).

5. *Common Law Procedure Act*, 17 and 18 Vict. ch. 125 (1854). Section 27: "Comparison of a disputed writing with any writing proved to the satisfaction of the judge to be genuine shall be permitted to be made by witnesses; and such writings, and the evidence of witnesses respecting the same, may be submitted to the Court and jury as evidence of the genuineness, or otherwise, of the writing in dispute."

6. Buquet, Alain, Handwriting Examination Background and Current Trends. *I.C.P.O. Review*, 1981 November; p 352.

7. *Reid v. Warner,* 17 L. C. (Rep., 485, 1867).

8. *Canada Evidence Act,* S.C., (1868) Chap. 76, adopting provisions of 1856 U.K., Chap. 113.

9. Wellman, Francis L., *The Art of Cross Examination* (New York: MacMillan Co., 1913), p 73, quoting Lord Campbell.

10. ibid. p 73, quoting from Taylor's treatise on *The Law of Evidence.*

11. Wrottesley, Frederic John, *The Examination of Witnesses in Court* (Toronto: Carswell Co., 1910). p 94.

12. Harris, Richard, *Hints on Advocacy* (London: Stevens & Sons, 1911), p 140.

13. ibid. p 141.

14. *Moody v. Rowell,* 34 Mass., 17 Pick. (1836) p 498.

15. *Mutual Benefit Life Ins. Co. v. Brown,* 30 N.J. Eq. 193, 201 (1878).

16. Risinger, D. Michael, Denbeaux, Mark P., and Saks, Michael J., Exorcism of Ignorance as a Proxy for Rational Knowledge: The Lessons of Handwriting Identification "Expertise." *University of Pennsylvania Law Review,* 1989; 137: 3.

A Handwriting Compendium for Document Examiners

2

4. What Is Handwriting?

Handwriting is an acquired skill and clearly one that is a complex perceptual-motor task, sometimes referred to as a neuromuscular task.

Skilled writing movements are so commonplace that one is inclined to overlook their complexity. Without exaggeration, however, writing is one of the most advanced achievements of the human hand.

The hand is an extremely complex and delicate mechanism, containing some 27 bones controlled by more than 40 muscles. Most of the muscles are situated in the lower arm and connect to the fingers by an intricate set of tendons. Their ability in manipulating a writing instrument is precisely coordinated by a timing system under a neural control of movements of the arm, the hand, and the fingers. The precise ordering and timing of the movements determines the structure of the pattern that is recorded by the pen or pencil.

The development of writing is complex because it is, in part, culture dependent, and cultures differ with locales and undergo constant change. The evidence of this dependence is manifest in class, system, or national characteristics.

Writing is a continuous or flowing task, not one of discrete or separated actions. There are apparent interruptions at word boundaries, but in many cases the pen movement may be continuous and uninterrupted, although not recorded as an inked line.

A feature of skilled performance, and certainly of handwriting, is that it involves the smooth execution of a structured sequence of coordinated movements in which each movement occurs at its proper time and place in the sequence.[1] The particular pattern of these movements constitutes the habitual aspects of writing that are peculiar to each individual. The fact that, with practise and skill, the execution of writing habits becomes more automatic, renders the writing process less subject to conscious control.

5. How Much Do We Know About Handwriting?

Much has been studied and written about handwriting in the last century, although for the first 90 years, the objectives were more practical than profound. Many studies pursued the correlation of writing features and various medical and mental conditions. Others sought to identify the affects of social status, self-esteem, and sex upon handwriting. Much work dealt with the pedagogy of writing and remedial approaches to improve its quality in the writing of children.

Perhaps the greatest effort was devoted to the correlation of writing features and particular personality characteristics, commonly called graphology or graphoanalysis. A large portion of this work sought to find evidence validating the claims of the vocation as a valid and reliable instrument for personnel selection, aptitude determinations, or as a psycho-diagnostic tool.

Many surveys of this work have been conducted over the years. Most have limited their scope to particular topics. Allport and Vernon[2] dealt with experimental work up to 1933. McNeil and Blum[3] dealt with methodology.

Fluckiger et al.,[4] reviewed the experimental research from 1933 to 1960. Almost simultaneously, Herrick[5] produced the most comprehensive bibliography on handwriting studies from 1890 to 1960 that listed 1,754 papers, books, and articles. Unfortunately, to that point, few of the studies were rigorous and experimental. Most were described as suggesting hypotheses rather than testing them.

Herrick and Okada[6] suggested the various directions that research, respecting handwriting, might pursue in the 1960s. Later Askov, Otto, and Askov[7] reviewed the research of that decade to assess the progress made along the lines suggested. They expressed some disappointment, commenting that handwriting instruction tended to follow accepted practises rather than be based on research findings.

A decade later, Peck, Askov, and Fairchild[8] reviewed the progress one more time and reported finding some encouraging signs. They mention the promising trend in experimentation on the handwriting of learning disabled and other atypical children. Their concluding comments should be of particular interest to handwriting examiners:

> "In an age of technical and mechanized communication media, from response-equipped cable television to computerized personal letters, it is pleasing to witness a continuing concern with handwriting. Although seemingly almost an archaic tool, handwriting remains one means of individualized expression. Its relationship to the development of the other language arts has been demonstrated…by research."

Huber[9] endeavoured to stimulate interest in the published literature on handwriting among document examiners and added some 200 titles of 1958 to 1983 to Herrick's survey of 1960. In 1985, 1986, and again in 1987, Baier, Hussong, Hoffman, and Klein[10] surveyed the material produced relative to questioned document examination from 1873 and have recorded some 5,871 monographs, articles, books, and papers, a substantial portion of which deal with writing.

A trend toward proper experimental investigation became apparent in the 1960s and 1970s,[11] but progress was slow. The International Workshop on the Motor Aspects of Handwriting in July 1982, brought together research scientists from the disciplines of experimental psychology, bioengineering, neurology and education, and gave birth to a new discipline of graphonomics. Not until then have the prospects for progress appeared so promising.

Perhaps for the first time, research is endeavouring to study and understand the development of handwriting as a perceptual-motor skill. It is seeking to discover the structures and processes operating at different stages, and the factors involved in their modification or change, according to Thomassen, Keuss, Van Galen, and Grootveld.[12] As these authors have told us, handwriting is a complex type of motor behaviour. The greatest difficulty in writing letters is not in the execution of their particular strokes but in the execution of complex combinations of strokes in ever-changing contexts. Furthermore, the practised writer does not simply follow a given trace to produce the required movements. Research has now shown that the writer retrieves the necessary information from an abstract motor memory. Handwriting involves a continuously proceeding output process that intrinsically intertwines the retrieval process, a buffer storage, and a monitoring action. Thus, the brain works like a computer — which it is.

The representation of motor acts in memory appears to be nonmuscle specific. Hence, writing follows similar patterns whether executed with an instrument in the hand, held by the foot, or in the mouth. The integrated sequence of movements is a hierarchical process. A combination of letters or a word may be executed as a unit. Thus, the execution of movement sequences appears to be far more independent of the monitoring of a feedback system than was once believed. Motor theories, however, are not yet completely developed.

As Thomassen and Teulings (1983), have elucidated in some detail, there are at least three different theories of how a skilled performance such as handwriting is achieved, and the role that feedback plays in it. The open-loop theory was described by Keele.[13] The closed-loop theory was developed by Adams.[14] A form of central motor program theory was proposed by Schmidt[15-16] under the name of schema theory.

It is not intended to dwell on these different theories and their differing approaches to feedback. Nevertheless, the involvement of a feedback mechanism cannot be ignored. To write satisfactorily requires the ability to distinguish visually between graphic forms of letters and other characters and to judge their correctness. Learning to write requires the ability to distinguish between the feedback provided by the senses associated with correct and incorrect movements. Modifying or controlling the movement of the writing instrument is also required.

Writing is described as a tool-using skill. Connolly and Elliott[17] have distinguished seven types of grip for tools, five of which they classify as power grips (as in holding an ice pick or screw driver), and two that they classify as precision grips (as in grasping a pencil or a pen).

The grip employed with a writing instrument may facilitate or inhibit certain types of strokes. The course of development in writing is a gradual improvement in control, especially of the more precise finger movements. This is reflected by a reduction in the size of writing and by a reduction in the number and extent of superfluous movements.

In the development of writing there are both qualitative and quantitative changes. Of the variables that can be more precisely measured, speed is probably the simplest overall measure of proficiency one can use. An increase in speed of writing as a function of increasing age has been described by Cormeau, Distrait, Toussaint, and Bidaine.[18] The rate at which the speed of writing increases is greatest between the ages of 7 and 9 years. It tapers off to 13 years, when there is little further increase.

As aforementioned, writing is a culture-bound activity, not only insofar as language and its orthography, but also in many motor aspects that are greatly influenced by culture and education. This is sometimes overlooked. Writing is spelling, as well as a perceptual-motor task; two quite different educational problems occurring coincidentally, that beg to be tackled at the same time. Teaching the motor preliminaries of writing involves the introduction of cultural standards such as regularity and neatness, the introduction of cultural biases such as slant, counter clockwise rotations, left to right transport. It also involve the introduction of various constraints such as posture, grasp, and which hand is being used. In different cultures (i.e., societies of the world) these standards, biases, and constraints may differ, producing different effects in the writing of their subjects.

It is also to be noted that in the development of writing or drawing, certain biases or rules have evolved for large numbers of the population. We have directional preferences of which we are not always conscious. These preferences prompt us, almost invariably, to execute vertical lines from the top down and horizontal lines from the left to the right. When these rules are broken, we look for reasons to explain them, such as the inverted hand position (IHP) in left-handed writers. It may also explain why there are many writers that tend to omit the upstroke in letters such as the "i," "t," "h," or "l," and commence the structure with simply a vertical stroke — from the top down.

With growth in age and development in handwriting, there is increased conformity to the rules, but the strength of one rule may decline while another increases, as Goodnow and Levine[19] observed.

6.   What Is the Origin of the Alphabet?[20]

The fabulous faculty of writing has prompted many to impute its origin to the gods. Assyrian, Chinese, Egyptian, Indian, and Scandinavian deities have all been credited with bestowing on mankind the knowledge of writing. In 1750, Champion wrote:

> "The origin of penmanship, or first invention of letters, has been much controverted; but next to God, the Author and Giver of all science, it seems rational to think it was derived from Adam."[21]

Neolithic man began written communication as long as 20,000 years ago, when he graphically represented objects and ideas in drawings on cave walls,[22-23] that are now referred to as iconographs. After these came the first pictographs or picture stories when action was added to the drawings of animals. To these were added figures of man, and the complexity of the depicted events gradually increased to become what were called ideographs or picture symbols.

Ideographs were simpler drawings, such as stick figures, yet more difficult to interpret. Then, iconographic symbols were combined with ideographs to provide more information. Particular combinations expressed ideas. The moon symbol and slashes might represent the lunar month.[24-25] The origin of the first systematic method for written communication is uncertain, but the evidence found in artifacts suggests that such a system began sometime after 3500 B.C.

In the initial development of writing in any culture, the symbols used represent objects rather than the spoken words. The linguistic elements followed. The phonetic use of symbols to represent syllables of words probably commenced with the endeavours to write foreign names, which conveyed no meaning other than identification. From this, syllabic usage spread into everyday words.

The earliest known forms of Egyptian hieroglyphics exhibited elements of a syllabic system. In fact, they exhibited elements of the final step from syllabic writing to true alphabetic writing in which symbols represented speech sounds and not just syllables.[26]

Early writings took on several forms. The Sumerians produced a cuneiform system when they conquered Mesopotamia, that dates back to 3200 B.C. and is perhaps the oldest. Later it underwent transition to ideographic and syllabic form.[27] With the introduction of clay as a writing vehicle, symbols were simplified and straight-line wedge shapes, made with broad tipped stylos, replaced round lines. Hence, the name *cuneiform* was coined to mean wedge-shaped.

Cuneiform was adopted by many Semitic tribes and evolved in different versions under the Acadians, Assyrians, Babylonians, Elamites, Hittites, and Kassites. The combination of ideographs and phonetic forms produced polyphones (symbols with more than one syllabic value), homophones (different symbols with the same phonetic value), and developed a need for determinatives to identify a word as being ideographic or phonetic, and/or its phonetic form. Phonetic symbols also served to sort ideograms with multiple meanings.

Various kinds of cuneiform writing survived throughout Egypt, Asia Minor, and Greece for over 2,000 years. The Persians adapted a mode of it for their use about 600 B.C. and then simplified it to about 40 signs, which may have been the beginning of a true alphabet. Cuneiform began its demise around 500 B.C. Although priests and astronomers continued to use it at the beginning of the Christian era, we have no record of it beyond 75 A.D.

Egyptian writing developed three different styles of symbol systems — hieroglyphic, hieratic, and demotic, each using the same combination of characters but in a different written form. Egyptian scripts were essentially national, living and dying only in Egypt. Egypt's hieroglyphics achieved early advancement over other systems, combining ideographs, syllabic forms, and even single letter symbols as well as determinatives. Despite its early growth and advance in development, it failed to become an alphabetic form. Hieroglyphics, which prevailed until after 500 A.D. was preferred while it lasted for royal and religious inscriptions.[28]

The introduction of the reed pen and papyrus around 2000 B.C. encouraged the development of hieratic writing that employed simpler forms to depict the same figures. As a result of its speed of execution, arising from the simplicity of some forms, hieratic became the choice for business and private documents.

A highly cursive form of hieratic, called demotic, developed about 700 B.C., but since it used the same system as hieroglyphics (ideograms, phonograms, and determinatives), it failed to spawn a true alphabetic system. Demotic symbols, however, were so cursive, and execution so much simpler, that it replaced hieratic and hieroglyphic styles, leaving them to religious and traditional transcriptions. The demotic system spread into general use in Egyptian writing, achieving the level of importance of hieroglyphics or Greek. Indeed, the Sumerian and this Egyptian system were probably the most influential upon subsequent developments.

The Cretan civilization, the Elamitic civilization, the Indus Valley civilization, and the Hittite civilization each developed their particular version of Babylonian cuneiform. This was later replaced by more cursive or pictographic systems.

The origin and development of Chinese writing is obscure. Semiphonetic forms date from about 1500 B.C.,[29] but it cannot be related to any particular foreign system. Chinese writing has endured primarily as a syllabic system, although some change has occurred to the physical appearance of figures and forms.

Japanese writing, like Chinese writing, has advanced little in centuries. Neither has seen profound changes to the underlying phonetic systems for inscribing thoughts and ideas. While dissimilarities in pronunciation produced differences in some forms, in many respects, Japan can be considered a colony of China.

These many languages and their writing systems had virtually no influence on the origin and development of the first alphabet. Their account here only lends some historical perspective to the search for better methods of written communication. Writing systems came and went more as the trappings of victors over vanquished rather than because of inherent efficiency or inefficiency.

The First Alphabet

Precisely when, where, and by whom, the first alphabet was developed is not known. Theories are numerous, and new archeological findings give birth to new theories or the modification of the old. The Phoenicians, the merchants of the Mediterranean from 1200 to 900 B.C., are credited with the spread of the first alphabetic system through their constant business travels from Palestine to Gibraltar.[30]

There are reports that the first true alphabet surfaced between Egypt and Mesopotamia in the years 1730 to 1580 B.C.,[31] perhaps in the Sinai Peninsula (1600 B.C.) where Hebrew-Egyptian script was used to write a Hebrew-Semitic language. The language needed only the development of basic linguistic sounds rather then syllables.[32] Others say Canaanites (i.e., Phoenicians) combined Egyptian and Semitic systems, eliminating everything but the fundamental sounds.[33]

A third theory suggests that since Palestine's culture was known to be highly developed, and an active international trading centre situated between the two great cultures of Egypt and Mesopotamia, it is a likely location for the origin of the alphabet.

In any event the first alphabet was largely a northern Semitic development. The north Semitic true alphabet can be traced to Byblos, Phoenicia[34] about 1100 B.C., but may have begun in Gebal, Phoenicia, 200 years before.[35] While the sounds of the alphabet remained stable, its physical appearances changed significantly. There were three styles of the early script:

1. The Phoenician script proper, with Cyprian, Sardinian, and Carthaginian varieties
2. The Libyan and Iberian scripts, that evolved from the Carthaginian
3. The Aramaic, that developed as an offshoot, about 1000 B.C.

Because of the Aramaeans control of the Damascus area and the retention of the system to the time of the birth of Christ, the Aramaic style acquired some importance for Western civilizations. Another system of note derived from the Aramaean was Arabic. The spread of Islamic with the Arabic alphabet eventually displaced the Aramaic language. A south Semitic alphabet al.so developed independently with many derivatives.

The Greeks derived and developed their own alphabet from the Phoenician system, introducing vowels to accommodate the Greek language. Other consonants not peculiar to Greek were dropped, resulting in the formation of the Greek alphabet. Evidence of this derivation can be found in the letter names.[36] The names of the letters of the Phoenician alphabet were of things: *aleph* (ox), *beth* (house), *gimel* (camel), *daleth* (door), etc., but the names of Greek letters have no other significance than as names of letters, e.g., *alpha*, *beta, gamma, delta.* There were changes, in the tenth to fifth centuries B.C., in the methods of writing, particularly in its direction. Those methods went through stages, first right to left, then alternating with each line (sometimes called ploughing style or boustrophedon) and finally left to right. By 350 B.C. the writing in all Greek states was standardized and Athens had adopted a fixed form for Greek letters.[37]

To facilitate the freehand execution of forms, the Ionic Greek alphabet was modified by the scribes. The writing of capitals with ink on papyrus and vellum provided a slight rounding effect that became known as the Greek uncials.

Two classes of writing evolved — calligraphy, which used book-hand forms, and tachygraphy, which used document-hand forms. The former sought clarity, precision, regularity, and beauty and was used to transcribe literature of importance. The latter sought speed and efficiency, and was the style for workaday documents. Calligraphy maintained a fairly stable design of uncials that became known as book-hand cursive. Tachygraphy allowed changing cursive forms to alter the appearance of the letters. After 250 B.C., rounder forms permitted ligatures to link letters and gave writing more speed. The trend continued until the seventh or eighth centuries A.D. when a new design of handwritten Greek emerged called minuscules. Some previous uncial forms recombined with it and a formal minuscule evolved between 1000 and 1400 A.D. The forms of letters in this system does not differ significantly from modern Greek printing.

A derivation of the Greek alphabet was that of the Etruscans in northern Italy, who, around 800 B.C., combined Semitic and Greek letters to create their own alphabet. Its final form remained in use from 400 B.C. until displaced by the Latin alphabet of the Roman Empire in the first century A.D. Another derivation of the Greek was the Messapian alphabet, which is thought to date from 800 B.C. when its people lived in the heel of Italy.

The last link between ancient and modern alphabets is the Roman alphabet. Before the Roman Empire peaked, Italy was dominated by the Etruscans in the north and the Messapii in the south, both of whom used alphabets garnered from the Greeks. Consequently, in about 70 to 0 B.C., when a script was selected for adaptation to the Latin language, the Romans understandably chose a Greek derived design. The first Latin alphabet consisted of 21 Greek letters from the Etruscan alphabet.[38]

Then, after 600 years of changes and additions to accommodate differences in pronunciation, the Roman alphabet was established. When the Romans conquered Greece in the first century B.C., two more Greek symbols ("Y" and "Z") were added. The medieval addition of three more modifications of existing Latin letters ("U," "W," and "J") brought the total to the current 26 letters.

The Romans also developed new forms for the letters, the first of which was called lapidary capitals. The Romans introduced graceful, rounded curves, and tapered stroke endings. A finishing line, called a serif, across the end of some strokes became popular in stone inscriptions during the first century.

As the use of pen and parchment increased, Square Capitals, or Book Capitals that were slightly rounded forms of the lapidary styles evolved. These more freehand formations provided a written rather than a drawn characteristic. At the same time, a second design emerged that sacrificed small details in favour of speed. Serifs became a last turn of the pen rather than a separate stroke. Pen lifts were avoided when possible. The resulting, somewhat casual design became known as Rustic Capitals.

The execution of these styles with a broad, flat-tipped pen, held at an acute angle to the line of writing, gave the strokes of the letters varying thicknesses. For the Square

Capitals, vertical strokes tended to be broader than the horizontal strokes, but for the Rustic Capitals, the converse was the case. Both forms were majuscule, that is, the entirety of the letters could be contained between two parallel, horizontal lines. This is roughly equivalent to the meaning of the words *capital letter* today. Rustic Capitals, popular for literary works until 600 A.D., appeared thereafter only in titles until their demise in the twelfth century.

The everyday Roman writing, used for business during the first century A.D., was called "cursive capitals". Made with a sharp pointed instrument and fewer pen lifts, the writing line was more uniform in width and connected. Some letters of the style became "minuscule", that is, containing strokes that extended above or below the main body of the letter (e.g., "h" or "g"). This is not precisely the meaning that the word currently carries.

Tannenbaum,[39] reports that Julius Caesar wrote in old Roman cursive, of which there are very few specimens in existence. It is of great historical importance and helps to explain the origin of modern scripts. Several of our minuscular letters are traceable to the forms of Roman cursive script found on wax tablets (libelli), discovered at the site of Pompeii in 1875. When this script was formalized, it became the ordinary diplomatic hand of Italy and France, until about the ninth century.

The development of writing styles is somewhat obscure in the second, third, and fourth centuries A.D., although it became evident that in this interim two new book hands and a new business hand came into use.

The older book hand, the Roman uncial, used the broad-tipped pen, but after 500 A.D., the pen tip was turned to an angle more parallel to the line of writing. Most of the forms were majuscule, but a few were minuscule. The newer of the book hands, called Semi-Uncials, was written with a parallel pen tip. It was almost entirely of cursive origin and minuscule form.[40]

The Uncial system faired well until the seventh century A.D. After 800 A.D. it was restricted to titles and disappeared in the twelfth century. The Semi-Uncial system had a more limited use in common literature and died about 1000 A.D.

The fourth century saw the introduction of the new business hand called Cursive Minuscules. It employed a pointed pen like the Cursive Capitals but utilized minuscule forms like the Semi-Uncials, with a high frequency of connecting ligatures. Their importance in later developments should not be underestimated. They were the basis for the eighth century Caroline Minuscules that dominated Europe for 700 years. The Gothic Cursives of the thirteenth to fifteenth centuries that also evolved, yielded to a revival of the pure Caroline Minuscules.

Development in writing systems was encouraged by development in writing materials, all geared to produce speed and efficiency. The domination of Rome produced vellum and the quill pen, but after Rome's decline and the loss of a centralized influence, a new influence surfaced — nationality. From then until today, national characteristics became the major factor in writing styles.[41]

Cursive Minuscules were the basis for many national business hands. Uncials and Semi-Uncials were perpetuated in religious texts. An Italian semicursive minuscule of the seventh to ninth centuries was one of the first predominant national styles. From it sprang other national styles such as Lombardic Minuscule (tenth to eleventh centuries), Beneventan (eighth to thirteenth centuries) and a pre-Caroline book hand of northern Italy.

There were numerous other national styles: Merovigian script (sixth to eighth century, France), Visigothic script (seventh to ninth century, Spain), and Germanic pre-Caroline (eighth to ninth century, central western Europe). The most important of the new developments were the Insular or Anglo-Iris hands developed by the church, as were most writing systems of the Middle Ages. Of these there were two groups, the Irish hands and the Anglo-Saxon semi-uncial. The former is generally attributed to St. Patrick and Irish missionaries, who, using Latin hands, spent countless hours copying Biblical texts. In the struggle for beauty and clarity, new forms of these letter styles surfaced.

The seventh to eighth century Anglo-Saxon hands, a more orderly derivation of the earlier Irish, were employed for Latin until about 940 A.D. and continued in use for Anglo-Saxon literature. During their time, three new letters were introduced for the sounds of "w," "th," and "dh," but only the "w" survived.[42]

Around 800 A.D., Charlemagne of France and his Holy Roman Empire became the major centralized influence in western Europe after the fall of Rome. He learned that many errors had been made in the Biblical texts copied over the previous decades and proposed to correct them. In 781 A.D., he persuaded Alcuin of York, a foremost Biblical scholar, to undertake the revision and rewriting of all the church literature. At a school set up in Tours, at the Abbey of St. Martin, Alcuin provided special training for scribes. He introduced a minuscule letter style designed from a combination and modification of the Anglo-Saxon script, Irish semi-uncial script, and other early Germanic Caroline scripts. The emphasis was on simplicity and clarity. Letters were joined for speed in writing, but not at the expense of clarity. The use of some punctuation and of capitals for titles was standardized.

By about 850 A.D., the Caroline developed by Alcuin replaced most of the national hands of Europe, and for 300 years was virtually the only book hand of western Europe. By the tenth century, however, the Caroline style had experienced various national modifications. German Caroline became conservative, the Italian version became a round book hand and eventually the Italian Gothic. English Caroline and that of northern France was beautiful and regular and served as the base for German Gothic.[43] The business hands of western Europe of the ninth to twelfth centuries were almost exclusively Caroline. There were national and personal variations, but all became increasingly connected.

During the twelfth and thirteenth centuries a number of factors influenced the development of writing styles. There was an increase in the level of literacy. The use and development of alphabetic systems had become established. Literacy was no longer exclusive to the Church. Changes in alphabets dealt less with basic concepts and more with the design of forms. Styles for artistic purposes were born. The shortage of writing materials could not meet the demand for written works and, consequently, writing was compressed into less space which necessitated some style alterations. Perhaps the greatest factor influencing changes in letter designs was the advancement of printing and the invention of moveable type.

As a result of these factors, German Gothic rose to prominence during the thirteenth and fourteenth centuries. Its narrow angular letters allowed for words to be compacted. As a book hand, it was popular with the scribes who had taken over much of the copying task from the churches. The business of this era also approached this sharp, angular style in the form of Gothic cursive minuscule, but it took longer to exhibit the broad lines of book hand Gothic. Gothic became the first widely used printing design to be spread by the emerging printing industry.[44]

Gothic letter styles, like the Caroline, experienced national variations, and had replaced most of the previous national Caroline styles by 1300 A.D. Gothic, in one form or another, became the major hand of Europe.[45] Italy was an exception. Though much of Italy used a Gothic cursive, by about 1350 A.D. that style's illegibility and lack of aesthetic appeal prompted the development of new styles.

The new styles were an attempt by some to revive a simple form of the Caroline minuscule.[46] The first of these, a new book hand, was the product of Poggio Bracciolini who introduced a new humanistic round hand in Florence. This began to replace Gothic as the standard type for books by 1500 A.D.

A comparable humanistic cursive was originated by Niccolo Niccoli, an official scribe of the Vatican, which helped to popularize the style. This cursive style, thinner in line and greater in ligature connections than Bracciolini's, was adapted to typeface by Aldus Manatius in Venice in 1501. Originally called Aldinian, it soon became known as italics and, as a running hand, became the standard for writing in most of Europe.[47] Cancellaresca, an important variety of italics, became the style of the manual of handwriting *La Operina*, printed in 1522 by Lodovico Arrighi.

From this point on, the progress of printing and the development of paper manufacture forced scribes and their book hands to yield to printers and their typeface designs. From the German Gothic and Italian fonts, numerous national styles emerged, some transient, some enduring, some ornate, and some extremely simple.[48]

At the same time, the role of business and personal handwriting also experienced change. The art began growing beyond its restraints. Writing masters, whose primary employment was teaching writing, began to develop individual systems and styles in an effort to compete with each other. The upper class, who wrote at their leisure, developed their own personal styles according to whim or fashion. Although, generally variations of the Gothic and/or Italian hands, the disregard for calligraphic rules often produced designs that defied classification.

One of the more significant variations of the Gothic cursive minuscule to emerge was called the Secretarie hand in England, around 1550 A.D.[49] Derivations of this design were used by many other countries as well. In France and Spain, the varieties of Ronde that surfaced were based on the Secretarie hand, with some influence from the humanistic cursive. Kurrentschrift, a variety of Gothic cursive that was the everyday hand in Germany until after World War II, was based on the Secretarie hand and the Gothic cursive hand of Holland.[50]

A lighter, more cursive style of the aforementioned Cancellaresca became the basis for a manual printed by C.A. Hercolani in 1574. His use of copper plates for printing, instead of wood blocks, allowed more delicate lines for the ascenders and descenders of the letter forms. Between 1680 and 1700, Colonel John Ayres of London worked on a merging of the Cancellaresca hand and the Secretarie hand. He introduced a slant to the right and gave delicate loops to the ascenders and descenders. The new vogue formed the basis for many of today's styles. Ayers' variation of what had previously been called testaggiata became known as copperplate, of which there were two designs: Round hand, a bold business hand, and Italian, a delicate ladies' hand. By the beginning of the nineteenth century, this English Hand was in general use in England, France, Spain, and Italy.

In 1809, Joseph Carstairs introduced a system in England that required the movement of the whole forearm, not just the fingers. Many of the current systems are modelled after the Carstairs system.[51]

The Recent Writing Systems

On this continent, the early colonists used designs that generally relied on the same hybrids of the Italic and Secretarie hands, as in Britain. Later, derivatives of the German Kurrent hand appeared as the style of the Pennsylvania Dutch. In Boston, in 1791, John Jenkins published one of the first American copybooks, which was based on a contemporary English Round hand.[52] After about 1830, a variety of the Carstairs system developed called Spencerian. This was the first major system native to the United States and was later imitated in Britain. Several current United States styles (Zaner-Bloser, Palmer, and others) used the wide swinging style of Spencerian as their basis, but replaced the contrasting thick and thin strokes with lines of more uniform dimensions.

In 1913, largely due to a mistake at a London teachers' conference, printing or manuscript writing, called printscript, was introduced.[53] This style found use in the United States as an introductory form for children learning to write. It became a final system of its own in some schools.

In the United States and Canada today, there are a number of commercial handwriting styles that have been advocated by major companies and school districts — perhaps 20 to 25. The emphasis is generally on speed and legibility. The student is exposed to one of these copybook designs, but the emphasis on clear and efficient execution soon acquiesces to the eccentricities of the pupils own needs, as long as they do not interfere with legibility. The need that causes these minor deviations from the copybook examples is generally the same need that brought the alphabet to its present form — the need to simplify the physical motion required to execute the letter designs.

Studies have suggested that current designs, although graceful and legible are not the most efficiently executed. They incorporate motions that are difficult manipulations, increasing individuality and illegibility. Whether future handwriting trends will result in more easily executed patterns is unknown. In any event, the problems of tomorrow that may emerge for the handwriting examiner are open to speculation.

7.   What Is the History of the Teaching of Handwriting?[54]

The earliest culture that possessed formal schools was that of ancient Egypt. Private schools and private tutors taught children of the nobility, as the ability to read and write was a necessary complement to their social status. Working class children who showed some signs of intelligence were sent to district schools where they were taught to read and write by old pedagogues. Trade schools were available to teach job skills to the young.[55] Those educated in district schools might become apprentices in scribe offices. After years of training they could enter the profession of a scribe, a highly regarded position. Scribes escaped the physical torment that the working class normally received. They could become notaries, writing letters and contracts for the illiterate, or even achieve a position in administration, or in the house of a wealthy person.

Teaching and training methods were not highly developed. Students memorized the names of designs of the written symbols and were given samples to copy. The copies were corrected and returned to the students who continued to practise until they mastered the art. There is no evidence that any other methods were ever employed or attempted for the teaching of handwriting.[56]

These methods were used for the teaching of the hieratic or demotic forms of Egyptian writing. Hieroglyphic inscriptions, that were matters of drawing and carving rather than writing, were also taught, but their use was restricted to the priestly or royal classes for official works.

Various cultures were propagated over the next few centuries, and with them went organized education. Greece was the next major culture, however, to display an educational system of any merit. While the elements of physical education were the focus of the Spartan civilization, Athens concentrated on education in the areas of language and thought. One of the first things taught to any student, in the three major areas of language and grammar, mathematics, and gymnastics, were letters. Earliest teachings in Athens (700 to 650 B.C.) were likely limited to professional schools for priests and poets. These scribal schools were limited to the wealthy and operated within a system of individual tuition.[57-58]

Solon, an early Greek lawmaker, made the learning of letter forms compulsory in the early sixth century B.C. The financial contribution of the parents determined the rate and extent of education for the student.

With the expansion of Greek trading, a wider need for reading and writing developed, particularly among the merchants, for the keeping of records and accounts. The teaching of other subjects began to be combined with the teaching of letters. By the end of the fifth century B.C., a knowledge of his letters became a man's irreducible minimum of education.

In school, students, who were generally boys seven years old, were required to memorize the names of each of the letters, learn the appearance of the letter forms, and how to spell certain syllables. The syllables grew in complexity and eventually were combined into words. The students learned to form letters with a stylus on tablets of wax, following a light outline prepared by the schoolmaster. When familiar with the movements necessary to execute the letter forms, the student was given a sample of good penmanship to emulate and was required to practise repeatedly, not unlike the requirements of present day copybooks. Speed and quality were encouraged.[59-60]

When the Romans conquered Greece and eventually adopted much of the Greek culture, they assumed many of the educational methods for writing as well. Reading and writing in Rome became much more commonplace than in any previous culture. Literacy became accessible to the common man, owing to the low cost and availability of reading and writing materials.

With the decline of Rome and the onset of the medieval ages, the churches became the last stronghold for formal education.[61] Book learning and the ability to read and write were, almost exclusively, the property of the church schools. Rome's stabilizing central force dwindled. Barbarians and kingdoms came and went. Learning received no encouragement and was of little use, except in the church. Even among the clergy, it was by no means universal.[62]

Prior to 800 A.D., the ability to write, outside of the clergy, was limited and existed almost exclusively within the upper class or their scribes. Even then, contracts and the like were often made verbally for want of notaries. The clergy discouraged education outside of church dogma; the warfare of the nobles didn't require it, and the masses were ignorant of it.

The sole bright spot in education during the Dark Ages was Charlemagne. His work and that of Alcuin, whom Charlemagne recruited around 800 A.D., saved much of the world's literature and the art of writing. Not until the late twelfth century, however, did order begin to arise out of the chaos of the Middle Ages. Political stability became established. The emphasis on chivalry encouraged a higher moral standard and increased manners, courtesy, and literary taste. Among the nobilities emerged a desire and use for the ability to read and write.

Municipalities emerged from the confusion of the feudal system. In more secure surroundings, industry and trade increased and brought a need for better education. By the thirteenth and fourteenth centuries, the magistracy of many cities established schools to teach the basics: reading, writing, and reconing. Although it still taught in Latin, the church opened its writing schools to some laymen.

From the fourteenth to sixteenth centuries education experienced a renaissance, as did most other aspects of culture; yet in all these years of development and growth, writing was still being taught in much the same way it had been taught 2,000 years earlier.[63] The only major differences were in the designs of letters (national hands replaced hieratic or Greek majuscules) and in writing materials (ink, quill pens, and parchment instead of wax tablets and papyrus). Although great strides were made by the educators of the Renaissance in the instruction of the arts and sciences, handwriting was still taught by the tracing and copying method.

The first writing manual entitled *La Operina* was printed in Italy by Lodovico Arrighi in 1522.[64] While providing little in new teaching methods, it introduced the prospective writer to two basic strokes with which to begin any letter, and then introduced the letters in groups of physical similarity. It was, however, the first formalized copybook.

The end of the sixteenth century saw the development and rise of the modern current hand, replacing the previous disjointed cursive writing. Instruction in handwriting began to vary, but primarily by style of letter design rather than method of teaching. Consequently, an educated Englishman, for example, would be master of two hands — an indigenous running Secretarie hand and an italic. From this evolved the writing master, each with his own preference in copybooks, or possibly with his own, more or less unique, copybook.

One of the first copybooks used on this continent was published in London, in 1570, by John de Beauchesne and John Baildor. This endeavour, entitled *A Booke Containing Divers Sortes of Hands, as well as the French Secretarie with the Italian, Roman, Chancelry, and Court Hands*, illustrated 37 diverse styles, including such extravagances as Secretarie, written in reverse to be read with a mirror.[65] About a dozen different copybooks were printed during early colonial times.

The earliest record of the teaching of writing in America was by William Brewster. He was the only member of the Pilgrims with a university education. Accordingly, he was given responsiblty for the education of the Plymouth children. He taught them an italian script, that he learned at Cambridge, by the outmoded methods of tracing and copying. The Massachusetts Bay colonies were conducting similar practises. The major problem of the schoolmasters in teaching handwriting was to bridge the gap between the handwriting of their forefathers, that exhibited variations and hybrids of the Italic and Gothic hands, and the Roman letters being used in printing fonts.

A hybrid called new mixed current, speedy Italian, or Italian Bastarde was the next major copybook style to emerge. The copybooks of Gianfrancesco Cresci and Lucas Materat spread the usage of this style throughout Britain and the colonies, with the assistance of the publishing efforts of Edward Cocker. Again, this publication championed a new letter style but no new teaching procedures.

By the middle of the seventeenth century, the Italic form became the form of choice. Secretarie had all but disappeared and Gothic was maintained for decorative purposes only. Instruction was conducted by writing specialists called writing masters, who gave lessons in public or private. They taught how to sit, how to position the paper, and how to hold and move the pen. They demonstrated the strokes of letters, the designs of letters themselves, and eventually, words and sentences. The master would set the copy in the student's book by writing an example for that lesson at the top of the page, which the student was required to copy repeatedly as well as he could.

The acquisition of the skill was held in sufficiently high esteem to foster separate schools for the art of writing. Boston had one public writing school by 1684. By 1720, it had two grammar schools and three writing schools. The maintenance of materials and the setting of copy, however, generally made such demands on the writing master's time that it precluded any great measure of individual attention, especially in public schools. The development and spread of ruled paper, steel pens, printed copybooks, and tax-supported schools, however, soon helped alleviate some of the problems.

With the spread of printed copybooks, new teaching ideas emerged, and the first self-help writing manuals appeared. The earliest copybook published in America was printed in Philadelphia by Franklin and Hall in 1748. It was called *The American Instructor* or *Young Man's Best Companion*. An earlier edition, by George Fisher, was well known in England. The first truly American copybook offered was Isaih Thomas's *The Writing Scholar's Assistant*, published at Worcester in 1785. It was aimed principally at those wanting to develop a useful round hand. In 1668, in London, one of the earliest attempts at a systemized method of teaching writing was published by Edward Cocker and called *England's Penman*. This book broke the letters down into strokes between turns or breaks. These strokes were practised separately first and then combined into whole letters. In 1714, John Clark authored a book that advocated another system. Clark pointed out that the Round hand forms were composed of the oval and the straight line, and that "l," "o," "n," and "j" were the fundamental letters.

The most original handwriting teaching system to appear, however, was that by John Jenkins, which emphasized the idea of principal strokes, not full letters and not strokes between turns and breaks. In *The Art of Writing*, published in Boston in 1791, Jenkins offered a system of six strokes that could be combined in various orientations and combinations to create almost all of the alphabet.[66] This was the core of his system and the highlight of its originality. Jenkins would drill his students on the execution of these principal strokes, then on the combination of them into letter forms. In the teaching of handwriting, this systemization marked one of the first truly original and significant changes in over 2,000 years. Offshoots of the Jenkins system appeared later, including Henry Dean's *Analytical Guide to the Art of Penmanship* (1804) and Allison Wrifford's *A New Plan of Writing Copies* (1810).

The next substantial change in the teaching of writing occurred in 1809 with the development of the flowing forearm style by Joseph Carstairs.[67] In this system, writing was not just the movement of the hand or fingers but was taught primarily as a movement of the whole arm. This movement took precedent over letter forms. Among the claims for the system were the freedom from writer's cramp, and an effortless, tireless writing. In the teaching of this method, the fingers were first taped into position around the pen, and the basic strokes and letter designs were practised. Once the strokes and designs were mastered, the hand was freed to allow the better execution of details. It was advertised as being possible to learn in 20 one-hour lessons, if the pupil practised 6 to 12 hours per day.

In the United States, the foremost advocate of the Carstairian system was Benjamin Franklin Foster. His work, *Practical Penmanship Being a Development of the Carstairian System*, published in Albany, N.Y. in 1830, was a significant influence in both America and Britain. He recommended the instruction of fundamental movements (arm, forearm, and hand) separately first, and then their combination into the writing movement. During the 1850s, however, Foster switched his allegiance from Carstairs to the system of Henry Dean, a Jenkins disciple.

The 1820s and 1830s saw an increase in the emphasis on legibility and efficiency. The increased importance of writing for strictly business affairs made perseverance and speed more desirable qualities. There was a greater emphasis on "mercantile" penmanship, sometimes referred to as the *scientific, practical, business,* or *commercial* hands. Exploitation began to be exhibited in this field, as was evident in the following advertisement from the *American Traveler* in 1832, placed by a Mr. Duhertis:

> "(Writing) taught with certainty and ease in six lessons of one hour each (that is in as long a time as is perfectly possible with due reason, regardless thereby of the insinuation manifested by prejudice or slander)…. Strangers…can be finished in two days by taking three lessons a day, or in one day, by attending for the space of six hours!!!"[68]

The exception to the emphasis on legibility and efficiency in the business hands was that made for ladies writing and for ornamental writing, but these writings were also taught by the copybook system.

The 1840s introduced a new emphasis and a new term: muscular movement. This system emphasized forearm movement. The arm rested on the muscle pad below (i.e., distal to) the elbow. Its use was continued through the 1850s and has even influenced many modern systems. In the late 1840s, Platt Rogers Spencer, a self-taught writing master, proposed a flowing swing to what was primarily a Fosterian system and thus, introduced the first Spencerian system, which he had been designing and developing since 1820.[69] Assisted by Victor M. Rice, Superintendent of Public Instruction for New York State, the Spencerian system gained widespread popularity, and became the basis for many of America's present systems.

This Spencerian system was the major system taught in America, until about 1890. The course of instruction began with the introduction of the student to the letter designs and names. As they memorized the names, the students also became familiar with the designs by tracing over large copies of the letters with their finger. The first skills taught were fundamental strokes and movements for the pen. The letters, except for the flourished capitals which required a free arm, were taught to be executed with a free forearm movement while resting the arm on the edge of the desk. When the fundamental strokes were mastered, the students were required to copy the letter forms in the copybooks. To aid the learning writer, horizontal guidelines (like a musical staff) and vertical sloping lines were sometimes printed on the practise paper

Starting in about 1890 and lasting for about 10 years, a new system sprang up across the country — vertical writing. Its advertised merits, probably the reason for its fast spread and wide acceptance, were claims to better hygiene for the writer. It was said by proponents of the vertical writing system that slanted writing, with its complex forms and flourishes, induced the pupil to sit crooked and to crane his neck. The simple design and nonslanted style of the vertical system were claimed to assuage the bad posture and poor eyesight caused by the slanted systems. In a few years of use, these claims were found to be totally untrue, and the vertical system was dropped almost as quickly as it had been accepted.

Shortly after 1900, most schools returned to teaching a kind of slanted or semislanted writing, frequently Spencerian, with or without a supplementary vertical system. The continued emphasis on speed in business writing, however, re-established an old and familiar problem. The elegant flowing forms of the Spencerian system, although somewhat simpler than formerly, could be gracefully formed only when drawn. Under the pressure of the speed required in business writing, they tended to be somewhat distorted and difficult to read and write. This led to the last major profound development in cursive handwriting systems of the twentieth century — the Palmer system.

A. N. Palmer had been trained in writing at the G. A. Gaskell Business College, that taught a Spencerian-type system. In about 1880, after teaching penmanship at a business college, he entered the business world. Thereupon, Palmer encountered for himself the problems of speed and legibility. Dissatisfied, Palmer went back to the teaching world with an idea for a new and better business handwriting system. Although based largely on Spencerian, he designed a hand in which the flourishes and shading were quite moderate. He emphasized a free lateral motion of the muscular movement, but reduced excess arm movement in the vertical direction. He implemented finger extensions for lengthened stems and loops. After a period of testing, the Palmer Business Hand was adopted by New York City in 1905 and soon spread across the country.

Since then many new writing systems have been published and adopted around the country. With the exception of the addition of some imposed rhythm, none of these systems have exhibited any significant or fundamental differences from the teaching methods of Palmer.

In 1960, Virgil Herrick conducted a study of 19 commercial systems of handwriting instruction that represented over 95 percent of the systems in use in the United States at that time.[70] These systems generally reflected common agreement on methods and objectives. Almost all employed a systematic introduction and practise of the letter forms, and employed some drawing experience to lead into writing tasks. There was only some variation in the order of systematic introduction to the various letters.

Herrick's study found that writing was taught as a tool for communication, not as an end in itself. Motivation for performance was provided by linking the handwriting task with work in other subjects. Legibility and speed were found to be emphasized, with little stress on letter quality beyond simple legibility. The parts of the letters were generally introduced and practised so that the student could recognize similarities in letter forms. Tracing and copying were still the most commonly found practise methods employed.

Herrick noted that the greatest dissimilarity in the systems occurred in the designs of the cursive forms of capital letters. There were as many as 10 designs for the same letter. (e.g., "F" and "R") For the most part, however, the differences were minor.

Even since Herrick's study, a number of additional systems have been recognized in the United States and Canada. In 1965, Beacom[71] catalogued 10 not mentioned by Herrick. In 1975, Towson[72] identified three others (MacLeans, Bailey and Stothers, and Trusler) that were extensively used in Canada. Their differences in form or teaching procedures from the previous systems, however, have been minor, and no new major variations have arisen and received widespread use. Most of the techniques for teaching handwriting have not changed significantly over the last 70 years. Purtell[73] described eight rather novel ones. Nevertheless, a great deal of information has been obtained in the fields of learning and skill acquisition, particularly handwriting skills. It is this plethora of new knowledge that has engulfed the field of handwriting instruction for most of the twentieth century, and promises to bring about the next significant changes in teaching methods.

8. What Systems of Writing (and Writing Systems Publishers) Are Known to Have Existed in the United States and Canada in the Last Half Century?

In our collection of material, 76 different systems or publishers of systems have been described or referenced. Samples have not been obtained for all of them, but in the group that we have seen the differences between many of them are not pronounced. The numbers of persons that may have been exposed to or taught any one of the systems is unknown and impossible to determine. Suffice it to say, the possibility of identifying, today, the particular system behind the writing of any individual of North American origin is extremely remote, if possible at all. The 76 different systems or publishers of systems are as follows:

The American Book Company
J. J. Bailey (Sir Isaac Pitman & Sons (Canada) Ltd.)
The Beckley-Cardy Company
The Bélanger System (Province of Quebec)
W. S. Benson & Company
Beta Books (publication used by Colorado private schools)
The Bobbs-Merrill Company
Bowman Noble (formerly Noble and Noble)
Cavanaugh-Myers
City of New York, Board of Education
Colonial, (American Southern Publishing Company)
Courtis-shaw
Creamer
D'Nealian (1978) (Scott, Foresman & Company)
C. E. Doner's Everyday Writing (Zaner-Bloser Co.)
Ecoles Chretiennes (Province of Quebec)
The Economy Company
The Forest-Ouimet System (Province of Quebec)
Frank Schaeffer Company
Freeman
Freres Maristes System (Province of Quebec)
Goodfellow
Graves
Graves-Prewitt
Haan-Wierson (Allan & Bacon Publishing Co, Boston)
I. Z. Hackman Company

Hall & McCreary Company
Hall-Savage
Harcourt Brace Jovanovich (HBJ) Publishers
Harlow Publishing Corporation
Harr Wagner Publishing Company
Hausam
Hayes Publishing Ltd. (Burlington, Ontario and Niagara Falls, N.Y.)
Jenn (Jenn Publishing Co., Louisville, KY)
Kelly-Morris
Kirk-Freeman
Kittle
Laurel Book Company
Lister
Locker
Lyons and Carnahan (Lyons & Carnahan, Meredith Corp. Chicago)
McGraw-Hill (Webster McGraw-Hill Book Co.)
H. B. MacLean Method
McDougal Little & Company
E. C. Mills System (Rochester)
New Laurel
Noble & Noble Publishers, Inc. (Later Bowman Noble)
Nystrom
A. N. Palmer Company
Peed
The Peterson Directed Handwriting System (MacMillan Publishing Co.)
Pitman Publishing Company (Also produced Bailey System)
Public School Publishing Company
Putnam-Mills
Reason to Write (A publication used by Colorado private schools)
Reid-Crane
Rice
Rinehart
R. E. Rowe
Scott, Foresman Company (publishers of the D'Nealian System)
Chas. Scribner's Sons
E. G. Seale and Company
Self Development (Educational Self Development Inc., Greensburg, PA)
Les Soeurs de la Congregation system (Province of Quebec)
Silver Burdett (Silver Burdett Co., Morristown, NJ)
Spirit Masters
A. F. Sprott's Metronomic System (Sir Isaac Pitman & Sons (Can.) Ltd.)
SRA (Science Research Associates, Inc., Chicago)
Steckbaugh (A publication used by Colorado private schools)
Steck Company
Steck-Vaughn (formerly the Steck Company)
Stone, Smalley & Cooke, (The Bobbs-Merrill Company)
C. E. Strothers & J. W. Trusler

Tamblyn
Waldorf (their own system, in Colorado)
Zaner-Bloser Company

Members of the American Society of Questioned Document Examiners have, on occasion, canvassed the state schools in the United States to compile a record of the writing systems adopted for use within the schools. Nine of the 28 states responding to the last survey (1993) reported that no specific system was then required to be followed by the teachers of the state schools. The other 19 states cited a wide assortment of the systems named above as the systems they recommended.

References

1. Thomassen, A.J.W.M. and Teulings, Hans-Leo H.M., "The Development of Handwriting" *The Psychology of Written Language*, M. Martlew, ed. (New York: John Wiley & Sons, 1983), p 181.

2. Allport, G.W. and Vernon, P.E., *Studies in Expressive Movement* (New York: Macmillan, 1933).

3. McNeil, E.B. and Blum, G.S., Handwriting and Psycho-sexual Dimensions of Personality. *Journal of Projective Techniques,* 1952; 16: pp. 476-484.

4. Fluckiger, Fritz A., Tripp, Clarence A., and Weinberg, George H., A Review of Experimental Research in Graphology 1933-1960, *Perceptual and Motor Skills,* 1961; 12: pp 67-90.

5. Herrick, Virgil E., *Handwriting and Related Factors, 1890-1960* (Washington: Handwriting Foundation, 1960).

6. Herrick, Virgil E. and Okada, Nora, "The Present Scene: Practices in the Teaching of Handwriting in the United States," *New Horizons for Research in Handwriting.* Virgil E. Herrick, ed. (Madison: University of Wisconsin Press) 1963, pp 17-32.

7. Askov, Eunice, Otto, Wayne, and Askov, Warren, A Decade of Research in Handwriting: Progress and Prospect. *Journal of Educational Research,* 1970; 69: pp 100-111.

8. Peck, Michaeleen, Askov, Eunice, and Fairchild, Steven H., "Another Decade of Research in Handwriting: Progress and Prospect in the 1970s," *Journal of Educational Research,* 1980; 73: pp 283-298.

9. Huber, R. A., *Quarter Century Search and Survey.* Presented at the annual meeting of the American Society of Questioned Document Examiners (Crystal Bay, Nevada, 1983).

10. Baier, Peter E., Hussong, Jürgen, Hoffman, Elisabeth, and Klein, Michaela, *The Mannheim Bibliography of Questioned Document Examination, 1987 (1986 and 1985)* (Mannheim University).

11. Herrick, Virgil E., ed. *New Horizons for Research in Handwriting* (Madison: University of Wisconsin Press, 1963).

12. Thomassen, A.J.W.M., Keuss, P.J.G., van Galen, G.P., and Grootveld, C.C., eds. Motor Aspects of Handwriting — Preface, *Acta Psychologica,* 1983; 54: p 1.

13. Keele, S.W., Movement Control in Skilled Motor Performance, *Psychological Bulletin,* 1968; 70: pp 387-403.

14. Adams, J.A., Issues for a Closed-Loop Theory of Motor Learning. G.E. Stelmach, ed., *Motor Control Issues and Trends* (New York: Academic Press, 1976).

15. Schmidt, R.A., A Schema Theory of Discrete Motor Skill Learning. *Psychological Review,* 1975; 82: pp 225-260.

16. Schmidt, R.A., The Schema as a Solution to Some Persistent Problems in Motor Learning Theory. G.E. Stelmach, ed., *Motor Control: Issues and Trends* (New York: Academic Press, 1976).

17. Connolly, K. and Elliott, J., The Evolution and Ontogeny of Hand Function. N. Burton Jones, ed., *Ethological Studies of Child Behaviour* (Cambridge: Cambridge University Press, 1972).

18. Cormeau, Veighe-Lenelle M., Distrait, V., Toussaint, J., and Bidaine, E., Normes de vitesse d'écriture. Étude statistique de 1844 écoliers Beiges de 6 à 13 ans, *Psychologica Beigica*, 1970; 10; pp 247-263.

19. Goodnow, J.J. and Levine, R.A., The Grammar of Action: Sequence and Syntax in Children's Copying. *Cognitive Psychology*, 1973; 4: pp 82-98.

20. Rhodes, Edward Franklin, "The Implications of Kinesthetic Factors in Forensic Handwriting Comparisons," (graduate thesis for the University of California, 1978).

21. Champion, Joseph, *The Parallel of Comparative Penmanship Exemplified*, 1750.

22. Diringer, David, *The Alphabet, A Key to the History of Mankind*. 3rd Ed., Vol. 1. (London; Hutchinson & Co. Ltd., 1968, pp 473.

23. Diringer, David and Freeman, H. *The Alphabet Throughout the ages and in All Lands*. Staples Alphabet Exhibition (London: Staples Press Ltd, 1953).

24. Ogg, Oscar, *The 26 Letters* (New York: Thomas Y. Crowell Co., 1959).

25. Diringer, David, 1968. Op. Cit., pp 473.

26. Humphreys, Henry Noel, *The Origin and Progress of the Art of Writing* (London: Day & Son, 1855), pp 178.

27. Diringer, David, 1968, op. cit.

28. Humphreys, Henry Noel, 1855, op. cit.

29. Diringer, David, 1968, op. cit.

30. Ogg, Oscar, 1959, op. cit.

31. Diringer, David, 1968, op. cit.

32. Mercer, Samuel A. B., *The Origin of Writing and our Alphabet, (A Brief Account)* (Luzac & Co. Ltd., 1959).

33. Diringer, David, 1968, op. cit., p 145.

34. Mercer, Samuel A. B., 1959, op. cit., p 23.

35. Irwin, Keith Gordon, *The Romance of Writing, from Egyptian Hieroglyphics to Modern Letters, Numbers and Signs* (New York: Viking Press; 1967), p 32.

36. Fairbank, Alfred, *A Book of Scripts*, 3rd ed. Harmondsworth (Middlesex Eng: Penguin Books, 1955), p 7.

37. Diringer, David, 1968, op. cit.

38. Humphreys, Henry Noel, 1855, op. cit., p 110.

39. Tannenbaum, Samuel A., *The Handwriting of the Renaissance* (New York: Columbia University Press, 1930).

40. Thompson, Edward Maunde, *Handbook of Greek and Latin Palaeography* (London: Kegan Paul, Trench, Trubner & Co. Ltd, 1893), p 200.

41. Diringer, David and Freeman, H., 1953. Humphreys, 1855. Ogg, 1959. op. cits.

42. Diringer, David, 1968, op. cit., p 425.

43. Ogg, 1959, op. cit., p 174, and Gard, Carroll, "Writing, Past and Present." *The Story of Writing and Writing Tools* (New York: A. N. Palmer Co., 1937), p 321.

44. Gard, 1957, op. cit., p 39, and Ogg, 1959, op. cit., p 177.

45. Diringer, David, 1968, op. cit., p 426, and Ogg, Oscar, 1959, op. cit., p 174.

46. Tannenbaum, Samuel A., *The Handwriting of the Renaissance* (New York: Columbia University Press, 1930) p 111.

47. Ogg, Oscar, 1959, op. cit., p 184, and Humphreys, Henry, 1855, op. cit., p 153.

48. Thompson, Edward Maunde, *Handbook of Greek and Latin Paleography* (London: Kegan Paul, Trench, Trubner & Co, 1893). p 279.

49. Dawson, Giles E. and Kennedy-Skipton, Laetitis, *Elizabethan Handwriting 1500-1650* (New York: W. W. Norton & Co. Inc., 1966), p 7, and Tannenbaum, Samuel A., *The Handwriting of the Renaissance* (New York: Columbia University Press, 1930), p 13.

50. Tannenbaum, 1930, op. cit., p 13.

51. Dougherty, M. L., History of the Teaching of Handwriting in America. *Elementary School Journal,* 1917; 18: pp 280-286, and Nash, Ray, *American Penmanship 1800-1850.* American Antiquarian Society (Worcester, 1969).

52. Nash, Ray, *American Writing Masters and Copybooks, History and Bibliography Through Colonial Times* (Boston: The Colonial Society of Massachusetts, 1959).

53. Fairbank, Alfred, *The Story of Handwriting, Origins and Development* (Faber & Faber 1970) p 59.

54. Rhodes, Edward Franklin, "The Implications of Kinesthetic Factors in Forensic Handwriting Comparisons" (graduate thesis for the University of California, 1978).

55. Gillett, Margaret, *A History of Education, Thought and Practice* (Toronto: McGraw-Hill Co., 1966), p 19.

56. Bowen, James, *A History of Western Education, Vol. 1, The Ancient World: Orient and Mediterranean, 200 B.C. to 1054 A.D.* (London: Methuen & Co, 1972), p 15.

57. Beck, Frederick A. G., *Greek Education 450 to 350 B.C.* (London: Methuen & Co., 1964).

58. Smith, William A., *Ancient Education* (New York: Philosophical Library Inc., 1955) p 129.

59. Bowen, James, 1972, op. cit., p 80.

60. Cole, Luella, *A History of Education: Socrates to Montessori* (NY: Rinehart & Co., 1950), p 26.

61. Bowen, James, 1972, op. cit., p 315.

62. Williams, Samuel G., *The History of Medieval Education* (Syracuse, NY: C. W. Baedcen, Syracuse, 1903).

63. Cole, Luella, 1950, op. cit., p 213.

64. Fairbank, Alfred, *The Story of Handwriting, Origins and Development* (London: Faber & Faber Ltd., 1970) p 48.

65. Nash, Ray, 1959, op. cit., p 3.

66. Jenkins, John, *The Art of Writing* (Cambridge: Flagg & Gould, 1813).

67. Dougherty, M. L., History of the Teaching of Handwriting in America *Elem. Sch. J.,* 1917; 18: pp 230-286.

68. Nash, Ray, *American Penmanship 1800-1859* (Worcester: American Antiquarian Society, 1969), p 55.

69. Ibid., p 65.

70. Herrick, Virgil, Comparison of Practices in Handwriting Advocated by Nineteen Commercial Systems of Handwriting Instruction. *Committee on Research in Basic Skills, University of Wisconsin* (Madison, Wisconsin, July 1960), pp 111.

71. Beacom, Mary S., *A Survey of Handwriting Systems by States and Territories in the U.S.A.* Presented at the meeting of the American Society of Questioned Document Examiners (1965).

72. Towson, C. S., *Handwriting Instruction in Canada* (a paper distributed internally by the R.C.M.P. Crime Detection Labs, 1975).

73. Purtell, David J., Modern Handwriting Instructions, Systems and Techniques. *Journal of Police Science and Administration,* 1980; 8: 1: pp 66-68.

The Discrimination of Handwriting

3

9. What Is Handwriting Identification?

There are two fundamental fields of study pertaining to handwriting:

1. The study of handwriting as a neuromuscular activity, its development as a skill and the effect upon it of various internal and external factors.
2. The study of handwriting identification as a discriminatory process.

The second uses knowledge acquired through the first, but is entirely independent of it, therefore:

Handwriting identification is a discriminatory process.
Fingerprint identification is a discriminatory process.
Firearms identification is a discriminatory process.
Blood grouping is a discriminatory process.
DNA analysis is a discriminatory process.

Each is a discipline designed to study the respects in which human or material substances are similar or different in their chemical, biochemical, physical or psychological composition, or behaviour. Each studies a different kind of evidence to make discriminations.

Handwriting identification is a discriminatory process that derives from the comparison of writing habits, and an evaluation of the significance of their similarities or differences.

What has been commonly and frequently referred to as characteristics or writing features, or qualities are simply manifestations of the habits formed. They are the discriminating elements of handwriting.

Writing characteristics (i.e., habits) have been commonly described as being of one of two types: class characteristics (the products of prescribed writing systems) and individual characteristics (the particular idiosyncracies of the individual). Class characteristics were predominant in the writings of the first half of this century, when adherence to prescribed writing systems was strongly promoted in the educational programs. But the current move to mechanical and electronic communicative processes and the concurrent loss of concern

33

for writing excellence has meant that class characteristics are progressively less discernible and identifiable in the inscriptions of present day writers. Thus, writings have become largely a composition or combination of individual characteristics. Thus, it is claimed that they should be more readily discriminated from one another than when copybook was the writing design that everyone struggled to emulate.

All recognized authorities define a handwriting identification as, for example, the finding of "…the same distinctive personal writing characteristics … in both known and unknown writing in sufficient number that the likelihood of accidental coincidence is eliminated…," as Hilton[1] expressed it. Such definitions invariably contain a rider or condition to the effect that "…and there are no basic or fundamental differences between the two sets of writing…," as Hilton's does. This, of course, raises the question, what constitutes a fundamental or significant difference? Presumably, it would indicate that two writings, despite other similarities, would not have been executed by the same person. We have sought to answer this question, in part at least, in Section 16 that follows in this chapter.

These comments notwithstanding, the answer to the present question is: handwriting identification is a comparison of habits in writing behaviour and performance.

10.   What Is the Process Underlying Identification?

The careful and systematic use of evidence, which is common to the many disciplines of forensic science is directed toward the identification of an unknown. The process involves three distinct steps or stages,[2] although routines are so well engrained into the practises of some disciplines that the existence of the three divisions, and our progress through them often passes unrecognised. It has been tagged the Law of ACEs.

Analysis or Discriminating Element Determination.   The unknown item and the known items must, by analysis, examination, or study, be reduced to a matter of their discriminating elements. These are the habits of behaviour or of performance (i.e., features or characteristics and, in other disciplines, the properties) that serve to differentiate between products or people which may be directly observable, measurable, or otherwise perceptible aspects of the item.

Comparison.   The discriminating elements of the unknown, observed or determined through analysis, examination, or study, must be compared with those known, observed, or recorded of the standard item(s).

Evaluation.   Similarities or dissimilarities in discriminating elements will each have a certain value for discrimination purposes, determined by their cause, independence, or likelihood of occurrence. The weight or significance of the similarity or difference of each element must then be considered and the explanation(s) for them proposed.

This process underlies the identification of any matter, person, or thing, by any witness, whether technical, forensic, or not. It is present in the recognition of personal property, familiar objects, friends, or relatives, although its conduct is so automatic that we are seldom aware of its existence. In determining the identity of unfamiliar substances or items, different scientific disciplines study different materials, or different aspects of the same material. Thus, the analysis, the examination, or the study differs with the discipline, and sufficient knowledge of the discipline is needed to appreciate what information the analysis, the examination, or the study should seek.

The comparison of elements, attributes, properties, characteristics, or qualities of items is probably within the competence of most literate people to conduct. Whether the data is numerical, chemical, physical, or graphical, the comparison is likely to be visual. Where populations of items are large or the data to be considered is extensive, modern technology may be engaged to assist.

The task of comparison, however, is more complex than it may seem to be. Any matter must be compared with like matters, apples with apples, oranges with oranges, so to speak. In handwriting examination, this means that discriminating elements must be compared with like discriminating elements. These are elements that are not only covertly similar in form or design, but rendered under similar circumstances. Handwriting executions are subject to change under the influence of different writing circumstances and conditions (see Chapters 8 and 9). Moreover, any discriminating element of handwriting may be influenced by the particular allographs (letter designs) and/or characters surrounding it. Consequently, comparisons of writing elements must take into consideration the influences of the pen movements (or pencil movements) preceding and succeeding them, or such other circumstances as may be responsible for or expected to produce subtle or gross changes in execution.

The evaluation of the significance of the similarities or differences observed in the comparison is, however, a matter that is peculiar to the particular discipline. It is the product of proper training and experience. It is the aspect of the process that distinguishes one discipline from another. It is the reason why an individual trained in one discipline is not necessarily competent to make judgments of evidence that may be pertinent to another. It is the essence of the argument as to why graphology and writing identification are not synonymous terms.

Evaluation is the target of much of the criticism of handwriting identification by lawyers and judges who are sceptical of the reliability of the process, as it is presently conducted. It is the reason underlying the call for empirical data to confirm the subjective judgments of practising examiners. It is a subject deserving of a reasonable and intelligent deliberation.

There is an absence of enough empirical data to assess the significance of a writing element, in terms of its expectancy in the writing of other persons. Because of this absence, examiners employ a set of homespun statistics that their study of writings and experience in writing examinations have provided. On the basis of these statistics, they make discreet judgments. The assessment of this significance, however, is not a simple matter of numbers reflecting the frequency of occurrence of a given feature in samples of writing.

Two properties, if not present and they frequently aren't, may alter evaluations substantially. They are fluency and intricacy of movement. When fluency is absent, the attributes of a signature may exhibit the symptoms of spuriousness. When intricacy is absent, the signature may be deceptively duplicated more easily. Intricacy, in the sense in which it is being used here, is what others[3] have referred to as complexity, with respect to pen movement or signature pattern. The importance of these properties of fluency and intricacy arises from the fact that the risk of spuriousness escaping detection in a signature or writing varies inversely with the magnitude in which fluency and intricacy are present. Intricacy in the writing movement is critical to the reliability of the process. Certainly, oversimplification of one's signature pattern reduces it to a series of loops or ovals, or to something that is little more than undulating horizontal lines. This is not uncommon with some writers inclined to stylize their executions. From the viewpoint of security in the signature, however, it provides models that have little in them to complicate the task of duplication.

Intricacy of movement or complexity of pattern is an aspect of writing identification that is seldom mentioned in books on the subject, but is potentially important. It is a reason why simple tabulations of the frequency of occurrence of the various discriminating elements of a signature cannot be used in probability calculations. They must first be weighted according to their contribution to a signature's self-defense. It is a factor affecting significance.

Its absence from the literature may be due to the lack of a method that may be employed to measure intricacy or complexity. How does one evaluate its quality, judge its degree, or appraise whatever it must have to support the assessments that an examiner has made respecting the significance of similarities or differences in intricate or complex movements?

It is axiomatic that complexity or intricacy provide evidence in support of genuineness, when comparison with standards reveals similarity. It provides evidence in support of spuriousness, when comparison with standards reveals difference. In both cases, however, the evidence must be appraised in conjunction with the presence or absence of fluency. It follows that significance in the evaluation of discriminating elements should vary directly with the intricacy or complexity of the element of writing being considered.

Judgments of intricacy are, at present, subjective assessments for which there have been no guidelines. Under these circumstances, two or more examiners may not judge the intricacy of an element or of the signature in its entirety quite the same. Furthermore, one examiner's judgment may not be consistently the same on subsequent occasions. Accordingly, we would suggest five respects in which a signature, or a writing, may be judged to rate its intricacy or complexity:

1. *The aggregate line length.* Generally speaking, the longer the line the more complex the design. There are, of course, some stylized signatures that contain lengths of strokes of no purpose. We are not referring to these.
2. *The number of pronounced directional changes in the line.* When directional changes are angles in the vicinity of 180° they constitute retraces. When less than 90° they may be departures in straight line movement or the commencement of curves. Many, if not most, of the directional changes in a writing will be due simply to allograph design, but here we are interested in those that are not attributable to copybook prescription.
3. *The number of overwritings.* Overwritings can be misleading as to stroke direction, and thus, confusing as to allograph construction. They may be one of two kinds, and for clarity, a distinction should be made between a retracing and a superimposition. We define a retracing as a line that is situated over another line, but is generated by pen motion in the opposite direction. A superimposition is defined as a line that is situated over another line and is generated by pen motion in the same direction. The stem of an "i" and the staff of a "t," when properly written are retracings. The tendency of some European writers to overwrite the bowls of letters in a circular pen motion (see Figure 9) is a superimposition. Both kinds of overwriting are common in the execution of capital letters in some signatures, although precision in the overwriting is not usually sought.

4. *The continuity of the pen movement.* The interruptions to continuity of the pen are pen lifts that are usually an advantage to the simulator as they provide a legitimate place to pause and consider the next move. However, a pen lift that reflects motion continuity, will have a tapered ending and beginning to the pen stroke as the instrument rises from and returns to the paper surface, without a distinct break in its travel (some call it a hiatus). This is more difficult for a simulator to duplicate in accurately aligning the elements of the stroke with one another and, at the same time, graduating the deposits of the medium used to generate the stroke.

5. *The repetition of well-segregated, complex pen motions.* Fluent and complex pen motions can be executed with ease, but only when natural and/or practised. Flawless replication of them is even more dependent on nature and/or practise. Complex pen patterns of the same design that are superimposed upon one another often conceal the evidence of spuriousness that would otherwise be available to consider. The segregation of complex patterns ensures that evidence of genuineness or spuriousness can be judged from the quality of the product.

Found and Rogers have suggested a seven-point criteria for judging intricacy or complexity that is, in some respects, comparable to ours. Readers will have their own views as to what makes a writing or signature complex or intricate and should endeavour to develop their own criteria. The objective is to construct a scale that will assist in the evaluation of similarities and differences observed in the signatures or writings, a scale that might supplement the conventional assesments.

The process of identification (the Law of ACEs) is a principle that the present authors have been espousing for nearly 40 years. It was advanced first in 1959,[4] and on four occasions since then. Essentially, the same process is delineated in different words in the description by Found and Rogers[5] of their model of the forensic comparison method, as conducted by their Australian laboratory. They use the terms *Subjective Feature Extraction* in place of our *Analysis.* They use *Comparison* and *Decision as to Similarity or Difference* for our *Comparison,* and *Propose Possible Explanations* and *Complexity Decision* rather than our *Evaluation.* Hardy and Fagel[6] in their description of the three phases of the identification process, followed by laboratories in the Netherlands, employ the language *Analysis of traces or objects, Comparison of the analysis results,* and *Determination of the relative individuality of the characteristics.* This is language more like ours.

It is frequently asked, Can writing identification be refined to be a more objective study? This is a question that many examiners have avoided and perhaps for good reason. Writing is a dynamic aspect of human conduct, undergoing constant, but not always discernable change, subject to numerous influences and differing degrees of natural variation. In this ever-changing world, empirical data respecting the writers of today, if it was available, may not be precisely applicable to the writers of tomorrow. Every population of significant size alters daily.

The pursuit of objectivity, that Hilton[7] described as "the calculation of a measure of reliability" in writing studies, is beset by at least three hurdles (1) natural variations, (2) the unknown interdependence or independence of discriminating elements, and (3) the absence of scales for the measurement or classification of some elements, such as writing quality, fluency or line quality, pen pressure, and some movements. At present and at best, these matters can only be subjectively estimated over some broad categorization.

Harrison[8] seems to share Hilton's views and goes so far as to condemn schemes for "the comparison of writing based on measurement of general features or on some system of scoring points for and against" as being worthless. In his view, such schemes will fail to appropriately consider differences, if and when present, that can be vital to the assessment of writings. Nevertheless, the pursuit of objectivity should not be thought entirely futile. It seems so only because, until the arrival of the computer in the last 20 years, little thought and endeavour had been applied to a task that appeared formidable.

We have cited Trueblood elsewhere as saying:

"The fact that we do not have absolute certainty in regard to any human conclusions does not mean that the task of enquiry is fruitless. We must, it is true, always proceed on the basis of probability, but to have probability is to have something. What we must seek in any realm of human thought is not absolute certainty, for that is denied us as men, but rather the more modest path of those who find dependable ways of discerning different degrees of probability.[9]

Our own comments, made in 1972, ran along the lines:

"Modern technology and recent advances in scientific fields have done no more and no less than enable us to make closer approximations to the truth, whatever it may be."

Further thoughts on the subject are contained in Section 73: Science and Scientific Method and are offered to stimulate thought and to prompt action.

11. How Is Handwriting Identification Taught?

There are four instructional methods that have been employed either discretely or in combination to develop handwriting examiners: self instruction, correspondence courses, apprenticeship programs, and university courses.

Self instruction was the process, and the only process available, by which most of the practitioners of pre-World War II (1939) learned the business. It launched the likes of Hagan, Ames, Frazer, Hingston, Osborn, Zinnel, Stein, Tyrrell, Harris, Walters, Cassidy, and others on their careers, with some help accruing from the fact that many of them were accomplished penmen or penmanship teachers to begin with. Certainly, as Hilton[10] pointed out, self instruction is the most arduous and least reliable learning process over short periods of time.

Correspondence courses have been the means by which most persons learn the field of graphology. From this, many have subsequently branched out into the arena of handwriting identification or even the broader field of document examination, with or without further instruction. This too, is an unreliable process of learning handwriting identification and subject to many pitfalls. As we stated earlier, the two fields are not synonymous.

University courses directly related to handwriting identification are offered by some European universities, frequently within the schools of psychology. The programs currently offered by universities on the North American continent are not specifically directed at handwriting identification or document examination, but some do offer what has been described as introductory courses. There are good reasons why programs have not been developed, most of which arise from the limited job opportunities for interested students and the absence of funding for an academic program. Others have argued for the need of active case work on which the apprentice can hone his skills, and the problems arising from the handling of physical evidence within an academic facility. This argument may not now be entirely valid, however, as the program of fabricated tests, developed by the Collaborative Testing Services over recent years, have proven to be practical and representative of the questioned document field. They offer a credible alternative to actual cases that can duplicate most case situations other than the unpredictable.

Apprenticeship was the process that started the practitioners like Ordway Hilton, Donald Doud, Albert S. Osborn, Paul Osborn, Jim Conway, and others in the post-World War II era. It continues to be, almost exclusively, the process by which the current crop of document examiners have grown, developed, and matured. It is invariably the process, combined with university courses. Courses, by themselves at this point, do not provide a complete program.

In the apprenticeship system, handwriting identification is currently learned through programs that invariably have six standard components:

1. A reading component, during which the student is required to read for him/herself the standard texts of Osborn, Harrison, Hilton, Conway, and perhaps a few others.
2. A writing component, requiring the student to produce essays on prescribed topics, the nucleus for which is found in the texts and in published and unpublished papers of examiners, many of which have been presented at national and international meetings of examiners.
3. A practical component, during which the student is required to conduct examinations of actual or fabricated cases, to render conclusions and write reports, all of which is conducted under the direct supervision and regular review of a competent practitioner.
4. A mock trial component, during which the student is required to present a finding orally, to defend the results he/she obtained, and to demonstrate his/her ability to express him/herself convincingly.
5. An examination or test component, in which the student is required to undergo an examination to measure the scope and depth of his/her understanding and knowledge of the subject.
6. A court introductory component, in which the student gives testimony that is corroborated by the testimony of a mentor or examiner who has examined the same material and reached the same conclusions.

Many writers have bemoaned the lack of standardization in the training programs offered,[11] but little has been done to correct it. Few training programs include formal lecture components. Several reasons are offered for this. More often than not, training classes consist of one to three persons, and formal lectures do not seem to be appropriate under such circumstances. Moreover, formal lectures are thought to take much more of the lecturer's time, both in preparation and presentation. Manuscripts of lectures are not something that are produced or circulated. Another reason is likely to be that few of the accepted texts spell out the fundamentals of the work in a systemic fashion that articulates the rules, principles, concepts, and definitions, and provides the arguments or grounds in support of them. Indeed, the lack of unified articulation is one of the discipline's most serious shortcomings, a fault that this dissertation has been conceived to overcome.

Insofar as the apprenticeship programs with which we are familiar, the tendency is to outline a calendar of assignments, headings, or topics, that may be as few as 1 or as many as 25 in number. Perhaps, also, to identify certain resource material from which the apprentice is expected to extract and assemble information respecting a particular topic that is assigned. In this process, direction is limited, and the apprentice may not know whether the right information has been extracted from the resources until an examination or test or written requirement of some kind is imposed.

Furthermore, it is likely to be the case that tutors and their laboratories will possess different libraries of material. The information to be extracted will, therefore, vary from place to place. Without a consolidation or summary of the knowledge of the field, such as we are endeavouring to provide in this dissertation, neither the apprentice nor the tutor is aware of what or if important aspects of the subject are missing.

Almost invariably, these course outlines stipulate a time frame that should be devoted to the topic that may be a matter of hours, days, or weeks. There is little to indicate whether the time frames correlate with the complexity of the subject or with the extent of the resource material that the candidate is expected to cover. For example, one outline might suggest:

Handwriting Identification — 1100 Hours

The apprentice will learn the basics of handwriting identification ... to use the stereo microscope ... to take request handwriting standards ... to understand the procedures necessary to make accurate handwriting comparisons.

Another program outline, with a different breakdown, might stipulate:

Introduction, testing and orientation.	2 weeks
History, scope, examiner qualifications, current practitioners	
History of handwriting.	3 weeks
Alphabets, writing systems, teaching methods, noteworthy cases	
Class characteristics.	3 weeks
Influence of systems, nationalities, environment and occupation	
Handwriting terminology	
Individual characteristics.	4 weeks
Causes, variation, disabilities and other influences, features of writing identification, marks and signatures, lettering and numerals	
Identification.	4 weeks
Scientific method, the law of ACEs, inductive and deductive reasoning	
Proof of identity, and of non-identity, qualified opinions, foreign languages and alphabets	
Standards for comparison.	4 weeks
Types of standards, acquisition of specimens	
Microscopy.	2½ weeks
Instrument types, magnification and enlargement, lighting techniques	
Evidence of genuineness.	2 weeks
Indicative characteristics, external conditions	
Evidence of spuriousness.	4 weeks
Forgery methods and characteristics of signatures and extended writings	
Disguised and Miscellaneous writings.	5 weeks
Disguise, assisted signatures, initials, anonymous letters	
Graphology.	2 weeks
Basis, application, practitioners, organizations and Societies	

Without the benefit of much direction, the training enunciated by these programs, on paper, is little better than a correspondence course, although the time frames and course content may be different due to the accessability of a tutor and of a library of resource material.

Few training programs conduct closed-book examinations. It is generally thought that the subject is too broad, too varied, or too complex to expect a candidate to convert all that has been written to memory. It is also argued, that for practical reasons, supervised examinations without access to books are more inconvenient to conduct. Whether or not this open-book policy has any bearing on the calibre of the graduate is a moot point. Certainly there are facts and fundamentals of handwriting identification that should be well ingrained in the mind of the student of the discipline to which closed-book examinations might be directed. Furthermore, in the course of giving testimony there are questions from counsels and courts that are frequently encountered and oral answers will be expected that are clear, comprehensible, and convincing. These answers must be given without reference to a book. Accordingly, they must be learned well in training.

The apprenticeship system of industrial training seems to have originated in the Middle Ages. It was the recognized system of training for all skilled trades in England as early as the thirteenth century. It fell into disuse and was not revived until the era of World War I developed the need for skilled labour. As labour became organized, standards of training and programs of apprenticeship were developed for the evolution of trades and skilled crafts.

Apprenticeship is not a term normally encountered in the professions, although working experience arranged by some academic institutions is sometimes referred to as pupil apprenticeship. The association of apprenticeship with the trades and crafts rather than the professions, the limited involvement of lectures and academic instruction in these fields, and the sparsity of textbooks to facilitate the learning process may betoken the kind and magnitude of the task in the conversion of handwriting identification to a scientific pursuit, if conversion is possible at all.

The apprenticeship system of training document examiners has not been without its critics. Leson[12] maintained that it suffers from a major disadvantage in that without a standardized curriculum there is no guarantee that apprentices are being correctly taught or similarly taught. Without some means of qualifying the instructor and the course, the training process lends itself to the perpetuation of poor training methods. Baxter[13] went on to say that not only does the period of training vary from individual to individual, but also from the practise of one office or laboratory to another, because it is largely dependent upon the staff, the facilities, and the cases available for training purposes.

Many have written on the subject of the training and qualifications of the document examiner[14-25] and many of them have itemized a desirable course content, insofar as the topics to be included. Some of these papers have covered the selection of candidates and the skills required. None of these papers and presentations that have listed the topics have stated what particular knowledge is intended to be imparted to the apprentice within each area. Several persons have attempted to select and assemble courses from university curricula that might constitute an ideal background program, without suggesting which institutions may be in a position to offer such a program (see also Section 77: What must be done to make handwriting identification a science?).

Even the duration of the training program for document examiners lacks some consistency and varies from one and one-half to two and one-half years. By contrast, apprenticeship in many skilled trades runs two to five years and raises the question as to whether document examiners don't have as much to learn. This variation in the training program for document examiners is due, in part at least, to the time that the apprentice must spend on photography and miscellaneous subjects such as the various printing processes, photocopiers and facsimile reproductions (fax machines), and ink chemistry that different programs may include.

The manifold papers and publications that we have cited here exhibit a significant level of consistency in the scope of the recommended training program. A report (circa 1975) by a committee of the Southern Association of Forensic Scientists prescribing an In-Service Training Program for Document Examiners is as complete as any other in listing the topics to be covered and the time to be devoted to each. The apprentice, however, is simply referred to a collection of publications without specifying the issue, the book, the chapter, or the page wherein the particular knowledge he/she should be seeking may be found. Thus, the knowledge the candidate is expected to acquire is without perspective or direction. Other programs afford little more in delineating the principles, the concepts, the fundamentals, and the ideas that should mould the student's course of thinking, respecting the tasks of the handwriting examiner and their solutions.

We make our own suggestions as to the academic background that is useful to aspiring document examiners or students of handwriting in Section 77 (What must be done to make handwriting identification a science?). We offer this tome in which these suggestions will be found, together with the fundamentals of the work set out in a systemic fashion articulating the rules, principles, concepts and definitions, and providing the arguments or grounds in support of them, as the first of what is hoped will be many endeavours to articulate the facts and fundamentals of handwriting identification.

12.   What Are Class or System Characteristics in Writing?

> Definition: Class characteristics are those aspects, elements, or qualities of writing that situate a person within a group of writers, or that give a written communication a group identity.

The group of writers or writings in any given class may vary in size from small numbers to continental populations. It may have geographic, religious, national, academic, or political boundaries by which its writing can be related to some recognizable common content. Traditionally, class characteristics in writing have been conceived as limited to national and/or system characteristics, the latter being more often a subdivision of the former. The current concept, however, is much broader, as in the case of European writing or Hispanic writing. Furthermore, the writing systems that these classes represent (and there may be several) are more difficult to define and to discriminate between, if distinguishable at all.

Not too long ago, it was said that national characteristics constituted those class characteristics that serve to differentiate between the collection of systems that are popular in or peculiar to different countries. In view of today's constantly changing borders it may be preferable to say peculiar to different areas of the world. Remarkably enough, where languages and alphabets are similar, if not the same, one finds much similarity in the class characteristics of the writings. Thus, Russian and Ukrainian writings have much in common. German and Austrian writings have much in common.

When the quantities of a foreign writing being scrutinized are sufficient, one finds that the national characteristics within a class often give the material a distinctive pictorial countenance ensuing from the collective effect of its common characteristics. The precise causes of its appearance are sometimes difficult to determine because the effects are cumulative rather than particular.

To carry our exegesis a step further, in the traditional sense, class characteristics within a handwriting are those writing habits or features that emanate from the published and/or prescribed method (i.e., system) of writing that has been utilized in the learning process. In the more distant past they have been of two kinds (1) unique characteristics or features that serve to distinguish one method or system from another, and (2) common characteristics such as slope, spacing, height, proportions, and letter designs that are shared with other systems.

More recent practises have lead to greater duplicity in writing systems through the use of optional forms, rendering them more difficult to differentiate from each other. Then too, the liberties allowed in adherence to any prescribed system result in letter forms that may be readable, but not identifiable, with any particular system source. Consequently, the role of class characteristics in the agenda of handwriting identification, because of form differences prescribed and exhibited by different systems, has been greatly diminished if not completely demolished.

There are, of course, within many systems of writing employed on this continent, three distinct styles of writing: cursive, manuscript or script, and block lettering. If the cursive styles have tended to duplicate one another with optional forms, there is an equal amount of duplicity within the script and lettering styles.

Tytell[26] has gone to some length to summarize and to consolidate the definitions that examiners nurse regarding class and individual characteristics. Haywood[27] devotes time to defining the terms presumably for the purpose of determining which category the black "J" and "W" would occupy, about which McCarthy had written.

Found and Rogers[28] question the orthodox theory that the validity of a document examiner's opinion is based on his/her ability to distinguish between class and individual characteristics. They maintain that the basics of the "class/individual" theory hinges on the notions of (1) a copybook form, (2) a divergence from the form, and (3) an evaluation of the uniqueness of that divergence derived from the experience of the examiner. With this one might agree, if the theory is still applicable, but it isn't except in isolated instances.

The latitude now allowed in the learning and conduct of writing renders the class/individual theory almost impossible to apply, certainly insofar as signatures are concerned. This is not news. Harrison, and then Miller, told us 25 years ago or more that it is virtually impossible to correctly identify the system taught. Indeed, the more handwriting we see, the more we are inclined to believe, except for a few elements of some letter forms, most if not all discriminating elements of writing on this continent now fall within the old category and definition of individual characteristics.

There are some features that still reflect the attributes of particular writing systems. The structure or design of the capital letters "F," "B," "P," "R," "T," "W," and "Y" exhibit as many system variations as any letter, but the designs and shapes of the lower case letters "e," "i," "l," "s," and "t" provide little latitude for variation between systems. The majority of class differences are found in the designs and shapes of capital letters. Capital letters, however, constitute a small portion of the writings that come into question.

Accordingly, except for some general features that may differentiate the writings of different parts of the world, class characteristics are a thing of the past. They are seldom recognizable aspects of today's writings present in copious quantities, and particularly in signatures. The approach to writing examinations must be modified accordingly. The problem, respecting system characteristics, issues from the task of estimating the significance of these elements of a writing if and when appearing. This has always been a problem, even when system features were more exclusively the symbol of a particular writing method. The appropriate data (e.g., the popularity of the system) is no longer of great value. Admittedly, then, system and national attributes have some influence upon populations of people, but, except for a few letters, the influence is indeterminable.

The claim of Found and Rogers that, "There is no evidence that experience improves competence in or validity of judgments (of handwriting)," is surprising. There are numerous disciplines and activities that provide support for the hypothesis that competence or skill that requires an element of judgment is a function of experience. The landing of an aircraft and the parking of an automobile are examples. Admittedly, these activities involve different skills to those employed in handwriting studies, but as in any skilled performance, competence in judgment is simply possession of a certain knowledge and an ability to employ it. The point we would make is that if experience improves judgments in other disciplines, there is no reason why it would not do so in the judgment of matters pertaining to writing.

The validity of judgments of handwriting has been substantiated frequently and regularly by the practical examinations undertaken by candidates for membership in the American Society of Questioned Document Examiners, candidates for certification by the American Board of Forensic Document Examiners and other bodies, and the practical examinations afforded by other similar organizations around the world. These examinations, despite their lack of standardization, are designed to test the candidate's ability to differentiate and identify writers in fabricated situations in which the correct answers are known. Whether candidates are relying on class or individual characteristics or some combination of them, the success rates achieved are evidence that the process, poorly articulated as it may be, has some validity worthy of consideration.

Their final point is that the class/individual theory is not applicable to many signatures. This is not news nor cause to condemn the theory. It is an observation that signature identification, for a number of reasons, must be based frequently on individual characteristics alone. Poor quality extended writing may suffer from the same malady. Notwithstanding the absence of recognizable class, system, or national characteristics within a signature, however, the writing may well be identifiable with a particular individual. There is no practical reason for not doing so. Furthermore, although they may not be numerous, or present in many cases, there are still some system and national characteristics that are quite distinctive, that, if present, would provide some evidence of writers originating from the same or different locations.

Our interest in class characteristics, however, is precautionary. We are endeavouring to avoid overestimating or underestimating the value of these features. Despite the lack of precise information and the consequent need to judge any discriminating element conservatively, it is difficult to see where any error in the recognition of a particular class characteristic would significantly alter results.

The kinsmen to class characteristics are, of course, individual characteristics defined as those aspects, elements, or qualities of writing that distinguish between members within a group.

13.   What Are National Characteristics in Writing?

Definition: To the extent that writing systems within a country share common features and induce class characteristics in the writing of its people, that are different from the products of writing systems of other countries, such features are referred to as national characteristics.

Few document examiners have a large library of books on the writing systems of the different countries of the world. Yet, it would seem that a library of some sort is necessary if we are expected to know what the class characteristics are of systems taught on this continent and how they differ from other systems taught elsewhere. Although the subtle differences between systems are becoming more obscure because of present teaching practises, there are some more pronounced disparities between regions of the world of which one should be aware. We have listed some of them as factors influencing handwriting in Chapter 8, Section 37.

A number of authors from the U.S. Immigration and Naturalization (INS) Lab and the U.S. Postal Inspection Service Labs have recently reported on studies conducted of some 20,000 lettered samples from writers emanating from 77 countries, in an endeavour to provide some empirical data respecting as many as 62 different features of handlettering, including seven numerals.[29-32] The intent of the studies was to determine whether any of these features was peculiar to particular nationalities, or conversely, whether they were notably foreign to a given country.

The preliminary discussion of this research and of the reference material used in the INS (Immigration and Naturalization Services) collection provides an excellent comment regarding the impact of current immigration policies and practises on American handwriting. To this is added some recent data respecting the population of foreign nationalities and of persons using foreign languages in the U.S.A. The discussion also cites several recognized authors that have expressed themselves on the need for this kind of information.[33]

We note that the citations provided in support of the work refer to cursive writings. We have little information as to how or if lettering or hand printing varies from location to location. Among the 62 features considered, there are some 11 features that exhibited a cursive nature (in the letters "B," "C," "E," "G," "J," "Q," "R," "T," "V," "Y," "Z"), and seven numerals (1, 2, 4, 5, 7, 8, 9). These normally fall within the scope of cursive writing styles. Consequently, some useful information is provided that relates to the frequency of occurrence that might be expected of some of these features in the letterings and writings of persons of foreign nationalities.

The caution frequently expressed in the reports of these studies is that the information does not justify its use as a reliable indicator of the nationality of the author of a questioned text. No single feature or combination of features was found to isolate any particular nationality reliably. Furthermore, the samples were prepared on INS Forms I-94 by persons entering the United States. The circumstances under which this takes place are seldom ideal for the execution of writing or lettering. Variation from that which might be considered normal for the individual can be extreme.

14.   What Are Individual Characteristics in Writing?

Definition: As was said earlier, in general, individual writing characteristics are
defined as those discriminating elements that serve to differentiate between members within any or all groups.

Ordinarily, individual characteristics are thought of as those particular aspects or
features of writing that are peculiar to a specific writer.[34] In this sense, they possess a
character that is infrequently encountered. There are, however, a large number of more
commonly encountered elements of writing that may be described as the designs, inventions, and developments of the writer that, when considered in combination as a group,
give to a writing a uniqueness.[35] In this sense, it is the composition of the combination
that is responsible for the individuality the writing acquires. Although the expression is
broadly used and presumably understood, few authors have bothered to define it, perhaps
because the need has not been apparent.

Individuality is probably more often exhibited by writers in the execution of the more
complex letter forms. Some letters of our alphabet require complex movements of the pen
that many writers find somewhat difficult to execute. As a result copybook, or model letter
forms, are often slightly altered by the individual to a structure or shape more conveniently
performed. These modifications, sometimes subtle, sometimes profound, are the individual characteristics of that writer.

Because writing must be read, some conformity to copybook design must be furnished
which places limitations on the extent of divergence from accepted forms. The result is
that similar individual features may be found in the writing of other persons,[36] although
a particular group of such features is not likely to be duplicated. It is the group or
combination of such features, rather than any specific feature, that serves, ordinarily, to
distinguish one writer from another.

15.   What Are Accidentals in Writing?

There are occurrences in writing that may have little or no plausible explanation. They
may be unusual forms, shapes or movements, breaks in the writing line, even the doubling
of some letters or parts of letters. They are more often minor in nature, infrequent, and
of insufficient concern to the writer as to warrant attention or correction.

Definition: Accidentals are isolated, brief, or temporary digressions from normal
writing practises.

It is seldom that accidentals are noted or observed in writing standards. Rather, it is
a designation or label given to an element of a questioned writing that digresses significantly
from the normal and natural writing practises observed in the writing standards, and for
which there is no other plausible explanation. Its only qualification for receiving the
designation seems to be that it is different.

Some examiners have been known to refer to accidental occurrences as accidental
characteristics. This is, of course, a self contradiction, for their occurrence is not likely to
be repeated in a similar fashion, and thus, it is not representative or characteristic of any
aspect of a writing.

In the section to follow respecting fundamental and significant differences, we note and quote the general principle advanced by several of the accepted authorities. The principle is that as few as a single difference can offset the weight of a number of similarities in writing examinations and studies. Given the definition we now have for *accidentals*, we are pressed to resolve the question as to whether a single disparity between questioned and known writings constitutes an accidental in the writing of the same person or a dissimilarity indicative of a disparate writer.

The answer may rest in the opportunities the questioned writing provides for the occurrence to repeat itself. If opportunities are present and the occurrence is not repeated, the occurrence may be considered to be an accidental. If opportunities are present and the occurrence is repeated, it must be considered to be behaving as a writing habit, and thus, constitutes a dissimilarity. Obviously, the resolution of the question will hinge largely on the nature and extent of the questioned writing, in which the discrepancy occurs.

If, however, the nature and extent of the questioned writing is limited and opportunities for the occurrence to be repeated are not available, how does the examiner categorize and/or allude to the occurrence? In Section 30, the various aspects of writing that are considered and studied in writing examinations are listed and described. These are designated as the discriminating elements of writing that serve the purpose of a writing study whether for or against the identification of a given person with a particular written execution (because their meaning is often imprecise the use of terms such as *characteristics*, *qualities*, and *features* is avoided whenever possible). Elements of writing that cannot be categorized as to their evidential usefulness are indeterminable elements and remain so until additional writings clarify their character. Such is the destiny of accidentals and/or dissimilarities as long as their true character is in doubt.

16.   What Is a Fundamental or Significant Difference in Writing?

In a world of material things, virtually all things are different, if the examination of them is carried out at an appropriate level of precision. This is particularly so in the comparison of handwritings, for no two samples of the same text, by the same individual, with the same writing instrument, on the same date, and under the same writing and writer conditions will be identical in all respects. Such being the case, the document examiner or handwriting expert is constantly challenged by the same provocative questions, What is a difference and when does it become significant?

Much has been written on the subject of differences, but as McAlexander[37] points out, little has been provided to clearly establish for us what a fundamental difference is and what makes a difference significant. None of the widely recognized authorities on handwriting, Osborn, Hilton, Conway, Harrison, or Ellen, each of whom has spoken of differences and of the consideration they must be given, has provided definitions of the terms with which examiners might work. Osborn spoke of "divergences in amount and quality beyond the range of variation and not attributable to writing or writer conditions." He later says that writings by different persons will differ in some of the 27 particulars he lists. He then states that divergences in two specimens of writing may be found in "repeated individual or general characteristics" that will be indicative of different writers. None of the other authorities has been more precise.

Whiting[38] lamented the absence of adequate definitions in the literature and the imprecision of those that are offered to properly describe a fundamental difference, the term
that is only too often used. While we would agree with his criticisms, he has not provided
a better definition with which to work. We will make little progress, we submit, until the
topic of differences has been more completely addressed.

Differences in writing are one of two kinds. There are what we may call *lucid* differences: those that are markedly distinct in quality or character. They are obvious. Among
other things they include differences in allographs (i.e., letter designs), dimensions, slant,
or letter construction. There are also *elusive* differences: those that are much less pronounced, more subtle, that do not reflect basic changes in design or structure.

There is merit in referring to lucid differences as disparities and in addressing elusive
differences as divergences. Lexical definitions of these terms seem to make this selection
appropriate. A *disparity* then, is a more pronounced difference in writings, while a *divergence* is a less pronounced or more subtle difference. Osborn used the word *divergence* in
this fashion.

In Chapter 6, Section 30, we go to some length to list, organize, and describe all of the
21 aspects or attributes of handwriting that are employed in the identification of handwriting. We speak of and designate these 21 aspects or attributes of writing as being its
discriminating elements, an element being defined as anything that is a part of a complex
whole. Discriminating elements, then, are those parts of the complex whole of one's writing
that can serve to differentiate between writers.

We also find that of these 21 discriminating elements, at least 17 of them may be
segregated into one of two prime groups. First, there are seven elements of style, that
include arrangement, class of allographs, connections, construction (including design and
selection of allographs), dimensions, slant or slope, and spacings. Second, there are
10 elements of execution, that include abbreviations, alignment, commencements and
terminations, diacritics and punctuation, embellishments, legibility or writing quality
(including letter shapes or forms), line continuity, line quality, pen control, and writing
movement.

Elements of style are those aspects of writing that are usually subject to direction in
the learning or vocational process. Consequently, they are the aspects that may change
with location, change with the school or the teacher, or change with the occupation of the
writer. Elements of execution, on the other hand, are those aspects of writing in which
personal idiosyncrasies usually develop as a result of personal preferences, personal circumstances, and/or personal skills.

In a review of what has been said about differences, we find that *lucid* differences, or
disparities, occur largely in the elements of style, whereas *elusive* differences, or divergences,
occur largely in the elements of execution. It is also apparent that *lucid* differences, that
we now call disparities, occur in those aspects of writing that are more fundamental to the
writing process, whereas *elusive* differences, or divergences, are more personal aspects of
the writing.

Disparities, when they occur, are more often attributable to a difference in writers.
They are the distinctive and usually observable dissimilarities that emanate from different
teachings, different backgrounds, or different practises. They include changes in allographs.

On the other hand, divergences, when they occur, are often the products of variation
in the same writer, that may be either natural variation or variation due to some special
cause. Divergences may also be simply the respects in which two individuals, subject to

the same influences, teachings or backgrounds, may differ from each other in the manner in which they execute a writing movement or manipulate the writing instrument, without actually changing the basic forms or letter structures. They are the subtle mutations observed in the graphs within writers or between writers. It might be said that disparities are differences that discriminate between groups, whereas divergences are differences that discriminate between members of a group.

Fundamental differences, then, will be disparities, which are dissimilarities that occur with respect to the elements of style, rather than the elements of execution. Accordingly, a proper definition of the term *fundamental difference* should narrow its perspective to the elements of style. In practise, one finds that changes in the elements of style are often accompanied by changes in patterns of execution. To avoid confusion, the assessment of differences should consider first the disparities that may be present in the elements of style. If they exist, they might constitute fundamental differences. If and when there are dissimilarities present in the elements of style, divergences in the elements of execution may be expected and placed in proper perspective as additional evidence of a different writer.

With these interpretations in mind a useable general meaning for a handwriting difference may be offered as follows:

Definition: In a comparison of questioned and known writings, a difference in a (questioned) writing is (1) a disparity in one of its discriminating elements of style or (2) a divergence in one of its discriminating elements of execution; either of which exceeds the expected range of natural variation for these elements within the writings with which it is being compared. In either case, the difference is otherwise inexplicable.

While this definition tells us what a difference is, it does not suggest why it is. Differences that are found must be studied and considered with respect to possible causes. They may be due to causes that tend to affect the elements of execution, such as those (1) due to writing conditions or other external factors, or those (2) due to internal factors such as age, illness, drugs or medications, or they may be (3) due to some attempt to disguise or to deliberately alter normal writing habits. They may, on the other hand, be true differences that are attributable to some fundamental discrepancy emanating from a different writing hand, more often observable in the elements of style.

There are differences, then, and there are fundamental differences, that make writings dissimilar from one another. Both must be considered insofar as the aspects of writing in which they are found.

Our definition of fundamental difference would be:

Definition: In a comparison of questioned and known writings, a fundamental difference in a (questioned) writing is a disparity in one of its discriminating elements, within the elements of style.

We might have qualified this definition and said, usually within the elements of form to allow for those few occasions in which there may be special differences in elements of execution. For example, in such features as the location of quotation marks, that would normally fall within the category of punctuation, we find that in some countries, these may be aspects of the system of writing taught.

If we are now better equipped to identify or describe a difference, what then is a significant difference?

Significance with respect to similarities, which is the evidence required to facilitate an identification, is determined by the frequency of occurrence of a feature or writing element in the writing of different persons. Significance, then, is a function of its rarity or uniqueness. It is a circumstance that has a potential for measurement, simply by collecting the empirical data relative to that frequency. There is no empirical data to be collected, however, that provides corresponding information respecting differences. What would we seek to count to measure the importance of a difference? What continuum or scale could be used on which to rank differences? How, then, can a difference, any difference, be classed as significant? Are not all differences of equal significance?

Much of what has been written respecting differences by the recognized authorities on handwriting identification has sung a somewhat similar tune with which most examiners are familiar: that even a single difference can outweigh a number of similarities. Hilton[39] stated:

"It is a basic axiom of identification in document problems that a limited number of basic differences, even in the face of numerous strong similarities, are controlling and accurately establish nonidentity."

Then, he goes so far as to say:

"A single significant difference between the (known and unknown) specimens is a strong indication of two writers, unless the divergency can be logically accounted for by the facts surrounding the preparation of the specimens."

Harrison[40] made similar comments:

"...the fundamental rule which admits of no exception when handwritings are being compared...is simple — whatever features two specimens of handwriting may have in common, they cannot be considered to be of common authorship if they display but a single consistent dissimilarity in any feature which is fundamental to the structure of the handwriting, and whose presence is not capable of reasonable explanation."

Then later, the point is reiterated:

"The rule that a single consistent dissimilarity, irrespective of the number and nature of the similarities which are demonstrable must exclude any possibility of common authorship may seem harsh, but in practise, it is exceptional for handwritings by different authors to be found to differ in but one material particular."

Conway[41] expressed the same theme when he wrote:

"A series of fundamental agreements in identifying individualities is requisite to the conclusion that two writings were authored by the same person, whereas a single fundamental difference in an identifying individuality between two writings precludes the conclusion that they were executed by the same person."

The common thread that these writings seem to exhibit is the importance attributed to a limited number of differences, perhaps only one. In the views of these authors, all and any fundamental difference (i.e., disparity) appears to carry the same weight, the magnitude of which is sufficient to offset the weight of a number of similarities, regardless of their respective importance. Therefore, all differences must be deemed equally important and equally significant. If this line of thinking is correct there seems little need to pursue the question, What is a significant difference? Some differences, however, if not more significant are at least less disputable as being indicative of production by different writers.

17. What Circumstances or Conditions Might Contribute to the Production of Apparent Differences in Handwriting?

Osborn and others have generally agreed that despite numerous similarities in two sets of writings, a conclusion of identity cannot be made if there is one or more differences in fundamental features of the writings. Such statements have prompted the discussion above, in which we attempted to define a difference. If there are differences between writings, however, can we properly conclude that the writings are the products of different writers. Or, is it possible that some apparent differences are not true differences indicative of different authors, but simply variations of the same author resulting from extenuating circumstances?

The simple answer is, of course, yes. There are a number of extenuating circumstances that could be responsible. McAlexander and Maguire[42] have suggested a few. They, like most writers on handwriting identification have commented on the numerous changes in circumstances or conditions that may influence the written product, but few have ventured to say in what particular manners. To some extent this can be explained by the fact that, in the human experience, different factors can influence different people in different fashions. There are, however, some generalities that can be stated.

Adequacy of standards. In the pursuit of a reasonable explanation for the existence of an apparent difference in the comparison of questioned and known writings, the first consideration must be given to the adequacy of the standards to ensure that the full range of variations of which the writer is capable is represented. Not only must the standards be adequate in quantity, but they must be as contemporaneous as possible with the questioned writing. This is in order that the variables, due to conditions, circumstances, date, development, and maturity, of the writing will be controlled.

The contemporaneousness of the standards is the point most often proffered as the reason for apparent differences occurring in two writings. Because writing is susceptible to internal and external influences, the matching of circumstances between the questioned and known writings is vitally important. It can account for a difference in shape, in quality, or in particular movements.

Accidental occurrences. There are occurrences in writing that may have little or no plausible explanation. They may be unusual forms or movements, breaks in the writing line, even the doubling of some letters or parts of letters. They are more often minor in nature, infrequent, and of insufficient concern to the writer to warrant attention or correction. They are, frequently, completely erratic movements and may reflect a momentary interruption in neuromuscular coordination. Thus, accidental occurrences are best described as brief, temporary digressions from normal writing practises (see Accidentals in Section 15).

Alternative styles.   There are individuals that are said to be versatile writers, that have more than one style of writing, perhaps cursive and script or cursive and lettering. The second may be prompted by a particular type of occupation such as architecture that requires lettering. On occasion, relapses occur wherein a change will be made in a letter or a word. More often than not, these incidents will be observed in reasonably skillful executions of extended writing. Changes to a second distinctive style are not normally expected in writings, but are found in signatures on infrequent occasions, as Hilton illustrated. Other instances have been reported, as well, wherein such changes were accomplished. Whiting[43] describes and illustrates the differences in two styles of writing and signing executed by one individual using two identities. Confirmation that the two identities were, in fact, the same person was provided by a fingerprint comparison.

Without elucidating further on what was meant by *styles* or how they differed, Bohn[44] reported that the FBI Laboratory (or himself) had encountered "…frequent instances where one person can adopt or employ two or more entirely divergent styles or systems of writing…." He cautioned that for this reason the examiner "…must make a careful evaluation to determine whether an apparent difference is truly a fundamental difference…."

McCarthy[45] claimed that it is easier for a poor writer to consistently change letter forms while printing than it is for a highly skilled cursive writer, since habit is not so intrinsically established. For the unskilled person who prints, the act is not fluent but more in the nature of drawing.

Ambidexterity.   Some, but not many individuals, especially among those persons that have converted from sinistrals to dextrals at some point, have the ability to write with either hand with almost equal dexterity. In most respects, the written products are similar. Muscular coordination of the two hands and arms may not be precisely the same, however, and differences in fluency and some movements may be noted.

Since society and its educational systems now tolerate left-handed writing in children, the expectation is that in the future there will be a reduction in the number of ambidextral writers. Whether this occurs we will probably never know, for we lack the necessary data to tell us.

Carelessness or negligence.   Most writers have occasions when their writing degenerates to a scrawl or scribble due to haste, carelessness, or particularly poor writing circumstances. These executions are usually confined to short notes, addresses, and telephone numbers. Often they are inscribed on small note pads, envelopes, and segments of paper. They frequently contain elements of a person's writing that are unusual or accidental. They may never appear again in another example. They are unreliable indicators of normal writing habits or of a writer's normal range of variation.

Changes in health condition of writer.   Depending on its nature, changes in health may affect the fluency, rather than the designs of writing. The changes can be expected to be temporary, however, and writing facility will likely return with the recovery of health. The deterioration of health generally is another matter and its progress may vary with the individual. Its effect is usually observed in a loss of control and the introduction of more erratic movements. This is one of the aspects that has a bearing on the adequacy of standards.

Changes in physical condition of writer — fractures, fatigue, and weakness.   Fractures of the hand and arm, requiring restraints on mobility that inhibit the grasp of the instrument or the movement of the pen will, of course, alter the written product. When movement has been restricted for long periods, the full use of the member, when restrictions are removed, may not be immediately regained.

Our experience has included instances in which individuals suffered such serious injury to the writing hand or arm that he/she was obliged to rely on whatever ability could be developed hastily with the nondominant hand and arm. The quality of the writing is poor in such cases, but depending on the duration of the incapacitation, a measure of skill can be acquired. The differences in the writing should be obvious, of course, but as we have said elsewhere there are numerous writing habits that will persist in the writing of the nondominant hand.

Studies have also shown that fatigue and weakness have their effects upon the control of the writing instrument and its performance may be altered in unpredictable fashions. These too, are aspects that have a bearing on the adequacy of standards.

Changes in the mental condition or state of the writer.   As we have noted elsewhere, schizophrenics and/or persons with multiple personalities can exhibit major changes in their writing on different occasions corresponding to the mental state at the time. These are changes not so much in kind as in quality. A change to a childhood state will be accompanied by a corresponding childlike or immature quality of writing (see Influences on Writing: Instability).

Concentration on the act of writing.   Concentration on the writing act will, of course, render it to be a more conscious process, and consciousness steals from fluency. The action becomes more deliberate and slower. The change will be noted in line quality unless the reason for concentration is due to uncertainty as to the letters or text to be written that may interrupt the writing process more profoundly.

It is said that for some people the nature of a document can have an effect upon the writing of signatures applied to it. Certainly wills, mortgages, large contracts, and real estate transactions are significant events in the lives of many persons, and it is understandable that the signing of such documents will be a more conscious act than it is in signing many others. Nevertheless, no one ventures to describe precisely what that effect may be. In our casework experience, it has been similar to the effect of tension, duress, or concentration on the writing process that is evident largely in some loss of fluency and line quality. When care is exercised, there can be a greater respect shown for copybook styles (see Section 38: Intrinsical Influences).

Disguise or deliberate change.   Disguise or deliberate change will produce the more pronounced results. This will not be an isolated change, however, but will be the kind of modification that tries to exhibit itself throughout the writing. It is frequently suggested as an explanation for differences, but since it is an intentional change it is questionable whether it belongs in this particular part of our dissertation. We have chosen to deal with it in Section 52: The Disclosures of Disguise.

Drugs or alcohol.   See Section 38: Intrinsical Influences.

Influence of medications.   See Section 37(F): Extrinsical Influences.

Intentional change for later denial.   This subject has been dealt with under the caption of Autoforgery (see Section 49). There we describe the remoteness of an occurrence of this kind. Nevertheless, and notwithstanding the few instances in which a person might be disposed to fabricate an irregular signature of this kind, there are numerous other instances in which a faulty memory coupled with a minor irregularity in the writing may induce an individual to honestly or dishonestly deny its execution. The handwriting examination on these occasions must address the issues of natural variation, accidental occurrence, deliberate modification, and true difference.

Nervous tension.   See Section 37(H): Extrinsical Influences — Emotional Stress.

Natural variations — beyond those of standards.   This is the reason that the adequacy of standards is particularly important. Limited standards may not contain the full range of natural variations peculiar to a given individual simply because some variations are the products of the time, the text and the circumstances involved in their production. The fewer the standards, the more likely that this situation will occur.

Writing conditions — place or circumstances (moving vehicles).   There is wide variation in the circumstances under which legitimate signatures are written and almost equal variation in the results. Recipient signatures for deliveries received are invariably executed in a standing position without adequate support for the writing surface. Furthermore, they are confined to small spaces on forms quite inadequate for the majority of writers. The result is a pronounced change in execution, often so altering the signature that it is beyond a subsequent identification.

Although it is true that these signatures are executed with less care and concern for the final product, the affect that these unusual circumstances may have upon the writing is more severe than that which carelessness and negligence normally generates. Harrison expounds that:

> "…it is not surprising that when specimens of the handwriting of one person written under different conditions are compared, there should be a doubt expressed that one individual was responsible for writing all the scripts, so different do they appear."[46]

Signatures executed at counters may have similar effects. Tables and chairs provide a reasonably consistent set of circumstances for the signing of documents, although there are exceptions to the rule. Counters, however, do not. They vary in height, as do the people attempting to write on them. They are sometimes narrow and restrictive for the writing process. Consequently, the writer's stance with respect to the document is subject to wider variation and the results can be a loss of some quality or control.

Related to this are the situations in which a writer, because of ill health, endeavours to execute a signature when confined to bed (see Section 57, Signs of Senility or Age). In other situations, an individual may attempt to write or sign a document on his/her knee or lap. For some writers, even the environmental circumstances can have some affect upon the nervous state of the individual and fluency in the writing may suffer.

Writings in moving vehicles of all kinds are remarkably numerous or at least claimed to be so. Depending on the nature of the vehicle, the influence of its motion may be minor or extreme. When extreme the writing may be quite erratic. Whichever it is, the effect will be general and likely apparent throughout the writing rather than localized to one or two elements. While writings in moving vehicles and other extreme circumstances do occur, it is more often a claim made to explain deficiencies or disparities in spurious signatures in an argument for their being genuine (see Section 38(2): Intrinsical Influences — Circumstantial).

This is another important aspect of writing that has a bearing on the adequacy of standards.

Writing instrument.   See Section 38(2): Intrinsical Influences — Circumstantial.

Writing position — including stance.   See Writing Conditions.

Writing surface.   See Section 38(2): Intrinsical Influences — Circumstantial.

Writing under stress.   In this we differentiate, as we must, between the effects of emotional stress and those of physical stress. The former is dealt with under the caption Mental State of the Writer Section 37(H). The latter is more often described as fatigue, and cases involving the writing of documents while suffering from extreme fatigue are rarely encountered. Physical stress is dealt with in detail in Section 38(C).

18. Is It Possible, Then, to Eliminate a Person as Being the Writer of an Inscription or Signature on a Document?

Writing examinations usually have one of three objectives: identification, elimination, or differentiation. Identification is a process that associates writings, for a purpose. Elimination segregates writings, for a purpose. Differentiation segregates writings, for no particular purpose, beyond making the distinction.

Differentiation is a seldom-mentioned process that lies at the root of studies to establish whether or not writings are the products of two or more persons, as they may purport. Marked ballots, testimonials, voter's lists, and other documents are often involved. In these cases, differentiation, when achieved, usually attests to genuineness. On the other hand, common authorship, when established, may be cause to reject a document as invalid, without any necessity to pursue its authorship further.

Differentiation is the objective that proves the heterogeneity of writing and the ability of the present processes to demonstrate it. Thus, it is a key to the validity and reliability of handwriting examination.

The term *nonidentity* is often used interchangeably with *elimination*. Differentiation, however, is also a matter of nonidentity. Thus, while elimination may be a matter of nonidentity, nonidentity is not solely a matter of elimination. Accordingly, it is more fitting to say that nonidentity is the all-inclusive parent of both elimination and of differentiation.

An identification is based on evidence that is quantitatively and qualitatively sufficient to support such a conclusion. The elimination of a writer may be based on what is quantitatively less evidence, or on an absence of evidence of identification in the documents at hand. It embraces speculation as to what other documents by the same writer might reveal, if they were available. Eliminations are broad and all-inclusive statements, that a given writer could not, under any circumstances, have executed a given writing. Identifications are particular and demonstrable. Eliminations are general and speculative.

An important key in the elimination of a writer rests in the contemporaneousness of the standards. Because writing is dynamic and subject to change over periods of time, it is crucial to have within the standards some samples of writing that are contemporaneous with the questioned document.

Because an elimination is such an all-encompassing statement it has been recommended that the conclusion, when expressed, should always be qualified. Rather than a bold statement that "K" did not write "Q," it is suggested that the finding should read in words to the effect that, "In the writing standards at hand there is no evidence that "K" was the writer of "Q.""

There are situations in which unqualified eliminations seem to be justified. An individual cannot be considered a potential author of a writing that exceeds the level of skill of which he/she is capable, providing the standards reliably attest to that level. Nor should an individual be considered for authorship of a writing that contains numerous fundamental disparities in the basic system followed that indicates a difference in national or system attributes, providing the standards are contemporaneous. It is also reasonable to exclude a person as the author of a tracing of his own signature, but while tracings usually mitigate against a conclusion of auto-forgery, grounds are insufficient to say that it couldn't happen.

It has been implied that the processes of identification and elimination are the same. With this we would agree, but only in the sense that the same discriminating elements, sought and appraised in the Analysis and Comparison, will provide the evidence of sameness or difference in the writing comparisons. The analogy between the two tasks, however, stops there. Although, in practise, the approach to both tasks may be the same, the physical evidence to be considered and its assessment is distinctly different. Identification is an evaluation of similarities. Elimination is an evaluation of differences.

Differences found in writing studies cannot be underestimated. On the other hand, the contention that a single or a few basic differences are controlling and can offset the weight of several similarities may be an overestimation of their role. Although basic differences are frequently considered to constitute adequate grounds for the "elimination of a writer" or a conclusion of "nonidentity," such findings may be more complicated than the simple tabulation of a few disparities between two sets of writings. As Dick[47] stated, and Dibowski[48] and Miller[49] reiterated, a conclusion of elimination may be more difficult, more complex, or have greater risks than that of identification.

It must be emphasized that the apparent differences in two sets of writings that might be indicative of writings originating from different sources (writers), are seldom found in isolation. If one is present, a thorough examination will likely reveal others. An isolated difference is more often due to one or more of the circumstances and situations suggested in Section 17: What circumstances or conditions might contribute to the production of apparent differences in writing.

The position taken by most authorities is that to properly support a conclusion of nonidentity or elimination, differences must be fundamental and repeated. Accordingly, such conclusions can seldom be justified respecting limited textual material as the opportunity for differences to be repeated may not be provided. Disparities in writing can occur for numerous reasons, and the consideration of all of those reasons is what makes eliminations a more complex matter than identifications may be.

When differences are numerous and persistent, and the standards in which they are present are adequate quantitatively and qualitatively, such differences must be entertained as evidence in support of the elimination of the writer. Osborn went so far as to say that, "If two writings cannot be identified as the same then, necessarily, they must be identified as having been written by different hands." In our view, whether an elimination is definitive or qualified must remain a subjective judgment on the part of the examiner. The benefit to the court, the counsel, or to the investigator should be virtually the same in both instances, and the qualified conclusion will avoid indeterminable risks.

References

1. Hilton, Ordway, *Scientific Examination of Questioned Documents*. Revised Ed. (New York: Elsevier/North-Holland Inc., 1982). p 161.

2. Huber, Roy A. and Headrick, A.M., *The Identification Process*. Presented at the 11th meeting of the International Association of Forensic Sciences (Vancouver, 1987).

3. Found, Bryan and Rogers, Doug, *The Forensic Investigation of Signature Complexity*. (Victoria Australia: La Trobe University, an unpublished interim report on work in progress, 1996).

4. Huber, R. A., Expert Witnesses. *The Criminal Law Quarterly,* 1959 November; 2: 3.

5. Found, Bryan and Rogers, Doug, Contemporary Issues in Forensic Handwriting Examination. A Discussion of Key Issues in the Wake of the Starzecpyzel Decision. *Journal of Forensic Document Examination,* 1995 fall; 8: pp 1-31.

6. Hardy, H. J. J. and Fagel, W., Methodological Aspects of Handwriting Identification. *Journal of Forensic Document Examination,* 1995 Fall; 8: pp 33-69.

7. Hilton, Ordway, The Relationship of Mathematical Probability to the Handwriting Identification Problem. *Seminar No. 5, R.C.M.P. Crime Detection Laboratories,* 1958, pp 121-130.

8. Harrison, W. R., *Suspect Documents: Their Scientific Examination* (London: Sweet & Maxwell Ltd, 1966). p 343.

9. Trueblood, E., *General Philosophy* (New York: Harper, 1963).

10. Hilton, Ordway, Education and Qualifications of Examiners of Questioned Documents. *Journal of Forensic Sciences,* 1956 October; 1: 3: pp 35-42.

11. Behrendt, James E., The Status of Training for Document Examiners in the United States. *Journal of Forensic Sciences,* 1989 March; 34: 2: pp 366-370.

12. Leson, Joel L., *The Education and Qualifications of Questioned Document Examiners.* A study submitted to the faculty of the Forensic Science Department of George Washington University, in fulfillment of the requirements for the degree of Master of Science in Forensic Science (Washington, 1974).

13. Baxter, P. G., The Training of Questioned Document Examiners. *Medicine Science and Law,* 1970; Vol X: p 76.

14. Hilton, Ordway, Education and Qualifications of Examiners of Questioned Documents. *Journal of Forensic Sciences,* 1956 Oct; 1: 3: p 41.

15. Cabanne, Robert A., *Recruiting and Training Document Examiners for United States Postal Inspection Service Identification Laboratories.* Presented at the ASQDE/RCMP joint meeting (Ottawa, 1965).

16. Mathyer, Jacques, *A Few Remarks Concerning the Training of a Document Expert.* Presented at the ASQDE/RCMP joint meeting (Ottawa, 1965).

17. Sellers, Clark, *The Qualifications of an Examiner of Questioned Documents.* Presented at the meeting of the American Society of Questioned Document Examiners (1966).

18. Caponi, Antonio I. and Berardi, Luis Alberto, *Training and Education of Questioned Documents Examiner in Argentina.* Presented at the 2nd International Meeting of Questioned Documents (Copenhagen, Denmark, 1966).

19. Purtell, David J., *Curriculum for a Document Examiner.* Presented at the meeting of the American Society of Questioned Document Examiners (Toronto, Canada, 1969).

20. Miller, James T., *Training and Certification.* Presented at the meeting of the American Society of Questioned Document Examiners (1972).

21. Miller, J. T., Professionalization of Document Examiners: Problems of Certification and Training. *Journal of Forensic Science,* 1973 Oct; 18: pp 460-8.

22. Greenwood, Bruce R., *Proficiency Standards for Document Personnel (Abilities, Duties, Knowledge and Skills).* Presented at the meeting of the American Society of Questioned Document Examiners (Lake Tahoe, CA, 1983).

23. Behrendt, James E., *The Status of Training for Questioned Document Examiners in the United States.* Presented at the meeting of the American Academy of Forensic Sciences (Philadelphia, PA, 1988).

24. Epstein, Gideon, Larner, James F., and Hines, Mark, *Forensic Document Examination Training in the United States.* Presented at the meeting of the American Academy of Forensic Sciences (New Orleans, February 1992).

25. Fisher, M. Patricia, Proposed Curriculum for an Apprenticeship as a Forensic Document Examiner in Private Practice. *Journal of Questioned Document Examination,* 1992 Sept; 1: 2.

26. Tytell, Peter V., *Defining the Terms "Class Characteristic" and "Individual Characteristic:" A Progress Report.* Presented at the meeting of the American Society of Questioned Document Examiners (Orlando, FL, 1991).

27. Haywood, Charles L., *Continuing the Search for the Black "J" and "W,"* presented at the annual meeting of the American Society of Questioned Document Examiners (Orlando, FL, 1991).

28. Found, Bryan and Rogers, Doug, Contemporary Issues in Forensic Handwriting Examination. A Discussion of Key Issues in the Wake of the Starzecpyzel Decision. *Journal of Forensic Document Examination,* 1995; 8: pp 1-31.

29. Berthold, Nancy N., and Wooton, Elaine X., *Class Characteristics of Latin American Hand Printing.* Presented at the meeting of the American Society of Questioned Document Examiners (Ottawa, 1993).

30. Ziegler, Larry F., and Trizna, Lurline A., *African Hand Printing.* Presented at the meeting of the American Society of Questioned Document Examiners (Long Beach, CA, 1994).

31. Trizna, Lurline A. and Wooton, Elaine X., *Asian Hand Printing.* Presented at the meeting of the American Academy of Forensic Sciences (Seattle, WA, 1995).

32. Trizna, Lurline A. and Wooton, Elaine X., *Hand Printing of the Middle East and the Subcontinent.* Presented at the meeting of the American Society of Questioned Document Examiners (Washington, DC, 1996).

33. Wooton, Elaine X., *A Preliminary Discussion of Research and Reference Materials Using the U.S. INS Collection of Handwriting from Other Countries.* Presented at the meeting of the American Society of Questioned Document Examiners (Long Beach, CA, 1994).

34. Hilton, Ordway, *Scientific Examination of Questioned Documents.* 2nd ed. (New York: Elsevier, 1982), p 160.

35. Osborn, Albert S., *Questioned Documents.* (Albany, Boyd Printing Co., 1929), p 219.

36. Hilton, Ordway, How Individual are Personal Writing Habits? *Journal of Forensic Sciences,* 1983 July; 28: 3: p 683.

37. McAlexander,, Thomas V., Assigning Weight to Handwriting Differences for Elimination Purposes. *International Journal of Forensic Document Examiners*, 1997 Jan/Mar; 3: 1: pp 4-7.

38. Whiting, Floyd I., The Application of Reasoning to the Evaluation of Fundamental Differences in Handwriting Comparison. *Journal of Forensic Sciences*, 1996 July; 41: 4: pp 634-640.

39. Hilton, Ordway, *Scientific Examination of Questioned Documents*. Revised Ed. (New York: Elsevier/North Holland Inc., 1982), p 10.

40. Harrison, Wilson R., *Suspect Documents* (New York: Frederick A. Praeger, 1958), p 343.

41. Conway, James V. P., *Evidential Documents* (Springfield: Charles C Thomas, 1959), p 65.

42. McAlexander, Thomas V. and Maguire, Kathleen B., Eliminating Ill-Founded Eliminations in Handwriting Comparison Cases. *Journal of the Forensic Science Society*, 1991; 31: pp 331-336.

43. Whiting, Floyd, Alternate Handwriting Styles — One Writer or Two. *International Journal of Forensic Document Examiners*. 1997 April/June; 3: 2: pp 167-175.

44. Bohn, Clarence E., *Fundamentals Pertaining to Signature Exemplars*. Presented at the meeting of the American Academy of Forensic Sciences (Dallas, 1974).

45. McCarthy, John F., *Problems Involved in Eliminating Authors*. Presented at the meeting of the American Society of Questioned Document Examiners (September, 1988).

46. Harrison, Wilson R., *Suspect Documents* (New York: Frederick A. Praeger, 1958), p 297.

47. Dick, Ronald M., *Handwriting Identification vs. Elimination*. Presented at the meeting of the American Society of the Questioned Document Examiners (New York, 1966).

48. Dibowski, James R., Proving Negative Conclusions, *I. D. News*, 1975 Oct; pp 11-13.

49. Miller, Lamar, *The Elimination of Suspects in Criminal Cases*. Presented at the meeting of the American Academy of Forensic Sciences (Las Vegas, 1985).

The Premises for the Identification of Handwriting

19. Is There a Requirement in Writing Identification to Have a Minimum Number of Points of Similarity, as in Fingerprint Identification?

To begin with, let us clear up a general misconception that exists respecting fingerprint examination. At the present time, there is no stipulated number of points of similarity that is statistically supported, for the identification of a fingerprint, that we know of anywhere in the world. The International Association for Identification, at its meeting in Jackson, Wyoming, August 1, 1973, based on a three-year study by its Standardization Committee, stated:

> "No valid basis exists at this time for requiring that a predetermined number of friction ridge characteristics must be present in two impressions in order to establish positive identification."[1]

There are individual practises of fingerprint technicians, departmental policies and recommended criteria that call for certain levels of similarity to support positive conclusions, 6, 8, 10, 12, or even 14 points, but they are practises, policies, and recommendations. The question as it has been posed here, and asked by some judicial officials, implies that there is a universally accepted or statistically supported number of points of similarity that will serve to discriminate one fingerprint from all others, but this is simply not the case.

In the field of chemistry there are analytical procedures, based on the current knowledge of the chemical composition of compounds, that allow an analyst to advance along a program that progressively reduces the number of possible substances that an unknown might be until a single substance remains. There is no point count, however, as the program of analysis varies with the substance being pursued.

Extensive DNA studies have accumulated hordes of information from which the probable occurrence of two persons being the same DNA genotype may be calculated. The levels of probability so calculated are sufficiently low that, for practical purposes, the uniqueness of the genotype is accepted as a certainty.

In fields such as physics, chemistry, and biochemistry, the evidence being sought is thought of as being, for the most part, invariable. Because of its stability, it has been and will continue to be the same for an indeterminate length of time. If it can be found in sufficient quantity it can be identified with known standards, even after long periods. This, however, is not entirely true. The evidence is invariable only if certain conditions are controlled as they usually can be, particularly purity, temperature, and atmospheric pressure. Variables influencing handwriting cannot all be controlled.

The point-count policy, publicly attributed to fingerprint identifications and followed by its technicians, has other inherent errors in it. It implies that each characteristic of the print is of equal significance, which is to say that its frequency of occurrence is the same as for any other. This we know is not true for all fingerprint characteristics, but the empirical data has not been broadly studied to determine relative values of significance.

In situations of this kind, science looks closely at the weight to be attached to each of the factors being considered, something that frequencies of occurrence might sustain. Weight, however, is also contingent upon the independence of any factor from any other. Some writing characteristics may be related to the system of writing that was learned. Consequently, some letter designs may exhibit similarities because of a relationship in their background. Point counts, then, are not simple numbers, but are more complex calculations.

The magnitude of the error that a simple point count produces in fingerprint examinations, and the direction in which it may lie is not known. It is assumed, however, that as long as the number of points of similarity is sufficiently large, ample allowance will be made for the inaccuracies that an arbitrary equalization of weights in assessments may generate.

Handwriting is not the same as the subjects of focus in these other fields. It is subject to variation from one occasion to the next and even the range of variations differ with the individual and with the element of writing. Furthermore, writing must be read. It is not free, like DNA, to vary from one subject to another without impairing recognition. It must be reasonably legible in order to be readable. Then too, there are limitations to the manner in which some elements can be varied or changed. How many ways can one write a lowercase, cursive "e" or an "i"? Consequently, insofar as some particular elements of writing, there is greater opportunity for writers to duplicate one another. For this reason, larger combinations of similarities may be required to support conclusions of identity.

How large a combination? This will depend upon the uniqueness of the features within the combination. How does one assess uniqueness? Without empirical data one must resort to experience, his/her own and that of others. In that regard, handwriting identification is not unlike fingerprint identification, which, although it has the empirical data, chooses not to use it. The difference between them is that handwriting examiners have not yet collectively selected any fixed group of points of similarity as a base. One reason for this is that the significance of points of similarity can vary substantially.

Handwriting, being what it is, may never permit precise determinations to be made of the value or significance of any particular writing characteristic or the probability of occurrence level for any combination of characteristics. Nevertheless, approximations are possible that, when used perspicaciously, can be sufficiently reliable for identification purposes.

If then, the analogy to fingerprint identification is not cogent, what analogy can be made to a process that is reasonably reliable and publicly acceptable? We need not leave the courtroom. In any civil or criminal litigation, the triers of fact take into account various elements of evidence, each having its own significance as a factor in determining the issues of guilt or responsibility. The assignment of significance to each factor is subjective and dependent upon the intelligence, training, and experience of each of the triers of fact, whether they be judge or jury.

The determination that is made is not based on any point count, but it is not less reliable for want of it. Perhaps, having given science and fingerprint identification too much credit for precision, the legal profession has been unaware that its process for reaching conclusions is, in principle, the same as that of the scientist. The court's own criterion for establishing the guilt of a person — beyond a reasonable doubt — discreetly avoids stipulating with certainty or even beyond any doubt.[2]

"The scientist, too, never proves everything with certainty or beyond a doubt; the best he can hope to say is that he has established a fact beyond a reasonable doubt. The difference between the scientific and the legal situations is that the scientist has learned to calculate the probability of the doubt. This has been the contribution of statistics."[3]

So, the short answer to the question posed is that the question is invalid for two reasons: (1) There is no minimum point count for fingerprint identification that is supported by statistics, (2) A point count cannot be applied as a primary determination in a matter wherein the factors being counted vary in their respective significance, without them being appropriately weighted.

20. What Information Relevant to a Case or a Questioned Writing Does an Examiner Need to Know to Conduct a Proper and Complete Examination?

There are at least two schools of thought on this subject. Some examiners maintain that to ensure impartiality and to avoid influence, one should not have any background information that might suggest a preferred conclusion or a conclusion consistent with that intimated by other evidence. They need know only what writing is questioned and what writings are known or are standards, and perhaps which standards may be doubtful as to their proof.[4]

On the other hand, there are those who argue that because handwriting is subject to the influence of many factors, from failing health, injury, and circumstances to intoxication, that sufficient information respecting the writer and the writing occasion is required. This is in order that due allowances may be made for these conditions, if necessary. Only then can true differences be properly discriminated from natural or unnatural variations. The reader is referred to the comments made respecting the effects of arthritis on the act of writing (Section 37.E.2.d) as an example of a situation in which information respecting the writer's state of health could be important to the examiner.

For such reasons, in our view the latter position is preferred, but it is accompanied by certain risks. It is difficult for the providers of such information, who cannot avoid being prejudiced to some extent, to supply information that is wholly impartial. Conversations normally ensue that may be brief or lengthy during which biased comments are difficult to preclude. If it was convenient to do so, and continuity could be preserved and not complicated, it might be suggested that a third party, knowledgeable in writing identification, might be the recipient of material that would be subsequently turned over to the examiner. Necessary and appropriate information might then be solicited from the submitter, and prejudicial statements filtered out of the conversations when relayed to the examiner. Under these arrangements undue influence could be avoided.

21. What Part Does Statistical Inference Play in the Identification Process?

The task of drawing conclusions from data on hand (i.e., a number of standards) about other data (i.e., an unknown) is a matter of statistical inference. Statistical inference, that is, statistical proof, underlies all scientific investigations in some manner, and in order to be a scientific pursuit, the identification of handwriting must, knowingly or unknowingly, engage statistical proof.

When one brings common sense to bear upon a problem, a mixture of experience and intuition is used. Inferential statistics employ a similar process, substituting data for experience and formula for intuition. Hence, in practise, statistical methods require us to do, in a more formal and rigorous way, the things that are done, informally, countless times each day.

Whether definitive (i.e., positive) or qualified (i.e., something other than positive), any conclusion of identification, derives from statistical inference and is an expression of probability having an arithmetic value somewhere between 0 and 1. In the vocabulary of probability, conclusions of absolute certainty, if such there be, have a value of 1.0.[5] Matters that are totally improbable, that is to say are impossible, have a value of 0.0. Any other conclusions, which includes all those respecting handwriting, are matters of probability that lie somewhere in between.

The use by handwriting examiners of statements of probability, commonly referred to as qualified opinions in reports or in testimony, has been debated for some time without a clearcut decision as to their legitimacy.[6-7] However, proponents of qualified opinions have not attacked the issue from a legitimate platform of statistical inference.[8-11] On the other hand, opponents to probability statements have not attempted to review the principles underlying the identification process.[12-13]

Taroni, Champod, and Margot,[14] report that Alphonse Bertillon, in his review of handwriting examination,[15] held that "only statistical and correlation analysis, based on an adequate sample of data describing the various forms of letter formation could justify the existence of the field." This was the substance of the criticisms of Kirk[16] more than 50 years later, and the gist of our comments made in 1980.

Osborn[17] suggested a statistical basis to handwriting examination by the application of the Newcomb rule of probability:

> "The probability of occurrence together of all the events is equal to the continued product of the probabilities of all the separate events."

Osborn was endeavouring to demonstrate how a combination of similar writing habits in two handwritings would occur with the frequency ratio provided by multiplying together the respective ratios of frequencies of occurrence of each of the habits. Furthermore, if a sufficient number of habits were involved, the frequency ratio of their combined occurrence would be such that they could be possessed by only one person in a given population.

Unfortunately, perhaps in his desire to be simplistic, Osborn neglected to qualify the events, in his statement of the Newcomb rule, as independent events, which is the only condition under which the rule is valid.

Nevertheless, some 40 years ago the rule was adapted to constitute the principle of identification, with its application to document examination particularly in mind. It is generally stated in the form:

"When any two items possess a combination of similar and independent characteristics, corresponding in relationship to one another, of such number and significance as to preclude the possibility of coincidental occurrence, without inexplicable disparities, it may be concluded that they are the same in nature or are related to a common source."[18]

For the application of the principle to be valid in any discipline, some data must be available to demonstrate the independence and the significance of the characteristics of the items that are under study. In some disciplines that fall within forensic science, the necessary data has not yet been accumulated and/or organized systematically.

A number of papers have been written in recent years relative to the application of statistics, particularly the Bayesian theorem, to handwriting examination, few of which have been very helpful to writing examiners. The subject is not that new, however. An excellent account of earlier attempts to apply the theorem to writing cases, of which Bertillon's was one of the first (1898), will be found in the study by Taroni, Champod, and Margot (1997). It is not our intention to devote excessive time and space to a review of the Bayes theory, other than to say that it allows the examiner or the triers of facts to take into account the relevant population of persons that circumstances and other evidence circumscribes in some practical fashion as encompassing the potential authors of a questioned writing. Thus, if a finding is not definitive, i.e., it is a qualified opinion, these other factors may provide sufficient information to render the finding more definitive than it is.

Souder[19] was one of the few and perhaps the first handwriting examiner to employ the likelihood ratio, that is a progeny of the Bayes theory, to assess the evidence in the identification of writing:

"...in handwriting we do not have to push the tests until we get a fraction represented by unity divided by the population of the world. Obviously, the denominator can always be reduced to those who can write and further to those having the capacity to produce the work in question. In a special case, it may be possible to prove that one of three individuals must have produced the document. Our report, even though it shows a mathematical probability of only one in one hundred, would then irresistibly establish the conclusion."

Once rebuffed and rejected, the Bayesian approach now has strong advocates for its use in forensic science. Aitken[20] wrote that "the Bayesian approach (is) the best measure we have for assessing the value of evidence." Gaudette,[21] without identifying its Bayesian basis, wrote on the "Evaluation of Associative Physical Evidence." Good,[22] a prolific writer on the topic, referred to it as the "weight of evidence." See also Hill[23] for a general review.

Alford, perhaps unwittingly, initiated the use of the Bayes Theorem and the likelihood ratio in handwriting case work in 1965. On the strength of a paper read at the meeting of the American Academy of Forensic Science by Olkin,[24] Hilton explained,[25] that the likelihood ratio statistic is the ratio of: the probability calculated on the basis of the similarities, under the assumption of identity, to the probability calculated on the basis of dissimilarities, under the assumption of nonidentity. Accordingly, the probability of identity in a population of five persons, on the strength of what Hilton calls the joint probability of three writing features, would be 1/5 to the power of 3, or 1/125. Then the probability of nonidentity would be 4/5 to the power of 3, or 64/125, (approximately 1/2). The ratio of 'identity' to 'nonidentity' in this case is 1/125 divided by 64/125 and equals 1/64. It is considered to be a measure of the likelihood of 'chance coincidence', (not our words). Hence, the smaller that this fraction is, or if you prefer, the larger the denominator relative to a numerator of 1, the less likely is coincidence and the stronger is the identification.

The likelihood ratio is a statistical means of testing a calculated value derived from a statistical sample. Relative to handwriting examinations, it is the means of determining whether the probability of identity and the probability of nonidentity are significantly different. In other contexts, we frequently use the term *odds*. We invert the likelihood ratio (that we determined above in our example to be 1/64), and say that the odds favouring the identification of this subject are 64 to 1.[26] Readers should note that it is the likelihood ratio that is inverted to produce the odds, not the joint probability of a number of similarities, that in our example was 1/125.

Others have written on the consideration to be given to the question of relevent populations that may strengthen the findings of a writing examination. Kingston's[27] view was that it was the role of the judge or jury, not the writing examiner, to apply the modification to the handwriting evidence that other evidence may justify. The question arises, however, as to who would be the most competent for the task: the judge? the jury? or the writing examiner?

But, to return to the question posed: statistical inference has a vital role to play in writing identification, greater, perhaps, than many examiners recognize.

22. What is the Logic and Reasoning Underlying Handwriting Identification?

The argument for the identification of a handwriting is an inductive argument. Any argument is inductive if it may be stated as "it is probable that...." Such arguments simply claim that its conclusion is reasonable to believe in view of the facts set forth as evidence. Deduction is a matter of recognizing valid logical forms, but induction is a matter of weighing evidence. Although inductive reasoning, unlike deductive reasoning, cannot be reduced to precise rules, there are certain important general principles that must be kept in mind.

Induction is a way of reasoning, as is deduction, yet quite different. Whereas deductive conclusions necessarily follow from their reasons, inductive conclusions are either (1) generalizations, or (2) hypotheses.

Suppose we taste a dozen Florida oranges, each of which is sweet. On the basis of this information we may conclude that all Florida oranges are sweet. The conclusion goes beyond the reasons given. Twelve oranges were offered in evidence but the conclusion is more general than the evidence. It is a generalization.

The second kind of inductive argument leads to a hypothesis. It is the character of scientific investigation. It is not a statement about a class, but about an individual, an event, or a state of affairs. A man named "A" murdered Miss "B" and then shot himself, or "X" wrote the anonymous letter "Q." These are inductive conclusions drawn from evidence. The truth of these statements is not established by direct observation. They are hypotheses.

In this kind of inductive argument, there are three elements:

1. A number of facts that are the data of the argument (e.g., "X" exhibits certain writing habits. There is a similarity between the writing habits of "X" and features of the writing "Q." There are no observable differences).
2. A hypothesis: that "X" wrote the anonymous letter "Q."
3. Certain generalizations connect the hypothesis with the facts:
   a. Handwriting is unique to each individual.
   b. Writing is habitual and, therefore, consistent from one execution to the next.
   c. Differences in media or time will not significantly alter writing habits to preclude identification.
   d. Differences between writers are such that, given sufficient writing standards, we can discriminate between the products of most writers.
   e. A sufficient number of facts (similarities), in combination, affirms that the hypothesis is acceptable.

As any hypothesis should, this hypothesis derives its convincingness from its ability to account for all of the facts. This is the reason why differences or disparities observed in a handwriting comparison must be accounted for before conclusions as to identification can be reached.

The underlying principle is clear. Assuming that the generalizations are true, every known fact that can be accounted for by the hypothesis is evidence that the hypothesis is true.

While we may have facts that are accounted for by the hypothesis, and that, therefore, constitute evidence, when it comes to the question whether to believe an inductive conclusion, the problem is more complex.

To begin with, any particular fact (e.g., a similarity in a discriminating element in a questioned and known writings) may be an instance of many possible generalizations. For example:

1. In order to be read, any writing will resemble another in some respects.
2. Pupils of the same teacher will write alike.
3. All systems of writing that are taught are similar.

As aforementioned, a hypothesis accounts for facts by being connected to them through known generalizations. This is the way lawyers build their cases. It is the way a scientific theory grows and becomes accepted. But, no matter how convincing a hypothesis may be, it is always conceivable that a new discovery will cripple or destroy it. Thus, a hypothesis wears a tentative provisional air. We accept it, we act upon it, but only until a better one comes along.[28]

When we have such strong evidence for a hypothesis (e.g., that "X" wrote the anonymous letter "Q"), that we no longer fear (or hope for) any further evidence that would be incompatible with it, we say the hypothesis has been proved. The practical question is, of course, at what point are we justified in regarding a hypothesis as proved? In writing identification terms, that is, asking the question as to how many or what kind of similarities must we have?

A simple and universal reply cannot be given, for many reasons. Still, there is a key principle that provides a rough estimate of the reliability of a hypothesis.

Generally speaking, a fact or a collection of facts can be accounted for by more than one hypothesis. The facts in a writing comparison matter, for example, may be accounted for by either of the hypotheses:

1. "X" wrote the anonymous letter "Q."
2. "X" was taught to write by the same teacher as "Y," that "X" has developed the same writing skill as "Y," that "X" was in the same locale as "Y" at the time "Q" was written, but that "Y" actually wrote the anonymous letter "Q."

Whenever we accept a hypothesis as true, therefore, we are, indeed, preferring it to alternative hypotheses, which may account for the same facts. Seldom can we find one and only one hypothesis. If we want to be reasonable, we must always choose the best of a number of hypotheses. This is the root of the problem. How do we determine when one hypothesis is to be preferred to another? What makes it better?

One feature should always be considered when comparing alternative hypotheses to decide which is the more convincing. This is the simplicity of the hypothesis. Other things being equal (a qualification that covers a number of delicate considerations), the simpler of two alternative hypotheses is the preferable one.

Obviously, in the situation suggested above, Hypothesis 2 requires us to suppose a longer chain of events than Hypothesis 1. Thus, Hypothesis 1 is simpler. Since both may account for the same facts, it is more reasonable to believe 1 than 2. This is not to say that we can be certain that Hypothesis 1 is true. All we can be sure of is that as an explanation of known facts, it is better than 2, and thus, would be preferred to it.

The *principle of simplicity* is an important and helpful consideration that avoids the *fallacy of unnecessary complexity.*[29]

If this sounds overly academic and seems unnecessary, it may be appropriate to mention that if the discipline of handwriting identification is to qualify as a science, and its practitioners are to deserve inclusion in the professional community, it requires that they understand not only how things are done but why they are done that way. This makes the distinction between the intelligence of the scientist and the mechanics of the technician, a distinction that this dissertation is endeavouring to engender.

23. How Does the Identification Process Impinge on Training?

If we reflect for a moment upon the elements of the identification process we realize that analysis and evaluation are the two aspects of it that make formal training necessary, the personal presence of a competent teacher essential, and the accumulation of experience mandatory. One must acquire a knowledge of what to look for in writing and how to assess its significance. It is of even greater importance to those who aspire to become document examiners or handwriting experts to recognize the fact that, because analysis and evaluation varies with the particular case material under examination, neither of these facets of the process can be learned completely from books. They simply aren't there now, and it is unlikely that they ever will be. Evaluation, particularly, must be learned through training and experience. Sufficient empirical data has not yet been accumulated from which probability of occurrences respecting particular writing habits may be calculated. Their significance must be subjectively judged on the strength of the experience of the examiner and his or her tutors. Thus, one's ability to judge the significance of a feature of writing is an element of one's competence that the self-taught novice has difficulty developing. It is an ability not easily learned by correspondence, and without it, the accuracy of the findings of a tyro examiner are at considerable risk.

On further reflection, it becomes apparent wherein the value of a competent expert lies. The trained mind conducts the more thorough and efficient analysis, seeking the more credible evidence, disregarding the trivial, unearthing that of which the lay mind is unaware. In comparisons, experience and familiarity enables one to make far more delicate and precise distinctions. For example, one of oriental extraction has far less difficulty in distinguishing between his/her own kind than most Occidentals. But it is probably in the area of evaluation that knowledge, training, experience, and skill make their greatest contribution. What analysis has found and comparison has revealed, only proper evaluation can make useful.

Once this process of identification is understood and appreciated, progress may be made in identifying matters not within one's normal purview. Thus, problems involving Chinese or Eskimo writing may be intelligently tackled by persons who don't speak the languages. Typewriters may be identified by persons never employed in a typewriter factory. Printing methods may be differentiated by persons never engaged as printers. Counterfeit currency can be identified reliably by document examiners who never made a dollar.

24. Is There Such a Thing as Handwriting Expertise?

In so many words, Risinger, Denbaux, and Saks[30] inferred that handwriting identification was unable to prove its worth, and until it did, it should be regarded as a con job.

The profession of the document examiner, the handwriting examiner, or the handwriting expert has been around the western world for more than a hundred years and probably for just as long in Europe. Its practitioners and their labours have been accepted as reliable, and their findings have been considered believable by the judiciary, the courts, and the layman for as many years, notwithstanding the fact that, as with many developing professions, there have been those within it whose services have not been of the highest calibre. The need for these services within the criminal justice and civil litigation systems, the remuneration that seemed warranted, and the absence of a standard to be met, were often the reasons that less qualified individuals were persuaded to become involved, and the process undoubtedly produced some errors.

With the passage of time and the growth of the profession, better methods of training, broader consultation and discussion, and the sharing of knowledge that stems from experience have evolved to furnish greater consistency in methods and more reliability in results. Nevertheless, an apprenticeship process tends to underlie the training of neophytes in handwriting identification. Although numerous books have been written on document examination, we are, as yet, without a true textbook that spells out clearly and concisely, and in some organized fashion, the fund of knowledge that the practitioner should have at his disposal.

It is not surprising then that the question should be raised as to whether any empirical data exists to support the claim that handwriting specialists possess a handwriting expertise, an expertise that laypersons do not normally acquire. Prior to 1990, there were only a very few studies that examined the reliability of handwriting identification by document examiners, a fact that was reported by Risinger et al., after what they claimed to have been an exhaustive literature search. Understandably, the report put document examiners everywhere very much on the defensive.

One might have expected the profession to hasten to rectify the situation, but instead one sensed a reticence to deal with the implications of the report and some trepidation respecting the outcome. Offers made to organizations of questioned document examiners to conduct appropriate studies have been declined and opportunities to conduct studies having some special potentials were lost.

As might have been expected, however, others interested in the subject pursued the task, and to some extent at least, have addressed the matter. Kam, Wetstein, and Conn,[31] in a study of small samples (seven professionals from a single source, i.e., the F.B.I. Laboratories, and 10 nonprofessionals) clearly confuted the null hypothesis suggested by Risinger et al. that there was no difference between professed handwriting examiners and lay persons in the examination of writing samples. While these results are encouraging, other studies are being and will be conducted to permit generalizing beyond the boundaries of the F.B.I. Laboratories and very small samples. Kaye[32] has commented on the shortcomings of the study and the difficulty in generalizing from the information provided by the limited sample size.

The fact remains, however, that some reliable and acceptable evidence has now been provided to dispute the Risinger et al. disparaging indictments. Further studies of a similar calibre can be expected to expand the perspective suggested by these results. If and where the differences between lay persons and professionals are not of the same magnitude as this investigation has disclosed, a more detailed study of the professional subjects and their backgrounds may be indicated.

There may be some examiners that feel that in studies of this kind the handwriting expert or document examiner must achieve near perfect results, whereas the lay person should be expected to achieve only the level of chance. This may explain the reluctance of some to submit to such studies and risk a reflection upon their competence and/or on the discipline at large. A properly conducted study, however, designed to confirm or to dispute the allegations of Risinger et al., needs only to reveal a statistically significant difference between the scores of the professionals and of the laypersons to prove the hypothesis that there is such a thing as handwriting expertise. This approach can economize on the time required for each examination within the test procedure and allow for a much greater number of examinations to be conducted, thereby, vastly improving on the reliability of the results.

References

1. Franck, Frankie E., *Objective Standards: Fingerprint Identifications vs. Handwriting Identifications.* Presented at the meeting of the American Society of Questioned Document Examiners (Chicago, 1996).

2. Huber, R. A., The Philosophy of Identification. *Royal Canadian Mounted Police Gazette,* 1972 Jul/Aug; 34: 7/8: pp 8-14.

3. McElrath, G. W. and Berman, J. E., Letters to the Editor. *Science,* 1956 Sept; 24: pp 589-590. With permission.

4. Stangohr, Gordon R., *Elusive and Indeterminate Results.* Presented at the meeting of the American Society of the Questioned Document Society (Nashville, 1984).

5. Bergamini, David, Mathematics. *Life Science Library* (New York: Time Inc., 1963), p 130.

6. Hilton, Ordway, Is There Any Place in Criminal Prosecutions for Qualified Opinions by Document Examiners? *Journal of Forensic Sciences,* 1979 July; 24: 3: pp 579-581.

7. Cole, Alwyn, The Search for Certainty and the Uses of Probability. *Journal of Forensic Sciences,* 1980 Oct; 25: 4: pp 826-833.

8. Cole, Alwyn, Qualified vs. No Conclusion Reports. *Identification News,* April 1962; 12: 4.

9. Cole, Alwyn, *Qualifications in Reports and in Testimony.* Presented at the meeting of the American Society of Questioned Document Examiners (Denver, August, 1964).

10. Schmitz, Philip L., *Should Experienced Document Examiners Write Inconclusive Reports?* Presented at the meeting of the American Society of Questioned Document Examiners (1967).

11. Duke, Donald M., *Handwriting and Probable Evidence.* Presented at the meeting of the International Association for Identification (Ottawa, 1980).

12. Dick, Ronald M., *Qualified Opinions in Handwriting Examinations.* Presented at the meeting of the American Society of Questioned Document Examiners (August 1964).

13. McNally, Joseph P., *Certainty or Uncertainty.* Presented at the meeting of the International Association of Forensic Sciences (Wichita, KS, 1978).

14. Taroni, F., Champod, C., and Margot, P.-A., *Forerunners of Bayesiansism in Early Forensic Science* (unpublished paper prepared at the Institut de Police Scientifique et de Criminologie/Faculté de Droit — Université de Llausanne (Switzerland), 1997. (Received in personal correspondence).

15. Bertillon, Alphonse, *La Comparaison des Écritures et l'identification Graphique* (Paris: Typographie Chamerot et Renouard, tiré à part de la Revue Scientifique (Revue Rose) des 18 Décembre 1897 et 1er Janvier 1898).

16. Kirk, P. L., *Crime Investigation* (New York: Interscience Publishers, 1953), pp 475-476.

17. Osborn, A. S., *Questioned Documents.* 2nd Ed. (Albany: Boyd Printing Co., 1929), p 226.

18. Huber, R. A., Expert Witnesses. *Criminal Law Quarterly,* 1959; 2: 3: pp 276-295.

19. Souder, Wilmer, Merits of Scientific Evidence. *Journal of Criminal Law and Criminology,* 1934-35; 25: pp 683-4.

20. Aitken, C. G. G., The Use of Statistics in Forensic Science. Commentary to the Editors. *Journal of the Forensic Science Society,* 1986 August, pp 113-118.

21. Gaudette, B. D., Evaluation of Associative Physical Evidence. Guest Editorial. *Journal of the Forensic Science Society,* 1986; 26: pp 163-167.

22. Good, I. J., Weight of Evidence: A Brief Survey. *Bayesian Statistics 2,* J. M. Bernardo, M. H. DeGroot, D. V. Lindley, A. F. M. Smith, eds. (Elsevier Science Publishers B.V. North Holland 1985), pp 249-270.

23. Hill, Bruce M., Bayesian Statistics. *Encyclopedia of Physical Science and Technology. Vol. 2* (New York: Academic Press Inc., 1992).

24. Olkin, Ingram, *The Evaluation of Physical Evidence and the Identity Problem by Means of Statistical Probabilities.* Presented at the meeting of the American Academy of Forensic Sciences (Cleveland, February 1958).

25. Hilton, Ordway, The Relationship of Mathematical Probability to the Handwriting Identification Problem. *Proceedings of Seminar No. 5*, Roy A. Huber ed. (Ottawa: Queens Printer, 1958), pp 121-130.

26. Evett, E. W., What is the Probability That This Blood Came From That Person? A meaningful question? *Journal of the Forensic Science Society*, 1983; 23: pp 35-39.

27. Kingston, Charles, A Perspective on Probability and Physical Evidence. *Journal of Forensic Sciences*, 1989 Nov; 34: 6: pp 1336-1342.

28. Beardsley, Monroe C., *Thinking Straight* (New York: Prentice Hall, 1954), p 244.

29. Beardsley, Monroe C., op. cit., p 246.

30. Risinger, D. Michael, Denbeaux, Mark P., and Saks, Michael J., Exorcism of Ignorance as a Proxy for Rational Knowledge: The Lessons of Handwriting Identification "Expertise." *University of Pennsylvania Law Review*, 1989; 137: p 731.

31. Kam, M., Wetstein, J., and Conn, R., Proficiency of Professional Document Examiners in Writer Identification, *Journal of Forensic Sciences*. 1994 January; 39: 1: pp 5-14.

32. Kaye, D. H., A Commentary on "Proficiency of Professional Document Examiners in Writer Identification" (*Journal of Forensic Sciences* 1994 Jan; 39: 1: pp 5-14), Letters to The Editor. *Journal of Forensic Sciences*, November; 39: 6: 1994.

The Fundamentals of the Identification Process

5

25. What Makes Handwriting Identification Possible?

Handwriting identification is based on two accepted premises or principles and a corollary to one of them.

First: habituation. Confucius philosophized, eons ago:

"Men's natures are alike, it is their habits that separate them."

People are primarily creatures of habit and writing is a collection of those habits. A habit hierarchy of at least three levels: the letter habit, the word habit, and the phrase habit are employed according to the degree to which the action process is subjugated to the thought process.

Writing habits are neither instinctive nor hereditary but are complex processes that are developed gradually. Handwriting, or indeed footwriting, mouthwriting, or typewriting, is a neuromuscular behaviour that develops as an acquired perceptual-motor skill. It involves successively higher stages of integration as learning proceeds.

It is a fact that in every language there are certain words, usually short, of frequent occurrence that have only syntactical significance that contribute little to the conveyance of ideas. In the English language such words include:

- articles: "a," "an," "the"
- conjunctions: "and," "but," "for," "or"
- subordinating conjunctions: "if," "that," "as," "than," "when," "where"
- prepositions: "at," "by," "in," "for," "from," "off," "to," "of," "on," "after," "before," "over," "until," "with"
- personal pronouns: "I," "you," "he," "she," "it," "they," "we," "them"
- demonstrative pronouns: "this," "that," "these," "those"
- relative pronouns: "who," "which," "what," "that"
- interrogative pronouns: "who," "which," "what"
- indefinite pronouns: "one," "none," "some," "any," "each," "both"

Because of their frequency of occurrence, their shortness, and their relative insignificance, they exhibit a greater degree of unconscious characterization or individuality than other words may. In accordance with what has been said above, it has been claimed that such words, insofar as the mental process of the average penman goes, are not words in the usual sense of the term, but are symbols. They are put on paper not as a successive series of letters, but are executed as single units.[1]

Thus, in handwriting comparisons, letters, combinations of letters, words, or phrases must be considered according to the degree to which they constitute a collective habit. It is a classic example of synergism in which the whole constitutes more than its parts. Accordingly, the influence of adjoining letters upon one another will vary according to the role these letters play in words or phrases that have become writing habits as units, rather than as individual letters. Variation in shape and movement can be expected to change in relation to this factor.

Along these lines two reported studies of the writing of 61 right-handed subjects by Eldridge, Nimmo-Smith, Wing, and Totty[2-3] attempted to measure what was called the Association Index (AI), to describe the degree of association between different features of handwriting. In this they found higher indices in letters or parts of writing sharing common elements in their design and advocated that they be evaluated collectively, or globally over all letters, rather than as independent factors in a writing examination and study.

Second: the individuality or heterogeneity of writing. Handwriting identification is predicated on the belief that handwriting is unique to the individual, and every document examiner must subscribe to this. Years ago, the argument in support of this contention stemmed largely, but simply, from the truism "nature never offers her handiwork to us in facsimile." Thus, people were likened to leaves or to stones, no two of which have been found to be precisely the same. Isaac D'Israeli is quoted as saying, more than a century and a half ago, "To every individual, nature has given a distinct sort of handwriting, as she has given him a peculiar countenance, voice and manners."

It is axiomatic that any two items of nature may be differentiated, provided the scale of judgment is carried out at a level of sufficient precision. But while there may be no such thing as true identity, the real question for handwriting examiners is whether or not, in writing discrimination, the judgment of the examiner and his instrumentation is capable of such precision as to make the necessary distinction. It is not sufficient, and hardly scientific, to argue that because some writings are obviously different, no two writings from different writers can be so coincidentally similar as to be wrongly judged as the product of one person.[4]

This point was highlighted by Harris[5] in his account of the similarity he found in signatures or writings of the same names, particularly those consisting of six letters or less. His study also disclosed that some letters provide less variation in shape or design from one writer to the next, and that other, more peculiar letter forms can become popular and appear more often than one might expect. Harris[6] described the coincidental similarity found in writers of bubble writing, the teenybopper style that enjoys popularity among adolescents.

Munch[7] reported on the resemblances between the writings of a mother and daughter that must be as close as one may expect to find anywhere. The features by which the two writers could be differentiated were subtle and might well have escaped detection in a hasty comparison or one in which the questioned material was textual and limited.

These reports do not dispute the hypothesis that handwriting is unique to the individual, and that the written products of different individuals can be differentiated from one another. They simply point up some of the risks involved in working within restrictive parameters in time or material.

In all cases, discriminations were successfully made, however, they argue for the exercise of caution because of the dangers they demonstrate. At the same time they should not be allowed to rest on the record without some indication of the frequency with which such cases might be encountered. While experience tells us that these cases are rare, as yet, we have no empirical data to indicate how rare.

Hilton[8] made the point years ago that the principle of heterogeneity "pertains to the whole of a person's writing" and cannot be proven or demonstrated on the strength of small samples. What is less certain, and at this point the more subjective aspect, is the size of the sample required to allow one to generalize to "the whole of a person's writing."

The heterogeneity of people in respect of the behaviour of handwriting is a matter that may never be proven empirically, but will have to be, to some extent, assumed and accepted, much like fingerprints. It is not practical to obtain standards of either writing or fingerprints from the world populations. Fingerprints, however, do have a system of classification that enables the millions of prints recorded so far to be studied for duplicity, and the data is growing daily. Instances of duplicity, if and when such occur, can be tabulated and their frequency of occurrence, together with other information that may have a bearing on duplicity, can be readily compiled. With such information and data, the quality or level of duplication and the impact of duplicity on the reliability of the process can be calculated. Handwriting identification does not yet enjoy this luxury.

Support for the claim of individuality in handwriting and the human ability to perceive it can be established with some confidence by a proper, scientifically-conducted study of the writing products of those persons in whom genetic or external influences are controlled to the extent possible. Pophal and Dunker[9] demonstrated the highly individualistic character of the movements of the hand in the air in the course of the writing process, by the use of slow motion photography. The studies of Norinder[10] and others on twin differences in writing performance disclosed that slant, minuscule height, supralinear heights, and regularity are not, to any significant degree, genetically determined. However, these endeavours and those of others[11] have not yet taken their place in validating the foundation upon which the work of the document examiner is dependent. Rather, for many examiners, the study of many writings within their personal experience induces belief in the uniqueness of writing without further proof, just as the observation of physical features persuades us that if we examine with care we are able to discriminate between any two individuals.

The Dionne quintuplets of Canada provide as reliable evidence as may be found anywhere of the fact that the discriminating elements (characteristics) of handwriting are not genetically determined. Being one of the first sets of quintuplets known to survive, and only the third set of identical quintuplets known to medical science, responsibility for their welfare was assumed by the government almost within hours of their birth. Under these circumstances, all of the variables respecting the development of their writing habits that could be controlled were, in fact, controlled.

They shared the same prepared environment constantly, the same influences which were so restricted as to exclude siblings and parents for nearly nine years. They shared the same experiences, they ate together, slept together, travelled together, had the same teachers, nurses, food, cooks, clothes and, until the age of eighteen, were not permitted to exist for any period of time in isolation from each other.

Sample writings exist, of which we have photographs, that were taken during the quintuplets' formative years. While these writings may not be fully representative of their executions after maturity they do demonstrate the individuality of the writings at this age. It is only reasonable to expect that with time, the disparity became more, rather than less, pronounced.

While this may constitute evidence that handwriting habits are not genetically determined, or totally dependent upon environmental influences, the feasibility of any particular group of habits serving to distinguish one writer from all others within a given population has yet to be fully explored or established. We are still without empirical data to tell us how significant particular writing habits may be, and how large a group of habits must be considered.

In the absence of such data, we are constantly facing the question as to whether the writing we are studying, at any given point in time, is one of these rare instances. Could there be another writer, whose execution of this quantity of questioned writing, would be so similar to that being studied that such a quantity may be insufficient to permit a reliable discrimination? And if it is one of those rare instances, how will we know?

A step in this direction was taken by Twibell and Zientek[12] in a study of the writing of three signatures "John P. Smith" by 130 subjects. Only two writers produced signatures that were deceptively similar, and even they could be discriminated when examined carefully. Whether or not this work contributes significantly to the larger question of the heterogeneity of the writing of the population generally, it does support the cautions of Harris, that care must be exercised in the examination of limited writings with few particularly distinguishing features.

Welch[13] has offered what he considers to be "compelling evidence for the individuality of handwriting" in his account of four cases in the United Kindom occurring within the last 25 years. In the first case, Harvey and Mitchell[14] reported that, on the strength of six writing features, a sample of 1,046 writings was searched to find the writer of a questioned cheque. A single writer was found that a more complete examination confirmed to be the writer of the cheque. In the second case, Baxendale and Renshaw[15] reported that, on the strength of "a few single features," a sample of 600,000 writings was reduced to 4,900 for further study. While a few of these aroused sufficient suspicion to warrant obtaining additional writing standards, ultimately, all were eliminated as potential writers of the questioned document. The writer responsible was eventually found in another geographic location by further police investigation.

In an earlier case, again on the strength of an initial study of six writing features, 100,000 writing samples were screened, some of which were duplicates, in an endeavour to identify a particular writer. As in the previously mentioned case, none of the writers were associated with the unknown writing when a full comparison was conducted.

In the fourth and most recent case that Welch describes, 10,000 writers were screened on the strength of five writing features, and any writing exhibiting three or more of these features was selected for further study. Some 1,300 writings had been screened when the writer responsible surfaced in the search. The identification was confirmed by a full examination of the writings, the admission by the suspect and a plea of guilty at trial.

At the same meeting of the American Society of Questioned Documemt Examiners, Shiver[16] cited a 1996 case involving 13 spurious cheques passed at two military bases in the western United States. Information on the cheques suggested that the perpetrator was associated with a particular military unit of nearly 1,000 persons. An examination was conducted of postal locator cards for all personnel of the unit. From a short list of three persons exhibiting some lettering and numeral similarities, one individual was selected and approached for additional request writings, with which a definitive conclusion of identification was reached. The result was confirmed by the admission of the soldier involved.

This case was also offered as argument in support of the contention that writing is unique to the individual. Otherwise, correct discriminations such as this would not be possible.

The validity of the argument that any or all of these cases demonstrate the uniqueness of writing is difficult to judge. While identifications and eliminations have been determined by full examinations we are without information as to which and how many *discriminating elements* were involved, and whether the same battery of elements would be employed in all cases. We surmise that it was, but until confirmation is available, we are only assuming that the criteria in any one case was much the same for the others.

Corollary: the discriminative reliability of the identification process. This pertains to the accuracy of judgments made across samples of writing from different persons, including those that are simulations of another person's writing, by whatever process of imitation may have been employed. In one sense, it is a corollary to the principle respecting the uniqueness of writing to the individual. We are concerned, however, with the capability of the technique that is being employed to discriminate between any two writers.

It might be expressed in an interrogatory form: given that no two writings by different persons are identical, are the elements of writing considered in the identification process adequate and reliable grounds for the making of discrete discriminations?

We must bear constantly in our minds this corollary that, until we have established the discriminative reliability of the process that we use to differentiate between the writings of any two persons, we are unable to prove, indubitably, the heterogeneity of writing. If writing is not heterogeneous, or if our capability to discriminate is unable to prove, without exception, that it is heterogeneous, how will we know whether our examination and study is being deceived?

We cited above the reports of several cases in which large numbers of writings were successfully sorted and studied in search of the identity of a particular questioned writer. These cases are classic examples of the ability of the process and the people using it to differentiate large numbers of writings correctly, despite the lack of empirical data that critics claim is necessary. Notwithstanding this failing, one has to allow that the risk of deceptive duplicity in large samples of the population, some as large as 600,000, that may escape the discriminating process(es) employed, is extremely low. It might then be argued that the probability of a wrongful identification is so remote as not to warrant practical consideration.

Although we have suggested a compilation of 21 elements of writing that are or may be involved in the writing examination process, we require some more or less universal agreement that these, and perhaps only these, are the elements of writing that would be involved. Following that, we must provide some reasons for believing that these aspects of writing will serve to discriminate between any two writers of a given population, and to differentiate between the genuine and spurious executions of any single writer.

The accuracy of the process of discrimination will hinge largely on the heterogeneity of writing. If the process does not discriminate in all cases, some revision or refinement of our 21 elements, or of an examiner's capabilities and facilities, may be required.

The practise of saving handwritten addressed envelopes, that we have received over many years, has provided us with examples of essentially the same textual material from upwards of a thousand different writers. When appropriately considered, these writings, that now number 2,000 or more in total, can provide some empirical support for the hypotheses that (1) handwriting is sufficiently unique to the individual to permit discrimination between writers, and (2) competent examiners, employing the 21 point criteria (or a better one), are sufficiently capable of discriminating between writers with acceptable low levels of error — to sanction the acceptance of both hypotheses (see Section 35).

The study by Harris,[17] made of certain surnames in signatures, *Smith, Shaw, Harris, Dybdahl,* and *Dye,* taken from the Los Angeles County Registrar of Voters, illustrated the deceptive similarity that can be found between writers insofar as certain writing features. The intent of the paper was to caution examiners against over-evaluating the significance of certain features that were responsible for the pictorial similarity between different writers, especially in the study of short names and single examples. As Harris pointed out, most signatures displayed differences in subtle features that should not be disregarded, as well as similarities in some more striking respects.

On the other hand, Harris has alerted us to the similarity he found in signatures of the same names, particularly those consisting of 6 letters or less. His study also disclosed that some letters provide less variation in shape or design from one writer to the next, and that other somewhat peculiar letter forms can become popular and appear more frequently than might be expected.

Accordingly, the discriminative ability of the writing examination process must be considered with regard to the kind and quantity of writing to be involved in the study, if valid results are to be obtained.

Unfortunately, Harris' statement that so many of these signatures lacked individuality and looked alike that they were not worth photographing, has been criticized for implying that similarities between substantial numbers of the population do not merit serious consideration by document examiners.[18] We are inclined to the view that Harris' comment regarding the worth of the similarities was with respect to their value as additional illustrations of the substance of the paper. It emphasized the fact that short names, not written as signatures in the customary fashion and comprised of certain letters, may afford limited evidence by which writers can be reliably discriminated.

The fact that some writings in small quantities, under certain circumstances, seem similar should not surprise us. To be usable, writing must be read. To be read, writing must conform in some degree to standards of size and design that are recognizable. These standards are provided by copybooks or writing manuals. While individuality modifies the styles of these manuals, it does so within limits, if the writing is to be comprehensible. Furthermore, writing is still subject to some social forces that set penmanship (in terms of quality and consistency) as a desirable attainment. Consequently, small segments of the writings of many persons will afford little evidence by which they can be discriminated. This is particularly because of the fact that the natural variation of any handwriting works against the virtues that discrete measurement might otherwise afford.

Indeed, knowing that you are dealing with a writing that consists of habits in number and nature that are less discriminatory, and thereby, may be misleading as to their significance, is the reason for having competent and experienced examiners. These examiners advise the courts as to the conclusions to be drawn from the similarity or difference observed. All of which brings us back to the topic we were discussing a moment ago.

Handwriting identification is a process of Analysis, Comparison, and Evaluation. What Harris has illustrated is simply one of the situations in which evaluation is vital and not likely to be within the competence of the court or jury to judge.

Perhaps at this point it is useful to re-emphasize the argument stated earlier that all conclusions in handwriting identification, indeed in all branches of forensic science, are matters of probability. There is a risk of error in all findings, even when positive conclusions are reached. The intent of the examination process is to minimize that risk to the extent possible and/or to reduce it to a level below which it is impractical to consider. The question, then, as to whether we are dealing with a writing that two or more persons may execute very much alike, is a question that arises in every case under examination and study, though it may seldom be expressed.

While we may not yet have the empirical data of the kind and quantity that science would prefer, experience and case histories have demonstrated that, given adequate samples, a careful study and an appropriate examination, the principle of the uniqueness of handwriting is believable.

26. What Makes Handwriting Identification Different?

Because it is a member of the family of forensic sciences that is encountered on the investigative scene every day, there is an expectation by some that document examination, and, in particular, writing identification, can be as precise and positive in its findings as other branches, such as blood identification, drug identification, or that assumed for bullet identification. Perhaps too, because its focus is on handwriting, many presume that there is considerable correspondence between handwriting identification and graphology. Both concepts are fallacious.

To understand its differences, we must first review what handwriting identification is in order to draw comparisons with other vocations.

Handwriting is an acquired skill and clearly one that is a complex perceptual-motor task, sometimes referred to as a neuromuscular task. But it is more than just a skill. It is a skilled behaviour or performance. Its identification (or elimination) ensues from a study of habits — habits of behaviour.

Writing identification is a process of analysis, comparison, and evaluation, wherein an endeavour is made to apply appropriate principles of science and logic (the science of reason) in accordance with scientific method. It presupposes the heterogeneity of writing on the strength of the volume of evidence now available. It allows for natural variation of a range, peculiar to the individual, that diminishes according to the level of skill of which the writer is capable. A resolution respecting identity is founded on the presence or absence of a combination of significant and independent similarities and the presence or absence of a number of inexplicable disparities.

The focus of a handwriting examination, that is the physical evidence, is the conscious and deliberate issue of an animate body — a human being. In this, it is not unlike two other kinds of study of recent inception having forensic application, i.e., voice identification and linguistics. Notwithstanding the gross differences in the parts of the anatomy involved, these three fields pertain to the conscious and at least partially controllable issues of animate bodies — human beings.

The materials other forensic sciences examine, e.g., fire and explosive residues, blood, urine, glass, hair, or paint, are inanimate, or are the involuntary issues of an animate body.

From the perspective of forensic analysis, the principal difference in the products or issues of animate and inanimate bodies rests in the voluntary control that the body can exercise over its issues. Animate bodies voluntarily control such issues as its communications, its voice, or its grammar, but not the biochemical composition of its blood, urine, or hair at any given moment in time. Inanimate bodies, of course, exercise no voluntary control.

In other fields of forensic science such as physics, chemistry, and biochemistry, the evidence being sought, because of its inanimate nature, is considered to be, for the most part, invariable. Once recovered, because of its stability, it has been and will continue to be the same for an indeterminate period of time, as long as several months or even years. If it can be found in sufficient quantity, it can be identified with today's known standards, even after long periods of time. This, however, is only true if certain conditions are controlled, as they usually can be, particularly purity, temperature, and atmosphere. The variables that influence handwriting cannot all be readily controlled. Time itself constitutes a variable. Consequently, known standards often need to be contemporary in age.

Then too, findings in other scientific studies have a bottom line below which results are not determinable, i.e., certain steps in a process must be completed. The findings in writing examinations may vary to a substantial degree, with the quantity and quality of the material submitted for examination.

The phenomena of any two writing dilemmas are never precisely the same. Hence, the evidence available to resolve writing identification questions varies quantitatively and qualitatively. The essences of the analyses are seldom consistent. The essences of other analyses can be refined to amazing consistency, the point and purpose of purification. Thus, writing identification differs profoundly from other forensic science determinations.

The principal respect in which writing identification differs from graphology is that it does not interpret the writing elements that the examination discloses, as graphology attempts to do. Moreover, identification requires an adequate sample of writing bestowed with writing habits to render a determination. Graphologists may work from limited samples, sometimes from only a single signature. For them, writing habits are an ancillary consideration. Natural variation is not a matter of great concern. Scientific principles, logic, and scientific method are not a professed part of graphology.

It is argued that knowledge of graphology is beneficial in writing examinations for identification purposes, as both fields of endeavor are studying the same elements of writing, albeit with different objectives. The graphologist's objective is to interpret what he/she sees in terms of personality traits. The writing examiner's objective is to evaluate what he/she sees in terms of evidence of authorship. The two tasks, interpretation and evaluation, are based on different premises, and have different requirements. Even the treatment of writing elements that may be studied is different. Graphology tends to treat all elements as independent aspects of writing. Writing examination seeks signs of inter-dependence commonly referred to as "class characteristics," or simply "consistencies," that may alter the evaluation of the elements. Thus, the two fields of endeavor are in conflict and neither can succeed within the preview of the same person.

Experimental support for the assertions of graphology is extremely limited and books offer little empirical data in defense of any of the relationships between elements of handwriting and personality traits, that proponents claim for them. On the other hand, writing identification has much material from which to draw and on which to build.

Thus, handwriting identification is different, very different, and if the discipline is to serve society properly and appropriately, its differences must be appreciated and respected.

27. What Makes Handwriting Identification Difficult?

There are a number of circumstances or conditions that have an affect upon the conclusions which can be drawn in handwriting studies and examinations. These include:

- the qualitative insufficiency (lack of significance) of the habits exhibited by the questioned material, i.e., a predominance of letters that provide less opportunity for individualization
- wide variation in the standards from one writing occasion to the next
- the quantitative insufficiency of the habits that the questioned material contains
- poor writing skill and the degeneration of letter forms
- the unrealiability of reproductions, as a record of writing habits, and of the character of the original document (e.g., consistency of inks and of papers, the sequence of strokes), when examination of the originals is not possible
- the deliberate distortion or disguise of the questioned writing or of the writing standards
- an anomalous condition of the writer or circumstances of writing of the questioned document

28. What Are the Axioms, Maxims, Principles, or Laws that have Evolved that Guide the Examiner in the Study of Handwriting?

For many of us, discrimination between the terms *axiom, maxim, principle, theorem, theory,* and *law* is difficult, and their proper application to the circumstances of writing is not always clearly understood. McCarthy[19] claimed that the basic axiom of handwriting identification was that "no two writings by the same or different persons are identical." At the same time, he argued that heterogeneity **and** natural variation were its fundamentals and went on to say that, "there are no other axioms or corollaries involved in the process effecting handwriting identification."

It must be reiterated that habituation and the heterogeneity of writing are the two principles or premises on which identification is predicated. They are much more than axioms. They are the basis on which other propositions are made, and thus, by definition, they are principles. To these principles is attached a corollary, as yet unproven by appropriate empirical data, that, given an adequate sample, the discriminatory process employed (our 21 discriminating elements) is capable of making the necessary distinction between any two writers.

We hold a distinctly different view to that of others respecting natural variation (q.v., Section 30.C.18). Variation is an attribute of writing that has been observed. It is a reflection of the degree of consistency between or within standards or rather between samples of the discriminating elements present in the standards. As such, it constitutes a condition observed, an attribute of each discriminating element of writing that may be great for some and less for others, rather than a principle as others have asserted. Variations in writing cannot be completely controlled. Hence, we refer to them as natural variations.

Hilton[20] provided us with 10 rules and 13 corollaries, thereby, introducing these two terms to identify some general truths, respecting writing identification, that have evolved.

To ensure clarity in our use of the terms, we employ the following definitions to assist us in sorting and establishing the facts and the fundamentals respecting handwriting and handwriting identification:

- Axioms are well established or universally conceded propositions that are self-evident, not requiring demonstration, including some maxims.
- Laws are (1) particular phenomena deduced from facts, expressible by the statement that it always occurs if certain conditions be present, or (2) the conformity of individual cases to a general rule.
- Maxims are propositions expressing general truths of science or experience.
- Principles are (1) truths or propositions on which other propositions depend, or (2) assumptions forming the basis of a chain of reasoning.
- Theories are (1) systems of ideas that account for facts or phenomena, or (2) general principles offered to explain something.
- Theorems are universal or general propositions that are demonstrable.

There is another fine distinction that has to be made in this discussion. There are axioms, maxims, and principles, etc., respecting writing, and there are axioms, maxims, and principles, etc., respecting writing identification.

With the exception of the two principles and one corollary on which writing identification is predicated, the majority of the other statements that are made respecting writing or writing identification are axioms or maxims according to our definitions.

Insofar as writing, the following assertions may be made:

1. Writing is an acquired skill that is a complex perceptual-motor task (a fundamental principle).
2. The execution of writing is a voluntary act that follows behaviour patterns learned as habits (a fundamental principle).
3. As a complex perceptual-motor task, writing is heterogeneous (a principle).
4. Writing is comprised of gross elements, that are more consciously executed and conspicuous, and fine elements, that are less consciously executed and inconspicuous (a maxim).
5. With practise, writing becomes automatic (an axiom).
6. With automation, writing becomes more skillful (an axiom).
7. With improvement in skill, writing becomes less variable between executions, although some natural variations are inevitably present (a maxim).
8. Natural variations are the imprecisions with which the habits (discriminating elements) of the writer are executed on repeated occasions (a definition).
9. Natural variation is an attribute of each of the habits (discriminating elements) of an individual's writing. Its range varies with the skill of the writer and the particular allographs (letters) being executed (a maxim).
10. Owing to natural variations, no two writings of the same material by the same person are identical (a maxim).
11. Natural variations in writing diverge with the writer's condition, the writing conditions and may diverge with the nature of the document. When conditions are controlled, there is less variation between executions (a maxim).

12. Natural variations in writing are usually less in synchronous writings than in asynchronous writings (a maxim).
13. Handwriting changes progressively over the lifetime of the writer. The change is greater during the earlier and later stages of life, however, the nature and extent of the change is peculiar to the individual (a maxim).
14. Deterioration in writing for any cause affects all of its elements (a maxim).
15. The rate of progression in the deterioration of writing varies with individual circumstances (a maxim).
16. Temporary physical or mental conditions can produce transitory or temporary changes in writing that leave with the departure of the condition (a maxim).
17. A writer cannot ameliorate his maximum writing ability or skill without effort, practise and/or training over a period of time (a principle).
18. Quality in any human endeavour, and particularly in writing, is its own best defence against simulation, forgery, or counterfeiting (a principle).
19. The keys to synchronism versus asynchronism are found in the attributes of consistency and continuity (a principle).

Relative to writing identification, the following assertions may be made:

1. Handwriting identification is a study and comparison of habits (a law or definition).
2. Handwriting identification is a process of Analysis, Comparison, and Evaluation (Huber's law of ACE's).
3. What Analysis has found and Comparison has revealed, only proper Evaluation can render useful (a principle).
4. Any conclusion of identification derives from statistical inference and is an expression of probability having an arithmetic value somewhere between 0 and 1 (a law or a principle).
5. The identification of a writer is particular and demonstrable; the elimination (nonidentity) of a writer is general and speculative (a principle).
6. The identification of a writer is a consequence of the evaluation of similarities; the elimination of or differentiation between writers (i.e., nonidentity) is a consequence of the evaluation of differences (a principle).
7. The significance of a discriminating element in a handwriting varies inversely to its frequency of occurrence in similar text material in the writing of different persons (a principle).
8. The elements of writing are reasonably stable from one writing occasion to the next (a principle. The consequence of habituation).
9. No two writings of the same material by different persons are identical (a principle. The consequence of heterogeneity).
10. Age and sex cannot be precisely determined from an examination and study of a writing (a maxim).
11. A simulation of another's writing will resemble it to some extent, depending on the skill of the simulator (a maxim).
12. Intricacy of pen movement or complexity of writing pattern provides evidence in support of genuineness, when comparison with standards reveals similarity; and provides evidence in support of spuriousness, when comparison with standards reveals difference (an axiom).

13. One cannot exclude from one's own writing those discriminating elements of which he/she is not aware, or include those elements of another's writing of which he/she is not cognizant (the principle of Exclusion and Inclusion).
14. It is a greater task to duplicate another's writing habits that are similar to, but discriminable from one's own, because of the difficulty of maintaining subtle or minor changes to one's normal writing habits (the principle of Interference).
15. Simulated signatures can rarely be associated with the writing of the simulator (a maxim).
16. Traced signatures can rarely be associated with the the writing of the tracer (a maxim).
17. Disguise is the consequence of any deliberate effort to alter the discriminating elements of one's own writing (a definition).
18. Attempts to disguise the less conspicuous features of one's writing for which there are few readily conceived alternatives, are less subject to change and may, therefore, be of greater identification value (a maxim).
19. Attempted disguise produces an inferior quality of writing (a maxim).
20. The level of deception attained by an attempt at disguise will vary with: (1) the skill of the writer, (2) the perceptive ability of the audience, and (3) the nature and amount of writing involved (a maxim).
21. Articles, conjunctions, prepositions, and pronouns in the English language exhibit a greater degree of unconscious characterization or individuality than other less frequently used words (a maxim).
22. In writing identification, the natural variation of discriminating elements mitigates against the virtues that discreet measurement might afford (a maxim).
23. There is no alternative available to us other than numbers to define precisely what we mean by *probability, strong probability,* and *very strong probability,* or any similar expression, to indicate the respective levels of certainty that each represents (a maxim).
24. When any two items possess a combination of independent discriminating elements (characteristics) that are similar and/or correspond in their relationships to one another, of such number and significance as to preclude the possibility of their occurrence by pure coincidence, and there are no inexplicable disparities, it may be concluded that they are the same in nature or are related to a common source (the principle of identification).

References

1. Quirke, Arthur J., *Forged, Anonymous and Suspect Documents* (London: George Routledge & Sons, 1930), p 57.
2. Eldridge, M. A., Nimmo-Smith, I., Wing, A. M., and Totty, R. N., The Variability of Selected Features in Cursive Handwriting Categorical Measures. *Journal of the Forensic Science Society,* 1984; 24: 179-219.
3. Eldridge, M. A., Nimmo-Smith, I., Wing, A. M., and Totty, R. N., The Dependence Between Selected Categorical Measures of Cursive Handwriting. *Journal of the Forensic Science Society,* 1985; 25: 217-231.

4. Huber, R. A., *Handwriting Identification — Facts and Fundamentals. A Potpourri of Comments Intended to Educate, Consolidate, Stimulate, and/or Substantiate.* Presented at the meeting of the American Society of Questioned Document Examiners, 1982.

5. Harris, John J., How Much Do People Write Alike? *Journal of Criminal Law, Criminology and Police Sciences,* 1958; 48: 6.

6. Harris, Patricia R., *Disguise, Forgeries and Look-Alike Writing.* Presented at the meeting of the American Society of Questioned Document Examiners (Vancouver, Can., 1980).

7. Munch, Andre, *The Comparison of Very Similar Handwriting — Reflections on the Real Value of Handwriting Analysis,* Presented at the meeting of the International Association of Forensic Science (Vancouver, Can., 1987).

8. Hilton, Ordway, Some Basic Rules for the Identification of Handwriting. *Medicine, Science and the Law,* 1964; 4.

9. Pophal, R. and Dunker, E., Zeit lupenstudien des Schreibvorganges (Slow Motion Studies in Handwriting Movements), *Zeit schrift fur experimentelle und Angewandte Psychologie,* 1960; 1: pp 76-99.

10. Norinder, Ynge., *Twin Differences in Writing Performance.* Lund, Hakan Ohlssons Bodtry-ckeri, 1946 (see also the work of Francis Galton, in Huber, Phillipp, "Sickness and hand-writing," *Kriminalistic,* 1960; 14: 9).

11. Talmadge, Max, Expressive Graphic Movements and Their Relationship to Temperament Factors, *Psychological Monographs: General and Applied,* 1958; 72: pp 16-46.

12. Twibell, J. M. and Zientek, E. L., On Coincidentally Matching Signatures. *Science & Justice,* 1995; 35: 3: pp 191-195.

13. Welch, John R., *A Review of Handwriting Search Cases as an Indicator of the Individuality of Handwriting.* Presented at the meeting of the American Society of Questioned Document Examiners (Washington, 1996).

14. Harvey, R. and Mitchell, R. M., The Nicola Brazier Murder: The Role of Handwriting in a Large Scale Investigation. *Journal of Forensic Sciences Society,* 1973; 13: p 157.

15. Baxendale, D. and Renshaw, I. D., The Large Scale Searching of Handwriting Samples. *Journal of Forensic Sciences Society,* 1979; 19: p 245.

16. Shiver, Farrell C., *Case Report: The Individuality of Handwriting Demonstrated Through the Field Screening of 1000 Writers.* Presented at the meeting of the American Society of Questioned Document Examiners (Washington, 1996).

17. Harris, John J., How Much Do People Write Alike? *Journal of Criminal Law, Criminology and Police Science,* 1958 Mar/Apr; 48: 6: pp 647-651.

18. *United States v. Roberta and Eileen Starzecpyzel,* 880 F.SUPP. 1027 (S.D.N.Y. 1995).

19. McCarthy, John F., *The Axioms of Handwriting Comparisons.* Presented at the meeting of the International Association of Forensic Sciences (Wichita, KS, 1978).

20. Hilton, Ordway, Some Basic Rules for the Identification of Handwriting. *Medicine, Science and the Law,* 1964; 4.

The Discrimination and Identification of Writing

29. What is the Language of Letters?

In espousing new ideas respecting the study of writings and letterings we must begin by defining the terms that will be used, to avoid confusion and to foster understanding.

When we speak of letter designs we tend to think only of the Roman alphabet. Writing examiners, however, are frequently involved in the examination of writing in other languages and alphabets in which there is remarkable variety, not confined simply to the formation of characters, but variation also in the number of characters employed. We find, for example, that to suit their alphabets to their sounds, languages require different numbers of characters or letters. English requires 26, Hebrew and Italian use 22 characters, Arabic employs 28 and Russian, 36. The alphabets of other European languages are equally diverse: Polish, 45; French, 25; Danish, 27; Spanish, 29; Hungarian, 38; and Albanian, 33. Eastern dialects are even more diverse: Tibetan, 35; Telugu, 48; and Japanese, 73.

Under these circumstances, the term *letter* is in some ways an imprecise one. Is the printed (uppercase) "L," the printed (lowercase) "l," and the handwritten (cursive) "*l*" the same letter, or are they different letters? And if they are the same letter, what term is to be used to distinguish between the three designs? Linguists interested in written language have proposed a number of new terms that are enjoying a significant degree of acceptance and use within the new discipline of graphonomics and in its current publications of research conducted.

Ellis[1] proposed a three-tier system that recognizes the grapheme as the most abstract unit. Hence, the English alphabet comprises 26 graphemes, of which "*l*" is one. In fact, there are more than 26, for there are a number of signs and symbols, such as "$" and "&," that are customarily included with the characters of the alphabet. When writing a word, one has to know the identity and the order of the component graphemes. Spelling processes specify this orthographic structure in terms of graphemes. Thus, a grapheme is the abstract representation of a letter, and a word is spelled as a string of graphemes.

Each grapheme is represented at the next level by a number of allographs, e.g., "L," "l," and "*l*." Systems of cursive writing, of manuscript, and of lettering or printing within a society are found in copybooks, manuals, and printing publications. These prescribe the particular designs of the allographs (and their uppercase or lowercase designs) for each

Figure 1 Varieties of upper and lowercase letter designs for the letters "p," "r," and "t" suggested in writing manuals.

style, to be used in certain positions within a given word. Some systems offer optional allographs for the same grapheme. Thus, in cursive writing we have two commonly used designs for the letters "r," "t," and "b," and as many as three designs for the "P," "B," and "R" (Figure 1).

Then too, as expounded below, individuals develop their own habits of mixing allographs (cursive, script, and/or lettered) depending upon the position of the grapheme within a word, or upon the allographs that precede or succeed the particular grapheme.

The third level in the descriptive hierarchy is the actual graph — the pattern of ink on the paper representing, for that writer, a particular allograph. Any given allograph will be produced and perceived, in grossly or minutely different fashions, in the writing of different individuals, or of the same individual on different occasions. These comprise the normal and natural variations between and within writers.

The graph, then, (i.e., a written pattern or form) is a writer's rendition of an allograph (i.e., a particular letter or character in cursive, script, or lettered style, in uppercase or lowercase design), respecting a particular grapheme (an abstract entity of a particular alphabet).

This language for reference to handwriting has now been adopted by scientists and academics around the world in reporting research studies. As Brault and Plamondon[2] expressed it:

> "...for any given word, each letter appears after having gone through three levels of representation: the grapheme (a concept of a letter without a precise form); the allograph (representing a precise type of letter); and the graph (representing the sequence of appropriate movements for the formation of the letter)."

There is, of course, a physical and final step that activates the specific muscles, in sequence, required to effectively form the graphs (letters) for the word.

We need not abandon the term *letter* when a precise descriptive level is not involved. The system is offered, indeed recommended, for use when clarification of the nature of the character in a process or occurrence is needed.

Handwriting examination is a study of graphs, that are the writer's graphic representations of a certain set of allographs. Different writers may have different concepts, or choices of the options for the allographs the text of the writing requires. Obviously, an identification of a writing implies that the graphs in the questioned and standard material derive from the same concept or choice of the allographs, comprising the written word.

30. What Are the Discriminating Elements of Writing that are Habitual, Individual, and of Potential Value in Writing Identification?

Numerous aspects of writing become habitual with practise, and execution becomes more automatic as the writing process subjugates itself to the thought process. The individual is more concerned with what is being written than how it is being written. Coincidentally, due in part to the complexity of the writing process, the individual develops his/her own idiosyncrasies in both the shape or form of letters and the fashions in which they are combined, all of which become habitual with practise. All of these habits, considered in combination, constitute the means by which the handwriting of one may be discriminated from that of another, or associated with a writing in dispute.

As previously mentioned, much like fingerprint identification, handwriting identification presupposes that handwriting is unique to the individual. While the empirical data to prove such a hypothesis is not yet considered sufficient by the adversaries of handwriting examination, handwriting examiners have, for many years, allowed their experience and that of other examiners to supply the confidence needed to assume the hypotheses to be true to the extent that, within limited populations, serious errors will not occur.

If handwriting is unique, then it is only reasonable to conclude that its individuality lies in the habits that are developed and become fixed to some degree in the writing performance. If individuality was to manifest itself in some more variable aspects of the writing, whatever they might be, the potential for and probability of duplication of these features in some other person's writing would increase, and discrimination between individuals would be less likely.

The study of writing is fraught with many problems. There are innumerable variables for which to account. Perhaps the most pressing problem, however, is that there is neither common terminology to describe or identify writing components, nor a consensus on the factors or aspects of which handwriting is comprised, that serve to distinguish between writers. This was called *conspect reliability* by Klimoski and Rafaeli[3] in their five-point criteria for the acceptance of a discipline by the scientific community. It was also the concern of a study by Blake.[4] It was a priority in the six-point criteria suggested to achieve scientific status for writing identification,[5] that we have chosen now to call conspectus reliability.

Without implying credence to their discipline, we must allow that students of graphology have made greater efforts to identify significant handwriting variables. If we do not embrace their objectives, we can at least recognize that, for the most part, their discipline and ours are focused upon the same elements of the writing process, but for different reasons. Accordingly, we might benefit by their work in this area.

Lewinson[6] itemizes 15 aspects of writing that early graphologists sought to measure. Lorr, Lepine, and Golder[7] measured 16 characteristics. Lemke and Kirchner[8] claim to have measured 47 handwriting characteristics with a ruler and magnifying glass. Peebles and Retzlaff[9] selected and studied 25 of these 47 features to determine whether even smaller groups of characteristics might serve to discriminate between writings. It was their finding that the factors of heights, widths, and angles could be used to greatly improve the reliability of handwriting measurement.

Strangely enough, the attendees at a meeting in 1931 of the forefathers of the American Society of Questioned Document Examiners were each asked to describe and illustrate 20 of the most significant individualities in handwriting. The reason for selecting the number 20 is not known, but the diversity in the recorded results of some of the participants is remarkable. Certainly, consistency in thinking was needed then, but the little that has been achieved in 67 years furnishes some justification for this attempt to articulate the topic.

Our own consideration of the matter over a number of years has lead us to the conclusion that there are 21 elements of writing that we employ, as a matter of practise, in the task of identifying or discriminating between handwritings. This is dependent upon how one classifies these elements. Furthermore, it is not surprising that there is considerable correspondence between our list and others, although the terminology and consolidation may differ. The consolidation of terms is probably the principal virtue in the catalogue we are advancing.

Osborn used the terms elements, qualities, and characteristics of writings without clearly differentiating between them, and others followed his example in their use without clarifying the issue for us any further. Many examiners use the term *characteristics*, while others use the term *individualities* or the expression *identifying individualities*, as Conway was inclined to do.

We have chosen the term *discriminating elements* as the most appropriate expression to use in reference to the aspects of writings that are involved in their identification or differentiation. The so-called standard texts employ various terms, such as *characteristics*, *qualities*, *features*, and *elements*, and go to some length clarifying the difference between them without attempting to define each of them precisely. On the other hand, the term *discriminating element* lends itself to definition in a particularly simple and understandable form.

> Definition: A discriminating element is a relatively discrete element of writing or lettering that varies observably or measurably with its author and may, thereby, contribute reliably to distinguishing between the inscriptions of different persons, or to evidencing the sameness in those of common authors.

There might be some merit in employing a term that is somewhat more or less vernacular that might develop a relationship with handwriting much as the term *symptom* has grown to acquire with respect to medical conditions. At this point, we are unable to offer an acronym or some other term likely to acquire general usage.

Only one other dissertation[10] of which we are aware has attempted to consolidate and delineate the discriminating elements of handwriting in a collection of some 17 points, organized in four categories, that we find somewhat vague and imprecise. Since it is a program followed by forensic laboratories in the Netherlands, it may have suffered in translation. As might be expected, there is some correspondence between their list and ours, but there are a number of elements that will be found in our inventory that don't appear in the Netherlands catalogue.

In organizing one's thoughts on this topic, it helps to segregate the discriminating elements of writing into two principal categories and two others:

A. Elements of style consisting of arrangement, connections, construction, design, dimensions, slant or slope, spacings, class, and choice of allograph(s). With the exception, perhaps, of construction, these are the aspects of writing that play a significant role in creating a pictorial, or general or overall effect. Differences in construction, of course, do not necessarily alter the overall effects.

B. Elements of execution consisting of abbreviations, alignment, commencements and terminations, diacritics and punctuation, embellishments, line continuity, line quality or fluency (speed), pen control (which includes pen hold, pen position, and pen pressure) writing movement (including angularity), and legibility or writing quality (which includes letter shapes or letter forms for any given allograph).

C. Consistency or natural variations and persistency.

D. Lateral expansion and word proportions.

Elements of execution are the aspects of writing that are the less obvious, more subtle elements, that frequently require the microscope or other technical assistance to fully assess. In large measure, they are the personal idiosyncracies of writing in which we find the subtle dissimilarities between the writing of one individual and the next.

Thus, without implying their relative importance by the order chosen, it can be stated that writing habits having identification value consist of the following. We feel they can be appropriately entitled the Discriminating Elements of Handwriting.

A. Elements of Style

1. Arrangement

Arrangement is a group of habits that are influenced by the writer's artistic ability, sense of proportion, and the instruction received. It may be evident in:

- the placement and balance of text
- the dimensions and uniformity of all four margins
- the interlinear spacing
- the parallelism of lines
- the character, position, and perhaps frequency of interlineations
- the depth of indentions
- the paragraphing
- the use of numerals and symbols in monetary amounts
- the location and nature of headings, salutations, introductions, and conclusions
- the location of signatures, relative to margins, rulings and constraints
- the style, size, and position of addressing on envelopes.

Arrangement can be a matter of considerable importance in the identification of authors of extended writings. Not all aspects of arrangement that we have itemized above will be available to study in every case. The type of document and the extent of the text will determine the factors that might be considered.

Matters of arrangement are taught in many business schools, but the number of graduates from these schools is relatively small. For the most part, people grow into, rather than consciously acquire, arrangement habits. It was Osborn's view that no other characteristic in handwriting was more indicative of literacy or illiteracy than habits of arrangement.[11]

The placement and balance of text.   This aspect of arrangement is closely allied to, if not a product of, the matter of margins. We tend, however, to think of the balance of text as respecting the left and right margins of the page principally, and give less thought to the dimensions of the top and bottom margins. To be precise then, marginal dimensions (all four of them) are the cause, placement of a text is the consequence, and balance (in any direction) is a judgment of the result.

Writers that are inclined to dispense with a right margin, are often seen to compress writing to ensure its fit within the edge of the sheet or space available. If compression of many lines of the text occurs, the result is that the text may appear to be imbalanced in that more writing in letters or words is present on the right side of the document than on the left. Balance, however, can be overlooked.

The dimensions and uniformity of margins.   It is not uncommon for left margins to be pronounced and consistent and for right margins to be completely disregarded. On ruled paper, left margins will be influenced by the location of a vertical rule, if one is present. There are writers that provide substantial margins in every direction, and subsequently, are not adverse to using the space to finish the communication if some space is needed, but not enough to justify another sheet.

Of particular interest in the study of arrangements is the disinclination of the writer to utilize hyphens and to split words out of deference to a particular dimension of margin on the right side of the text. If a right margin of any width has been established, it will be found that many, if not most, writers will violate the margin rather than hyphenate the word.

Another aspect of margins that has been frequently observed is that the top and bottom margins are of a smaller dimension than the side margins. Indeed all four margins may exhibit different dimensions. Unquestionably, margins merit attention and should not be disregarded.

The interlinear spacing.   Interlinear spacing is usually predetermined by ruled paper. Individual spacing tendencies or habits become apparent only in writing on blank or unruled sheets. Generally speaking, on unruled paper, interlinear spacing for most persons is slightly greater than the approximately 7 to 9 mm in which ruled paper is inscribed. For some whose writing is relatively small, the spacing can be apparently great. For some others whose writing is relatively large, it is not uncommon for the lines to be or seem to be crowded, and for the loops or staffs of infralinear and supralinear letters to intersect.

The parallelism of lines.   If we define parallelism as being the quality or state of being parallel, and we allow, that on unruled paper, writing lines may not be consistently parallel, we come to realize that the condition we are appraising is the overall alignment of each line of writing relative to its imaginary baseline. Indeed we might look at the matter from the perspective of alignments, except that in the present sense we are suggesting that all of the line alignments be viewed in a comprehensive fashion, in order that the cumulative effect of a sequence of lines, if there is one, can be observed, studied, and appreciated.

In this respect it will be noted that alignments may decline progressively, and it is not unusual to observe some effort to correct the situation as the writing nears the bottom of the page.

The character and position of interlineations.   Interlineations tend to be of two kinds: (1) words or short groups of words inserted into a sentence that alter the context to some extent. This is the short form interlineation; and (2) whole sentences inserted into a document where space is available to inject additional conditions, provisions, or requirements that alter the terms or the context of the document to a significant extent. This is the long form interlineation.

The short form interlineation is usually preceded by the insertion of a caret. A caret is a mark in the shape of a small inverted "v," the name of which was derived from the Latin for something lacking. The size, shape, and position of the caret can vary somewhat with the individual. The principal dispute respecting short form interlineations is whether they are changes made at the time of the creation of the document or some time after its completion and issue.

The key to the determination of the origin of the short form interlineation lies in its consistency: the consistency in the inks involved, in the writing instrument, and/or in the writer. In this last respect, the nature and execution of the caret should not be overlooked. The study of the points of intersection of writing lines was also recommended by Osborn, but the sequence of the textual writing and the short form interlineation is rarely an issue.

Long form interlineations are not usually accompanied by carets. The intention is to make them appear to be original components of the document. Here again, consistency in the ink, the instrument, and/or the writer will be key to determining whether the material was a later insertion.

Other aspects of the questioned material in suspected long form interlineations, however, must also be considered. If, in fact, it was a later addition to the document, then depending on the amount of text involved and the space available for it, there may be evidence of compression of the writing to render it appropriate for the space. Furthermore, under these circumstances the sequence of the writings of intersecting lines of the questioned material and the text of lines below it, and only below it, may be a factor of considerable significance.

Handwritten interlineations in typewritten text usually eliminate consideration of the consistency of the inks involved, unless there are other handwritten material or signatures on the document with which a comparison may be made.

The depth of indentions.   A review of available literature has not revealed a source that stipulates what the depth of indentions for paragraphs in extended writings should be. Examples that are provided in penmanship courses range from no indention at all to an indention of half of a line length. The inference to be drawn from instructions that are given is that the writer is at liberty to choose an indention of any length that is pleasing to the eye and conforms to or provides a balance to the text.

Our experience has exposed us to examples of both extremes on the scale (none to one-half line) with a majority that fall into the group with a dimension between one-half and one and one-half inches. We note, too, that the omission of an indention seems to be more common of late. When that occurs it is usually accompanied by some increase in the interlinear space immediately above to identify the commencement of a new paragraph.

Obviously, it is an element of writing that can be considered principally in the study of extended writings, such as anonymous letters. Both Osborn and Harrison comment on its usefulness as a discriminating element, but that purpose is served when the depth of the indentions are extreme variations from the norm, in either direction. Admittedly, it is a feature of writing to which few persons give much thought, and that has a bearing on its usefulness in the study of disguised or anonymous writings.

The paragraphing.   The word *paragraph* was at one time simply the name given to the mark ¶ written in the margin of a manuscript where a unit or subdivision of the text was to begin. The signal we currently use for that purpose is to indent the first line, however the pilcrow, the formal name of the mark ¶, is still used in legal literature to mark or identify paragraphs, and is generally employed as a proofreader's mark to indicate a paragraph beginning.

As a signal, then, and an aid in the comprehension of text, we can think of the indention of the beginning of a paragraph as a kind of punctuation. The rules for the application of that kind of punctuation vary substantially with the nature of the text to be punctuated. Consequently, we have little information as to what would constitute normal paragraphing (i.e., the copybook style), and what practises would be unusual or individual.

Communications that are extended writings, such as are encountered in anonymous letters or disguised writings, are usually classed as expositions. Generally in expositions, a paragraph is defined as a related group of sentences, with or without a summarizing sentence, but the extent to which this rule is consciously followed in personal communications is quite limited. There are some individuals that never paragraph from the beginning to the end, and there are others that tend to make paragraphs out of every sentence.

As with many other elements of writing, greater discriminative value in the examination and study will occur when the writer diverges distinctly from what intelligence tells us should be the norm or that which conforms with our definition.

The use of numerals and symbols in monetary amounts.   Over the years, various endeavours to classify writings have begun with the classification of writing on cheques. Prominent in this work were the manners in which numerals were written and how they were used in the inscription of monetary amounts. Horan and Horan[12] saw fit to include the frequency with which zero's are connected to one another in their study of numerals. They reported that 18 percent of their population of 700 subjects joined two or more zeros together at the tops. Related to this is the manner in which some individuals employ the "x" or simply the dash in place of the zeros in round figured monetary amounts.

The location and nature of headings, salutations, introductions, and conclusions. There is little that needs to be said on this subject. There are few standards against which the practises of a given writer can be judged. Individual idiosyncracies frequently appear that are almost self-evident as unusual practises.

The location of signatures.   There was a time when the signature to a letter was invariably placed below and to the right of centre of a text, but that is no longer the case, and signatures may occur in various locations. Their relationships to text, to margins, and to rulings, if any, may all warrant study. The manner in which they occupy a confined space may also be noteworthy.

The style, size, and position of envelope addresses.   Few people are aware of their habits in respect of arrangements or to appreciate how their habits differ from those of others. Yet their habits may be distinctive as in the extent of indentions at the beginning of lines, the spacing of address lines without the benefit of rulings, and the position of the material relative to the envelope edges.

Harrison points out the value in the arrangement of envelope addresses in the study of anonymous letters. As a common act, it becomes quite automatic and is one in which the attention of the writer is directed at legibility rather than arrangement protocol. For this reason writers develop a style for themselves from which they rarely depart.[13]

What must be borne in mind, in the course of obtaining request writings from a possible author, is that in order for the standards to be useable they must be furnished from dictation that is carefully prepared and discretely administered. There must be no external influence insofar as any of the 11 factors of arrangement above mentioned that the writer might exhibit.

2. Class of Allograph — The Four Styles of Allographs

Style is a term that has been applied rather loosely to apparently different patterns of writing habits executed by individuals under different writing circumstances. For many persons, there seems to be a difference in writing practises between the writing of formal letters and the scribbling of notes. Whether these differences should be identified and described as different styles of writing or whether they are simply alternatives to some gross features, such as slope and lettered capitals that have become the writer's practise in less formal executions or on certain special occasions, is a moot point that only a careful study of adequate writing standards can resolve. They may be simply a brief disregard for care and quality often described as scribbling. Shaneyfelt[14] commented on the variety of styles of writing exhibited by some individuals in the signatures appearing on FBI (Federal Bureau of Investigation) fingerprint cards. The writing involved is limited to one or two signatures per card, however, and on the strength of these it is difficult to discriminate normal, natural writing from a short-term or long-term disguise, or from a deliberate modification. Persons in police custody may have good reasons for making at least pictorial changes to their writing. While Shaneyfelt's comments are a caution against the impulsive elimination of a writer as a probable author of a given questioned signature in any examination, we are unsure as to the frequency with which we may expect to encounter one of Shaneyfelt's versatile writers.

In the sense in which we are employing the term, there are four principle styles or manners in which people using the Roman alphabet endeavour to communicate with the pen. They are, in fact, the four general categories into which all allographs may be segregated. Care must be taken that changes in writing quality, due to haste, negligence, or deliberate writer action, are not improperly perceived as changes in writing styles or allographs, which are as follows:

a. Cursive writing, in which letters are connected and are designed according to some commercial system.
b. Manuscript or script writing, in which letters are disconnected and are designed similar to upper and lower case printing characters.
c. Handlettering, sometimes referred to as handprinting or block lettering, in which letters are separately structured and more often are designed as upper case printing characters.
d. Composites, of cursive writing and handlettering, of cursive writing and script, and somewhat rarely of handlettering and script.

Osborn credited England with the origin of manuscript writing,[15] but Marjorie Wise is credited with the development of the first manuscript alphabet for use in the United States in 1921, according to Anthony.[16] Osborn considered it to be a fad that, like most fads, would pass in time. Now, more than 75 years after its introduction, it is still with us, although its popularity may have waned.

Many producers of commercial cursive writing systems offer a method of manuscript writing for use in early grades of schooling, and some go so far as to recommend its use at each grade level. The American Book Company states: "Manuscript writing is four times easier and 20 percent faster than cursive writing…."[17] There is usually a transition point in the school system, however, at which a change from manuscript to cursive writing is arranged. This is frequently at or about Grade 3. There are also a few companies that produce commercial systems, and a few school systems that use them, who pursue the pre-World War II policy generally followed on this continent in which cursive writing is the sole system advocated. In these circumstances, manuscript writing is reserved for adults with special reasons for adopting a more distinctive style, such as architects and engineers.

Anthony attributes the development of the D'Nealian script writing system to Donal Neal Thurber, who used the letters of his given names to create the acronym. Thurber, a Michigan educator is reported to have begun development in the 1960s in an attempt to ease the learning of writing for the very young and to facilitate the transition to cursive writing later on. Simplicity and legibility were his goals. As in other recently developed systems, slant is not important so long as it is consistent. The publisher, Scott, Foresman and Company, claims this to be the first new writing system offered in the years since 1931.

Many different forms of the same grapheme or symbol are taught in both manuscript and cursive letters and numerals. Greater variation in shape is found in uppercase cursive letters and numerals, while less variation is found among lowercase cursive letters.

Handlettering is a style that individuals tend to develop for themselves. Perhaps because the lowercase forms of many print characters do not adapt well to execution by hand (e.g., "a," "e," "f," "d," "r"), there is a preference to use capital letter forms only. It might be argued that this style is simply a limited or modified version of manuscript writing or vice versa.

Where manuscript writing or handlettering becomes an individual's preferred style, and is used constantly, connections between letters frequently develop as speed of execution is improved. In this process, numerous individual characteristics can evolve. From the standpoint of writing identification, however, the disconnection of letters eliminates several features or writing habits, and evidence that might be utilized is, therefore, diminished.

Some examiners have argued that style characteristics are useless for the identification of a handwriting but allow that they may be indicative of nationality or the writer's country of learning. This then, is to admit that they serve as class characteristics which are very useful evidence in identification, although the weight to be given them must be appropriately modified. They must not, however, be totally disregarded.

3. *Connections*

    a. Intraword, i.e., between letters, of particular types, not necessarily related to or arising from the writing system.

    b. Interword, i.e., between words, if, when and where they occur.

The evolution of cursive writing from lettering to facilitate speed and ease lead to the introduction of connecting strokes between letters. Then, as Harrison puts it, "From time to time, attempts were made to purify handwriting by the elimination of these modern interlopers — the connecting strokes." Such a philosophy may have been responsible for the birth of manuscript writing of 50 years ago.

Harrison writes that in the civil service writing of England the connecting strokes are curved and relatively lengthy, unlike the straight angular connecting strokes of the American Business Hand. This was because of the abnormal separation of the letters in a word. Osborn says that the degree of curvature and the slant of connecting strokes is one of the most significant variations in handwriting. Ellen describes some of these variations, but beyond these three authors little has been written on the subject. Lee and Abbey,[18] under the caption of Connections, speak of the importance of disconnections as a writing characteristic, that in their time, of course, were digressions from the copybook style and were infrequent occurrences. Quirke (1930), placed importance on the forms of connections, categorized them in nine fashions and maintained that they were the progeny of speed, lateral expansion, and spacing. Spacing is, of course, one of the two integral parts of lateral expansion. He asserted, almost as a contradiction of Lee and Abbey, that except in the writing of master penmen, "one never encounters a writer who observes the conventions of copybook connections in their entirety." In recently written material Hayes[19] is the only examiner of whom we are aware that has dealt with the subject.

Osborn, Harrison, and Ellen all speak of the amount of retracing of the upstroke or lead-in stroke to letters having a bowl or circular component, such as the "a," "c," "d," "g," "o," and "q." All of them consider connecting strokes valuable in the identification process. All of them note that they are frequently overlooked in the simulation of a writing, and all of them comment that the task is more difficult in the examination of writing that is devoid of connecting strokes. We are, however, without a comprehensive treatment of the subject.

Connections are the unions of two or more letters. In cursive writing they are prescribed, merely by illustration in copybooks, to occur between any two lowercase letters. Some manuals also prescribe, again by illustration only, the connection of certain uppercase to the lowercase letters that follow, but this varies with the design of the uppercase letters that the system advocates. The "boat" letters, "B," "G," and "S" are invariably connected to following letters, but seldom the "I," even in a "boat" configuration. On rare occasions, connections may occur between two uppercase letters or between the characters of block lettering. Only the Zaner-Bloser company is known to have offered any actual direction as to the manner in which connections of any kind should be executed.

Psychologists have long referred to the upstroke to bowl type letters as secondary strokes, in that they are not essential to the recognition of the letter (Figure 2). Letters that are not bowl type, but that are loop type, trough type, or arch type, do not have secondary

Figure 2 Examples of lowercase cursive allographs without secondary (up) strokes.

strokes. They commence with an upstroke, described as a primary stroke, necessary for their recognition. Furthermore, according to the copybooks for writing systems, with the exception of the letters "b," "o," "v," and "w" that terminate with a horizontal bar, all other letters terminate with an upstroke that leads directly into the primary or secondary strokes of all other letters. The horizontal bars of the "b," "o," "v," and "w," or spurs as Harrison calls them, lead directly into modifications of the primary strokes or secondary strokes of the letters that follow, all of which eliminate the necessity for the initial upstroke. The particular modifications of the succeeding letters, or to their initial strokes that bars or spurs may induce, may provide some of the most unique and, therefore, useful discriminating elements of a given writing.

The point of this is that while there are unions of letters, or connections of one kind or another, actually, between lowercase letters, there are no such things as connecting strokes. To use the term *connecting stroke* implies that there is a distinct entity, identifiable as a pen or pencil stroke, that occurs between two written characters. What is being referred to as connecting strokes are the many manners in which unions are made between terminal strokes, bars or spurs, and initial strokes, irrespective of whether that initial stroke may be of a primary or secondary nature.

Worth noting is that in simulation of signatures, connections may be particularly important. The simulator may copy the letter designs but overlook a reasonable duplication of the manners in which letters are connected.

Few writing systems prescribe a method for the connection of capital letters to other capital letters. In these relationships one encounters true connecting strokes, that are distinct and recognizable entities quite foreign to the design of either letter. As a result a great deal of individualism can occur in these unions and the consistency of them that is of value in a study of the writing.

Furthermore, it is not too uncommon for a writer to connect words together, and the mere occurrence of these kinds of unions can provide a worthy contribution to the assembly of writing habits of a given individual. Interword connections are not suggested by copybook and, consequently, the pattern of practise in this respect is entirely individual. The practise of connecting words and the consistency in doing so may depend on the letters involved, the words involved or the writing situation, all or any of which may be difficult to determine, particularly if the text material is limited.

Thus, interword connections may not appear at first glance to be consistent practises of the writer, except for the fact that they are present. They do not necessarily correlate well with speed. Of some importance to the writing examiner is the fact that in disguised writing they may not always be omitted.

The other side of the coin is, of course, the matter of disconnections, that can be of equally great significance as the peculiarities of connections. Because disconnections are seldom, if ever, prescribed in writing systems on this continent, because they frequently constitute evidence of spuriousness, and because they are often referred to as pen lifts, it is our view that they warrant separate consideration that might better be dealt with under the caption of line continuity to be discussed.

4. Designs of Allographs and their Construction

In this category, we endeavour to include the factors related to the graphic forms of the particular letters of a writing. Elsewhere (Subsection 2, Class of Allograph) we speak of style as being either cursive, script, lettering, or mixtures, that are, in fact, four types of allographs for a set of graphemes. There, we are dealing with the forms of letters generally. Here we are dealing with some factors that relate to the system learned, some to structure of the character, and some to the patterns or styles selected, including the idiosyncracies of some writers insofar as the use and misuse of capitalization:

a.	correspondence to foreign/domestic or particular writing systems
b.	number, nature, position, sequence, and direction of strokes in allograph (letter) construction
c.	use of two or more designs for the same allograph
d.	capitalization — divergences from standard practises
e.	allograph (letter) combinations — wherein one allograph's design influences the structure or shape of its neighbour

To facilitate the discussion of the written characters of the alphabet, we must proceed from certain general ideas about the Roman hand that we presently practise. In this, we can benefit from Tannenbaum's[20] classification of cursive English writings executed during and after the time of Shakespeare. For him there were four varieties of cursive letters:

- Linear letters are those lowercase letters having no ascending loops or stems, (i.e., not supralinear) or descending loops or stems (i.e., not infralinear), sometimes called minuscules, consisting of "a," "c," "e," "i," "m," "n," "o," "r," "s," "u," "v," "w," and "x." There are no capital letters in this class.
- Supralinear letters are those letters that extend a distance vertically above the linear letters and include "b," "d," "h," "k," "l," and "t." Most capital leters, sometimes called majuscules, are included in this class.
- Infralinear letters are those letters that extend a distance vertically below the baseline of the writing or of the linear letters, and include "g," "j," "p," "q," "y," and "z."
- Double-length letters are those few letters that extend a distance vertically both above and below the linear letters, such as the "f," the "Y," and "Z" and in some systems the lowercase "p."

Writing systems.   Letter forms (i.e., allographs) are the principal fashions in which systems of writing, advocated by different schools of penmanship, choose to distinguish themselves. Older systems also differed from one another in proportions or relative heights, but dimensions are comparable in most of today's systems.

Letter forms (i.e., allographs) are also the principal means by which nationalities can be broadly discriminated, even today. Numerous other characters or symbols also assist in indicating the part of the world in which a writer developed his writing style. For more information on this topic see Writing Systems, National, Cultural, and Occupational, Section 37.A.

Some rather unusual letter forms and designs (i.e., graphs and/or allographs) have been observed and reported in the literature. Some of these are peculiar to certain occupations[21] and some are peculiar to certain populations (see class characteristics and national characteristics, Sections 12 and 13).

Allograph construction.   Winchester and McCarthy,[22] then later McCarthy and Williams[23] reported on unorthodox structures of the uppercase cursive letters "J" and "W" among black students in southern states of the U.S.A. In these instances the "J" is formed by executing the lower loop first and extending the upstroke from it to form the upper loop in a counterclockwise direction. The "W" is formed by executing a large numeral "3" in lieu of the initial and usually straight downstroke of the letter.

Daniels[24] described a very unorthodox structure of the lower case "p" that is without explanation. Normally the "p" is constructed by executing the staff or lower extension element first followed by the forming of a circular bowl in a clockwise direction. In Daniels' example, the bowl has been formed first in a counterclockwise direction that leads into the execution of the staff. When the stroke of the staff returns to the bowl, it proceeds to retrace the lower sector of the bowl, then moves on to connect to the subsequent letter.

Similar to Daniel's discovery, there are numerous unusual structures employed in cursive writing that seem to contradict the teachings of copybooks. The clockwise bowls of the letter "b," and the execution of the bowl after the staff of the letter "d" are two examples. The construction of block or capital letters in the process of hand lettering provides variations that are more frequently encountered. For example, there are as many as four sequences in which the horizontal bars or arms of the letters "E" and "F" may be added. The upper arm of the letter "K" may be either an upstroke or a downstroke. The "M" and "W" may be constructed of a single stroke or of as many as four. Even the "O" is sometimes made from two strokes rather than one. Similar variations can be found in numerals, particularly the "4," "5," and "8."

Multiple designs.   Wing[25] and later Wing, Nimmo-Smith, and Eldridge[26] endeavoured to determine whether the position of the letter or grapheme in a word had any effect upon the allograph selected. More recently, Van der Plaats and Van Galen[27] studied the affect of a preceding letter (i.e., "a" or "o") upon the selection of or consistency in the allograph. These authors point out that problems can arise in studies of allographic choice owing to the somewhat vague distinction that can occur between the allograph and the graph when the range of natural variation is broad. They found that greater variation occurs when the letter is located in the initial position than in the medial or final positions, and that the connection to or terminal stroke from a preceding letter might automatically lead to the selection of a particular allograph or letter design. Studies of letter designs employed in medial or final positions of a word should, therefore, be conducted with due regard to their immediate neighbours.

Capitalization.   Oddities in capitalization in cursive writing can occur in one of two fashions. Enlarged lowercase letters may be used as capitals, or uppercase letters can be used within words as common alternatives for lowercase letters. Letterings in lowercase styles, rather than block lettering, can produce a mixture of designs, the patterns for which, if there are any, may be difficult to fathom.

Allograph combinations.   Just as positions of a letter within the word (i.e., initial, medial, or terminal) may influence the allograph selected, so also may the nature or structure of its neighbouring allographs (letters) exercise some influence upon a character, if not in its shape at least in its size. In such instances, relative sizes can become important discriminators.

Note that, in keeping with lexical and other authorities, we use the terms *form, shape,* and *graph* as synonyms. Likewise, the terms *allograph* and *design* are used synonymously. Accordingly, shapes may vary substantially without entailing a change in design (Figure 3). This is done to achieve greater lucidity in the language respecting writing. The terms *form*

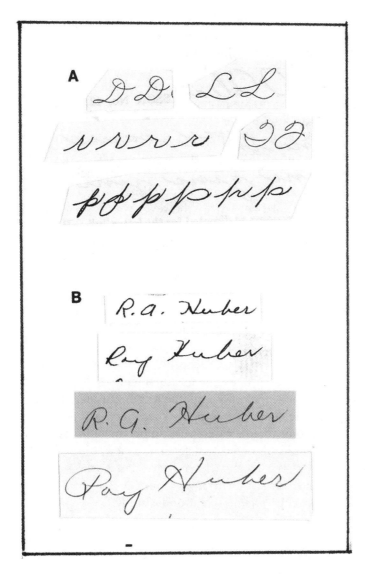

Figure 3 An illustration of the variation in shapes of letters that may occur without altering the design of allographs. Group B are the writings of one person. Group A are not.

or *letterform* in the broad customary sense are less specific as to whether reference is being made to aspects of the letter design, or to aspects of the shape (or graph) of a letter of a given design.

A letter design or an allograph may have a shape that is quite distinctive for a given writer. The shape will be a product of its dimensions, or the regularity of the curves in the principle strokes with which it is constructed.

5. *Dimensions*

There are a number of expressions that are used to refer to the physical measurements of writing, without an apparent clear distinction between their meanings, that can lead to confusion. These include such terms as *proportions, relative heights, size, relative sizes,* and *ratios*. Add to these such terms as *slant, slope, incline* and *lateral expansion* and we find we have a multitude of expressions without guides as to their particular applications. Different authors and examiners use different terms to refer to the same thing, or the same term to refer to different things. We are lacking the rules necessary to ensure that there will be some consistency between examiners in the meanings of the terms employed and their application to the study of writings. To clarify the situation we should begin by sorting out the principal linear measurements that are involved in the study of writing. Angular measurements will be dealt with later.

Individuals differ in their writing insofar as its vertical dimension and/or its horizontal dimension. Copybooks and writing instruction give us general parameters within which the writing should be executed and prescribe certain consistencies that should be observed. Nevertheless, many writers develop their own practises, some of which are quite distinctive and unique. Perhaps a majority of writers, however, will display a degree of similarity in these dimensions.

For starters we should clarify that vertical dimensions are measurements or judgments taken or made along a single vertical axis or two or more vertical and parallel axes. Horizontal dimensions are measurements or judgments taken or made along a single horizontal axis. Vertical is understood to mean at an angle of 90° to the baseline of the writing, and horizontal is understood to mean parallel to the baseline of the writing. The baseline of the writing may or may not coincide with ruled lines on the document.

The designs of most letters (with the exception of "M," "m," "N," "n," "W," "w," and perhaps the lowercase "k" and "q") can be considered to have a single vertical axis, that is to say that a single linear rule can provide the measurements of all the essential components in the letter's design (e.g., the length of a loop, the length of a staff, the height of a bowl, the height of an arch, and the depth of a trough). The letters "M," "m," "N," "n," "W," and "w" require us to employ two or three separate rules to obtain all the appropriate information.

Furthermore, it should be noted that from the viewpoint of writing identification, there are two aspects of dimensions in which we are interested: (1) their absolute measures, and (2) their relative measures. Which of these measures will be important and pursued will depend on the particular writing habit under study.

Proportions. The term *proportions* is used to describe, insofar as some aspect of size, the relationship of elements of letters to each other, i.e., of bowls to staffs (as in the "d," "p," "P," and "R"), of bodies to loops (as in the "z"), of upper loops to lower loops (as in the "f"), of bowls to loops (as in the "b" and "g"), of arches to loops (as in the "h"), of troughs to loops (as in the "y"), of bowls to bowls (as in the "B"), of staffs to arms or legs (as in the "k" and "R"), of upper loops to base elements (as in the "G" or "S"), of upper curve to lower curve (as in the "E"), or simply the relationship of small letters to tall letters.

Osborn[28] spoke of proportions frequently, in the sense of a class characteristic by which the writing system taught and followed might be identified. He differentiates between systems according to the relationship of short to tall letters as being, for Vertical writing (1:2), Old Round Hand (1:2½), Spencerian (1:3), Old Spencerian (1:4), and others (1:5). In this fashion, Osborn was using the term respecting the heights of letters relative to one another. In a second and less precise fashion, he speaks of the proportion of parts of a given word.

Osborn was dealing with writings executed when penmanship was in vogue and there was greater adherence to copybook standards. When writers varied notably from these proportions, significant individual characteristics developed.

Few of Osborn's contemporaries discuss proportions. Lee and Abbey (1922) mention proportions briefly, and like Osborn, for the purpose of making distinctions between the systems of Spencerian and Modern Vertical writing. They do, however, report on the process of graphometry, developed by Dr. Locard of France in which measurements of letter heights are taken to calculate proportions of letters to each other. Others would refer to this in the term *relative heights*. The results are alleged to provide convincing proof of nonidentity or strong corroborative evidence of identity.

Ellen speaks of proportions in block lettering in terms of height versus width of particular letters, much as Harrison used the term *relative sizes*. He then mentions *proportions of letters within a word* as others would describe *relative heights*. Hilton speaks of the proportional size of various letters and parts of compound letters, such as "k" and "g," that he says are matters of variation among writers.

Harrison[29] uses the term *ratio* almost interchangeably with *proportions* to refer to the relative heights of short letters, such as the "a" and "o" versus the tall letters, such as the "h," "b," and "l." He asserts that, to a great extent, the ratios of letters are maintained despite changes in size, speed, or intent of the writing (normal or disguised). Nevertheless, he holds that a similarity in ratios cannot, alone, be considered a reliable indicator of common authorship, but that a difference in ratios is a safe indicator of different authors.

Relative sizes of letters is a separate topic for Harrison, wherein he discusses the height versus the width of a letter. Osborn, in his list of points of consideration in the examination of documents, includes proportions of individual letters to each other, (and) proportions of parts of the same word, without elaborating on the proportions that he had in mind. In our view, these are matters of size, and we too believe that size and relative size should be dealt with separately from proportions. For us, they have distinctly different meanings. Obviously, there is a need for guidelines for the terminology to be used to achieve a measure of consistency and uniformity. Some definitions may help.

Definition: Proportion is the relation to each other of at least two measures along a single axis of a single entity, i.e., one letter or character.

Lexical sources define it as the ratio between two quantities of the same kind (e.g., vertical dimensions) and is the relation that one quantity bears to the other, the one being a multiple or part of the other, as in the relation of a part to the whole.

We think of the two quantities as being measured along the same axis, so that one quantity is clearly a multiple or part of the other. It should be employed, then, in the sense of the measure of a part relative to another part or to the whole. It would apply to the measurement of one element or component of a letter having two or more components, ("b," "d," "f," "g," "h," "j," "k," "p," "q," "y," "z," "B," "E," "G," "K," "P," "R," "S," "Y," and "Z") relative to its full vertical dimension, or to another component of the same letter (e.g., the two bowls of the "B").

Thus, the height of the arch of the "h" relative to the height of its loop, and the size of the bowl of such letters as the "d," "b," "p," "q," or "g" relative to their ascending or descending stems or loops, are aspects of writing that should be referred to as proportions in accordance with the definition provided above, because the measurement of their components can be made along a single axis.

The relation that the vertical dimensions of the arches of the "m" or "n" have to one another, or that the elevations that the sides of the "u," "w," and "y" might have to each other, cannot be included within our category and definition of proportions. The term should be reserved for measurements that can be made along a single axis in the vertical direction. Obviously, the measurements one would make, insofar as these letters are concerned, would have to be made along two or three parallel axes to ensure accuracy.

It might be argued that the measurement of the arches and sides of these letters along parallel axes should qualify them for inclusion within our definition. Copybook designs, however, almost invariably prescribe that arches and sides of troughed letters should be of equal height. When we think of relationships of a part to the whole, to which our definition pertains, we encounter a problem deciding which component of these letters is the part and which is the whole. The more appropriate and less confusing term for such measurements is relative heights.

Finally, proportion should not be applied to the relationship of a letter's vertical dimension to its horizontal dimension (two measures). This may be confusing, since many use this relationship as the basis for judging size.

If an extended amount of writing or a line of writing is to be considered as the single entity, then, as Osborn did in his time, there is only the measure of the average height of the small letters to the measure of the average height of tall letters that one might consider as a useable factor within the definition of proportion. A single, vertical measurement might then establish the proportions of the writing. However, because each of these averages is established on the strength of two or more independent measures of letter heights, it can be argued that relative heights is the more appropriate term to be applied. In either case, however, these measurements are less precise in many writings and the evaluation of similarity or difference must be more judiciously made.

Relative heights.   Some examiners use the term *relative heights* in reference to those letters in some writings that tend to be oversized for unknown reasons. We have observed, however, that such letters usually display an increase in their horizontal dimension as well as their height or vertical dimension, the two segments of size. In our view, they are, therefore, candidates for consideration under the category of relative sizes. For this discussion a definition may help.

> Definition: Relative heights is the relationship of the measures, along separate axes, of the vertical dimensions (only) of two or more discrete entities or components to each other.

Examples are the height of a "t" relative to the height of an "h" in *the, that,* or *this,* or of the "M" relative to the "rs" in "Mrs." It might be used to refer to the vertical dimensions of the arches of an "m," an "M," or an "n," or "N" relative to each other, or two of any other components of a letter having independent vertical dimensions (the sides of the "u," "w," or "y").

Absolute size.   The absolute size of writing is an aspect that, like many other writing habits, is of greater value when it exceeds the normal range of writings by being overly large or unusually small. Because we are taught to do so, and because the spacing of lines provided for writing on printed forms tends to be a constant frequently based on copybook dimensions, many of us tend to develop a size of writing that is similar. Accordingly, that which is unusual will be of much greater significance.

The subject of absolute size of writing is, however, more complex than it appears. Before writing can be judged as to size, we must agree as to which elements of the writing will be measured or considered in our estimates. Do we measure the linear letters? Do we measure the supralinear letters? Or do we measure from the tops of the tallest supralinear letters to the bottoms of the longest infralinear letters, that is from the tops of the "h" or "l" to the bottoms of the "y" or "g"? Writings do vary in their proportions of linear letters to the heights of ascenders and the lengths of descenders, and we must decide which letters are going to be subject to judgment or measurement.

> Definition: Absolute size is an approximation of the average heights of the linear letters of a writing, based on the measurements or judgment of their vertical dimensions, presuming that there is sufficient consistency to permit a reasonable approximation to be determined.

This is not to deny that ascenders and descenders have a bearing on size but simply to point out that their vertical dimensions are of greater service in the study of relative heights (and lengths) and proportions.

These judgments or measurements, however, are measurements in a single direction, vertically, and we must ask ourselves what bearing the width of a letter or of the spacing between letters has on our judgment of size. Certainly it has some, but how does one handle it?

Osborn evidently relied on linear letters only, for the application of measuring grids to determine size in writing. His illustrations of the use of the grids, however, were somewhat idealistic in that they made the task appear simple in measuring consistent writings in which all linear letters were of the same height. Both arches of the "m" were of the same height and the central elements of supra-linear letters such as the "h," "d," or "b," or of the infralinear letters such as the "g," "j," "q," or "y" were consistent with the size of the linear letters.

In this day and age, however, writing is not that consistent and the varying sizes of linear letters and the central components of other letters raises the question of how any scale might be applied to determine reliable and useable estimates of size. Obviously, an arbitrary procedure must be introduced that will vary with the textual material under examination. A particular allograph or allographs must be selected that appear in the text frequently and consistently enough to serve as the base for judgments. Obviously, too, in comparisons with a questioned writing, the same allograph must be selected for analysis.

The absolute size of a writing that is above average (whatever that is) is usually reflected in both its vertical and horizontal dimensions. Thus, a larger writing will be taller and wider. On the other hand, a smaller writing that is below average in size is invariably shorter, but may or may not display a similar or corresponding reduction in line length for the same text. This seems due to the fact that smaller writing frequently displays relatively greater lateral expansion (see below).

It should be noted that absolute size is a feature of writing that can be somewhat divergent under varying conditions.[30] Harrison argued that because handwriting size is controllable by the writer, "it cannot be regarded as an identifying feature of any great value." He does allow that normal and unrestricted writing is of a preferred size for the majority of persons. This seems to be his way of saying that size can be a useable feature when the normality of the writing is not in question. He goes on to say that an increase or decrease in size can be indicative of disguise, that, in our view and contrary to his earlier statements, makes it a feature of value but for another reason.

Harrison claims that fatigue can be responsible for a reduction in size, the omission of letters or of words, or even of groups of words. He maintains that fatigue can be responsible for the tendency of certain letter groups, such as "ing," to become thready or slurred.

He also argues that a reduction in size is the usual consequence of an increase in speed in writing. Speed, he says, is determined by the horizontal motion of the writing instrument and that vertical motion is counterproductive and, therefore, diminished as a result.

Greater space or the absence of ruled lines often induces a larger execution. A number of studies have endeavoured to determine the correlation, if any, between signature size and status or self-esteem, but the matter continues to be disputed.[31-39]

There are occasions when writing must be compressed in order to be accommodated in limited spaces, but as Morton[40] points out, this reduction is accomplished without fundamental alteration of the writing habits. Hence, she cautions against crediting divergences in writings to contractions due to space limitations.

Relative size.   Relative sizes of letters is a separate topic for Harrison, as it should be. He notes that copybook requires that many short letters, such as the somewhat circular structures of the "a," "c," "d," "g," "o," "q," and perhaps the "p" be of equal width, but this is rarely followed. Many will exceed or fail to match the normal dimensions of linear letters. He goes on to say that the absolute size of a writing varies with circumstances, but that this does not affect relative sizes. However, constancy in relative sizes of the letters is lost when the writer is experiencing either mental or physical stress.

Of considerable assistance in cursive handwriting studies is the relative sizes of letters or of elements of letters. Herein, one finds greater variation from one writer to another as well as within the writing of the same individual. Some writers will vary the size of a letter with the position it occupies in a word or with the particular letters with which it is combined. In other cases, certain letters will be persistently large or small regardless of location.

It is to be noted that block lettering is not immune to variation in the relative sizes of letters. In practised hands that prefer or need to use lettering, significant size relationships can be observed in the executions of many persons.

There are many cursive writers that vary the size of a letter. Sometimes the variation is related to its position within a word, or with respect to another particular letter. Some tend to enlarge letters that are the first in a word, for no special reason. Not infrequently, the lower case letter "r" will be found enlarged, especially when it is the first letter in the word. The study of the relative sizes of letters within a writing must take these practises, if they exist, into account to ensure that comparisons with questioned writings are valid comparisons.

Furthermore, to avoid some confusion, the examination must isolate the study of relative sizes of letters from studies of relative heights of letters, that was defined and discussed above.

> Definition: Relative size is the judgment of one letter against itself in other locations, or against the apparent standard size for other letters within the writing, whereas relative height is the judgment of the vertical dimension of a particular letter against the vertical dimensions of other particular letters.

Relative size implies a two-dimensional consideration of the letter, i.e., its height and width, both of which tend to increase or decrease correspondingly when the given letter varies from others in being enlarged or diminished.

We have spoken about *relative sizes* and *relative heights* of letters in writing almost exclusively with respect to lowercase letters, and their components relative to one another. In so doing, we may seem to have been dwelling on the relationships of linear letters to infralinear and supralinear letters, that is, those with ascenders and descenders. We cannot leave the topic, however, without noting the many other relationships that occur in writing that have a bearing on writing identification.

There are height relationships of specific letters with respect to other specific letters, according to their positions in a word or regardless of their location. There are height and size relationships of uppercase letters to lowercase letters, of letters to numerals, and of numerals to other numerals, all of which can be peculiar to the individual writer and, therefore, of assistance in his/her identification. For the most part, all of these judgments will be made on the vertical dimension of the characters, with the exception perhaps of the numeral zero ("0"), that is often found to be diminished in both height and width relative to other numerals.

Lateral Expansion. There is another linear dimension that is variable between the writings of different individuals that is referred to as lateral expansion. It is the product of letter formations, letter sizes, and the spacing between letters and words. Because interletter and interword spacing is the greatest contributor to variation in lateral expansion between writers, it seems more appropriate to discuss it further as a topic under the category of spacing.

6. *Slant or Slope*

    a. of the writing in general
    b. of letters or parts of letters in particular

Hilton defines slant in writing as "the angle or inclination of the axes of letters relative to the baseline." It is a matter that varies with different writers from a pronounced backhand to a sharply inclined forehand slope, with most angles between well-represented in the population. Indisputably, and in accordance with this definition, a slant of about 60° forehand, prescribed by most writing systems, is by far the most common.

Before going any further, however, there is good reason to rethink our definition of slant. When the angle of inclination is related to the baseline, problems in semantics arise. A change in slant to something more pronounced is spoken of as an increase in slant, when, in fact, it is actually a decrease relative to the baseline. It is an increase only in its relationship to the vertical, which is the perpendicular to the baseline. Osborn speaks of backhand slopes of ≤15° that can only be thought of as relative to the vertical, which is indeed the slope of one of the systems of writing of his time. Harrison speaks of enhanced slopes that one might interpret to mean greater slopes to the right. If slope is related to the baseline, however, these greater slopes are actually lesser.

As a solution to the confusion, we propose that slant or slope be related to the perpendicular or to the vertical. Lexical definitions of these terms suggest that vertical refers to a line upwards to some zenith point whereas perpendicular refers to a line that meets with another line at a right angle, such as the baseline of the writing. Accordingly, we offer:

Definition: Slope is the angle or inclination of the axes of letters relative to the perpendicular to the baseline of the writing.

This definition allows for the fact that some writings have ascending or descending baselines that can have an effect upon the slopes of letters. It can be readily understood, then, that as writing slopes lean further to the right or to the left, the angle increases and so the slope increases. No accommodation in our thinking is necessary.

Using the slope of the stem of the capital "T" as the determinant, Wing and Nimmo-Smith[41] observed, in a study of 61 subjects, that there was a statistically significant difference between the sexes, in that females wrote more upright (0.09 radians or $\approx$ 5.1525 degrees) than males (0.24 radians or $\approx$ 13.74 degrees). If the former is the more upright, then the angle of inclination must be considered relative to the perpendicular.

This study is somewhat in contrast to comments made in manuals of writing-system publishers that now place less emphasis upon slant. Stone, Smally & Cooke[42] state, "The slant (whether forward, vertical, or backhand) should be one which the pupil has success in keeping uniform." Purtell[43] noted that newer commercial systems considered slant in writing as not of major importance.

Osborn treated the matter of slope extensively as a means of distinguishing between the principal writing systems of his time and as a useable feature for distinguishing in many cases between writers. There was, of course, on average, greater quality and consistency in writing at that time than can be found among today's writers, and the indicators of writing systems are now seldom seen. In place of consistency in any respect, writing has become irregular for many persons and the value of measurement in the study of slopes in these cases is questionable.

On the other hand, a regular and consistent slope contributes substantially to the appearance and beauty of a writing. In mature writings, it remains fixed once it has been developed. Contemporary writers display a variation in the slope of their executions over a range of 50° extending from ±40° forehand, to a backhand slope of ±10° left of the perpendicular.

At the same time, slope can affect legibility. Backhand slopes are more often foreign to normal experience and greater effort may be needed in reading the writing. On the other hand, the eye and the mind can more readily adapt to an enhancement of slope in the forward direction.

Harrison claims that experiments have shown that small changes in slope are virtually impossible to achieve and maintain without impairing fluency, over a quantity of extended and reasonably skillful writing. Consequently, slope has been considered an important feature of writing identification.

Osborn maintained that a consistent difference of 15° or less in the slopes of two writings was indicative of different authorship. Harrison qualified this rule by arguing that speed of execution must be considered. In his view, fast and undisguised writing will exhibit a small increase in forehand slope, from the vertical.

One should not confuse any discussion of slope by using the term *slope* to refer to ascending and descending alignments of words or lines of writing, as some authors (e.g., Harrison) have done. For the purpose of writing identification, the definition of alignment as being the relation of successive letters of a word, signature, or line of writing to an actual or imaginary base line, is more accurate and appropriate, and less likely to be misunderstood.

While slope has lost its former significance as a system or individual characteristic, it continues to be a useful tool in the study of disguise. As we have indicated elsewhere, changes in slope are a favoured process for affecting a disguise. Not surprisingly, it has been reported that a change from forehand to backhand is seven times more popular as a means of disguise than a change from backhand to forehand or from forehand to an enhanced forward slope from the vertical. This is understandable in that an increase in the forehand slope seems to have less affect upon the appearance of a writing than a change in the opposite direction, and an alteration in appearance is the change intended.

Although a change in slope affects the pictorial appearance of a writing it is accomplished at the expense of fluency and rhythm. Few writers are able to maintain, deliberately and extensively, a small change in slope. Furthermore, to defeat recognition, in many cases, a profound change in slope is all that is considered necessary to accomplish disguise.

While change in slope is difficult to maintain deliberately in the course of disguise and considerable variability may result, it must be noted that variable slope is not always evidence of disguise. Writings of poor quality usually exhibit variation in slopes. Other factors such as variation in size, spacing, and letter forms, that may accompany variability in slope, can be strongly indicative of a lack of skill or of incompetence rather than of disguise.

From the viewpoint of writing individuality, where this discussion began, slant or slope of writing can be a significant consideration. As with size and spacing, we find that slant must be approached in both its absolute and relative respects, absolute being an estimation of the general slant of tall letters usually, and relative being the relationship between the slants of any two letters or parts of letters. We also find that not all people are consistent in writing slant. Some develop idiosyncrasies of slant insofar as particular pairs or groups of letters. As a result the relative respect of slant will be the more significant characteristic of the writing to be studied.

One of the problems in the study of writing slant or slope is the basis on which slant is to be judged, particularly insofar as bowl type letters ("a," "c," "g," "o," "q"), complex letter forms, ("r," "z"), and some numerals. Obviously, as others have suggested, one must reasonably, but arbitrarily judge the axes of bowls, loops, arches, and troughs in the vertical direction.

As in many aspects of handwriting, there are extreme diversions from the norm in slant that tend to be the more obvious cases. Of some import to the examiner is the fact that because slant is a more obvious feature of writing it can be the subject of more voluntary control. It may change in minor respects as a result of writing circumstances. As is noted elsewhere, a pronounced alteration in slant, e.g., forehand to backhand, is a device commonly used for the purpose of disguise. Such a change is invariably blatant. On the other hand, unless writing circumstances may have a bearing on it, as Osborn maintained, a lesser but consistent difference in slant between two sets of writings is likely to be indicative of a difference in authors. Harrison cautions, however, that an increase in the speed of execution of a writing correlates with an increase in its forward slope and the disparity in slopes must be carefully assessed.

7. *Spacings*

  a. interword and lateral expansion (between)
  b. intraword and lateral expansion (within)

There are several aspects of spacing within writing that become habitual with the individual and of value in the identification process. These include the wide, narrow, mixed, or uniform spacing between letters, words, and between lines on unruled sheets sometimes referred to as interlinear spacing. Habits of some significance also develop in the spacing between capital letters and lowercase or small letters in the same words.

Two other aspects of extended writing that might be included within this category are the dimensions and uniformity of margins, and the parallelism of lines on unruled paper. We choose to deal with these aspects as elements of the arrangement of writing on the page.

Some authors have contended that spacing between letters and words is affected by the slant of the writing, but we are without data to confirm this.

Copybooks prescribe uniformity in spacing between letters in the execution of writing that is currently found only in better quality writing. At other levels of writing skill, habits of spacing evolve with pairs or groups of letters. Spacing and letter forms then combine to become units of habit and must be considered in that fashion rather than as separate forms or characters. Examples of this are frequently found in word endings such as "er," "ly," or "ing." Other letter combinations worthy of note are the "th" and the "wh." The result is an unevenness in the writing that can be found to vary widely from writer to writer. The extremes in this variation are significant personal habits.

As we mentioned above in the discussion of writing size, there are occasions when writing must be compressed in order to be accommodated in limited spaces. Such restrictions and accommodations tend to have greater effects upon interletter spacing than they have on letter forms or letter sizes, at least initially in the process of compression. The reason for this is simply that in order for the writing to be read, letter forms and sizes must be preserved to the extent possible. Of even greater import is the fact that, as Morton[44] points out, this reduction is accomplished without fundamental alteration of the writing habits. She cautions, therefore, against attributing divergences in two writings to contractions due to space limitations.

Spacing is a matter that is not appreciably different in the writings of many people. There are writers, however, that deviate from the norm noticeably, and the value of this aspect of writing in writing studies increases accordingly. It is surprising that interletter and interword spacing is a topic that has not received more attention in some of the widely recognized books on document examination.

One of the difficulties in the study of spacings lies in the method employed for judging its dimensions. A variation in the size of the writing will exhibit a corresponding variation in interletter spacing, making linear measures unreliable in writing comparisons. Harrison suggests that linear dimensions of writing should be judged in terms of letter-widths, a measurement that will reflect the proportionate contribution of spaces when the overall size of the writing is diminished. The exception to this will be writings that are insertions in restricted spaces, that tend to sacrifice interletter space in the interests of legibility.

B.   Elements of Execution

8.   *Abbreviations*

    a.   word contractions that eliminate letters
    b.   letter combinations that sacrifice form in favour of speed

Within all of the books that have been written on writing identification, few authors have mentioned the topic of abbreviations. Osborn and Harrison speak briefly of the abbreviations of the titles "Mister," "Mistress," and "Doctor" but there are numerous other titles and words that are contracted and subject to individual methods for so doing. Police and military ranks are almost invariably abbreviated. Political offices are frequently abbreviated and business positions are reduced to Mgr., for manager; Dir., for director, etc. There are a multitude of others many of which have been products of the current popularity of acronyms.

Of import to the examiner of handwriting is that the contemporary styling of abbreviations is, to a large extent, inconsistent and arbitrary. Among the masses of contractions, reductions, and abbreviations now employed, no set of rules can hope to cover all the possible variations encountered in the written and printed word. As Webster's (1993) has said:

> "The styling of abbreviations — whether capitalized or lowercased, closed up or spaced, punctuated or unpunctuated — depends most often on the writer's preference or the organization's policy."

How abbreviations are styled, then, can become a significant individualizing feature of writing. Among the many that examiners are likely to encounter will be abbreviations of the following:

Agency, Association, and Organization names
Company names (including Co. for company and Inc. for incorporated)
Compass points
Computer terms (e.g., CPU, RAM, ROM, OEM, DOS)
Contractions employing apostrophes (sec'y, ass'n, dep't)
Country names (U.S.A., CAN, U.K.)
Days of the week (Sun., Mon., Tues. or Tue., Wed., Thurs. or Thu., Fri., Sat.)
Degrees (academic)
Geographical and topographical names (St., Mt., Pt., Ft., and postal addresses)
Latin words and phrases (etc., i.e., e.g., viz., et al., pro tem.)
Military and police ranks (Cpl., Sgt., S/Sgt., CSM.)
Months of the year (Jan., Feb., Mar., Apr., Jun., Jul., Aug., Sept., Oct., Nov., Dec.)
Personal names (Geo., Marg., Marj.)
Special characters (ampersand "&," dollar sign "$," octothorpe "#," pound "£")
Structural locations (Apt., Bldg. Ct.)
Thoroughfare designations (Ave., Blvd., Cres., Pkwy., Rd., St.)
Titles (including Hon., Rev., Sen., Mr., Mrs., Ms.)
Units of measure (cu. ft., sq. yd., km., Kilo., sec., min., hr.)
Words and word groups (c/o, w/o, w/w, c.c., c.o.d.)

In what are said to be carry-overs from the Secretarie System of 400 years ago, there are some variations in the alignment or manner in which abbreviations are written that become habitual with current writers. It was the practise in that system to omit letters and elevate the last letter or letters of the word to indicate that a reduction had been made. The elevation of the "r" in M^r or the "rs" in M^{rs} are examples. Teachers in scientific fields are known to write "sol^n" for solution.

The special characters included in the list of abbreviations mentioned above are worth noting. They are not contractions of words as other abbreviations are. They are symbols that are used to represent words and, thereby, to economize on space or writing. In that sense, they have the same purpose in their use and for that reason we include them here. Some writers use them frequently, particularly the ampersand (Mr. & Mrs.) in addressing envelopes.

There is little or no instruction given in writing books governing the form, size, or structure of these special characters. Without guidance or restriction, individuals are left to develop these characters for themselves, and consequently they vary substantially from writer to writer. The result is that they become highly individual elements of writing.

Signatures are often illegible but are not normally abbreviated in the usual sense. What serves as an abbreviation of a signature is the inscription of sets of one or more of the initial letters of the name. When referred to collectively as a person's initials, they are ascribed some of the attributes of personal identity that the signature enjoys. These may, however, display little of the normal characteristics of the signature they are intended to represent. Because of their widespread use in authenticating, validating, and authorizing documents, a writer's initials can take on a character of their own that can be, in some cases, just as reliable and useable a means of identification as the signature itself. For many writers, initials tend to diverge more drastically from copybook prescription than extended writing. On the other hand, some initials are over simplified to little more than a single letter. The difficulty that initials present for writing examiners lies in the quantity and quality of evidence of similarity or dissimilarity, of genuineness or of spuriousness, that such limited writing may contain. Notwithstanding the fact that, for many writers, initials can be distinctive and unique, caution must be exercised in the comparison and evaluation processes, for the less writing involved, or the more inconsistent its execution, the easier the task of spuriously reproducing it.

There are numerous fashions in which letter forms and structures are abbreviated by the omission of elements, usually in the interests of fluency or speed. Initial upstrokes are frequently sacrificed (particularly in the "i," "t," and "h"), loops are reduced to single downstrokes (particularly in the "f," "h," "g," and "y"), retracings of staffs (as in "t," "B," "P," "R") are not performed. There are also writers (this author is one) that are aware of these omissions that they are making and will occasionally return later to repair the deficiency by adding strokes. In these kinds of abbreviations, it will be noted that almost invariably it is the upstrokes that are sacrificed while the downstrokes, that are the more dominant strokes with right-handed writers, are retained.

9. *Alignment*

This concerns the relation of successive letters of a word, signature, or line of writing to an actual or imaginary baseline.

With or without the benefit of ruled lines, the majority of people exhibit an ascending (i.e., rising) baseline in their writing. Some maintain a horizontal baseline, while the baseline of others tends to descend. But whatever the tendency is it will likely be fixed. Some authors employ the term *line of writing* to describe a writing's conformity to this real or imaginary line.

Alignment habits may be general and occur insofar as a signature, a word, or a group of words. They may also be specific to a letter and/or relative to a neighbouring preceding or succeeding letter.

One of the few studies of alignments conducted was reported by McClary,[45] respecting the writing of signatures and extended text by 200 subjects on both ruled and unruled paper. His findings were that:

> "The study confirmed that baseline alignment is a repetitious writing habit and reliable factor in handwriting comparisons for the purposes of identification or elimination. This is true more so with respect to signatures that are the more habitual of one's handwriting skills."

In addition to alignments, fixed habits will also be found, insofar, as the location of signatures and other material written within a limited space. It is as though the width of the left margin, or the space to be left preceding the entry, was as fixed a practise as other habits might be.

10. *Commencements and Terminations*

a. their length, direction, and path
b. their taper (the abruptness with which the instrument approaches and leaves the paper)

Lowercase letters, particularly those following a capital letter, are frequently commenced with an initial stroke that is long and often intersects with the terminal stroke of the capital letter that precedes it. This is a common occurrence in the writing of the "r" in the abbreviations "Mr." and "Mrs." It is perhaps even more common in the writing of signatures. A long initial stroke, usually a secondary stroke, can occur, of course, with any lowercase letter in any initial position in extended text.

Furthermore, while copybook prescribes for termination in an upwards direction for all lowercase letters, the strokes with which terminal letters in a name or a word are finished are found to vary substantially in the writing of different persons, if indeed, they are executed at all. Frequently, the terminal stroke will return to cross "t"s, apply accents, or simply to inscribe a characteristic underscore or rubric. This tendency seems to correlate with the fluency or speed of the execution of the signature.

Thus, we find that the strokes with which lowercase letters are commenced and terminated, vary in both length, the direction of their paths, and their tendency to intersect with the strokes of other letters, according to the personal habits of the writer. Therefore, they can be significant individualizing elements of writing.

Another aspect of initial and terminal strokes that must be studied, although only indirectly as a point of identification, is the abruptness with which the strokes start or finish. In normal, natural, and reasonably fluent writing, these strokes exhibit a degree of taper, owing to the fact that they are created by a writing instrument that is in motion as it approaches or departs from the surface of the paper. Handwriting examiners have long referred to these tapered strokes as flying starts or flying finishes and have relied upon them as evidence of fluency and, therefore, evidence of genuineness. In spurious simulations of another's writing or signature, these strokes are found to commence and terminate abruptly, having noticeably blunt endings, as the application of the instrument to the paper is a more deliberate and conscious act.

In summary then, initial and terminal strokes to letters, words, or names must be considered insofar as their length, their direction, and/or their path, and their degree of taper, all of which will be present — if indeed, such strokes are present.

11. Diacritics and Punctuation — Presence, Style and Location

Punctuation marks are used in the English writing system to clarify the meaning of sentences by attempting to control the reading of a passage to correspond to certain elements of the spoken language. They also serve to clarify meaning by organizing certain grammatical elements in the structure of the sentence, regardless of how those elements might be spoken. Punctuation is intended to indicate pause, pitch, volume, and stress.

Two terms that are frequently used regarding the comma to describe patterns of punctuation are *open* and *close*. An open pattern is one in which the comma and other marks are used sparingly. A close pattern makes liberal use of punctuation marks, often putting one wherever grammatical structure will allow. In the examination of extended writing, an awareness of these two patterns of practise can be helpful.

Diacritics, or diacritical marks, are marks that are used with a letter or group of letters to indicate a sound value that is different from that of the letter(s) without it. Although the English language doesn't use diacritics, the French language and many others do. In the sparsely written material on the subject, some authors have referred to the "i" dot as a diacritic, but since the "i" has no alternative sound without the dot it fails to qualify for the term. It is an integral component of the letter much like the crossbar to the "t." It was introduced to distinguish the "i" from the numeral "1." In earlier writing (circa 1500), the "1" and the "y" had their vertical stems dotted, but the practise was switched in the seventeenth or eighteenth century.

Like some others, punctuation is an aspect of writing on which few of the recent authors have seen fit to comment. For Osborn, it was one of 16 features considered under the general heading of Arrangement, and in that respect, location of the punctuation relative to baselines was important. He cites a case in which the apostrophe was consistently but improperly used in many words in which it didn't belong. This evidence supported the identification of the writer. He cites another case to illustrate the precision with which punctuation was reproduced in tracings that would not occur in natural writings.

Harrison also comments on the location of "i" dots as being of some potential value in writing comparisons since few writers place them precisely over the staff. But there are other respects in which a study of the dot form or structure may be helpful. The "i" dot may be round, a stroke, a tick, or small "v," sitting upright or lying on the horizontal. In bubble writing, the dot is frequently executed as a small circle and located rather precisely over the staff. In the case of some writers, the dot may be omitted completely, or applied only occasionally.

Similar variations will be observed in the study of accents or diacritics in other languages. Few correspond closely to the copybook styles. It will be found, however, that since "i" dots and diacritics are somewhat carelessly and speedily applied during the writing process, and perhaps because of their size, they may vary substantially in both style and location.

Commas and periods are, of course, the punctuation marks most frequently encountered in examinations. Here too, little correspondence is found between their forms, sizes, and locations and the copybook examples. For the most part, they are strokes that vary in length and direction, not dots, and are seldom curved. In the writing of many persons, little consistency in them will be found, but as with so many other writing elements, there are some individuals that are quite distinctive in the manners in which they punctuate and are reasonably consistent in their execution. Osborn suggested years ago, there can be consistency in the location of the comma relative to the word that it is inscribed to follow. Accordingly, this element of the study should never be overlooked.

While often a matter to be considered in signatures and extended writings, "i" dots and punctuation marks can be of particular assistance also in the study of envelope addresses. The writing of envelope addresses invariably provides ample opportunity for the writer to display his/her particular habits in this respect.

If the potential of diacritics and punctuation marks is to be realized in a writing examination and study, and request standards are likely to be available, it is important that those standards be prepared from dictation rather than from copy, in order that no assistance may be provided that might influence the use or location of dots, accents, commas, and periods.

12. *Embellishments*

Embellishments are flourishes, ornaments, paraphs, rubrics, and underscores.

Embellishment adds or extends strokes that are easily executed and are not essential to the recognition of the character or the word. It is the natural product of speed, fluency, or individual caprice. Although some terminal letters seem to lend themselves to embellishment, as the lower loops of the "y" and "g," the flourishes and ornamentation that a writer may develop for him/herself follow no particular patterns and are as individualistic as a writing element might be.

A particular kind of embellishment of some years ago was a complex design or symbol located under or after the signature or name. It evolved into a more simplified pattern and eventually into a single flourish or understroke. This was called a paraph that was sometimes more in the nature of an initial, and that, according to the Oxford dictionary, originated about 400 years ago as a kind of security against forgery. Ellen[46] claims that the same practise is followed even today by some writers for the same reasons. It may have been the forerunner to the current practise of initialling all pages of a document as protection against substitution or replacement. The underscore to a signature is often currently but improperly referred to as a rubric, for which Osborn may be given some of the credit as he gave both terms, *paraph* and *rubric*, the same meaning. Regardless of what term may be used to refer to them, underscores to signatures that we encounter today are not always limited to single lines, but may be double or even triple.

The rubric, in ancient documents, was an initial character or a heading, or underscore to such a character or heading, that was printed or inscribed in red or ocher ink to set it off as the beginning of the page or passage. More recently, it has been used to refer to marginal instructions or explanations in a manuscript that were invariably done in red ink. In the world of today, perhaps in the absence of employment as an embellishment to initial characters or headings, it is occasionally used to refer to the underscores that some writers apply to their signatures, or to some personal flourish that follows it.

In this discussion of the extraordinary strokes and patterns that are added to the writing of signatures, one cannot overlook the smaller but highly personal embellishments that are frequently executed in the first or final letters of words in extended writings that, for want of a better term, might be called ornamentations. The crossings of the "t" can also be somewhat ornate. These antics of the pen, as Osborn described them, are obviously intended to add a certain artistic quality to the writing. Of import to examiners of writing is that these ornamentations tend to be persistent habits of the writer. Writings with split nib or fountain pens, that allow for some noticeable variation in stroke width, exhibit more of this kind of characteristic than writings with other instruments may. The shading of the stroke, that flexible nibs allow, is an inducement to writers to exploit the potential for this kind of ornamentation.

13. *Legibility or Writing Quality*

We are not considering legibility from the viewpoint of the density of the written line relative to the substrate, that might be better described as visibility. Nor are we considering quality, as Osborn and Hilton have done, to refer to particular identifying factors or characteristics. We use either or both of these terms, legibility and writing quality, as closely related measures of the excellence of a writing, each being a product of the other.

> Definition: Legibility and writing quality are the ease of recognition of letters, usually stemming from the adherence to copybook designs, and to a lesser extent, to copybook size, slant, and spacing.

When one thinks of legibility or writing quality as measures of the excellence of writing, we realize that excellence must be considered from the standpoint of both the writer and the reader.

From the viewpoint of the writer, excellence is the efficiency of production. Efficiency has to be judged on the basis of the quality of the stroke, the smoothness of the movement, and the economy of the action of the pen, that is often developed at the expense of letter formation.

As a measure of efficiency in writing, speed does not correlate well either directly or inversely. That which a reader may judge to be better quality takes slightly more time to produce, but in many cases this is because the pen travels a greater distance to complete the letters. At the same time, that which takes more time to produce is not necessarily of better quality, for the writing may lose some of its smoothness as the action becomes more deliberate and conscious.

From the viewpoint of the reader we consider the ease of recognition, and it is from this perspective that we more often judge writing quality. One cannot judge writing excellence, however, without addressing the question as to what makes writing good or bad.

One of the aspects of writing by which its excellence is judged is its uniformity. The lack of uniformity affects appearance even to the point of the writing's legibility. Uniformity or the lack of it is observed in alignments, letter slopes, and the consistency of shape in repeated letters or in different letters having common elements: e.g., "a" and "d," "q" and "g," "y" and "j," "h" and "l, "m" and "n," "F" and "T," "P" and "R" (Figure 4).

In addition to uniformity, there are two other aspects of writing having a bearing on its excellence. These are the quality of the line or stroke producing the letters (see line quality) and the shapes of letter formations themselves. In the latter respect it cannot be denied that adherence to copybook design must contribute to excellence, if only because copybook styles have proven to be the least ambiguous designs for letters, which ensures their legibility. Nonetheless, there are handwritings that are quite legible that employ letter shapes that depart widely from copybook models. In these cases, it is found that the departure retains some of the basic elements of letter design, or the modifications are sufficiently distinctive from one another that confusion and misinterpretation is avoided.

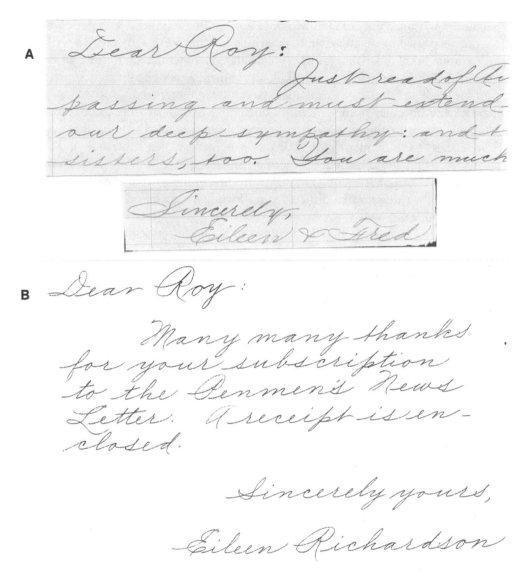

Figure 4 Writings of (A) Fred and his wife (B) Eileen Richardson, both master penmen who followed the Mills (Rochester) system. Both were 84 years old at the time of writing. Note the striking similarity in many letter shapes, but also the subtle differences in the proportions of the "p," the angularity to the "y" and the style of "t" when a medial letter.

Writing movements, particularly the garlanded movement, when allowed to dominate the writing execution severely, renders many of the linear letters difficult to differentiate. The "m" and "n" resemble the "u," "v," and "w" very closely, and words such as *minimum* are extremely difficult to recognize or distinguish.

Poor legibility can also result from wide ranges in natural variation that permit some letters to be mistaken for others. Thus, as was stated earlier, uniformity or consistency in the various elements of writing, whether it be shape, size, slant, spacing, or other aspects contributes substantially to writing quality and consequently to legibility.

The importance of distinguishing between levels of excellence in writing is primary to the application of one of the fundamental principles of handwriting: a writer cannot exceed his maximum writing ability or skill without effort and/or training over a period of time. This principle is used to advantage in handwriting identification. Obviously, a writer who possesses limited skill in writing cannot be considered a potential author of a writing that was executed with indisputably greater skill, unless there are extenuating circumstances to account for the lesser skill at the time that standards were prepared.

Remarkably little has been written by document or handwriting examiners on the topic of legibility or writing quality over the years. Osborn made the point that illegibility and carelessness were frequent indications of genuineness, that grotesque and illegible signatures were thought to be better protected against forgery. That, of course, is now not true. Harrison explains that legibility may be unrelated to the writing's artistic quality, that elegant and fluid writing may be difficult to read while irregular and unrhythmic writing may be read with ease.

Furthermore, consistency in letter designs and shapes fosters legibility. Wide ranges in variations confuse letter recognition and makes reading slow and laborious in deciphering words. Similarly extreme slopes, particularly backhand slants, introduce features that are foreign to a reader's normal experience to which the eye does not readily adapt and, thus, makes reading difficult.

For these same reasons, writing that is excessively arched or garlanded, such as the bubble writing of adolescents, can be quite illegible to many readers. More often, of course, the reason for illegibility is simply a lack of skill or carelessness on the part of the writer.

In one of the few research studies with which we are acquainted, Andersen,[47] in an investigation of the writings of 5,286 elementary and junior high school pupils, reported on five handwriting variables: legibility, size, slant, size uniformity, and slant uniformity. On average the quality of writing (i.e., legibility) of girls was better, and the writing was more vertical than that of boys. He also observed that legibility varied directly with uniformity in slant and with writing size. However, larger writings, while being more legible were less uniform in size.

14. *Line Continuity*

This concerns the interruptions in or discontinuity of the writing line, occurring as a result of pen stops, pen lifts, or disconnections.

Nineteenth century writing systems and some foreign systems made a practise of executing some letters independently of the letters preceding them rather than in the uninterrupted continuous pen motion that this century's systems prescribe. Consequently, disconnections occurred in specific places with specific letters. Today's systems, when they are followed meticulously, require that each word in lowercase be completed without the writing instrument leaving the paper. The crossing of the "t," the crossing of the "x," and the dotting of the "i" are acts that follow the completion of the word. Intraword disconnections, then, are elements of one's personal writing habits and vary profoundly from one to another.

Many foreign systems of writing are similar to lettering on this continent, in that letters are separately constructed. Oriental, Arabic, and East Indian scripts are of this kind, largely disconnected. North Americans do block lettering or pen printing with the same frequency of disconnections or pen lifts. When highly developed, disconnected writings of these kinds can display consistency and many features of individuality. When unskillfully produced, they can be spuriously reproduced more easily than connected writing.

Disconnections, or pen lifts as they are more frequently labelled, in the cursive writing of this continent, occur for several reasons. They may be due to a lack of skill in the movement control of the writing instrument. For some of this class, there is a need to interrupt the writing process to contemplate the next step. Erstwhile, writers of script experience difficulties with letter connections in converting to cursive writing styles. Circular or bowl type letters, such as the "a," "c," "d," "g," "o," and "q," seem by virtue of their design to prompt a lifting of the pen before commencing the bowl. Indeed, writers of the old Round Hand system of the turn of the century were taught to lift the pen before beginning the body or bowl of such letters.

Disconnection occurring before and after some lowercase letters, such as the circular or bowl type letters, may be so pronounced that there is no vestige to be seen of the secondary or terminal strokes to these letters or to the letters that precede them. When the interruption in the movement of the instrument is of this magnitude, the disconnection is usually referred to by United Kingdom examiners as a hiatus.

Under the circumstances, disconnections, when they occur in normal, natural, genuine writing of lowercase letters, usually occur between letters, or insofar as initial or terminal strokes, usually are few in number for the whole word or name. On the other hand, capital letters are often written in separate segments and in that sense similar to the process in block lettering. Letters such as the "B," "D," "P," "R," "T," and "F," can be constructed of two or more separate strokes despite the requisite of the copybooks to produce the letter in one continuous action.

Harrison[48] cautioned that in his view writing habits respecting hiatuses were not fixed. He commented that it is not uncommon to find that slow writing by some individuals will be liberally garnished with gaps (i.e., pen lifts or hiatuses), yet another specimen by the same author will be almost devoid of pen lifts, much less hiatuses. Thus, the value of pen lifts and hiatuses will depend greatly upon the letters between which they occur. Before the "c," "d," "g," and "o," they will be common. After the "p" and "s," they may be common when these letters are written with closed bowls. Before the "e," "i," and "v," they will be uncommon, and after the "w," they will be uncommon as well.

Disconnections in genuine writing, whether they be pen lifts or hiatuses, are frequently obvious and seldom, if ever, corrected. With fluent writers, the motion of the pen may be continuous even if the line is not, thus producing tapers to the ends of the strokes. On the other hand, disconnections in spurious writing are much less obvious, and often patched, repaired, or retouched afterward. Patching and retouching requires a second, third, or more applications of the writing instrument that are usually obvious in examination by microscope. In the examination and study of signatures, disconnections or pen lifts are classic symptoms of simulation by tracing methods. The reason claimed for this is that one who forges is the most severe critic of his/her own work and strives to perfect it.

The consequence of all of this is that dissimilarities in pen lifts can be of greater value in eliminating writers than similarities may be in writer identification, particularly in respect of circular or bowl type letters, unless the method of disconnection is very unusual.

The retouching of genuine writing, if it occurs at all, is clearly apparent and made with strokes that are obviously intended to improve only the pictorial effect or to dispel potential problems for the reader in comprehension.

Pen stops that may be defined as the abrupt cessation of motion of the writing instrument without its removal from the paper, are a distinctly different feature of writing on which little has been written. Our experience has revealed it to be a characteristic of schizophrenics experiencing a distorted perception of reality, during which they believe themselves to be another personality, or the same person but at an earlier time. In such cases, the writing instrument is brought to a full stop without being immediately removed from the paper. It occurs frequently at the finish of strokes before changing direction, at the ends of terminal strokes, or at the ends of "t" crossings. As in the case of disconnections that may be present in either genuine or spurious writings, pen stops can only be reliably confirmed by study under the stereomicroscope.

15. *Line Quality*

A. S. Osborn is credited with the introduction of the term *line quality*, but not all authors have understood it to mean the same thing. Others have described it as resulting from the level of freedom and the rate of velocity in the movement of the pen. For Harrison, it was better stated as quality of line. As indicated above, and as Hilton has used it, it has been suggested that line quality is the umbrella under which many elements of writing movement reside. To achieve much needed clarification, the terms should be divorced and separately defined.

> Definition: Line quality is the degree of regularity (i.e., smoothness and/or gradation) to the written stroke as may be judged from the consistency of its nature and of its path in a prescribed direction. It varies from smooth and controlled to tremulous and erratic.

Osborn used the term *writing movement* as a matter of several writing elements forming a component of line quality. In our view line quality, or alternatively, the quality of the line is a matter that is depicted by characteristics independent of form or routes of pen action. As is delineated by our definition the quality of the written line or line quality is the degree of regularity (i.e., smoothness or gradation) in the written stroke. It may be described as or judged from the consistency of its path in a prescribed direction. It varies from smooth to tremulous, from controlled to erratic. Its third dimensional characteristic, if it has one resulting from the application of pressure by the writing instrument, will vary from consistent, gradual, or rhythmic to irregular, sudden, or abrupt.

There is no doubt that many factors related to control (e.g., skill, state of health, age, velocity of the instrument, pen pressure, even quality of vision) are contributing factors to the quality of the line that may be produced. They are, however, contributors to line quality, and care must be exercised in the evaluation process to avoid improperly appending the evidence of line quality to the evidence of its contributing factors.

There are a number of other terms that presumably are used to reflect some level of line quality. Harrison uses the term *fluency* as something that is absent in the execution of disguise. Furthermore, he employs the expression *fluency and rhythm* that implies that they are somewhat different qualities. Osborn did not use the term *fluency* precisely, but has defined a flowing hand to be a coordinated succession of movement impulses that glide into each other with a rhythm which is the final perfection of fixed and cultivated habit. If fluency can be equated with a flowing hand, then Osborn's definition suggests that rhythm is an integral part of it. Osborn also speaks of skill and freedom and goes on to describe freedom in writing as that which is shown by the direction, uniformity, and clear-cut quality of the pen strokes.

What is apparent with these terms, their definitions, or descriptions, whether or not we are speaking of fluency, freedom, skill, or a flowing hand, is the critical fact, not always fully appreciated that they have limited application. They are references to conditions found only in better qualities of writing. One seldom speaks of fluency or freedom insofar as poor writings or simulations or disguises, for invariably they are not present. One should speak of line quality in these situations for, whether it is good or bad line quality, it will be present. Fluency, freedom, and other like terms simply refer to a generally higher grade of line quality, not always present, that is without any kind of tremour or erratic changes in direction or in pen pressure. Line quality then, being the more ever-present circumstance, is the preferred term.

16.   *Pen Control*

This concerns the management of the writing instrument by the hand in generating a writing line.

To organize information within the families to which they relate, point load (pen pressure), pen hold, and pen position are assembled as aspects of pen control.

a.   Point Load — the vertical component of the force applied to the nib, ball, or tip of the writing instrument, during line generation. Frequently called pen pressure, it may be (1) absolute: i.e., constant through all the writing, or (2) relative: i.e., greater or lesser in some strokes. In either case it will be evidenced by (1) shading and variations thereof, (2) the deposition of ink or graphite, and variations thereof, or by (3) the depression of the paper, and variations thereof.

It is called rhythm, or fluency or a flowing hand when it materializes as a harmonious and graduated recurrence.

b.   Pen Hold — the grasp of the writing instrument by the hand, mouth, foot or prothesis, determinable only (1) when the angle of the axis of a ball point pen and the plane of the writing surface is ≤45°, or (2) when shading is produced by a split nib pen.

c.   Pen Position — the orientation of the writing instrument relative to (1) the writing sheet or sustrate, (2) the writing baseline, or (3) the writing stroke.

Point Load (pen pressure and shading).   We begin the discussion of these aspects from the perspective of that which has generated the greatest interest within the published material over the longest period of time — pen pressure and shading, two facets of writing that at one time were considered to be separate entities but closely related.

Tytell[49] has provided an excellent account of the role and the course of shading over the eras of the quill pen, the steel nib, and the fountain pen to the arrival of the ballpoint pen in the late 1940s. In the transition from one kind of instrument to the next, the diminution of shading was seen as the demise of important qualities and characteristics of skilled penmanship. As Tytell describes it:

"Today's common perception…holds that the introduction of the ballpoint pen after World War II foisted upon the public a writing instrument unsuitable for proper shading. For the penman, the ball point was just another step in a steady descent of writing instruments. In the nineteenth century, the steel pen was compared unfavorably to the quill. In the twentieth, the fountain pen was criticized as inferior to the steel pen."

There has been some difficulty expressed in the early writings of this century in making a distinction, whether necessary or not, between shading and pen pressure. In consequence, terms like *unconscious emphasis* and *unconscious pressure emphasis* have been employed to clarify meanings, but not very well.

As Tytell reports, Osborn (1910) in his first edition of *Questioned Documents*, recognized a potential for confusion between pen pressure and shading.

> "No very definite distinction can be drawn between pen pressure and shading in writing…pen pressure refers…to the involuntary placing of emphasis, smoothness of stroke, and quality of line in writing, as distinguished from that deliberate and voluntary emphasis that is ordinarily described as shading…."

The confusion of terms was not fully resolved by Osborn in his second edition of the book when he wrote:

> "Without careful definition this term *pen pressure* means nothing, and a term which perhaps would more clearly express what is here called pen pressure, as compared with shading, would be unconscious emphasis. What is termed *shading* is that more obvious increase in the weight of strokes which in many instances are in conformity with and grow out of the system of writing followed. Shading itself in a mature well-developed hand is, however, largely unconscious, so that the term *unconscious emphasis* may be somewhat misleading in that it would suggest that what is called shading is always consciously done. It is seldom that a handwriting made up of the finest and most delicate lines does not show throughout consistent variations in line widths due to variations in pressure, and this emphasis is what is here described as pen pressure, or unconscious emphasis, as distinguished from pronounced and perfectly evident shading."[50]

Brewester[51] reiterated Osborn's words in saying:

> "Pen pressure may be defined as the weight or pressure, unconsciously applied to the pen during the act of writing, while shading is that conscious or voluntary pressure at first deliberately applied to certain parts, but afterwards becoming as much of an automatic act as any other unconsciously acquired writing habit."

As Tytell tells it, Osborn was still not satisfied with his definition of pen pressure, and in another effort to curb the misuse of the term he wrote in 1946:

> "…one of the most significant qualities in handwriting, (is) often inadequately described as pen pressure, which without accurate definition means nothing….
>
> "…there is in writing, a delicate inconspicuous and almost wholly unconscious variation in line quality, weight of stroke, location of emphasis, smoothness of line and manual skill that has high identifying value. This…is the result of the movement employed, the pen holding, body and arm position, and the habitual skill and speed that has been developed…the location and character of emphasis or unconscious shading, (and) the variation in this feature is one of the most important evidences of genuineness or forgery….
>
> "The mere habitual location of extra pressure or emphasis in a character often is highly significant and the force, freedom, and speed of the writing is clearly shown by the quality of line or control of pen pressure, or whatever it may be called.
>
> "The examination of line quality and unconscious pressure emphasis is especially important in alleged signature forgeries…."[52]

Some readers will recall that Osborn felt so strongly about shading and pen pressure that he had made for himself diagonal line measures, i.e., glass grids with which he could measure and compare stroke widths from 1/30 to 1/200 in.

Hilton in his collection of definitions lists pen emphasis as "the act of intermittently forcing the pen against the paper surface with increased pressure. When the pen point has flexibility this emphasis produces shading," and goes on to define pen pressure as "the average force with which the pen contacts the paper."[53]

Hagan made a similar distinction between average pressure and extremes of pressure in stating:

"In addition to the general measure of pen pressure found to occur throughout the writing of a signature, there must also be taken into account, in determining individual habit, the measure of comparative density occurring between the lighter and heavy lines of a signature, the points at which the shading emphasis commences and ends, and the facility with which it is accomplished."[54]

We should not disregard the admonition of Tytell that it would be wrong for us to suggest that persons as renowned as Hagan and Osborn, and as familiar with the calligraphy of their time, were off base or obsolete in their treatment of the subject of pen pressure and shading. Even Osborn, however, would allow that there might be something to gain from another perspective of the topic.

A review of these definitions and explanations raises some questions and prompts one to make some observations. Both Hagan and Hilton are saying that there is a general measure of pen pressure in any writing. It may range from light to heavy, but it is necessary to prompt the release of ink to the paper. Beyond that there may be localized variation in the application of this general measure of pressure that supplements the changes in stroke width at turning points that might emanate purely from the physical dimensions of the nib of the writing instrument and its orientation to the writing.

Osborn seems to have held the view, originally, that pen pressure was unconscious and involuntary, and that shading was deliberate and voluntary. He allowed that shading, initially induced by imitation, becomes, with practise, an unconscious and involuntary habit of the individual. The difference between pen pressure and shading, then, seems to be only in the magnitude of the effect attained.

In the Second Edition of his book Osborn defined pen pressure as unconscious emphasis. This term implies that shading, the alternative circumstance, is a relatively conscious act. Indeed, he says that shading is the more obvious and presumably deliberate and conscious increase in the weight of strokes. Yet, shading, he says, in mature writing is largely unconscious. Thus, the term *unconscious emphasis* for pen pressure can, by itself, be misleading.

We suspect that the crux of the problem which Osborn and others were endeavouring to resolve centred around magnitude, the magnitude of the variation in stroke width. The shading of writings of Osborn's era was extreme. It was decorative, and it was deliberate. To achieve it required a conscious effort. The literature says that it was much slower to perform. Mature writings, executed with speed and fluency, seldom displayed the same magnitude of variation in stroke width. Thus, when shading became less conscious, it also became less pronounced.

One might ask why a distinction between pen pressure and shading must be made at all. There is little ground for claiming them to be fundamentally different, other than in their visible properties. They are directly related in that they are cause and effect. Furthermore, it is virtually impossible to determine when shading would change from a deliberate act to one that is involuntary.

Shading, in its more extreme forms, is the product of pen pressure that is manifest in the widening or narrowing of the stroke, particularly with split nib pens, or in the production of impressions or troughs in the surface of the paper. Shading and indentations are the manifestations that can be observed, but the application of pressure on the pen, and consequently of the pen on the paper, is the action that becomes the habit of the writer. Therefore, shading is not the characteristic of the writer; pen pressure is. Shading is the manifestation, but pressure is the cause.

To be technically correct, pen pressure is not the term to be used, although it has been for a century. Point load, which is defined within the manufacturing industry of pens as the vertical component of the force applied to the writing tip during line generation is in fact what has been loosely referred to as pen pressure. Pen pressure has two components, a vertical component and a horizontal component, but only the vertical component is responsible for the shading of the line (Figure 5).

The application of pressure on the pen or the point load, then, which may result in shading, may be constant and heavy in the writing of some individuals, producing broad strokes throughout a writing, or constant and light. It may be rhythmic, occurring consistently with strokes moving in a particular direction, usually but not necessarily down strokes or strokes towards the wrist of the hand. It may be peculiar to particular elements of certain characters or it may be sporadic, having no apparent raison-d'être. It may be graduated or it may be impulsive.

What is being discussed here, and was by Hagan, Osborn and Hilton, is merely the two qualities of pen pressure or point load: absolute pen pressure and relative pen pressure. These are two qualities that are similar to those we spoke of with respect to size in writing, and with respect to slant. Absolute pen pressure is that which is constant through all of one's writing. It may not always be obvious but it will be there. It is necessary for the writing instrument to generate a line. Relative pen pressure is that which is greater or lesser at certain locations in some strokes. It is responsible for that property of writing that is commonly referred to as shading.

On reviewing the effects of modern writing instruments on the classic attributes of writing, we must acknowledge that the fundamentals of the movement of the instrument are essentially unchanged from the days of the nib pen. Only the visual track is different. Line quality is still a product of pen control, pressure variation and fluency. The evidence depicting it may be diminished but it has not been demolished.

Kinds of shading and its causes.   Shading should be studied in terms of its nature, consistency or graduation, intensity, skill, and location. If it is faulty, it can be evidence of spuriousness. If it is correct, it can testify to genuineness.

Shading occurs, for the most part, because of the separation of the nib points due to the application of force against the writing surface. The separation ensues because of the curvature of the nib, which gives each half of the nib its own, but a different arc. Each arc subtends an ordinate that runs at a small angle to the other. Pressure, or a point load upon

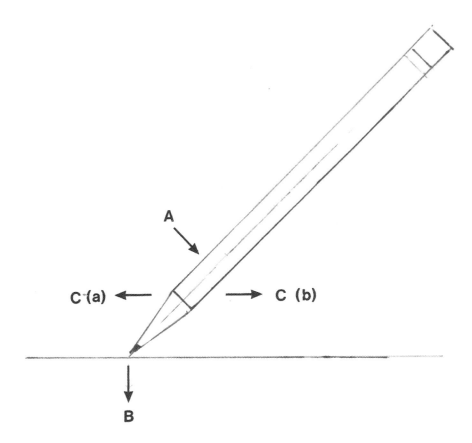

Figure 5 Forces exerted on and through the writing instrument:

Directional components

A. "Pen pressure" by the writer (exerted perpendicular to the axis of the instrument)

B. Point load
   – the vertical component
   – responsible for indentations and shading (i.e., the separation of nib points)
C. Travel action
   – the horizontal component
   – responsible for line generation
     (a) forward or sideward (as in upstrokes or crossings)
     (b) drag or backward (as in downstrokes)

the nibs causes each to bend along the lines of these ordinates, with the result that the tips move away from each other, thereby, widening the stroke they make.

The quill pen, the original split nib writing instrument, was frequently so resilient that evidence of nib tracks was difficult to find. The steel nib left no doubts. The gold pen or gold-tipped pen was a modification of the steel nib to overcome the corrosive action of the acids of ink on the steel. The softness of gold was overcome by the addition of iridium that greatly extended the life of the nib.

The reservoir pen was the forerunner to the fountain pen, in which an ink reservoir was attached to the back of the pen shaft to allow much more writing to be executed without requiring refilling or dipping the nib. Indeed, the length of the ink line without replenishing the supply in the pen is the principal means of differentiating the reservoir pen from the conventional steel pen.

The fountain pen extended the length of the written line between fillings to a much greater extent. It was initially more resilient and responded to pressure by broadening the stroke, but more recent products are not so reactive.

The greatly reduced use of split nib pens and the popularity of ball pens has correspondingly reduced the incidence of pronounced shading in writing of this era. Shading in older writings, or indeed in any writing, however, occurs for one or both of two reasons: the application of the vertical component of pen pressure that forces the separation of the nibs, and/or the use of broad tipped nibs that changes the width of the stroke according to the pen's orientation with reference to the generated line. When the principal ordinate subtending the full arc or curve of the broad tipped nib lies parallel to the direction of the stroke, the ink line will be broad, as broad as the width of the nib point, or greater with greater point load or pen pressure. When the direction of the ordinate crosses the stroke at right angles, the ink line will be narrow, as narrow as the thickness of the nib point, regardless of the pressure applied. In both cases, however, the point load (i.e., the pen pressure) could be the same. Between these extremes, the angle of the ordinate to the stroke of the writing and the pressure applied will determine the width of the written line. Thus, as a characteristic of writing or as a habit of identification value, it is preferable to speak in terms of pen pressure or point load rather than shading, and to avoid confusion with terms respecting the evidence of a particular pen hold or pen position, or the evidence of a choice of pen. Shading can be the product of one or more of these four factors.

We say "the product of one or more of these four factors" because it is possible to shade a stroke without any appreciable application of pressure or point load. This is due simply to the physical dimensions of the nib point that is usually, but not necessarily wider than it is thick. Consider the execution of a circle. From any fixed position there are two segments of the circle (usually but not necessarily top and bottom) at which the line width will conform to the thickness of the nib, thereby creating the pen's thinnest strokes. There are two other segments (the extremities of the circle, left and right) at which the line width will conform to the width of the nib, thereby, creating the pen's normally and naturally wider strokes. In the area of these latter segments of the circle, as the point load increases so does the stroke width.

No summarization of the topic of pen pressure could improve on the remarks of Tytell cited above, for which reason they are quoted here in their entirety.

> "A review of the patents granted for devices and methods, the scientific and technical literature, as well as the experimental data and findings all support the hypotheses that there are highly individual characteristics in (the) act of writing and that among the most individual and consistent of these is the pattern of pressure emphasis in writing a signature — the same conclusion found in the literature of document examination."
>
> "The basic principles of questioned document examination are explained fully in the various texts and articles studied by all students of the subject. It is not easy to reduce them to a few bare statements, like proofs in a geometry book, and any such attempt runs the risk of omitting a crucial detail. However, both the texts in document examination and the results of nondocument examiners working with dynamic handwriting analysis as a form of biometric identity verification support the following statements:

- Dynamic pressure patterns are an integral part of an individual's signature.
- Patterns of pressure emphasis show a high degree of interpersonal variation. They are highly individual to the extent that it would be exceptional to find two people with well-developed signatures of normal length and the same patterns.
- The pressure patterns of a well-developed signature or normal length are extremely difficult, if not impossible, to duplicate when imitating another's writing, especially when attempting to reproduce details of formation and method of production.
- As with all writing, there is some intrapersonal variation in these patterns from signature to signature.
- The amount of intrapersonal variation in pressure patterns is generally less than with other writing characteristics.
- In some individuals, these variations will be extreme, in others slight or virtually undetectable.
- For writing of individuals with a wide range of variation, more standards than usual may be required.
- As with all writing, there can be changes in these patterns over time.
- In some individuals these changes will be extreme, in others slight or virtually undetectable.
- Standards close to the date of the questioned material are generally preferable, especially where change over time is acute.
- The pressure distribution and pressure contrast of these pressure patterns can be considered along with other dynamic elements (the elements of line quality), such as speed of writing, for a fuller assessment of individuality."

Important to bear in mind in any study of shading is that the particular location of the shading of the stroke may be a function of the particular writer's pen hold, or the orientation of the instrument to the paper surface or to the writing line, that is called pen position. It might be also a function of the instrument employed. Together and in combination with pen pressure or point load they produced the result that was known as shading. Pen holds, that were previously taught with penmanship, now vary substantially with the individual. Some writers are known to hold a pen in such a position that the horizontal strokes are widened (i.e., shaded) rather than the vertical.

Pen Hold (grasp).   Insofar as any variation in width that might be observed in the writing line, the pen hold or grasp of the pen will make a difference. We note, incidentally, that grasp was a term used by early authors on handwriting to refer to the degree of rigidity or force with which the instrument was clutched, rather than simply the manner in which it is controlled within or by the hand. The various pen holds or grasps that are presently employed do not exhibit the same rigidity or force of former years. It has been observed, however, that individuals that hold the writing instrument in the more awkward fashion of a clenched fist tend to execute rounder forms of letters. Surprisingly, more recent studies show that, contrary to earlier teachings, unconventional pen holds do not necessarily slow the speed of writing execution.[55]

Nevertheless, variation in the grasp of the pen or pencil occurs in a fashion that is more extreme in the writing of sinistrals, or even dextrals, utilizing the inverted hand position (IHV) (see left-handed writing). In these cases, the slope of the instrument is in a direction away from the writer and the stroke on which greater emphasis might be placed will be in the direction of the wrist, and that is away from the writer. Consequently, if

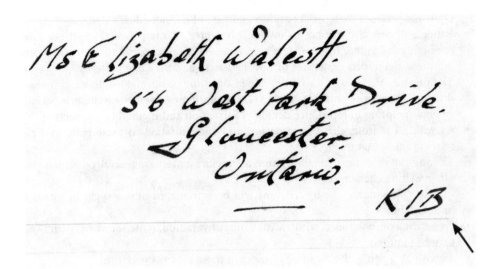

Figure 6   An envelope address executed with a broad-tipped flexible pen nib, from which an unusual pen position (note arrow) can be determined.

emphasis occurs it is likely to be found on what would otherwise be identified as upstrokes, rather than the downstrokes. This aspect of a writing is sought and studied if only to provide evidence of execution by a left-handed writer, or at least one using an inverted hand position.

Pen Position.   The pen position may also make an observable difference. Generally, we are speaking of the orientation of the instrument to the writing line, or the orientation of the document to the writer (Figure 6). In this latter respect, people are quite consistent in the orientation they prefer with respect to the document, but can be quite different from one to another. Modern ball point pens, however, provide much less evidence of the orientation of the instrument to the paper or to the writing line than their predecessors. Consequently pen hold and pen position are not aspects of a writing that the examiner will have an opportunity to consider in most cases.

Pen position, defined earlier as the orientation of the instrument to the paper surface or to the document, is usually thought of as being in reference to the line of writing. Another relationship pertains to the angle at which the axis of the instrument meets the paper surface. Its importance lies in the fact that ball point pens, roller pens, and perhaps others have limitations to these angles at which the housing of the pen contacts the surface. This seems to be, as Lyter and Nemecek[56] have reported, at about 45 degrees. At this angle, shadow and other lines created by the housing and writing substrate may appear. These conditions can be helpful in supplying evidence as to the writer's pen hold or grasp as well as the pen position that can be of some significance in certain cases.

In Summary.   It follows that if the writing is executed with a flexible instrument the shading observed can be a feature of some significance in the examination and study of handwriting for the purpose of its identification. The extent and location of shading depends upon the instrument, its grasp, and the manner of its manipulation. Pen pressure (and shading) tends to become more habitual and pronounced with signatures and other frequently executed segments of writing such as initials. Accordingly, its importance as a useful feature has been stressed.[57]

The fountain pen, the principal split nib writing instrument currently available, has not been completely replaced by the ball point pen. Indeed, reports indicate that its popularity may be regaining lost ground. Consequently, shading of the ink stroke may continue to be a factor to be considered in the identification of writing for some time.

Pen Performance. The effects of instruments on the evidence related to pen control.

Shading, or the variation in width of the line generated, is not the only consequence of variation in the point load. Depending upon the surface against which the writing is done, and the type of writing instrument, some degree of indentation or embossing of the paper can occur.

Ball point pens frequently produce a groove in the paper that is observable and, to some extent, able to be judged under examination with a stereoscopic microscope. As a result of variations in the point load or pressure, the depth of the groove will be seen to vary, even if the width of the line remains apparently unchanged.

In initial studies of the ball point pen, Mayther[58] suggested that the stroke width of the instrument might vary from very narrow when against a hard surface, to that which represented the width of the ball when writing occurred against a soft or resilient surface, and the ink was deposited in a trough in the paper. There are, of course, some differences in ball sizes between fine and broad instruments, but given a particular instrument and a particular writing surface, there is not likely to be any measurable difference in stroke widths that will correspond to the shading of the split nib pen. Point load, or pen pressure, then, must be judged on the basis of the indentation observable by microscope in the paper surface, if indeed, there is any.

In a later study of ball point pens by Lyter, Harris, and Greenwood[59] it was hypothesized that six factors affect the written line of ball point pens: the pen mechanism and ink, the writing speed, point load, writing angle, writing direction and writing surface, only the first of which is not controlled by the writer. These factors manifest themselves in the written line in three ways: the line width, the line density, and certain anomalies called gooping, splitting, dotting, skipping, starving, and blobbing. The study was directed at the affect of the pen, the writing angle and point load on the width, line density, and the occurrence of the anomalies of splitting and blobbing.

The results indicated that, insofar as the twenty different kinds of ball point pens employed in the study, stroke width, density, and anomalies are attributable to both the writing instrument and the writer. This combination of factors appears to be inseparable, however, and, therefore, their value in the identification of writers or instruments requires, that for comparison purposes, instruments and writing conditions, i.e., point load, writing angle, and paper type, must be duplicated.

Both line width measurements and line density measurements (i.e., the absorption of 580 nm light waves by inked line deposits) were ruled out as reliable factors for discriminating between either writers or writing instruments. As reported, fine point instruments could be differentiated from medium point instruments only at low angles of incidence to the paper surface.

Definitions of the technical terms used in this study report: ball point pen, point load, writing angle, blobbing, dotting, skip, directional skipping, starving, splitting, and gooping, are provided in the paper and are included in our glossary.

The porous point or fibre tip pen was the first to appear on the scene after the ball point pen. It delivers an aqueous ink through a feed system based on capillary action. Its relatively soft tip produces a flat ungrooved line. The ink deposits from this pen tend to be heavier than others and varies in dimension only insofar as the point type (fine, medium, broad) of the instrument selected. For this discussion, suffice it to say that pressure or point load makes no difference to the width of the written line.

In fact, there are two kinds of writing tips to these pens: one is made from a stiff perforated plastic and the other is a fibre or felt tip. The plastic is used in fine and most of the medium tips and the felt in broad tips. The porous tip tends produce a surplus of ink at stroke endings. Because of the aqueous nature of its ink, it may spread or bleed along the edges of the stroke, particularly on unsized paper. In these respects, then, it may create some apparent differences to writings executed with ball point pens, but not significantly greater than the differences that might occur in two writings with the same kind of pen.[60]

Variation in point load does not result in apparent variation in stroke width, although the broader stroke, and the bleeding that occurs, tends to fill the counters of narrow loops, acute angles, and small gaps between strokes. Hence, open bowls of the "o" and "a" may be closed. Tapered stroke endings do occur, but are less frequently observed than in writings with other kinds of instruments.

The roller pen is another instrument manufactured in the early 1950s using aqueous ink in a ball point pen design, of two sizes, that is now seldom seen. The pen produces a ball track or groove much like the ball point pen, and a more dense ink deposit much like the porous point pen. Against a soft surface variations in groove depth may be observed as with other ball point pens. Against a hard surface and with a lighter point load, the groove may not be observable and the stroke resembles closely that of the porous point pen.

In the late 1970s, the porous point pen was supplanted by the plastic-tip pen having a hard plastic tip or one of fibres encased in a plastic tube. The stiffness of this point is sufficient to create carbon copies, that the porous point pen could not do. Furthermore, against a reasonably soft writing surface, the firmness of the point is sufficient to produce grooves or furrows in the writing line where the point load is greater. In any event, it is not likely to be as pronounced an indentation in the paper surface as the conventional ball point pen produces. Like the porous point pen, the dimension of the writing line, regardless of the point load, changes only insofar as the point size of the instrument selected.[61]

Plastic-tip pens are capable of producing a fine writing line and, thereby, producing a slight groove or furrow even against a hard or less resilient surface. One instrument, the Pilot Razor Point was reported to produce a finer line than those of competitors and, consequently, were the most apt of its kind to emboss the paper. The Flair Hardhead produced a moderate width stroke, but, according to Hilton, no other plastic-tip pens were reported to produce the wide strokes of which some porous point pen were capable.

It can be stated, as Hilton did, that "fine pointed writing instruments are capable of reproducing the finer details of a person's writing. Broader points normally obscure these details with the result that certain significant aspects of fine line writing are lost in the broader, less distinct writing strokes."

The fountain pen has survived the invasion into the market by these other kinds of writing instruments, although not well. Some argue that it is recovering. It remains the only split nib instrument that is capable of the shading and pressure characteristics of the pens of the past. It is also the only conventional writing instrument that provides a reasonable indication of pen hold and pen position.

17.   *Writing Movement*

Writing movement is a term that is used in several different respects, and tends to adopt for itself a somewhat different meaning for each occasion. Traditionally, it is an attribute of writing that is observed in letter formations and intraword connections, that may be as follows:

a.   garlanded — counter-clockwise movements predominate.
b.   arched — clockwise movements predominate.
c.   angular — straight lines take precedence to curves.
d.   indeterminable — predominating movement uncertain.

Thus, we define it in this fashion:

Definition: Writing movements are (1) general variants in the predominating action of the writing instrument.

If differentiation can be made at all, these movements seem to fall into one of the three classes: garlanded, arched or arcaded, and angular. To be fully comprehensive, however, we must add the fourth class: indeterminable.

There are, as well, other more specific movements in the writing of a person that are particularly letter related. It may be the manner of combining the letters "of" to significantly modify the construction of the upper loop of the "f," the arching of the connection in "on," or any one of a number of methods of executing initial or terminal letters or of executing letter combinations that are more frequently present in the written language. Such movements tend to sacrifice form in the interests of fluency and speed. It is not uncommon to find signatures that exhibit particular movements in the production of certain letters that may, in fact, render the letters quite indiscernible. Because of their greater frequency of use these movements become more fixed and less consciously executed habit patterns. To be complete, then, our definition must have a second clause that reads:

Definition: Writing movements are (2) specific variants in the union of two or more particular letters.

To this point, we are describing what is a two-dimensional pattern of action of the writing instrument. In addition, variation in point load (i.e., the application of pen pressure) is also a part of the action of the instrument, and may be present and observable in any particular pattern of movement in forming a letter or combination of letters. Thus, we have provided ourselves with a three-dimensional pattern of the action of a writing instrument. All of this instrument action is what is included in the definition of writing movement.

Ames used the term *writing movement* to discriminate between the chief elements of the limb involved in the writing process: finger movement, finger and wrist movement, finger and forearm movement, or whole arm movement. These discriminations, however, are applicable to better qualities of penmanship that are seldom seen in the writing of current times. Osborn supports Ames' classes of movements and suggests five levels of quality that each kind of movement might attain. Harrison used *writing movement* to refer to the various patterns of motion of the writing instrument, but not necessarily the dominant patterns. Hilton[62] fails to define it precisely, but uses the term *line quality* almost synonymously with *writing movement* that is said to embrace several aspects of writing instrument performance, such as skill, speed, freedom, hesitation, and emphasis. Admittedly, these are factors that may contribute to the quality of the line, but there are other factors as well. It seems preferable to avoid a confusion of terms, to refrain from considering the terms to be interchangeable, but to allow them to enjoy distinctly different definitions.

C.   Attributes of All Writing Habits

18.   *Consistency or Natural Variation*

Definition: "Natural variation" is the imprecision with which the habits of the writer are executed on repeated occasions.

Natural variation is the current and popular alternative to the term *consistency* used in the old-fashioned penmanship classes. Consistency was an objective to be achieved. Natural variation was a condition to be avoided. Despite such teachings, mutability occurs and can be observed in any two or more examples of a person's writings, whether or not they are made on the same date, at the same time, in the same place. The reason for this mutability is simply that humans are not machines, and consequently, the executions of every writer vary to some extent from one occasion to the next. There is also variation occurring between writings made on different dates, on different documents and with different instruments. The difference between these variations is usually just a matter of degree and may be greater or lesser depending upon circumstances.

With practise, the acquisition of skill, and the application of control, these variations diminish in their range, but we are never totally without them. Skilled penmanship may exhibit the consistency that makes the imprecision difficult for the unaided eye to perceive, but a more precise method of judgment (e.g., a measuring microscope) will reveal it.

Natural variation is an attribute of every perceptual-motor task. There is natural variation to the basketball player's toss of the ball to the basket. There is natural variation to the shooting of a gun. Golf is a perceptual-motor skill to which there is natural variation, that golfers are incessantly trying to explain or to control. The decrease of natural variation in perceptual-motor skills is the mission and intent of practise and training.

Natural variation in writing has been spoken of as if it was a general attribute that affects all of the aspects of writing in some common fashion. Hence, the use of the singular number. This, however, is not quite the case. To resolve this issue we are prompted to ask the question: Variation? Variation of what? The answer is obvious: Variation in each of the discriminating elements of writing.

Some of the discriminating elements of writing may exhibit much wider variation than others. For example, the designs and shapes of the cursive letters "i" and "e" may be quite consistent. Indeed, there is little about them to vary. On the other hand the shapes and sizes of the loops to the cursive letters "g" and "y" and the formation of the capital letters "G" and "S," because of the number of curved strokes involved, may seldom be quite the same. Natural variation, then, must be thought of as an attribute of each element in the composition of a writing, having some cumulative effect upon the countenance of the total product. To be correct then, we should use the plural number and refer to them as natural variations.

Osborn contended that the important and often unappreciated fact is that the variations in a handwriting are themselves habitual.[63] Whatever the difference may be between variations affected by differing circumstances, for the most part, variations tend to lie within ranges peculiar to the individual and to the elements of a writing. Accordingly, these fluctuations in a writing are said to constitute a writer's range of natural variations.

The range of variations in writings of different dates or documents or instruments, appropriately called asynchronous writings, tends to be somewhat greater than that of synchronous (i.e., same date, place, and time) executions. Furthermore, while variation will occur in the consistency of the same letter form, (i.e., the graph), there may also be variation in the selection of the style (i.e., the allograph) employed. There are, for example, many writers that use two designs of the letter "r," one that has a cusp and a shoulder (the conventional form) and one that is a narrow "v" shape (the Palmer option), and each may have a use in particular letter combinations. Others have two methods of crossing the "t" depending on whether it is in a medial or terminal position within the word. Some writers vary the allograph in a more fundamental fashion going from one style of writing to another, if only for certain graphemes and then only in certain locations in a word. Thus, block lettering or script may be mixed with cursive writing.

The more practised the hand or the more skillful the writer, the more consistent is the product and the more limited is the range of these variations. But skill is not the only factor limiting or influencing variations, particularly insofar as the choice of design or allograph selected for many graphemes (i.e., letters). How much variation may occur will depend on the individual and the circumstances. Needless to say, standards for comparison may not always reflect the full range of variations of which the writer may be capable, or duplicate the circumstances responsible for some of the anomalies.

Speed and context can also be contributing factors to variation. Practised writers that write quickly often tend to slur the execution of some letter combinations, especially word endings, that can greatly affect the letter shapes, perhaps to the point of rendering them unreadable as individual letters. Recognition is achieved primarily by virtue of the context in which the words occur.[64]

Wing, Smith, and Eldridge[65] found that there is greater variation in an allograph (letter design) when it occurs in the initial position of a word than when it occurs in the medial or final positions of a word. Furthermore, an allograph is as consistent in the final position as in the medial position. The variation to which this study was directed is the more profound variation in allograph selection, not to be confused with the subtle changes occurring in the execution of the same allograph, to which natural variation normally refers. Thus, it was concluded, as Ellis[66] had concluded before them, that the selection of the allograph (design) of a letter depends on the position of the letter in the word and the letters that precede it, or perhaps succeed it.

Suffice it to say that variations, and the range of them, can be in some instances significant elements of the writing to be considered in both the identification or the elimination of a writer.

Natural variation, then, in the execution of writing, is a term respecting the consistency of the attributes of its many discriminating elements that observation and study have revealed. It is sometimes used in a collective sense to refer to the level of imprecision exhibited by the writing as a whole on repeated occasions. As such, a statement about it constitutes an observation rather than a principle. It is a reflection of the degree of consistency between or within standards, or rather of the degree of consistency between samples of the discriminating elements of the standards. It is often an explanation for a disparity between standards and the unknown. Collectively, it is a variable attribute of the substance (i.e., writing) or particularly of an element of the substance (i.e., any of the 21 discriminating elements of writing) under examination. It is a kind of attribute that fields of science such as chemistry and physics seldom have to consider, provided temperature, pressure, and purity are controlled.

In writing examinations, variation is an expected attribute of the standards, for which allowance must be made in the study of any apparent disparity between the standards and the unknown or questioned writing. The level of such disparity and the range of the writer's normal variation may be the principal factors on which the determination of authorship may turn.

Over many years, various claims have been made for natural variation as a principle on which writing identification is based. It will be obvious that with such claims we cannot agree. We only trust that this detailed explanation, respecting natural variation as we see it, will clarify the matter finally.

There are some examiners that tend to confuse persistency with natural variation. A writer that is inclined to employ two or more designs (allographs) of a letter, perhaps a block letter and a cursive letter, perhaps an epsilon "e" and a conventional one, is said to display great variation in his/her letter forms. It is our contention that while these different forms may be different styles in the construction of a letter, they are more correctly described as different allographs of the same grapheme. They are not the kind of subtle changes from one execution to the next to which natural variation is normally intended to refer. Natural variation is a property of a single allograph or design, a single method, a single writing movement, that experiences a change due to imprecision when it is repeated.

19. Persistency

This concerns the frequency with which a given habit occurs, when the occasion permits.

The term persistency tends to be applicable particularly to the selection of the allograph to be used in any particular situation. As has been observed in studies, and we have reported elsewhere, the position of the letter within the word may determine the allograph chosen. It may be simply the purpose the writing is intended to serve that will prompt the change or selection. The inscription of addresses on envelopes is a case in point.

It might be argued that persistency and consistency (see Element #18) are the same thing, and the use of both terms will be confusing. As aforementioned, *consistency* was the predecessor to the term *natural variation* in the language of penmanship, when excellence in it was being sought. Consistency was attained by the acquisition of skill that refined the execution of a character, a feature or writing element, without altering or modifying its design. Persistency pertains to the more allographic or profound changes in an element of writing than natural variation does, and so the use of the two terms, *persistency* and *consistency* is justified.

D. Combinations of Writing Habits

20. Lateral Expansion

Definition: Lateral expansion is the horizontal dimension of a group of successive letters and words.

It is the product of letter formation, letter sizes, and the spacing between letters and words. It ranges from contracted to expanded.

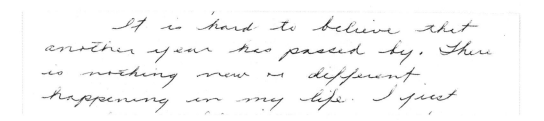

Figure 7   An example of considerable lateral expansion, the product or interword spacing, interletter spacing and in some cases letter widths.

Although letter forms and letter sizes contribute to lateral expansion, the principal contributor tends to be the interletter and interword spacing. This is an aspect of writing that is frequently distinctive and remarkably consistent with some individuals (Figure 7).

Consequently, lateral expansion is not a writing characteristic, per se, and may be difficult to judge for comparison purposes, except in special cases. Precise judgments can only be made on similar text material, and that is seldom available except in signature comparisons. Its particular advantage in the study of writings and especially signatures lies in its being cumulative. Minor disparities in the dimensions of letters and of spacing are accumulated across a signature, across several words or across a line of writing, that confirms the similarities in size and space aspects, if such are present, and renders differences more pronounced, if differences exist.

Some writers exhibit considerable lateral expansion. When this occurs, it is to be noted that an increase in interletter spacing correlates well with interword spacing. An increase in the vertical dimension or the size of the writing does not necessarily ensue. An increase in the vertical dimension of the writing, such as occurs with an increase in the size of letters, frequently results in a decrease in the space between letters or an apparent crowding of the writing.

21.   *Word Proportions*

   a.   vertical dimension versus horizontal dimension.
   b.   the product of size and spacing.

Osborn wrote:

> "Genuine writing or genuine signatures show a certain definite and fixed proportion of height of letters to length of words. This is another of the distinctive ways in which the general appearance of a page of writing is changed by a different system of writing. This change may be very slight although in combination it changes the general appearance of writing in a striking manner."[67]

Osborn is saying that the subtle or minute differences in writing, between systems or indeed, between persons, have a cumulative affect that is more obvious when greater quantities of writing (such as a page) can be considered. Of some import to document examiners is the correspondence between Osborn's comments respecting word proportions and the approach of one of the schools of graphology called graphoanalysis. This approach, introduced by Bunker in 1929, known as the holistic or global personality pattern, advocates the study or consideration of the general appearance of a page of writing as a whole, judged at arm's length if necessary, as well as the consideration of its particular elements.

The study of word proportions is not a topic on which others have commented. It is a circumstance that we have observed in some cases, however. It arouses an early reaction in the mind of the examiner and prompts a further investigation as to its cause.

E.   Final Comment

Artistic Quality

We might be challenged for not having included artistic quality in this catalogue of writing features by which writing might be identified or differentiated. Admittedly, artistic quality is a term sometimes used in reference to writing in which many of its aspects, such as arrangement, size, proportions, line quality, and writing quality are of such kind and consistency as to be pleasing to the eye. It cannot be simply defined, however, any more than beauty can be defined, for it rests largely in the eyes of the beholder. Consequently, it is not an aspect of writing, or a writing habit of itself, that can be easily defined, described, or utilized in the identification process.

Summary

Briefly, then, and in summary, the aspects of writing that become habitual with each and every writer, that are its discriminating elements, and that are the subject of examination and study in the process of handwriting identification or elimination are 21 in number, including two combinations of habits and two common properties of habits, as follows:

The 21 Elements in Review

A.   Elements of Style

1.   Arrangement

- influenced by artistic ability, sense of proportion and instruction received.
- the product of a group of habits.

2.   Class of Allograph

The four styles of allographs.

3.   Connections

a.   interword.
b.   intraword.

4.   Designs of Allographs and their Construction

a.   correspondence to foreign/domestic or particular writing systems.
b.   number, nature, position, sequence, and direction of strokes in letter composition.
c.   use of two or more forms for the same letter.
d.   capitalization — divergences from standard practises.

5. *Dimensions*

- proportions of elements of letters, i.e., of bowls to staffs, of bodies to loops, of arches to loops.
- absolute sizes.
- relative sizes – of specific letters to specific letters,
             – according to position in words.

6. *Slant or Slope*

a. of the writing in general, and,
b. of letters or parts of letters in particular.

7. *Spacings*

a. interword.
b. intraword.

B.   Elements of Execution

8. *Abbreviations*

a. word contractions that eliminate letters.
b. letter combinations that sacrifice form for speed.

9. *Alignment*

The relation of successive letters of a signature, a word or line of writing to an actual or imaginary base line.

10.   *Commencements and Terminations*

a. their length, direction, and path
b. their taper (the abruptness with which the instrument approaches and leaves the paper)

11.   *Diacritics and Punctuation — presence, style, and location.*

12.   *Embellishments*

Including flourishes, ornamentation, rubrics, and underscores.

13.   *Legibility or Writing Quality*

Ease of recognition of letters or adherence to copy-book form.

14.   *Line Continuity*

The presence/absence of pen stops, pen lifts, or retracings.

15. Line Quality

The degree of regularity (i.e., smoothness and/or gradation) to the writing stroke as is judged from the consistency of its nature and of its path in a prescribed direction. It varies from smooth and controlled to tremulous and erratic.

16. Pen Control

a. Pen Hold
b. Pen Position
c. Point Load (pen pressure)
   • to be considered if and when determinable.
   • evidenced by shading, greater deposition of ink or graphite or by the depression of the paper. Called rhythm, or fluency or a flowing hand when it materializes as a harmonious and graduated recurrence.
   • absolute — occurring in all writing.
   • relative — greater or lesser in some strokes.

17. Writing Movement

• variants in the predominating action of the writing instrument. May be three-dimensional.
• observed in letter formation and interword connections that may be:
  a. garlanded — anticlockwise movements predominate.
  b. arched — clockwise movements predominate.
  c. angular — straight lines take precedence to curves.
  d. indeterminable

C. Attributes of All Writing Habits

18. Consistency or Natural Variation

The precision with which the habits are executed on repeated occasions.

19. Persistency

The frequency with which a given habit occurs when the occasion permits.

D. Combinations of Writing Habits

20. Lateral Expansion

• ranges from contracted to expanded.
• the product of spacing and letter formation.

21. Word Proportions

a. vertical dimension versus horizontal dimension.
b. the product of size and spacing.

Were the profession of handwriting identification or of document examination to agree universally on these twenty one aspects of writing as the targets of study in writing examinations we would achieve conspectus validity, or conspect validity, the first step in the rise to science.

References

1. Ellis, Andrew W., Slips of the Pen. *Visible Language,* 1979; 13: 3: p 273.

2. Brault, Jean-Jules and Plamondon, Réjean, A Complexity Measure of Handwriting Curves: Modelling of Dynamic Signature Forgery. *IEEE Transactions on Systems, Man and Cybernetics,* 1993 March/April; 23: 2.

3. Klimoski, R. J. and Rafaeli, A., Inferring Personal Qualities Through Handwriting Analysis. *Journal of Occupational Psychology,* 1983; 56.

4. Blake, Martha, *Are We Seeing the Same Thing? Results of a Survey Presented to Forensic Document Examiners.* Presented at the meeting of the American Society of Questioned Document Examiners (Long Beach, CA, 1994).

5. Huber, Roy A., *Handwriting Examination as a Scientific Discipline.* Presented at the meeting of the American Society of Questioned Document Examiners (Chicago, 1995).

6. Lewinson, Thea Stein, Classic Schools of Graphology. *Scientific Aspects of Graphology.* Baruch Nevo ed. (Springfield: Charles C Thomas, 1986), pp 5-46.

7. Lorr, M., Lepine, L., and Golder, J., A Factor Analysis of Some Handwriting Characteristics, *Journal of Personality,* 1954; 22: pp 348-353.

8. Lemke, E. and Kirchner, J., A Multivariate Study of Handwriting, Intelligence and Personality Correlates. *Journal of Personality Assessment,* 1971; 35: pp 584-592.

9. Peeples, E. Edward and Retzlaff, Paul D., A Component Analysis of Handwriting. *The Journal of General Psychology,* 1991; 118(4): pp 369-374.

10. Hardy, H. and Fagel, W., Methodological Aspects of Handwriting Identification. *Journal of Forensic Document Examination,* 1995 fall; 8: pp 33-69.

11. Osborn, Albert S., *Questioned Documents.* 2nd Ed. (Albany NY: Boyd Printing Co., 1929), p 139.

12. Horan, James J. and Horan, George J., *A Study of Numbers.* Presented at the meeting of the International Association of Forensic Sciences (Oxford, 1984).

13. Harrison, Wilson R., *Suspect Documents, Their Scientific Examination* (New York: Frederick A. Praeger, 1958), p 337.

14. Shaneyfelt, Lyndal L., *The Versatile Writer.* Presented at the meeting of the American Academy of Forensic Sciences (Dallas, TX, 1974).

15. Osborn, Albert S., *Questioned Documents.* 2nd Ed. (Albany: Boyd Printing Co., 1929), p 188.

16. Anthony, Arthur T., *D'Nealian: A New Handwriting System.* Presented at the meeting of the American Society of Questioned Document Examiners (Nashville, TN, 1984).

17. Herrick, Virgil E., *Comparison of Practices in Handwriting* (Madison: University of Wisconsin, July, 1960), p 32.

18. Lee, C. D. and Abbey, R. A., *Classification and Identification of Handwriting* (New York: Appleton & Co., 1922).

19. Hayes, James L., *Connecting Strokes.* Presented at the meeting of the American Society of Questioned Document Examiners (Vancouver, 1987).

20. Tannenbaum, Samuel A., *The Handwriting of the Renaissance* (New York: Columbia U. Press, 1930), p 16.

21. Masson, Janet Fenner, *A Look at the Hand Lettering of Draftsmen.* Presented at the meeting of the American Society of Questioned Document Examiners (San Jose 1990).

22. Winchester, Janis M. and McCarthy, John F., *Data Obtained from a Survey of the Handwriting of Black Students in Grades One Through Twelve in a Study of the Letter Forms "J" and "W."* Presented at the meeting of the American Society of Questioned Document Examiners (Seattle, 1971).

23. McCarthy, John F. and Williams, Thelma, *A Second Survey of the Handwritings of Black Students in the United States in a Study of the Black "J" and "W."* Presented at the meeting of the International Association of Forensic Sciences (Vancouver, 1987).

24. Daniels, James, *Unusual Formation of Cursive Lowercase Letter "p."* Presented at the meeting of the American Society of Questioned Document Examiners (San Jose, 1990).

25. Wing, A. M., Variability in Handwritten Characters, *Visible Language.* 1979; 13: pp 283-298.

26. Wing, A. M., Nimmo-Smith, I., and Eldridge, M. A., The Consistency of Cursive Letter Formation as a Function of Position in the Word, *Acta Psychologica,* 1983; 54: pp 197-204.

27. Van der Plaats, Rudolph E. and Van Galen, Gerald P., Allographic Variability in Adult Handwriting. *Human Movement Science,* 1991; 10: pp 291-300.

28. Osborn, Albert S., *Questioned Documents.* 2nd Ed. (Albany: Boyd Printing Co., 1929), p 143.

29. Harrison, Wilson R., *Suspect Documents* (New York: Frederick A Praeger, 1958), p 312.

30. Osborn, A. S., *Questioned Documents.* 2nd Ed. (Albany: Boyd Printing Co., 1929), p 140.

31. Zweigenshaft, Richard L., Signature Size: A Key to Status Awareness. *Journal of Social Psychology,* 1970; 81: 1 pp 49-54.

32. Swanson, Blair R. and Price, Raymond L., Signature Size and Status. *Journal of Social Psychology,* 1972; 87: 2: p 319.

33. Zweigenshaft, Richard L., and Marlowe, David, Signature Size: Studies in Expressive Movement. *Journal of Consulting & Clinical Psychology,* 1973; 40: 3: pp 469-473.

34. Maloney, E. R., Signature Size and Self Estimation: A Brief Note. *Journal of Psychology,* 1973; 84: 2: pp 223-224.

35. Stewart, Robert A., Effects of Self-Esteem and Status on Size of Signature. *Perceptual & Motor Skills,* 1977; 44: 1: pp 185-186.

36. Zweigenshaft, Richard L., The Empirical Study of Signature Size. *Social Behaviour and Personality,* 1977; 5: 1: pp 177-185.

37. Jorgenson, Dale O., Signature Size and Dominance: A Brief Note. *Journal of Psychology,* 1977; 97: 2: pp 269-270.

38. Aiken, Lewis R. and Zweigenshaft, Richard L., Signature Size, Sex and Status in Iran. *Journal of Social Psychology,* 1978; 106: 2: pp 273-274.

39. Lester, David and Meyer, Donna, Two Studies on Handwriting: Correlates of Signature Size and Slant. *Perceptual & Motor Skills,* 1979; 48: 3 Pt 2: p.1278.

40. Morton, S. E., How Does Crowding Affect Signatures? *Journal of Forensic Sciences,* 1980; 25: 1: pp 141-145.

41. Wing, A. M. and Nimmo-Smith, I., The Variability of Cursive Handwriting Measure Defined Along a Continuum: Letter Specificity. *Journal of the Forensic Science Society,* 1987; 27: pp 297-306.

42. Anon., *Teacher's Guide for Basic Handwriting* (Stone, Smally & Cooke, 1962), pp 2-13.

43. Purtell, David J., Modern Handwriting Instructions, Systems and Techniques. *Journal of Police Science and Administration,* 1980; 8: 1: pp 66-68.

44. Morton, S. E., How Does Crowding Affect Signatures? *Journal of Forensic Sciences,* 1980; 25: 1: pp 141-145.

45. McClary, Carl R., A Study of Baseline Alignment in Signatures and Handwritten Sentences, *International Journal of Forensic Document Examiners,* 1997 Jan/Mar; 3: 1: pp 35-44.

46. Ellen, David, *The Scientific Examination of Documents: Methods and Techniques* (Chichester, Eng: Ellis Horwood Ltd, 1989), p 41.

47. Andersen, Dan W., *Correlates of Handwriting Legibility.* Presented at the meeting of the American Academy of Forensic Science (Chicago, 1964).

48. Harrison, Wilson, *Suspect Documents* (New York: Frederick A. Praeger, 1958), p 322.

49. Tytell, Peter V., *Pen Pressure as an Identifying Characteristic of Signatures — Verification from the Computer.* Presented at the meeting of the American Society of Questioned Document Examiners (Chicago, 1995). Excerpts used with permission.

50. Osborn, Albert S., *Questioned Documents.* 2nd Ed. (Albany: Boyd Printing Co., 1929), p 128.

51. Brewester, F., *Contested Documents and Forgeries* (Calcutta: The Book Company, 1932), p 39.

52. Osborn, Albert S., *Questioned Document Problems.* 2nd ed., revised (Albany: Boyd Printing Co, 1946), p 292.

53. Hilton, Ordway, *Scientific Examination of Questioned Documents.* Revised Ed. (New York: Elsevier/North-Holland, 1982), p 20.

54. Hagan, William E., *Disputed Handwriting* (Albany: Banks & Brothers, 1894), p 68.

55. Sassoon, Rosemary, Nimmo-Smith, Ian and Wing, Alan M., An Analysis of Children's Penholds, *Graphonomics: Contemporary Research in Handwriting.* H. S. R. Kao, G. P. VanGalen, R. Hoosain eds. (Elsevier Science Publishers B.V. North Holland, 1986).

56. Nemecek, Joe, *Ball Point Pen Oddities.* Presented at the meeting of the American Society of Questioned Document Examiners (Milwaukee, WI, 1974).

57. Moore, D. S., The Importance of Shading Habits in Handwriting Identification, *Journal of Forensic Sciences,* 1983 Jan; 28: 1: pp 278-281.

58. Mathyer, Jacques, Ball Pens and the Expert Appraisal of Written Documents. *International Criminal Police Review,* 1950 Dec; 43: pp 357-360.

59. Lyter, Albert H. III, Harris, John J., and Greenwood, Bruce R., *The Ball-Point Pen — Nomenclature, Definitions and Writing Characteristics.* Presented at the Meeting of the American Society of Questioned Document Examiners (Lake Tahoe, CA, 1983).

60. Hilton, Ordway, Effects of writing instruments on handwriting details. *Journal of Forensic Sciences,* 1984 Jan; 29: 1: pp 80-86.

61. Hilton, Ordway, *Distinctive Qualities of Today's Pens.* Presented at the Meeting of the American Society of Questioned Document Examiners (Vancouver, 1980).

62. Hilton, Ordway, Line Quality — Historic and Contemporary Views. *Journal of Forensic Sciences,* 1987 Jan; 32: 1: pp 118-120.

63. Osborn, Albert S., *Questioned Documents* (Albany: Boyd Printing Co., 1929) p 208.

64. Wing, Alan M., Variability in Handwritten Characters. *Visual Language,* 1979; XIII: 3: pp 283-298.

65. Wing, Alan M., Nimmo-Smith, M. Ian and Eldridge, Margery A., The Consistency of Cursive Letter Formation as a Function of Position in the Word. *Acta Psychologica,* 1983; 54: 197-204.

66. Ellis, Andrew W., Slips of the Pen. *Visible Language,* 1979; 13: 3: pp 265-282.

67. Osborn, Albert S., *Questioned Documents,* 2nd Ed. (Albany: Boyd Printing Co., 1929), p 141.

Special Problems in the Discrimination and Identification of Writing

7

31. Are Initials Identifiable with a Writer as Are Other Handwritings?

In this discussion it must be understood that we are speaking of initials as an incidence of writing separate and apart from the execution of a signature. It is rather an execution in lieu of a signature, usually comprised of the first letters of some or all of the names involved.

Business practises in recent years have made the use of initials a standard procedure in the authentication of documents, the approval of amendments thereto, or the authorization of the action to which the document pertains. It has been suggested that initials are utilized in these instances simply as an abbreviated signature. This explanation for their wide use is not to suggest that initials will resemble any part of the signature of that individual in every case. In fact, the disparity may be surprising. In the majority of instances, however, a close study of one's initials will disclose at least some basic correspondence with the first or capital letters of the individual's signature.

Some writers adopt distinctive styles in their initials, and sufficiently so, that they provide ample evidence by which the writer can be identified. Authorizing or approving initials by persons in some authority are frequently accompanied by other abbreviations of the individual's rank or position, such as "A.B.C./R.N." or "D.E.F./Mgr.," "G.H./Sgt," "I.J./Sec'y" or "K.L./Dr," with or without punctuation or the slash shown here. The manner of punctuating and appending the rank or title can be, of course, quite individualistic and a significant element in the identification or elimination of a potential writer. In the majority of cases, however, the evidence within initials themselves, alone, is qualitatively limited and quantitatively insufficient.

Initials are sometimes elaborately embellished, or hastily scrawled such that the letter forms they are expected to contain are unrecognizable. It is not uncommon to find that initials are underscored and underscores may not be the practise of the individual when executing a signature.

The initials of persons having less need to write them may display little consistency. Frequently, they are used simply to acknowledge receipt of an item, or an agreement to terms on a document (that may not be read or fully understood), and are commonly executed under a wide range of writing conditions and writing positions. For these reasons it is often stressed that when possible "request" writing standards for use in comparisons should be prepared under similar writing circumstances, however, inconvenient or perturbing that may be.

In some lines of employment, the initializing of documents as an authorizing or authenticating exercise is a frequent daily requirement and, consequently, becomes a well practised movement that reflects much greater consistency, greater perhaps than the signature. In one of the few properly conducted studies of natural variation, Widla[1] collected writing samples from 30 extramural students at law at the Silesian University (Poland) who, by virtue of their employment, were required to sign and to initial documents many times a day. It was reported that, over a period of six months, initials proved to be a more stable graphic product than signatures. This finding was based on the initials displaying, on average, a smaller standard deviation in physical dimensions than that of signatures from the same individuals. The results of this study are said to support the findings of Wallner.[2]

The potential for identification of the author will depend on the number of letters involved in the execution, the complexity of the movements, and the skill and consistency with which it is performed. The use of the microscope or of photographic enlargements, in the examination or illustration of evidence the initials may contain, is a recommended practise.

Although not numerous, cases are known to have occurred wherein initials, and in some instances signatures, have been deliberately written carelessly and illegibly to supply a plausible pretext for the eventual repudiation of the writing, that is, a later denial that the writing is genuine. As has been said elsewhere, disguise and distortion is a deed affecting the gross or more obvious elements of writing because they are the more consciously executed structures. Initials are, for the most part, a group of such gross features of an individual's writing. Consequently, disguise and distortion affects a more substantial portion of the limited amount of writing that initials provide. The examination and study of illegible initials and signatures must be conducted with such possibilities in mind.

One of the few writers on the subject, Galbraith[3-4] conducted two studies of initials and their relationship to the signatures of the same persons. She reports that size and relative heights may change, and that spacing usually changes by diminishing, displaying more crowding or less lateral expansion to the writing. It was found that punctuation, not present in the signature is often added to the initials. Even letter forms may be modified. The majority of her subjects in both studies (72 percent and 69 percent) disclosed some change in the initials as compared to the signatures, suggesting that they should be considered a special category of handwriting.

A wider range of variations is expected to be found in initials from people not required to use them on a daily or routine basis. This is probably due to the fact that there is no necessity to conform to any standards, thereby, allowing more freedom and individuality in developing the design of the final product.

Although initials may display much fluency they may also display a great deal of variation from one execution to the next. Because of their brevity, a deceptive simulation of the initials is much easier to achieve. Only a general outline of the genuine product is required to be reproduced to pass normal scrutiny, without regard to details. Consistency in the known standards of the initials, however, such as may emanate from the more practised hands, is an indication of the range of variation within which a set of questioned initials may be expected to fall if they are genuine.

32. Do Numerals or Symbols and Other Nonalphabetic Characters Play a Part in the Writing Identification Process?

Numerals and other nonalphabetic compositor's job case characters are those characters that normally occupy a space in the type case that was used for many years in the days when compositors set type by hand. This group of characters, plus the letters of the alphabet in both capital and small letter size came to be known as the font of any style and size of type. The term *font* is unrelated to any particular, typeface, a word we use interchangeably with type style. Modern usage tends to associate font improperly with the name of a typeface, as in a Bodoni font or a Times Roman font. Being somewhat old-fashioned we prefer to think of the font as the complete collection of characters and letters (uppercase and lowercase) that one might receive if one was to purchase or procure a particular typeface, or type style.

There are, however, other characters that appear in conjunction with handwriting, such as check marks, cross marks, arrows, and other symbols of various shapes that are currently offered as type characters for the computer and are collectively called *dingbats* or iconic symbols.

Numerals and Textual Symbols

With respect to numerals and other nonalphabetic "compositor's job case" characters there is little in the available literature that has been written lately on the topic of numerals and other characters, and even less on the differences between domestic and foreign systems in numerals and other "compositor's job case" characters. Hilton[5] provided a general coverage of the subject of numerals, going so far as to suggest that a writer may be identified from the habits acquired in the writing of numerals alone. Horan and Horan[6] reported on the correspondence they found between 675 (American) subjects and the review of numerals by Ansell and Strach.[7] In a later paper, Hilton[8] describes some of the features that he noted in the Austrian writing of numerals.

Osborn, Hilton, and Conway have each made the point that numerals, and the signs and symbols associated with and frequently accompanying numerals, possess similar discriminating elements to those of the alphabetical cursive characters. Consequently, the examination and study of numerals does not differ fundamentally from that of any other aspect of writing. Numerals and other characters are found to vary with the writer insofar as structure, dimension, slope, spacing, system (in some cases), varieties of styles and shapes utilized, and even connections, although they are primarily independent executions.

Because of this independence, variations due to the influence of a preceding or succeeding character or numeral are limited. Distinctive relationships in dimensions of two or more numerals (i.e., relative heights or sizes) do occur, particularly respecting the cipher (zero), but the quantity of evidence of individuality is considerably reduced by the independence of the numerals.

For the most part, there is greater consistency in the writing systems followed on this continent in the designs and structures of numerals and other characters than there is in the designs and structures of upper and lowercase letters of cursive writing. Furthermore, there are fewer, if any, optional forms for any numerals or characters suggested by any of the published systems, and less time is devoted to their development. Some pronounced differences are to be noted in the construction of other characters, such as the ($) dollar sign, the (¢) cent sign, the (%) percent sign, the (c/o) "in care of" sign, the (&) ampersand, the (@) "at" sign, and the writing of fractions, 1/2 or ½. Numerals themselves, however, are much less distinguishable with any given system.

As a consequence of this greater consistency in writing systems, and the lesser influence of other numerals or letters or characters with which the numeral may be associated, it might be expected that there are fewer variations in the products by different writers. Indeed, one would expect that some numerals by design (e.g., the "0" and the "1") allow for little to be done as personal modifications. In a study of the numerals executed by approximately 110 writers, Giles[9] found that the numerals "1" and "6" afforded the fewest number (three) of classifiable variations in design, and the "2" the greatest (eight). In fact, the "0" afforded as many variations in design (five) as the "8" and "9." The numerals "3," "4," "5," and "7" varied in (six) classifiable fashions. Among other things respecting the frequency of occurrence of some forms, Giles comments that the presence or absence of a crossbar to the numeral "7" divided her sample in half. Furthermore, she reports that this numeral and the numeral "1" were the most consistent in design among the writers of her sample.

While Giles' study records three to eight variations in design for each numeral, there are numerous subclassifications in most classified variations that are not reported. For example, the cross stroke to the "7" is a single category among six for this numeral, although it was apparently present in 50 percent of her sample. Cross strokes, however, may vary in length, position on the staff, and in angle of intersection.

For some writers, consistency in shape and design doesn't always prove to be the case. In normal written communications for these people, numerals are infrequent inclusions and for this reason are less practised habits. Accordingly consistency in their execution can be poorer than that of textual material from the same individual. In her study, Giles found that significant numbers of persons (as many as 48 percent) employed two or more forms for any given numeral.

At the same time there are numerous occupations, including architects, engineers, and draftsmen, that are taught to write numerals in a prescribed fashion. Then too, there are lines of work that generate documents bearing numerals, symbols, or combinations of the two to express monetary amounts, dates, times, or prices, that become targets of dispute in civil and criminal litigation. These include accounting records, inventories, stock records, bank deposit slips, drawings, records of time, records of distance, logs, and even betting and gambling records. In many of these cases, by virtue of the nature of employment, the writer of the records may be sufficiently practised to display much consistency in his/her writing of numerals. Consequently, the role of natural variations in the study of numerals will vary with the writer's personal background and experience.

These circumstances prompted Ansell and Strach (1975) to study the classification of numerals as a first step in the future classification of block lettering (capitals) and ultimately cursive writings. In a report of their study of 1,080 (British) subjects, they have provided frequency of occurrence data (in percentages) of four to eight distinct variations in structure and/or design for each of the numerals "0" to "9." This differs only slightly from the aforementioned results obtained by Giles.

In their study, Horan and Horan (1984) examined the numerals of 675 (American) subjects, using the Ansell and Strach system of classification and obtained corresponding results. As these authors point out, however, in the categories of variations in structure and design for each numeral, one category represented a clear majority of the subjects in each case. As a classification system, this circumstance tends to limit its usefulness in the discrimination process. It also furnishes a caution to the evaluation of similarities in numerals in the approach to their identification.

Other studies have shown (Section 34: Can Handwriting be Usefully Classified) that the writing of monetary amounts on cheques has been usefully classified to narrow populations of writers that may be potentially authors of questioned writings, usually on cheques. Although these studies are few in number, and their use by examiners is not broad, they still constitute evidence in support of the argument that there is some empirical data available that can be applied to handwriting cases under certain circumstances.

Because of the wide diversity in the situations in which numerals and other characters may play a part, in addition to the 21 discriminating elements of writing, generally, the study of numerals and other characters, frequently, must consider many matters: the manners of ornamentation, the manners of simplification, the manners of utilizing the virgule or slash "/," the caret "∧," the octothorpe "#," the plus sign "+," the minus sign "-," the equals sign "=," the percentage sign "%," the "in care of" sign "c/o," the methods of space filling (with straight lines or undulating lines), the alignment of digits in amounts or quantities, the writing of fractions, the underscoring of digits in some sets of numerals, the manners of writing monetary amounts with dollars "$," pounds "£," cents "¢," and the manner of writing ciphers "0" in pairs or triplets.

Alford[10] provides us with a classic example of the case in which the discrimination between the numerals of a small population of writers is possible. In this case, other circumstances narrowed the population of possible writers to four persons whose habits in executing the numerals "0" to "9" were sufficiently distinctive from each other to permit proper conclusions of authorship to be drawn. This was the first application of the Bayes Theorem and the likelihood ratio to writing examination that we are aware of.

As others have expressed, numerals, and this wide assortment of other characters, are matters that are given less consideration in the disguise or distortion of one's writing, or in the simulation of another's, when circumstances call for their inclusion in the questioned document. Their usefulness in writing studies and examinations, therefore, should not be overlooked or underestimated.

Although disguise in the execution of questioned numerals is less frequently encountered, Kelly[11] has drawn attention to the fact that disguise in the execution of numerals may be attempted in the preparation of standards or request writings, for use in comparisons with questioned writings consisting largely of numbers.

In Kelly's study of the methods of disguise employed by 200 subjects in the writing of numerals, she identified five techniques and reports their frequency:

1. The use of an alternate form for the numerals "2," "4," "7," "8" and "9" (45 percent to 62 percent depending on the numeral).
2. An increase in the size of the numerals (20 percent).
3. The adoption of a more formal version of the numeral (15 percent).
4. A change in slant, but not well maintained (10 percent).
5. A change in pen direction in the structure of the numeral (5 percent).

Numerals are the means of recording telephone numbers, illicit drug deals, bets or wagers, and the monetary amounts of debts, cheques, and other transactions. In such cases, the quantity of questioned writing is often limited, the size of the document is often small, and the records on a given document may be the product of two or more persons. Thus, the examination warrants considerable care.

Dingbats and Iconic Symbols

Within the general category of dingbats or iconic symbols there are *check marks* and *cross marks*. These are two of the other manually-executed characters that often enough become matters of dispute, and consequently, are subject to examination and study by handwriting examiners. Unlike numerals and other characters that are usually executed in conjunction with textual material of some sort, check marks and cross marks are seldom a minor part of a larger problem of writing identification. More often they are the principal issue in dispute and their identification, without the help of other material, is sought to establish the validity of a document or documents as it/they now exist. They frequently occur with typewritten or printed text and may be the only handwriting on the document.

Cross marks are the usual essence of disputes respecting ballots in election processes. They are usually one or two stroke structures situated with their components running roughly vertically and horizontally, or with two feet on the baseline and their components running diagonally. In both cases, the intention, if not the tendency, is for the strokes to intersect one another approximately in the centre. The precision with which the intersections are made in the middle of the strokes can be a matter that varies between individuals, and serves to distinguish the products of some writers from each other. The orientation of the strokes to the baseline, be it vertical or diagonal or some position in between, may also be peculiar to the individual and of discriminatory value.

The strokes of cross marks seldom meet at right angles to one another, and the angle itself may exhibit some consistency worth consideration. Furthermore, while the ideal structure is for the strokes to intersect in their middles, this is often not the case, and the pattern of balance, if there is one, may be of some significance. The quality of the lines, of course, can indicate the fluency with which the character was executed. Alternatively, a more slow, drawn, deliberate production may say something about the act of writing or the writer.

It is generally presumed that cross marks are executed as two separate downstrokes, although on infrequent occasions when the character is small it has been noted that hastily executed cross marks may exhibit a pen drag from the bottom of the first stroke to the top of the second. Certainly, this is the structure prescribed by copybook, as a survey by Doud[12] disclosed.

We can be reasonably certain that forgers of cross marks seldom or never work from masters. If and when known standards are available for comparison the questioned cross mark(s) can exhibit differences in skill or fluency, differences in movement or angles of intersection and differences in pen position.

Legitimate cross marks are, frequently, the extent of the writing ability of illiterates and bedridden individuals. The amount of evidence that they can provide will be limited in any case and the task of identification or elimination is especially difficult. We must bear in mind that the identification process is based on the study and comparison of habits. Illiterates and bedridden individuals are rarely sufficiently practised in the execution of cross marks to have developed consistent habits in their production.

Check marks must be studied in a fashion similar to cross marks. The usual structure is comprised of two strokes meeting at an acute angle much like a printed "V," the first stroke of which is shorter than the second. The axis of the angle normally is vertical or slanting slightly to the right.

The conventional style of check mark varies with the writer in several respects: the size generally, the relative lengths or balance of the strokes, the slant of the axis of the angle, the placement of the mark with respect to the line or item of the text to which it refers, and the curvature or straightness of the strokes, particularly, the second. It has also been observed that some sinistrals (left-handed writers) reverse the orientation of the check mark such that the longer and final stroke extends off to the left. These aspects of the mark can serve to distinguish reasonably well between the products of different writers, although the degree to which a finding must be qualified depends on the case circumstances.

The inversion of the check mark "∧," called the *caret*, is a symbol employed regularly as a direction along the baseline to indicate the location for the insertion of additional text. It should not be overlooked when the examination of the handwriting of the material to be inserted is being conducted. Much like the check mark, an insertion mark can possess its own style of individualization. While the conventional design of the check mark "√" is that which comes readily to mind when the subject is mentioned, there are numerous other methods of checking off articles in a list of items. The dash or hyphen "-" may be used. The period may be used. A short inclined line or diagonal may be employed, or even an arc or circle. Other symbols sometimes appear in questioned documents not always as check marks, but of some importance to the resolution of the matter in dispute. Arrows, brackets, and some styles of parentheses are but a few. These kinds of marks may afford fewer attributes to study and consider, but the approach in doing so remains the same. Indeed, one can move from these kinds of iconic marks to music symbols, mathematical symbols, and the like.

What must be scrutinized carefully is the consistency between the standards and the questioned marks. If consistency does exist the weight of the evidence of common authorship may still be dubious. If consistency is blatantly absent a conclusion of nonidentity or elimination may be more demonstrable. In many cases, it will be found that the task of the examination is not unlike that of synchronous and asynchronous writings. The key lies in the consistency of the executions.

We would make a final observation respecting the various marks of this nature. The circumstances of the matter under investigation frequently limits the population of possible or potential writers to be considered, and this may have a bearing on the merit in any conclusion reached. If and when we allow it to, we have applied, knowingly or unknowingly, the Bayesian Theorem to handwriting identification.

33. Does the Quest for Anonymity in Writing Alter its Examination and Study?

Anonymity in a writing is an author's device employed to prevent the association of the writer with the document, or the comments expressed on it. It may involve some method of disguise, some method of simulation, the inclusion of some method of deception or misdirection, or simply the omission of any conventional method of recognition of its source. Elsewhere, we deal with disguise in the section captioned Disclosers of Disguise and with simulation in the section captioned Flags of Forgery. Methods of deception or misdirection may go well beyond the realms of disguise and simulation. The omission of conventional methods of recognition of its source, usually limited to the omission of a signature or the adoption of a fraudulent or ambiguous identity, may involve a change in traditional or practised methods of communication. A typical example would be a change from cursive writing to typewriting and delivery in some unorthodox fashion.

Invariably, these are attributes of anonymous letters, but they may also be aspects of the preparation or issue of fraudulent cheques, hold-up notes, hotel registrations, and a multitude of other documents that may have the potential to identify and/or incriminate an individual in some manner. Anonymous letters as a group can usually be classified, according to their purpose. Casey[13] and Harrison[14] both suggest seven categories, although their breakdowns into different categories are not quite the same. Casey lists them as threatening, obscene, extortion, nuisance, stool pigeon, racial, and guilty conscience. Harrison, on the other hand, lists them as threatening, indecent (obscene), blackmailing (extortion), practical jokes (nuisance), disparagement/recommendation (racial or stool pigeon), revenge and spitefulness. Although the anonymous letter may be intended to serve one of seven or more different purposes the general techniques for concealing the identity of the source remain the same: disguise, simulation, deception, or omission of identifiers.

In these cases, the examination and study of the handwriting, per se, does not necessarily change from that of other cases. What does change are the circumstances prevailing, and these may have a bearing on the examination.

1. Cursively-written anonymous letters, of a kind other than nuisance, guilty conscience, revenge or spitefulness, tend to be reasonably lengthy productions. Handprinted communications and paste-ups tend to be shorter, principally because their production is more labour intensive. For the same reason, typewritten letters may be shorter, unless typing is not strange to the typist. Frequently, limited hand printing is added to commercially printed greeting cards bearing some comment or verse that can be modified to suit the communication's objectives, that are usually obscene or offensive.

    Longer handwritten letters, wherein disguise of one's writing or the simulation of another's has been attempted, may exhibit relapses to the author's normal or natural writing habits for short intervals, after which the disguise is resumed. Unfamiliar writing practises are difficult for most persons to maintain.

    Furthermore, in anonymous letters a page or more in length, it is frequently observed that as the writer approaches the end of his/her discourse, the disguise employed is not as assiduously pursued and more normal or natural writing ensues. Consequently, this is the segment of the document that should receive the examiner's particular attention.

2. Anonymous letters are usually intended to generate some kind of response on the part of the recipient that the sender often delights in observing. If the response is pleasurable to the sender, or if there is no indication of the letter having been received or of having elicited any response, the sender is frequently encouraged to issue another or a series of additional communications.

    The greater the number of anonymous letters issued, the greater the potential for collecting evidence indicating or identifying the source. Disturbing as these kinds of communication may be to the recipient, authorities and writing examiners advocate strongly the taking of such action or of no action. This will encourage the production of further letters that may afford additional evidence.

It is usually the case that the method of disguise employed in a first anonymous letter will not be consistently followed in subsequent letters. What was changed and how it was changed will escape the writer's recollection. This may benefit the writing examination in two respects. First, it is an indication of the elements of the writing that are not to be trusted as evidence of normal writing habits, and second, it provides an opportunity for normal writing habits to occur in subsequent letters that may have been concealed by disguise in earlier products.

3. Envelopes in which letters are sent may be as useful in writing examinations as the letters themselves.

Writers develop habits in the manner in which they address an envelope, which evidence can seldom be found in the documents it contains. Occasionally, instances are encountered in which the letters and the envelopes are the products of different writers, particularly in those cases in which the assistance of a second party is obtained to write the letter, as a technique of deception.

4. Anonymous letters containing obscenities and profanities are as often the products of female writers as male writers, perhaps more often.

Until recent times, a judgment might be made as to the sex of the writer based on the manner in which obscenities and profanities were expressed. It was generally believed that women were much less practised in these conventions and more awkward in their use. The current generation of the western population makes such judgments more precarious.

5. Notwithstanding the lack of consistency within a single anonymous letter that one usually finds in disguised writing, there may be an abundance of consistency between letters executed on separate occasions.

Although the particular effects of the method(s) selected for altering one's writing may be difficult for an individual to maintain consistently without practise, there is likely to be some consistency in the selection of the method(s) employed on repeated occasions. Parker (1989) reported on the similarities to questioned disguised writings found in court-ordered request writings, when the subject was required to disguise his executions. There are, obviously, limits to an individual's knowledge of and familiarity with the techniques that might affect an appropriate change.

6. On infrequent occasions, anonymous letters contain indications of the nationality, age, education, or occupation of the author.

Assessment of these attributes is sometimes based on the study of sentence structure, grammar, idioms, spelling, division of words, and other such aspects of the text. Osborn[15] suggested 53 of them in what he called "The Analysis of Language as a Means of Identification." There is no doubt that similarities and dissimilarities in these aspects of a text are difficult for an examiner to ignore, but the danger in infringing on the domain of the linguistic analyst without adequate academic qualification should not be disregarded.

7. A recipient of an anonymous letter (perhaps one of several) is, frequently, the author of the letter or instigator of the act. This is done for various reasons on which we need not elaborate.

From the viewpoint of the writing examination, all recipients of anonymous letters should be included in the circle of potential authors.

As was intimated earlier, there are numerous anonymously written documents other than letters, or various types of personal communications. Hold-up notes are a classic example. Because of the limited written material that they contain, a first step in the course of investigation is usually an attempt to associate the writing with that of other similar documents appearing in other crimes or cases. The accumulation of written material improves the potential for the identification of the author.

The quest for anonymity in letter writing is invariably coupled with a sense of compulsion to repeat the act. The purpose of the anonymous communication will usually indicate to an investigator whether the recipient will be the same or different in a subsequent letter, and whether the number of communications is likely to be large or small.

Books on document examination frequently describe the techniques that might be employed in associating documents of this kind with others, or in relating them to particular sources. These techniques range from watermarks to paper cutters, to paper types, to inks, to commercially printed inscriptions, to paper stains, to indentations in the paper surface. Other documents that share similar properties may assist significantly in identifying the sources of them. Notwithstanding the wide range of aspects of a questioned document that may contribute to its identification or the determination of its origin, the process of study and examination of the writing or handlettering thereon remains essentially the same.

34.   Can Handwriting be Usefully Classified?

Numerous attempts have been made to devise classification systems for handwriting over the past 100 years. When one reviews these endeavours, one is struck by the changing goals of classification that underlay the efforts.

Initially the objectives were vague, but were generally in pursuit of greater knowledge of handwriting to facilitate the identification of it, or simply to organize the knowledge already possessed by classifiers. It might be argued that classification was expounded by early examiners as a means of demonstrating their erudition of handwriting without actually putting classification to work in any given case.

Ames[16] and Osborn[17] classified handwriting according to the involvement of the fingers, hand, and arm in the action of writing, usually one of four categories: finger movement, wrist movement, forearm movement, and whole arm movement. Neither of these authors provided a system for discriminating between the products according to the different movements. Indeed, the whole arm movement is an action that is almost exclusive to blackboard writing, or to some of today's graffiti writing, the circumstances of which will alone suffice to distinguish the movement. With the exception perhaps of graffiti or writing and painting on walls, the whole arm movement is seldom a matter to be considered in the process of writing identification.

Furthermore, we have little information as to the extent to which these classifications served any purpose in actual handwriting examinations, except perhaps to differentiate writings in some general pictorial fashion that might otherwise have been more precisely attributed to writing quality, writing movement, consistency of shape, and consistency of slope.

Blackburn and Caddell[18] claimed that all writing could be placed in one of 10 classes or categories. The system included the making of some measurements that may have been more practical insofar as the writing of their time than it is for current writings. Lee and Abbey[19] devised a system of classification utilizing the criminal record forms of their days. It endeavoured to tabulate eight factors of handwriting, each of which had as many as three subdivisions. As a system, it has been criticized as being too imprecise, providing merely dumping grounds for large numbers of writing samples.

Quirke[20] developed what he referred to as his "Practical Scheme of Handwriting Analysis" in which he described 16 general qualities or features of writing followed by some 100 or more examples of each lower case letter of the alphabet, then 13 points for attention in examining upper case letters, 13 points for attention in examining numerals, 24 points for guidance respecting block letters, and 3 points respecting Roman numerals. It was hardly a system for classification and because of his interest in and acceptance of graphology it was generally disregarded. We cannot deny, however, that there is some correlation between Quirke's 16 general features of handwriting and our own suggested 21 discriminating elements of writing that are or should be part of the identification process.

The last 50 years has seen several systems of handwriting classification develop, principally in the law enforcement field with a distinctly different objective in mind. Their application has been, and still is, to facilitate the identification of the writers of fraudulent cheques, hold-up notes, and anonymous letters, as an assistance to investigators. The observation had been made in the early 1940s that paper hangers, i.e., cheque forgers, were frequently quite consistent and distinctive in their manners of writing bad cheques.

The first published attempt on this continent to classify elements of writing for this purpose was made by Livingston[21] for the benefit of the Milwaukee Police Department beginning in 1944. The system grouped and filed the manners in which monetary amounts of the cheque were inscribed. Alignment and slant were also recorded. Other breakdowns were created in aspects such as writing skill, and material was classified simply as poor, medium, or good. The use of chequewriters and typewriters were given separate categories, as were names used.

By 1952, other law enforcement agencies had established "Fraudulent Cheque Files" that endeavoured to classify material according to the following:

- the manner of writing sums
- the method of production: written, lettered, or typewritten
- the names used
- selected individual handwriting characteristics
- idiosyncracies, e.g., the use of "only," "and," and "&," etc.
- other peculiarities in production or passing of the cheques

In 1954, T. L. Smith,[22] a pupil of Robert Saudek in London, published a procedure for the classification of handwriting based on variations in six aspects of writing: pressure, form, speed, spacing, size, and slant, that were broken into 59 subclassifications. While the claim was made that the categories of the classification were measurable discriminations, the language used is not convincing. For example: *spacing* is subdivided into *perfect, good,* and 12 divisions (4 each) of *fair, poor,* and *bad.* The objective of the classification process is not clear, but may be simply a method of organizing the information sought and accumulated in the course of a handwriting examination. It was, of course, one of the earliest attempts at classification since the writings of Quirke in 1930.

In a subsequent paper, Smith[23] elaborates on her classification system by adding seven more aspects of writing to the previous six as further divisions. They are loops, t-bars, capital "I," word units, mistakes, signature position, and special peculiarities, each of which is broken down into from eight to twenty subdivisions. From this it is clear, that what is offered is not a system of classification for the filing of writing samples, but rather, as we suspected, a delineation of the features of a writing that might be sought and studied in the course of a routine examination, whatever the reason for that examination may be.

In 1955, Livingston put his classifications on McBee Punch Cards to facilitate searching and sorting, and in 1959, he published an illustrated article entitled *A Handwriting and Pen Printing Classification System for Identifying Law Violators.* By 1962, Livingston's system had expanded to include other breakdowns and the fraudulent cheque files of other agencies were exploring new ideas. Wrenshall and Rankin[24] noted that classification had taken two forms:

1. The classification of inherent characteristics of handwriting, e.g., skill, letter forms, etc.
2. The classification of variations in the arrangement of handwriting on a document, particularly the manner of completing a cheque form, sometimes referred to as *the completion method.*

The first of these two was the more desirable, but the second had proven more popular and practical, if only because it was less subjective and provided greater consistency between classifiers. Problems developed, however, when the completion method, which offered few subclassifications, produced unsearchable large collections of material in the more common categories. Further, criminals were found to change their method of completing a forged cheque from time to time, which frustrated the search for them from their products.

Interestingly enough, Wrenshall and Rankin in 1965 foresaw the use of the computer in handwriting classification and search at a time when information retrieval was, apparently, not a primary pursuit of computer programmers. Research into computer retrieval, however, had to be prefaced by research into the features of handwriting that might be classified for search purposes.

Schroeder[25] described his procedure which tried to include some writing aspects into a system devoted largely to the completion method. It is not unlike the system R. Mally devised in Switzerland in the 1960s. Schroeder, too, apparently saw the value of the computer in classification, but when his system was revised,[26] it had reverted to the use of card wheels that had been discarded years before. Rather than employ the burgeoning electronics field to expand the system's potential, classification was considered to be merely an aid to the searcher's memory, which is the most efficient means of connecting new incoming checks with those already on file.

Despite the lack of optimism for handwriting classification expressed in the writings of Baxter,[27] the last 20 years have witnessed many changes in the approach to the subject. Initial studies suggested that all capital letters of the alphabet might be placed in one of 12 groups, which allowed for a degree of commonality between letters such as "F," "T," "M," "N," and others. Then the observation was made that some letters, e.g., "Z" and "X," seldom appeared on cheques while others were infrequent enough to question their value as classification categories within the system. The Metropolitan Police Lab in London in the late 1970s designed a simple system around the word *Pounds* that invariably appeared in British cheques. The number of subclassifications were too few, however, and the numbers of writers falling into some categories became unmanageable for manual searching.

A system unrelated to cheques and their completion method but directed at the inherent writing characteristics was developed at the Zurich Kantonpolizei Laboratory, and described formally in a report by Angst and Erismann.[28] It employed a large number of writing features, selected from a prescribed one paragraph sample of writing, that were classified by a document examiner. The results of classification were entered into a computer to become the data bank against which unknown writings could be checked in a search for correspondence. A simple "yes" or "not present" approach was taken in the system procedure to objectively classify and search for writings.

Some nine aspects of writing were recorded in the data bank, including:

1. Writing skill
2. Line quality
3. Slope
4. Size
5. Width (lateral expansion?)
6. Angularity
7. Type and degree of connection
8. Position of diacritics
9. Construction of cursive and block letters

Noticeable in this is that these nine constitute almost half of the 21 single discriminating elements (two of which are combinations of two elements) of writing that this dissertation maintains to be the basis of the writing identification process.

Harvey and Mitchell[29] describe a one-time classification sort and search system designed to scan samples from 1,046 writers to assist investigators in their quest for a particular murder suspect. The process involved three features related to the completion method of fraudulent cheque files and three additional features that would qualify as inherent writing characteristics that were present in a cheque involved in the commission of the crime. The combination was sufficient to permit a positive identification to be made. The authors of the paper spend some time reviewing the use of the X^2 statistical test to assess the significance of two or more of these features occurring together. As it happened, and almost contradictory to their findings, the X^2 values obtained were too high to permit the acceptance of a null hypothesis: that two of the apparently unrelated features in the completion of the questioned cheque (the use of = between the numbers of pounds, shillings, and pence, and the indentation of the writing on the amount line), were in fact independent of one another. The suggestion is made that a larger data bank may have been helpful.

Ansel and Strach[30] attempted to classify the methods of 993 individuals in writing the numerals "0" to "9" in an exploratory study that would qualify as related to inherent writing characteristics. Their method provided four to eight subclasses for each numeral, but soon revealed that the "1" had little or no discriminatory value, the "2," "3," and "7" had only limited value, and the "0," "6," "8," and "9" provided the best division of samples. As it happened, using the X^2 test, as Harvey and Mitchell had done, the classification of "0" and "8" could not be established as independent of one another.

The process of classification was highly subjective and dependent on the judgments of the classifiers. While other studies were proposed by these authors, for example the interdependence of all numerals and the consistency of the frequencies of occurrence found for all subclasses, no further information is available as to whether they were pursued.

With a similar objective in mind, Allan, Pearson, and Brown,[31] in a study of extended writing from 52 subjects, attempted to use measurements to obtain data that might be computerized to discriminate between the subjects and determine the consistency of the data in specimens taken a year later and in specimens that were disguised.

Eight measurements were taken, including:

1. The number of lines taken to write a given passage
2. The margin widths
3. The paragraph indentions
4. The length of the last 10 spaces
5. The length of the last 11 words and spaces
6. The length of the first 10 spaces
7. The length of the first 11 words and spaces
8. The ratio of relative heights of letters with ascenders

The rationale for selecting these particular measurements, and the application of study results to actual case work, is not explained or suggested. While margin widths, paragraph indentions, and relative heights may be matters to be considered in case work, items 4 to 7 are much less likely to prove useful in the examination of other texts, and causes a reader to wonder about the point and purpose of their inclusion.

A second study by Allan and Pearson[32] attempts to subjectively classify the upper case "D" in the specimens obtained and to add this information to that provided by the previously taken eight measurements. The study results are difficult to comprehend and the task is not made easier by use of the terms *crime specimens* (to refer to what others would call questioned writings), *questioned specimens* (to refer to what others would call known writings of a particular writer, e.g., K1), and *file specimens* (to refer to what others would call known writings of 51 other writers, e.g., K2 to K52).

These authors were likely influenced by Kind, Wigmore, Whitehead, and Loxley[33] who advocated the use of such terms in an attempt to consolidate the proliferation of terms employed in forensic science literature. The task of the document examiner is not likely to be greatly eased by the terms proposed.

Ansell[34] reviewed a number of the classification programs developed to that point, including unpublished work that he conducted with H. Prichard at the Metropolitan Police Forensic Science Laboratory in London. Eighteen parameters were used to classify samples of block lettering from 134 subjects, that was successful in discriminating between all but three pairs of subjects. The 18 parameters are summarized as concerning:

- the design and shape of the "A"
- the commencement of the "A," "B," "D," and other letters
- the termination of the "G"
- the number of strokes in the construction of the "K"
- the centres of the "M" and "W" (long or short)
- the termination of the "U"

A radically different approach to handwriting identification was taken by the Bundeskriminalamt at Wiesbaden employing computerized image processing and pattern recognition. As described in Klement's report (1983) the more objective process of feature extraction by the computer supplants the more subjective study and classification of writing features by human beings, with apparent success.

The research program, which acquired the title FISH (Forensic Information System of Handwriting) has captivated the interest of a group of scientists at the German Bundeskriminalamt (BKA) Laboratory for more than 10 years and after an investment of more than 12 million dollars has produced many publications, Hecker and Eisermann,[35] Bross, Eisermann, and Klement[36] to cite just a couple.

The German endeavour has proven to be as successful as any other, if not more so. Its greatest failings are the cost of the equipment involved and the technical competence required to run the system. The duration of the necessary six months of training seems to be greater than that of the computer programs pursued in the United Kingdom and elsewhere. The Dutch government and the United States Secret Service have each acquired operational versions of the FISH system, the Secret Service having the only English version.

The Secret Service has established two databases, one in 1991 for protective intelligence, respecting the president, vice president and public officials, and a second, authorized in 1995, to assist law enforcement agencies in cases respecting missing and exploited children. As Maguire and Moran[37] have reported, the system is proving its worth in a manner that continues to grow. Apparently 33 "hits" were scored in the first 6 months of 1996.

Nicholson[38] reported at the I.A.F.S. meeting in Oxford on progress in the system of the Metropolitan Police Forensic Science Laboratory that is much like that described by Ansell above. As is common to many manual systems, problems had emerged:

1. The same character may be classified differently by different classifiers or by the same classifier on different occasions.
2. Tolerance must be provided in the system for natural variation from one occasion of writing to the next, the range of which varies with the individual writer.

Nicholson's system concerns itself with block lettering of all characters of the alphabet excluding the "C," "L," "O" and "S," and is based on (1) the number of pen strokes, and (2) the particular pen paths followed in the letters "E," "H," and "N."

Variation is accommodated by permitting letters to be classified in each of two sub types, if necessary. Some provision is made for cursive forms and the tendency of some writers to interconnect certain printed letters.

Nicholson's project had two stated objectives:

1. To permit linking crimes to one another and to known perpetrators
2. To accumulate quantitative information respecting frequency of occurrence of the features classified.

At the same time, he hoped to improve on previous systems by reducing the number of misclassifications due to ambiguities and felt that fewer categories for each letter would reduce the misclassification due to natural variation. In this system, letters were classified according to the number of pen strokes in letter construction and their order of execution. In a few cases, classification was made according to pen paths rather than pen lifts as the former was considered to be less variable.

A pilot study of 140 subjects was conducted and while high frequency was encountered in some categories for some letters that seemed to reduce their discriminating value, it is reported that computer calculations confirmed that useful discriminating power had been achieved. It is not clear, however, whether the frequency of occurrence of certain letters in the English language was fully factored in these confirmatory calculations.

In a further study, Nicholson[39] sought to determine whether pen path habits are less variable than construction habits involving pen lifts. This study was confined to samples of the block letters "B" and "E" taken from a standard passage of text prepared by 100 dextral subjects. The results apparently confirmed the views previously held that pen path habits are less variable than pen lift habits.

It was also observed, rather incidently, that the letter "B" varied with its position within a word. Similar observations have since been made by other investigators respecting a number of other letters.

Hardcastle, Thornton, and Totty[40] pursued the matter of classification of block lettering on cheques employing 32 features of each of 2,000 samples. These features included 18 of the letters of the alphabet, 10 numerals, and 4 general features (relative heights, style of date, sex and identity of writer if known). Only the manner of writing the date was carried over from earlier trial schemes as it was found that other completion practises varied or changed over periods of time.

The classifications for each feature were coded and filed on a computer under a program that permits the operator to search the data by way of a single feature or any combination of features. The latter facility is reportedly used routinely with reasonable success.

Taylor and Chandler[41] described a relatively simple classification program created for the Arkansas State Laboratory. It was based on the writing of eight lowercase cursive letters, to which was added categories for race and sex. Although it showed some promise it was limited to 500 files, which was the storage capacity of the home personal computer on which it was run.

Of particular interest in the report is the statement that "classification is not the same thing as identification." The former is said to distinguish authors on the basis of handwriting patterns, whereas the latter is concerned with handwriting patterns plus individual characteristics "as well as a host of other features."

We would contend that the "handwriting patterns" described in this, or in fact employed in any system, and used to classify writings, are simply some of the discriminating elements, occurring in isolation or in combinations, that constitute handwriting habits, i.e., arrangements, designs and styles of allographs, unorthodox shapes, styles of diacritics, etc. Classification systems generally discriminate between writings on the basis of gross or lucid features, but identification requires the consideration of other more subtle or elusive and individualistic discriminating elements of the writing as well, not in place of, but in addition to the gross features. These more subtle and individualistic features simply do not lend themselves readily to classification.

Hardcastle and Kemmenoe[42] sought features of cursive writing that would discriminate effectively between writers, and that occur frequently enough in the writing of cheques to yield some investigative assistance. They selected 21 features including 6 lower case letters ("d," "f," "i," "p," "t," and "u"), 2 upper case letters ("C" and "F" as in "Cash" and "Fifty"), 15 numerals and general features taken from the scheme of classification for block lettering developed by Hardcastle, Thornton, and Totty (1986). At the time of writing (1990) there were 1,000 samples in the test collection.

In summary, it may be said that classification began as a means of providing investigative leads respecting unknown authors of fraudulent cheques by associating the handwriting with that of a known writer living or moving within a given area, or with other cheques. The systems endeavoured to record and to group in some prescribed fashion all of the fraudulent cheques passed or uttered within the area. If the system was well-designed, the groups were small in size and writers within the group could be quickly and conveniently differentiated.

It worked well as long as the collections were relatively modest, as long as the perpetrators of this type of crime made few changes to their writing, and as long as their activity was confined to limited areas. But collections grew large and unworkable, perpetrators did change their manners of writing, and they became exceedingly transient. Other equipment such as typewriters, cheque writers, copiers, and printers became involved, and file classifications had to be expanded to accommodate such features appropriately. Other instruments of the criminal have begged to be included, such as anonymous, threatening, crank, obscene and insulting letters, false identification and travel documents, and hold-up notes as reported by Williams[43] and by Noblett.[44] The last mentioned were used in a study of San Francisco's collection reported by Blake,[45] although the systems of classification for them are not described. In addition, any negotiable document having a monetary value (e.g., postal money orders, cash grain tickets, or poultry tickets) that has been repeatedly falsified has warranted some classification consideration and classification systems have been constantly challenged and taxed.

The advent of the computer and its potential for use in the analysis of handwriting was described generally at some length by Teulings and Thomassen.[46] The particular application of the computer to handwriting recognition insofar as the more recent developments (1) in digital image processing (Kuchuck, W., Rieger, B., and Steinke, K.;[47] Steinke, Karlof;[48] Klement, Volker[49]), (2) in pattern recognition (Klement, V., Naske, R.-D., and Steinke, K.;[50] Impedovo, S. and Abbattista, N.[51]), (3) in sonar analysis (de Bruyne, Pieter and Mesemer, Paul[52]), (4) in prototype deformation (Naske, R.-D.[53]), has obviously wetted the appetite of a number of scientists, particularly European. The International Graphonomics Society (IGS) has stimulated and surfaced virtually hundreds of papers and publications related to the study of handwriting by way of computer applications. The objective underlying many of these studies has been the search for a validation process that would serve to verify the identity of the individual executing a signature,[54] from which better methods of handwriting classification may ensue simply as a by-product. Nevertheless, this work elevates the prospects that the near future will afford an almost limitless means for recording, classifying, and cataloguing handwriting aspects such that subjectivity can be replaced by objectivity for the most part. Although much progress has been made in achieving success rates in sorting and searching test files of classified samples of writing or lettering well in excess of 90 percent, the objective of reaching very low numbers of matches or misses in very large collections has not yet been achieved.

Some of the impediments to progress lie in the differences between handwriting systems and practises in different parts of the world. Furthermore, the standards that might be accumulated for comparison with extended writings, e.g., anonymous letters, are less suitable for comparison with the writings on fraudulent cheques, or with spurious signatures.

Consequently, what may be a discriminating feature in one locale or in one kind of document may not be as helpful in another.

It must also be noted that frequency of occurrence statistics that classification systems might generate are not necessarily transferable over long distances, particularly between populations that are less transient. And, of course, technology and its necessary components are still beyond the reach of most and available only to the fortunate few. Additionally, all of the work performed to date seems inclined to carry a rider, either stated or implied, that reads: "All identifications made by machines require confirmation by competent humans." It may be surprisingly useful to simply ask ourselves *why*.

35. What Data Is Available to Establish the Significance of Writing Habits?

Handwriting identification has been criticized for a hundred years for the absence of statistical data to support its conclusions. The renowned French criminologist Alphonse Bertillon[55] said, "The investigation by the handwriting expert in the court will, in fact, only deserve to be referred to as a science from the day he creates tables of probability for the various letter shapes...." Kirk[56] and Rhodes[57] were equally critical. Thorton and Rhodes[58] described document examination (and must have meant handwriting identification) as a field "which has progressed more by judicial acceptance than by any attempts to elevate the practise to a more scientific discipline."

If empirical or statistical data is what Thornton and Rhodes were looking for they must have overlooked a number of publications in German, the writings of Popkiss and Moore,[59] Livingston;[60] the studies of Muelberger, Newman, Regent, and Wichmann;[61] Ansell;[62] Eldridge, Nimmo-Smith, Wing and Totty;[63] and of Nicholson;[64] all being work that was designed, as Nicholson described it, "...(to) permit the linking of crimes to each other, and to their perpetrators, and to provide the means to accumulate quantitative information which document examiners can draw on when reaching their conclusions." Blake[65] proposed the taking of objective measurements of stable handwriting forms in an attempt to validate methods, and completed a study for presentation in 1994.[66] If progress has been slow in this regard, as indeed it is in most scientific pursuits, at least some progress is being made.

Over a greater period of time forensic scientists in Europe have shown considerable interest in objectivity within the discipline. As Böhle[67] has reported it, Meuller[68] attempted to determine the frequency of occurrence of particular versions of seven letters, letter elements, and one numeral. Reitberger[69] conducted similar studies that deviated greatly from Meuller's. A feature catalogue, developed in the former German Democratic Republic in the 1950s, failed to produce acceptable results. Bein[70] criticized the practises of that time and called for objective rates of evaluation in handwriting expertise. Solomon and Lissner presented a proposal to objectivize the evaluation of features of handwriting at the 9th International Criminal Symposium of Socialist Countries in East Berlin in 1973. A research team was formed that issued a catalogue of significant features of lowercase letters of handwriting in 1977, that has been revised and developed throughout the 1980's. It provides frequency data respecting segments of the German population.

After some twenty years of research this feature catalogue shows promise, although its application seems to be tedious and time consuming. It tends to deal with letters in isolation whereas we know that some of the most significant features of handwriting are found in particular letter combinations. Furthermore, it would have to be revised for application to other populations. Mathematical methods, however, are undoubtedly a method of making the analysis of handwriting more objective. Although they are not likely to replace fully the current working methods of the handwriting examiner, Böhle contends "Mathematical methods can back up some logical and theoretical methods used to recognize individualization in handwritings and extend the practical experience of the expert."

In the last decade (1984 to 1994) an increasing number of studies have been conducted in England and the Netherlands in attempts to produce empirical data and to apply measurement and statistical analysis to it that will expand our understanding of handwriting and supplant subjectivity with some degree of objectivity.[71-75] A measure of success has been achieved in the computerized classification of block lettering and cursive handwriting employed on personal cheques.[76-77] The size of the files that have been created, however, is not large and accordingly their usefulness is limited. Other reports respecting the frequency of occurrence of particular handwriting features have been mentioned within the topic of handwriting and handlettering classification above.

Much of the early work done relative to the classification of writing suggests an attempt to provide frequency ratios that could assist in the evaluation of the significance of writing features. However, the study by Muehlberger, Newman, Regent, and Wichmann[78] was the first to clearly state it and pursue it as an objective. The study involved an examination of request writings of 100 subjects and nonrequest writings of a similar number. The study was focused on the letter combination "th" as appearing in words such as "that," "this," and "the." The work classified and counted letter forms, relative sizes, proportions and positions of elements, and the alignment of the letters in the combination.

The data is provided and a number of observations respecting forms and correlations are made, although, as the authors point out, the sample size is too small (200 persons) to generalize from these results. This, however, is one of the better studies of writing frequencies that have been conducted, and it is unfortunate that the work was not pursued by these and other investigators.

As aforementioned, Nicholson[79] reported at the I.A.F.S. meeting in Oxford on progress in the system of the Metropolitan Police Forensic Science Laboratory at that time. Nicholson's project had two stated objectives, one of which was to accumulate quantitative information respecting frequency of occurrence of the features classified.

In this respect, a pilot study of 140 subjects was conducted and while high frequency was encountered in some categories for some letters that reduced their discriminating value, it is reported that computer calculations confirmed that useful discriminating power had been achieved.

Giles[80] provides a further report on the program of the Metropolitan Police Forensic Science Laboratory in London mentioned earlier. The data base that is searched along the lines of the program developed by Totty, Hall, Hardcastle, and Brown[81] respecting type styles, but dealing with the stroke structure of upper case block letters, has been expanded to 1,100 files. It is reportedly not used to search for specific individuals but principally to provide some insight into the process of evaluation by offering actual data on feature frequencies. Thus, it functions in a support role in casework, if not in direct evidence.

Huber[82] suggested that examiners might provide themselves with some statistical information respecting the handwriting features contained in their own mailing addresses by retaining and filing the handwritten envelopes received daily in their personal and business mail. The import of this that has escaped attention is that the combined endeavours of examiners could produce a very large sample of writings from which frequency of occurrence counts could be made relatively easily. As long as they are pursued in isolation, however, writing collections of this kind have limited value owing to the narrow scope of their text material.

Kroon-van der Kooij[83] reported on a five-year-old project of the Netherlands Institute for Forensic Examinations and Research (NIFO) to develop a computer-assisted method for filing and searching handwriting as an investigative tool. Preliminary research is being conducted on a collection of 500 writing samples of extended cursive text. Twenty two items of the writing have been selected for measurement and coding and although detailed information has not yet been provided it is said that most of the categories relate to proportions.

In this project, as in others, statistical evaluations of the items selected is a stated objective, although a search and selection (i.e., identification) system for a large collection (35,000) of writing samples, presently held by the Dutch police is currently considered to be of primary importance.

Horton[84] attempted a strictly statistical, and as yet unpublished, study of the frequency of occurrence of arbitrarily selected aspects of writing including slope, alignment, particular letter forms, diacritics, numeral structures, and dollar and cents symbols. The author concedes that the study is not as profound as it might have been and it has been criticized on several counts.

Unfortunately, his study of frequency is mixed with an attempt to tabulate methods of disguise employed by each of the 580 subjects, but nothing more than changes in slant, shape, size, and hand used are noted.

The randomness of the sample may be open to question. All were military personnel, civilian employees of the military, or family members, 98.6 percent of whom had 12 years of education or more, and 82 percent of whom were 20 to 39 years of age.

Horton notes that five (0.9 percent) of his subjects commenced and terminated "0"s at the bottom. It might have been helpful to have information supplied as to whether the stroke direction is clockwise, and whether the writers are sinistrals.

Of particular interest to the present authors is the finding that 11 percent of the subjects were sinistrals, an estimation we have made for populations generally. Other statistics of some interest include:

b	clockwise bowl	16%	8	two circle "snowman" 8	14%
d	backward d	3.8%	$	two bars	77%
e	epsilon e	1.2%	S	lettered	6.7%
r	Palmer r	3.1%	W	three stroke style	0.7%
7	European 7	18%	J	two stroke	0.7%
i	circular dots	2.8%	5	one stroke	17%

In summary, the search for empirical data on the significance of writing features as might be found in frequency of occurrence studies, was foreseen to be a reasonable offshoot from and/or a target of classification. It began with Livingston's (1963) tabulation of characteristics in the lettering of 200 subjects, and was continued in the spirit of the reports and papers of Muehlberger, Newman, Regent, and Wichmann (1976), Huber (1990), Giles (1990), Horton (1992), and others.

Perhaps because there has been a continuing need to attempt to correlate the writings on fraudulent cheques as an assistance to criminal investigators, the study of completion methods in the writing of fraudulent cheques has continued to attract the attention of government examiners. This is illustrated by the work cited above of Hardcastle, Thornton, and Totty (1986); Hardcastle and Kemmenoe (1990), and by the most recent survey of Crane and Crane.[85] Tangential to these studies has been the search for information respecting the frequency of occurrence of the elements of writing with which the studies have dealt.

Data has also been pursued at length in Europe. The aforementioned German endeavour to produce a feature catalogue of significant features of Latin handwriting, under development for 20 years, has been described by Böhle.[86] Based on a sample of 1,000 writings, 1,485 features of 20 minuscules, 532 features of 20 majuscules, and 207 features of the numerals "0" to "9," have been combined to create a record of 2,224 features in total.

The usefulness of the catalogue lies in determining within a questioned writing and a group of known standards whether they contain a corresponding combination of a number of the 2,224 features that have been catalogued. The respective values or levels of significance for each feature (i.e., frequency of occurrence) can then be used to calculate the significance of the feature combination.

The question as to the number of significant script features required to support an identification was initially thought to be 26, on average, that, by employing a particular and somewhat complex formula, yields an identification value of 40.9. Recent studies suggest that this identification value might be set at a level as low as 20.4, by reducing the number of similarities required to support an identification.

Böhle feels that the number of features catalogued (2,224) is too large for the system to be workable. The suggestion is also made that the sample size on which it is based (1,000) should be increased to 5,000 to provide greater reliability.

As we stated earlier, among the problems encountered with the frequency of occurrence statistics that may be generated by these classification systems is that these statistics are not necessarily transferable over long distances, particularly between populations that are less transient or that have different origins. What may seem to be a discriminating feature between writers in one locale or in one kind of document may be less discriminating in another. Consequently, assessments may have to be modified in the light of certain circumstances.

Further prudence is warranted, however. The frequency of occurrence statistics that classification systems may produce cannot be applied as a rudimentary calculation of probability respecting any particular combination of writing elements. When the respective significance of the discriminating elements varies from one to another, as they do in writing, each element must be appropriately weighted to determine the composition of the combination of elements necessary to support any conclusion of identity.

We mention in Chapter 12, Section 74, that Welch (1996) has provided the details of four cases in the United Kingdom in which large numbers of writing samples were manually scanned in search of as few as five or six particular elements of writing. Although these cases are offered as evidence of the heterogeneity of writing, they are limited evidence, but evidence nevertheless, that discriminating elements of handwriting can be employed to search and segregate masses of writers (as many as 600,000) into workable numbers for further more detailed study. This is all that any system of classification is designed and intended to do.

Classification systems that may afford some evidence of frequency of occurrence deal primarily with gross features. Needless to say, these are measurable features, and refinements of the classification process and the utilization of computers will make the systems increasingly discriminating. The identification of writing, however, involves additionally and particularly the study of subtle features that may change with certain letter combinations, certain writing circumstances or certain writer conditions, features that we are not yet able to classify. Two aspects of writing identification that undoubtedly will be difficult to classify or to measure, beyond general subcategories such as good, poor, and average, will be writing movements and line quality (see Sections 30.B.15 and 30.B.17).

The difficulties in measuring all aspects of handwriting should not be allowed to stand as an excuse for not attempting to do so. There is much that can be done, and in the process of doing so, the areas that now seem impossible to resolve may be gradually diminished. Reasonable progress in a foreseeable future will require the commitment of time, talent, and funds that few sources can supply. Nevertheless, the search for sources should be conducted.

36. Can Synchronous Writings be Distinguished from Asynchronous Writings?

Few have written on the subject of distinguishing between writings or signatures executed at one and the same time, and those executed at different times. Comments offered have been, largely, descriptions of specific cases and the knowledge gained, perhaps owing to the diversity of situations requiring such studies.

Diversity notwithstanding, like many other questioned document problems the question is usually one of authentication, fabrication, or alteration. This requires a study in search of evidence that signatures, writings, or entries, purportedly made on different and separate occasions were, in fact, written at one and the same time. Or the study may be in search of evidence that signatures, writings, or entries, purportedly made on a single occasion were, in fact, the products of separate writing instances.

The particular circumstances will vary with the case, of course, and the resources available to establish the genuine or spurious nature of a document, or simply its history of production is seldom the same twice. Writings, typewritings, inks, papers, and writing instruments can all play a part in the study.

There is also some diversity in the manner in which authors refer to the two writing circumstances. Some use the terms *single entries* and *multientries*, others use *same time* and *different time*. Some call them *periodic entries*, others prefer to say *made separately* or *made sequentially*. Even the more ambiguous terms like *continuous* and *uninterrupted* and their antonyms are occasionally employed.

For the purpose of this discussion we use *synchronous* and its antonym *asynchronous* in the sense of the Oxford dictionary that defines *synchronous* as: "happening at the same time, coincident in time, contemporary in occurrence, related to different events of the same time or period," but not simultaneous in the strictest sense as in a stroke by stroke reproduction. That would involve a mechanical or electronic device to create two or more writings from the same singular movement of the hand. Accordingly, we must broaden our understanding of *at the same time* to refer to writings normally occurring:

- on one occasion
- in the same writing position (sitting, standing, or leaning over)
- with the same media (pen and paper)

- on the same surface (table, counter, lap, or other)
- for the same purpose (two or more copies of the same document)
- by the same person
- in the same mental and physical state

These circumstances, insofar as the writings of signatures are concerned, are considered to be conditions exercising control of the internal and external influences on the writing. Moreover, as we are using the terms, writings executed after an interval or interruption of as little as an hour or less are not always thought of as happening at the same time. Interruptions in the writing process of even a quarter or half hour are likely to be accompanied by some adjustment in the writing position and/or in the orientation of the documents to the writer, that may have some affect upon the products written.

Although circumstances vary widely in matters in which this question arises, the issue of synchronous writings frequently centres around two or more signatures or sets of initials that are required to be executed in the completion of the same transaction. Or it may involve notes or records (e.g., medical records, inventory registers or research logs) written in the course of some continuing, but short term action, examination, or study. Contracts consisting of a number of handwritten or typewritten provisions may also be subjects of dispute. On the other hand, the question of asynchronous writings more often is challenged insofar as the extended writings of the entries of records, diaries, logs, and the like, normally prepared over a period of days or weeks, that are alleged to have been rewritten or amended to conceal an act of omission or to materially alter the record of events.

The matter of synchronous and asynchronous writings is closely related to the dating of documents or of writings on which Osborn, Hilton, and Harrison have written at some length. The difference in the two approaches lies chiefly in the time frames that are usually involved. Dating studies are more often conducted on writings divided by substantial periods of time, often years, where paper and watermarks, aging or decrepitude of writing, and changing of writing styles, and changing of machines (typewriters) or instruments (pens) can play a greater role in establishing periods of production of documents. On the other hand, synchronous or asynchronous issues tend to relate to time frames no longer than days, weeks, or months, for which the methods of Osborn, Hilton, and Harrison seldom suffice.

The point to be remembered, however, is that the kind of evidence sought to differentiate documents in a broader time frame, e.g., dates of introduction (DOIs) of pens, machines, or materials, can sometimes be helpful in the study of documents within narrower time frames, when the circumstances happen to straddle pertinent DOIs.

In summary, it may be said that these studies invariably involve:

1. Records, such as tally sheets, compiled by inserting tally marks vertically (opposite particular names) or horizontally (to register a predetermined number).
2. Time books or time cards on which hours of work or days off and sickness are inscribed according to dates.
3. Log books and records of an occupational specialty — ship's logs, medical logs, or records.
4. Ledger sheets recording money transactions, formal or informal.
5. True diaries of a personal or official nature.
6. Pocket notebooks.

The key to many of these handwriting studies is the matter of consistency. Synchronous writings are almost invariably consistent executions. Asynchronous writings are as frequently not.

Synchronous writings are consistent in writing quality, line quality, size, slope, spacing, letter forms, pens, inks, and arrangement. If inconsistencies do occur there is often an apparent reason for them, for example a change in writing instrument due to pen or ink failure. Unless they are particularly skilled executions, asynchronous writings should almost invariably display inconsistency. Such inconsistency can be expected to be of a magnitude comparable to the range of natural variation observed in collected writing standards of the author, for that, indeed, is what they are. Writings found to be synchronous or asynchronous, particularly in the creation of medical records, however, cannot be prejudged as to their pertinence or legitimacy without fully investigating the record keeping practises of the institution or the individual.

In the study of these cases other factors may be available for consideration. Greater consistency may be evident in letter forms in synchronous writings or signatures of an individual that normally uses alternative or optional forms or structures for some letters. Intersections of the strokes of writings with one another may support or dispute the sequence in which questioned writings purport to have been produced. Document dates may not be consistent with the date of introduction of the printed form, or the particular kind of paper. Cards or sheets of paper allegedly taken from stocks serving various purposes over periods of time may be found, by aging characteristics or guillotine (paper cutter) characteristics too similar to one another to be consistent with their selection from stocks over long periods of time. Furthermore, surface indentations on one document may provide evidence of having been present and in a close relationship beneath another document when the latter was being prepared.

Keeler[87] described the evidence she found in tally marks, tabulating election results, indicative of marks having been made in groups with greater speed, as opposed to the more deliberate writing of other tally marks, made separately and somewhat unpredictably, in disparate locations on a tally sheet. The former displayed *drag tracks* or connecting strokes between tally marks, whereas the latter marks were more irregular and unrelated to one another with typical blunt endings. The drag tracks of the former reflect a continuity of pen motion from one mark to another, and for such reasons, continuity is allied to consistency as keys to synchronousness. Marks may also be related by regularity in spacing, slant, and pen pressure. The irregularity of asynchronous writings is attributed to the necessity to change position of the arm or hand between the execution of each mark. Regularity and irregularity seem to have been the chief discriminating aspects of the writings to sort the synchronous from the asynchronous.

Errors may also be helpful. In synchronous writings, they may be repeated in columns or rows, whereas, in asynchronous writings they tend to be singular and/or isolated.

Harris and Mills[88] summarized their findings as evidence of alteration ("The Expanded Record"), or fabrication ("The Substituted or Rewritten Record"). Alteration is, of course, the objective of an asynchronous production, whereas, fabrication is the usual objective of a synchronous preparation. The third line of forensic pursuit, that of authentication, might be investigated, of course, from the perspective of either a synchronous or asynchronous parcel of writing.

Under the category of alteration, they noted as evidence:

1. The crowding, squeezing in or fitting of insertions around other material.
2. Irregularities (i.e., inconsistencies) in slant, pressure, and quality.
3. The occurrence of erasures, eradications, or obliterations.
4. Irregularities (i.e., inconsistencies) in inks, writing instruments, typing ribbons or machines.
5. The behaviour of lines intersecting with other lines, folds, perforations, tears or holes in the paper.
6. The presence or absence of indentations in subsequent pages.
7. Inconsistencies in alignments.

Under the category of fabrication, they noted:

1. Remarkable (i.e., unusual) consistency in writing quality, ink, margins, spacing, arrangement, and alignment.
2. The bleeding of ink strokes, purportedly of different dates, into one another at intersections.
3. Variation in preternatural paper characteristics between undisputed and disputed pages of the same record.
4. Errors in the writing of dates in advance of their occurrence.
5. The use and dating of forms in advance of their dates of introduction.

Doud[89] reviewed the frequency of occurrence of forms for the letter "e" ("*e*" vs. "*ε*") and the numeral "4" (closed vs. open) in an allegedly asynchronous record. He compared these frequencies to those displayed by standards that were indisputably asynchronous. Again, the evidence was that the questioned material displayed consistency in forms that was not present in the normal, natural writing of the individual.

Beck[90] summarized his review of diary entries as matters evaluated in terms of (1) consistency with statements made about them and, (2) consistency of entries with each other.

In the latter respect, he notes that synchronous writings "Tend to be more like each other in quality, size, shape, etc. than samples done at different times," which is simply the evidence of consistency that may also be found in the writing instrument employed, in arrangement and alignment, and in size, proportions, slant, pattern of letter forms, and the use of options.

As others have done, Beck mentions other evidence to be considered as including erasures and obliterations, ink offsets, and ink trails between entries, as well as aging or the soiling of pages.

Foley[91] differentiates between the two basic situations as *single entries* (that we call asynchronous writings) executed independently of one another, and *multientries* (that we call synchronous writings) executed with little or no interruption or alteration of the writing position. He describes single entries as slower, more deliberate executions than multientries. The slower, more deliberate writings exhibit the classical symptoms: abrupt commencements and terminations of strokes, less slant, larger letters, shorter word length, heavier and wider strokes, and greater legibility. Multientries offer classical symptoms of greater speed: greater slant, poorer letter construction, tapering stroke endings, decreased pressure, greater word lengths, perhaps greater variation and decreased legibility.

Foley found that progressive increase or decrease in marginal alignments occurred in multientries or synchronous writings, whereas single entries seemed less influenced by the alignments of other entries. Single, asynchronous entries displayed greater randomness, as Kelly (1978) had reportedly communicated to him, respecting the placement of hand-written notations on calendars synchronously and asynchronously. Foley's study also confirmed the work of Doud insofar as the frequency of occurrence of optional letter and numeral designs or design variations.

McCarthy,[92] in three case illustrations, reiterates what others had said, that asynchronous writings display:

1. Greater variation:
   a. In writing styles
   b. In arrangement or location of written material
   c. In the use and manner of abbreviations
   d. In methods of record production
   e. In writing angles and in pen pressures
   f. In writing inks, instruments and pen performance
2. Less evidence of progression in left hand margins
3. Less evidence of prior knowledge of text to be written
4. Less or no evidence of relatable indentations on pages behind or (in page substitutions) from pages above

Despite the finding of this kind of evidence in each of his cases, McCarthy declines to commit himself to positive statements respecting the production of the writings as being asynchronous or otherwise. Rather, he seeks to find a unique feature to contradict the nature of production purported by the text itself.

Foley[93] repeats that synchronous writings display greater consistency than asynchronous executions and cites several cases that illustrate his point. In conclusion, and contrary to McCarthy, he suggests that, on this evidence "along with other relevant document evidence," whatever that may be, an examiner may reasonably conclude that writings or signatures were executed coincidentally.

Foley[94] addresses the subject again with particular respect to signatures and states that signatures, whether synchronous or asynchronous, are normally expected to display a lesser degree of variation, although this is dependent upon the writer. Variation is greater, he maintains, where the "external and internal influences or both" change. Variation is lesser where "external and internal influences" are controlled or constant.

That having been said, external influences should include:

1. The writing instrument
2. The writing position
3. The writing media (pen or pencil and paper)
4. The paper position relative to the writer
5. The writing space

On the other hand, internal influences should include:

1. The writer's state of mind
2. The writer's state of health
3. The formality or informality of the act
4. The level of trauma or pleasure to the act
5. The writer's state of intoxication or psychosis

Foley's study of some 400 signatures revealed, as expected, that signatures signed when documents were stacked and writing was "synchronous and sequential," displayed the greatest consistency in alignment and size. Single or asynchronous signatures exhibited more variation, less speed, and greater legibility.

In summary, we would emphasize, as others have done, that adequate writing standards of a similar kind, e.g., diaries or logs, are important to these examinations but difficult to find, if they exist at all. Many factors may contribute to a study. including examination of the media (i.e., pens and papers), indentations of and on other pages of the record, statistics (frequencies of occurrence of writing idiosyncracies), and offsets of ink or pencil on facing surfaces. Information respecting record-keeping practises is almost invariably helpful. Stains, soils, tears, staple holes, and other preternatural characteristics of the record must also be duly considered to ensure that the implied chronology of events in the history of the record is completely plausible. To begin with, however, as we stated earlier, the key to synchronism versus asynchronism is found in the attribute of consistency, considered in conjunction with continuity.

References

1. Widla, Tadeusz, The Influence of Spontaneous Writing on Stability of Graphic Features. *Forensic Science International,* 1990; 46: pp 63-67.

2. Wallner, T., Die Relative Konstanz der Handschrift. *Zeitschrift für Menschenkunde,* 1975; 3-4.

3. Galbraith, Nanette G., *Initials: A Question of Identity.* Presented at the meeting of the American Society of Questioned Document Examiners (Vancouver, 1980).

4. Galbraith, Nanette G., *Initials: A Special Category of Handwriting.* Presented at the meeting of the American Academy of Forensic Sciences (Cincinnati, OH, February, 1983).

5. Hilton, Ordway, Identification of Numerals. *International Criminal Police Review,* 1970 Oct; 241: 25: pp 245-250.

6. Horan, James J. and Horan, George J., *A Study of Numbers.* Presented at the 10th meeting of the International Association of Forensic Sciences (Oxford, 1984).

7. Ansell, M. and Strach, S. J., *The Classification of Handwritten Numerals.* Presented at the 7th meeting of the International Association of Forensic Sciences (Zurich, 1975).

8. Hilton, Ordway, *Individual or Class Characteristics in Foreign Numbers.* Presented at the meeting of the American Society of Questioned Document Examiners (location unknown, circa 1986).

9. Giles, Audrey, *Figuring It Out.* Presented at the meeting of the American Society of Questioned Document Examiners (Washington, 1996).

10. Alford, Edwin A., Identification through Comparison of Numbers. *Identification News,* 1965 July; pp 13-14.

11. Kelly, Jan Seaman, *The Examination and Identification of Numbers*. Presented at the meeting of the American Academy of Forensic Sciences (San Fransisco, 1998).

12. Doud, Donald, *X Marks the Spot*. Presented at the meeting of the American Academy of Forensic Sciences (Las Vegas, 1985).

13. Casey, Maureen A., *The Anonymous Letter Writer — A Psychological Profile?* Presented at the meeting of the American Academy of Forensic Sciences (Cincinnati, 1983).

14. Harrison, Wilson R., *Suspect Documents* (New York: Frederick A Praeger, 1958), pp 469-493.

15. Osborn, Albert S., *Questioned Documents*. 2nd Ed. (Albany: Boyd Printing Co., 1929), p 397.

16. Ames, D. T., *Ames on Forgery* (New York: Ames-Rollinson, 1900), p 43.

17. Osborn, A. S., *Questioned Documents*. 2nd Ed. (Albany: Boyd Printing Co., 1929), pp 102-106.

18. Blackburn, D. and Caddell, W., *The Detection of Forgery* (London: Layton, 1909).

19. Lee, C. D. and Abbey, R. A., *Classification and Identification of Handwriting* (New York: Appleton, 1922).

20. Quirke, A. J., *Forged, Anonymous and Suspect Documents* (London: Routledge, 1930).

21. Livingston, Orville B., Bogus Check File Classified by Trademarks. *Journal of Criminal Law, Criminology and Police Science*, 1949 Mar/Apr; 39: 6: pp 782-789.

22. Smith, Theodora LeH., Six Basic Factors in Handwriting Classification. *Journal of Criminal Law, Criminology and Police Science*, 1954; 44: 6: pp 810-816.

23. Smith, Theodora LeH., Determining Tendencies, The Second Half of a Classification for Handwriting. *Journal of Criminal Law, Criminology and Police Science*, 1964; 55: 4: pp 526-528.

24. Wrenshall, A. F. and Rankin, W. J. T., *Automation and the Cheque File or Document Searching and the Push Button Age* (an unpublished paper of the Royal Canadian Mounted Police Fraudulent Cheque Section, 1965).

25. Schroeder, E. H. W., Checlass: A Classification for Fraudulent Checks. *Journal of Forensic Sciences*, 1971; 16: 2: pp 162- 175.

26. Schroeder, E. H. W., A Revised Method of Classifying Fraudulent Checks in a Document Examination Laboratory. *Journal of Forensic Sciences*, 1974; 19: 3: pp 618-635.

27. Baxter, P. G., Classification and Measurement in Forensic Handwriting Comparisons. *Medicine Science and the Law*, 1973; 13: 3: pp 166-184.

28. Angst, E. and Erismann, K., Auswertung von Anonymen und Pseudonymen Handschriften mit Electronischer Datenvarbeitung, *Kriminalistic*, 1972; 2: p 60.

29. Harvey, R. and Mitchell, R. M., The Nicola Brazier Murder. *Journal of the Forensic Science Society*, 1973; 13: 157.

30. Ansell, M. and Strach, S. J., *The Classification of Handwritten Numerals*. 7th Meeting of the International Association of Forensic Sciences (Zurich, 1975).

31. Allan, A. R., Pearson, E. F., and Brown, C., *A Comparison of Handwriting Characteristics, Part I*. 8th Meeting of the International Association of Forensic Sciences (Wichita, 1978).

32. Allan, A. R. and Pearson, E. F., *A Comparison of Handwriting Characteristics, Part II* (unpublished, October, 1978).

33. Kind, S. S., Wigmore, Rosemary, Whitehead, P. H., and Loxley, D. S., Terminology in Forensic Science. *Journal of the Forensic Science Society*, 1979; 19: pp 189-191.

34. Ansell, Michael, Handwriting Classification in Forensic Science. *Visible Language*, 1979; XIII: 3: pp 239-257.

35. Hecker, M. and Eisermann, H. W., *Forensic Identification System of Handwriting (FISH)*. Presented at the 44th meeting of the American Society of Questioned Document Examiners (Savannah, GA, 1986).

36. Bross, F., Eisermann, H. W., and Klement, V., *Experiments on the Writer Recognition With Interactively Measured Features* (publication details not known, circa 1987).

37. Maguire, Kathleen B. and Moran, Traci L., *Identification of Written Text Writings by the Forensic Information System for Handwriting*. Presented at the meeting of the American Society of Questioned Document Examiners (Washington, 1996).

38. Nicholson, P. J., A System for the Classification of Block Capital Handwriting. *Journal of the Forensic Science Society,* 1984; 24: pp 415.

39. Nicholson, P. J., *The Relative Variability of Pen Lift and Pen Path Habits in Block Capital Writing*. Presented at the 11th Meeting of the International Association of Forensic Sciences (Vancouver, 1987).

40. Hardcastle, R. A., Thornton, D., and Totty, R. N., A Computer-Based System for the Classification of Handwriting on Cheques. *Journal of the Forensic Science Society,* 1986; 26: pp 383-392.

41. Taylor, Linda R. and Chandler, Howard "Bear," A System for Handwriting Classification. *Journal of Forensic Sciences,* 1987 Nov; 32: 6: pp 1775-1781.

42. Hardcastle, R. A. and Kemmenoe, D., A Computer-Based System for the Classification of Handwriting on Cheques. Part 2: Cursive Handwriting. *Journal of the Forensic Science Society,* 1990; 30: pp 97-103.

43. Williams, Richard M., *The Bank Robbery Note file, An Automated Approach to Document Screening*. Presented at the meeting of the American Society of Questioned Document Examiners (Montreal, 1985).

44. Noblett, Michael G., *Storage and Retrieval of Individual Writings in Large Databases of Handwriting*. Presented at the 49th Meeting of the American Society of Questioned Document Examiners (Orlando, 1991).

45. Blake, Martha, *Are We Seeing the Same Thing? Results of a survey presented to forensic document examiners*. Presented at the 52nd Meeting of the American Society of Questioned Document Examiners (Long Beach, CA, 1994).

46. Teulings, Hans-Leo H. M. and Thomassen, A. J. W. M., Computer-Aided Analysis of Handwriting Movements. *Visible Language,* 1979; XIII: 3: pp 218-231.

47. Kuckuck, W., Rieger, B., and Steinke, K., Automatic Writer Recognition, *Proceedings of the 1979 Carnahan Conference on Crime Countermeasures* (Univ. of Lexington, 1979).

48. Steinke, K., Recognition of Writers by Handwriting Images. *Pattern Recognition,* 1981; 14: p 357.

49. Klement, V., An Application System for the Computer-Assisted Identification of Handwritings. *Proceedings of the 17th Carnahan Conference on Security Technology* (Zurich, 1983).

50. Klement, V. R., Naske, R.-D., and Steinke, R., The Application of Image Processing and Pattern Recognition Techniques to the Forensic Analysis of Handwriting. *Proceedings of the 1980 International Conference on Security through Science and Engineering* (Berlin, 1980).

51. Impedovo, S. and Abbattista, N., Handwritten Numeral Recognition, The Organization Degree Measurement. *Proceedings of the 6th Internal Conference on Pattern Recognition,* IEEE (Muenchen, 1982).

52. de Bruyne, Pieter and Messmer, Paul, Authentication of Handwritten Signatures with Sonar. *International Conference: Security Through Science and Engineering* (Berlin, 1980).

53. Naske, R.-D., Writer Recognition by Prototype Related Deformation of Handprinted Characters. *Proceedings of the 6th International Conference on Pattern Recognition,* IEEE (Muenchen, 1982).

54. Watson, R. S. and Pobgee, P. J., A Computer to Check Signatures. *Visual Language,* 1979; XIII: 3: pp 232-238.

55. Bertillon, Allphonse, La Comparison des Ecritures et Identification Graphique. *Revue Scientifique* (Paris Dez, 1898 January).

56. Kirk, P. L., *Crime Investigation* (New York: Interscience Publishers, 1953), pp 475-476.

57. Rhodes, Henry T. F., *The Principals of Identification Application to Handwriting.* Presented at the 1st International Meeting in Questioned Documents (London, April, 1963).

58. Thornton, J. I. and Rhodes, E. F., Brief History of Questioned Document Examination. *Identification News,* 1986 January; p 12.

59. Popkiss, A. and Moore, J., Handwriting Classification. *Police Journal,* 1945; 18: pp 39-55.

60. Livingston, Orville B., Frequency of Certain Characteristics in Handwriting, Pen-Printing of Two Hundred People. *Journal of Forensic Sciences,* 1963; 8: 2: pp 250-259.

61. Muehlberger, R. J., Newman, K. W., Regent, James, and Wichmann, J. G., A Statistical Examination of Selected Handwriting Characteristics. *Journal of Forensic Sciences,* 1976; 22: pp 206-215.

62. Ansell, M., Handwriting Classification in Forensic Science. *Visible Language,* 1979; 13: pp 239-251.

63. Eldridge, M. A., Nimmo-Smith, I., Wing, A. M., and Totty, R. N., The Variability of Selected Features in Cursive Handwriting: Categorical Measures. *Journal of the Forensic Science Society,* 1984; 24: pp 179-219.

64. Nicholson, P. J., A System for the Classification of Block Capitals. *Journal of the Forensic Science Society,* 1984; 24: p 415.

65. Blake, M., *Handwriting Individuality, Can We Prove It?* Presented at the meeting of the American Society of Questioned Document Examiners (1977), p 7.

66. Blake, Martha, *Are We Seeing the Same Thing? Results of a Survey Presented to Forensic Document Examiners.* Presented at the meeting of the American Society of Questioned Document Examiners (Long Beach, 1994).

67. Böhle, Karlheinz, Cataloguing Significant Features of Handwriting as an Aid to Objectivising Evidence in the Investigation of Handwritten Script. *Journal of Forensic Document Examination,* 1993 Fall; 6: pp 41-58.

68. Mueller, B., Zur Frage des Beweiswertes der Schriftgutachten nebst Statistischer Untersuchungen über die Häufigkeit einiger Schriftmerkmale, *Archiv. f. Kriminologie,* 1939; S. 104.

69. Reitberger, L., Zur Frage des Beweiswertes der Schriftgutachten nebst Statistischen Untersuchungen über die Häufigkeit einiger Schriftmerkmale, *Archiv. fur Kriminologie,* 1941; 108: S. 130 ff.

70. Bein, W., Statistische Häufigkeitsuntersuchungen. *Krim und forens. Wiss., Berlin,* 1967; S. 89-96.

71. Eldridge, M. A., Nimmo-Smith, I., and Wing, A. M., The variability of selected features in cursive handwriting: categorical measures, *Journal of the Forensic Science Society* 1984; 24: pp 179-219.

72. Evett, I. W. and Totty, R. N., A Study of the Variation in the Dimensions of Genuine Signatures. *Journal of the Forensic Science Society,* 1985; 25: pp 207-215.

73. Wing, A. M. and Nimmo-Smith, I., The Variability of Cursive Handwriting Measures Defined Along a Continuum: Letter Specificity. *Journal of the Forensic Science Society,* 1987; 27: pp 297-306.

74. Wann, John and Nimmo-Smith, Ian, The Control of Pen Pressure in Handwriting: A Subtle Point. *Human Movement Science,* 1991; 10: pp 223-246.

75. Eldridge, M. A., Nimmo-Smith, I., Wing, A. M., and Totty, R. N., The Dependence Between Selected Categorical Measures of Cursive Handwriting. *Journal of the Forensic Science Society,* 1985; 25: pp 217-231.

76. Hardcastle, R. A., Thornton, D., and Totty, R. N., A Computer-Based System for the Classification of Handwriting on Cheques. *Journal of the Forensic Science Society,* 1986; 26: pp 383-392.

77. Hardcastle, R. A. and Kemmenoe, D., A Computer-Based System for the Classification of Handwriting on Cheques. Part 2: Cursive Writing. *Journal of the Forensic Science Society,* 1990; 30: pp 97-103.

78. Muehlberger, R. J., Newman, K. W., Regent, James, and Wichmann, J. G., A Statistical Examination of Selected Handwriting Characteristics. *Journal of the Forensic Sciences,* 1976; 22: pp 206-215.

79. Nicholson, P. J., A System for the Classification of Block Capital Handwriting. *Journal of the Forensic Science Society,* 1984; 24: pp 415.

80. Giles, Audrey, *Increasing the Level of Objectivity in Handwriting Examinations.* Presented at the meeting of the American Society of Questioned Document Examiners (San Jose, 1990).

81. Totty, R. N., Hall, M. G., Hardcastle, R. A., and Brown, C., A Computer-Based System for the Identification of Unknown Typestyles. *Journal of the Forensic Science Society,* 1982; 22: pp 65-73.

82. Huber, Roy A., *The Uniqueness of Writing.* Presented at the meeting of the American Society of Questioned Document Examiners (San Jose, 1990).

83. Kroon-van der Kooij, Leny N., *Computer Supported Analysis of Handwriting.* Presented at the meeting of the American Society of Questioned Document Examiners (Milwaukee, 1992).

84. Horton, Richard A., *A Study of the Occurrence of Certain Handwriting Characteristics in a Random Population.* Presented at the meeting of the American Society of Questioned Document Examiners (Milwaukee, 1992).

85. Crane, A. C. J. and Crane, S. L., A Frequency Study of Cheque-Writing Styles. *Canadian Society of Forensic Science Journal,* 1997 September; 30: 3: pp 113-126.

86. Böhle, Karlheinz, Cataloguing Significant Features of Handwriting as an Aid to Objectivising Evidence in the Investigation of Handwritten Script. *Journal of Forensic Document Examination,* 1993 Fall; 5: pp 41-58.

87. Keeler, Katherine, A Study of Documentary Evidence in Election Frauds. *Journal of Criminal Law, Criminology and Police Science,* 1934-35; 25: pp 324-337.

88. Harris, John J. and Mills, Don Harper, Medical Records and the Questioned Document Examiner, *Journal of Forensic Sciences,* 1963; 8: 3: pp 453-461.

89. Doud, D. B., *Letter Form Variations as Related to Suspect Calendar and Diary Entries.* Presented at the meeting of the American Society of Questioned Document Examiners (San Francisco, 1967).

90. Beck, Jan, *Evaluation of Handwritten Diary Entries.* Presented at the meeting of the American Society of Questioned Document Examiners (Milwaukee, 1974).

91. Foley, B. G., Handwritten Entry Research. *Journal of Forensic Sciences,* 1979 April; 24: 2: pp 503-510.
92. McCarthy, John F., *Were These Entries Made in the Normal Course of Business?* Presented at the meeting of the American Academy of Forensic Sciences (1981).
93. Foley, Robert G., *Nearly Identical Signatures — A Supplemental Exposition.* Presented at the meeting of the American Society of Questioned Document Examiners (Montreal, Canada, 1985).
94. Foley, Robert G., Characteristics of Synchronous Sequential Signatures. *Journal of Forensic Sciences,* 1987; 32: 1: pp 121-129.

The Extrinsical Factors
Influencing Handwriting

8

As an introduction to the factors to be discussed in Chapters 8 and 9, the following general comments are warranted.

The Variables of Handwriting

There are numerous conditions and circumstances that contribute to the nature of normal writing and the quality of the writing performance.

Some of these factors are variables that are extrinsical and, for the most part, not within our voluntary control. They belong to the nature of the writer and include those factors that are physical in kind while others are mental. Age and infirmity are invariable extrinsical influences. Sinistrality (left-handedness) is another frequently encountered. Adherence to a particular writing system or skill in penmanship are two others.

Other variables are intrinsical and somewhat circumstantial. They are factors over which we might exercise some control, if we chose to do so. The imitation of family and other practises, or the grasp of the writing instrument are two such factors.

Included within these intrinsical factors are that set of temporary conditions, derived from hallucinogens, alcohol, hypnosis, stress and fatigue, that exercise their influence upon writing, regardless of the form it otherwise takes. All are influences to which one voluntarily submits, for other reasons.

37. What *Extrinsical Factors* (i.e., Not Normally Within the Writer's Control, Not Matters of Choice) Influence Handwriting?

A. Writing Systems: National, Cultural, and Occupational

To some extent, the nature or appearance of our writing is predetermined. Since it is an acquired perceptual motor skill and there is nothing about it that is known to be instinctive or hereditary, it is primarily environment, experience, and culture dependent. The writing systems we are taught, that follow patterns popular within our country or our particular population provide some basic characteristics of form, slant, proportions, movement, and size.

A number of the earlier authors have placed emphasis on the importance of writing systems in the study of handwritings. Osborn devoted an entire chapter to the subject (37 pages) and stated, "Through all these changes (that a person's writing undergoes) the original system will to some extent visibly protrude."[1] Osborn argued, "Definite system characteristics and distinctive national handwriting characteristics must always be properly considered in any thorough handwriting investigation." He claimed further, and Hilton[2] agreed, that evidence of the system learned may serve as "a fairly accurate gauge of his (the writer's) age," since there have been definite periods during which particular writing systems were taught. Almost every writer on the subject has maintained that handwriting identification is based on the finding of a combination of similarities in class and individual characteristics, and class characteristics (see Section 12) are invariably defined as those characteristics that result from such influences as: the writing system taught, trade training, and education.

Prior to the time when the typewriter and the now common electronic printer began to dominate, our communication methods and records were dependent upon calligraphy. Numerous occupations developed distinctive characteristics. There was a *small literary hand* with wide word spacing, the *strong railroad style* having a fixed number of words per line, the compact writing of the *bookkeeper's hand*. There was the modified *Round Hand* with vertical slope, having wide spacing between letters that was known as the *Civil Service hand,* and there was also a large awkward, angular hand that was taught in certain exclusive schools for women.[3]

More recently Masson[4] reported on the lettering of draftsmen, architects and architectural engineers, that follows prescribed patterns of design or construction and can greatly limit individualization. The patterns of construction are sufficiently distinctive that the occupational influence upon a writer may be recognized. For example, all strokes are executed in a downward direction. Circular letters such as "O," "Q," and "C" are formed using two or more strokes all of which are executed in a prescribed sequence. Furthermore, engineers are allowed even less freedom to individualize letter styles than architects, it seems.

Herrick[5] published a comparative review of some 19 commercial systems being followed by schools of the United States in 1960. Beacom added 10 others to it in 1965.[6] Towson[7] compiled a similar, but less detailed, review of the five systems being taught in Canada during the period 1960 to 1970. Moon[8] provides a slightly different list of 16 systems being offered in 39 states of the United States. However, the 1980s marked the beginning of the demise of stipulated policy respecting handwriting in the schools, and we are now without a prescribed writing system in many areas. Vastrick's report[9] is testimony to this. His survey, to which 28 states responded, revealed that 9 states had no specific system to offer pupils. The balance of 19 states identified 14 different systems that were being taught.

The role of penmanship in the development of the individual has changed substantially over recent years, as many examiners have observed, and adherence to any writing system has not been aspired or required. Harrison[10] recognized that a great deal of change from the system a person has been taught is to be expected. He comments:

"By the time adolescence is past and the handwriting has assumed the character it will certainly retain until senility or ill-health takes their toll, it may well be that comparatively few letters will conform at all closely to the original copybook design."

Miller[11] conducted a study of a selected sample of specimen writings from 128 former students of various ages of a specific school that had been in existence since 1909, that had taught the Palmer writing system exclusively until 1936 and the Zaner Bloser system since that time. In his report, he makes a rather profound declaration:

> "Perhaps the most significant outcome is the demonstration that it is virtually impossible to give a correct opinion regarding the system of handwriting a mature person was taught."

Because the evidence of the writing system to which the individual was subjected in his or her formative years is becoming that unclear, we are now compelled to omit reference to it as a class characteristic to be considered in the comparison of many if not most writings. Its value may only lie in the study of writings of nearly a century ago.

1. *(North) American Writing Systems*

Herrick, in his aforementioned study of the 19 writing systems in use in the United States in and about 1960, found that the greatest dissimilarities in the systems were the letter forms advocated, and the use of manuscript writing. In the cursive designs of the capital letters suggested by these systems, there were as many as 10 designs for one allograph (e.g., "F" and "R"). Most of the differences in these designs, however, were minor, and less than a dozen of the cursive capitals showed any really significant formation differences in even as few as two forms. The lowercase cursive letters showed even less variance.

The teaching of manuscript writing to the students, before their introduction to cursive writing, was the other major dissimilarity. While manuscript was employed in a large number of systems, it was not universal. Manuscript writing was introduced in United States schools around 1920, and in the 1980s a majority of schools still taught it before they taught the cursive style, because the strokes involved are simpler and less varied.

Moon[12] surveyed the systems being taught in schools in the United States with a view to relating them, if possible, to geographical locations. In 39 states, some 15 different systems were being followed. Some states employed two or more systems. The conclusion drawn was that it was not possible to determine the geographic origin of a person by the style of handwriting he or she was taught.

In a review of 35 of the commercial systems offered in various locations in North America, Regent[13] took a different approach in search of the elements of upper and lowercase letters of the alphabet that all systems had in common, rather than those by which they might be differentiated. His objective was to catalogue the aspects of writing that should not be construed or considered to reflect class or system characteristics. Divergences in these aspects can then be rightfully categorized as individual characteristics.

This study of cursive systems, coupled with our own observations, revealed a number of common elements, including:

1. The uppercase letters "D," "L," and "Q" have an eyelet at the heel, of similar size, the axis of which runs parallel to but slightly above the baseline.
2. The descending loops of the uppercase letters "J," "Y," and "Z" are similar in shape and size, and the axis of each parallels the slope of the writing generally.
3. The centre trough of the uppercase letter "G" forms a cusp with the final lower curve, which cusp is never as tall as the initial loop.
4. The loops of the uppercase "J" are executed in a clockwise direction.
5. The bowls of the lowercase letters "a," "d," "g," and "q" are similar elliptical or oval shapes that are closed at the upper right point of the ellipse.

6. The descending loops of the lowercase letters "g," "j," "y," and "z" are similar in shape and size, and the axis of each parallels the slope of the writing generally.
7. The loops of the lowercase "f" are executed in a counterclockwise direction.
8. The loops of the lowercase "f" do not intersect with one another or meet at a common point on the staff.
9. The loops of the lowercase "h" and "k" are similar in shape and length.
10. The arches of the lowercase "m" and "n" are rounded and of equal height and width.
11. The top of the lowercase "r" commences from a cusp on the upper left and proceeds as a descending compound curve to fashion a round shoulder on the right from which the stroke returns to the baseline.
12. The apex of the lowercase "s" is a cusp.
13. The stem of the lowercase "t" is a retrace.

Regent quotes Osborn as stating, "The most significant handwriting characteristics of form are those that most diverge from the design that was followed as a learner." Osborn's assumption seems to have been that most writers follow copybook designs closely, which may have been the case in his time. In another location, Osborn states, "…those identifying or differentiating characteristics are of the most force that are most divergent from the regular system or national features of a particular handwriting."

These statements of Osborn imply that significance varies directly with divergence from copybook form or system style. Conversely, it might be held that the least significant characteristics are those that most closely resemble the prescribed copybook form. Huber,[14] in a study of the writings of 227 subjects, reported that neither of these tenets could now be supported. Copybook writing, that is penmanship of quality, is a rarity nowadays, and accordingly, copybook forms are of greater value in the identification process. So much so that quality in writing has become a writer's best defence against forgery.

It was also observed in this study that some writers utilize some letter forms in, and perhaps only in, certain written text, such as the writing of "USA" on envelope addresses, that is developed as a unit of habit. The form(s) may not appear frequently in any other text or when these letters are isolated from one another.

As a law or fundamental principle, then, it is obviously more correct to say that the significance of a discriminating element of handwriting (a characteristic) varies inversely as its frequency of occurrence in similar text material in the writing of different persons.

It is generally presumed, as most writing systems tend to prescribe, that certain consistencies will prevail in the common elements shared by some letters. For example, the uppercase "P," "B," and "R" can be expected to display some similarity in the structure of the staff and the bowl. Consistency can also be expected in some elements of the uppercase "M" and "N," the uppercase "F" and "T," the uppercase "I" and "J," the uppercase "V" and "W," and the lowercase "a," "d," "g," and "q." It might also be expected that some consistency would be found in the loops of the lowercase "l," "h," "b," and "k," or in the commencement of the uppercase letters "U," "Y," and "Z." These assumptions can be important in cases where limited standards do not contain samples of all of the allographs present in a questioned writing.

While similarities in the common elements of such allographs may prompt an examiner to presume that, in the general case, there would be similarity in another allograph sharing these elements if a sample were available, this assumption may not be invariably valid. Consequently, it may not necessarily follow that a difference in, say, the design of the "P" is indicative of a difference to be found in the design of the "R," if such an allograph was available to compare.

Kiser and Torres[15] in a study of a sample of 588 incarcerated individuals, of both sexes and of Caucasian, Negroid, and Latin extraction, also found that these assumptions are not fully supported. Inconsistencies occurred in these sets of letters in as many as 40 percent of their sample in some cases. However, as indicated elsewhere in this dissertation, the present writers have some reservations about generalizing from prison inmates to the general population. Kiser and Torres discreetly make no comments, whatsoever, respecting the reliability of the data they collected.

Systems may develop within systems and can be far more localized than national, provincial, or state boundaries might suggest. Bellomy[16] describes the nature of Mexican-American communities, called *barrios* that have developed in Arizona, Colorado, New Mexico, Texas, and particularly in southern California. For various reasons, these communities have produced street gangs, known as *vatos* that have been a part of the social structure of those areas for some 75 years. Part of a gang's guise or identity is the adoption and use of its own distinctive style of lettering referred to as *Barrio Script* that is a particular modification of conventional handprinting, employed by the vato in gang writings on the walls of structures. Bellomy provides four examples.

Additionally, influences can be exhibited with respect to particular letter forms, without altering the designs of any other letters of similar structure. Because of their prevalence among the coloured student population in Florida, the McCarthy papers mentioned earlier (see Section 30.4) refer to the unusual letter forms of the "J" and "W" as the black "J" and "W," but as Haywood[17] has pointed out the generalization to the black population may not be fully justified. Certainly, it is found among coloured students in Florida, but Haywood's review of FBI fingerprint forms reveals that users of these letter designs are widely dispersed throughout the United States. A majority of these individuals claim the state of New York as their place of birth, but the reliability of this data is uncertain. The examples that the study surfaced were indeed coloured persons, which represented about 5 percent of the population of coloured subjects in the sample.

Little can be concluded regarding these letter formations on the strength of the information at hand. The origin of the forms is still unknown. They may be simply imitations of writing characteristics of other older students. The authors of this work hold a sample of writing containing the "black W" that is identified only as originating in Brazil (Figure 8). Haywood's study provides evidence that these designs persist throughout the adult life of the writer, that was not the situation suggested by the earlier McCarthy studies.

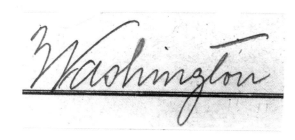

Figure 8   The "Black W" or "3-W," written on an envelope received from Brazil.

2. *Aruba/Curacao Writings Systems (see A.21. Various Writing Systems)*

3. *Belgian Writing Systems (see A.21. Various Writing Systems)*

4. *English (U.K.) Writing Systems*

A review of notes and writing samples collected over 45 years yields a few particular
observations respecting English writing systems worth considering in writing studies.

1. English writing tends to be more vertical.
2. The "M" and "N" is frequently of a Spencerian style, and similar to the styles of the
    English Civil Service Hand, that was a modification of the old Round Hand.
3. English writers frequently add a period or a comma after the house number in a
    street address and after the abbreviations "Mr" and "Mrs."
4. English writers frequently introduce an eyelet to the union of the vertical and the
    horizontal strokes in the numeral "4" (see also A.21. Various Writing Systems).

5. *French Writing Systems*

In a study of the signatures of 16 female youths from France, ages 11 to 24, 12 of whom
were adolescents aged 15 to 17, Bolsover[18] reported that 15 of the 16 writers exhibited one
or more of three particular characteristics: 13 writers added a rubric, 9 writers superimposed an initial with the capital letter of the surname, and 9 writers exhibited a distinctive
ascending baseline. The study of two additional signatures from older persons having an
origin in France revealed similar features, suggesting that the features noted are not necessarily peculiarities of the adolescent.

   The explanation offered is that writing systems taught in schools in France tend to be
fancier and that, consequently, signatures are fancier. An element of the writing that may
contribute to the fancier assessment of French writings is the inclusion of a small eyelet,
often blind, to the commencement of the uppercase letters "H," "I," "J," "K," "V," "W," and
"Z," executed in a counterclockwise direction. It produces a short, trough-like, horizontal
beginning to the letter. Large commencement curls are characteristic of other uppercase
letters (see also A.21. Various Writing Systems).

   The addition of a cross stroke to the stem of the digit "7" is common in French cursive
writings taught in France and in other French communities (e.g., in Canada). The use of
guillemets, i.e., horizontal chevrons «...» to enclose a quotation, rather than quotation
marks, is another practise of old France.

   The observation has been made, and we have no reason to doubt it for our exposure
to writings originating in France is limited, that the writings of France tend to be smaller
than those of their neighbours, Germany and Spain.

6. *German Writing Systems*

Features of the German cursive writing systems can be found often in the writing of
neighbouring countries such as Austria, Switzerland, and Poland. The Netherlands and
the Scandinavian countries of Denmark, Norway, and Sweden share many of these features,
that include (see also A.21. Various Writing Systems):

1. In any quotation, the first set of quotation marks are located on or below the baseline. The last set are elevated.
2. Salutations are usually followed by an exclamation mark "!" rather than a colon ":".
3. Apostrophes are not always used to indicate the possessive forms of nouns or pronouns, except when the name ends in an "s."
4. A small u-shaped diacritic is placed over the letter "u" to distinguish it from the letter "n."
5. German writing is frequently larger than that of other countries, just as French writing tends to be smaller.
6. The bowls of cursive letters in German writing tend to be broader or more circular than those of English or North American writings, which are more oval shaped. As in other Cyrillic European writings the bowls may be overwritten by the same stroke (Figure 9).
7. Younger German writers tend to use the printed style of a letter as a capital. Older writers are more ornate in their executions.
8. Many German writers add an approach stroke to the figure "1," a cross bar to the figure "7," and commence the figures "2" and "9" with an inside curl or hook.
9. A medial or terminal lowercase "t" is frequently crossed in a continuous motion that begins at the base of a straight stem or staff, rises and loops in a counterclockwise direction to the left of the staff, and crosses it, usually at midpoint. Some copybooks omit the execution of the complete loop or buckle.
10. Large initial loops are omitted in the execution of the uppercase "I" and "J" in favour of a smaller single arch connected to the apex of the letter with two acute angles. Similar movements are employed to commence the "H," "K," "V," and "W."
11. The uppercase "G" is designed as an enlargement of the lowercase "g."
12. The contour of the arch of the uppercase "N" and the second arch of the uppercase "M" is interrupted by a shallow trough at the apex.
13. The shoulder of the lowercase "r" is troughed rather than rounded.

7. Hmong Handwriting Systems

Tweedy[19] reports that Hmong people (pronounced "Mong") originated in the northern portions of Laos, Thailand, and Vietnam, and in southern China. Many have moved, by way of refugee camps, to the United States after the war in Vietnam, and have located in Minnesota where they now number (1995) over 27,000.

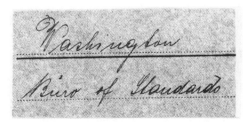

Figure 9 Writing from Germany, illustrating the tendency for some European writing to retrace the bowls of cursive letters, such as "a," "g," "q," and "d."

The Hmong people did not have a written language of their own until 1953, when one was developed for them by missionaries, that was called the Romanized Popular Alphabet (RPA). This alphabet was designed to use all of the letters of the Roman alphabet. On the heels of the RPA, another system of writing was developed that was called Pahawh Hmong, and used symbols created specially for the system rather than the Roman alphabet and letter forms. According to Tweedy, other systems or scripts have appeared on the scene since the late 1950s but none have become popular or survived.

Tweedy's study of 107 samples of Hmong writings (68 males, 37 females, and 2 unknown), most of whom were taught to write before moving to the U.S.A., failed to reveal any particular national characteristics that might serve to suggest a person of a Hmong background. There was a tendency (83 percent) to execute a lowercase lettered style for the allograph "b" (with a clockwise bowl and no loop). There was, however, a much greater tendency for Hmong writers to use lettered styles and fewer connections between letters. Frequently, not more than two letters would be joined. Beyond that the writings disclosed no particular class characteristics of value to a writing examination.

8.   Ideographic Writing Systems: Chinese, Japanese, and Korean

Caywood offers two examples of the English writing styles offered to Chinese, Japanese, and Korean students in the process of their learning to speak English. These copybook examples are not readily identifiable with known systems currently in use in North America, probably because both have been stripped of embellishments and flourishes, to facilitate the learning process. In this respect, they may correspond to the D'Nealian system as closely as to any other. Beyond that their usefulness is uncertain.

9.   Indian Writing Systems (see A.21. Various Writing Systems)

10.   Italian Writing Systems (see A.21. Various Writing Systems)

11.   Jamaican Writing Systems

In a study of the handwritings of 90 Jamaican women, Anderson[20] reported a number of features that were common to many writers:

1. The lower case "a" and "d" and the upper case "A" commenced with a small internal curl within the bowl.
2. The lower case "c" and the upper case "C" commenced with a small curl.
3. The majority (62 percent) used lettering as opposed to cursive writing.
4. The majority (90 percent) printed the capital letter "E," and at least half of those executed the bottom arm with an undulating stroke.
5. The majority (80 percent) used an enlarged lower case style for the capital "G," and located the bowl above the baseline. As in the "a," "c," and "d," the letter was commenced with a small curl within the bowl in most cases.
6. A number of writers (38 percent) formed the loop of the capital "I" by adding a downstroke to the front of a staff. Similarly, the majority of writers (61 percent) added a downstroke to create the upper loop of the capital "J," as has been observed in "the black J," and in the capital "J" written by many Newfoundlanders.
7. Some writers (40 percent) used the lower case "i" for the personal pronoun "I."
8. No cursive forms of the letters "K" or "k" were found.
9. The majority (90 percent) used the Palmer "r."

10. All writers formed the upper and lower case "X" as two circle sectors, back to back, as is common in German writing.
11. Half of the writers commenced the numerals "2" and "9" with a small curl or hook within the upper curve, much as many German writers do.
12. Some writers execute a cross bar to the numeral "7" (36 percent), and a majority (66 percent) undulate the top bar.
13. It is also common for Jamaican women to use lower case letters to begin proper names of the days or months or for middle names or initials.

12.   Latin American (Hispanic) Writing Systems

Muehlberger[21] has written on the class characteristics of Hispanic (i.e., Latin American) writers, large numbers of which have migrated to the southern United States, particularly from Cuba and Mexico. He has observed that there is a distinction between the older generations of Hispanics, who were educated in private schools that provided instruction in penmanship, and the younger generations whose education was obtained in state-run schools that offered little in penmanship training. In consequence, older generation Hispanics frequently display a better quality of writing often based on the Palmer system, whereas, younger generation individuals exhibit a lesser quality of writing not readily associated with any particular writing system. It is reported that good penmanship acquired a status in years gone by that became a matter of personal pride. Then too, due to the level of technology, and the quality of record keeping in the Latin American countries, there is little doubt that penmanship was put to greater use by the educated portion of the population.

Evidently, many Hispanic writers share a tendency to ornateness in the formation of capital letters that produces embellishments and disproportionate increases in size that may reflect a European influence. The mixture of simplistic or lettered forms with cursive writing is not unusual. Whether it is due to the tendency to embellish or not, disconnections, hiatuses or pen lifts between letters are not uncommon. Mixtures of writing movements (e.g., garlanded with arcaded) have also been noted in the work of some writers, but this lack of consistency has not been explained. All of this may give Hispanic writings a character that is somewhat different from the normal writings of the United States and Canada. The geographical source of the influence, however, is not likely to be determinable.

Caywood's study[22] of the impact of foreign education on handwriting illustrates a number of samples of writing purportedly receiving Spanish influence, from such countries as Mexico, Cuba, and other Hispanic countries. The copybook style for Spanish writings that he provides is, with a few minor exceptions, the Palmer Method.

13.   The Netherlands Writing Systems (see A.6. German Writing Systems and A.21. Various Writing Systems)

14.   Nigerian Writing Systems

Ziegler[23] provided a few samples of Nigerian handwriting that is mostly lettering and some signatures, with few comments as to the source of his material or the frequency of occurrence of the features that are illustrated. One feature noted is the profuse use of periods before initials and after signatures and numerical dates (e.g., 8/15/85.). He also notes that the cent symbol "¢," is frequently used with the dollar symbol (e.g., $15:25¢), and that colons are used in amounts ($15:25¢) and dates (e.g., 10:17:53). He provides samples of signatures with underlining. Little else is offered that might be particularly characteristic of the writing of the Nigerian population.

It was reported (1987) that the Metropolitan Police Forensic Laboratory has assembled a collection of Nigerian writings in an endeavour to recognize the Nigerian nationality, where appearing, in the study of documents involved in criminal cases, but we are without further information on its success.

15. Norwegian Writing Systems (see A.6. German Writing Systems).

16. Portuguese Writing Systems

Behrendt[24] reported that in a study of Portuguese writings he found that 6 of 14 subjects commenced the upstroke to the loops of the lowercase "l," "b," and "h" and to the staff of the "t" at a point well above the baseline, thereby, disconnecting the letter from any preceding letter. Breaks preceding other letters such as the "a," "c," "g," and "m" were also common occurrences. Behrendt attributes these breaks to a Portugese writing system that teaches the commencement of these letters from an elevated point, and so considers it to be a class characteristic.

17. Spanish Writing Systems

Strangers to Spanish writing systems may not be familiar with their practise of using an inverted question mark "¿," to open an interrogative statement in extended texts (see also 12. Latin American and A.21. Various Writing Systems).

18. Surinam Writing Systems (see A.21. Various Writing Systems)

19. Swedish Writing Systems (see A.6. German Writing Systems)

20. Vietnamese Writing Systems

In a continuing study of the writings of Vietnamese that have immigrated to the United States since 1970, Torres[25] provides a number of worthy observations in the nature of national characteristics. Vietnamese use the Latin alphabet in systems handed down under French rule. Correspondence with French writings can often be found. There are, however, other idiosyncracies that may constitute national characteristics of their own. For example:

1. Signatures are highly stylized and written without breaks between the first, middle, and last names. It is typical of Vietnamese to place the signature in the middle of the signature line.
2. The "1" is frequently executed with an approach or secondary stroke.
3. The "2" is frequently executed with an initial curl within the upper curve.
4. The terminal stroke of the "3" is frequently without curvature.
5. The bowl of the "5" is often angular rather than all curved.
6. The staffs of "4," "7," and "9" often descend below the baseline.
7. The "6" commonly commences with a small hook.
8. Fewer than 50 percent of writers place a cross stroke on the "7."
9. The staff of the "9" frequently descends below the baseline, the bowl rests on the baseline with the resulted appearance of a letter "g."
10. Block letters frequently replace cursive capitals.

11. Lower case letter forms frequently replace capitals.
12. The lower loop of the "f" is executed clockwise.
13. The upstrokes to "b," "h," "l," and "k" frequently commence part way up the letter.
14. The bowl of the "p" is often open.
15. Terminal "t"s are often Palmer style. In other cases, the cross stroke is located to the right of the staff.
16. The "W" is sometimes formed by the overlapping of two separate "V"s.

21. Various National Writing Systems

Within the published and unpublished material written by document examiners it is frequently mentioned that writing systems are as nationalistic as languages, that the writing of a person taught to write in a foreign country retains a foreign accent. Hilton claims, "The presence of foreign writing characteristics is a strong indication of foreign background and particularly of foreign education." Among these authors, however, Hilton[26] is the only writer who describes and illustrates a few of the foreign characteristics to be found in French, German, and Italian writings. Osborn provides a few samples of English writing without comment. Stangohr[27] provides some 98 samples of writings or of portions of samples of writings from around the world, but abandons the reader with the comment: "No attempt is being made at this time to make a detailed comparison of writing from one country to the next, and the noting of various likenesses or differences is left to the reader." This is difficult to do as the illustrations have been greatly reduced photographically.

Caywood[28] provided samples of writing from 15 transient individuals that had been educated in one country and were living in another, usually an English-speaking country. Their origins were mixed and included Ceylon, Greece, Persia, West Germany, Japan, India, Pakistan, Croatia, French Canada, and France. The samples are not accompanied by guidance as to what specific writing features may indicate the individual's country of origin or adoption. Similar criticisms may be made of his 1995 publication.

McCarthy,[29] under the promising title *A Collection of Modern European Handwriting Systems*, describes a program for the assembly of samples of European writings to be pursued by the Forensic Document Laboratory of the Immigration and Naturalization Service, but offers only two samples of Cyrillic (Russian) writing for us to see, without further comment. Sommerford and the United States Post Office Department[30] produced a useful collection of standard alphabets most of which are in cursive writing styles from 28 nations around the world, other than the U.S.A.

Work by Kroon-Van der Kooij[31] provides us with five samples of four letters and two numerals (the uppercase "F" and "J," the lowercase "d" and "g," and the "7" and "8"), written by individuals from 10 different national backgrounds: the Netherlands, Surinam, Aruba/Curacao, Belgium, France, the United Kingdom, India, Western Germany, Italy, and Spain. From these charts, certain national characteristics seem to emerge.

1. The Netherlands changed the system of writing taught in their schools in 1950 from a somewhat ornate style to one that is quite simplistic. Most capital letters are now quasi-printed forms without secondary strokes. The "F" is one such character in which the upper horizontal arm extends well to the left of the staff. This printed style is apparent in younger writers in the Netherlands. Surinam and Aruba/Curacao, both former colonies of the Netherlands, did not follow the 1950 change promptly as copybooks were evidently not available. France, the U.K. and India also

use a printed style, without the projection of the upper arm to the left of the staff. There is also a tendency to connect the strokes. West Germany is more cursive in style.

2. The "J" is a lettered style in the samples from France, the U.K., and India.

3. The slope of the letter "g" tends to be vertical or backhand in the writings from France, the U.K., and India.

4. The "7" is invariably crossed with, perhaps, the exception of India. The staff runs well through the baseline in the Netherlands, Surinam, and Aruba/Curacao, that is not surprising since the latter two are colonies of the Netherlands. The numeral sits on the baseline in all other country samples. The cross stroke in the Italian samples is quite consistently sloped downward to the baseline.

5. Construction of the numeral "8" seems to differ distinctly in the Netherlands and its colonies in that it commences with the counterclockwise formation of the lower bowl and ends with the clockwise formation of the upper bowl. The Surinam writings, however, include some samples in which the movement of the strokes appears to be in the opposite direction. The U.K., West Germany, and Italy writings disclose a tendency to pirouette the structure of the figure so that its beginning and its end meet at the centre top.

6. The slope of the writing in the France, U.K. and India samples tends to be vertical or even slightly backhand. The samples from West Germany, on the other hand, are clearly forehand leaning.

7. Insofar as the Belgium writings are concerned, it should be noted that the country is bilingual, French and Dutch. Belgian writings may follow the patterns afforded by either of these nationalities.

B. Physiological Constraints

1. *Use of Foot or Mouth*

Those that are not familiar with actual cases of it find the ability of people to write with a foot or the mouth almost incredulous. Equally incredulous is the fact that the written product may not be distinguishable in any particular fashion from the writings of any other person produced with a fully enabled hand. There are, of course, a number of convenience factors involved. The individual that writes with the foot or the mouth does not have the facility of the hands to uncap the pen, hold the paper, turn over the page, manipulate an eraser, or the capacity to write on a horizontal surface at the elevation of a bank, business, or store counter. Nevertheless, persons incapacitated in this fashion from birth are capable of developing remarkable facility for adapting to the situation. The point is that when conditions are appropriate the writing itself resembles in many respects the general characteristics of the writing of any other individual.

The fact that this is the case might constitute evidence that, in the mechanism of human writing, the mind may be the principal component of this neuromuscular process. The literature on the subject is sparse, but the unpublished work of Raibert[32] respecting foot-writing and mouth-writing has been commonly cited as supporting the concept of writing system independence in the motor process. Wellingham-Jones[33] has reported a case of an individual who became a quadriplegic at the age of 26 as a result of spinal abscesses around the fourth and fifth cervical vertebrae of unknown etiology. Samples of postparalysis writing with an instrument held in the mouth are remarkably similar in letter forms, slant, loops, and proportions to samples of writing taken two years prior to the onset of the illness. The circumstances prompt the article's author to suggest, "Handwriting is brainwriting."

Wann and Athenes[34] describe a single case study of an individual with congenital absence of both arms who had 16 years experience at foot-writing and was employed in a clerical position. After a study of numerous aspects of the individual's writing, including form, pressure, speed, and velocity/curvature dependence the authors report that "…there is little to distinguish the foot-script from normal handwriting either in size or form." However, interesting anomalies in letter formation were present. The directional preference for the formation for letters such as "e" and "o" was clockwise, contrary to all current writing practises of manual writers, the findings of Thomassen and Teulings,[35] and the samples of foot-writing held by the present authors. Writing speed was on average 60 percent slower than manual writers on similar tasks, but on the other hand, pressure and other aspects of writing performance were surprisingly similar (Figure 10).

This evidence tends to support the conclusion that the normal development in the use of an alternative motor system for writing will produce a script exhibiting the same control features observed in manual writing.

2.   Use of Artificial Aids (Protheses)

Artificial aids have been developed by talented individuals to satisfy the writing needs of particular individuals. More often than not, these are cases of persons that have lost the use of the dominant hand or arm due to accident or injury, or the inability to grasp the writing instrument owing to arthritis. These devices may be engineered to operate from the affected member (the arm or hand), from the head, or from a prosthesis designed to replace a lost hand or arm.

Studies have disclosed that after a period of practise with the artificial aid the ability to write reasonably well can be reacquired.[36] This is not unlike the acquisition of skill in writing with the subdominant hand when circumstances make it necessary to do so. A common attribute of the writing produced with artificial aids may be observed in the lack of pen pressure that can be applied, so much so that ball point pens exhibit poor ink flow. Not surprisingly then, the preference of these writers seems to be the fibre-tipped pen. Furthermore, as in other situations in which new writing skills must be learned, the writing tends to be larger than normal, at least until the finer manipulations of the pen are accomplished.

3.   Deafness and Sightlessness

The writing of the deaf or hearing impaired individual has not been the subject of frequent study. Indeed, it may be that it has been presumed that one's inability to hear would have little or no effect upon one's ability to communicate by pen and ink. This, of course, is not so. It may be also that we have overlooked the numerous situations of a civil nature, e.g., property transactions, wherein the validity of a signature of a hearing impaired individual has been brought into question. We are fortunate, then, that Savage[37] saw fit to address the matter in some depth and to provide a fairly comprehensive report on the various kinds of hearing loss and what might be expected of them in written products.

Hearing is a precious capacity that most of us take for granted. Only when we lose it, or begin to lose it do we fully appreciate its value. Unlike vision loss which we can simulate

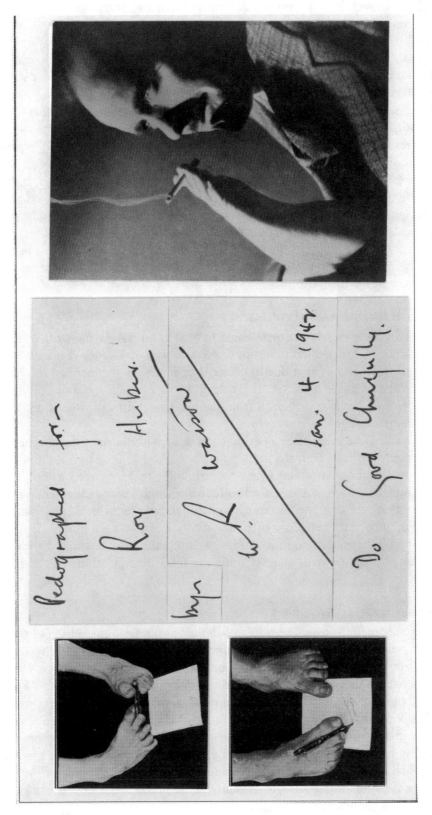

Figure 10   An example of footwriting with a fountain pen, displaying all of the attributes of good handwriting, particularly fluency.

and experience simply by closing our eyes, hearing ability impairment cannot be completely and conveniently simulated.

Hearing impaired individuals are one of two classes: the hard of hearing, or hearing impaired, and the deaf. The hard of hearing are those who can identify through hearing, (without visual receptive communication, e.g., speech reading or lip reading), enough of its distinguishing features to permit at least partial recognition of the spoken language. With lip reading, the individual may comprehend more of the language that is furnished by vocabulary and syntax if it is a part of his or her linguistic code, i.e., understanding of language.

A deaf person, on the other hand, is one who cannot identify enough of the prosodic and phonetic features of speech to permit recognition of word combinations. This individual relies mainly or entirely on speech reading or some other type of visual receptive communication. He/she may understand language in many instances, but his/her linguistic code will be much less developed, especially if hearing impaired or deaf from birth.

As Savage tells us, traditionally there has always been a distinction made between the congenitally deaf (those who are born deaf), and the adventitiously deaf (those who are born with normal hearing that becomes nonfunctional through illness). Adventitious deafness is now less frequent since medical science has been able to treat and control illnesses such as rubella, meningitis, chronic respiratory infections, and otitis media, all of which caused deafness in the past. Thus, the congenitally deaf seem to command more of our attention.

To the number of adventitiously (illness-related) deaf persons must be added the large numbers of individuals that suffer hearing impairment with advancing age. These numbers are being constantly increased by the benefits of medical science in prolonging life, generally. The growth in the population wearing hearing aids is a reasonable indicator. Canada reported statistics showing that, in 1991, 5.3 percent (1.59 million) of the Canadian population (30 million) suffered from a hearing disability. However, statistics that reflect the constant change to the numbers of persons experiencing hearing impairment are not readily available, and consequently, there may be a higher frequency of hearing impairment in our society than we realize. In the same year, the United States reported 24 million.

Years ago the term *deaf and dumb* was encountered in reference to the deaf, particularly among the younger age group. Use of the term, however, indicated a serious lack of understanding of the problem. Hart and Rosenstein[38] demonstrated that deaf children are endowed, according to most psychometric test measurements with normal intelligence and abilities. The deaf child, however, is maturing in a world that is stimulus-rich for others but is lacking in meaningful sound for him. Thus, he is compelled to master one of life's most vital tasks, language, without helpful aural experience. Under these circumstances, the deaf child was more often mute, a condition for which the term *dumb* was commonly substituted, along with its conventional, but, in this case, improper meaning.

The child, whether deaf or able to hear, is required to learn how to respond to and produce patterns of phonology, meaning, morphology, syntax, and function words. When language must be acquired by vision alone it is much more difficult to master without the benefit of linguistic stimuli. It is not surprising then that the hearing-disabled child is slower by some three years or more in his acquisition of language and educational attainment than his hearing-enabled counterpart. As a teenager, his reading vocabulary may be even further behind. Because of its importance as an educational tool, his underdeveloped vocabulary will greatly influence his academic progress, but this is not a valid reflection of his intellectual ability. Accordingly, the fallacy that the deaf are dumb should be completely dismissed, as Vernon's study[39] clearly demonstrates.

Savage's study did not reveal any particular handwriting feature(s) or general property or properties common to the writing of the hearing impaired, by which their executions as a group might be distinguished. There is as much variation in writing habits, style, and system as is encountered in the writing of the hearing-capable population.

The principal characteristic by which the writing of the deaf deviates from that of the hearing-capable individual rests in the field of linguistics. Every language evolves a criteria governing sentence structure, word order, grammar, and punctuation under the general umbrella of syntax. Furthermore, in language there are lexical meanings to the separate words and structural meanings to word combinations. Both lexical meanings and structural meanings must be present and correct for an utterance to be intelligible. It has been held that deaf children acquire lexical meanings more readily than structural meanings, and it is this delayed mastery of morphology, syntax, and function words (verbs) that retards the development and utilization of proper sentence forms.

For the most part, the deaf child develops language through lip reading, but by this process he/she does not perceive every word of an utterance. The key words are caught or perhaps only the root words, e.g., *man* instead of *men*, *work* instead of *worked*. Words not understood are ignored, as are function words that tie a communication together. To achieve meaning, the deaf child forms links between the words he/she has lip-read and fills in with nonverbal clues derived from the situation, the gestures and facial expressions of the speaker. Thus, there are two points to watch for in writings of the deaf: (1) emphasis on the use of key words, often leading to improper use of singular or plural forms, and (2) the omission of function words, such as definite and indefinite articles, e.g., "the" or "a," and others like "for," "to," "by," "at," "in," etc. that serve to tie sentences together.

Studies have shown that while word knowledge increases with time for the deaf, word usage progresses more slowly. At any age they display a persistency in the use of certain phrases, indicating an inability to apply normal variation and flexibility to written language. Furthermore, two types of errors are common to their written communications: one of substitution and one of addition. Substitution produces sentences like "A boy will running" rather than "is running," whereas, addition creates sentences like "A dog is be barking." Remarkably, the frequency of these errors persist, notwithstanding any growth in the person's vocabulary.

An error that does tend to diminish with age and vocabulary is that of word order, seen for example in verbs: "A girl playing is," and in noun/adjective relationships: "A dog brown." Studies of punctuation in the writings of the deaf from the perspectives of addition, omission, and substitution have revealed that the hearing impaired are equal to or superior to the hearing abled in this respect.

Some general observations regarding the writing of the deaf include:

1. a greater inclination at all ages to use nouns, rather than pronouns,
2. A greater inclination to omit verbs.
3. If articles such as "a," "an," and "the" are used, they are used in greater number than the hearing population.
4. Greater difficulty is encountered in the use of prepositions, adverbs, adjectives, and conjunctions.

5. A greater inclination to write short (but more) sentences of simple construction, employing limited vocabulary.
6. A greater tendency to commit errors in verb tenses, and lexical substitutions, e.g., family for familiar or vice versa.

While these points are admittedly matters of linguistics, and some may argue that they are beyond the purview of the handwriting examiner, their inclusion here has been prompted by the intent to provide some insight for the examiner into the potentials of the subject for the identification or elimination of hearing-impaired individuals from their handwriting. Indeed, the points are not so complex that they cannot be appreciated by any reviewer without the aid of special knowledge of linguistics or the involvement of statistics.

Progress in the social acceptance and treatment of deaf persons in recent years has had its implications for handwriting examiners. The teaching of visual gestural language known as American Sign Language (ASL) has modified our understanding of what to expect in the writing of the deaf.

The native language of the deaf person is not English, but ASL. ASL is a unique and distinct language that has its own principals of syntax, its own idioms, and its own problems in translating the English language, all of which can be helpful in determing whether a writing was executed by a person so restricted. ASL, however, is not so much a language as it is a code, one of several that have been created to teach English to deaf children. As a code or set of principles, ASL dictates rules for the sign language content of a communication that may also be evident in the extended writings of the deaf person. Kerr and Taylor[40] have provided an outline of some of the characteristics of Sign Language (ASL), that such writings may exhibit and the reasons for them.

Points that they mention include:

1. In ASL, syntax is described as sign-order rather than word-order. Signs are arranged in the order in which the events they represent occur or occurred.
2. Signs are repeated to show plurality, for *few, many, some.*
3. Tenses are not incorporated in verb signs.
4. Verbs differ according to directionality.
5. In ASL, one sign is used for all forms of be. Signing frequently omits them.
6. There are no articles in ALS ("a," "an," or "the").
7. First and second persons singular pronouns tend to be left to the end.

Kerr and Taylor summarize that the ability of the deaf person to use the English language in writing (or speaking) varies with the individual. Many documents written by them will exhibit linguistic evidence indicative of membership in the deaf community. Determinations that the author is deaf, however, should not be based simply on the fact that the quality of English seems poor.

Studies of sinistrality in the handwriting of the deaf by Boyd[41] have indicated that there is a lesser degree of dominance of one hand over the other, regardless of the hand preferred. This being the case, if evidence, such as that delineated above, is present in a questioned document that would indicate that it may be the execution of a hearing-impaired individual, the examination of samples from both hands of a hearing impaired suspect may be warranted.

Another matter of interest to those who examine handwriting is in the observation that has been made that sinistrality is more common among the hearing-impaired population than among others. Studies of deafness due to external causes at or near the time of birth, of the prenatal and postnatal exogenous groups, disclosed that 16.7 percent were left-handed in writing, as opposed to 11 percent of the population, generally. Among the hereditary deaf group, the endogenous group, 30 percent were found to be sinistral (see Chapter 11.58 Symbols of Sinistrality).

In summary then, the manner in which a handwriting by a hearing-impaired person may be expected to differ from that of the normal hearing person must involve the field of linguistics. Under these circumstances, a single signature or a few words of text are not likely to provide adequate material for the purposes of indicating hearing impairment from an examination of the handwriting.

The writing of the blind or visually-impaired individual is quite a different matter. The characteristics it may exhibit will diverge to some extent depending on whether the vision loss occurred prior to the point in the individual's education when writing is normally taught, or after some experience in the writing process had been acquired. Then too, the written product will vary with the degree of the vision loss.

The terms *legally blind, functionally blind, industrially blind* or *partially blind*, each of which is used relative to visual impairment, do not all mean the same thing to all persons. Legal blindness is defined as the condition of having not more than 20/200 corrected vision in the better eye. Partial blindness is the condition of having between 20/70 and 20/200, that also includes functional blindness and industrial blindness. Furthermore, there is a variety in kinds of visual impairment some of which have a bearing on one's writing ability. These encompass:

1. Congenital blindness — total blindness from birth.
2. Myopia — near sightedness. Good vision, but only at short range.
3. Hyperopia — far sightedness. Good vision, but only at long range.
4. Optic atrophy — damage to the optic nerve resulting in a small field of vision, restricting areas useable for reading and writing.
5. Retinitis pigmentosa — night blindness. Difficulty seeing under reduced illumination, particularly in artificial light.
6. Retinal detachment — separation of the retina from the choroid behind. A portion of the central field of vision is obstructed.
7. Cataracts — clouding of the lens resulting in a loss of detail.
8. Glaucoma — an elevation of pressure within the eye that may destroy side or peripheral vision.
9. Retinopathy — a swelling and leaking of retinal blood vessels. May cause blurring or obstruction of vision. Common among diabetics.
10. Macular degeneration — three types from different causes: the thinning or atrophy of the macula, the abnormal growth of blood vessels behind the retina, or the blistering of the retina. Principal effect is the distortion of the image in the field of vision.

Various writing aids have been offered to the visually impaired from time to time, none of which have been widely adopted. Templets have been designed as a column of long windows to accommodate lines of writing or lettering on a reasonably-sized sheet of paper, and others provide windows within which a signature might be executed. Templets provide problems for the execution of lower loops and descending staffs. Some templets employ elastics or wires to represent rulings or baselines. Still other techniques for the production of folds in a sheet of paper have been suggested. For example, the rolling of the sheet around a pencil, withdrawing the pencil and flattening the paper tube against the table surface to create parallel creases about one-half inch apart, is intended to provide tactile but not restrictive guides for the baseline of the writing. Related to this is the Marks System of Writing that teaches the subject to locate the writing well above the guide lines to accommodate downward extending letters. Other instructional techniques encourage the production of letters in rectangular forms.

Understandably, as these types of writing aids imply, one of the principal disadvantages of a visually-impaired writer is the lack or loss of feedback information that the writer with normal vision experiences with each and every movement of the writing instrument. Without that information, the visually impaired must judge the form, length, and location of strokes without references. Partial vision can provide a few guides and the availability of these references or reference points may determine the quality of the writing or lettering that the subject is able to produce.

Understandably too, a well practised signature may represent the best quality of writing of which the subject is capable, and this quality may supply little evidence of the nature or extent of the impairment, particularly if the vision loss occurred long after writing habits had been established.

There are cursive writing systems offered that prescribe the construction of nearly all letters without the necessity to lift the pen from the paper. Cross strokes are formed as retracings ("t," "F"), or as a result of the retracing of other strokes ("H"). Where pen lifts must occur, as in "i" dots or "j" dots, the index finger of the other hand is employed to mark the position of the writing instrument at the point of leaving the paper, to which point the instrument is returned after the dot has been made.

Thus, the characteristics of the extended writing of the visually impaired or totally blind person that occur to a greater or lesser extent according to the degree of sight loss, the writing aids employed and the type of instruction received, if any, are likely to include:

1. The misalignment of letters with respect to one another, of words with respect to one another, and of writing with respect to a ruled or implied baseline.
2. The inconsistency of spacing between letters and between words.
3. The intersection of writing with other writing or printed material.
4. The overlapping of letters or of words, sometimes making reading or decipherment difficult.
5. The flattening of letter bases, and the flattening and extending of connections in cursive writing, indicative of the use of a visual or writing aid.
6. The execution of squared letter forms, particularly in handprinting, if certain kinds of writing instruction have been received.
7. Infrequent pen lifts in cursive writing, and connections, frequently longer than necessary, employed to assist in positioning the succeeding letter.
8. The absence of "t" crossings in cursive writing, or alternatively their construction as a continuous motion of the pen.

9. The absence of "i" dots or "j" dots in cursive writing, or their consistent application and location over the stem of the letter, indicative of the employment of some means of assistance, such as another finger.

10. The stunting of letter designs, particularly the upper and lower loops.

11. The unrepaired or unretouched occurrences of pen failure creating voids in ink deposits in the strokes of ballpoint pen writing.

12. A lack of fluency, or the appearance of tremour in strokes, owing to an uncertainty in the formation of letters or in the writing process.

13. The infrequent introduction of hesitation marks or scratches at the beginning of letters or commencement strokes.

14. Some increase in letter sizes from that of previous practises, if writing had been learned prior to the onset or occurrence of the impairment.

15. A likely increase in vertical spacing between lines of writing.

Aside from the effects of restrictions imposed by writing aids, studies have not revealed consistent characteristics that can be associated with vision impairment of any particular origin or nature. The only observation that might be made is that, at the outset of the degeneration of visual ability, writings of the individual may acquire attributes easily confused with symptoms of spurious writings.

The examination of the writing of the blind or visually impaired by questioned document examiners seems, for the most part, to be directed toward the identification of signatures as genuine executions of a given individual, or toward a reliable decipherment of executions that are difficult or impossible to read or to understand. In the latter cases, confusion occurs from the overlapping of words and letters and the extreme misalignments and irregular spacing of them relative to one another. The task then becomes one of identifying letters individually, and combining them appropriately to create words that can lead to sentences. While not an impossible task, it may be and usually is extremely time consuming.[42-46]

Further to what has been said above, and particularly to Item 5, individuals have been encountered whose sight is not significantly impaired but who practise straightedge writing, or what is referred to as *blind-man's writing* (Figure 11). These individuals employ some device, such as a card or ruler, that is positioned along the baseline of the writing to provide a buffer against which the writing instrument is deliberately run to inflict a horizontal but quite unnatural characteristic upon the execution. The intent of the writer is to give the writing an attribute that is both neat and unusual. A danger to the writing examiner lies in misinterpreting this characteristic as evidence of vision impairment.

The technique of producing simulated blind-man's writing of this kind usually requires some ensuing action by the writer to add the lower loops and extenders to staffs that the straightedge device obstructs. The accuracy with which the elements are added is evidence of the ability of the individual to see reasonably well. The manner of executing and adding the descending elements can be of considerable value in writer identification. Some writers add one element at a time, some add the elements for a line of writing at a time, and others will complete the additions for a page of writing, at one and the same time. The regularity of straightedge writing in letter and word spacing, letter slopes, and letter forms is usually a reliable means of distinguishing between the products of individuals with and individuals without the ability to see. Morgan and Zilly[47] have provided excellent examples of straightedge writing and some of the techniques employed to accomplish the effect.

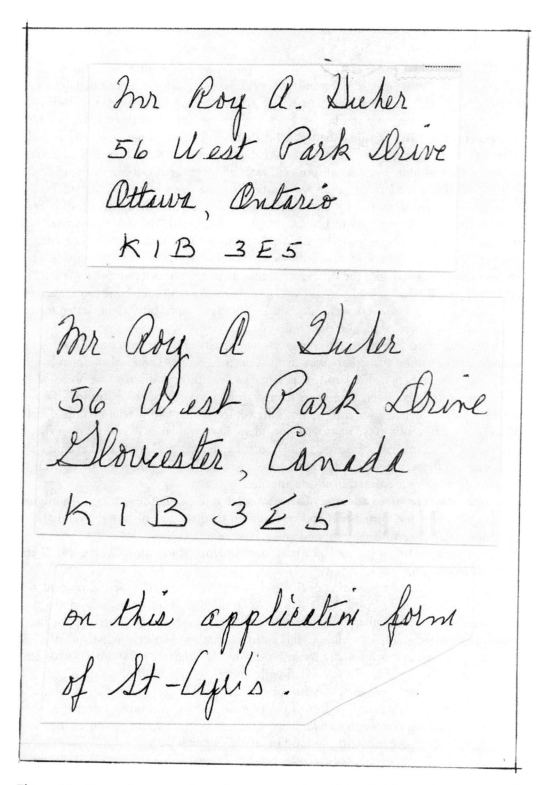

Figure 11 Illustration of a writer who uses a writing aid (a ruler) for aesthetic reasons. She is without visual impairment. Even textual material is written the same way. All lower loops are added later.

C.   Genetic Factors

1.   *Familial Relationships*

The earliest published comment respecting the possibility of writing similarities due to familial relationships is one in the December 2, 1911 issue of *Scientific American* that reports an article by R. H. Chandler. The article was printed earlier in an issue of *Knowledge*, describing Family Likenesses in Handwriting. The article illustrates three cases in which some general similarity is noted between brothers, sisters, or father and son, but the similarity is not so great that current and competent examiners would be easily deceived. Comments on this topic by other authors are rare, however. Even Osborn omitted it.

Stevens[48] noted the lack of published material on the resemblance in the writings of siblings as compared to that found in nonsiblings. It was felt that the influence of genetic factors, if any, upon the writings of siblings should be addressed. The study conducted was a comparison of the writings from three control groups with the writings of eight members (seven female) of one family, all of whom were dextral writers, taught in the same school by the same teachers and with the Palmer writing system. The control groups were matched as closely as possible in age and sex, but were unrelated to each other. Nine elements were said to have been considered including stroke endings, continuity, slant, letter forms, proportions, size, speed, skill, and pictorial appearance.

The results indicated that there was greater similarity and less variation between the members of the family than there was in the control groups. The level of resemblance between some members of the family was remarkable, although discrimination could be made. One control group, eight inmates from a women's correctional institute, disclosed the greatest variation from writer to writer. Suffice it to say that family relationships, locale, and schooling can result in writings with considerable resemblance to one another that is greater than might otherwise be expected. Unfortunately, Stevens leaves us to examine the photocopies of the writings included in the paper to establish for ourselves the respects in which the family writings resembled one another.

Münch (1987) reported on the similarity found in one case in the writings of a mother and daughter. The questioned material was limited to three sets of initials. While there were disparities between the questioned and known writings they were not so consistent or so fundamental that they could not have been attributed to natural variations, if the examination and study was not fastidious.

In our discussion of the writing of sinistrals, we pointed out that there is no evidence that left-handedness in writing can be related to familial sinistrality (i.e., left-handedness in brothers, sisters, and other relatives). Nevertheless, there are grounds supporting a relationship between sinistral children and sinistral parents. Maternal left-handedness is significantly associated with sinistrality in both sexes of children, although paternal left-handedness can be significantly associated with sinistrality in sons, but not in daughters.

Beyond these affects on the incidence of sinistrality in writers, and the resemblances that can occur to varying degrees from imitation, schooling, and other external factors, there is no evidence that family relationships influence the discriminating elements of handwriting in any particular manner and on any significant scale.

2.   *Multiple Births*

In the accepted books on document examination, virtually nothing is said about the possibility that twins, triplets, quadruplets, or quintuplets, by virtue of their genetic background, might develop or possess very similar writing habits that could make discrimination between them difficult. Thorndike (1915) and Kramer and Lauterbach (1928) wrote on the subject of similarity in the writing of twins, but not from the point of view of writing identification. None of the authors were document examiners or professed to be handwriting examiners. Thorndike, however, does point out the dissimilarity in the writing of twins, and goes so far as to say, "Twins are probably distinguishable by their handwriting oftener than by their physical appearance."

Multiple births are classed as identical, i.e., the products of the same egg, or fraternal, i.e., the products of two or more eggs fertilized at the same time. Fraternal twins are stated to be no more alike than any other two siblings from the same parents. On the other hand, identical or same egg twins are likened to the left and right halves of one individual's body.[49]

Beacom,[50] a former handwriting teacher, was the first of the document examination profession to tackle the subject. It was her recollection that the writing of twins differed sufficiently for discrimination purposes, but she was without empirical data to support her position. In a study of the writings of 50 pairs of twins, 19 pairs were identical and 31 fraternal. Twenty pairs were both male, 22 pairs were both female and 8 pairs were mixed as to sex. The identical twins were always, of course, the same sex.

Four pairs of identical twins were mixed as to handedness, one dextral and one sinistral, a circumstance that prompts some to classify them as mirror twins. Three pairs of fraternal twins were similarly mixed as to handedness. Forty-three pairs were both dextral, and of some import is the fact that no pairs were both sinistral (see section 58: Symbols of Sinistrality).

Writings were assessed with the assistance of the Ayers scale for writing quality on the basis of legibility, relative sizes, spacings, slant, and line qualities. Although some pairs received similar scores, this did not reflect similarity in their writings as different ratings were received by each member of the pair for different aspects of their writings, but sometimes resulted in a similar cumulative total.

Twins displayed comparable abilities to their siblings in cursive writing, lettering, and script writing. Notwithstanding their similarity in schools attended, teachers, and family environments, the writings of twins could be discriminated from one another without great difficulty given adequate specimens. Basic differences could always be found.

Beacom also found some progression in the differences between siblings, probably resulting from differences in occupations as adults. There were no particular deviations in writing quality related to sex that were unlike other populations.

In an endeavour to determine whether twins displayed greater resemblance to one another in their writings than other siblings, Kramer and Lauterbach (1928) studied the products of 205 pairs of twins and 101 pairs of siblings. It was their finding that twins showed a greater degree of resemblance than other siblings, that alike sex twins displayed a greater resemblance to one another than unlike sex twins, and, like Beacom, resemblance does not increase with age. Where greater resemblance occurs, however, there may be factors other than genetics at work.

Gamble's study[51] of 58 pairs of identical twins, 24 pairs of males and 34 pairs of females, claimed that this work established that no matter how closely two persons are alike and related to one another, their handwriting allowed them to be differentiated. He found 42 of his sets of twins were dextral writers, 15 sets were mixed and 1 set was sinistral. These stats are slightly different to those of other studies, but the number of subjects is not large in any case and this may account for it.

Gamble's study was directed at seven elements of writing (1) pictorial effect, (2) size, (3) slope, (4) speed, (5) writing quality, (6) proportions, and (7) letter forms. His finding was that identical twins can exhibit greater similarity in their writing than might otherwise be expected. Nevertheless, similarities in letter forms and general appearance are accompanied by a sufficient number of differences to allow an examiner to discriminate between individuals.

Beacom claims to have studied the writings of triplets, quadruplets, and quintuplets with similar results, that is, that the issue of multiple births develop writing habits that are distinctive from one another and evidently independent of their genetic backgrounds. In Section 25, we offer some evidence of this from our examinations of the writings of the Dionne quintuplets.

3.   Sex

The possibility of distinguishing the sex of the writer from his/her handwriting has been the quest of many investigations. It has been suggested as a primary step in the validation of graphology. If handwriting is related to different personality traits then it is argued that there may be no greater personality distinction than the distinction between male and female. It is also argued that the lack of success in these investigations may be due to the fact that some males are more feminine than masculine, and some females tend to display pronounced masculine personality characteristics. To date, however, these studies have not been productive beyond making the general observation that, on average, female writers are more skillful at writing than are male writers.

For more information on this topic see Section 59, The Symptoms of Sex.

D.   Physical (Normal)

1.   Maturity, Practise, and Development

This caption is directed at the normal and natural changes, if any, that occur to handwriting over the period of a lifetime. It is a topic about which very little has been written. The terms are not found in the material produced by any of the leading authorities, except that Harrison comments (@ p 341) along the lines that a developed handwriting has the potential for identification. This is the more remarkable as many have had something to say respecting the writing of adolescents and senility in persons of advanced age.

The development and progress of one's handwriting passes through four stages in the course of a lifetime: (1) the formative stage, (2) the impressionable or adolescent stage, (3) the mature stage, and (4) the stage of degeneration. The development we are speaking of is really a matter of control. During the first two stages, the writing act is more deliberate and under greater voluntary control. During the latter two stages, the act is more involuntary and under progressively less control.

From these premises, it becomes obvious that the changes that will occur during the first stage will be seen in structure, fluency, and consistency. It is the learning stage for all persons, when letter designs are being developed and skills are being mastered. The changes occurring in the second stage may be quite pronounced in form or style, depending on the source of the influence responsible for the change. The desire to imitate another style may stem from many exogenous factors, both aesthetic and identification related.[52-53] Writing of the third stage is more consistent over longer periods of time, and likely to change only in fluency or design; the former usually being the result of writing frequency, and the latter usually being the product of a particular occupation. The fourth stage, associated with endogenous factors, is prompted largely by neurophysical degeneration, the onset and the magnitude of which varies with the individual. It is the stage in which line tremours become evident, shapes, slopes, and sizes become less consistent, and quality or skill in writing becomes progressively poorer.

2. Handedness

a. Dextrality (i.e., right-handedness). The best estimate that one can make is that 89 percent of the population are right-handed insofar as handwriting is concerned. This is not to suggest that the same percentages will be found in the handedness of golfers, batters, sewers, rifle shooters or in any other activity in which a limb or an eye on a particular side of the body is chosen to direct or to execute the action. For many years, instruction in penmanship was tailored to the right-handed individual. The grasp of the writing instrument was prescribed and the orientation of the paper to the writer was directed. Notwithstanding these facts, right-handers appeared in small numbers that preferred the inverted hand posture (IHP) in which the axis of the pen or pencil was directed upwards and away from the writer rather than towards the writer. A much greater number of sinistrals use the inverted hand posture as has been noted elsewhere in this dissertation. For more information respecting handedness, see Section 58: Symbols of Sinistrality.

b. Sinistrality (i.e., left-handedness). See Section 58: Symbols of Sinistrality.

c. Ambidexterity. Some writers have been observed with the ability to write reasonably well with either hand. They are not great in number and among the recognized authorities only Harrison[54] has seen fit to comment on the circumstance. In his view, the individuals exhibiting this ability are probably persons who were sinistral in their early years, but who were persuaded to change to dextral in handwriting during the course of their schooling. Suffice it to say that, in most cases, the executions by the two hands will be similar in many respects, but divergences between them will be found in fluency or writing quality. The reason for this is suggested to be the lack of practise that one hand will experience owing to the writer's inclination to use the other hand as a matter of personal preference.

d. Grasp. The two postures of grasp are: (1) normal posture (writing instrument directed away from writer's body), and (2) inverted posture (writing instrument directed towards writer's body).

For information on this topic see Section 30.B.16: Pen Control, and Section 58: Symbols of Sinistrality.

E. Physical (Abnormal State of Health)

1. Handwriting as a Diagnostic Tool

Some, but not many, researchers have investigated the affect of particular illnesses upon handwriting.[55] Interest in this aspect of human conduct sprang from endeavours to employ handwriting as a diagnostic tool. Few of these studies have proven to be useful, largely due to the fact that, with the exception of one condition, i.e., Parkinson disease, the effects of illness upon handwriting have not been found to predate the occurrence of other symptoms of a disease that are more specific in their diagnostic values.

For the most part, the effects of an illness upon one's handwriting stem from and portray a loss of control or fluency. The result is a more erratic execution, exhibiting omissions, distortions (particularly in the formation of loops and compound curves), irregularities in the application of pressure, and general illegibility. There is a loss in such consistency as the writing previously had.

While writing skill and quality deteriorates progressively there are some recognizable aspects (i.e., habits) of the writing that persist. There is no logical reason for fundamental changes in writing habits to occur. Although the act of writing may involve a degree of effort, it is not deliberate and pressure controlled in the usual sense. It is never drawn.

Claims have been made that a change in writing can occur prior to the observation of other symptoms of a developing illness, but reliable, empirical data to support most of these claims is not available at present. On the other hand, in an attempt to develop a theory of handwriting deterioration that correlates with particular illnesses, a number of studies have been conducted.

Where correlations have been found, the usual medical symptoms of the condition are invariably present. The principal exception to this is the occurrence of micrographia in writing, that is a reduction in size, as much as two years prior to the onset of Parkinson disease in some 10 percent to 15 percent of the cases. Micrographia has also been observed in a few cases of cerebral syphilis and of schizophrenia, but there is no data respecting its relative frequency or its ability to predate the occurrence of other symptoms. Otherwise, writing has not yet provided reliable grounds for utilizing handwriting as a diagnostic tool.

Furthermore, while the deterioration of handwriting is an accepted consequence of many kinds of illness, and simply of ageing itself, there are few characteristics of this deterioration that may be identified with any particular illness, or family of illnesses. Age and illness eventually affects the neuromuscular coordination which alters the writer's ability to control the writing act. But the effect on the neuromuscular system is largely the same, regardless of the cause.

While a decline in writing ability and a loss of vigour is expected during illness, it is a fact that some signatures written during an illness do not reflect the expected writing weaknesses. This may be the case, particularly with illnesses of short duration and those that don't limit the individual's mobility or confine the person to bed. Being the most automatic element of a person's writing, signatures tend to be the most resistant to change. Consequently, some signatures written during an illness or recuperation are not altered sufficiently to hamper or to alter handwriting examinations.[56]

2.   *Illnesses — Organically Related*

a.   **Agraphia, aphasia, and dyslexia.**   Agraphia, aphasia, and dyslexia are closely-related conditions: *aphasia* is understood to be impairment of the power to use and understand words, although some definitions are broad enough to include impairment of all means of communication including speaking, reading, writing, and ciphering. We shall use the word in this latter sense. To be precise, however, *agraphia* is the term that identifies the inability to write, or to write in an orderly fashion, as the result of brain lesions. *Dyslexia* is a more limited disturbance of the ability to read.

Aphasia usually stems from head injuries, strokes, brain infections, and tumours. It is frequently accompanied by paralysis (hemiplegia) from which the upper limbs recover more slowly than the lower limbs. More often, paralysis will affect the right side of the body rather than the left requiring dextrals to learn to write with the left hand in the recovery process, and reportedly as many as 90 percent of them succeed, over a period of six months. Furthermore, improvement in writing seems more difficult to achieve than improvement in speech. Ordinarily, as might be expected, the skills in writing do not fully return.

Most forms of aphasia affect one's ability to write and abnormal genuine writing is often disputed, particularly with respect to wills and financial transactions. Furthermore, senile aphasics are frequently the victims of fraud or miscreant influence. Accordingly, the correct interpretation of the symptoms of aphasia may be helpful in the study of aphasic's writing and the peculiar manners in which the writing process can be impaired, when such cases arise. Furthermore, the current increase in life expectancy, the concomitant increase in strokes and the increase in motor accident injuries bodes a corresponding increase in the number of cases in which the writing of aphasics will be the centre of argument.

Unfortunately, the mass of literature, the special vocabulary, and conflicting medical theories make the subject difficult for the lay person to understand. Harris, however, has provided an excellent coverage of the disorder and its effects upon motor skills such as writing.

Aphasics do not seem to be effected by a single symptom, but experience a combination of disorders involving reading, writing, and speech. Cases of pure motor agraphia (i.e., able to read and speak, but unable to write) are rare. The disorder attacks a person in a highly individual manner, and generalizations are seldom possible. Recovery is equally diversified. Persons afflicted at an age under 50 make more progress than others, but it is never possible to forecast the results of therapy. Suffice it to say, recovery is never complete.

Writing suffers in either execution or composition or both. *Motor agraphia* is an inability to write due to an inability to form letters, but ability to spell is retained. *Amnesic agraphia (or agnostic agraphia)* is an inability to spell, but ability to manipulate the writing instrument is retained. *Paragraphia* is an inability to write the correct words, but the ability to copy text is retained.

When aphasia is accompanied by a degree of paralysis (hemiplegia), the individual must learn to write with the other hand. Recovery in penmanship ability varies but generally finds a plateau beyond which little improvement occurs.

Writing ability is not always effected by aphasia. Mental skills may suffer more than motor skills. Accordingly, the writing itself is not always a reliable indicator in recovered aphasics. The context, syntax, spelling, and repetition of names or words has to be considered. Peculiarities in arrangement and inconsistencies in spacing may also prove helpful.

As Harris reports, Head[57] classified aphasic disorders into four groups with symptomatic handwriting observations for each:

1. Verbal Defects — the person knows what he/she wants to say but is unable to express correct words. May not be able to write, but writing of signature is last ability to disappear and first to return upon recovery.
2. Syntactical Defects — the person speaks in a jumble of brief phrases, is confused and only isolated words are understandable. Composition is affected more than manual ability. Able to execute a letter, but unable to read it. Always executes a recognizable signature after experiencing the initial shock.

3. Nominal Defects — able to describe an object, but unable to name it. May be able to write his/her name. Can copy text but unable to compose.
4. Semantic Defects — may talk coherently in short phrases. Unable to compose or comprehend paragraphs. No gross effects on handwriting. May write in fast scrawl to avoid losing train of thought. Context may be confused, but writing is otherwise normal.

Although writing skill is often effected, one's inability to compose thoughts on paper is more frequently observed. The individual may be able to copy a text and produce a legible script, but writing from memory (e.g., the days of the week) may display great deterioration. It may result in the omission of small words such as articles, prepositions, and conjunctions, in accelerating the writing process sometimes to the point of skipping words, or in producing mirror writing. The execution of proper letter forms can be difficult. It seems that the capacity to manipulate the writing instrument can be retained, but there is a loss in the mental capacity to know what to write.

When writing is affected, and particularly in the case of the agraphic, the forms of letters may be irregular, and mistakes are made that may or may not be corrected. Alignments of letters and proportions are irregular that Neudert[58] attributes to disturbances of coordination.

Some individuals have difficulty with numbers, but others that are unable to speak, read, or write may be able to solve mathematical problems. Some can count in proper sequence, but are unable to comprehend the meaning of the numerals.

As aforementioned, the extent of the disorder varies greatly with the individual. From the reader's viewpoint a written product can be confusing owing to the interchanging of words with similar sounds, usually rendering the sentence meaningless at first glance. Beacom,[59] one of the few writers on this subject, offers several examples:

| beat — heat | stamp — damp | hair — chair | locks — socks | gun — pun |
| pair — fair | sty — sly | tool — cool | wet — met | take — cake |

Also provided are examples of misspellings of words containing double consonants, e.g., *leter* for *letter*, *hamer* for *hammer*, *mater* for *matter*, *seling* for *selling*.

Vowels may be changed and phonetically similar letters may be substituted: e.g., *watur* or *watar* for *water*, *fathur* or *fathar* for *father*.

Intermediate syllables may be omitted in long words, e.g., *rember* for *remember*, or *infortion* for *information*.

Occasionally, consonants are omitted, e.g., *quater* for *quarter*, *coner* for *corner*, or *kitche* for *kitchen*.

Questions of mental competence are difficult to decide. There may be a tendency to classify all aphasics as the same or equal, that is fundamentally wrong. It has been recommended that if an individual is capable of signing his/her name in a semilegible manner he/she should be allowed to do so, if the need for a signature arises.

Harris[60] also noted that speech therapists consider writing to be an important kind of therapy for aphasics, and for that reason often retain dated exemplars in a patient's file, thus, providing a ready source of specimen material, if needed, for handwriting comparisons at some later date.

Dyslexia, on the other hand, is a learning disability that becomes apparent in children as a difficulty in learning to read and later as a problem with spelling. It is thought to be a maturational defect that lessens as the child grows older and is capable of improvement or correction, especially with the proper remedial assistance. It is usually a genetically-determined condition, appearing to affect more boys than girls, that is unrelated to intelligence, teaching methods, emotional factors or sociocultural circumstances.

Probably because dyslexics usually respond to proper training and treatment during the period of maturation, the writing of the dyslexic is not frequently encountered in forensic handwriting identification. McCarthy,[61] one of the few document examiners that has written on the subject, did so principally because the matter was raised in cross-examination in a case in which a dyslexic was accused of an offence and the issue of dyslexia and disguise in the writings standards became of some significance.

The condition becomes apparent when children experience difficulty in learning to read, because for a percentage of them some letters may be reversed, (e.g., "b" for "d") or wrongly interpreted, (e.g., "cut" for "cat"). Difficulties in learning are increased in developing writing skills. Because it is a problem, handwriting is, invariably, slowly and carefully executed to achieve legibility and accuracy. Consequently, the child suffers scholastically in traditional schools where time is limited or essay type of answers to questions are often required.

The slow, careful writing process results in large, well formed letters with an almost vertical slant. Interletter spacing tends to be greater, reversals of letters sometimes occurs and "i" dots and "t" crossings are carefully formed and positioned, however, in some cases, these elements of the letters will be omitted completely. Misspellings and malformation of letters can make extended writings more difficult to comprehend. Dyslexics may err in transcribing words that sound the same but which have different meanings, such as *read* and *red*. Because of the difficulties experienced in writing, vocabularies in written text tend to be more limited, and the text itself tends to be brief.

Dyslexics sometimes make phonetic substitutions in their writings, producing *cum* for *come* or *rite* for *right*. Reversals are another common problem, in which *dog* is written as *bog*. Vertical reversals also occur in which letters such as "y" and "h" are exchanged, with the result that *yard* becomes *hard* and *hat* becomes *yat*. Reversals in sequence also occur, in which *rat* becomes *tar* and *form* becomes *from*. Mirror writing, in which the letters of an entire word are reversed, is also known to happen, but it is reported that it only occurs in sinistrals and only in cursive writing. Words with double letters are sometimes abbreviated by omitting one of the double letters. In other cases, all letters will be present but in improper order, or the spelling of the word may be completely irrational.

Dysgraphia is a severe writing problem related to dyslexia in which writing may be illegible, erratic, misshaped, and cramped. Cramping of writing is thought to be an endeavour to mask spelling errors. Copying is often a difficult task for the dyslexic or dysgraphic individual. He/she is prone to make the same types of errors in copying that are made in reading including reversals, omissions, and substitutions.

The acts of disguised and spurious writings require much more attention and concentration than is normal. The result is a decrease in writing speed, characterized by blunt initial and terminal strokes, heavy and even pen pressure, awkward movements, tremour, and irregular pen lifts. What should be of particular interest to examiners is that, as Hicks[62] reports, many of these characteristics can be exhibited by the normal writing of dyslexics.

In the taking of writing standards from the dyslexic, the difficulty they have in writing from dictation rather than from copy must be fully appreciated. The labour exhibited by the individual may be wrongly interpreted as an effort to disguise the writing act.

With specialized training over a period of time, many of the problems can be overcome and the effects of the disorder upon the individual's writing will be significantly diminished. This suggests, that in the study of dyslexic's writing, the need for contemporary standards is particularly important, and the significance of evidence of a slow, drawn execution must be properly assessed.

A number of well-known individuals have been reported to be dyslexics, including Nelson Rockefeller, Winston Churchill, Thomas Edison, George Patton, and Agathe Christie.

b. Alzheimer's Disease.   Alzheimer's Disease is an inexorable, degenerative, neurological disorder for which there is currently no known method of prevention or cure. It seems clear that the illness is not caused by hardening of the arteries. Nor is there any evidence that it is contagious. Studies have indicated that there might be a slight hereditary disposition in some families, possibly combined with undetermined environmental factors.

Between 2 to 3% of the population over the age of 60, and from 7 to 10% of those over 65 are believed to be affected by this illness. In the aging population in which we live, the numbers of diagnosed cases can be expected to double by early in the next century.

Behrendt[63] claims that Alzheimer's Disease accounts for 50 percent of all senile dementia cases. It is further subcategorized as (1) Senile Dementia Alzheimer's Type (SDAT), (2) Alzheimer's Related Dementia, and (3) Alzheimer's Disease.[64] Alzheimer's Disease is said to be senile dementia occurring before age 65, sometimes called presenile dementia. SDAT is said to refer to senile dementia occurring after age 65, a boundary that is an arbitrary one. Both conditions are pathologically similar. Alzheimer's Related Dementia refers to senile dementia arising from different causes, but sharing the same symptoms.

Alzheimer's Disease robs its victims of that which separates them from the lower orders of animal life — the complex memory bank that is the human brain. Losing memory doesn't simply end intellectual growth; It reverses the learning process. When memory fails us, we revert eventually to childhood and ultimately to infancy.

The symptoms are usually progressive, but the rate of memory loss varies from person to person. Infrequently, there is rapid deterioration. More often there are long periods in which little change is obvious.[65]

As one loses memory, one's ability to read and to write is also diminished. Words are forgotten, the thread of a conversation is lost, and there is a tendency for one to repeat him/herself endlessly. As the disease progresses, the individual finds it difficult to concentrate on and finish a given task, even one as straightforward as writing his/her own name. For a while, the individual may succeed if given a model to follow, and then the process becomes too complex for him/her to decide how to start.

Behrendt[66] reports that many persons experience the initial stages of mental degeneration, but retain physical strength and health such that their writing may display some symptoms of age, such as the omission or repetition of letters, the improper connection of words, but reveal no noticeable loss of writing skill or fluency. It seems that only when the mental ability to direct the motion of the pen is no longer available will the writing cease to be performed. Writings may be executed in any direction, but exhibit some evidence of strength and skill in the movement.

Diaz de Donoso[67] provides two sets of samples of the writing of persons with Alzheimer's Disease that illustrate the progressive loss of control over a period of time. As in many other situations, this loss of control affects the execution of curves initially, resulting in the production of angles or abrupt changes in direction in the writing line, and eventually in the demolition of recognizable forms.

As the condition progresses Alzheimer's patients experience emotional and personal changes in addition to cognitive impairment. They become confused, depressed, irritable, restless, anxious, and agitated. Drugs are administered to offset these symptoms, most frequently Librium and Valium. The examiner of a handwriting from an Alzheimer's patient must, therefore, ensure that standards are obtained that reflect, if possible, the medical and mental state of the individual at the time a questioned handwriting is alleged to have been executed.

c.   Amyotropic Lateral Sclerosis (ALS or Lou Gehrig Disease).   Literature respecting the effect of Amyotropic Lateral Sclerosis on writing is extremely limited. Information reported here has been gleaned largely from Conway's[68] report of a single case.

ALS is a degeneration of the muscles of the body resulting from a disorder of the nervous system. It is characterized by muscular weakness and atrophy, among other things, that are first evident in the hands and forearms in at least one-third of the cases. A progressive twitching is a common symptom, but one that does not necessarily affect the writing act as the twitching is spasmodic rather than constant, and not entirely beyond control by the individual.

ALS is progressive and continuous, and the increased weakness produces an increased inability to do simple things efficiently, such as writing. Progression of the disorder is relatively rapid, leading to paralysis and death in two to five years.

Physical pain is not symptomatic. Mental ability, intelligence functions, and awareness are preserved even to the terminal stages. Frustration and stress are experienced due to the inability to direct the muscular system.

The cause of ALS is unknown. The number of cases is estimated to be as many as 50,000 in the U.S.A. and Canada. It strikes more men than women and usually at the ages of 50 to 70 years. An exception to this was Lou Gehrig, of baseball fame, who contracted the disease in this thirties and died from it at the age of 38. In consequence, ALS is still commonly referred to as *Lou Gehrig Disease*. Occasionally, ALS occurs in families in a manner that suggests that there could be a genetic transmission.

Some variation in writing ability may be seen in subjects during the early stages of the disorder. With progression, the subject's ability to form and to connect letters is affected. Malformations and some illegibility occurs. The writer's intellectual function, however, may not be impaired. When difficulties in pen movement are encountered and malformations ensue, little attempt is made to conceal or correct the mistake.

d.   Arthritis.   Many physical factors may alter a person's writing, injuries and deformities to the hand and arm particularly. There are also diseases and injuries affecting the central nervous system; diseases and afflictions affecting muscles, ligaments, and joints of the writing hand that may temporarily or permanently alter one's writing. Perhaps the most common physical anomaly that tends to accompany age is arthritis and its related conditions.

Many millions of people suffer from more than one hundred different kinds of arthritis, and the number of victims increases annually with the extension of the normal life span. These ailments create degenerative changes in articular cartilages, particularly of the phalanges, resulting in pain and swelling of the joints. In advanced stages, they may lead to deformities in the hands and feet. Stiffness, discomfort, or pain may last from a matter of hours to one of days. Characteristic of the malady is that it afflicts more women than men.

Obviously, it is a condition that will have its effects upon writing, and one that may be encountered by the document examiner in the study of wills, deeds, bank documents, and perhaps in suicide notes. The question of import, in all cases in which alterations to the writing act may result from medical circumstances, is whether the effects may be misinterpreted as indications of a spurious execution of one kind or another.

Miller[69] studied the writings of 420 subjects suffering from a diagnosed intermittent arthritic condition whose ages ranged from 56 to 78 years of whom 72 percent were female. Writing samples were taken from each subject while not suffering from an arthritic episode and able to write in a normal manner. A second writing sample was taken from each while enduring an arthritic episode during which they experienced difficulty. A third and a fourth sample was also obtained under similar sets of circumstances.

The study of these samples disclosed that changes occurred at least 48 percent of the time in each of 12 writing indicia that were claimed to be the aspects of writing that would be closely examined in cases of suspected forgery. These included (1) line quality, (2) pen lifts/separations, (3) retouching/patching, (4) angle/pitch, (5) pen pressure, (6) size/proportions, (7) alignment, (8) diacritic placement, (9) stroke formation, (10) loop formation, (11) beginning/ending strokes, and (12) circle formations.

It was reported that significant changes were noted in the afflicted writings of arthritics, particularly insofar as:

- line quality, (97 percent of samples)
- size/proportions (93 percent of samples)
  - size was pictorially larger
  - spacings increased (greater concentration on letter forms rather than words, more deliberate or conscious writing)
- retouching/patching (82 percent of samples)
- loop forms wider, squared, shorter, with broken connections (78 percent of samples)
- terminal strokes, heavier pressure, blobbed endings (48 percent of samples)

Noteworthy is the author's explanation of the frequency of retouching and patching as attempts in the arthritic writing of signatures to match the quality of normal signatures. We would expect that corrections made of this sort would be crude and obvious, and more likely to reflect the writer's concern for readability rather than writing quality. If an inability to control the writing instrument was responsible for the error that needed correction, then the retouching or patching would be conducted with the same lack of control and would likely achieve the same cumbersome results. On the other hand, retouching and patching done in the course of simulations (forgeries) tends to be less obvious, more subtle, often requiring examination by microscope to confirm its existence.

It has been observed that in some cases, the discomfort of writing for arthritics is sufficiently severe that the grasp of the writing instrument is changed. It is clutched rather than held, and its orientation to the paper surface and the line of writing may be profoundly changed.

More significant findings in Miller's study respected the examinations of signatures, that were initially conducted without the extended writings or any knowledge of the malady suffered by the writers. In this case, 81 percent of the arthritic signatures were found to possess characteristics indicative of forgery. Of the signatures, 68 percent were classed as forgeries, and 32 percent were classed as inconclusive. However, when examiners were provided with all of the extended writings that accompanied the signatures, 92 percent of the findings were changed to authentic with the qualification *attempted to disguise*, presumably as an endeavour to account for the differences observed in the two sets of writings.

The results of the study prompted the author of the report to caution that, without the benefit of standards that are contemporaneous insofar as the state of the illness affecting them, differences in writings might be wrongly interpreted. Obviously, in cases involving arthritic writings, standards written a day before or a day after the date of execution of a questioned writing or signature, or of an arthritic episode, may not be completely satisfactory. He then uses these results as an argument in support of his contention that the examiner should be provided with as much information as possible respecting the writer's physical and mental health prior to an examination or study.

The results of Miller's study raise a number of questions, one of which would relate to the competence of the examiners that conducted the examinations and misinterpreted the arthritic signatures as "found to possess characteristics indicative of forgery." As we have stated elsewhere, there are differences between spurious writings of signatures and ailment altered executions by persons afflicted with such things as arthritis. The discomfort experienced by the act of writing, the effects of rigidity of the hand and fingers, the loss of fluency and speed of writing is evidenced in all elements of writing. The results are capricious and involuntary. The erratic movements produced are irregular, awkward, and unpredictable. On the other hand, spurious writings exhibit some intent to achieve a sufficiently fluent product to avoid attracting undue attention to its execution.

In most cases, the pain of arthritis is severe enough to discourage the individual from doing any writing, whatsoever, during an arthritic episode, unless absolutely necessary. Accordingly, the occasions on which severely-affected arthritic writings will come into question are extremely infrequent. Furthermore, we are aware that different writing instruments have a bearing on the discomfort the writer experiences, the smoother pens requiring the application of less pressure resulting in less discomfort.

e. **Cerebral palsy.** Mary Beacom,[70] to whom much is owed for the knowledge and examples that we have of the writing of (1) the blind, (2) the sinistral, (3) aphasics, (4) twins and quintuplets, provides a definition of cerebral palsy as "an abnormal alteration of movement or motor function arising from defect, injury, or disease of the nerve tissues in the cranial cavity."

Beacom claimed that it was estimated that there was a million cerebral-palsied individuals in the United States, and that a New Jersey study of 1,265 cases revealed that 46 percent of them were sinistral. Causes of cerebral-palsy include birth injuries, meningitis, encephalitis, or any other ailment that carries a very high fever. Many cerebral-palsy patients have learning disabilities, or hearing or sight disabilities, but the greatest incapacities experienced occur in the fingers and toes.

There are a lot of cerebral-palsied persons that are gainfully employed, even in the professions. While many are badly incapacitated, training and education for them is possible and available, and the signing of wills, credit card transactions and the writing of cheques are among the functions that some can perform.

Beacom's examples disclose lettering and cursive writings of varying qualities. Erratic movements and angularities are common. Consistency in form and in many other aspects of the writing is difficult for them to attain. Lettering or cursive writing tends to be large, in many cases. Better writing, however, can be achieved with practise and instruction. An example of excellent penmanship in the Palmer method from one case is included.

f. Diabetes Mellitus. Remarkably little has been written on the affects of diabetes mellitus and particularly low blood/sugar levels on writing performance, notwithstanding the fact, that it is a condition believed to be experienced by at least five percent and perhaps as much as eight percent of the populations of Canada and the United States, whether the persons afflicted are aware of their condition or not. Diabetes is an inability of the pancreas to supply sufficient insulin to maintain normal sugar concentrations in the blood stream to meet the body's needs for energy.

When sufficient insulin is not supplied by the pancreas, the concentration of sugar (glucose) in the blood increases progressively to the point where the individual becomes comatose. To prevent this, individuals may be injected with insulin subcutaneously to augment the supply from the pancreas and control the blood/sugar levels. While the body has a mechanism (a homeostatically regulated system) for ceasing the supply of insulin when not required, such a brake is not available to insulin that is injected and it continues to work regardless of the need for it. As a result, blood/sugar levels may move below the norms (hypoglycemia) and offsetting action must be taken by the individual in the form of the ingestion of food to moderate the sugar levels in the bloodstream.

Very low blood/sugar levels are known to affect human behaviour in many respects, sometimes resulting in serious accidents or even death. There are blood/sugar levels below the normal, but above the level of complete loss of personal control at which people can function sufficiently well to execute signatures and some writing or initials. These levels are usually of relatively short duration, i.e., 10 to 60 minutes, after which they progress to the point where control and consciousness are completely lost.

Towson[71] studied the effects of low blood/sugar levels on handwriting. The study endeavoured to find the kind of impairment of the writing that results. It also researched the ability of handwriting examiners to identify correctly the writing products under these circumstances with their proper authors. Writing samples were obtained from 28 subjects at normal blood/sugar levels and at two levels of hypoglycemia induced by insulin injections.

Towson's findings were that there is a highly significant correlation between low blood/sugar levels and writing impairment. Furthermore, when impairment occurs competent writing examiners (13 RCMP Lab personnel) were able to make a significant number of correct judgments as to writing impairment. Notwithstanding the impairment that occurred, examiners were able to correctly associate the writing samples with their proper authors more than 98 percent of the time.

Impairment of the writing was exhibited by the following:

- A deterioration in line quality
- An uncertainty of letter forms, overwriting and wrong letter forms

- Deterioration of and abbreviation of letter forms
- Failure to maintain alignment or a consistent baseline
- An increase in pen lifts, pen stops and hesitations
- An increase in the overall size of the writing
- An inconsistency in writing slant

Of interest to this particular investigator was the fact that three of his subjects proved to be reactive hypoglycemic patients that tend to register abnormally high or low blood/sugar levels three to five hours after the ingestion of food. Reactive hypoglycemia is a condition of fluctuating blood/sugar levels that may occur in some cases in the early stages of the development of the disease. It can result in impairment of the handwriting, seemingly in a contradiction of the blood/sugar levels the subject may experience.

Apart from reactive hypoglycemia, the impairment of writing will occur with diabetics almost exclusively in connection with low blood/sugar levels, known medically as hypoglycemia. Elevations of blood/sugar levels, known as hyperglycemia, have no particular effect upon writing other than that which might be expected as the individual progresses slowly into a comatose or sleep-like state.

g. Multiple sclerosis (MS).   Multiple sclerosis (MS) is a widespread neurological disorder, a chronic progressive disease, with a variety of symptoms, some of which are noticeable in handwriting. Eighty-five percent of those with the disease are first diagnosed between the ages of 20 and 40 years of age. Sixty percent of the victims are women. Duration of the disease may be more than 25 years, and is increasing as technology increases life spans. MS follows a ritual of remissions and exacerbations in which the time between exacerbations decreases as the illness progresses. It is believed that the target of MS is myelin in the central nervous system, the fatty insulating sheath surrounding the axons (long single nerve-cell process) of many nerves in the body.

In a study of the writing of 23 MS patients, Wellingham-Jones[72] found that the disorder did, in fact, alter the writing of the subjects in a measurable fashion. Writings displayed irregularity, angularity, decreases in lateral expansion, a decrease in speed of execution, tremour, and distortions. Word spacing and alignment were also affected. Fewer flourishes and narrower left margins were also noted. The study suggested that patients had difficulty in manipulating the pen and making flexible formations and connections. In general, it may be said that control and fluency are diminished.

Wellingham-Jones' subjects were 7 men and 16 women, from the United States and Canada, between 29 and 75 years of age, that had been medically diagnosed as having MS. The writing samples were collected over a period of five years and consisted of extended writings of the subject's own generation. In descending order of frequency of occurrence, their physical symptoms included leg and arm weakness, coordination problems, tremour, fatigue, and visual problems. Obviously, the effects upon handwriting are consistent with the physical symptoms that the individuals experienced.

h. Ailments procreating tremulous writing.

- Parkinson's disease
- Acquired agraphia
- Linguistic agraphia

- Nonlinguistic agraphia
- Spatial agraphia
- Progressive supranuclear palsy
- Huntington's disease
- Essential tremour

Parkinson's disease (PD) is considered to be a disease of the middle and older ages. The affect of the ailment upon handwriting is frequently profound, but equally profound is the affect of medications upon the uncontrollable tremour that is characteristic of the advanced stages of the disease.

Two other less-common conditions produce tremour, Progressive supranuclear palsy and Huntington's disease. These, with Parkinson's disease and Essential tremour, are classed as extrapyramidal disorders to identify them with the part of the neural system within the brain to which they are attributed.

Progressive supranuclear palsy is much like akinetic Parkinson's disease, but has other characteristics observed in the face and eyes including the paralysis of eye movements.

Huntington's disease is hereditary and is characterized by large jerks of the arm or hand occurring at random. It is called *choreic* because the legs are always moving as if dancing.

Essential tremour is a monosymptomatic illness that is common to all age groups and equally distributed between the sexes. It is considered to be a *postural tremour* (i.e., present but much less noticeable during the maintenance of steady posture) that is accentuated by voluntary movement creating disabilities during activities such as writing. The handwriting is typically large and tremulous in contrast to the effects of the tremour of Parkinson's disease. It is unlike the tremour of PD that is referred to as a *resting tremour*, present when the limb is at rest, but disappearing during action (see Section 57: Signs of senility).

In a study by Boisseau, Chamberland, and Gautier[73] of the writings of 35 individuals suffering from these disorders, no particular characteristics were found in the handwriting that could be associated with any one of the four disorders. The administration of drugs was seen to affect a few letters or the general quality of the writing but the majority of the elements of writing were not significantly altered. In their view, tremours due to neurological conditions tend to be more gross and erratic changes to or interruptions in the pen movement, that become more obvious with the progression of the responsible disorder.

To fully understand Parkinson's disease and its effects upon handwriting we must try to grasp some of the neurological thinking of the last two decades. To do so, we must acquaint ourselves with the extrapyramidal system and the affect upon it of neuroleptics, that we have tried to describe under Section 37.F.: Medications.

Parkinson's disease is a degeneration of cells within the brain in an area called substantia nigra. As a result, there is a decrease in the amount of the neurotransmitter dopamine present in the cells that causes disturbances of a particular function and results in interference of motor control. The principle symptoms of the disorder are (1) akinesia — the loss of muscular power, (2) bradykinesia — abnormal slowness of movement and fatigue, (3) rigidity — resistance to muscular action, and (4) tremour — oscillations of the hand at frequencies of three to five oscillations per second (some sources report 2 to 3 per second) when the limbs are at rest. One of the classic features of this tremour is its presence during rest and its disappearance on purposeful movement. The tremour usually is aborted by the initiation of any willed act, but tends to reappear a few moments later, despite the continuation of the action. In most cases, the tremour is less pronounced during action than it is during rest.

Clinically speaking, Parkinson's disease is described as a disorder of the scaling of movements that are slow, but do not exhibit obvious problems in the selection and sequencing of muscle activity. Patients have normal patterns of muscle activation, but require more cycles of muscle activity to produce their movements.[74]

Males and females are equally affected by the disorder that tends to run in families 10 to 15 percent of the time. Its characteristic tremour is said to be asymmetrical, affecting one hand or both hands or both hands and the trunk. The disorder is progressive over periods of 10 to 20 years and, although manual skills are gradually lost, senses and intellect are not damaged.

Handwriting difficulties have been suggested as one of the earliest symptoms of the disease. Patients have been observed to have problems with the size or speed of writing and report difficulties in the writing of signatures, as on cheques. It appears that the effects are exhibited principally by the motor programs, since spelling and letter formation are not usually impaired.

Acquired disorders of handwriting are subjects that have not been extensively studied except, perhaps, insofar as their relationship to Parkinson's disease. Furthermore, Acquired agraphia, a decline of writing performance, and, in the extreme, an inability to write at all, has not been accounted for as a primary sensory or motor dysfunction like blindness or paralysis. Agraphia is most often associated with lesions of the cerebral cortex, but no writing centres have been clearly identified.

According to Margolin and Wing,[75] linguistic agraphias are essentially disorders in spelling portrayed by letter omissions, substitutions, additions, and letter reversals, although letter morphology (i.e., forms) is preserved according to Marcie and Hecaen.[76] Nonlinguistic types of agraphia entail the production of faulty letter forms with intact spelling, and may entail a breakdown in morphology and in the sequencing of movements. Neither of these occur with PD.

As noted by Hecaen, Penfield, Bertrand, and Malmo,[77] some instances of agraphia are due to perceptual disturbances, caused by brain lesions, and may produce a particular combination of writing changes termed *spatial agraphia*. These changes include ascending or descending alignments, widening of the left margins and letter repetitions, but these also are not characteristic of PD.

Handwriting disturbance is frequently an early manifestation of PD and is widely accepted as a part of its clinical picture. The incidence, severity, and modifying features of the phenomenon are now becoming better understood. Certain characteristic size changes have led to the use of the term *micrographia* to identify and describe the condition in the writing of some Parkinsonian patients.

Micrographia, described as a reduction in the size of letters that is often progressive along a line of writing and/or down a page of writing (Figures 12 and 13), with no higher-order problems such as spelling or stroke errors, was first noted by Pick.[78] Several other investigators, most of whom published their results in German in the early 1920s, have studied the phenomenon from the viewpoint of its etiology, i.e., its cause or origin, and its effects in the writing of Parkinsonian patients.

Kinner,[79] in suggesting possible causes, reported the occurrence of micrographia in cases of cerebral syphilis and central arteriosclerosis. Gilmour and Bradford[80] reported two cases in a study of 17 patients undergoing drug treatment for schizophrenia.

Figure 12 Micrographia in Parkinson's Disease. In 10 to 15 percent of patients their writing progressively diminishes in size and lateral expansion, with years of duration. In this case: A — 1984, B — 1987, C — 1992, D — 1996, E — 1997, F — 1998. The 1997 and 1998 writings were made following a change in medications. PD was confirmed in 1993.

McLennan, Nakano, Tyler, and Schwab[81] tried to describe the phenomenon more precisely and establish its incidence among patients with PD by studying the records of 800 Parkinsonians from which 95 cases exhibiting micrographia were selected. From this the incidence of micrographia was estimated at 10 to 15 percent.

Cheque signatures proved to be the standard source of writing samples executed prior to the diagnosis of PD. The study disclosed that patients with micrographia are unable to sustain normal sized writing for more than a few letters, if at all. The tendency was obvious to write progressively smaller as the end of the line approaches. Renewed effort produces temporarily larger writing, but this soon diminishes to even smaller writing than previous

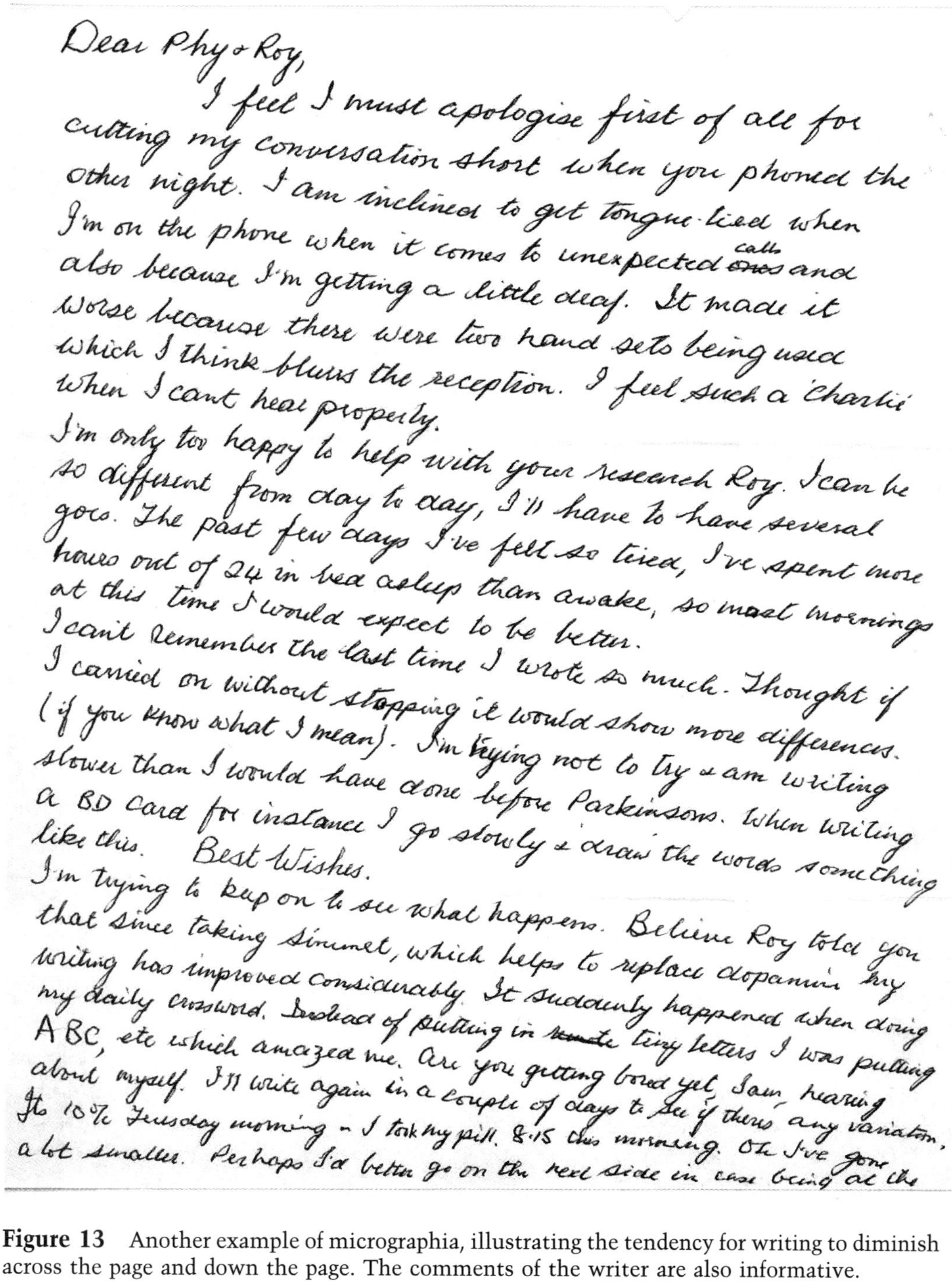

Dear Phy & Roy,
I feel I must apologise first of all for cutting my conversation short when you phoned the other night. I am inclined to get tongue-tied when I'm on the phone when it comes to unexpected calls and also because I'm getting a little deaf. It made it worse because there were two hand sets being used which I think blurs the reception. I feel such a 'Charlie' when I cant hear properly.
I'm only too happy to help with your research Roy. I can be so different from day to day, I'll have to have several goes. The past few days I've felt so tired, I've spent more hours out of 24 in bed asleep than awake, so most mornings at this time I would expect to be better.
I cant remember the last time I wrote so much. Thought if I carried on without stopping it would show more differences (if you know what I mean). I'm trying not to try & am writing slower than I would have done before Parkinsons. When writing a BD card for instance I go slowly & draw the words something like this. Best Wishes.
I'm trying to keep on to see what happens. Believe Roy told you that since taking Sinemet, which helps to replace dopamine my writing has improved considerably. It suddenly happened when doing my daily crossword. Instead of putting in tiny letters I was putting ABC, etc which amazed me. Are you getting bored yet, I am, hearing about myself. I'll write again in a couple of days to see if there's any variation. Its 10% Tuesday morning – I took my pill. 8.15 this morning. Oh I've gone a lot smaller. Perhaps I'd better go on the next side in case being at the

Figure 13 Another example of micrographia, illustrating the tendency for writing to diminish across the page and down the page. The comments of the writer are also informative.

executions. Occasionally, patients can write larger with the assistance of guidelines, but without such guidelines the writing becomes small.

McLennan and his associates charted the course of the changes in the writing of 17 patients from 6 years before and after the onset of PD. This study revealed that changes were observed at least one and sometimes two and three years in advance of the onset and diagnosis of the disorder, and that micrographia developed in some cases four to five years following. Micrographia appears to be a very definable symptom in at least 5 percent of all PD patients, and in as much as 30 percent of those patients who will later develop more advanced micrographia.

No correlation has been found between micrographia and the side of the body affected by PD. Neither is it related to the handedness of the writer. Furthermore, tremour and rigidity that are two of the four principal attributes of PD show no correlation with micrographia. Former writing characteristics are reasonably well preserved. McLennan reports that many samples of micrographic signatures would, if enlarged, superimpose well on other earlier written signatures. Suffice it to say that the phenomenon of micrographia remains unexplained. It can only be said that it originates within the central nervous system.

Tarver[82-83] on the strength of a study of 16 PD subjects claimed that he found no support for the existence of micrographia in the writing of his subjects. At an occurrence rate of 10 to 15 percent that McLennan reported, out of an examination of the writings of 800 Parkinson's disease patients, it is not surprising that small samples might contain no evidence of its existence. Furthermore, there are sources[84] other than McLennan that have confirmed its actuality (for a personal encounter by this author, see Figures 12 and 13).

There are few instances wherein handwriting may be used as a diagnostic tool by medical practitioners in advance of other symptoms. Parkinson's disease is one of the exceptions. Although the percentage of patients displaying micrographia is small, it may serve as a specific prodrome of what is developing or will develop in a period of up to four years.

The administration of L-dopa makes a greater amount of dopamine available to the brain, a therapy that can have spectacular results permitting those otherwise disabled limbs to function near-normally for 10 to 20 years, although in some cases the efficacy of the drug can decline in 5 to 7 years. In a study of 91 patients by Stellar, Mandell, Waltz, and Cooper,[85] 75 percent showed marked or partial improvement. They reported that mild tremour was lessened in a small number of cases, and that rigidity, bradykinesia, facial masking, voice, gait, and handwriting disturbances were often greatly diminished, although toxic side effects occurred in a high percentage of patients.

Patients with Parkinson's disease, however, may experience dyskinesia (excess, unintentional or involuntary movement) as a side effect of drug therapy. These unwanted movements can occur in the process of handwriting and interfere with letter formation. Problems of letter formation and spelling are also observed in other disorders and must be carefully judged if to be used as indicators of PD.

Much research has been and continues to be conducted in an endeavour to better understand the difficulties experienced by Parkinsonian patients in the execution of writing. Teulings and Stelmach[86] attempted to quantify writing deficits in Parkinson patients through the use of signal-to-noise analyses. Phillips, Stelmach and Teasdale[87] endeavoured to study the extent to which several measures of handwriting quality might discriminate between the handwriting of two control groups (young adults and elderly) and Parkinson patients, particularly as a result of the tremour that Parkinson patients usually experience.

While not yet too productive from the viewpoint of the handwriting examiner, these studies need to be monitored for the knowledge they provide respecting the neuromuscular process that underlies the writing act.

F. Medications

Although medications have been suggested as the cause of changes in writing by many authors, little literature that describes their effects precisely crosses the desks of handwriting examiners. Gilmour and Bradford (1987), cited in the discussion of Parkinson's disease, found that neuroleptic drug treatments for schizophrenia did produce changes in individual writings, but the nature and extent of these changes were quite variable between subjects. Furthermore, the nature of the change insofar as line quality varied from an improvement to a deterioration.

It was their conclusion that:

"The effect of drugs (i.e., medications) on handwriting is dependent on the type of drug administered, the individual's sensitivity to it, and the points at which the handwriting is sampled during drug treatment."

Neuroleptics, that are drugs used in psychiatric treatment of some disorders can cause a reversible Parkinson-like state, exhibiting the characteristics of rigidity, akinesia and tremour at rest. The principal medications used to treat *Parkinson's disease* are (1) L-Dopa, to control the motor abnormalities, and (2) anticholinergics, to control the resting tremour. The first can cause choreic movements called Dopa-induced dyskinesia. The second may result in impairment of recent memory.

The principal medications used for Essential tremour are propanolol and primidone, that decrease the amplitude of the oscillations during movement. In Huntington's disease, neuroleptics are said to slightly relieve the frequency and amplitude of choreic movements, but at the expense of some Parkinson-like symptoms.

In what Gross claims to be, "The most sophisticated, significant and replicated research in the area of drug-induced handwriting changes," Haase[88] studied the relationship between the therapeutic response to a neuroleptic agent and the handwriting changes that are produced. For some time prior to his study, antipsychotic drugs were and still are frequently administered to patients with mental illness (e.g., schizophrenia) to render them more amenable to psychotherapy. Sometimes there is a slowing of the motor activity typically found in patients with Parkinson's disease.

It was Haase's theory that small doses of neuroleptic drugs produce fine motor changes often not apparent to the clinician. These changes manifest themselves in the handwriting of the patient. Haase suggested five primary handwriting changes indicative of fine motor neuroleptic effects: stiffening, cramping, size reduction, a lessening of slant, and shakiness. His terms, however, warrant some thought. Stiffening and cramping are certainly conditions of the hands, but say little of the effects manifest in the writer's script. Shakiness presumably produces a degree of tremour in the written line that may be the meaning the author intended.

Beginning in 1954, Haase demonstrated that the efficacy of chlorpromazine, reserpine, and analogous drugs is associated with their effects on fine extra-pyramidal movements as seen in handwriting. Studies of other drugs with similar actions have confirmed his findings.[89] The neuroleptic effectiveness of a drug depends on the affinity the drug has for the extrapyramidal system and on the dose given. But let us be clear as to what the extrapyramidal system is.

The term *extrapyramidal system* was first used in 1912 by S.A.K. Wilson to refer to those parts of the central nervous system (CNS) that were concerned with motor disorders. The term is used clinically and anatomically to refer to one of the three principle motor systems in humans: the pyramidal system, the cerebellar system and the extrapyramidal system. Each is thought of as a separate entity and considered to be an independent structure. Lesions (abnormal structural changes due to injury or disease) within each of these systems result in distinctive disturbances in motor activity.

The fibres of the pyramidal system pass through the medullary pyramid. Injury to this tract produces paralysis of voluntary movement. The cerebellar system comprises the cerebellum and the pathways to and from it. It is believed to be concerned with the coordination of movements as opposed to the initiation of voluntary movement. Lesions of this system result in tremour with movement, incoordination, dyssynergia, and ataxia. The extrapyramidal system is made up of a number of paired nuclei and associated pathways. The term *basal ganglia* is often used as an alternative term. Lesions of the extrapyramidal system often result in abnormal movements (e.g., tremours) that usually are present at rest. There are also abnormalities of station and postural reflexes. This system is thought to be concerned particularly with the maintenance of posture as opposed to initiation or coordination of voluntary movement.

The term *extrapyramidal disease* ties together a number of clinically defined disease states that share a number of related symptoms. The clinical signs and symptoms that help to tie these disease states together fall into four groups: (1) hyperkinesia (abnormal involuntary movements), (2) akinesia (slowness or poverty of spontaneous movement), (3) rigidity, and (4) loss of normal postural reactions. The principle disorder within this group was described by James Parkinson, after whom it was named, as: "Involuntary tremulous motions with lessened muscular power in parts, not in action and even when supported with a propensity to bend the trunk forward and to pass from a walking to a running pace, senses and intellect being uninjured."

The Haase study compared the action of four stronger neuroleptic drugs to chlorpromazine insofar as their effects upon handwriting. These included prochloperazine, trifluoperazine, fluphenazine and thioperazine. The results were essentially the same for all drugs and were observed to be the extrapyramidal handwriting manifestations of (1) stiffening, (2) diminution (reduction in vertical dimension), and (3) narrowing (reduction in horizontal dimension). Weeks after treatment with the drugs, the writings of the patients returned to normal fluency and dimensions.

Hart[90] outlined some of the adverse effects of three groups of drugs: antipsychotic drugs, tranquilizers of the phenothiazine type, and potent synthetic analgesics. Of the first group, lithium is mentioned as one having adverse effects upon muscular coordination that may be accompanied by tremour. Tranquilizers may have adverse effects depending upon the dosage of the drug and the duration of administration. A central nervous system disorder called *tardive dyskinesia* may occur that is characterized by involuntary movements of the extremities, among other things. These involuntary movements may result in a jerky writing that is abnormal in appearance. This may be accompanied by blurred vision that would also have its effects upon writing. The effect of drugs within the third group, classed as potent analgesics, is not as great upon the central nervous system as the first two, but blurred vision or double vision can occur that will have a detrimental effect upon handwriting to varying degrees.

The point of Hart's paper is that the effects of these drugs may resemble the characteristics of disguised writing, and need to be carefully studied. They are drugs that can be easily obtained and may be taken for maladies other than those for which they are usually prescribed. She lists the drugs within the three groups as taken from the *Physicians' Desk Reference, 1985*, available to any examiner.

The importance of discriminating accurately between disguise and the effects of these drugs stems from the position taken by the courts in the United States that the presence of disguise in court-ordered writing samples is tantamount to contempt. This places an onus upon the examiner to responsibly determine whether a disguise has been deliberately attempted.

Concern respecting the risk of misinterpreting the effects of drugs and some medical conditions on handwriting is often expressed. The risk is admittedly present when the material under examination and/or the competence of the examiner is limited. Hopefully, the treatment of disguise (q.v., Section 52) provides some of the guidelines by which reliable discriminations can be made.

It has been reported that a study, by Glogowaski[91] at the Orthopedic Department of the University Hospital in Munich, of the affect of treatment with Valium on the handwriting of 27 patients, aged 8 to 16 years, resulted in a demonstrable improvement in coordination of the handwriting mechanism. While the changes are described as, "An objective qualitative improvement in handwriting," we have little information as to the nature of the illnesses for which the subjects were being treated or precisely what changes were responsible for the improvement.

G. Infirmity

1.   *Time Changes or Age and Senility*

It is an accepted fact that an individual's handwriting changes throughout a lifetime. As we stated earlier (see Section 37.D.1.: "Maturity, Practise, and Development), handwriting progresses through four stages in the course of a writer's life. It begins with (1) the formative or learning stage, that is followed by (2) the impressionable or adolescent stage, sometimes called *the puberty stage.* The third stage is (3) the maturity stage that is the longest and in which the writing is most consistent. The fourth stage is (4) that of degeneration, sometimes referred to as *the senility stage,* during which writing quality, pen control, and fluency suffer progressively. Changes may occur during any of these stages depending on circumstances, but particularly so and understandably during the early stage when it is developing, and the late stage when it is deteriorating. The progressive deterioration of writing skills in the elderly, i.e., the fourth stage, is the topic that has been covered in response to the question: What are the signs of senility and age (see Section 57)?

There are also temporal or short term changes occurring in handwriting resulting from illness, disease, or injury, the effects of which diminish or disappear completely with recovery from the condition.

In recent years (1970s and 1980s), a style of writing has been noted, particularly among adolescents, that has been given the name *bubble writing* largely because of its predominant roundness. In addition to being round, it is usually large, vertical, and compacted in that little space is provided between letters for connections. Relative heights of letters or of elements of letters are also distinctive in that supralinear and infralinear letters (those having ascenders and descenders such as "d," "f," "g," "h," "j," "k," "l," "p," "y," and "z") do not have vertical dimensions that are not much greater than linear letters (i.e., "a," "c," "e," "i," "m," "n," "o," "r," "s," "u," "v," "w," and "x"). The staffs of the letters "d" and "t," that tend to be looped by many other writers, are retraced as copybook prescribes. The letter "b" frequently exhibits a clockwise structure in the bowl, giving it a printed appearance. Other tendencies that seem to be associated with bubble writing include the construction of the "8" as two separate circles, the dotting of the "i" with a small circle, and the production of punctuation marks as circles. It is a writing style popular with over 40 percent of the female subjects, all of whom were adolescents, in studies reported by Masson[92] and Cusack.[93]

Some bubble writers are consistent and characteristic, and are readily identified with the class. There are also numerous other writings that are described as a modified round style or modified bubble writing, that are not as clear and distinct a group of variations from conventional writing practises, and exhibit greater individuality than the classic bubble writing tends to do.

While little information is available on the subject, it is suspected that bubble writing may be a passing phase in the maturation of the writing of adolescents and particularly females. It occurs at a stage in writing development when experimentation is common. Individuals that use it are known to be able to revert to a more conventional writing style at will. Its origin is vague, but its transmission among adolescents is undoubtedly a matter of intentional imitation. Noteworthy is the fact that bubble writings by different individuals may have a great deal of resemblance and their differentiation can be extremely difficult and precarious.

A Canadian study of the writing of adolescents within the native populations of Saskatchewan by MacInnis[94] failed to find any significant evidence by which native and nonnative adolescents might be distinguished from one another. Some distinction was observed, however, between male and female subjects of his study that may be related to the prevalence of a roundness in the writings of females of both natives and nonnatives, not unlike the modified bubble writing mentioned above.

2.   *Guided Hands*

a.   Deathbed Signatures.   With the decline in writing ability, illness effects the writing consistency. Because of a decline in coordination, signatures will vary between themselves in somewhat erratic manners. There may be the occurrence of extraneous, false strokes. As quality diminishes, letter designs, relative heights, slant, and alignments lose their former stability. The product may appear deceptively false.

The affect of a terminal illness upon writing may not be consistent. Relapses occur even at times close to death when, for unknown reasons, or due to medication, spells of writing control may return, perhaps to be lost again hours or days later. As illnesses progress, however, and death approaches, one's ability to control a writing instrument diminishes to the point where little that is legible can be executed. Normally, there are few signatures written when in this condition, but almost too frequently, it is at this stage when wills are made or revised and the choice of beneficiaries and bequests become subject to dispute.

Terminal illnesses, in their last stages of progress, produce signatures that are often accompanied by false starts. The writing is erratic and letters are poorly formed. Terminal strokes and final elements of these signatures may display more fluency than any other part as though there was some relief from a strenuous ordeal. The study of these signatures for the purpose of identifying the handwriting is made more difficult by the lack of contemporaneous standards, that is usually the case.

b. Guided-Hand or Assisted Signatures. Often enough it is alleged that a second party endeavoured to assist the testator in executing a signature by holding the hand and guiding it through the movement. For a broad treatment of this topic, see Section 51, respecting the attributes of assisted-hand and guided-hand signatures.

Some recent studies have been directed at the corrective effects upon a subject's handwriting ensuing from drugs and other medications administered to the patient. There are, for example, drugs that will suppress the tremours characteristic of Parkinson's disease for periods of time but not permanently. For further information see Section 37.F: Medications.

H. Mental State of the Writer

1. Emotional Stress

Most of the leading document examiners have allowed that emotional stress can have an effect upon one's handwriting but little has been written to describe precisely what the effect may be. McNally[95] depicted it as a condition that interferes with fluency in that it makes the process a more conscious endeavour, increasing care and attention to details. The product is more drawn than written. In short, it possesses many of the characteristics that are observed in spurious writings or signatures, and for that reason, caution in its study must be exercised.

The element of emotional stress is not only a condition peculiar to the questioned writing, but can enter into the execution of the so-called request writings of a subject. Its effects can be noted in some exaggeration of the range of natural variation that a writer may exhibit. It has been suggested that stress in some degree has a part in most of the cases that an examiner studies. Girouard[96] notes that research has demonstrated that stress affects both our physiological functioning and our psychological health. She states, "For this reason it is difficult to isolate the effects of stress, for it has an influence on the organism as a whole."

Frederick[97] sought evidence of stress in the writings on suicide notes and employed graphologists to distinguish genuine suicide notes from fabricated productions. If differentiation could be made, some indications of the evidence for doing so might be available. Three sets of judges were used, graphologists, detectives, and secretaries, to examine 45 sets of notes. The results disclosed that the detectives, and secretaries were not significantly better than chance in selecting true suicide writings, but the graphologists did achieve a significantly better score.

Of import to us is the fact that none of the five graphologists that achieved the better scores was able to identify the particular aspects of the genuine suicide notes that prompted their selection. Reactions to emotional stress, then, vary with the individual and no predictions can be made as to the impact of its influence.

For further information respecting the effects of physical stress or fatigue the reader is referred to Section 38.C.4.

2. Nervousness

Although nervousness has been suggested as a cause of fine tremours or some lack of fluency in writing, no particular studies have been conducted on its effects of which we are aware. Understandably, the induction of a nervous state in a subject in a test situation may not be easily accomplished.

According to Carney,[98] the authors Elble and Koller discuss task specific tremours such as orthostatic tremour and primary writing tremour. Primary writing tremour is defined as a tremour that is induced primarily, but not only, by the act of writing and other similar motor activities, such as handling a knife or screwdriver. Carney also notes that alcohol, inderal, and mysoline all reduce primary writing tremour, but they are ineffective upon other tremours such as that of Parkinson's disease. Whether primary writing tremour is, in fact, a consequence of a state of nervousness in some individuals is not known, but might warrant further investigation.

3.   *Instability (Mental Illness)*

In studies to test the hypothesis that patients' signatures may have a useful potential in the making of psychiatric diagnoses, some evidence has been found that the signature size in the manic group and in the organic mental disorder group of patients at one hospital was significantly larger than that of control groups.[99]

To our knowledge, little has been reported respecting the writing of individuals experiencing Multiple Personality Disorders (MPD). This is a psychopathological and psychophysiological phenomenon that is offered with increasing frequency as an explanation for certain kinds of conduct or actions. It is described by Schwid and Marks[100] as a dissociative disorder in patients that have experienced childhood abuse or neglect and that are dissociation-prone.

MPD is defined as two or more distinct personalities that exist in one person, each of which is dominant at a particular time. Switching from one personality to another occurs when the subject has difficulty dealing with specific conflicts, and feels threatened by a particular situation. Of importance to document examiners are the reports that the handwriting of the subject changes notably when the individual switches from one personality to another.

In view of this change, problems arise for document examiners in ensuring that questioned and specimen writings are executed under the same prevailing personality. Our experience has included cases in which an examination and study of handwritings was required to determine which of the personalities indicated by the writings was likely to be the executions of the normal or nonafflicted personality. The psychiatrist's interest in this determination rested in the desire to administer medication for the condition only during the normal nonafflicted state of the patient.

It is reported that, according to material offered by Cohen and Giller,[101] people with dissociative disorders tend to be intelligent, creative, resourceful, and articulate. Authorities agree that multiple personality patients suffer a great deal and are generally relieved when their disorder is diagnosed.

Schwid[102] provides examples of the writing of four of some nine personalities of one subject, in which there are size changes, proportion changes, quality changes, and changes in lateral expansion. Despite such changes, in the cases of which we are aware, given adequate standards, document examiners have been able to associate the writings of the various personalities of a subject as the products of one and the same physical being.

I.   Injury

The effects of injury upon one's ability to write are as practical as one might expect. Injuries that impair the movement of the writing arm or hand will afflict the control of the writing instrument. The result, usually, is erratic movements or sudden changes in direction, or an obvious inability to execute some finer or more complex maneuvers of the pen or pencil.

It is important to bear in mind that injuries are usually temporary. Unless some permanent damage to the arm or hand has occurred, writing ability will be regained over a period of time, although depending on the injury recovery may not be 100 percent. The dates on which the injury occurred and on which the questioned or standard writings were executed may become important and should be noted. The quality of the questioned writing must be consistent with the ability of the writer on the particular date of its purported execution.

It is also possible for a person to suffer mentally, if not physically, from an injury. Mental injury will be evident in tremour in writing, usually of a fine nature. Its duration is not likely to be as long as a physical injury, if one accompanies it.

References

1. Osborn, Albert S., *Questioned Documents*. 2nd Ed. (Albany: Boyd Printing Co, 1929), p 168.

2. Hilton, Ordway, *Scientific Examination of Questioned Documents*. Revised ed. (New York: Elsevier/North-Holland, 1982), p 144.

3. Osborn, Albert S., *Questioned Documents*. 2nd Ed. (Albany: Boyd Printing Co., 1929), p 191.

4. Masson, Janet Fenner, *A Look at the Hand Lettering of Draftsmen*. Presented at the meeting of the American Society of Questioned Document Examiners (San Jose, 1990).

5. Herrick, Virgil E., *Comparison of Practices in Handwriting Advocated by Nineteen Commercial Systems of Handwriting Instruction* (Madison, Wisconsin: School of Education, University of Wisconsin, 1960).

6. Beacom, Mary S., *A Survey of Handwriting Systems by States and Territories in the U.S.A.* Presented at the meeting of the American Society of Questioned Document Examiners (Ottawa, 1965).

7. Towson, C. S., *Handwriting Instruction in Canada*. Private communication (1975).

8. Moon, H. W., A Survey of Handwriting Systems by Geographic Location. *Journal of Forensic Sciences*, 1977; 22(4) pp 827-834.

9. Vastrick, Thomas A., *1993 ASQDE Handwriting Systems Survey*. Presented at the meeting of the American Society of Questioned Document Examiners (Ottawa, Canada, 1993).

10. Harrison, Wilson R., *Suspect Documents*. (New York: Frederick A Praeger, 1958), p 296.

11. Miller, J. T., Departure from Handwriting System. *Journal of Forensic Sciences*, 1972 16:1: pp 107-123.

12. Moon, H. W., A Survey of Handwriting Styles by Geographic Location. *Journal of Forensic Sciences*, 1977 22; 4: pp 827-834.

13. Regent, James, *The Significance of Characteristic Uniformity in the Identification Process*. Presented at the meeting of the American Society of Questioned Document Examiners (Arlington, VA, 1989).

14. Huber, Roy A., *Interpolating First Principles of Handwriting Identification*. Presented at the 1st International Meeting on Questioned Documents, i.e., the 3rd meeting of the IAFS (London, 1963).

15. Kiser, Roy F. and Torres, Barbara, *"Like" Letter Substitution — How Dependable?* Presented at the meeting of the American Society of Questioned Document Examiners (Colorado Springs, CO, July 1975).

16. Bellomy, David A., *Barrio Script Mexican-American Gang Writing*. Presented at the meeting of the American Society of Questioned Document Examiners (Savannah, GA, September, 1986).

17. Haywood, Charles L., *Continuing the Search for the Black "J" and "W"*. Presented at the meeting of the American Society of Questioned Document Examiners (Orlando, 1991).

18. Boisover, Gale, *Signatures of Teenage French Girls*. Presented at the meeting of the American Society of Questioned Document Examiners (Ottawa, Canada, 1993).

19. Tweedy, Janis S., *A study of Hmong Handwriting*. Presented at the meeting of the American Society of Questioned Document Examiners (Chicago, 1995).

20. Anderson, Diane J., *Foreign Influence and Identifying Characteristics of Writing Systems*. Presented at the meeting of the Canadian Society of Forensic Science (Halifax, 1982).

21. Muehlberger, Robert, *Class Characteristics of Hispanic Writers in the Southeastern United States*. Presented at the 40th annual meeting of the American Academy of Forensic Sciences (Philadelphia, February, 1988).

22. Caywood, Douglas A., *The Impact of Foreign Education on the Handwriting of Individuals Learning English as a Second Language* (Ottawa Canada: Shunderson Communications, 1997), 280 pages.

23. Ziegler, Larry F., *Nigerian Handwriting*. Presented at the joint meeting of the American Society of Questioned Document Examiners and the Southwestern Association of Forensic Document Examiners (Aurora, CO, September 1988).

24. Behrendt, James E., *An Examination of Exemplars Taken from Nonenglish Speaking Writers*. Presented at a meeting of the American Society of Questioned Document Examiners (unknown date).

25. Torres, Barbara, *A Study of Vietnamese Class Characteristics*. Presented at the meeting of the American Academy of Forensic Sciences (February, 1987).

26. Hilton, Ordway, *Scientific Examination of Questioned Documents*. Revised ed. (New York: Elsevier/North-Holland, 1982), p 145.

27. Stangohr, Gordon R., Comments on the Determination of Nationality from Handwriting. *Journal of Forensic Sciences,* 1971 July; 16; 3: pp 343-358.

28. Caywood, Douglas A., *Handwriting Styles Based Upon Cultural Education*. Presented at the meeting of the International Association of Forensic Sciences (Wichita, KS, 1978).

29. McCarthy, William F. Jr., *A Collection of Modern European Handwriting Systems*. Presented at the meeting of the American Academy of Forensic Sciences (Orlando, 1982).

30. Sommerford, Albert W., *A Manual for Examiners of Questioned Documents*. United States Post Office Department, 1953.

31. Kroon-van der Kooij, Leny N., *Differences Between Handwriting Characters in Relation to Various Nationalities*. Presented at the 11th meeting of the International Association of Forensic Sciences (Vancouver, 1987).

32. Raibert, M. H., *Motor Control and Learning by the State Space Model*. (MIT: unpublished doctoral dissertation, 1977).

33. Wellingham-Jones, Patricia, Mouth-Writing by a Quadriplegic. *Perceptual and Motor Skills,* 1991; 72: pp 1324- 1326.

34. Wann, John P. and Athenes, Sylvie, Structural Influences in Writing Script: An Analysis of Highly Skilled Footwriting. *Proceedings of the 3rd International Symposium on Handwriting and Computer Applications* (Montreal, 1987).

35. Thomassen, A. J. W. M. and Teulings, Hans-Leo H. M., The Development of Directional Preferences in Writing Movements. *Visible Language,* 1979 XIII: 3: pp 299-313.

36. Kelly, James H., *Effects of Artificial Aids and Prostheses on Signatures.* Presented at the meeting of the American Society of Questioned Document Examiners (Colorado Springs, CO, 1975).

37. Savage, G. A., *A Study of the Handwriting of the Deaf and Hard of Hearing.* A paper produced for the Crime Detection Laboratories of the Royal Canadian Mounted Police (October, 1977).

38. Hart, Beatrice Ostern and Rosenstein, Joseph, Examining the Language Behaviour of Deaf Children. *The Volta Review,* 1964 January; pp 17-27.

39. Vernon, M., Fifty Years of Research on the Intelligence of the Deaf and Hard of Hearing. *Journal of Rehabilitation Deaf,* 1968(b); 1; pp 1-11.

40. Kerr, L. Keith and Taylor, Linda R., Linguistic Evidence Indicative of Authorship by a Member of the Deaf Community. *Journal of Forensic Sciences,* 1992 November; 37: 6: pp 1621-1632.

41. Boyd, John, Comparison of Motor Behaviour in Deaf and Hearing Boys. *American Annals of the Deaf,* 1967; 112; 4: pp 598-605.

42. Todd, Irby, Handwriting of the Blind. *Identification News,* 1965 January: pp 4-9.

43. Beacom, Mary S., Handwriting of the Blind. *Journal of Forensic Sciences,* 1967 January; 12; 1: pp 37-59.

44. Bleuschke, A., *Handwriting of the Blind.* (Royal Canadian Mounted Police Crime Detection Labs: unpublished paper 1968), p 59.

45. Lindblom, B., Identifying Characteristics in the Handwriting of the Visually Impaired. *Canadian Society of Forensic Science Journal,* 1983 December; 16: 4: pp 174-191

46. Duane, William D., *Macular Degeneration (A Low Vision Impairment) and its Effect on Handwriting.* Presented at the meeting of the American Society of Questioned Document Examiners (Arlington, 1989).

47. Morgan, Marvin and Zilly, Pam, Document Examinations of Handwriting with a Straight-edge or a Writing Guide. *Journal of Forensic Sciences,* 1991 March; 36: 2: pp 470-479.

48. Stevens, Viola, *Similarities in the Handwriting of Members of One Family as Compared to Unrelated Groups* (unpublished paper, February, 1964).

49. Dahlberg, Gunnar, An Explanation of Twins. *Scientific American,* 1951 January.

50. Beacom, Mary S., A Study of Handwritings by Twins and Other Persons of Multiple Births. *Journal of Forensic Sciences,* 1960 January; 5: 1: pp 121-131.

51. Gamble, D. J., *The Handwriting of Identical Twins* (unpublished paper prepared for the Royal Canadian Mounted Police Crime Detection Laboratories, 1978).

52. Hecker, Manfred R., *The Change of Handwriting as a Process of Identification.* Presented at the meeting of the International Association of Forensic Sciences (Bergen, Norway, 1981).

53. Bellomy, David A., *Barrio script.* Presented at the meeting of the American Society of Questioned Document Examiners (Colorado Springs, CO, 1975).

54. Harrison, Wilson R., *Suspect Documents.* (New York: Frederick A Praeger, 1958), p 450.

55. Wellingham-Jones, Patricia, Characteristics of Handwriting of Subjects with Multiple Sclerosis. *Perceptual and Motor Skills,* 1991; 73: pp 867-879.

56. Hilton, Ordway, Consideration of the Writer's Health in Identifying Signatures and Detecting Forgery. *Journal of Forensic Sciences,* 1969 April; 14: 2: p 159.

57. Head, Henry, *Aphasia and Kindred Disorders of Speech* (New York: Hafner Publishing Co., 1963).

58. Neudert, Gerth, *The Importance of Agraphia in Expert Opinions on Handwriting.* Presented at the 1st International Meeting in Questioned Documents (April, London, 1963).

59. Beacom, Mary B., *Handwriting by Aphasics* (an unpublished paper, probably presented at the meeting of the American Society of Questioned Document Examiners, 1970).

60. Harris, John, *A Questioned Document Examiner Looks at Aphasia, Its Accompanying Handwriting Disorders, and Resulting Case Problems.* Presented at the meeting of the American Society of Questioned Document Examiners (Toronto, Canada, 1969).

61. McCarthy, William F. Jr., *Dyslexia and Its Effect on Handwriting.* Presented at the meeting of the American Society of Questioned Document Examiners (Nashville, 1984).

62. Hicks, A. Frank, *Dyslexia: Its Effect Upon Handwriting.* Presented at the meeting of the American Society of Questioned Document Examiners (Washington, August 1996).

63. Behrendt, James E., *Problems Associated with the Writing of Senile Dementia Patients.* Presented at the meeting of the American Society of Questioned Document Examiners (Boston, 1982).

64. Strub, R. I., Alzheimer's Disease — Current Perspectives. *Journal of Clinical Psychiatry,* 1980 April; 41: 4: pp 110- 112.

65. Trueman, Peter, When Memory Disobeys. *Ottawa Magazine,* 1991 May; pp 13 and 14.

66. Behrendt, J. E., Alzheimer's Disease and Its Effect on Handwriting. *Journal of Forensic Sciences,* 1984 January; 29: 1: pp 87-91.

67. Diaz de Donoso, Gladys Ruiz, *Alterations in Handwriting Caused by Alzheimer's Disease and Abuse of Drugs.* Presented at the meeting of the American Society of Questioned Document Examiners (Ottawa, Canada, September 1993).

68. Conway, James V. P., *Effects of Aging and Physical/Mental Disorders on Handwriting, Part 1 — Amyotropic Lateral Sclerosis.* Presented at the meeting of the American Society of Questioned Document Examiners (Montreal, September 1985).

69. Miller, Larry S., Forensic Examination of Arthritic Impaired Writings. *Journal of Police Science and Administration,* 1987; 15: 1: pp 51-56.

70. Beacom, Mary, Handwriting of the Cerebral-Palsied. *I. D. News,* 1968; 18: 11: pp 7-15.

71. Towson, C. S., *Low Blood Sugar Levels and Handwriting.* (Ottawa: an unpublished report of a study conducted at the Royal Canadian Mounted Police Crime Detection Lab, 1970).

72. Wellingham-Jones, Patricia, Characteristics of Handwriting of Subjects with Multiple Sclerosis. *Perceptual and Motor Skills,* 1991; 73: pp 867-879.

73. Boisseau, M., Chamberland, G., and Gauthier, S., Handwriting Analysis of Several Extrapyramidal Disorders. *Canadian Society of Forensic Science Journal,* 1987; 20: 4: pp 139-146.

74. Phillips, J. G., Steimach, G. E., and Teasdale, N., What Can Indices of Handwriting Quality Tell Us About Parkinson's Disease? *Human Movement Science,* 1991; 10: pp 301-314.

75. Margolin, David I. and Wing, Alan M., Agraphia and Micrographia: Clinical Manifestations of Motor Programming and Performance Disorders. *Acta Psychologica,* 1983; 54: pp 263-283.

76. Marcie, P. and Hecaen, H., Agraphia Writing Disorders Associated with Unilateral Cortical Lesions. *Clinical Neuropsychology*, K. L. Heilman and Valenstein (eds) (Oxford: Oxford University Press, 1979), pp 92-127.

77. Hecaen, H. W., Penfield, W., Bertrand, C., and Malmo, R., The Syndrome of Practagnosia Due to Lesions of the Minor Cerebral Hemisphere. *Archives of Neurological Psychiatry*, 1956; 75: pp 400-434.

78. Pick, A., Ueber Eine Eigentumliche Schreibstorung. Mikrographie in Folge Cerebraler Erkrankung. *Prag. med. Wschr.*, 1903; 23: pp 1-4

79. Kinner, Wilson S. A., The Croonian Lectures on Some Disorders of Mobility and of Muscle Tone with Special Reference to the Corpus Striatum. *Lancet, ii*, 1925; pp 1-10.

80. Gilmour, C. and Bradford, J., The Effect of Medication on Handwriting. *Canadian Society of Forensic Science Journal*, 1987; 20: 4: pp 119-138.

81. McLennan, J. E., Nakano, K., Tyler, H. R., and Schwab, R. S., Micrographia in Parkinson's Disease. *Journal of the Neurological Sciences*, 1972 15: pp 141-152.

82. Tarver, James A., *Micrographia in the Handwriting of Parkinson's Disease Patients*. Presented at the meeting of the American Society of Questioned Document Examiners (Aurora, CO, 1988).

83. Tarver, James A., *Micrographia in the Handwriting of Parkinson's Disease Patients*. Presented at the meeting of the American Academy of Forensic Sciences (Las Vegas, 1989).

84. Margolin, David I., The Neuropsychology of Writing and Spelling: Phonological, Motor and Perceptual Processes. *The Quarterly Journal of Experimental Psychology*, 1984; 36A: pp 459-489.

85. Stellar, Stanley, Mandell, Stanley, Waltz, Joseph M., and Cooper, Irving S., L-Dopa in the Treatment of Parkinsonism. *Journal of Neurosurgery*, 1970 March; 32: pp 275-280.

86. Teulings, Hans-Leo and Stelmach, George E., Control of Stroke Size, Peak Acceleration and Stroke Duration in Parkinsonian Handwriting. *Human Movement Science*, 1991; 10: pp 315-334.

87. Phillips, J. G., Stelmach, G. E., and Teasdale, N., What Can Indices of Handwriting Quality Tell Us About Parkinsonian Handwriting? *Human Movement Science*, 1991; 10: pp 301-314.

88. Haase, Hans J., Extrapyramidal Modifications of Fine Movements — A "Conditio Sine Qua Non" of the Fundamental Therapeutic Action of Neuroleptic Drugs. *Revue Canadienne de Biologie*, 1961 June; 20: 2: pp 425- 449.

89. Simpson, G. M., Controlled Studies of Antiparkinsonism Agents in the Treatment of Drug-Induced Extrapyramidal Symptoms. *Acta Psychiatry — Scandinavia Supplement*, 1970; pp 44-51.

90. Hart, Linda J., *Illusions of Disguise*. Presented at the meeting of the American Society of Questioned Document Examiners (Montreal, 1985).

91. Glogowski, G., Aktuelle Probleme der Spastischen Extremitätenlähmung. *Münchner Mediz-inische Wochenschrift* (Jahrgang, 1963), p 2448.

92. Masson, J. F., A Study of the Handwriting of Adolescents. *Journal of Forensic Sciences*, 1988 January; 33: 1: pp 167-175.

93. Cusack, Christine T. and Hargett, John W., *A Comparison Study of the Handwriting of Adolescents*. Presented at the meeting of the American Academy of Forensic Sciences (Philadelphia, 1988).

94. MacInnis, S. E., Adolescent Handwriting — Native Versus Nonnative. *Canadian Society of Forensic Science Journal*, 1994; 27: 1: pp 5-14.

95. McNally, Joseph P., *Signatures Under Stress*. Presented at the meeting of the American Academy of Forensic Sciences (Dallas, TX, 1974).

96. Girouard, Patricia, *The Influence of Stress on Writing*. Presented at the meeting of the International Association of Questioned Document Examiners (Toronto, 1986).

97. Frederick, Calvin J., An Investigation of Handwriting of Suicide Persons through Suicide Notes. *Journal of Abnormal Psychology*, 1968; 73: 3: pp 263-267.

98. Carney, Brian B., *A New Tremor in Handwriting*. Presented at the meeting of the American Society of Questioned Document Examiners (Ottawa, 1993).

99. Baig, Mizra S. A., Shen, Winston W., Caminal, Edouardo, and Huang, Tsung-Dow, Signature Size in the Psychiatric Diagnosis: A Significant Clinical Sign. *Psychopathology*, 1984; 17: pp 128-131.

100. Schwid, Bonnie L. and Marks, Lynn Wilson, Forensic Analysis of Handwriting in Multiple Personality Disorder. *Advances in Handwriting and Drawing: a Multidisciplinary Approach*, Faure, Keuss, Lorette, and Vinter, eds. (Paris: Europia Press, 1994), pp 501-513.

101. Cophen, B. and Giller, E. eds. *Multiple Personality From the Inside Out*. (Maryland: The Sidran Press, 1991).

102. Schwid, Bonnie L., *Forensic Case Study: Multiple Personality*. Proceedings of the joint meeting of the International Graphonomics Society and the Association of Forensic Document Examiners (London Canada, 1995).

The Intrinsical Variables of Handwriting

9

The reader is reminded of the comments respecting "The Variables of Handwriting" that will be found as an introduction to Chapter 8, Section 37.

38. What Are the *Intrinsical Factors* (i.e., Those Within a Writer's Control, Adopted by Choice) Influencing Handwriting?

A. Imitation

Beyond the various writing systems to which we are exposed, we are influenced by what we see and like in the writing of others. In many cases, our tastes turn us in certain directions, or our artistic sense expresses its preferences. Imitation is probably one reason why the handwritings of classmates, close relatives, and those who have lived together for a long period of time, often have so much in common.[1] Certainly, as we have noted elsewhere, sinistrality and the adoption of the inverted-hand posture, have some factors to them that may be hereditary or be simply the imitation of parents or siblings.

Hecker[2] described the changes that occurred in one 16-year-old German female's writing that occurred coincidentally with her development of interest in the black civil rights movement in America. Her fixation with the problems of the blacks was expressed by a change to an Afro hairstyle, a change in tastes in music, and a change in social relationships to those involving coloured Americans. Hecker suggests that the change in writing is a product of a personality change produced by a problem of the time.

It is typical of the acquired handwriting styles occurring in particular teacher-pupil relationships, in professional and social groups, and in the fashionable or popular writings of a social strata at a particular time. The permanence of the changes will likely depend on the duration of the interest in the group or individual adopted as the model.

B. Circumstantial

There are factors influencing writing that vary with circumstances under which the writing is executed. Osborn, Harrison, Hilton, and Ellen have each commented on the affect that circumstances may have upon writing, usually under the broad caption of "writing conditions." For the most part, these comments have dealt with extreme circumstances and the claims that have been made in defence of unskillful simulations.

For example, the writing is claimed to have been executed against walls, on the roofs of cars, in moving vehicles, upon one's knee, or on a clipboard held in the hand. It is well-known that writing up against walls, on the roofs of cars, in moving vehicles, writing on one's knee, or while standing without stable support for the document, or in a confined space at the bottom of a document are conditions that often occur with genuine executions of *recipient* or attesting signatures. Consequently, the use of these conditions as excuses for apparently poor writing is understandable.

It is also well-known that writings under these circumstances may be badly distorted, erratic, and imprecise. Retraces are difficult to execute, bowls of letters are not carefully closed.

There are other circumstances, or variations in normal circumstances, such as changes in the nature of the writing instrument or changes in the nature of the document being signed are less extreme and, accordingly, their effects upon the writing may not be as pronounced.

There are six circumstantial factors that an examiner should consider:

1. The writing media employed,
2. The writing posture, including stance and orientation to paper,
3. The writing purpose,
4. The writing space available and location,
5. The writing surface and support
6. The writing environment

1.   The writing media employed.   Osborn[3] devoted a full chapter to "The effect of the writing instrument upon writing as a means of identifying it (i.e., the instrument)," and discussed the products of various types of split nib pens and pencils of the time. Insofar as their effects upon the writing of an individual, he had only to say that the flexibility of the split nib permitted one to consider pen pressure and pen position relative to the written stroke as significant matters of habit for the writer and, accordingly, important elements in the study of writing for the purpose of identification.

His comments respecting pencil writing dealt particularly with the fact that it tended to conceal many aspects of writing that were important to consider in the process of identification, including line quality (tremour and fluency), line continuity, pen lifts, pen position, retouching, overwriting, and even pen pressure. Furthermore, pencil writing, particularly with hard leads, usually requires more pressure, that is a greater point load, than split nib pen writing to produce a pronounced line, and allowance must be made for this in the handwriting study and comparisons.

The split nib, but less flexible, fountain pen has replaced Osborn's steel nib pens, and technology has provided a plethora of other kinds of writing instruments for today's use that range from ball point pens (using viscous ink), porous point pens having felt, fibre or plastic tips to roller ball pens (using less viscous or fluid inks). The pencil is still with us, but its use in documents falling under the scrutiny of forensic science is undoubtedly less frequent than a century ago.

More recent studies by Mayther[4] and Hilton[5] of the writing produced by these relatively new instruments have enabled us to discriminate reasonably well between their products. The task of handwriting identification is not assisted, however, as the softer but more stable instrument points tend to conceal matters of line quality (tremour and fluency), line continuity, pen position, pen pressure, pen lifts, and even overwriting. Thus, in many respects, the problems provided by the pencil have been revived. And the absence of a pen track, as occurs with felt tips, is reminiscent of the old quill pens.

In two short studies (34 subjects and 19 subjects) of the work of felt tip pens of different widths, Masson[6-7] has reported that the affect of this instrument upon the writing is merely superficial. In a few cases, however, in which a very broad-tipped pen induced the writer to increase the size of his/her writing, although the increase was not extreme. More substantial problems arose from the difficulty in following the continuity of the line made by the felt-tip pen, and establishing unequivocally the occurrence of pen lifts or disconnections.

Of importance to us in this dissertation is that, as Mayther pointed out, the influence of the writing instrument upon the writing of an individual is rarely very significant. If there is an observable difference between the writings of a given person made with different instruments, it may be due as much to that person's personal preference for, or comfort in using, a particular instrument as it is to the effects of the instrument itself.

2.   The writing posture.   The affects of extreme conditions are highly variable and little can be proffered as to what may be expected in any given situation. Nevertheless, Grant[8] reported on a distorted writing alleged to have been written under unusual circumstances. It was claimed that it was written while standing at a cluttered counter when the writer was holding a weight of unwieldy tools in the other hand. Standards were obtained when circumstances were duplicated and a remarkable correspondence in the writings was revealed.

3.   The writing purpose.   The writing of signatures is a more conscious act when being inscribed on formal or legal documents of some significance. More care is exercised in the site of the signature, if only because the act is at least witnessed if not directed by other parties. For some people, care is simply warranted, and given to the execution of the signature, that results in a better quality of writing, pictorially, than it might otherwise exhibit. Consequently, the care that the writing of the signature receives usually improves letter forms and regularity at the expense of fluency.

Case experience seems to be the source of evidence in support of these statements. Osborn, Harrison, and Hilton barely mention the fact that the purpose of the document may have an affect upon the writing. Nevertheless, it is only reasonable to assume that, for persons not frequently required to sign formal documents, the act of doing so will be a matter or greater importance and, consequently, a more conscious endeavour.

4.   The space available and location on the document.   There is a normal assumption made that writing within a confined space will have an affect upon the writing, but surprisingly few studies have been conducted to determine precisely the manner or manners in which confinement alters the written product. It is a question that arises more frequently, and for obvious reasons, with respect to signatures that are required to be applied to printed forms of various kinds that seem to exhibit little respect for people with longer names. There are other occasions when extended writings are voluntarily confined by their nature when they are executed as interlinear insertions in a handwritten or typewritten document.

Morton's study[9] of signatures provides some empirical data that indicates that a limitation of space may affect a signature in one of two fashions: (1) a reduction in lateral expansion only, that is, a compaction of the writing length with little change in vertical dimension, or (2) a miniaturization of the writing in both vertical and horizontal directions, particularly if a vertical limitation was imposed upon the signature. Although inter-letter spacing is shortened when lateral expansion is reduced and long commencement and terminal strokes may be altered, there is little change to other aspects of the writing such as form or relative heights and no evidence of a significant change in writing fluency. On the other hand, as might be expected, miniaturization has little affect upon any of the writing aspects other than absolute size. Horizontal limitations did not result in miniaturization in all cases, however, vertical limitations invariably did.

A recent study of the signatures of 62 subjects by Bey and Ryan[10] may be in conflict with Morton's findings. The report of these authors indicates that a reduction in the vertical space available does have an affect upon the relative heights of some letters, that they say was to be expected. They also report that they found a strong relationship between the space available and "the occurrences of variation in a person's signature." This is not variation in the sense in which the term is normally used, but rather an observable change in five writing characteristics: letter spacing, legibility, relative heights of uppercase to lowercase letters, relative heights of uppercase to uppercase letters, and change in baseline tendencies.

Like Morton, these authors were endeavouring to identify some of the changes that might occur in signatures written in a confined space, for which allowance must be made in the study and comparison of handwriting. When due allowance is made, neither of these studies suggest that the task of identification is made overly difficult or impossible.

5.   **The writing surface/support — stability, smoothness, and resilience.**   Many claims have been made in defence of poor simulations that the questioned writings, usually signatures, were executed under extreme conditions, but little research has been conducted to dispute these claims, except as might be demanded by particular cases. For the most part, the circumstances of these cases are extreme, as in writings on the flesh of dead bodies.

There are, however, numerous other sets of circumstances, closer to the norm for writing, that may alter the written product. In one of the few studies of which we have record, Hecker[11] examined the effects of four writing instruments, ball point pen, pencil, fibre-tipped pen, and felt-tipped pen, against ten difference surfaces and using two different weights of paper, copy paper (25-39 g/gm) and typing paper (60-90 g/gm).

As might have been expected, his results showed that effects depended upon:

- the thickness of the paper
- the type of writing instrument employed
- the hardness of the supporting surface

He observed that, with thinner papers, the structure of the supporting surface was more apparent in the writing, but depended to some extent on the nature of the writing instrument. He also noted that sharply-pointed instruments (pencils) pierced papers more frequently on soft support surfaces than others.

The fine structure of a support surface became particularly obvious when a soft pencil was used. On the contrary, fibre-tipped pens provided the least evidence of the nature of the support surface. When the "amount of relief" to the surface is near negligible there is little deflection of the instrument and the surface structure is not well reproduced, but hard pencils may enhance it. Regularly-patterned surfaces tend to produce regularly-patterned marks in the paper as the instrument runs across it.

Fibre-tipped pens were found to provide fewer clues to supporting surface characteristics and felt-tipped pens provided the fewest, as one might have expected. Coarse-structured surfaces interfered with the movement of the writing instrument to the extent that, on occasion, garland movements were converted to arcadic. Extremely coarse structured support surfaces such as corrugated cardboard provided different effects depending on the orientation of the writing to the direction in which the ribs of corrugation run.

Hecker cautions against misinterpreting deflections in pen movement that may be simply accidental characteristics as indications of irregularity in support surfaces. He also notes that embossing on the reverse (back) of the document viewed with oblique lighting may yield evidence as to the surface structure on which the document was written.

Major irregularities in surface structure, such as cracks in a table top, can cause the writing instrument to change direction and follow the irregularity some distance. Such is a localized or isolated circumstance that may not be repeated if the writer takes evasive action. Hecker's studies were made of general conditions of surfaces, that might affect any or all lines of writing across them.

Other reports in our collection by Leung[12] and Totty[13] describe the examination of lettering (and Chinese writing) on the soft skin surfaces of corpses. Taylor and Hnilica[14] describe the examination of lettering present on a corpse that they found to be self-inscribed prior to death. Brown[15] describes the examination of writing on the hard metal surfaces of fairly large copper tubing (2-in. diameter). In all cases, some evidence was found by which the lettering could be associated with the authors, although not definitively. Many factors had a bearing on these examinations, including the effects of the movement of the flesh with the writing instrument, and the curvature of the pipe. A principal obstacle in all cases was in obtaining appropriate standards for comparison. The reader is left to consider the methods he/she might devise to overcome such an obstacle.

6. The writing environment, — lighting, temperature, and wearing apparel. Numerous environmental circumstances are suggested or claimed as conditions responsible for changes in writing, particularly of signatures. Frequently, the condition alleged must be considered, not in isolation, but in combination with some other condition. Subdued lighting may have little effect on the writer, unless he/she suffers from impaired vision. Low temperatures may have little effect, unless writing is executed while wearing apparel on the hands that is heavy or restrictive, or unless body temperature is diminished and shivering is induced.

Canadian winters provide ample opportunity for these environmental conditions to be studied, and we have found that the general effect is a matter of writing instrument control. When finger movement is restricted, the control of fine writing movements is restricted, and some change in their fluency or quality of execution will occur. Writing becomes more of a whole hand or forearm movement that is often unfamiliar to the writer and may, therefore, have its effects upon the fine movements that are required, until some adjustment to the circumstances is made by the writer in the course of longer texts or successive signatures.

C. Temporal States (Induced Conditions) of the Writer

In an excellent, if academic, review of 30 papers on the subject of drug induced changes to handwriting, Gross[16] describes, and criticizes when necessary, the work of different investigators, including Purtell and Hilton. His introduction sets out the reasons for the interest in the subject as being the tangible and measurable effects of many pharmacological agents in altering the user's muscular coordination:

> "…complex motor skills, including handwriting, have frequently been utilized to assess these temporal malfunctions. There are several advantages in utilizing handwriting…. First, the analytic sample is easily obtained and provides a permanent record. Second, since handwriting is one of the most complex, coordinated human activities, intrusions upon the nervous system should logically produce alterations in one's usual writing pattern. Finally, since it is such a well-habituated act, handwriting should provide a conservative measure of the actions of pharmacological agents."

The potential of handwriting in research involving therapeutic administrations of antipsychotic and anti-Parkinsonian drugs has become evident. The use and abuse of many different pharmacological agents in contravention of the law and the consequences of such abuse within a forensic arena has stimulated the interest of handwriting examiners called upon to identify the writings of the users that become the perpetrators of other crimes. It comes as no surprise, then, that the drug most often studied in relation to handwriting changes has been alcohol.

Gross's criticisms of the studies conducted are directed largely at the methods employed. They deal with design components that work of this kind should address. First: many of the studies were conducted without the administration of placebos, necessary to verify that effects are legitimate, not psychosomatic or resulting from other variables. Second: few studies employed the double-blind technique in which neither the subject nor the investigator is aware of whether treatment or placebo is being administered, to control expectation effects. Third: the statistical analyses of data were often descriptive rather than inferential. Thus, the differences in the effects on handwriting could not be accurately or objectively assessed.

These criticisms notwithstanding, there is a degree of consistency in the results reported respecting the effects upon handwriting that serve as a guide to examiners. This guide encompasses where and what changes occur, whether or not such changes are measurable at low, or indeed, any level of drug influence. Furthermore, as Gross himself advances, "It appears that psychological stability influences the degree and direction in which one's handwriting is apt to change following drug ingestion." Despite the variation in the location and extent of change, however, the discriminating elements involved remain the same.

1. Alcohol

For reasons that we need not explore, volumes have been written on handwriting and alcohol (perhaps test subjects are easy to find). The fact remains that questions frequently arise in matters under litigation respecting the effects of drugs, particularly alcohol and hallucinogens, upon the writing of the individual, that has prompted numerous studies to be conducted.

There may be no other aspect of handwriting identification that has received as much attention and undergone as much research, so called, as the affects of alcohol on handwriting. It may be because it is so frequently proffered as a prevailing condition at the time of signing a document, when the writing itself becomes the centre of dispute. The argument contending that the writer was intoxicated at the time is proposed to contest the writer's knowledge and responsibility for his/her actions.

It could be that in research on alcohol and writing, it is not difficult to muster a body of willing subjects not wanting financial remuneration for their time or talents. Furthermore, in recent years we have seen the introduction of instruments for the testing of breath alcohol levels in vehicle operators. Understandably, the need has emerged to train users of the equipment in real life situations to develop their skills in order to obtain valid and reliable results from test processes. This has made available a body of subjects whose capabilities in numerous other tasks, such as writing, can be conveniently and coincidentally tested or measured.

Whatever the reason for the interest in the subject, the question respecting the influence of alcohol on writing continues to be posed and examiners should be prepared to deal with it.

Initially, we should clarify certain facets. Alcohol is a toxic substance. It is a poison to the human body. When ingested in any amount (e.g., the first social drink) it results in a state of intoxication (i.e., poisoning), almost immediately. This is not to say that, at this point, intoxication affects behaviour. Nor is it to say that the level of intoxication is detectible to an observer or is a fact of which the subject is conscious. Furthermore, drunkenness is a state of impairment of the faculties, not too precisely defined, usually applied in a nontechnical sense to high levels of intoxication.

Ethanol, the kind of alcohol that is consumed as a beverage, is a reasonably moderate poison and one that the body can tolerate or contend with in limited quantities. While in the body, it is a depressant drug affecting the central nervous system much like anesthetics such as ether or chloroform. The alcohol, of which we are speaking, ethanol, is often referred to in the vernacular as *grain* alcohol. The more lethal kind of alcohol found in many household items, and sometimes consumed by addicts with devastating if not deadly results, is methanol, referred to in the vernacular as *wood* alcohol.

Alcohol, almost the entire dose of alcohol in a beverage, is absorbed through the walls of the gastrointestinal tract within 30 to 75 minutes of consumption. It is distributed throughout the body by the blood system. It resides in the tissues of the body in proportion to their water content. It is eliminated from the body by metabolism (95 percent) and as a relatively unchanged component of urine, sweat, and expired breath (5 percent). It leaves at a rate of about one ounce of liquor per hour for a 160-lb male. Digestion is not required. Food in the stomach, particularly starches and fats, may serve to slow the rate of absorption somewhat.

The blood alcohol concentration (BAC) is the amount of alcohol in blood, expressed in various ways, at any point in time. The same amount of liquor will produce a lower concentration of alcohol to blood (BAC) in a large person than it will in a small person, simply because the larger person has more water in the body in which the alcohol is distributed.

In order to attain higher BAC levels, one must consume a number of ounces of liquor within a relatively short span of time, to offset the body's natural rate of elimination of one ounce per hour, and to build the concentration.

Alcohol is metabolized in the body by an oxidation process involving enzymes. The enzymatic systems reduce the level of BAC in chronic drinkers at a faster rate than non-drinkers. An alcohol tolerance can develop, in some cases. These enzymatic systems may be responsible for the greater ability of some chronic drinkers to carry out complicated tasks while under the influence. This retention of capabilities is the reason chronic drinkers can exhibit fluent, normal writing at BAC levels higher than nondrinkers.

Tolerance is a word with many meanings in technical alcohol discussions. *Blood alcohol tolerance* usually refers to the concentration of alcohol (BAC) needed to produce measurable changes in particular behaviour or performance (e.g., vehicle operation or handwriting). This is a tolerance that varies with different individuals or with the same individual on different occasions. It is the tolerance that induced lawmakers to limit BACs to certain levels for motor vehicle operation, as deterioration in performance was measurable at those levels. The performance of neuromuscular tasks by many persons, particularly those requiring high levels of muscular coordination (such as handwriting), may be measurably altered at BAC levels as low as ≥ 0.05 percent.[17]

Then there is *body tolerance*, that is the amount of alcohol required to affect different people (or the same person on different occasions) to the same degree or to the same change in performance (e.g., the ability to stand without wavering, to walk a straight line or to bring the ends of two fingers together with arms outstretched). This is a tolerance that varies with the individual owing to differences or variations in the rates of absorption, metabolism, and elimination. It is the sense in which the layman uses the term *tolerance for alcohol*.

The literature on alcohol and writing tends to classify people in one of four categories: nondrinkers, social drinkers, chronic drinkers, and alcoholics. The lines of demarcation between the last three groups are not always clear, at least in the minds of the drinkers. Then too, the first three groups are often referred to as normal drinkers, distinct from alcoholics. Perhaps some elaboration is needed here as well.

Alcoholism is a disease, the nature and origin of which has long been debated. The prevailing view for years was that it was an emotional disorder that when treated and resolved allowed the individual to return to normal drinking practises. The newer and more enlightened view is that alcoholism is a disease entity in itself that is physiological in origin. This school holds that the behaviour pattern of the alcoholic is the result rather than the cause of the disease that can be arrested only by total and continued abstinence from alcohol.

Beck (1982), has provided an excellent description of the alcoholic and his/her attendant problems giving us some explanation for the tremours occurring in the patient's writing, and some insight into the improvement in writing performance that accompanies the alcoholic's first drinks after a spell of sobriety. Beck explains, "While the normal drinker has two states of handwriting, sober and intoxicated, the alcoholic has three states: sober, intoxicated, and in withdrawal."

The studies conducted are attempts to answer a few fundamental questions:

1. Does handwriting contain evidence of a writer's consumption of alcohol within a certain time period prior to execution? If so, what evidence?
2. Does this evidence, if any, correlate reliably with the writer's blood alcohol concentration (BAC)?
3. Could the evidence of intoxication in handwriting be mistaken for another condition/circumstance, or vice versa?

We can begin with the comments of Dr. Emil Bogen[18] who summarized a chapter from a manual then in preparation for the American Medical Association and systematically outlined the several changes that occur in writing, speech and behaviour in the course of progressive intoxication. He stated:

"The choice of words and subjects in writing shows the same loss of inhibitions which may be noted in speech and actions. Handwriting at an early stage is apt to be larger and heavier and more ornate than usual. There may be a tendency for the writing to rise or fall, and to vary in the size of letters. Later, the changes become more marked and the letters less legible, with more misspellings, crossing outs or erasures, overwriting, and with excess duplications, insertions, omissions, or transpositions of strokes, letters, or words similar to the corresponding changes in the enunciation of spoken language. The writing becomes more scrawling and illegible and eventually merely a sprawling line before the person becomes entirely unable to scribble."

We can recap the findings of the several investigators with which we are familiar, including Nousianen;[19] Rabin and Blair;[20] Tripp, Fluckiger, and Weinberg;[21] Resden;[22] Packard;[23] Duke and Coldwell;[24] Doulder;[25] Hilton;[26] Anderson;[27] Doud;[28] Beck;[29] Galbraith;[30] Goyne and Kittel;[31] Conway;[32] and Watkins and Gorajczyk[33] as being consistent with one another in a number of respects.

1. The ingestion of alcohol results in handwriting impairment, although the BAC at which it becomes apparent, and the elements of writing affected varies with the individual, his/her drinking practises or history, and the circumstances under which the writing is done.
2. The quality of one's writing deteriorates progressively with the elevation of BAC, and more profoundly in extended writing than in signatures.
3. The legibility of one's writing deteriorates progressively with the elevation of BAC, partially due to the distortion of letter forms.
4. The dimensions of one's writing increases with the elevation of BAC. A given word or text will occupy more space.
5. The lateral expansion of one's writing increases with the elevation of BAC.
6. The alignment of one's writing deteriorates progressively with the elevation of BAC.
7. The irregularity of letter slopes increases progressively with the elevation of BAC.
8. The point load of the writing instrument (pen pressure) increases or may become irregular with the elevation of BAC.
9. The speed of writing decreases markedly with the elevation of BAC.
10. Errors, letter omissions, and overwritings increase in frequency with the elevation of BAC.
11. Erratic movements or sudden changes in the writing line or tremours may occur with the elevation of BAC.
12. Abnormalities in allograph selection may occur with the elevation of BAC.
13. There is no particular residual evidence of impairment in the writing of a normal drinker during the period following the return to sobriety (the hangover period).
14. The influence of alcohol on writing can vary somewhat with the individual's temperament, state of health, emotional state, or with fatigue.
15. The quality of writing of an alcoholic may not be fully recovered during the withdrawal (sober or hangover) stage of his/her drinking behaviour.

16. The quality of writing of a sober alcoholic may be improved initially by the ingestion of alcohol.
17. Tremour is a likely characteristic of the writing or line drawing of chronic drinkers and alcoholics, drunk or sober, that may be reduced or eliminated at low levels of BAC.

In determining these fashions in which alcohol alters handwriting, the results of the studies are quite consistent, although the methods of judgment are somewhat imprecise and lack specificity. As Gross has done, the reliability of some studies has been challenged. Reports on some aspects of writing such as point load (pen pressure) and speed are less consistent with one another, perhaps because procedures and blood/alcohol concentrations are not entirely comparable.

The listing of these 17 changes that may be found in the writing performance of persons consuming alcohol is not to suggest that all will be present and to the same degree in any particular drinker's writing sample at any given BAC. The reason for changes at all is evidently due to alcohol's depressant action upon the central nervous system. Beyond that the similarity between individuals or between the effects on the same individual on different occasions diminishes.

Studies that have attempted to use changes in handwriting as a measure of the level of intoxication or BAC of a subject have not yet proven successful. Duke and Coldwell, did find a degree of correlation between them that has not been pursued, a task that would be complicated by differences in body tolerance.

The tendency for most persons to write larger, poorer, and with less regularity under the influence of alcohol suggests that alcohol inhibits the finer movements of muscular coordination or motor control. However, as Galbraith reported, a few individuals have been observed to write smaller, which seems to contradict the theory. The likelihood is that there are factors involved in these special cases that we don't yet fully understand.

A recent study by Stinson[34] endeavoured to validate selected prior studies of the effects of alcohol consumption upon handwriting. On the strength of a study of 26 subjects, agreement was found in changes observed as compared with the reported observations of earlier studies. Difficulty was encountered, however, in attempting to compare quantified results, owing to the vagueness of the language used in the previous works. Terms such as *few* or *increased, appeared more* and *did not appear to have an effect* were too imprecise to facilitate comparisons.

Purtell[35] is one of the few writers to mention the affect of alcohol when taken in conjunction with or in addition to some other forms of medication or drug abuse such as meprobamate (a tranquilizer). While other drugs and/or medications by themselves may not significantly alter a person's writing, when combined with the ingestion of alcohol they tend to potentiate the effects of the alcohol. On the other hand, it has been claimed that alcohol increases the sedative effect that any other drug may have on the central nervous system. We are limited in our information as to the consequences of the combination other than to note that the alterations to the writing are more pronounced at lower levels of BAC.

Brun and Reisby[36] conducted a study of handwriting changes resulting from the effects of alcohol, meprobamate, and their interaction. In two experiments involving 38 subjects (28 males), and 40 subjects (29 males), it was found that the interaction of alcohol and meprobamate produced more errors than either drug alone, while each drug produced more errors than a placebo.

The greatest measurable changes in handwriting occurred from the interaction of alcohol and meprobamate, however, there were few measurable changes resulting from meprobamate alone. While no single handwriting change was found to be drug specific, writing consistency and stability appeared to be most reflective of drug ingestion. Other reliable indices of drug effects were found to be fluctuations in letter size and pen pressure, as well as undulating baselines.

In the second experiment, the subjects were grouped by psychiatric interview into four categories using the Taylor Manifest Anxiety Scale. Interestingly, the handwriting of the subjects in the group displaying the fewest personality disturbances was the least affected under any of the drug conditions.

Tripp, Fluckiger, and Weinberg, demonstrated that normal persons possess superior writing ability to alcoholics in tests of pressure variability, ataxia, and speed, and further that the tougher the task the greater the difference. Under the influence of ethanol, however, the performance of normals was impaired while that of alcoholics showed marked improvement. To this extent, then, what happens to one's writing under the influence of alcohol depends upon the drinking history of the writer.

Hilton commented on the fact that the changes to writing that result from alcohol are, in the initial stages or at low levels of BAC, not unlike some symptoms of other conditions, of fatigue, carelessness, and even spuriousness. For this reason, hasty conclusions should not be drawn that alcohol is the only cause to be considered.

2. *Hallucinogens and Hard Drugs*

Much like alcoholics, persons addicted to hard drugs such as heroin, cocaine, and the many varieties of them experience, initially, a certain state of well-being with the ingestion of the drug during which performance in any neuromotor task is improved over that in a state of withdrawal or abstinence. Literature is somewhat limited on the subject, and fortunately so are the cases in which it is involved. Important to note, as well, is the fact that effects similar to those of alcohol are obtained in writing under the influence of other drugs such as lysergic acid diethylamide (LSD-25) and of BOL-148 (d-1-brom lysergic acid diethylamide).

Cases do arise, however, involving the writing of wills or other communications in conjunction with or prior to the taking of drug overdoses resulting in death. Cheques and receipts are sometimes signed while in a drugged state, after which, and on return to a normal state, the writer may have no recollection of the writing act. As with alcohol, it can be a defence offered by an accused person who has been linked to a document on the strength of writing, or other evidence.

Hallucinogenic and addictive drugs of most kinds, like alcohol, have an affect upon the neuromuscular system, and while the effects are somewhat varied there is some consistency in the conditions reported. In a well-conducted study of the effects of seven different drugs on the handwriting of five subjects, Hirsch, Jarvik and Abramson[37] compared the results obtained from the oral consumption of:

LSD-25 (lysergic acid diethylamide)
LAE-32 (lysergic acid monoethylamide)
BOL-148 (d-1-brom lysergic acid diethylamide)
Ethyl alcohol
Ergonivine (ergometrine)

Pervitin or Methedrine (methamphetamine hydrochloride)
Scopolamine (hyoscine)
No. 1 tap water placebo
No. 2 tap water placebo

Several precautions were taken. Each substance was given on a separate day. No two subjects received the same drug on the same day. About 4½ hours after receiving each substance, the subject was required to copy a poem one paragraph in length. Each drug was diluted in 200 cc of water and only the alcohol had a taste and an odour. The principal results are summarized as:

1. The effects of the different substances varied with the individual.
2. Under the influence of LSD-25, alcohol and BOL-148, three subjects wrote much larger, i.e., occupied more space, than after the placebos, and two wrote smaller. Under ergonovine, subjects generally wrote small.
3. The greatest number of errors and the greatest number of erasures, deletions, corrections etc., tended to occur under scopolamine. This drug produced feelings of extreme drowsiness that may have been responsible. No erasures, etc., were made after ergonovine, and only one erasure was made after BOL-148.
4. The greatest irregularity and carelessness in writing occurred after alcohol, scopolamine and LSD-25. The most noticeable effects followed LSD-25 ingestion. Irregularity in letter size, word spacing, slant, and lack of control characterized the writing of four subjects under the influence of LSD-25. One subject wrote smaller. The other drugs had no widespread marked effects.

Fisher conducted a number of studies alone and with others, the most interesting of which to us was the study of Fisher, England, Archer, and Dean[38] respecting the effect of the hallucinogen psilocybin on psychomotor performance, and particularly on handwriting. It was their finding that at peak levels of the drug on two male subjects, there were substantial increases in the size of writing, the rate of writing, and the pen pressure (point load) exerted. Other investigations of the effects of lysergic acid diethylamide (LSD) on an index of handwriting referred to as the handwriting pressure curve (HPC) by Thuring[39] proved less resultant.

Legień[40] employed a handwriting test with some success in the diagnosis of narcotic addiction.

Legge, Steinberg, and Summerfield[41] examined six measures of handwriting size as indices of the effects of different concentrations of nitrous oxide (NOH), the anaesthetic gas that is a central depressant drug. Nitrous oxide produced a systematic increase in the size of handwriting that varied with the concentration of the NOH. The six aspects of size that were measured consisted of (1) the number of words in two lines of writing, (2) the average baseline lengths (horizontal dimension) of 10 key words, (3) the average vertical dimension of minuscules in the key words, (4) the average vertical dimension of infralinear letters (e.g., "y" and "g") in five key words, (5) the average vertical dimension of supralinear letters (e.g., "l" and "h") in five key words, (6) the vertical dimension of the tallest supralinear letter.

The baseline length (horizontal dimension) of words was found to be the most sensitive and reliable index; it is relatively quick and simple to measure and might have some practical application. Why nitrous oxide produces a systematic increase in writing size that correlates with the concentration of the dose administered is not explained, but the suggestion is made that it acts on neuromuscular control in such a way that only relatively coarse movements can be made. The effect is not unlike that of alcohol.

In a later study of the same drug on handwriting, Legge[42] observed that the drug appeared to have acted on processes subserving judgment, and increased the subjects' tolerance for errors in alignment. Under the drug's influence, misalignments were accepted that were not tolerated when performing without the drug.

Dhawan, Babat, and Saxena[43] examined the effects of two stimulants (caffeine and methamphetamine), two depressants (chlorpromazine and phenobarbitone), and a placebo on handwriting in a double-blind test situation using the elements of writing employed by Legge et al. (1964). Briefly, they found that the time taken to copy a passage decreased under the influence of methamphetamine but increased under phenobarbitone. They found that the average length of words and the vertical dimension of key words increased under the stimulants caffeine and methamphetamine, but was unaffected by the depressants chlorpromazine and phenobarbitone. The authors felt that the tests were not sufficiently sensitive to differentiate reliably between the different types of centrally acting drugs.

Peters, Lewis, Dustman, Straight, and Beck[44] studied the influence of 9-tetrahydrocannabinol (THC), common name: hashish, the active ingredient of cannabis sativa, common name: marijuana, in a number of sensory, motor, cognitive, and perceptual tasks, but not specifically handwriting. The effect was minimal but consistent. Performance was less efficient and more variable. Even at high dose levels, THC failed to produce gross alterations, but there were consistent, subtle decrements on a variety of performance measures. Klonoff, Low, and Marcus[45] is reported as obtaining more pronounced results in other similar tests, which suggests that factors other than THC may be involved.

Many studies have been conducted of the effects of alcohol on performance when taken in conjunction with other drugs. Zirkle, McAtee, King, and Van Dyke[46] found that there was a greater (synergistic) effect on human performance and judgment from a combined dosage of meprobamate and alcohol than from either of these drugs taken singly. Indeed, the effects were greater than those found in an earlier study[47] of alcohol and chlorpromazine, that is generally considered to be a stronger drug.

Several studies have been conducted of the effects of cannabis sativa, common name: marijuana, or the active ingredient THC and alcohol in simulated driving tests. THC has been found to have a stronger affect on one's ability to estimate time and distance, but that both drugs slowed one's reaction time.

Few studies have been reported respecting the combined effects of THC and alcohol on handwriting. Foley and Miller[48] studied the handwriting of 12 individuals under the influence of marijuana, alcohol, and a combination of the two relative to control samples taken in advance. Of the 12 subjects, 8 were judged to be habitual users, smoking marijuana at least twice a week. The others were less frequent users.

These authors found that:

1. After smoking one marijuana cigarette, there was little or no change in the subject's handwriting.
2. After smoking three marijuana cigarettes, some changes were observed in the writing of subjects with little prior experience with THC. There was some increase in size and some alteration to letter forms.

3. After smoking five marijuana cigarettes, there was a general increase in letter sizes, some deviation in alignment and greater carelessness in execution.

4. After consuming three 12 oz. cans of beer, subjects increased writing speed, letter sizes, and lateral expansion. Some changes in relative heights of letters and letter slopes were also observed.

5. After consuming three 12 oz. cans of beer and smoking three marijuana cigarettes, subjects revealed changes to their writing similar to those observed after the ingestion of alcohol alone. The authors suggest that the gross changes observed when consumption of the drugs was combined was probably due, principally, to the affect of the alcohol.

6. Marijuana smoking in moderate amounts had less effect upon handwriting than did alcohol. The combined effects of alcohol and THC are evidently not synergistic.

Foley and Miller explain that the neuromuscular activity necessary to produce normal writing is directed by the central nervous system (CNS). The marked effect of alcohol on writing is due to its depression of the CNS. Although THC also affects the CNS, it does not greatly depress the activity that directs manipulative functions, such as handwriting. Thus, THC produces emotional or mood changes, a *high* for example, without impairing the individual's ability to write.

In the body of literature that we have available, there is some variation in the effects obtained by drugs upon handwriting. As Gross has so ably pointed out, "It appears that psychological stability influences the degree and direction in which one's handwriting is apt to change following drug ingestion. There is reason to believe that these drug-induced graphomotor reactions are proportional to one's psychological reactions."

A statement by Carl E. Anderson, neurologist, from Santa Rosa, CA, quoted by Wellingham-Jones[49] points out that, "Several classes of drugs interfere with neurotransmitter function, producing disturbances in handwriting as a result. These handwriting changes are nonspecific and not, of themselves, diagnostic of any one drug or combination of drugs. Yet, the knowledge of variation in handwriting due to drugs can be most helpful to document examiners...."

3. Hypnosis

Hypnosis is a trance-like condition or an induced state that resembles sleep in which the subject experiences diminished will power and is very responsive to the suggestions of the hypnotizer. Although we have no record of an actual case in which writing under hypnotic influence is alleged to have occurred, it is a possible circumstance that some document examiners have been curious to explore. Does handwriting change under hypnosis, and/or can it be made to resemble another individual's writing or signature. If it was so, the potentials for this as an argument in civil and criminal matters are copious.

K. S. Bowers[50] is quoted as saying that:

"A deeply hypnotized person experiences himself in some rather unusual ways.... His behaviour and perception are exquisitely sensitive to the hypnotist's communication."

"Becoming hypnotized is not an all-or-nothing proposition. While some people are able to achieve deep hypnosis with difficulty, others seem intractable to hypnosis, many more people are only moderately hypnotizable. Just why these differences in hypnotic ability exist is not entirely clear."

In a study of 17 subjects and of their ability to simulate or forge signatures when hypnotized, Nemecek and Currie[51] found that neither hypnosis nor posthypnotic suggestion improved the subject's ability to simulate or forge another's signature. In fact, most subjects reported that under hypnosis, the writer was more relaxed to the point at which writing was an effort. Obviously, interest in the task was lost.

Blueschke[52] claimed that judges in British Columbia have posed the questions:

Does hypnosis have an affect on handwriting?
Can hypnosis be used to write the perfect forgery?
Can hypnosis be used to disguise one's handwriting successfully?

His study of 26 subjects disclosed that in some cases handwriting under hypnosis deteriorated, but the degree of deterioration varied with the individual. Furthermore, the subject's ability to simulate another writing or signature did not improve. The question of disguise was not dealt with.

On the strength of the information that we have, we are without reason to believe that hypnosis will make a significant difference to a writer's ability with a writing instrument other than to diminish their own writing quality in some cases.

4.   Fatigue or Physical Stress

As we said earlier, there are two forms of stress that the human being may experience: emotional stress and physical stress. Fatigue is the physical form of stress. One can find mention of the effects of fatigue upon writing in papers dealing with alcohol, but little that describes in any detail what the effects are. Hagan, Osborn, and Harrison have commented briefly on fatigue, but the source of their knowledge is not indicated. Noustianen reports on the changes occurring in writing after the subject had run up four flights of stairs. In these, he observed that the lateral expansion of the writing had increased significantly.

Signatures are sometimes executed when the writer is fatigued, more often as an incidental record (e.g., in physical fitness centres) or a signature on a receipt, but seldom on more formal documents. The circumstances do not normally allow for it. There is usually ample time for the body to recover from the effects of fatigue before there is a necessity to write.

This may explain the paucity of information regarding fatigue and writing that exists in the literature. Of the earlier recognized authorities, only Hagan[53] and Harrison[54] mention it, but simply as one of several factors that may influence handwriting, without further elucidation as to how.

Nousianen[55] reported on the changes in the writing of one subject in executing a sentence of eighteen words after having run up four flights of stairs. He noted changes that resembled those produced by intoxication, particularly an increase in lateral expansion but without an apparent increase in height.

Roulston[56] reported on a study of 30 writers under extreme and moderate states of fatigue, and fatigue localized to the writer's forearm. His subjects were healthy males of similar age (early twenties) that were required to write a modified version of the London Letter under four different test conditions.

He observed an increase in vertical height (109 out of 120 cases) in both lowercase and uppercase letters, without a significant change in proportions or relative heights and an increase in letter width or lateral expansion (23 subjects out of 30). Insofar as the spacing between words, Roulston found both expansion and contraction (15 subjects out of 30), but noted that whichever tendency was exhibited it remained consistent. Slope was not significantly effected, nor was speed, rhythm, or fluency habits. Only minor deterioration was noted in writing quality, that tended to produce a scrawl and exhibit less care. In only one case was greater pen pressure displayed. No evidence of tremour was found.

Remarkably, fewer patchings and overwritings occurred in writing under fatigue. Minute movements tended to be enlarged, but there was no fundamental change to most writing habits. There was some propensity to abbreviate, to commit spelling errors, and to omit punctuation and diacritics ("i" dots).

There was no apparent difference between the effects of forearm fatigue and general body fatigue. In either case, however, there was some difference in the effects that varied with the severity of the fatigue. Roulston's data is fully reported in his treatise and while the effects of fatigue cannot be denied Harrison's statement that "...Fatigue and a poor state of health can have a most deleterious effect upon handwriting..." may be an exaggeration of the condition.

Remillard[57] in a study of 21 high school students endeavoured to determine whether there was a degree of impairment to a person's writing that would correlate with the pulse rate of the heart under different levels of exertion. He studied further what the nature of the impairment would be and whether stress-impaired writing could still be correctly associated with its author.

Remillard's results disclosed that physical stress, producing abnormally high pulse rates, did in fact impair the individual's writing performance, but the reading of pulse rates can only be considered an indicator of the level of stress being experienced by the subject. It cannot be construed from this study that pulse rates are totally responsible for the degree of impairment, although they may be a contributing factor.

Impairment of the writing in this case was judged on the strength of the following:

1. Deterioration in letter formation, coupled with overwriting and corrections.
2. An increase in lateral expansion, particularly of the spacing between letters, and a frequent misjudgment of the length of words at the ends of lines.
3. A tendency to write larger.
4. A reduction in the speed of writing, accompanied by an inconsistency in point load (pen pressure).
5. A failure to maintain good alignment or a proper baseline.
6. A general failure in writing quality and greater carelessness.

Notwithstanding the impairment of the writings in these fashions, a group of 15 competent writing examiners were able to associate the writing samples of each subject correctly (100 percent accuracy) at various levels of stress. These results are obviously consistent with the findings of Roulston that were reported above.

An interesting closing comment by Remillard was that the impairment of writing resulting from physical stress, produced by running various distances was generally similar to, but not as pronounced as, the impairment resulting from the ingestion of alcohol.

In summary, it may be said that extreme fatigue has some affect on the control of the writing instrument, that tends to increase the expansion of the writing both vertically and horizontally. This expansion may be noted in the enlargement of the more minute movements of the writing process and suggests a trend in the writing toward a scrawl. Needless to say, the effects are of relatively short duration and the writing returns to normal when the body has recovered its energy.

D. Literacy and Education

Part of this topic will be dealt with in response to the question: What are the indicators of illiteracy (Section 56)? Here we shall discuss education as an influence on handwriting.

To begin with, we note that Broom and Basinger[58] in an attempt to judge intelligence from samples of penmanship from 30 subjects, concluded that:

> "It is as easy to judge weight from penmanship as it is to judge intelligence; neither is judged correctly except by chance."

This may explain the paucity of information that is available respecting the relationship of any aspect of handwriting with either education or intelligence. Among the authorities on writing, identification, only Harrison has seen fit to comment, and then only briefly, on his view that skill in paragraphing reflects the educational status of the writer. He suggests further that punctuation and spelling, presumably when correctly done, may also be indicative of a reasonable level of education. We can hardly quarrel with his contention for it is only logical to expect an educated person to be more competent in the written language, and more capable of sorting and organizing thoughts, from which proper paragraphing and punctuation ensues.

Interestingly enough, as Harrison notes, correlation is not to be expected between artistic quality (i.e., writing skill) and education or intelligence, that has been the evidence proffered by written prescriptions executed by medical professionals, with which we are all familiar.

References

1. Harrison, Wilson R., *Suspect Documents* (New York: Frederick A. Praeger, 1958), p 297.

2. Hecker, Manfred R., *The Change of Handwriting as a Process of Identification.* Presented at the meeting of the International Association of Forensic Sciences (Bergen, 1981).

3. Osborn, A. S., *Questioned Documents.* 2nd ed. (Albany: Boyd Printing Co., 1929), pp 151-166.

4. Mayther, J., The Influence of Writing Instruments on Handwriting and Signatures. *Journal of Criminal Law, Criminology and Police Science,* 1969 March; 60: 1: pp 102-112.

5. Hilton, Ordway, Effects of Writing Instruments on Handwriting Details. *Journal of Forensic Sciences,* 1984 January; 29: 1: pp 80-86.

6. Masson, Janet Fenner, Felt Tip Pen Writing: Problems of Identification. *Journal of Forensic Sciences,* 1985 January; 30: 1: pp 172-177.

7. Masson, Janet F., The Effect of Fibre Tip Pen Use on Signatures. *Forensic Science International,* 1992; 53: pp 157-162.

8. Grant, Julius, *The Effect of Posture on a Signature.* Presented at the meeting of the International Association of Forensic Sciences (London, 1974).

9. Morton, S. E., How Does Crowding Affect Signatures? *Journal of Forensic Sciences,* 1980 January; 25: 1: pp 141- 145.

10. Bey, Robert F. and Ryan, Dennis J., *Limited Writing Area and Its Effect on a Signature — A Preliminary Study.* Presented at the meeting of the American Academy of Forensic Sciences (San Fransisco, 1998).

11. Hecker, Manfred R., *Effects of Unusual Paper Supports on Handwriting.* Presented at the meeting of the American Society of Questioned Document Examiners (North Lake Tahoe, NV, 1983).

12. Leung, S. C., *A Case of Lipstick Writing on a Body.* Presented at the meeting of the American Society of Questioned Document Examiners (Savannah, 1986).

13. Totty, R. N., A Case of Handwriting on an Unusual Surface. *Journal of the Forensic Sciences Society,* 1981; 21: pp 349-350.

14. Taylor, Linda L. and Hnilica, Violette, Investigation of Death through Body Writing: A Case Study. *Journal of Forensic Sciences,* 1991 September; 36: 5: pp 1607-1613.

15. Brown, Christopher David W. P., *The Identification of Handwriting on a Convex Surface.* Presented of the meeting of the American Academy of Forensic Sciences (Las Vegas, 1985).

16. Gross-Leon J., Drug-Induced Handwriting Changes: An Empirical Review. *Texas Reports on Biology and Medicine,* 1975; 31: 3: pp 371-390.

17. Baird, J. B., *The Pharmacological Effects of Alcohol.* Presented in a Breathalyser training course, given by the Crime Detection Laboratory of the Royal Canadian Mounted Police (Regina, Sask, April 1969).

18. Bogan, E., Handwriting, Speech and Behaviour Changes. *Journal of the American Medical Association,* 1958; 168: pp 48-49. With permission.

19. Nousianen, Hugo, Some Observations on the Factors Causing Changes in Writing Style. *Nordisk Kriminalteknisk Tidsskrift, (Northern Criminal Technical Journal)* Sweden, 1951; 25: 8: p 92.

20. Rabin, Albert and Blair, Harry, The Effects of Alcohol on Handwriting. *Journal of Clinical Psychology,* 1953; 9: pp 284-287.

21. Tripp, C. A., Fluckiger, F. A., and Weinberg, G. H., Effects of Alcohol on the Graphomotor Performances of Normals and Chronic Alcoholics. *Perceptual and Motor Skills,* 1959; 9: pp 227-236.

22. Resden, Rene, The Graph Test. *International Criminal Police Review,* 1959 October; 131: pp 226-236.

23. Packard, Royston J., Alcohol and Handwriting. *The Criminal Law Quarterly,* 1960; 3: pp 57-59.

24. Duke, D. M. and Coldwell, B. B., *Blood Alcohol Levels and Handwriting.* Presented at the joint meeting of the American Society of Questioned Document Examiners and the RCMP Crime Detection Laboratories (Ottawa, August 1965).

25. Doulder, Howard C., Examination of a Document Case. *Journal of Forensic Sciences,* 1965; 10: 4: pp 433-440.

26. Hilton, Ordway, A Study of the Influence of Alcohol on Handwriting. *Journal of Forensic Sciences,* 1969 October; 14: 3: pp 309-316.

27. Anderson, Gilbert J., *Varying Effects of Alcohol on Handwriting.* Presented at the meeting of the American Academy of Forensic Sciences (Dallas, 1974).

28. Doud, Donald, *Some Pitfalls in Testimony Relating to Alcohol Consumption and Handwriting.* Presented at the meeting of the American Society of Questioned Document Examiners (Colorado Springs, 1975).

29. Beck, Jan, *Handwriting of the Alcoholic.* Presented at the meeting of the American Society of Questioned Document Examiners (Boston, 1982).

30. Galbraith, Nanette G., *Alcohol: Its Effect on Handwriting.* Presented at the meeting of the American Society of Questioned Document Examiners (Nashville, TN, 1984).

31. Goyne, Thomas E. W. and Kittel, Hartford R., *Do "Hangovers" Impair Writing Ability?* Presented at the meeting of the American Society of Questioned Document Examiners (Montreal, 1985).

32. Conway, James V. P., *Effects of Alcohol on the Writing Process.* Presented at the meeting of the American Society of Questioned Document Examiners (Orlando, FL, 1991).

33. Watkins, Richard and Gorajczyk, John, *The Effect of Alcohol Concentrations on Handwriting.* Presented at the meeting of the American Academy of Forensic Sciences (Nashville, TN, 1996).

34. Stinson, M. D., A Validation Study of the Influence of Alcohol on Handwriting. *Journal of Forensic Sciences,* 1997; 42: 3: pp 411-416.

35. Purtell, David J., Effects of Drugs on Handwriting. *Journal of Forensic Sciences,* 1965 July; pp 335-345.

36. Brun, Birgitte and Reisby, Niels, Handwriting Changes Following Meprobamate and Alcohol. *Quarterly Journal of Studies on Alcohol,* 1971; 32: pp 1070-1082.

37. Hirsch, M. W., Jarvik, M. E., and Abramson, H. A., Lysergic Acid Diethylamide (LSD-25): XVIII Effects of LSD-25 and Six Related Drugs upon Handwriting. *Journal of Psychology,* 1956; 41: pp 11-22.

38. Fisher, R., England, S. M., Archer, R. C., and Dean, R. K., Psylocibin Reactivity and Time Contraction as Measured by Psychomotor Performance. *Arzneimittel-Forsch,* 1966; 16: pp 180-185.

39. Thuring, J. Ph., The Influence of LSD on the Handwriting Pressure Curve. *Advances in Psychosometric Medicine,* 1960; 1; pp 212-216.

40. Legień, Marek, Test Pisma Jako Metoda Diagnozowania W Toksykomanii (The Handwriting Test as Diagnostic Method in Narcotic Addiction) *Psychiatr. Pol.,* 1984. T. XVIII, Nr 3. pp 233-240.

41. Legge, David, Steinberg, Hannah, and Summerfield, Arthur, Simple Measures of Handwriting as Indices of Drug Effects. *Perceptual and Motor Skills,* 1964; 18: pp 549-558.

42. Legge, D., Analysis of Visual and Proprioceptive Components of Motor Skill by Means of a Drug. *British Journal of Psychology,* 1965; 56: 2 & 3: pp 243-254.

43. Dhawan, B. N., Bapat, S. K., and Saxena, V. C., Effect of Four Centrally Acting Drugs on Handwriting. *Japanese Journal of Pharmacology,* 1969; 19: pp 63-67.

44. Peters, B. A., Lewis, E. G., Dustman, R. E., Straight, R. C., and Beck, E. C., Sensory, Perceptual, Motor and Cognitive Functioning and Subjective Reports Following Oral Administration of δ^9-tetrahydrocannabinol. *Psychopharmacology,* 1976; 47: pp 141-147.

45. Klonoff, H., Low, M., and Marcus, A., Neuropsychological Effects of Marijuana. *Canadian Medical Association Journal,* 1973; 108: pp 150-156.

46. Zirkle, George A., McAtee, Ott B., King, Peter D., and Van Dyke, Robert, Meprobamate and Small Amounts of Alcohol. *Journal of the American Medical Association,* 1960; 173: 16: pp 121-123.

47. Zirkle, G. A., King, P., McAtee, O. B., and Van Dyke, R., Effects of Chlorpromazine and Alcohol on Coordination and Judgment. *Journal of the American Medical Association,* 1959 November; 171: pp 1496-1499.

48. Foley, Bobby G., and Miller, A. Lamar, *The Effects of Marijuana and Alcohol Usage on Handwriting.* Presented at the meeting of the International Association of Forensic Sciences (Wichita, KS, 1978).

49. Wellingham-Jones, Patricia, *Drugs and Handwriting* (Tchama, CA: PWJ Publishing, 1991).

50. Bowers, K. S., *Hypnosis of the Seriously Curious.* (Montgomery CA: Brooks/Cole Publishing Co., 1976).

51. Nemecek, Joe and Currie, Cuthbert, *Handwriting under Hypnosis.* Presented at the 6th meeting of the International Association of Forensic Sciences (Edinburgh, Scotland, 1972).

52. Blueschke, Arnold, *Regression and/or Attempted Simulation of Handwriting by Hypnosis.* Presented at the joint meeting of the American Society of Questioned Document Examiners and the RCMP Crime Detection Laboratories (Montreal, 1985).

53. Hagan, William E., *Disputed Handwriting* (Albany: Banks & Brothers, 1894), p 94.

54. Harrison, Willson R., *Suspect Documents* (New York: Frederick A Praeger, 1958), p 297.

55. Nousianen, Hugo, Some Observations on the Factors Causing Changes in Writing Style. *Nordisk Kriminaltekniak Tidsskrift, (Norther Criminal Technical Journal),* Sweden 1951; 21: 8: p 92.

56. Roulston, M. G., *The Fatigue Factor: An Essay Dealing with the Effects of Physical Fatigue on Handwriting Habits* (an unpublished report of a study conducted by the RCMP Crime Detection Laboratories, 1959).

57. Remillard, J. L. G., *Abnormal Cardiac Rhythm and Handwriting* (Ottawa: an unpublished study conducted at the RCMP Crime Detection Laboratories, May 1970).

58. Broom, R. H. and Basinger, M., On the Determination of the Intelligence of Adults from Samples of Their Penmanship. *Journal of Applied Psychology,* 1932; 16: pp 515-519.

The Requirements and the Results

10

39. What Standards Are Required for Handwriting Comparisons?

Writing standards, or exemplars as they are sometimes called, are of two kinds: collected standards or request standards. Collected standards are those samples of writing or lettering that have been executed in the normal course of business or social activity, and are usually unrelated to any matter in dispute. Request standards are those writings or letterings that are executed at the request of an investigator, a counsel, or some other person involved in the process under litigation.

From the viewpoint of the examiner of handwriting, collected standards are the preferred material to work with in most cases, for it is the more normal and natural product. Collected standards, however, consisting of similar texts to that of the questioned writing, such that they will contain similar letters, letter combinations and letter locations may not exist, or may be difficult to find.

Request writings, on the other hand, are frequently influenced by the circumstances and the knowledge that they are to be the subject of some examination. If the writer of the request writings is, in fact, the author of some writing in dispute, it is not unusual to find that the specimens are altered from the person's normal writing in some manner. If the writer of the request writings is not the author of the disputed material, the circumstances themselves may induce a degree of nervousness that may have some affect upon the fluency of the writing.

Handwriting comparisons require samples of writing from those individuals who are considered to be potential authors, that meet the following conditions:

1. They are sufficient in number to exhibit normal writing habits in executing the questioned text or parts thereof, and to portray the consistency with which particular habits are executed.

    Since humans are not inanimate machines operating mechanically within narrow tolerances, natural writing has in its elements a degree of variation from one writing occasion to the next, the range of which is peculiar to the person. Writing standards should be sufficient to portray the range of those variations. For skilled or practised hands, a half dozen signatures or one or two pages of extended writing might prove adequate. For others, the requirement might be greater. Suffice it to say, one can never have too much.

2. They include some samples in original ink.

    Original ink samples have a three-dimensional character to them, with which aspects of instrument control, particularly pen pressure (point load), and pen position, may be observed or calculated. These properties of the writing may be important in examinations or studies.

3. They consist of both collected and request samples.

    Collected standards, in addition to being more representative of normal writing habits, are also indicators of the degree of reliance that can be placed on request writings that may or may not be deliberately altered. Also, they can be more contemporaneous with older questioned documents. On the other hand, request writings can provide duplication of the letter combinations of the questioned material.

4. They duplicate the conditions or nature of the questioned writing.

    Many things may influence a person's writing, from the writing instrument and writing circumstances to the writer's age or temperament. The extent to which they can be duplicated in writing standards is the extent to which these variables can be controlled. Thus, the comparison should be made of like material, of similar age, similar letters or letter combinations, similar words, names or phrases, written under similar conditions, and with the same media (instrument and paper). Much that has been written on standards of comparison is directed at the control of these variables.[1-4] A comparison of general writing features, such as size, slant, and proportions, may not provide sufficient evidence from which definitive conclusions can be drawn.

Control of the variables, however, means having at least:

1. *Similarity of texts.* The comparison of writing habits necessitates having the same habits of form and other writing elements executed under the influences ensuing from the same level of habit hierarchy (i.e., letter, word, or phrase). To reproduce the influence of one letter or letter combination upon another one is compelled to duplicate the text.

2. *Similarity in writing circumstances.* It is common knowledge that variations in instruments, writing position, and writer's condition can have considerable effect upon the written product, that may complicate the identification process. This last factor underlies the requisite for comptemporaneousness in writing standards, if possible.

3. *Similarity in writing purposes.* The nature of the document, the intent of that which is written, and the audience to whom it is directed may make significant differences to the manner in which writing is executed. Personal notes and handwritten business communications may contain little that corresponds in these respects.

The control of variables arising from texts, circumstances, and purposes prompted this author to begin years ago to collect and file every handwritten address on envelopes containing mail directed to his residence. They are classic examples of writing in which variables are reasonably controlled. They are executions of a wide assortment of persons, bearing a similarity in text, probably executed under similar writing circumstances, and for the same purpose: to serve as an instrument of transit. As a collection, they facilitate the study of writings from a number of different perspectives. Accordingly, the creation of such collections of writings by document examiners has been strongly recommended.

40. What Quantities of Handwriting Standards Are Required?

There is no simple answer to this question. Osborn, himself, could not be specific, but he made some comments that are open to challenge. Respecting the examination of signatures he states that, "Five signatures constitute a more satisfactory basis for an opinion than one, and that 10 are better than five." Following this he cautions, "It is dangerous to base a positive and final conclusion that a suspected signature is genuine on a comparison of it with only one genuine signature, unless it is a highly individualized and skillful signature." He states further that, "A suspect signature…may contain so many inherent qualities indicating that it is not genuine that one good standard signature may be sufficient on which to base a positive opinion that it is not genuine." Clearly from this, one can reason that under certain circumstances he was prepared to reach positive conclusions of either identification or elimination on the strength of an examination of a single standard. Almost in contrast, he adds that it is not always helpful to examine more than 25 to 75 signatures except in unusual cases.

Insofar as extended writing is concerned he says, "For comparison with a disputed letter, one good complete standard letter may be sufficient, but even more writing should always be obtained if possible."

In an endeavour to provide some guidance to investigators, Hilton[5] went so far as to suggest that five or six pages of continuous writing should be adequate for comparison with questioned extended writings, and 20 or more separate signatures should be adequate for comparison with questioned signatures. Others have suggested less, perhaps only half those numbers. In practise, we have found that half of Hilton's quantities are all an examiner is likely to receive in most cases.

One should not try to answer the question of quantities until one has addressed the issue of the need for numbers in standards, whatever those numbers might be. This need stems from two factors of writing: habituation and natural variation.

The fact that we are dealing with habits says something about the standards we must have to conduct a study. Single or limited examples of any element of human conduct are insufficient to substantiate reliably that the conduct is habitual. Admittedly, in fluent and skillful writing we can presume, confidently, that another sample from this individual will look very much the same. It is a presumption, however, based solely on experience with other writers, not this one, and science avoids presumptions as a general rule. This brings us to the centre of the problem that standards frequently present.

The habits that we want to study comprise the discriminating elements of writing that are present in the questioned material. Many of these discriminating elements will involve specific letters or combinations of two or more letters in particular relationships to one another. As a result it is important, if not imperative, that the writing standards with which comparisons will be made consist of similar letters and combinations of letters as will occur in similar words, names, texts, or signatures written under comparable circumstances. Except in request writings, it is seldom that a few standards will meet these requirements, and, as was said before, request writings are not always trustworthy.

Furthermore, there is the matter of natural variations to contend with that may be broad or narrow, depending on the individual and the circumstances. Should they be broad, as occurs in less skillful writings, only greater quantities of standards, and particularly collected standards, will properly portray its nature and its range. The variables affecting writing have a greater influence on less skillful writing than on skillful writing. Larger quantities of collected standards afford a better opportunity to study writings in which the variables have been duplicated and are, thereby, controlled.

Notwithstanding such suggestions, sight unseen, there is no simple answer to the question as to how many writing samples will be required, and we doubt that there will ever be, as the requirement will vary with the writer and the circumstances. In the interests of practicality, Hilton's recommendations as to numbers may be a reasonable target even if somewhat ideal. Of one thing we can be certain, although we can have too few, we will seldom have too many.

41. Where Might One Find Suitable Samples of Signatures, Writings, and/or Letterings of a Collected Nature?

Given the time to think about it, there are a multitude of sources that may bear signatures, letterings, or extended writings suitable as standards for comparison. Frequently, some of these sources don't occur to someone in search of standards, but are readily recognized as sources with good potential when they are suggested. For that reason, the following list of possible areas of exploration are offered in the hope that if, in themselves, they don't prove to be productive, they may suggest other areas that will.

Accounts, charge	Bank deposit slips	Certificates of birth
Accounts, time payment	Bank money orders	Certificates of death
Address change forms	Bank safety box records	Certificates of marriage
Affidavits	Bank signature cards	Charge accounts
Agreements, business	Bank withdrawal slips	Charity pledge cards
Agreements, car rental	Bar chits	Chattel mortgages
Agreements, financial	Bibles, family	Cheques, bank, business
Agreements, rental	Bills of sale or lading	Cheques, bank, personal
Agreements, separation	Birth certificates	Chits, bar
Applications, bond	Birthday cards	Christmas cards
Applications, credit	Bonds, surety	Church records
Applications, employment	Book flyleaves	Club records
Applications, insurance, various	Business correspondence	Community service records
Applications, license	Car rental agreements	Contest entries
Applications, loan	Cards, bank signature	Contracts
Applications, membership	Cards, birthday	Cooking recipes
Applications, passports	Cards, Christmas	Corporate records
Applications, permit	Cards, credit	Correspondence, business
Applications, utility service	Cards, florist	Correspondence, personal
Assignments	Cards, get well	Courier receipts
Attendance records	Cards, greeting	Court records
Authorization letters	Cards, identification	Credit cards
Autograph books	Cards, membership	Credit card purchases
Automobile insurance applications	Cards, pledge	Currency exchange records
Automobile licenses & applications	Cards, report	Death certificates
Bank deposit authorizations	Cards, union	Declarations

Deeds	Military records	Records, attendance
Delivery receipts	Minutes, meeting	Records, bank
Depositions	Money orders, bank	Records, church
Diplomas	Mortgage releases	Records, convention
Discharge papers	Mortgages	Records, employment
Divorce documents	Naturalization papers	Records, library
Drafts, correspondence	Options	Records, political party
Driver's licenses	Orders, automobile service	Records, school
Employment records	Orders, bank money	Records, tax
Estimates	Orders, merchandise	Records, union
Examination papers	Orders, purchase	Records, voting
Family bibles	Orders, repair	Registers, funeral
Fingerprint records, civil	Passes	Registers, guest
Fingerprint records, criminal	Passports	Registers, hotel and motel
Foreign currency drafts	Pawnshop records	Registers, narcotic purchase
Greeting cards	Paycheques	Registers, poison purchase
Grocery lists	Payroll deduction authorizations	Registers, visitor
Guardianship papers	Personal correspondence	Rental agreements, automobile
Guest registers	Personnel records	Rental agreements, residential
Health cards	Petitions	Reports, accident
Hospital records	Pledge cards	Reports, committee
Hotel and Motel registers	Post cards	Reports, credit
Identification cards	Power of attorney	Reports, executor
Insurance applications, various	Premise access records	Reports, trustee
Insurance claims	Probate records	Requisitions, stores
Insurance releases	Proxies	Requisitions. supply
Investment accounts	Purchase orders	Requisitions, tool
Invitations	Real estate listings	Social security cards
Labels	Receipts, cash payment	Stock transfers
Leases	Receipts, courier	Tax returns
Letters	Receipts, delivery	Time sheets
License applications	Receipts, express	Travellers cheques
Licenses, automobile	Receipts, freight	Union records
Licenses, business	Receipts, personal property	Visitor registers
Licenses, drivers	Receipts, refund	Waivers
Licenses, fishing	Receipts, registered mail	Warrants
Licenses, hunting	Receipts, rent	Welfare records
Licenses, marriage	Receipts, storage	Wills
Marriage certificates	Receipts, telegram	Withdrawal slips
Membership cards	Receipts, witness fee	Work orders
Memoranda	Recipes, cooking	Working papers

42.   How Should Request Standards be Prepared?

Bearing in mind that, ideally, writing standards should reflect the normal, natural, unconscious writing habits of the individual, there are three key words that provide the necessary guidance in obtaining request writings: dictate, duplicate, and isolate.

Dictation

It is a cardinal rule that request writings should be prepared from dictation, leaving the subject free to make his or her own decisions as to how material is arranged or spelled.

Only the writing style, i.e., block letters, script or cursive writing should be stipulated. If the manner of signing or preparing particular kinds of documents, e.g., personal cheques, is of special interest, then blank documents of the same type should be supplied for completion.

The speed of dictation should prompt the subject to write as rapidly as he or she may do comfortably. In so doing, the writer is compelled to direct attention more so at what is being written rather then how it is being written.

Duplication

As the general rules for writing standards indicated, the duplication of the writing conditions and circumstances is a means of controlling the variables that may influence a writing. This control can be exercised conveniently in the production of request writings, whereas, duplication of writing conditions in collected samples is much more difficult to achieve. On the other hand, the variable produced by time cannot be controlled in request writings. If a questioned writing is alleged to have been executed at some time in the past, only collected standards of the same vintage will portray the writer's capabilities and practises of that period.

Isolation

To avoid biasing the standards in any fashion it is a basic rule that the questioned writing should never be exposed to the subject from whom writing samples are being taken. Depending on the individual and the instructions given, exposure of the questioned document may have one of two consequences.

1. It may induce the subject to imitate, unintentionally, the features of the questioned writing, which diminishes the significance of similarities found in a subsequent handwriting study. The danger is that evidence might be generated that could wrongly incriminate an innocent person.
2. It may induce the subject to modify or to omit features that he or she considers to be similar to the questioned writing, to avoid association with it, which diminishes the significance of differences found in a subsequent handwriting study. The danger is that evidence might be generated that could wrongly exonerate a guilty person.

If isolation of the questioned material is not maintained, the handwriting examiner, unaware of the circumstances under which the standards were obtained, would be at a distinct disadvantage in evaluating the evidence that has to be considered, and is likely to overestimate or wrongly estimate its worth in the identification process.

Not only should the questioned writing be isolated from the subject, but each sample of writing should be removed from view immediately upon completion, and thus, writing samples are isolated from one another. Deliberate alterations to writing, if they are attempted in the writing of the standards, are difficult to maintain consistently from one sample to the next, because they are unnatural and not habitual practises. Thus, their nature may become self-evident, and particularly so, if the alteration has to be repeated from memory and not from a model, that another sample might provide.

43. Are There Standard Texts for Request Writings?

A number of attempts have been made to compose a standard or universal text for request writings, that would contain two or more examples of each letter of the alphabet in upper and lowercase, all of the numerals and some of the various punctuation marks. Osborn provided what has come to be known as the *London Letter* in his first edition of *Questioned Documents*. It has been the standard and most widely used text in past years but is less popular now. It runs:

"Our London business is good, but Vienna and Berlin are quiet. Mr. D. Lloyd has gone to Switzerland and I hope for good news. He will be there for a week at 1496 Zermatt St. and then goes to Turin and Rome and will join Col. Parry and arrive at Athens, Greece, Nov. 27th or Dec. 2nd. Letters there should be addressed: King James Blvd. 3580. We expect Charles E. Fuller Tuesday. Dr. L. McQuaid and Robt. Unger, Esq., left on the 'Y. X.' Express tonight."

He later composed[6] the *Dear Sam* and *Dear Zach* letters, modifications of the *London Letter*, that also contained all of the upper and lowercase letters and the numerals of the English alphabet. The latter has also been referred to as the *Idaho Letter*. They read:

"Dear Sam:-

"From Egypt we went to Italy, and then took a trip through Germany, Holland and England. We enjoyed it all but Rome and London most. In Berlin we met Mr. John O. Young, of Messrs. Tackico & Co., on his way to Vienna. His address here is 1497 Upper Zeiss Str. care of Dr. Quincy W. Long. Friday, the 18th, we join C. N. Dazet, and leave at 6:30 A.M. for Paris on the "Q.X" Express and early on the morning of the 25th of June start for home on S. S. King.

"Very sincerely yours."

"Dear Zach:-

"Well, the old class of "16" is through at last. You ask where the boys are to be. Val Brown goes on the 24th to Harvard for law. Don't forget to address him as "Esq." Ted Updike takes a position with the N.Y. N.H. & H.R.R., 892 Ladd Ave., Fall River, Mass. and Jack McQuade with the D.L. & W. at Jersey City, N.J., 400 E. 6th St. Wm. Fellows just left for a department position in Washington; his address is 735 South G St. At last accounts Dr. Max King was to go to John Hopkins for a Ph.D. degree. Think of that! Elliott goes to Xenia, Ohio, to be a Y.M.C.A. secretary. I stay here for the present. What do you do next? How about Idaho?

"Yours truly, and Good bye."

Purtell and others have criticized these letters as not being too useful with subjects of limited education or lower intelligence. He found the names and passages too unusual for the average individual involved in criminal cases in the mixed populations of metropolitan areas: in a sense too foreign to foreigners.

In an endeavour to create a document with names more familiar to Canadians, and to add other writing features commonly encountered in questioned documents, the Crime Detection Laboratories of the Royal Canadian Mounted Police composed the *Canada Letter* in 1951. The text of 236 words of this letter is reprinted herewith.

Mr. & Mrs. W. E. James,   1953 51st Ave., West,
c/o X-Ray Department,   Toronto, Ontario,
Gold Medal Hospital,   Aug. 2nd, 1979.
Lincoln Road, Zone B,
New York City, N.Y., U.S.A.

Dear Vera and Eric:

We are enjoying a quiet and lazy Canadian holiday. Following a visit with Dr. Harry Young at Erie Beach from the 2nd to the 23rd of July we journeyed to Sarnia and London. After six days in that zone we went on to Niagara Falls via St. Thomas for a change of scenery. There we met John Oliver and Ken Green, both of whom are presently working for Upper Canada Insurance Co. Last time I saw Ken was in 1978, I believe. Do you remember him? He left the X-Ray field to become a salesman.

Quite recently we heard from "Madman" Murray Robertson. He is flying for United Airlines Ltd. now, Flight 600, out of New Zealand I think. Incidently Murray sold us his car for eight hundred dollars cash and seventeen monthly instalments of twenty-five dollars and fifty cents. (Total price $1241.50) His interest rate was 6 1/2 percent, which wasn't bad.

Remind George that we haven't heard from Jean or him for 7 or 8 months. Presently we will be at 246 Queen St., East, Apt. 16, Toronto, M5A 1S3. Our mail could be forwarded there for the next 2 or 3 weeks, if you wouldn't mind.

Very truly yours,

Bob

For the benefit of cases occurring in the French speaking areas of Canada a French version of this letter, *La lettre Canada*, was later composed, that we have modified to read:

M. & Mme W. E. Gendron,   1953 51ième Ave. Ouest,
a/s Hopital Jean Joseph,   Trois-Rivières, P.Q.
Département du Rayon X,
Rue Lionel,
Zone Postale 'B'
New York, N.Y., E.U.

Chers Victor et Emélie,

Nous nous réjouissons d'une vacance canadienne assez tranquille. A la suite d'une visite avec docteur Henri Yvon à la plage Erié du 18 au 20 juillet, nous avons été à Sarnia et Londre. Après six jours dans cette zone, nous allâmes aux Chutes Niagara en passant par St-Thomas pour un change de paysage. Là, ils recontront Jean Olivier et George Kirouac, le deux sont présentement employés par la compagnie d'assurance Union Viger Incorporé. La dernière fois que j'ai vu Kirouac était en 1939, je crois. Te rappelles-tu de lui? Il a déserté le département du rayon X pour devenir un voyageur.

Très recemment nous attendions parler de François Robert qui est parti en dessous. Il vole maintenant pour l'aviation, la compagnie Warwick, Vol no. 600, je pense, de Nouvelle-Zélande. Incidemment, Marie nous a vendu sa machine pour huit cents piastres comptant et soixante quinze et vingt cinq sous par mois. (Prix total $1241.50). Le taux d'intérêt est 6½%.

Dis à George que je n'ai pas reçu aucune nouvelle de Françoise depuis 7 ou 8 mois. A l'heure même, nous sommes à 6465 rue Brébeuf, Québec 4. Notre malle pourra être délivrée à cette place pour les 2 ou 3 prochaines semaines, si vous voulez.

Affectueusement,

Bernard.

It was reported by Hall and Hardcastle that in a study of European writing, Davies and Brown found that a text of 200 words executed once in block letters and once in cursive style was the most that could be obtained from subjects without them becoming uncooperative. Two samples of such a letter in either style is probably all the request writing of this kind that one could expect a cooperative subject to provide.

Other attempts at a universal or multipurpose text that might serve for different kinds of criminal cases have since been made. The most noteworthy of these is the study by Hall and Hardcastle[7] who have provided a draft of a new letter with certain reservations. It is a text of approximately 200 words that reads as follows:

Dear All,

I'm sorry that I haven't written to you for quite a long time but I have been very busy since April. I enjoy this new job more than the old one and it's only about an extra hundred yards or so for me to walk up the road from the station. What I don't like though is that my employers are paying my wages by cheque into my bank that is way across town. Cash every week would be so much easier because you know how lazy I am without a car. On Friday it took us no less than fifty minutes getting to the bank and back. There were six people in front of me in the queue — two with jumbo size zip up bags of money for paying in. The first of them was fairly quick but the next one hadn't sorted his out properly so it took absolutely ages for the cashier to serve him. I don't know why she couldn't refuse and make him go away and do it all again.

Anyway, how is Mr Pounds getting on? He was very lucky he did not receive a major injury when that big box of equipment fell and knocked him out at work. And they all said he just got up after as if nothing had happened!

Well, must stop now. See you soon.

The text was composed after a study of 42 passages of varying length from 21 authors, totalling 69,340 words, to determine average word lengths, letter frequencies, letter pairs, and common words. The 200 word text then reflects what this study revealed.

It was their view that texts such as this might be used in cases involving anonymous letters, that a design might be deliberately biased to serve cases of cheque fraud, or cases concerned with signatures. An appropriate text sample, however, could not be designed to reconcile these three different types of questioned writings. Hence, they concluded, "The Universal Specimen is not a viable proposition."

Given the wide variety that exists in the nature and kinds of questioned documents, this conclusion is not surprising. No single letter model can contain all of the possible letter combinations or other features of writing, such as those related to arrangement or the methods of writing cheques, that may be present in the disputed material. The methods of writing signatures are, for many people, distinctively different from textual writing.

Universal or standard letter formats, however, should not be expected to reflect all writing possibilities. Their purpose is to provide an adaptable vehicle, a document whose elements such as names, places, words, or phrases, even the expression of monetary amounts, should be replaced by those occurring in the disputed material, and a more normal and natural execution of the writing can be obtained. Request writings in the form of word lists, alphabets, and isolated names tend to produce a more deliberate and artificial product, in which writing habits may be less fluently performed.

Nevertheless, many law enforcement agencies and forensic document laboratories have designed forms for the taking of request writings. Purtell[8] while working in the Chicago Police Scientific Crime Detection Laboratory was one of the first to publish useable formats. They sometimes consist of individual upper and lowercase letters of the alphabet, they usually include a list of names, that might correspond to questioned signatures, and occasionally a passage of extended text. No serious attempt is made to cover all possible requirements but they evidently are considered to serve some purpose.

44. What Legal Requirements do Writing Standards have to Meet?

In Canada, the *Canada Evidence Act* permits testimony to be given respecting comparisons of questioned or disputed writings with writings proved to the satisfaction of the court to be genuine. This is not unlike the rules of evidence regarding admissibility in the United States, and in both countries one of four conditions usually serve to qualify a writing standard for acceptance.

1. The standard is acknowledged by the writer, to the court or to another party who is prepared to testify to such acknowledgment.
2. The writing of the standard was witnessed by a party who is prepared to testify to the action.
3. The standard is identified as the product of the writer by a party who is familiar with his or her writing through some business, social, or family relationship.
4. The circumstances surrounding the standard make a conclusion that a particular person executed the writing to be the only reasonable conclusion that the court may reach.

Obviously, the latter two methods of proof are open to challenge more so than the former two. Furthermore, greater latitude is allowed in civil cases than in criminal matters. The requirements of the law, however, must be borne in mind, for a denial by the court to admit any of the standards may significantly alter the findings of the handwriting examiner based on the remainder of the writings.

If the proof of a particular standard is likely to be challenged or is doubtful for other reasons, and these circumstances can be anticipated, the examiner should be advised so that the writing examination can be conducted in stages that will determine first, the results that can be supported by the more limited material, and, subsequently, the results that are supported by the standards as a whole.

45. What Results can be Expected from Handwriting Examinations?

Insofar as handwriting examinations are concerned, the results of an examination are dependent upon the amount and significance of the evidence that the study discloses. This may be hampered by restriction to photocopies or inadequate standards. It may also be that the questioned writing is too brief to contain a sufficient combination of writing habits to support a conclusion, as is frequently the case with initials or numerals. Given the appropriate material in both nature and amount, definite conclusions are normally achievable. Unfortunately, such circumstances are not always encountered.

Photocopies, etc.

When dealing with reproductions of questioned or disputed handwriting, such as photocopies or facsimile transmissions, care must be exercised in the manner of reporting results. When a handwriting examiner identifies a writing appearing in a photocopy, he or she is, in fact, identifying a writing that is not on the paper of the photocopy, but on another document that the examiner has not seen. Whether writing appearing in the reproduction is an actual inscription on the document on which it purports to reside, only an examination of the original document will determine. Learned examiners are aware of the ease with which photocopies can be falsified. Findings must be so worded, then, that they clearly indicate:

1. The identification is of a writing on a document of which the material at hand purports to be a trustworthy reproduction.
2. The findings are subject to confirmation of their existence as original writings, upon examination of the original document.

Conclusions vs. Opinions

Some controversy has been noted in the views of examiners as to whether the results of their examinations should be expressed as conclusions or as matters of opinion. It may be that the legal need for a definition and classification of the kind of testimony that an expert gives, that might otherwise be considered inadmissible, has contributed to some confusion in nonlegal minds.

The Shorter Oxford English Dictionary defines *opinion* in the traditional legal sense as:

"The formal statement by an expert or professional person of what he (she) thinks, judges or advises upon a matter submitted to him (her)."

This then, is the name given to the kind of testimony that a professional might provide. It says nothing about the substance of that testimony or the basis on which that statement has been established. It suggests that it is deemed to be advice. Some examiners, in response to the challenge that their testimony is merely an opinion, have argued that they offer a considered opinion.

In the nonlegal sense Oxford defines *opinion* as the following:

- an estimate of a person or thing
- a belief, a view, a notion
- something seeming to one's own mind to be true
- a belief of something as probable
- a judgment resting on grounds insufficient for complete demonstration

This suggests clearly the basis for the opinion, from which its reliability may be judged.

The attributes of this definition tend to be completely incongruous with the concept that competent/experienced expert witnesses hold of the task they have performed, the findings it may yield, and the testimony they may offer in the legal context. It is not a belief, or something seeming to be true, or a judgment resting on insufficient grounds for demonstration. There is much more physical evidence in support of the findings than these expressions convey.

On the other hand, Oxford defines *conclusion* as the following:

- an outcome
- a final determination
- a judgment arrived at by reasoning
- an inference, induction, or deduction

These terms are far more appropriate to describe the results of a handwriting study or document examination. Handwriting examiners, as do persons engaged in other forensic science pursuits, make judgments or determinations by reasoning and inductive inference. Accordingly, they reach conclusions, that, when reported as testimony in courts of law and other public forums, qualify for admission under the terms prescribed for a class of testimony inappropriately captioned, perhaps for want of a better title, *opinion evidence.*

Some examiners believe that their findings must be expressed as opinions to comply with their understanding of the law respecting expert witness testimony. The rules of law do not govern how expert evidence is determined or expressed, however, but only how it will be received. The issue over opinion evidence arose many years ago, and provision was made to allow it in the courts in hypothetical situations in which there was no factual or physical evidence before the court. In such cases there would be an estimate, a belief, a view or a something seeming to be true, based on no actual grounds or grounds insufficient for demonstration. There is no analogy to the current situations in which physical and factual evidence is an essential element of the expert witness' testimony.

Qualified Opinions

When definite conclusions cannot be reached, qualified opinions are sometimes expressed. In the light of what has just been said it is clearly more correct to refer to them as *Qualified Conclusions*. They are in the form of statements of probability such as "There is a very strong probability that writer A wrote Q."

Statements of this kind are supposedly statistical inferences, but are semantically untenable. The statement that anyone "probably wrote" anything has no sensible meaning. Only two semantically tenable statements can be made about writing: (1) that writer A wrote Q, or (2) that writer A did not write Q.

The objective of a probability statement respecting the identification of a writing can be only to signify that, if we accept the proposition that A wrote Q and act accordingly, the risk of error is low, although the statement may not indicate precisely how low. Probabilities are measures of the likelihood of either one of the two statements, (1) or (2), being correct. The probability cannot be attached to the action, i.e., the act of writing, of the statement itself.

A semantically tenable *qualified opinion* would be written in the form:

> The probability that a person selected at random would possess the correspondence in writing habits found in this questioned and known material is remote, very remote or extremely remote.[9]

Because it is not the common language of the layman, this wording lacks the ostensible strength of the semantically incorrect or untenable probability statements, that have been and are being employed. On the other hand, there is no reason why a finding cannot be expressed in terms that both justify and explain the reason for a modification to the wording, such as:

> "To be semantically tenable, only one of two statements can be made respecting the relationship of writer A to the questioned writing Q: (1) that writer A wrote Q, or (2) that writer A did not write Q. On the strength of the evidence in the documents at hand, there is a strong probability that the statement (1) is that which is correct."

When the correspondence between the questioned and known material is of such magnitude or significance that the probability of another person's writing exhibiting such correspondence is too remote to warrant practical consideration, a definitive conclusion of identification is justified.

Probabilities derived from statistical data, as these statements imply, are expressed mathematically as a ratio of likely occurrences of any event divided by the number of possible occurrences of the same event. So, we might ask, given that we have found a number of similarities and no disparities between questioned and known writings, how many other persons might exist in a population of, say, 1,000, that would have the same quantity and quality of similarities as the known writings exhibit? If our expectation is fewer than 10 persons, then, if we resolve that the given writer executed the questioned document and act accordingly, the risk of error is less than 1 percent, or the likelihood of our being correct exceeds 99 percent.

$$P = \frac{\text{number of likely occurrences}}{\text{number of possible occurrences}} \times 100\% = \frac{10 \times 100\%}{1000} = 1\%$$

As the likely occurrences of other persons with similar writing habits approaches zero, the ratio of likely occurrences to possible occurrences also approaches zero so that $P \approx 0$ (that which never happens). Conversely, as the likely occurrences approach the number of possible occurrences (that which happens every time), i.e., the finding of these similarities to a questioned writing in that of any person selected at random, the ratio nears the value of 1. Thus, probability values range from 0 (that which is impossible) to 1 (that which is a certainty).

Probabilities are measures of the risk of error in positive statements, or the likelihood of an alternative explanation for a given set of circumstances. Since the only two semantically tenable statements one can make about a writing are (1) that the writer of A wrote Q, or (2) that the writer of A did not write Q, then the task of the examination is a matter of determining which of these statements is likely to be correct, on the strength of the physical evidence that has been found.

To each of these statements there is always a risk of error or a likelihood of an alternative explanation. In the first case (the identification statement), insufficient evidence may enhance the risk of error. In the second case (the elimination statement), unusual writing circumstances may be misinterpreted or overlooked and result in an error: document Q may have been written when A was ill, or when A was intoxicated, or when A was writing against a wall, etc. Whenever these measures, i.e., the risk of error or likelihood of a plausible alternative explanation, are small but not inconceivable, we reach qualified conclusions and express qualified opinions, as legal minds would refer to it. When these measures are very small and too remote to be practical considerations, we reach positive conclusions.

It has been argued that examiners making statements of probability should be prepared to translate them into mathematical values. There is no other way to explain or to describe in precise terms what is meant by *a strong probability* or *a very strong probability* to an intelligent audience. Only mathematical numbers will indicate the relative certainties intended by the two expressions. Despite the reluctance of some handwriting examiners to involve statistics in their work Hilton pointed out:

"When the examiner states that in his opinion two writings were written by the same person, he has actually applied the theory of probability (without mathematics)."[10]

Statistical proof underlies all scientific investigation, and the tool is the same for all disciplines. As Dixon and Massey[11] stated:

"There does not exist a theory of statistics applicable only to economics or only to education. There is a general theory of statistics which is applicable to any field of study in which observations are made."

The allegation has been made, frequently, that sufficient data has not been assembled to establish the frequency of occurrence of any particular discriminating element of handwriting, from which its significance for identification purposes might be calculated. There is a line of argument, however, that supports the view that some arbitrary values can be ascribed to probability statements to reflect the magnitude of the risk of error the statement is intended to represent.

The risk of error that might be implied by *a strong probability* may be judged, arbitrarily, to be less than 1 percent. How much less need not be expressed. The examiner is saying the chance of encountering another individual with as much similarity in their writing in a random selection from the same population is fewer than one in a hundred persons. The estimate of that probability is based solely on his/her experience, which is comprised of what has been observed or read or heard.

Similarly the risk of error implied by the expression *a very strong probability* might be judged, arbitrarily, to be less than 0.1 percent. The intended meaning is that the chance of encountering another writer with the same degree of similarity in a random selection from the same population is fewer than 1 in 1,000 persons.

Admittedly, such statements are founded entirely on an experience based judgment, and while their accuracy cannot yet be statistically demonstrated, at least they reflect the level of confidence that the examiner has in his or her finding. One should also be confident that the error in the statements will be an underestimation of the level of probability that the evidence supports. The examiner, however, is left to him/herself to set the figures that reflect what he/she has in mind when qualified opinions are expressed.

Obviously when the risk of error exceeds five percent and the chance of encountering another writer with the same degree of similarity is thought to be equal to or greater than 1 in 20 persons, the conclusion pointing to an identification is not very strong. In this respect, the numbers speak for themselves.

46. What Then, Are the Levels of Certainty Achievable in Handwriting Identification?

The principle of identification that we have followed for many years was stated earlier[12] as:

"When any two items possess a combination of independent discriminating elements (characteristics), that are similar and/or correspond in their relationship to one another, of such number and significance as to preclude the possibility of their occurrence by pure coincidence, and there are no inexplicable disparities, one may conclude that they are the same in kind or have a common source."

While this principle provides a general criteria for drawing a definitive conclusion, it does not stipulate how many characteristics or what level of significance is required. At this point in time it is virtually impossible in some fields of forensic science to state arbitrarily how much evidence and what kind is necessary to reach a certain conclusion. How many striations on a bullet or in a tool mark does one need? How many similarities in the discriminating elements of a handwriting does one need? These are subjective judgments that have been conscientiously made by examiners who are usually fully cognizant of the dangers involved.

In the absence of an appropriate formula and in the interests of reliability, it is the rule of competent writing examiners to limit one's conclusions to those that may be drawn by any other equally competent examiner after a study of the same material. Although this rule is not overly explicit, it introduces an element of conservatism, or a caution that may serve to avoid serious error.

To put matters into proper perspective respecting the certainty of conclusions, Elton Trueblood[13] is quoted as saying:

"The fact that we do not have absolute certainty in regard to any human conclusions does not mean that the task of enquiry is fruitless. We must, it is true, always proceed on the basis of probability, but to have probability is to have something. What we must seek in any realm of human thought is not absolute certainty, for that is denied us as men, but rather the more modest path of those who find dependable ways of discerning different degrees of probability."

There is little difficulty in finding examiners that will agree on definitive or positive conclusions. Nonetheless, no one will state precisely what their respective level is that a positive conclusion would represent on a probability scale, other than to hold that the quantity and quality of the evidence of similarity precludes the possibility that it would occur in the writing of another randomly selected person by pure coincidence. In fact, there are differences in the levels at which certainty is reached by each examiner. As long as personal experience prescribes, simply, that conclusions exceed the level of certainty at which the risk of error would give any examiner cause for concern, no attempt is made to define the levels precisely. The argument is closed in the form of a question. What would be gained? Perhaps only the satisfaction of consciously moving in the direction of orthodox scientific method, but this should be reason enough.

Obviously, there is little to be gained when the evidence is overwhelming, It is only when evidence nears the lower limits for positive conclusions that examiners have arbitrarily set for themselves, that we see divergence occurring in the findings of examiners. As the strength of the evidence diminishes, conclusions such as "a very strong probability…," "A strong probability…," "It is highly probable…," "It is probable…," "There is evidence to indicate…," and a multitude of others make their appearance in reports and testimony.

Whittaker[14] challenged, yet cautioned, criminalists:

> "It is the responsibility of the criminalist to command the written and verbal skills necessary to make crystal clear to his listener of what exactly the probative strength level of the identification consists."

There are few topics respecting writing identification on which more has been written by a greater congregation of persons than on the subject of probable conclusions or qualified opinions. Whether or not qualified opinions should be expressed at all is an issue that has long been debated. Those that oppose their use may do so from a lack of understanding of statistical inference and may wish to avoid discussions of it from a witness box. There are, however, good reasons for the use of statements of probability.

Principal among them is the fact that, as Trueblood stated, all conclusions, whether positive or not, are expressions of probability and it is important for this to be recognized. Moreover, we are no better equipped to articulate the level of probability chosen for a positive conclusion than we are for a qualified one.

Then too, as this author wrote 35 years ago, the legal profession should be made aware that their process of reaching conclusions is, in principle, the same as that of the scientist. The court's own criterion for establishing the guilt of a person — "beyond a reasonable doubt" — discreetly avoids stipulating "with certainty" or "beyond any doubt."

> "The scientist, too, never proves everything "with certainty" or "beyond a doubt;" the best he can ever hope to say is that he has established a fact "beyond a *reasonable* doubt." The difference between the experimental and the legal situations is that the scientist has learned how to calculate the probability of the doubt. This has been the contribution of statistics."[15]

Advances in scientific fields have done no more and no less than enable us to make closer approximations to the truth, whatever that may be. The search for truth seems reason enough for handwriting examiners to engage statistics to assist them in the definition and clarification of the levels of certainty, confidence, or probability, in order that conclusions being drawn are more precise reflections of the truth.

Hilton[16] wrote an excellent dissertation on the relationship of mathematical probability to handwriting identification, but confined his remarks to cases in which unqualified opinions were expressed. His comments were directed particularly at the criticisms of Kirk[17] respecting the absence of probability data in published material, that had prompted Kirk to say:

> "Handwriting analysis, despite statements to the contrary, cannot be truly "scientific" until such serious omissions as these are repaired."

Hilton pointed out some of the difficulties in collecting and classifying the writing data that Kirk insisted someone should assemble. Not the least of these is the allowance to be made for natural variation in the measurement of discriminating elements, the uncertainty of the degree of independence between elements and the unsuitability of some elements to any process of measurement. In this regard Hilton mentions such aspects as skill, speed, shading (i.e., pen pressure), and writing quality.

McAlexander, Beck, and Dick,[18] in a review of some 60 different manners of enunciating conclusions, has suggested nine expressions (*identification, strong probability, probability, evidence to indicate, no conclusion, indications did not, probably did not, strong probability did not, elimination*) to reflect levels of certainty without locating them precisely on the continuum of probability from 0 to 1. Ellen[19] has proposed a scale of five expressions (*identification, high probability, could or consistent with, inconclusive, no evidence and likely to be by different persons*) and argues that fewer divisions on the scale permits them to be more easily defined. The problem with these expressions is that they mean different things to different people. Both authors attempt at some length to explain exactly their intended interpretations. Terms suggested for forensic odontologists[20] are even less precise.

If, in the past, there has been a reluctance on the part of examiners to express qualified opinions, or on the part of lawyers and the courts to use them, this seems to be the case no longer. Scott[21] cited several cases in which testimony of writing examiners was expressed in a wide variety of manners, some very poorly, and each was accepted by the courts.

Leung and Cheung[22] have thoroughly reviewed the practises and views of some 40 examiners worldwide. Their survey provides 16 divisions and the probability levels (in percentages) for many of them. Noteworthy in their report is the variation in the zero points on the scale, and the directions in which the scales run.

This survey disclosed that there is much diversity in the use of percentages as measures of certainty. Confusion stems on occasion from the placement of the zero and the 100 percent points of the scale. Some run levels of certainty in descending order from 100 percent for definite-positive, to 0 percent for definite-negative. Others used percentages as indicators of the degree of certainty in opposing scales of identification and elimination, starting from 0 percent for the level of an inconclusive finding.

The latter practise introduces another uncertainty into the process, for the point of inconclusiveness is not precisely determined, regardless of the direction that the scale is running (i.e., towards an identification or an elimination). In our view, it is preferable to think in terms of a single scale for identification respecting any particular writer, wherein levels approaching 0 percent are indications that it is almost an impossibility for this writer to have executed the questioned material. In statistical language, the level of inclusiveness is 0.5 or 50 percent, and a level of 50 percent means that the toss of a coin would be as reliable an indicator of the writer's involvement as is the handwriting.

As has been maintained in other writings,[23] the only means that is available to us to convert observations and evaluations (or judgments such as conclusions) that are qualitative, subjective, and private, to forms that are quantitative, objective, and public, is by means of numerical values that are communicable. Not surprisingly, criticisms are now being voiced in different locales. For example, McKenna[24] and Found and Rogers,[25] have commented respecting the vagueness of the expressions used and advocated, and their interpretations.

Brown and Cropp[26] ventured to propose conversions for the findings in all fields of forensic science in suggesting four levels of approximate probability commencing from 0.5, the statistical level of chance. These consisted of Possibly (0.5-0.9 or 50-90 percent), Probably (0.9-0.99 or 90-99 percent), Very Probably (0.99-0.999 or 99-99.9 percent) and Almost Certainly (>0.999 or >99.9 percent).

Any attempt to use probabilities (statistics) to reflect the likelihood of things happening in the real world requires that we understand certain statistical terms, and three of them in particular: *Randomness, Independence*, and *Clustering*.

Randomness.   When we say that there is a strong probability that writer A wrote Q, we are, in fact, implying that the chances of *selecting at random* another person in the same population with similar writing characteristics (i.e., discriminating elements) is very low.

Randomness is the property of the process of selection that gives each person in the population possessing a particular combination of a number of items (e.g., writers with 10 particular discriminating elements) the same chance of being the sample selected. In the toss of a coin, randomness ensures that heads and tails have equal opportunities to occur, but it does not guarantee that a head (or if you wish a tail) will occur every second time.

Randomness allows us to calculate the approximate predictability of occurrences by relative frequencies, the degree of approximation depending, by the Law of Large Numbers, on the number of observations (i.e., features) being considered.

Independence.   Events are said to be independent if the probability that one of them will have a certain outcome is the same no matter what the outcome of all the other events may be. For example: the occurrence of an Epsilon "ϵ" in a person's writing should be independent of the occurrence of a Palmer "r" or a Palmer "t".

In writing examinations, the matter of independence means that a number of class, national, or system characteristics cannot be considered to be as many separate pieces of evidence, but can only be considered collectively as one.

Clustering.   Many events in the real world seem to happen in clusters: accidents, deaths, successful rolls of the dice. We've heard it said, "I'm on a roll." We even wager on this basis. It seems that clustering affords a basis for forecasting the observations in an otherwise random sequence. The more often that "black" pays the more likely "red" will appear in the next event. Nonetheless, as long as the events are independent of one another and the selection is random, the likelihood of a particular result, like the ones on which we may wager, aren't improved one iota.

One of the impediments to progress in our understanding of the application of statistical inference to writing examinations is in the conflict between the meaning of *probability*, as a statistician might use it, and the more vernacular sense of the layman. As has been pointed out,[27] to be semantically tenable one cannot say, "There is a strong probability that writer A executed Q." One can only say, "Writer A did or did not write Q."

In fact, what we are saying when we use probability expressions is that if we act on the assumption that "writer A wrote Q" the likelihood is that we will be correct. Indeed, Webster defines *probability* as "a likelihood, something that, judged by present evidence, is likely to be true." But how likely? To paraphrase Oxford's definition of *probable*, if we say, "Writer A probably wrote Q" we are making a statement that is worthy of belief. But how worthy? And how much more worthy (or likely) is a strong probability than a probability?

There is no alternative to numbers that is available to us to define precisely what we mean by *probability, strong probability, very strong probability,* or any similar expression, to indicate the respective levels of certainty that each represents.

If we think of percentage probabilities in the lexical sense that Webster has suggested, rather than the statistical sense, that of representing "the likelihood of being true," it may help to understand the proposals of Brown and Cropp, whom we cited earlier. These authors have suggested that expressions of *probability* should be considered as lying between the 90 and 99 percentages, which is to say that the risk of error in identifying the wrong person is no greater than 1 in 10 and may be as small as 1 in 100. They suggest that an expression of *very probably* should be considered as lying between the 99 and 99.9 percentages, which is to say that the risk of error in identifying the wrong person is no greater than 1 in a 100 and may be as small as 1 in 1,000. A finding of *almost certainly* is anything greater than 99.9 percent, that is a level at which the risk of error in identifying the wrong person is less than 1 in 1,000. These are ratios that should be within the comprehension abilities of most examiners and may be worthy of adoption, at least until more reliable data is available.

In our earlier writings, we suggested that percentages such as these might be thought of as risks of error or duplicity. A statement of a 90 percent probability means that the chance of finding in another sample of writing as much correspondence in writing features as these known writings exhibit would be 1 in 10, if a writer was selected at random from the same population. Similarly a 99 percent probability lowers the odds to 1 in 100, and a 99.9 percent probability represents a chance of 1 in 1000 of encountering another writer in the same population with a similar combination of writing characteristics.

At the same time, because of the clustering phenomenon that we mentioned above, one must use caution in applying this kind of probability thinking to particular cases. A chance of one in a thousand does not mean that there can't be two or three writers exhibiting the same degree of correspondence in a particular sample of one thousand persons.

In some respects, however, this provides a better concept of the ballpark we are playing in. If more than 10 percent of a population would display as much similarity in writing characteristics (i.e., a less than 90 percent probability respecting the known writer) the risk of error or duplicity is high, the likelihood of a conclusion of identification being true is low, and the evidence of identity cannot be very strong. If more than 1 percent of the population would display this degree of similarity (i.e., a less than 99 percent probability), the risk may be lower because the evidence is stronger but not overwhelming. Suffice it to say, any qualified opinion that is thought of or translated into a probability of identification of a magnitude of less than 0.9 or 90 percent says little for the strength of the evidence, the risk of error or the likelihood of being true. The writings of Brown and Cropp implied as much.

Attempts have been made by knowledgeable people to apply the various probability theories to handwriting examination with little success.[28] Two of the reasons for this is the lack of empirical data respecting the frequency of occurrence of writing elements, and the absence of apparent concurrence as to what aspects of a writing constitute significant elements of identification value.

Leung and Cheung, cited earlier, have suggested an 11-point scale running from a midpoint 0, for inconclusive, to ±5 for positive identifications or eliminations that might be used somewhat arbitrarily to clarify the level of certainty in the mind of the examiner. Such a scale implies that the differences between the levels of the scale are more or less uniform. It also implies that the difference between an inconclusive finding and the lowest level of a significant probability is not particularly great. This is not the picture we are attempting to portray. As the Brown and Cropp scale intimates, the term *probable* should be applied to levels ≥0.9 or ≥90 percent, and allowed to move rather exponentially up the scale from there.

Herein lies the difference in the approaches to probability scales, as conceived by the layman and the statistician. Probability applied to writing identification should not be thought of, necessarily, as a linear regression in which changes between levels are uniform or regular. It may run exponentially, on a scale in which the levels of probability (or risks of error) constantly change. The change in probability at any point is proportional to the level of probability already attained. This is *curvilinear regression* in which probabilities follow a curve rather than a straight line, similar to compound interest.

In writing studies this means that at higher levels of probability on the scale, a small quantity of additional evidence would contribute greater towards an identification than the same quantity would contribute at lower levels. This approach may reflect more accurately what we have in mind in our conclusions.

Even if qualified opinions are defined in these very broad terms some progress will have been made in the direction of greater consistency between examiners, the comprehension of findings and the examiners intended meanings. When examiners begin thinking and speaking alike, we can presume that they are playing the game in the same ballpark.

Thornton[29] admonished forensic experts when he wrote:

> "We have tended to reject statistics and probability because we generally don't understand them, and to concede their validity forces us to admit to our ignorance as to how they would be implemented…. To master statistical models to explain much of our evidence may be a slow, reluctant march through enemy territory, but we must begin to plan for that campaign."

47. If and When Errors Occur in Handwriting Examination, Wherein Lies Their Likely Cause?

It cannot be denied that handwriting study and examination, that is, as yet, a largely subjective assessment of writing elements, has on rare occasions been known to err. Osborn, Harrison, Hilton, and others have commented on the circumstances that lead to erroneous conclusions. More recently, Beck[30] has dealt particularly with three of them. In summary these circumstances include:

1. Inadequate, fallacious or self serving standards for comparison.
2. Quantitative insufficiency of questioned writing.
3. Lack of comprehension respecting the discriminating elements of writing.
4. Lack of appreciation for the writing movement underlying the form.
5. Improper assessment of divergences.
6. Over-evaluation of class or system characteristics.
7. Overlooking or ignoring disparities.
8. Omission of intercomparison of standards to confirm common authorship.
9. Influence of external information respecting the matter.
10. Incompetence on the part of the examiner.

Other factors have also been suggested, including a suspicious attitude or predisposition towards the matter and the documents. Owing to the fact that in North America, cases are submitted to examiners from sources that represent one side of an issue or the other, it is difficult for the examiner to avoid the prejudice that accompanies the submission of material. Objectivity is then put at risk and every component observed in the questioned document may be approached as suspicious.

Some of the circumstances responsible for errors are classed as human factors, such as competition, dishonesty, recognition, or ego. The misinterpretation of facts and the misapplication of scientific principles have also been cited. These can occur in any field of forensic science, and on this, Howard[31] has written, suggesting the establishment of an independent testimony review board.

Gencavage[32] draws attention to the need to examine extended writing closely for the subtle evidence that may exist in a word, a line, or a paragraph having been inserted in a document by a second writer. While evidence of another author can be quite pronounced, every examination should be thorough enough to avoid the errors that haste and assumption can create.

It has been said that handwriting and handlettering identification lends itself readily to unintended bias on the part of the examiner, and bias can lead to error. It is, admittedly, one of the few disciplines of forensic science that depends primarily on a subjective analysis and evaluation of evidence. Most questioned document examiners are aware of this and attempt to be as objective as possible, using sophisticated measurements when they can. Complete objectivity is difficult to achieve, however, particularly in civil cases, because of (1) the circumstances under which the examiner is summoned, and (2) the fact that the identification process is precariously subjective.

Nisbett and Wilson,[33] and Miller[34] reported that there were unconscious factors at work on human behaviour that could account for bias, prejudice, fear, stereotypes, and the like. Applying social-psychological schools of thought to bias among document examiners, it can be seen that a subjective conclusion by the examiner may have been influenced by social interaction, situation, and/or past experience. In a criminal situation, the police may be convinced of the guilt of the accused. Their preoccupation is with procuring sufficient evidence to obtain a conviction. Knowingly or otherwise, the police may communicate their belief to the document examiner in a social interaction. The examiner may assume the existence of other evidence to indicate the guilt of the individual and such unconscious beliefs have the potential to create bias. In a civil action, an attorney may provide the same bias influence on the examiner in expressing his own conviction of his client's innocence. This bias may receive support if the questioned and known writings/letterings exhibit some pictorial similarity. The expectation of payment for an opinion may also have a subtle influence.

Miller attempted to test the hypothesis that document examiners are influenced by the social interaction between themselves and the police or attorney requesting their services and by the situation in which they were requested to do the examination. Twelve college students, trained in the forensic examination of questioned documents, were divided into two groups and provided with fictitious evidence of a case of forgery of cheques. The first group was provided with (1) a synopsis of facts concerning the investigation, (2) the suspect's name and his handwriting examples on a request exemplar form, and (3) three cheques allegedly written by the suspect. Group One was advised that the police had two witnesses that would testify that they saw the suspect write and pass the checks. Group Two was supplied with the same three questioned checks and writing exemplars from two additional suspects. They were not advised of expected witness testimony and were simply asked if any of the three suspects wrote any of the questioned cheques. In fact none of the suspects had written any of the cheques.

The conclusions reached by the examiners supported the bias hypothesis. Four of the examiners in the first group wrongly identified the suspect as the writer of the cheques. One examiner was inconclusive and one examiner was correct. All six of the examiners in Group Two correctly eliminated all three suspects.

Miller admits that his experiment was superficial. His examiners were university students and the questions are left unanswered respecting their course of training, their trainers, or their experience. His point is simply that bias is difficult to control and offers three suggestions to limit its effects. First, information should not be provided regarding a writer's possible involvement with a written document. Second, writings from more than one suspect should be submitted, and thirdly, when possible, collected specimens from writers should be submitted.

There are those that will argue these points: that some information is useful, or that the examination of the writings of a second or third subject would be an unnecessary waste of time and trouble. No one will argue, however, that collected specimens are not vital to any examination of handwriting.

It seems fitting to end this discussion of the reasons for and means of avoiding error with the comments of Alwyn Cole who wrote:

> "The standard or base of experience to which the document examiner refers every new examination does not remain static. It is subject to small changes day by day, especially in the early years of experience. A period of success will tend to make the standard more liberal. A single error or near miss will raise the standard as a protection against repetition. Over a long period of time, the standard becomes more efficient and permits the greatest number of useful judgments with the best protection against error." [35]

References

1. Hilton, Ordway, The Collection of Writing Standards in Criminal Investigation. *Journal of Criminal Law Criminology and Police Science*, 1941 July-August; 32: 2: pp 241-236.

2. Hilton, Ordway, A Further Look at Writing Standards. *Journal of Criminal Law, Criminology and Police Science*, 1965; 56: 3: pp 382-389.

3. Hilton, Ordway, *A Second Look at Signature Standards*. Presented at the meeting of the American Society of Questioned Document Examiners (San Francisco, 1967).

4. Hodgins, J. H., Request Specimen Writing for Comparison Purposes. *Royal Canadian Mounted Police Gazette*, 1967 March; pp 15-16.

5. Hilton, Ordway, *Scientific Examination of Questioned Documents*. Revised edition 1982 (New York: Elsevier/North-Holland, Inc.) p 316.

6. Osborn, Albert S., *The Problem of Proof* (New York: Matthew Bender & Co., 1922), pp 50-51.

7. Hall, M. G. and Hardcastle, R. A., *Is a Universal Handwriting Specimen Feasible?* Presented at the meeting of the International Association of Forensic Sciences (Vancouver, 1987).

8. Purtell, David J., Handwriting Standard Forms. *Journal of Criminal Law, Criminology and Police Science*, 1963; 54: pp 523-528.

9. Huber, Roy A., The Quandary of "Qualified Opinions." *Canadian Society of Forensic Science Journal*, 1980; 13: 3: p 7.

10. Hilton, Ordway, The Relationship of Mathematical Probability to the Handwriting Identification Problem. *Royal Canadian Mounted Police, Crime Detection Laboratories, Seminar No. 5*, 1958; p 127.

11. Dixon, Wilfred J. and Massey, Frank J. Jr., *Introduction to Statistical Analysis* (New York: McGraw-Hill, 1951), p 2.

12. Huber, Roy A., Expert Witnesses. *Criminal Law Quarterly*, 1959; 2: 3: pp 276-295.

13. Trueblood, E., *General Philosophy* (New York: Harper, 1963).

14. Whittaker, Edward, The Adversary System: Role of the Criminalist. *Journal of Forensic Sciences*, 1973 July; 18: 3: pp 184-187.

15. McElrath, G. W. and Berman, J. E., Letters to the Editor. *Science*, 1956 September; 24: 589-590. With permission.

16. Hilton, Ordway, The Relationship of Mathematical Probability to the Handwriting Identification Problem. *RCMP Crime Detection Laboratories, Seminar No. 5*, 1958; pp 121-128.

17. Kirk, P. L., *Crime Investigation* (New York: Interscience Publishers, 1953), pp 475-476.

18. McAlexander, Thomas V., Beck, Jan, and Dick, Ronald M., The Standardization of Handwriting Opinion Terminology, in Letters to the Editor, *Journal of Forensic Sciences*, 1991 March; 36: 2: pp 311-319.

19. Ellen, D. M., The Expression of Conclusions in Handwriting Examination. *Canadian Society of Forensic Science Journal*, 1979; 12: 3: pp 117-120.

20. Dailey, John Curtis, Identification Strength Scale, in Letters to the Editor, *Journal of Forensic Sciences*, 1987 March; 32: 2: pp 317-318.

21. Scott, Charles C., *Inconclusive Opinions as Viewed by the Courts*. Presented at the meeting of the American Society of Questioned Document Examiners (Aurora, CO, 1988).

22. Leung, S. C. and Cheung, Y. L., *On Opinion*. Presented at the meeting of the American Society of Questioned Document Examiners (Aurora, CO, 1988).

23. Huber, Roy A. and Headrick, A. M., Let's Do it by Numbers. *Forensic Science International*, 1990; 46: pp 209-218.

24. *United States v. Starzecpyzel*, 880 F. Supp. 1027 (S.D.N.Y. 1995).

25. Found, Bryan and Rogers, Doug, Contemporary Issues in Forensic Handwriting Examination. A Discussion of Key Issues in the Wake of the Starzecpyzel Decision. *Journal of Forensic Document Examination*, 1995 Fall; 8: p 21.

26. Brown, G. A. and Cropp, P. L., Standardized Nomenclature in Forensic Science. *Journal of the Forensic Science Society,* 1987; 27: pp 393-399.

27. Huber, Roy A., The Quandary of Qualified Opinions. *Canadian Society of Forensic Science Journal,* 1980; 13: 3: pp 1-8.

28. Karlsson, J. E., What is the Probability that Jones' Signature is Genuine? *Canadian Society of Forensic Science Journal,* 1987; 20: p 114.

29. Thornton, John I., The DNA Statistical Paradigm vs. Everything Else, in Letters to the Editor, *Journal of Forensic Sciences,* 1997 July; 42: 4: p 758.

30. Beck, Jan, Sources of error in forensic handwriting evaluation. *Journal of Forensic Sciences,* 1995; 40: 1: pp 78-82.

31. Howard, Larry B., The Dichotomy of the Expert Witness. *Journal of Forensic Sciences,* 1986 January; 31: 1: pp 337-341.

32. Gencavage, John S., Recognition and Identification of Multiple Authorship. *Journal of Forensic Sciences,* 1987; 32: 4: pp 130-136.

33. Nisbett, R. E. and Wilson, T. D., Telling More Than We Can Know: Verbal Reports on Mental Processes. *Psychological Review,* 1977; 84: pp 231-259.

34. Miller, Larry S., Bias Among Forensic Document Examiners: A Need for Procedural Changes. *Journal of Police Science and Administration,* 1984; 12: 4: pp 407-411.

35. Cole, Alwyn, *Qualification in Reports and in Testimony.* Presented at the meeting of the American Society of Questioned Document Examiners (Denver, CO, 1964).

The Diagnosis of Writing Identification

11

48. Is it Possible to Produce a Perfect Forgery?

This question does not have a simple answer. What is considered to be perfect, and who will be the judge? If we are speaking of a quality of forgery that will deceive the lay person, then the answer is unquestionably "yes." It is a daily occurrence. If, however, we are speaking of a forgery that will not be detected as such by a competent examiner, then other questions arise. Are we dealing with a quantity of extended cursive writing, or handlettering, or are we dealing with a signature? And if a signature, is the name long or short? Is it awkward or fluent? And, regardless of its length, is it a recognizable writing or does it lack all sense of letter forms?

To answer the question as briefly as possible, there is no practical way of knowing whether or not perfect forgeries have been created. Being perfect, they necessarily escape detection. Forgeries that have been detected must be something less than perfect. Under certain circumstances, forgeries can and have been produced that have been exceedingly difficult for the most competent examiners to detect. Under most other circumstances, forgeries are frequently produced which, while not readily detected by lay persons, are within the capacity of the competent examiner to recognize as being what they are: spurious executions.

For a further discussion of this subject, the reader is directed to Section 50, respecting the existence of professional forgers.

49. Is it Possible to Produce An Autoforgery?

Normally, *autoforgery* would be defined as a forgery of one's signature created by oneself. This, however, is a contradiction of terms for a forgery must be, by definition, an execution performed by another person. The observation must be made, then, that there is no such thing as autoforgery. Thus, the question becomes: whether or not a person can so subtly alter his/her signature that its alteration will pass casual scrutiny and, under normal circumstances, will be accepted as genuine. At the same time, the signature will, by virtue of some omission, modification, or addition of a less conspicuous handwriting attribute, deceive handwriting examiners into concluding and believing that the signature is spurious.

In a study of twenty subjects, Cole[1] found it to be beyond the capacity of the persons in his study to accomplish the task posed by this question. He did, however, find that a few subjects revealed what he considered to be a potential for an appropriate handwriting change that a period of practise might develop. On the other hand, his subjects were given a week to practise and were asked to submit only their most successful efforts. One wonders, then, whether additional practise would significantly alter the results, and whether the subjects themselves would be able to appreciate the improvement. Furthermore, we have to assume that the subject is aware of the nature of the change to his/her handwriting that would be appropriate. This being the case, the ability of a person to develop their potential for autoforgery may not be a particularly practical possibility that the handwriting examiner needs to entertain.

The circumstances under which an individual might pursue this kind of action are unquestionably remote, but Cole describes two scenarios involving large sums of money in which the denial of signatures containing minor defects converts the question posed above from the hypothetical to the more realistic form. Notwithstanding the few instances in which a person might be disposed to fabricate an irregular signature of this kind, there are numerous other instances in which a faulty memory coupled with a minor irregularity in the writing may induce an individual to honestly or dishonestly deny its execution. The handwriting examination on these occasions must address the issues of natural variation, accidental occurrence, deliberate modification, and true difference.

50. Are There Such Persons as Professional Forgers?

McCarthy,[2] Buglio and Gidion,[3] McCarthy,[4] Lee and Scott (1998), have reported on the skill of a few known individuals at producing freehand simulations of various person's signatures. Some authors have suggested that there are others. The five individuals on whom these studies focused were relatively skilled, and with one exception, were noncriminal freehand forgers, who had only an avocational interest in simulating signatures that had prompted them to practise. None of the products of these persons was judged to be beyond the capacity of competent examiners to detect as spurious, given adequate standards. Osborn wrote, years ago, that it is "Fortunate that the rare one or two out of hundreds of thousands who might do this act well are seldom inclined to do it and that the one who attempts it is usually not well qualified."

Totty[5] investigated the ability of one individual who, by virtue of training and profession, might be expected to succeed in creating accurate reproductions of signatures. The subject was a graphic artist, with professional training at college and university in the field, and 10 years practical experience in the preparation of copy for advertisements, sales literature, and packaging. He was a skilled artist and accustomed to making accurate freehand drawings from sketches or outlines. He had no interest in the simulation of signatures and had never previously attempted to do so.

He was asked to copy the signatures of four individuals, working at his own speed, under his own conditions, using materials of his own choosing, without restriction as to time or extent of practise. The object of the exercise was to study the ability of a skilled person in copying signatures under optimum conditions.

The results were that overall pictorial accuracy and a high level of skill and fluency was achieved. The classic symptoms of forgery, i.e., tremour, poor line quality, hesitation, and pen lifts, were almost entirely absent although some pen lifts and blunt stroke endings did occur. The subject paid less attention to details of letter designs and it is to these more subtle features that the examiner's attention is directed when the work of a professional must be taken into account.

Ordinarily, however, this question seems to be seeking the existence of a market of competent people who are available to the public for illicit purposes and whose services may be engaged for a price. When considered in this light, the answer to the question is clearly no, at least as far as is currently known. If the services of a professional forger were available, the user of such services must be cognizant of the fact that, in so doing, he or she gains a dangerous ally, who could become a permanent blackmailer.

This being the case, the matter of considering the possibility that any given disputed signature might be the work of a hired penman possessing particular skill diminishes in its potential. While it cannot be ignored completely, the risk of error in disregarding such a proposition is, in most cases, extremely low. This low risk notwithstanding, the possible occurrence of a perfect forgery needs to be acknowledged. What is meant by *perfect* is really a subjective judgment of the forger's ability to deceive, and that will vary with the circumstances under which the forgery is scrutinized and the perceptivity of the scrutineer. It can also vary with the kind of signature involved. Shorter signatures, those in which letter forms have diminished to simply undulating lines, and those, wherein proper structure and design has been sacrificed in favour of embellishments that almost invariably suffer from great variation from one execution to the next, make a good reproduction more difficult to discriminate from the genuine. However, just as there are degrees of proficiency in the act of writing, there are degrees of proficiency in the act of executing forgeries, and it may well be that the fruits of some of the best have escaped detection, in the course of their examination or inspection.

Buglio and Gidion (1977) reported on the ability of one individual who displayed remarkable talent and speed in simulating the signatures of others. As a demonstration of his talent, he produced a simulation of the signature of each of 32 individuals that was combined randomly on a single sheet with 11 genuine signatures. These examples were employed in a study of the level of this simulator's competence in duplicating signatures.

The authors claim that the simulations are reasonably good reproductions. They can be distinguished upon careful and thorough examination by competent examiners, with the benefit of the 11 standards for comparison on the same sheet, notwithstanding the fact that the spurious signatures were randomly distributed among the genuine executions. This is a somewhat ideal situation in which a comparison might be made. What the results might be if one was to encounter a signature in isolation, or had less suitable standards for comparison, are questions to be considered. A further question is raised as to whether any of the spurious signatures could be positively eliminated.

As these authors point out, their single subject cannot constitute a threat to the profession of handwriting examination. Nevertheless, they do acknowledge that the finding of this one person with the prerequisite ability to simulate the writings of others reasonably well compels one to allow that there may exist others within the population possessing equal or greater skill. The likelihood of such a person being involved in a given and particular case is a proposition that depends on many ancillary factors, including accessibility, awareness, availability, and amenability to a fraudulent act. When all factors are considered, the likelihood of there being an involvement of a willing person, having the necessary qualifications, at the right time and place, seems extremely remote. Consideration of such a prospect is likely to be unwarranted.

A point that may be of some interest to readers is that the simulator is left-handed and professed to experience greater difficulty in duplicating the writings of the two left-handed persons among the group of 32. No reasons are offered for this.

The adept penman in this case was an individual with some drawing, if not artistic, ability. He is well educated, holding a Ph.D. in criminology and membership in the American Academy of Forensic Sciences. The authors leave us to ponder the question as to how many others there may be with equal or greater skill. Although the answer is speculative, it is reasonably safe to say that none are likely to profess the same personal attributes or qualifications.

Should an examiner be concerned about the prospects of a given questioned signature being the work of someone that is particularly adept at duplicating another person's writing? A few observations can be made that may be helpful:

1. Simulated forgeries of high quality will probably display little or no evidence of the slowness or lack of fluency that is normally one of the hallmarks of spuriousness.
2. Standard signatures of poor quality call for equally poor quality in their duplication, however, the simulation may, in fact, display a superiority in writing style or writing quality.
3. Writers are known to have deliberately altered their writing styles in their signatures with limited practise and in a limited period of time.
4. On questioned cheques, witnessed endorsements may be poorer than unwitnessed maker's signatures, even if both are in the same name.
5. In skillful simulations, the differences between the questioned signature and the known standards will be more subtle. Their study must be more carefully conducted, standards must be more contemporary in time and, if possible, should be prepared or produced under more comparable circumstances.

McCarthy's (1984) study of the work of two adept penmen provides a number of valuable observations respecting his two subjects that are worth bearing in mind should the possibility of this rare quality of simulation occur:

1. Deceptive simulations of unskilled writing can be accomplished with little or no practise.
2. Skilled simulations done from memory can be as deceptive as those made with a model at hand.
3. With proper standards the author of some simulations can be identified.
4. Simulations of signatures in a foreign alphabet may be difficult for a simulator to produce, but equally difficult for an examiner to detect.
5. Retouching of skilled simulations is a very infrequent occurrence.
6. Flying starts and finishes can occur in better quality or skilled simulations.
7. Reduction in the size of a simulation from that of a model is achievable, but requires some practise.
8. Simulations will equal the size of the model if there are no space constraints.

9. Two simulations of the same model by the same skilled simulator may be near superimposable.

10. Deceptive simulations may not provide sufficient evidence that they are spurious, but conversely, when doubt exists, it should not be assumed that they are genuine.

11. Deceptive simulations can appear among the standards for comparison.

12. Practise on several documents from which one is selected to be proffered will result in a better quality of what then becomes the questioned signature.

13. The methods employed by skilled simulators will vary.

14. The simulations of two different skilled simulators are distinguishable under optimum conditions.

15. Simulators of great skill have an unusual capacity to remember complex images and forms, but may not believe that they have special eidetic (power of recall) capabilities.

51. What Are the Attributes of Assisted- or Guided-Hand Signatures?

This is a topic that has provoked much interest and some controversy over the years. Much of that which has been written deals with isolated instances encountered by document examiners. Little that may be called true research has been conducted and this may be the reason for some of the controversy. Furthermore, it is not a subject that the examiner is required to deal with very often.

Invariably, the writing involved, when assistance is needed, is a signature, although there have been exceptions to this rule. Terms used to refer to the action include (1) *inert-hand,* (2) *guided-hand,* (3) *assisted-hand,* and (4) *forced-hand,* and are intended to reflect the different levels or degrees of voluntary action on the part of the signatory, or the requirement for help. The term *aided-hand* has been employed in lieu of *guided-hand* or *assisted-hand* but without further definition. The term *death-bed signature* has also been used, but it is even less specific as to the method of production and only indicative as to place and time. For clarification we would define these terms as follows:

The *inert-hand* is completely involuntary, incapable of motor activity and the signatory may be conscious or even unconscious. It has been suggested that completely illiterate persons might appear in this group when their ignorance of the document is being exploited. Foley and Kelly[6] describe the state as *total incapacitation.* These cases are rare.

The *guided-hand* and *assisted-hand* actions are attempts to define slightly different situations that may disclose slightly different characteristics. The *guided-hand* situation is one in which the person providing the guidance usually dominates the writing process and provides the greater portion of control. The *assisted-hand* situation is one in which the person assisting provides help to a lesser degree, perhaps only to the point of steadying a tremulous arm or hand, without actually directing the movement of the writing instrument.

These latter two terms refer to what Foley and Kelly called *partial incapacitation* and relate to a continuum of signatory abilities ranging from little or none to near normal. These cases are more common.

Signatures of *inert-hands, guided-hands,* or *assisted-hands* are often the products of a line of thinking that a writing instrument must be in the hand of the signatory, even if mentally or physically incapable, in order for a signature to be accepted as legally valid.

Occasionally, they appear as the products of young children in some expression of greeting or gratitude directed at family and relatives, where parents are, obviously, the guiders or assistants.

The *forced-hand* is a term that Locard[7] and Mathyer[8] employed to refer to somewhat, although not entirely, theoretical situations of a criminal nature in which the signatory is forced to write against his will, by threats, constraints or extortion. It is alleged to have occurred with people and prisoners in World War II (1939-1945) and more recently in the incarceration of hostages on the international scene. Understandably, few cases can be cited.

To avoid misunderstanding as to which of the individuals involved in the writing act reference is being made, authors resort to such terms as *guider* and *guided*, or *assister* and *assisted*. But *guider* and *assister* are not normally found within English lexicons. We choose to use the term *signatory* to refer to the person whose name is being inscribed upon the document, who is the individual requiring the assistance or guidance, and the term *coadjutant* to refer to the individual providing the enabling aid.

The *inert-hand*, by its very name and nature, provides no evidence to associate it with the signatory. On the other hand, the signature of an inert-hand may be identifiable with the person controlling the movement of the writing instrument. The impediment provided by the signatory's hand results in less regularity in the writing, greater angularity, pen stops (halts), and disconnections. It also effects the forms and locations of diacritics and "t" crossings. Locard (1951) cites a case of a quadriplegic who wrote well prior to incapacitation. As a product of entirely passive collaboration, the signature to a will was unlike the signatory's former writing or that of the guider, except for the fact that it reflected a writing style, Anglaise de Sacre Coeur, corresponding to that of the individual, i.e., the coadjutant, controlling the signatory's hand.

Almost invariably, the questioned writing or signature and the relevant action within this category is referred to as *guided-hand* or *assisted-hand* signatures. The guidance or assistance required ranges from minimal — the steadying of a tremour — to complete — the maneuvering of the hand through the course of the writing act.

The assistance provided and its effect upon the written product varies with the level of dominance of the coadjutant's hand that is assisting or guiding the signatory's hand. As may be expected, if the signatory is passive the coadjutant will dominate and the signature tends to acquire characteristics of the latter.

If the signatory is not completely passive and the coadjutant endeavours to dominate, conflicts occur in the execution of writing elements. If the assistance rendered is minor, the effect on the written product may be little, or indeed, unobservable.

Assistance at this level will amount to either a steadying of the arm, or a steadying of the hand, and the degree of interference with the writing process will differ somewhat from case to case. The steadying of the hand requires greater pressure and control, and consequently, the results will be more distorted. Needless to say, both steadying methods involve some conflict, but a steadying of the arm is less restrictive for the signatory and, accordingly, the product will be closer to the individual's writing prior to the onset of tremour or dehabilitation.

In the extreme, the participation of the signatory may be no more than a resting of the hand on the arm or hand of the individual doing the actual writing. Or it may be limited to a grasping of the end of the writing instrument. This is a practise having some historical significance in that it was followed a century ago in the application of signatures of Indian band leaders to treaties with governments. Hence, came the expression: "The laying on of hands."

Many cases, however, appear to be within the group where conflict is evident. Irregularities in the writing occurs due to a lack of harmony and coordination of movement impulses between the two hands involved.[9] As Osborn pointed out many years ago, guided-hand signatures exhibit uneven alignment and inconsistent spacing between letters, and these are two of the less conscious elements of handwriting. They also display abrupt changes in direction, disconnections, superfluous strokes, as in false starts, and a general decrepitude of the writing. These then, are the symptoms of genuineness.[10] Conversely, smoothness, continuity, shading, pen control, careful retouching, and the meticulous joining of stroke endings can be construed as evidence of spuriousness.

Such conflict tends to produce a more angular product and a reduction in writing size. Alignments that an unassisted writer has difficulty maintaining can be substantially improved. Furthermore, in situations of conflict, the coadjutant tends to anticipate the pen movement. Consequently, the level of conflict is greater and the influence of the coadjutant is more pronounced in the execution of more unusual or peculiar letter formations or writing movements.

It is to be expected that the speed of the writing act will be slowed because of the conflict. Letter dimensions are irregular, spacing is broader, pen pressure becomes greater than normal for either party and letter forms are generally larger. Ascending and descending strokes and loops tend to be longer than customary and executed with greater pressure. Foley and Kelly (1977), however, found, in their study, that assistance for their subjects tended to reduce writing size.

Contributions to the conflict of hands may result from differences in the normal and natural practises of the two parties, particularly where differences are pronounced in writing slants and in the progression and locations in which diacritics are applied. Some writers are in the habit of dotting the letter "i" and crossing the letter "t" immediately after completing the letter, whereas other writers apply them after completing a group of letters or the entire word.

Few of the authors of books on handwriting identification of a century ago, other than Osborn, have mentioned the subject of guided-hand signatures in their dissertations. Frazer[11] devoted several pages to the measurement of questioned signatures of this kind for the purpose of discriminating between the elements of the writing emanating from the guided and those emanating from the guider. This apparently proved to have limited results, quite out of proportion to the amount of work involved.

In our limited experience with these kinds of questioned writings, and as Sellers[12] maintained, where conflict between the hands is great, it may render the product almost unidentifiable with either individual. The signature produced will be erratic in size, in spacing, in slant, in alignment, in commencement and terminating strokes, in speed or fluency, and in skill. The opposition between the hands yields false starts, grotesque characters, deviating movements, and pen jabs into the paper that can be destructive. This latter feature, however, when present, can of itself be evidence that the signature was guided.

Different views have been expressed as to whether guided-hand signatures are valid or not. Sellers raises the issue as to whether unconscious individuals, incapacitated individuals unable to resist, illiterate individuals ignorant of the purpose of or need for the signature, and/or any individual lacking the mental, physical, or oral facility to register or indicate disagreement with the process should be protected from the assumption that the writing of their name attests to anything. Along this line of thinking, Mathyer[13] makes the point that the more evidence one can find in the questioned signature of the signatory's normal writing characteristics, the more evidence there is that the signatory participated voluntarily.

Skelly[14] argues that without any evidence of awareness or consent the matter must be left to the courts to decide. McNally[15] maintains, similarly, that guided-hand signatures are products of the person doing the guiding, the coadjutant, coupled with aberrations and distortions resulting from the particular writing conditions. Along the same lines Mathyer states that, in European countries, a signature created by or with an inert-hand, a guided-hand, or an assisted-hand would not constitute a signature, in that it is not the product of a series of more or less rapid reflex movements. Rather, it should be referred to more correctly and simply as a written name.

There is, however, an even more fundamental controversy. Notwithstanding the many pages that have been written on the subject, there are those that question whether an actual guided-hand or assisted-hand signature exists. Harrison[16] states that every guided or assisted-hand signature examined by him has been declared a forgery. It may be this experience that prompts him to stress the importance of obtaining, at the outset, precise details of the manner in which the questioned signature is alleged to have been inscribed in order that the evidence within the signature can be considered as to its plausibility under the claimed writing circumstances. His view of the dubious nature of guided-hand signatures was shared by Ruenes[17] who wrote in 1949 and later reiterated that:

> "The guided hand is only one of the many stories invented to explain the poor quality of a traced forgery or imitation, and as such it is inadequate."

It seldom occurs that more than a single signature of these kinds is disputed in a matter under civil or criminal litigation. Jones,[18] however, describes a case in which a claim was made that certain signatures written over a period of time were genuine but assisted, as the writer had suffered from an injury to the hand. The point of this paper is the contention that in cases where several signatures are involved, the effect of assistance should vary in location within the signature from one execution to the next. Control, under such circumstances, is never consistent or constant, but vacillates from guider to guided and signature to signature. Apparent defects in the signatures, then, are not likely to occur in the same manner and location over a purported period of time. When it does, the evidence it provides of spuriousness is impressive.

There is an aspect of these cases that must not be overlooked. It is the reconstruction of the circumstances under which the signature is purported to have been executed. Gähwiler[19] reported on it, Mathyer[20] experimented with it, and Sellers[21] recommended it: that is, the production of sample signatures while duplicating the circumstances that allegedly occurred. As we reported earlier, Grant described a classic example of a signature, the authenticity of which was disputed, written while standing at a counter holding a weight of unwieldy tools in the other hand, which circumstances significantly altered the execution of the signature. Circumstances must always be considered a variable influencing the written product.

In the majority of instances, the signatory will be in bed and semi-, or fully-reclined. Seldom will he/she be sitting upright. Support for the writing is frequently improvised.

Under these circumstances, it can be quite inconvenient for a second person, the coadjutant, using the same hand as the signatory, to control or conduct the movement of the hand and arm while writing. Frazer, in his comments referred to above, claims that assistance is usually given by "Passing the arm around the body of the invalid or otherwise incapacitated writer, and supporting the writing hand."

In one of the few research studies conducted and reported involving larger samples from actually incapacitated persons (53 subjects), Foley and Kelly (1977) noted the difficulties encountered in orienting the two parties to one another and reported that: "It was necessary to make several attempts on different days to obtain…samples." Obviously, circumstances will have a significant contribution upon the written product, which tends to justify Harrison's want of full details describing the writing act, that was mentioned earlier.

A point that most writers on the subject have made is that appropriate standards for comparison are seldom or never available. A person incapacitated in this fashion is unlikely to execute any other document without considerable difficulty and will avoid doing so. Examiners of handwriting must therefore extrapolate from standards of an earlier or later date, and such a process is sometimes difficult to do and frequently subject to challenge.

52. What Are the Disclosers of Disguise?

Writings are disguised, be they extended writings, letterings or signatures, with the sole objective of concealing the writer's identity. Disguised writings serve various purposes:

1. They may avoid recognition of the writer by the reader, as in the writing of both short and long anonymous communications, threatening or extortion letters, "hate" mail, "nut" mail, and obscene letters.
2. They may be subsequently denied by the author, more often involving the writing of one's own signature, as in autoforgery.
3. They may avoid association of the writer with the writing of an incriminating document as frequently happens in the production of court-ordered writing samples. They may be intended to avoid association with the writing of hold-up notes, or with the writing of fictitious cheques and endorsements on stolen cheques. They may be an attempt to conceal a relationship with the application of fictitious names or signatures to electoral documents, or other official records. Within this group are the writing standards obtained from charged or incarcerated individuals including fingerprint forms, bond forms, as well as exemplar forms and personal effects forms.

Each of these situations are sufficiently different that they produce evidence of somewhat different natures.

Generally speaking, that which is obvious and superficial is disguised while that which is done less consciously and is less conspicuous (and, therefore, may be more individualistic) is usually overlooked. Consequently, the more significant writing elements frequently escape disguise. The intent of the writer seems to be to alter the pictorial effect of the writing. When delicate inconspicuous parts of a writing are executed consistently on repeated occasions, and especially if they are written freely, it is safe to conclude that they are elements that are not disguised.

Disguise in writing is a topic on which much has been written and from a number of different perspectives. Our literature research has produced to date some 75 papers, articles, and books that deal with the subject specifically if not exclusively. A number of these use the term *intentional disguise* which is a redundancy of words since an intent is implied by the word *disguise*.

Osborn[22] contended that there are four changes to the writing that are popular in anonymous letters or extended writings, as methods of disguise: (1) a change in slant, (2) a change in size and/or proportions, (3) a change in style, usually from cursive to block lettering, and (4) the invention of unusual letter forms. It was reported by W. W. Mansfield that in 1925, Dr. Georg Mayer provided a list of 19 points in the disguise of German writing, set down in order according to increasing difficulty in applying them effectively. Saudek[23] who, like Mayer, wrote from the viewpoint of some value to graphology, reported a similar list of 17 points respecting disguise in English writing. Mansfield[24] followed with a list of 52 points, claiming that neither Saudek nor Mayer dealt adequately with the matter in a forensic sense. Each of these authors, has somewhat arbitrarily ascribed levels of difficulty in accomplishing certain changes to one's writing to effectively disguise it. None, however, have provided reliable information as to the kinds of changes that are more popular, more effective in achieving disguise, or more deceiving to the public or to the practising document examiner.

Harris,[25] in what has proven to be the vanguard of an army of more recent studies, reported that in an investigation of 100 disguised writings, 12 particular aspects of writing were altered, to which Harrison[26] added two more. Alford[27] in a study of 135 subjects, Herkt[28] working with 72 writers, Konstantinidis[29] with 98, and others have also reported on similar studies that can be consolidated into a list of 30 changes that may occur, singularly or in combinations, intentionally or as by-products of other changes, in writings wherein disguise has been attempted. These consist of the following:

Frequency of occurrence:		Nature of change:
1.	common	in slant
2.	common	in capital letter designs
3.	common	in lower case letter designs
4.	common	in commencement (approach) or terminating strokes
5.	common	in dimensions (size) of writing
6.	common	in style, i.e., cursive to lettering or script or vice versa
7.	common	in hand used
8.	common	in spacing
9.	common	in upper and lower extenders (stems, staffs, or loops)
10.	common	in speed or fluency of writing
11.	common	in movement to greater angularity
12.	common	to grotesque letter forms
13.	common	to flourishes or embellishments
14.	common	in pen stops
15.	common	in pen lifts
16.	common	in connections
17.	infrequent	in care or writing quality
18.	infrequent	to copybook style
19.	infrequent	in letter proportions
20.	infrequent	in an increase in pen pressure

Frequency of occurrence:		Nature of change:
21.	infrequent	in patching, retouching, or overwriting
22.	infrequent	in alignment
23.	infrequent	in arrangement
24.	infrequent	in diacritics and punctuation, being altered or omitted
25.	infrequent	in special characters, signs, or symbols
26.	infrequent	in numerals
27.	rare	to a previously learned system
28.	rare	to simulate age or illiteracy
29.	rare	in spellings and misspellings
30.	rare	in writing direction (to backward or mirrored writing)

Many of these changes occur in either of two directions: slant may change from forehand to backhand or vice versa, or simply to or from the vertical, size may increase or decrease, spacing may be enlarged or reduced, speed may be increased or decreased, pen stops and lifts may be more frequent or fewer. Writing quality, that usually tends to deteriorate, may on occasion improve with the care and/or consciousness that the act of disguise invokes. Individuals are known to merely change their writing instrument, presumably expecting it to have the desired effect.

In his summary, Alford stated that the elements most often changed drastically affected the pictorial appearance of the writing. Other changes that may occur are in writing elements such as the lower loops of "g" and "y" that simply lend themselves to modification or substitution. Somewhat remarkably, Alford, contrary to his expectations and the principle of escape for the inconspicuous, found that nearly 15 percent of his subjects altered their use of diacritics and punctuation. Konstantinidis found similarly in 19 percent of his Swedish subjects. Notwithstanding these findings, Alford and Bertocchi[30] make the point that disguise seldom results in an alteration to punctuation marks, diacritics, and symbols, and that in studies they conducted these features contributed substantially to the identification of disguised extended writings. This was consistent with the accepted principle that the less conspicuous features of writing, for which there are few readily conceived alternatives, are less subject to change and, thus, are of greater identification value.

Keckler[31] sought to deal with the possible criticism of other studies that results may be unreliable due to differences in the motivation underlying the action of real criminals and that of the socially well-adjusted subjects of academic research. In his study of the writings of 400 felons he found 16 modes of disguise, which corresponded closely to the 12 methods of disguise reported by Alford.

Herkt's study of disguise in the writing of signatures disclosed that twenty of the changes listed were observed. In summary, he, like Alford and others before him, reports that the most favoured methods of disguise were those that endeavoured to alter the more obvious features of the signature, such as slope, care, pictorial appearance, capitals, supra-linear and infralinear letters, and commencement and terminal strokes. Some of the conditions he observed, particularly hesitation and retouching, as well as changes to alignments, pen pressure, and pen lifts may have been unintentional by-products of the process rather than elements of the selected method or methods of disguise.

Two other observations were made that are worth noting. The length of the signature and the space available to execute it had no significant affect upon the method of disguise employed.

In 1987, Konstantinidis conducted a similar study of 98 subjects from a Swedish viewpoint, principally because national Swedish handwriting systems underwent changes in 1943, 1968, and again in the mid 1980s, each of which tended to simplify letter designs to facilitate the process of learning to write. While the popularity of some techniques varied from that found in other studies, the results were much the same.

Herkt and Konstantinidis both commented, rather incidentally, on the fact that some changes occurring in disguised writing may be the unintentional by-products of other deliberate action. Regent[32] and Jamieson[33] are two of the very few who have attempted to isolate the effects of a deliberate change in slant upon other aspects of the writing, without there being any particular intent to disguise.

Regent found that in changing slant, 50 percent of writers used less space, 10 percent used more space, and 40 percent were unaltered. Also, 82 percent displayed an increase in pen pressure, 7 percent a decrease, and 11 percent were unchanged. In writers changing letter forms there was a greater tendency to alter the capital "S" and the capital "Z." The tendency to loop the "t" staff was greater when the slant went from forehand to backhand, whereas retraced "t" staffs dominated any changes from backhand to forehand writing. The tendency to loop the staff of the "d" was greater when slant was changed in either direction.

Jamieson found, as expected, that letter forms did not change with the change in slant. Of his writers, 80 percent reversed the direction of their normal slant, and 20 percent increased the slant in its normal direction. There was no clear tendency in altering spacing between words or letters: 25 percent of the writings displayed a noticeable loss in line quality; 35 percent, an increase in the frequency of retouching; 65 percent, increased the size of loops (7 percent were smaller). On unruled paper, baselines ascended 67 percent of the time and descended 14 percent of the time. Finally, as others have contended, the adopted slope was not consistently maintained in 62 percent of the cases.

Related to these studies is another of more recent publication by Halder-Sinn and Wegener.[34] It reports the observation that a change in slant can be more pronounced and maintained more consistently if it is the only modification that the individual is attempting to pursue. If modifications to one or more additional features are attempted, the change in slant is modified and the writing becomes more vertical. This is attributed to the "Overtaxing of the control function in a multiple disguising task."

Kropinak's[35] study, primarily of the effectiveness of four particular methods of disguise: (1) change of pen hold, (2) change of slant, (3) change to lettering, and (4) change of writing hand, also revealed a relationship between some aspects of the results. Cramped pen holds affected writing quality but little else. Change of slant effected arrangements, and in some cases letter size, but little else. The change to lettering yielded a script rather than normal printing or block lettering. Printing tendencies in cursive writing, if and when they existed, went unchanged. Improper letter forms were common. Change in writing hand produced poorer writing quality, increased pen pressure and greater inconsistency. Connection practises were unchanged. There was a tendency evident to use copybook letter forms. Embellishments and diacritics did not change. Worth noting is that Kropinak and others have observed that there is less deterioration in writing quality when a normally left-handed writer changes to the right hand than conversely. The reason for this is, as yet, unclear, but it may be that many left-handers have received some instruction, at some time in writing, with the right hand without being permanently converted, and there are some residual effects.

Parker[36] made a further observation respecting signature disguise that is also worth bearing in mind. His experience suggested that the kind of disguise that an individual might employ tended to be consistent from one occasion to the next, as a request for disguised signatures evidently revealed.

The methods that one might employ in disguising one's writing are numerous and the manners in which the writing may be altered are equally numerous. The method selected is unpredictable and, as Galbraith,[37] Crane,[38] and Kechler (1988) have observed, there is no apparent correlation between education, sex, or motivation and the method chosen or the skill and success of the endeavour. Hull[39] has provided some evidence that the number of changes occurring in a disguised handwriting increases with the level of formal education of the writer. Persons with less education tended to change to lettering and changed arrangements, while more educated individuals changed a greater variety of writing aspects such as lowercase letters, speed, spacing, size, approach strokes, numerals, and special characters.

The effectiveness of any one method or combination of methods will depend to a large extent on the amount and nature of the writing being disguised and the talents of the particular writer. In these studies, it has been found that some individuals are much less capable than others, for no apparent reason.

Similarly, the prospects of identifying the author of disguised material also varies. While studies have revealed the competent examiner's ability to penetrate disguises in the majority of cases, it has to be admitted that in some cases it can't be done. We cited earlier the report of Whiting (1997) that one individual had succeeded in adopting two identities and two distinctly different writing and signing styles. Behnen[40] reported two cases, one in which an individual exhibited two styles for the writing of his signature, and another in which the writer exhibited five styles of writing of signatures, although some of these may be simply the effects of some consistency in a chosen disguise upon relatively short productions. Although these cases are rare, the fact remains that the interpretation of differences in some circumstances is precarious.

Insofar as the anonymous letter writer is concerned, it has been repeatedly observed that writing is so automatic that the author, particularly when the document is of some length and his or her attention is absorbed by the thoughts being expressed, almost inevitably lapses into his or her natural hand. This may occur intermittently throughout the document and frequently towards the end.

Osborn maintained further that illiterate anonymous writing frequently consists of a combination of script forms and Roman capitals, or pen or pencil printing, and that often this writing contains original or freak forms of letters, abbreviations, or punctuation marks that are individual creations and are of the utmost significance as evidence of individuality. At the same time, he cautioned that assumed illiteracy was often the disguise adopted by anonymous letter writers and that such cases warranted a thorough study.

It should not be overlooked that anonymous letters can sometimes be associated with individuals by the materials used, such as pens, inks, papers, writing pads, envelopes, as well as the writing. Even postmarks, traces of obliterated or erased writings and typings, or their impressions, left on the anonymous letter itself or on an underlying sheet, have proven to be helpful in tracking a document to source.

While under special circumstances handwriting may be successfully disguised, the disguises ordinarily adopted are ineffective. The author of an anonymous letter of any considerable length, and particularly a series of letters, can in most cases be identified, given adequate standards. In many serial cases, perhaps 20 percent of them, the writer is one of a number of supposedly innocent recipients of the letters, and perhaps more often than not the writer is female.

It also happens that in instances where a series of anonymous letters have been issued at intervals, the disguise employed is apt to be partially disregarded or almost entirely forgotten after the first few issues. There are also cases on record in which the only person to have received the anonymous letters is the writer him/herself.

Assumed illiteracy is sometimes encountered as a disguise in an anonymous letter. Further information on such attempts will be found in Section 56: What Are the Indicators of Illiteracy.

While document examiners have suffered with disguised writings for years and regarded the fact of disguise as simply an obstacle in the course of handwriting identification, recent decisions in case law respecting court-ordered exemplars have changed the role of the document examiner to a great extent. In *People v. Igaz*, 326 N.W. 2d, 420 (Mich. App. 1952), the U.S. Appelate Court ruled that:

> "Defendant, in an attempt to disguise his handwriting, in effect, refused to comply with the order requiring him to give exemplars..."

Thus, as Hart[41] has pointed out, a defendant who disguises court-ordered exemplars of writing provides grounds for contempt proceedings, the proof of which rests solely on the shoulders of the handwriting examiner. It has now become just as important to prove disguise as it is to prove the subsequent writing identification. Accordingly, there must be criteria developed to establish disguise and to eliminate other less incriminating explanations for changes in writings such as abnormal variations, writing circumstances, or the influence of drugs and medical ailments.

Coupled with the changes in aspects of writing listed above, the principal and most persistent distinguishing feature of disguised executions is likely to be inconsistency: in size and forms of letters, in spacing, and in writing quality, when compared to the normal natural writing of the individual. Obviously, inconsistencies will be more evident in longer writing samples.

Writers of articles on various topics, including arthritis and drugs taken as medications, have mentioned the risks of wrongly interpreting the effects of these conditions or circumstances as evidence of disguised writing or forgery. In some cases, however, the concern for misinterpretation may be unwarranted. There are principles and practises characteristic of disguise that make it recognizable from the normal, natural writings of other persons and from the normal, natural writing of its author, as the foregoing has endeavoured to delineate.

Furthermore, if drug- or ailment-altered writing can be improperly identified as disguise, and an author of court-ordered writing samples, thereby, wrongly incriminated as knowingly refusing to comply with the order of the court, then it must be allowed that disguised writing can be improperly identified as drug-affected writing and its author wrongly exonerated. Hence, the discipline must assume some responsibility for clearly discriminating between the written products of these two situations.

A novice examiner may well ask the question: where will one find, clearly articulated, the differences between disguised writing and the effects of other internal and external writing conditions? Regrettably, the answer is not in the works of any one of the commonly recognized authorities.

We do know that the loss of control, fluency, and consistency resulting from drug ingestion or medical ailment is evidenced in all elements of a writing. It is capricious and involuntary. A reduction in the speed of writing may be partially responsible. The changes to writing provoked by disguise are evident in gross features and escape the subtle features. They are deliberate and voluntary. The speed of writing and fluency is not necessarily affected. They frequently include extreme distortions of the writing movement. The erratic movements of drug- and ailment-altered writing are irregular and unpredictable, whereas the supposedly erratic movements that disguise may include have a more regular nature and location to them.

Misinterpretation of the evidence can occur, but should not occur when the amount of writing and, consequently, the amount of evidence is adequate.

53.   What Are the Discriminators of Devices?

The *devices* to which we are referring are manually-operated devices for inscribing a signature, such as rubber stamps, and mechanically-operated devices for inscribing a signature or any other writing, such as photocopiers, facsimile machines, or even printing presses. Each kind of device has its own particular characteristics, or "set of fingerprints" if you will, by which it may be discriminated from the normal and natural writing executed by persons with pens or pencils.

For the most part, manual, mechanical, and electronic devices produce images of a signature that are two-dimensional. If there is a third dimension, that is an impression into the paper, the point load observed in the writing line is constant. There is no evidence of the variation in pen pressure that normal, natural writing usually exhibits.

Most manual, mechanical, and electronic devices produce what is referred to as a *static* impression, created without (horizontal) movement in the direction of the plain of the paper. Actual writing is a *dynamic* impression, created only as a result of some horizontal movement of the writing instrument over the plain of the paper. Static and dynamic impressions differ particularly in the manner in which the writing media (ink or graphite) is deposited on the paper surface. While static impressions are without any directional evidence, dynamic impressions frequently, if not invariably, contain directional evidence. The reason for this lies in the fact that the fibres of the papers surface are being employed as a friction agent to drag ink or graphite from the instrument. As a consequence, ink or graphite tend to accumulate along the edge of the paper fibres facing the approach of the pen or pencil, to a greater extent than along the opposite sides.

Admittedly this kind of directional evidence, visible clearly with the aid of a stereomicroscope, is more pronounced with pencils and with some types of inks than with others, but it is a condition that should be studied. If there is an accumulation of ink or graphite deposits on either sides of the fibres, it may be evidence of a dynamic rather than a static impression.

Dynamic impressions by manual, mechanical, or electronic devices are found, in the production of multiple signatures by machines such as the Signo-graph for the signing and authenticating of as many as 20 stock certificates, bonds, and similar monetary or negotiable instruments at the same time. This is accomplished by coupling a number of writing instruments to a master pen that is manipulated by the signing official. Single enlarged or reduced reproductions of signatures may be created with the aid of a pantograph machine, but neither of these machines have the capability of duplicating the third (vertical) dimension of the writing, to replicate properly the pen pressure or point load throughout the signature.

A machine called the Autopen was invented in 1958 by R. M. de Shazo for the reproduction of signatures, one at a time, in a device in which a prepared matrix is housed that controls and maneuvers the pen. Signatures can be repeated by setting the speed of the machine as fast as an operator can insert and replace the documents under the pen. Dynamic characteristics are induced in the writing by the movement of the turntable beneath the pen, rather than a left to right motion of the pen across the paper.

The dynamic nature of the Autopen signature gives each product additional symptoms of an authentic execution. It has been a relatively common machine, used by many government officials, insurance companies, airlines, and fund-raising organizations. Because the movement of the pen is controlled by the matrix, each new signature executed will be a very close duplication of the last. Changes will only occur with the wear of the matrix, that is plastic or metal.

The more observable defects in the signature are the result of operator settings of the machine. These were described and illustrated by McCarthy and Winchester[42] that also dealt with such questions as whether the product of a robot writer is a legal execution, and whether a given execution can be associated with the matrix employed to produce it. Certainly, the signatures produced warrant close study and examination for many reasons.

Somewhat in the nature of a manual device, Radley[43] reported that he had encountered 10 presumably spurious signatures (eight executed with a ball-point pen and two with a felt-tip pen) that were evidently prepared with the assistance of a stencil. The stencil enabled the perpetrator to control the movement of the writing instrument and allow it to be manoeuvred through curves and loops at greater speed, to produce a more deceptive fluency. Radley found that usable stencils could be cut from reasonably thick material following the outline of a genuine signature. His observations of the results of this rather unusual production method were that (1) the signatures were quite superimposable executions, (2) there was a consistently heavy point load (pen pressure) within the strokes, and (3) there were irregularities in the lines at the point of stroke intersections that he called *kinks*.

The foregoing deals with devices designed for signature execution. For information respecting the devices and processes being studied for the purpose of signature verification, the reader is directed to Section 76: Where Does This Leave Handwriting Identification — Science or Art?

54. What Are the Flags of Forgery?

Generally speaking, criminal codes of western civilizations define *forgery* as the making of a false document with the intent that it should be used or acted upon as genuine, and, for the purpose of the law, "making a false document" includes altering a genuine document in any material part.

Forgery is probably not the oldest of crimes known to our civilization but there is no doubt that it has occurred ever since man first recorded his thoughts on papyrus. Whether or not forgery has always had something of the present definition, certainly in principal, it is the same. The public attitude toward it, however, has profoundly changed. Until the 1500s, and because of the illiteracy rates of the lower classes, forgery was more common among royalty and the upper classes. This era saw forgery flourish among the clergy since they constituted a significant portion of the people who could read and write. Consequently, the occurrence was tolerated and did not become a statutory offence in England until 1562.

To the forger of this century nothing is sacred, and given the necessary skill, time, and resources any document may be reproduced at a deceptive level. Absolute security is almost impossible to provide within the document itself. In forgeries, the workmanship, the modus operandi, or method of operation may vary from the clumsy and obvious endeavours of the inept to the almost undetectable productions of the adept, and the materials involved may be equally variable.

One of the more disturbing consequences of the forging of cheques is that many of the generally accepted security practises are now no longer trustworthy. Sophisticated and expensive printing formats, company stamps, cheque writers, cheque protectors, and bank certification stamps are all devices available to the forger and are capable of deceptive duplication. They may be used to give his or her work a more authentic appearance. As a means of protection, their reliability is, consequently, diminished.

Certainly, the signature is the principal target of the forger, and insofar as this element of writing is concerned forgeries tend to fall into one of four types; (1) the simply spurious execution, (2) the freehand simulation, (3) the traced simulation, and (4) the transferred signature. Although it is a less frequent occurrence the forgery of other extended writings, including letters, holographic wills, personal notes, diaries, and other handwritten records is also attempted and often receives greater publicity, perhaps because of the monetary aspects involved. The Howard Hughes Mormon will,[44] the Howard Hughes autobiography fiasco,[45] the Benito Mussolini diaries (1968) and the Adolph Hitler diaries (1983) are four of the more prominent cases in recent years. The task of forging extended writings is different in many respects from that of forging signatures and for that reason the evidence to be considered changes distinctly.

The Hughes' will, his autobiography, the Mussolini diaries and the Hitler diaries are instances that demonstrate the ingenuity and/or talent of the individual and the extent of the labour that the forger is prepared to devote to the production of extensive false instruments when the calculated financial return appears adequate. In each case, the documents were sufficiently deceptive to delude authorities and some reputable document examiners, but each had failings that a careful and appropriate examination of the handwriting and the paper on which it resided would disclose.[46-49] The eventual identification of the Hitler diaries as spurious documents proved to be a classic example of the difficulties one may encounter in the examination of writings in a foreign language, the need for a thorough investigation and confirmation of the reliability of the standards supplied, and the assurance of their adequacy in nature and contemporaneousness.

Forgery, however, is a legal term that, while it describes the act, also implies some illicit motivation. A didactic dissertation of a quasi-technical nature, that this presentation endeavours to be, should not concern itself with motivation, but confine itself to the matter of distinguishing spurious writing from the genuine, and *spurious* will be intended to refer to that which is not executed by its purported author. Accordingly, where understanding will not be impaired the term *spurious* will be used.

Spurious writings of all kinds usually exhibit at least one common symptom of their fraudulent nature: it is not so much their divergence in form from the genuine writing, but a drawn and hesitating quality of line, particularly at points that should be freely written. Furthermore, a simulation of another person's writing, be it extended writing or a signature, must in some measure resemble that which it is intended to duplicate. Osborn believed that most errors in identifying writing are due to the improper assumption that this general correspondence of writing characteristics is proof of genuineness.[50] On the other hand, it must be acknowledged that a simulation of another's writing may sometimes be produced that, while suspicious, cannot positively be declared to be spurious. Nevertheless, one of the writing features most characteristic of spuriousness and most often occurring is the lack of fluency.[51] Accordingly, it has long been held that it is easier to produce a forgery with a pencil than with pen and ink, for the pencil is less inclined to show the evidence of a halting, tremulous movement that lacks continuity. It may fail to disclose pen lifts, pen position, retouching, or overwriting as clearly as a pen.

Simply spurious signatures, are encountered in cases in which the perpetrator has no access to a sample of a genuine signature to use as a model. This happens when cheques are stolen. In such cases, there is usually little correspondence between the spurious signature and the genuine. There may be odd flourishes or embellishments to the writing, presumably added as a kind of disguise, or to give it an ambience of authenticity.

In other situations, perhaps after some previous study or practise in copying from a model, the simulation of the signature is attempted from memory, as in the case of an endorsement to a cheque written in front of a teller at a bank. Understandably, the product may be a mixture of some features of a writing that recollection can provide, together with such contributions as the writer's own habits or inventions may suggest to complete the enterprise. As may be expected, the components of a signature that are remembered sufficiently to be included are likely to be the gross or more obvious ones.

Depending upon their length, the letters involved, the quality of the writing and the writing circumstances, however, the simply spurious writing may, by coincidence, resemble the genuine products to a deceiving degree. Discrimination is even more difficult when the writing is limited to a matter of initials. For the most part, however, differences will be obvious and discriminations can be made. The argument often offered in support of the spurious is that it was executed under unusual circumstances (on a moving train, on the roof of an automobile, on one's knee) which accounts for its disparity from the normal genuine product.

The study of the differences must, therefore, be made as to whether they are differences in the fundamental aspects of the writing or simply in matters such as size and design that could conceivably fall within the wider range of variation that unusual writing circumstances might produce (See Section 16: What Is a Fundamental or Significant Difference in Writing?).

Perhaps the most telling characteristic of simulated signatures is poor line quality that reflects the level of consciousness in the writing act. Simply spurious signatures, however, are more often freely and fluently written and line quality can be misconstrued as indicative of genuineness. Then too, because most people's writing changes slightly but steadily with time, and signatures are known to be changed in style rather distinctly in many cases by choice of the writer, it is particularly important that handwriting comparisons be conducted with contemporary standards.

Although it is not often that a writer of a forged signature will include enough of his or her own writing characteristics in it to allow him or her to be identified with it, the potential for doing so is, understandably, greater in the execution of that which is simply spurious.

Freehand simulated signatures are the most common kind of signature imitations. While it is reasonable to expect that imitations will resemble in some ways the writing being imitated, they tend to deviate from the genuine in three principle respects: form, line quality, and stroke continuity.

The reproduction of letter forms suffers particularly in complex letter designs in which compound curves are involved. Because the simulation process requires reasonable attention to detail and form, and a consciousness of the writing act in attempting to follow an unfamiliar design, there is, frequently, a loss in the smoothness or fluency of the writing line commonly referred to as *tremour of fraud*. This lack of fluency may be discerned in abrupt changes in stroke direction.

In a recent study by Masson,[52] the loss in line quality occurred in the overwhelming majority of freehand simulations and resulted in a line quality that was inferior to both that of the model being simulated or that which was normal for the simulator. Worth noting is the fact that in some 50 percent of the cases the resultant line quality was no different whether the simulation was made freehand or by tracing. In the other 50 percent of the cases, the tracings were the poorer. Also worth noting is the fact that the line quality in some simulations and tracings produced in this study was only marginally diminished.

This loss in line quality and the reasons for it prompts some examiners to suggest that the more conscious and deliberate act of simulating tends to result in drawings rather than writings. With the reduction in writing speed or fluency and the resultant loss in line quality, there is, as might be expected, a tendency for initial and terminal strokes to exhibit blunt endings.

The poorer quality of line usually present in freehand simulated signatures, often described as tremour of fraud, may be accompanied by varying and abrupt changes in pen pressure, and an absence of any regular contrast in point load between upstrokes and downstrokes. There is likely to be unequal distributions of ink and interruptions in the movement of the writing instrument in the middle of curves or even straight lines. It must be distinguished from the tremour of age, the tremour of illiteracy, and the loss of control that may occur with certain illnesses.

Conway has commented on the not uncommon finding in simulations that they deteriorate and differ more from authentic signatures toward the end of the signatures.[53] In effect, the task of sustaining a good simulation is more difficult the longer the signature.

A hallmark of spurious simulations can be found in line continuity. Simulations frequently contain too many pen lifts or pen lifts in the wrong locations. Masson's (1996) study of simulations of signatures by 22 writers revealed that more than 60 percent of the freehand simulations contained at least one pen lift or area of patching (Figure 14). Pen lifts, however, are more readily seen in the strokes of fluid inks, whereas in pencil and ballpoint pen writings it may prove difficult to determine the location of pen lifts with certainty. Letter alignments is another less conscious element of the signature that frequently escapes the attention it deserves in the simulation process. Furthermore, spurious simulations may contain patching or retouching in some areas, to improve their correspondence to the master being copied, or to conceal errors in the imitation.

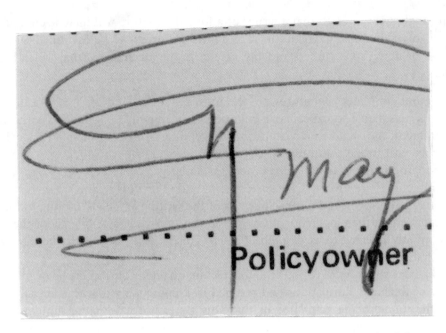

Figure 14 A freehand simulation of a signature in which there is a lack of fluency in the flourishes above, a discontinuity (pen lift) between the flourish and the commencement of the "M" and a retouching in the loop of the "y," all of which are symptoms of spurious writing.

The patching and retouching of a letter or part of a letter is not always evidence of spuriousness. Some persons are known to have contracted the habit of going over elements of what they have written to improve on imperfections, and the practise is repeated whether the retouching is needed or not. The examination of several samples of writing will likely indicate the consistency and nature of such practises. Then too, these patchings and retouching are seldom as subtle or inconspicuous as are found in spurious writings.

Complex or unusual letter structures and designs can be misinterpreted by one who is simulating (or tracing) a signature such that the particular movements of the writing instrument in the model or genuine signature are not duplicated. These conditions when occurring can be particularly significant.

Simulated forgeries involve a double process: the discard of one's own writing habits, most of which are unconscious acts, and the assumption of the unfamiliar characteristics of another writer, many of which are not fully perceived. This results in a mental and physical conflict for the individual, the magnitude of which will determine the success to be achieved. Furthermore, it has been commonly observed that, in simulations of signatures and writings, attention is directed at the obvious features of the writing rather than at the less consciously executed aspects. Recent experiments by Leung, Cheng, Fung, and Poon[54] and by Herkt[55] have now provided empirical data confirming the generally accepted viewpoints of the past. The examination and study of simulated signatures can continue to be conducted from these premises.

The writings of Osborn and Hilton on this subject and the findings of Herkt and Leung et al., are elucidations and evidence of the Principles of Exclusion and Inclusion, in handwriting identification. One cannot exclude from one's writing those habits or discriminating elements that he or she is unaware of possessing. Furthermore, one cannot include in

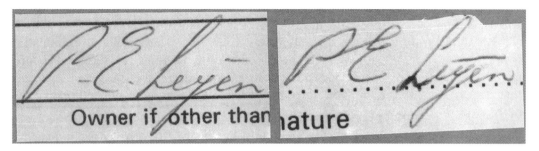

Figure 15 A genuine signature (left) and a freehand simulation of it, exhibiting the blunt endings, retouching, and lack of fluency, symptomatic of spurious executions.

one's writing those habits or discriminating elements of another's writing of which he or she is unaware as being present or significant.

Another fundamental related to freehand simulations that must be borne in mind is the Principle of Interference. This well-established psychological principle holds that it is more difficult, rather than easier, for an individual to duplicate (writing) habits that are similar to, but discriminable from one's own, because of the difficulty of maintaining a subtle or minor change to one's normal or natural tendencies. Subtle changes would be those related to proportions, relative heights, alignments and economies of movement. Less subtle changes that would be more easily accomplished and maintained would include those occurring in capital letter formations, slope, size, embellishments, and extremes of contraction and expansion.

Horan[56] reports that graphologists have maintained that "Forgers subconsciously shrink the size of their fabrication to avoid detection," apparently on the premise that a smaller writing will conceal evidence of spuriousness. This might be a valid contention if the reduction in size was being made photographically, but such testimony as pen lifts, retouching, loss of fluency, or tremours are just as evident in the writing regardless of the dimensions it happens to possess.

Horan's study of 482 samples of simulated signatures (i.e., forgeries), disclosed that fewer than 18 percent of them exhibited any significant reduction in size. In fact, a larger percentage (25.1 percent) exhibited a notable increase in dimensions.

In summary then, hesitation, unnatural pen lifts, patching, tremour, uncertainty of movement as exhibited by abrupt changes in the direction of the line, and a stilted, drawn line quality devoid of free normal writing movements combine to reveal the true nature of the spurious simulation of a signature[57] (Figure 15). In multiple forgeries, there may be less variation from one spurious signature to the next than there is in the collected signature specimens from the individual whose signature has been violated.

For the most part, the task of determining that a simulation is spurious is not insurmountable, but quite routine. The question frequently posed, however, is whether the author of simulated writings, particularly signatures, can be identified with his/her product. Obviously, the prospects will vary with the nature and amount of writing involved (i.e., extended writing vs. signatures), the respect for letter form in the writing being simulated, the level of penmanship that it reflects, and the quality of the simulation. Certainly, the closer the simulation comes to duplicating the writing being copied the less evidence it is likely to contain of the hand that engenders it. Conversely, poor simulations may be expected to contain features that reflect some of the natural writing habits of the author.

Whether or not the evidence will be sufficient from which to draw definitive conclusions will depend on the circumstances and the evidence in each particular case.

The model from which the simulation was made is rarely available for examination with the simulation. When it is, it can be of some assistance in extracting those features in which attempts have been made to duplicate the model, and focussing on the balance that is more likely to exhibit some correspondence to the writing of the author, as Muehlberger (1990) has pointed out.[58]

Traced simulations of signatures are almost invariably produced by techniques that yield drawings rather than writings. Only an exceptional individual can trace a signature accurately with a fast, fluent pen movement. A study by John Paul Osborn,[59] however, disclosed that the quality of line of the tracings varied somewhat with the nature of the writing instrument (ball-point pen, fibre-tipped or felt-tipped, and roller ball pen) that was employed. The tremour that is characteristic of tracings was more difficult to observe in products of the fibre-tipped pens. The wider line of this kind of pen, its handling characteristics and the manner in which the ink took to the paper were all considered factors contributing to the quality of the tracing.

In addition to its revealing line quality, the primary evidence of spuriousness in a tracing is its correspondence to the model from which it was created, or the correspondence of a number of tracings to one another. Absolute correspondence is not found in genuine signatures, even if they are the executions of a well practised writer.

Traced signatures usually depart from genuine signatures (1) in fluency that is the result of greater speed of execution in normal, natural writing, (2) in line quality that a tracing lacks, (3) the presence of pen lifts and/or retouching that is indicative of the uncertainty of the writing instrument movement, and (4) the attendance of guidelines in the form of graphite or carbon lines or indentations. Notwithstanding these respects in which the spurious tracing will differ from the genuine product, it has long been held that tracings, by their very nature, are not likely to contain sufficient evidence of the discriminating elements of the perpetrator's writing habits to allow the author to be identified.[60] Muehlberger and Vastrick,[61] however, provided an example of an instance in which the circumstances of the case limited the number of potential authors to a small population. Within these limitations it was possible to select the writer possessing the few discriminating elements within his/her writing that appeared in the questioned material, to support a conclusion of identity.

A typical tracing contains a rather uniformly heavy stroke without the variations in pen pressure characteristic of natural writing. Also symptomatic of tracings are frequent interruptions in the movement of the writing instrument that may be found as full pen stops or as pen lifts in abnormal locations that display some care and accuracy in the subsequent application of the instrument to the paper. These hesitations or interruptions provide the individual with a momentary opportunity to review and to plan the ensuing course to be taken by the pen. Imperfections in the product are often corrected or concealed by patchings or retouchings. Depending on the method of production, microscopic examination may disclose that tracings exhibit carbon traces, pencil traces, or simply indentations in the paper that do not precisely coincide with the ink strokes of the signature.

Generally speaking, tracings exhibit a reasonably close adherence to the letter forms and dimensions of the signature being duplicated. Complex or unusual letter structures may not be correctly interpreted, however, and a lack of correspondence in this respect may be significant in a study of genuineness.

There are a number of techniques that are employed in the tracing of signatures, none of which are particularly successful in producing deceptive products. Basically, they are variations of (1) a transmitted light technique, sometimes called direct tracing, (2) a carbon creation or pencil line technique, (3) an excessive pressure technique also called projection tracing, and (4) a tracing paper methd.

• In the first procedure, the document is appropriately positioned over the genuine signature being traced, and against a glass surface behind which a strong light source (such as a window, a headlight, a projector, a photographic printer, or a lamp) is situated. The outline of the genuine signature that can be seen through the spurious document is followed carefully with the writing instrument. A pen may be used to produce a final product directly or a pencil may be employed to create a light outline that is overwritten later and the outline erased. The quality of the product will depend upon: having reasonably translucent documents, having documents without interfering printing or writings on their backs, and keeping the spurious document tight against the genuine signature so that its image is clear and precise. The technique can leave indentations in and around the genuine signature used by which it can be associated with the tracing.

• In the second method, the genuine signature to be traced is positioned over the spurious document, a piece of carbon paper is inserted between them and the outline of the genuine signature is followed by overwriting with a pen or an inkless instrument. The carbon impression on the spurious document is then over-written with a pen after which the carbon deposits can be removed with an art gum or soft eraser. If the removal of the carbon is not complete, its presence can be seen under a microscope or detected with infrared photography and the process of production can be established.

• In the excessive pressure technique, the genuine signature is positioned over the spurious document on a somewhat soft surface, e.g., several sheets of paper or a writing pad, and the strokes of the signature are overwritten with a pen or similar instrument with sufficient pressure to create an observable impression in the document beneath. The impression is then inked in by following the course of the furrow with a pen. The impression in the paper of the spurious document remains obvious under oblique lighting and examination under a microscope usually discloses a failure of the ink and the impression to coincide at all points. The study of impressions in documents is sometimes facilitated by scrutiny of the reverse side with parallel or oblique lighting techniques. As in other tracing processes, the application of pressure and/or ink to the genuine signature provides evidence by which it might be associated with the tracing created.

In these three techniques, impressions or outlines may be produced that need to be removed, for, as Harrison claims,[62] the most devastating evidence of a tracing is the presence of a guideline or traces of it. The search for traces of guidelines should be concentrated around the ends of strokes, as graphite or other evidence in these areas cannot be as readily attributed to the instrument employed for overwriting. Pencilled guidelines, however, may be erased completely, in which case the close correspondence in design between the spurious and its master, together with the classic lack of fluency in the copy, may be the only evidence on which one has to rely.

Harrison also cautions that the presence of suspicious impressions alone is not reliable evidence that the signature is spurious. It may be simply that the signature bearing the suspicious impression is the genuine signature that was used as the model from which another signature, that is spurious, was traced. To be significant as evidence of spuriousness, the impressions should extend beyond the ends of the ink lines.

On rare occasions, genuine signatures have been overwritten on documents as a result of legitimate handwritten changes that were made later. The overwriting is simply an endeavour to achieve some consistency in the colour or kind of writing ink for all elements of the document. Overwritings have also been made to genuine signatures that have experienced ink failure or fading on the part of an exhausted writing instrument. In such cases, evidence of the progressive failure must be sought under the microscope in the traces of the original writing not completely concealed by the overwritings, perhaps with the help of the discriminating techniques of infrared radiation.

One should not overlook the situation in which several copies of a document or several documents require signatures on the same occasion, and genuine signatures are executed while the several papers are superimposed on one another. In such cases impressions of one signature may be left in the document beneath it. Depending on the consistency of the writer and the consistency of the signature locations on the sheets, innocuous impressions may be mistaken as grounds for suspicion.

• The tracing paper technique reported by Harrison[63] and Herkt[64] is an alternative to the carbon paper method for applying a carbon outline of the genuine signature on the false document. Tracing paper is laid over the signature to be traced and an outline is created on it by running a soft pencil or pen over the lines of the signature that can be seen through the tracing paper. Following this, the back of the tracing paper is given a graphite rubbing with the side of a sharp pencil and the tracing is laid over the spurious document. Overwriting the outline of the signature on the obverse with a suitable instrument will then transfer graphite on the reverse to the document beneath in the outline of the signature, that is then overwritten in ink to create the final product. While the method is more tedious than the others, it leaves no evidence behind on the genuine signature by which it can be associated with the tracing other than the correspondence in outline that there may be between the two.

A discourse on traced signatures should not overlook the fact that, when writing with ball-point pens, there are some circumstances that provide genuine signatures with the characteristics of traced executions. de la Pena[65] described a case in which ink failure in a genuine signature prompted an overwriting by the author using a second instrument, yielding close correspondence between the impression of the first execution and the ink of the second, suspiciously similar to the symptoms of a tracing. Walters and Flynn[66] reported that the metallic plating on the housings of some ball-point pens tended to be rubbed off and left along the ink lines of writing done on zinc-oxide photocopy paper, when the angle of the pen to the paper surface was low enough to permit contact. These deposits produced a guideline, shadow, ghost image parallel to the writing line that lasted for a few letters until the plating in that location was worn off. The shadow line could be misconstrued as evidence of a tracing process, if not studied closely. Vastrick[67] found other instances of what he called *sister lines* that might be observed under other circumstances, in which genuine writing might be mistakenly identified as spurious.

Notwithstanding what has been said of these four tracing techniques there is no reliable line of distinction between skillful freehand simulations and tracings in all cases. Some of the defects may be the same, and tracings may diverge from the model as much as dexterous simulations.

The transferred or transposed signature is the unwanted progeny of modern technology. Since the advent of Scotch tape, the development of dry transfer lettering, and the invention of the photocopier, document examiners have speculated on and studied the potentials for machines and materials to facilitate the transfer of genuine signatures from one document to another. While actual cases have not been numerous, the fact remains that it can be done and examiners are cautioned to study physical evidence with this possibility in mind.

The fundamental characteristic of transposed signatures is that they lack any evidence of pressure of the writing instrument into the paper. Furthermore, when dry transfer or photocopier techniques are employed, the ink of the strokes can be seen microscopically to be deposited, perhaps in some quantity, on the surface of the document rather than impressed into the substrate. In this respect, it has been likened to intaglio or "relief" printing, although the vertical dimension the ink deposit can acquire is considerably less. The materials used are recognizable and sometimes provide evidence by which the product can be identified with a source.

Transposition by transparent tape can be accomplished with pencil writings, but encounters problems with some ball pen inks. The release of the graphite or ink in the new location is usually encouraged by burnishing the back of the tape with a burnishing tool or ball-point pen, similar to the procedure for depositing dry transfer characters. Even when release of the graphite or ink can be achieved, the adhesive of the transparent tape is often reluctant to leave the paper surface and fibre disturbance or adhesive can remain as telltale evidence of the encounter. To prevent this, the document may be deliberately torn and the tape left on the paper to imply that it is there to repair the tear. In other cases the document is photocopied to conceal the presence of the tape and the original is then conveniently lost or destroyed. Solvents may also be used to separate the tape from the paper, but not without the risk of reaction with the ink.

Greater use of dry transfer lettering has been found in criminal cases in which attempts have been made to duplicate the printing of corporate or private negotiable instruments, such as payroll cheques. In most cases, however, the authenticating signatures to these documents are reproduced by other processes or are simply spurious executions.

Much has been written[68-75] to describe other techniques in detail. One technique that has been mentioned in papers is that of gelatin transfers. These differ slightly from other transfers in that the original signature is not totally removed from its document, but a quantity of its ink is lifted by a gelatin medium and deposited on the second document. The line is not as crisp or as deep in colour and the ink is different in its manner of bonding to the fibres of the paper.[76] Still another technique for producing a number of replicas of the same signature was reported by Radley and described in Section 53: What Are the Discriminations of Devices?, in which stencils, cut from plastic photocopying sheets or pantographs, were used as guides for the movement of the writing instrument.

55.   What Are the Guides to Genuineness?

Over many years the International Association of Master Penmen and Teachers of Handwriting have fought a losing battle for excellence in handwriting. Writing examiners shared their concerns, if only because excellence in whatever one does is its own best defence against duplication. It applies to any skill or personal performance. It pertains to the printed document or to the handwritten document. Thus, quality in writing is its own best protection against forgery, and quality in handwriting is reflected in fluency, forms or shapes, and consistency. Along the same line, Osborn maintained that the most effective protection of a signature is skill in that no one can successfully imitate a writing more skillful than his or her own.[77]

It follows then that where one finds fluency in the quality of the line, adherence to copybook form and consistency or uniformity in other aspects of the writing such as slope, size, proportions, and spacing, the conclusion is reasonable that the writing is genuine. One can expect these conditions to be accompanied by the application of graduating pressure on the nib, ball, or point of the instrument (point load), and some difference in it between upstrokes and downstrokes. Evidence of fluency is frequently found in the tapering of endings of commencement and terminal strokes, sometimes referred to as *flying starts* and *flying finishes.* Other evidence will probably include speed, carelessness, and inattention to detail, as well as delicate, inconspicuous movements, consistently repeated, especially if written freely (see also Section 30.B.13: Legibility and Writing Quality).

There are also occasions on which carelessness, speed, reasonable variation, and even illegibility are earmarks of genuineness. Obvious but inexplicable omissions may be further symptoms. The determining factor is the level of consciousness of the writing process that may be evident. Except in the executions of the aged or infirm, genuine writings more often reflect a concern for what is being written rather than how it is being written.

Errors made will be more obvious and corrections attempted less carefully performed, particularly so in the writing of the aged or infirm. Under these circumstances, elements of the writing may be clumsily overwritten. Indeed, physical infirmity may produce signatures that are broken, unfinished, and completely divergent from those written in a state of good health, but in these circumstances their very nature will be indicative of genuineness.

Questioned documents bearing writings of some length can introduce other factors that are indicative of genuineness, particularly natural variation. It must be present, and will be found to have a distinctive range peculiar to the writer, even in the short frequently occurring words such as "and," "of," "but," "the," "my," and other articles and possessive pronouns. These words warrant special study. In spurious handwritten documents words like these have been noted to take on a rubber-stamp effect due to their unnatural consistency. The same concern for natural variation must be directed at cases involving two or more signatures in the same name.[78]

Initials, individual letters, and even some signatures provide such limited material to study that the evidence available may not be so profound. Initials and signatures are sometimes allowed to degenerate into little more than a nondescript mark, the letters of which often cannot be positively deciphered. They may be executed, however, in a distinctive way with great fluency and speed that can distinguish them from the slowly drawn imitation. In the extreme case of the illiterate, unable to inscribe more than an "X," it has long been held that a cross mark by itself is insufficient to show evidence of genuineness or a lack of genuineness

Tangential to the study of the writing elements themselves, there are other aspects of the document worthy of the examiner's consideration. An obvious ink failure, particularly if clumsily rectified, or a failure wherein no attempt is made to complete the signature or writing, is often the kind of carelessness characteristic of genuineness. In extended writings, the study of composition, facts stated, idioms, grammar, division of words, titles, abbreviations, folds, aging, soiling, cut or torn edges, paper size or type, all may contribute something to the determination of the authenticity of the document, of the writing on it, or of the history of its production.

Since fluency is so important in the determination of genuineness it must be noted that the signature is the single element of one's writing that is done more automatically, hence more fluently, and with less awareness of the writing process. Even the poorest of writers of other material can have reasonable fluency in their signatures.

56.   What Are the Indicators of Illiteracy?

Since the comments of Osborn, penned in 1910, little has been written on this topic. It may be that it is a matter not frequently encountered, but there are kinds of illiteracy more common now than in Osborn's time.

Illiteracy in writing seems at the outset to be a contradiction in terms. It is usually one's inability to write at all which warrants him or her being labelled illiterate. The inability, however, may apply only to writing in other languages or in using non-Roman alphabets. For example, literate English-speaking people are usually illiterate in Arabic or the languages employing the Slovak alphabets. As a result of the movement of masses of immigrants, refugees, and international trade and communication, it is not unusual to encounter individuals of reasonable intelligence that are illiterate insofar as the Roman alphabet is concerned. This is not basic illiteracy, however, and the effects upon handwriting may not be the same.

The hallmarks of basic illiteracy are hesitation and a kind of tremour characterized by a general irregularity of the line that is due to a lack of skill and a mental uncertainty as to design and form, and to a general muscular clumsiness from unfamiliarity with the writing process. In tremour of illiteracy, the changes in direction are not apt to be as numerous or as abrupt as in tremour of age or of weakness. In the latter kinds, omissions of strokes or parts of letters are not common. Nevertheless, there have been cases in which the tremors of illiteracy, age, and illness have been difficult to distinguish from each other.

Basic illiterate writing, even on ruled paper, frequently shows a pronounced irregularity in alignment. On unruled paper, illiterate writing tends to go uphill across the sheet or page. Both conditions probably stem from the lack of practise and control of the movements of the writing instrument. In other cases, basically illiterate writers will press the pen or pencil too hard, cutting the paper or breaking the point. The pen strokes are strong but uneven, and few elements will be symmetrically designed.

Disconnections or pen lifts tend to be more frequent with illiteracy. These disconnections are more closely related to letter designs rather than writing movements. Fluent writers do not stop the motion of the pen each time it is raised. Its continuous motion will be noted in the tapered ends of strokes as it leaves or approaches the page, whereas the unpractised hand will begin or terminate strokes bluntly.

Frazer[79] observed in his time, and we have no reason to disagree, that signatures attempted by illiterate persons are comprised of separate strokes or letters. There is an apparent absence of any model as a whole in the writer's mind.

Bungling illiterate writers have been known to develop peculiar characteristics that are purely individual inventions, probably due to their lack of skill or their lack of familiarity with a proper letter form. Overwritings may occur in locations that make no particular sense. Osborn claimed that illiterate writers are not respecters of margins and write on both sides of a sheet, but this implies the production of more writing than that of which the basically illiterate person would be capable. He may have been referring to persons of limited literacy, of course, who could conceivably have occasion to execute a longer document.

Common indications of limited literacy are faulty arrangement of words, lines, paragraphs, and pages indicating general unfamiliarity with the writing process, and errors in punctuation. Variation in letter form is often much less in the writing of the less literate than in that of the practised writer, who may alter the form or allograph with the location of the letter in the written word. Osborn[80] claimed that looped letters in basic illiterate writing often tended to slant too much because the upstroke is made too nearly straight.

Less literate individuals may misspell the same word differently on different occasions. Misspellings sometimes follow pronunciation, especially in proper names. Uncommon names may be misheard, then mispronounced, then misspelled. It is claimed that anonymous letters have been traced to source through mispronunciations, evidenced through misspellings, that have later been recognized.

As previously intimated, writers initially taught to write in Arabic, Hebrew, or Yiddish, which languages are written right to left, may have difficulty developing fluency in writing English or other languages from left to right. If used only occasionally, their Roman alphabet executions may continue through a lifetime to be hesitating, conscious acts characteristic of the unpractised hand or of forgery. Where a supposedly "western world" style of signature, at least, is necessary to conduct business, a series of strokes may be developed that bear little resemblance to characters of the Roman alphabet, but which are sufficient collectively to be acceptable to the banking or legal fraternities.

Illiteracy has been successfully simulated in some of these respects and has sometimes been employed as a method of disguise in anonymous letters. When used it is evidenced by attempts to convey the impression of limited educational qualifications through:

- bad grammar (perhaps combined with the subjunctive forms of verbs)
- poor punctuation (perhaps combined with proper hyphenation)
- spelling errors in simple words (with proper spelling of difficult words)
- the use of "I is" or "you was," (with otherwise proper sentence structure)
- the use of "i" for "I"

Inconsistencies of these sorts do not support a pretence of illiteracy.

57. What Are the Signs of Senility or Age?

The writing of all persons changes progressively and steadily with the passage of time. The extent of the change will depend on a number of factors: the amount of writing done, the state of health of the writer, and the particular stage in life of the individual. Kapoor, Kapoor, and Sharma[81] found in a study of 50 subjects over a 10-year period that changes occurred in 40 percent of the writers, but that the changes were less marked and there were fewer of them in persons over the age of 45. The extent of change in signatures may differ from that in extended writings of the same individual. For these reasons, writing standards obtained for comparison purposes must be as comparable and contemporaneous as possible.

From a slightly different perspective, Lester, Werling, and Heinle[82] in a study of the writing of a sample of 2,168 subjects (20 to 69 years), in a search for indicators of age, observed that few measurable differences were found that might be reliably related to any age group in 40 aspects of writing.

The writing of older persons, the ill or the infirm is characterized by its evident lack of control of the writing instrument. Strokes of the writing tend to be rough and made with considerable pressure. They are likely to exhibit more breaks in line continuity. Letter forms may be awkward and in many locations it seems that the direction of motion of the pen is unpredictable. Lack of control is frequently evident at the point of application of the pen to paper.

Loss of control is usually progressive though not necessarily linear, and its onset may be heralded by tremour, that is simply a deviation from the normally smooth and uniform writing stroke. Natural tremour, being involuntary, is apt to be comparatively uniform along similar elements of the writing. It may be minor or severe. When minor, it may be prompted by the writing process much like a state of nervousness. When severe, the writing may exhibit considerable departures from normal letter designs.

Tremour, however, can be of different types having different characteristics. That which document examiners refer to as tremour of age or infirmity has been defined by Hilton[83] as "A writing weakness portrayed by irregular, shaky strokes." Harrison[84] defines it as "Frequent deviations and discontinuities in the smoothness of the line," and the tremour, if it is genuine, will be consistent and continuous throughout a writing. Hilton maintains, on the other hand, that a tremulous signature or writing may exhibit sporadic moments of freedom and fluency.

There are other causes and kinds of tremour besides the tremour of age or infirmity. Boisseau, Chamberland, and Gauthier[85] introduced us to the term *Essential Tremour* that they claimed to be a common neurological condition causing tremour of the arms often leading to difficulties with handwriting. Carney[86] reported that Elble and Koller[87] define tremour generally as "Any involuntary, approximately rhythmic and roughly sinusoidal movement." These authors go on to define Essential Tremour as a "Monosymptomatic illness" with a prevalence (4 to 60 per 1,000 persons) that increases with age, but is common to all age groups and equal in the sexes. It is considered to be a postural tremour (i.e., present, but much less noticeable during the maintenance of steady posture) that is accentuated by voluntary movement creating disabilities during activities such as writing. The handwriting is typically large and tremulous in contrast to the effects of the tremour of Parkinson's disease.

Evidently, Essential Tremour can begin at any age, even childhood. It is a much more benign and common disorder than Parkinson's disease. Its course is extremely variable. It begins insidiously and progresses slowly. Although Essential Tremour usually disappears during rest (sometimes said to be an active tremour) and appears with action of the limb, it may not always do so in advanced cases. On the other hand Parkinson's disease is said to be a resting tremour that is apparent when the limb is not in use, but disappears when put into action.

As we have noted elsewhere, there are two other conditions, much less common, producing tremour: Progressive supranuclear palsy and Huntington's disease, that, along with Parkinson's disease and Essential Tremour, are classed as extrapyramidal disorders that identifies them with the part of the neural system within the brain to which they are attributed. Progressive supranuclear palsy is much like Parkinson's disease but has other symptoms observed in the face and eyes. Huntington's disease is depicted by large jerks of the arm or hand occurring at random.

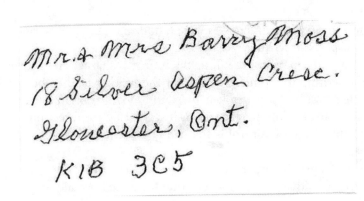

Figure 16　An example of the tremour of age. At the time of writing, this individual was 90 years of age. Note the erratic movements, particularly in what should be smooth curves.

According to Boisseau, Chamberland, and Gautier, in their study of the writings of 35 individuals suffering from these disorders, no particular characteristics were found that could be related to any of the four disorders. The administration of drugs was seen to affect a few letters, but the majority of the elements of writing were not significantly altered. Tremours, due to neurological conditions, tend to be more gross and erratic changes to or interruptions in the pen movement, that become more obvious with the progression of the responsible disorder.

According to Carney, the authors Elble and Koller also discuss task specific tremours such as orthostatic tremour and primary writing tremour. *Primary writing tremour* is defined as a tremour that is induced primarily, but not only, by the act of writing and similar motor activities, such as handling a knife or screwdriver. Carney also notes that alcohol, inderal, and mysoline all reduce primary writing tremour, but they are ineffective upon the tremour of Parkinson's disease.

It is also to be noted that tremours can be induced by the ingestion of numerous common drugs including nicotine, alcohol, lithium, caffeine, thyroid hormone, and cardiac antiarrhythmics. On the other hand, as Behrendt[88] reported, the affect of tremour on handwriting can be diminished by the administration of mild sedatives.

Tremour of age in signatures is often accompanied by uneven alignment or a signature may apparently disregard the writing baseline. Furthermore, tremours of age, weakness, and illiteracy are not always distinguishable from each other. Tremour of age and tremour of weakness, however, beyond their many similar characteristics that make them indistinguishable, have about them a certain carelessness or abandon that marks them as genuine.

Feebleness is characterized by a general lightness of the stroke, and much tremour. It is accompanied by a decline in the design of a signature, not to be confused with the kind of change that occurs with haste or negligence. Terminations of strokes are often accompanied by the application of pressure. Despite the loss of control, the correct ideas of letter forms underlie the writing.

In summary then, age and infirmity may be seen in the deterioration of one's writing quality over time owing to the gradual and progressive loss of control of the writing instrument (Figure 16). This becomes evident in the following:

1. A loss in fluency (i.e., skill) or in the smoothness of curves and lines
2. The appearance of fine tremour

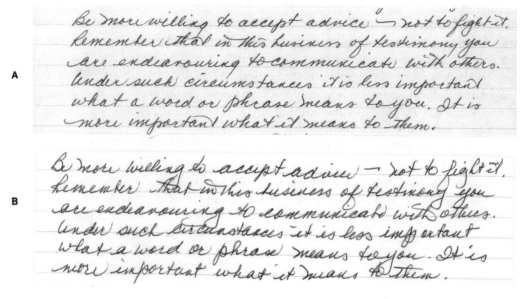

Figure 17   Changes in writing with age and/or time. Writing (B) was executed at age 77, 24 years after writing (A). Note the subtle changes that have occurred. (B) is less consistent in alignments, less consistent in letter sizes, and exhibits more angularity to troughs and arches. The slope of the writing of (B), relative to the vertical, is slightly less than that of the writing (A). Although fluency has been retained, these changes have resulted in some loss in skill or writing quality.

3. A deterioration in the quality and structure of letter forms
4. The irregularity of letter and word alignments
5. The irregularity of interletter and interword spacing
6. The irregularity of the widths of loops
7. The inconsistency in the locations of commencement strokes
8. The inconsistency in the direction and length of terminating strokes
9. The occurrence of erratic movements, and irregular, shaky strokes
10. The occurrence of "false starts" and inexplicable movements at the beginning of a signature or of a writing
11. The general reduction in pen pressure, but an application of pressure in terminal strokes

In a sense the progressive loss of control of the pen or pencil results in an expansion of natural variation in many of the aspects of writing that are here mentioned. The decline in form and skill or quality affects legibility. Erratic movements affect letter forms in manners that are beyond the ability of the writer to carefully and neatly correct.[89] In more serious cases, letters or parts of letters may be repeated without any apparent attempt to correct such occurrences.

The changes in the writing ability or quality are seldom extreme over short periods of time (Figure 17). Furthermore, writing ability can vary from one occasion to another such that relapses to better writing quality may sometimes be observed. Vision also can be a victim of age and some of the conditions that appear in writing may be due, in part at least, to the impairment of sight.

The deterioration of one's writing due to a particular illness, particularly if the individual is aged or infirm, is not likely to produce symptoms that can be associated with any particular illness. Loss of control in writing is simply that, and one can only speculate in most cases as to the cause. Nevertheless, it may have a trait to it that can distinguish it from the effect of attempts at spurious simulation.

When an individual suffers infirmity to the extreme, he/she is oftentimes confined to bed due to his/her inability to stand without support. Consequently, any writing one may wish or have to do must be executed under conditions that are bound to impair the quality of anyone's written product, and this too may have a bearing on the conditions noted above that may be observed.

When infirmity develops to the point where the ability to control the writing instrument is insufficient to produce an intelligible or decipherable inscription on paper, it is frequently necessary for another person to provide assistance in the control of the hand, and since these occasions usually involve the application of a signature to a document, they are referred to as *guided-hand-signatures.*

58. What Are the Symbols of Sinistrality (Left-Handedness)?

Second to sex, there is probably no other aspect of human behaviour that has experienced a more profound change in society's attitude toward it and understanding of it than left-handedness. But, similar to its attitude toward sex, the change is a relatively recent occurrence.

There has always been a small proportion of the population of humans that displayed a preference to perform certain manual tasks in a manner that seems to oppose that of the majority. When members of the left side of one's body tend to dominate the action it is called *sinistrality,* or left-handedness, and when, as with most people, the right foot, right leg, right hand, right arm, or right eye tends to receive some preferential consideration it is called *dextrality* or right-handedness.

The human phenomenon of handedness has been of interest to psychologists and pedagogues for many years. Its definition in the broadest sense as the preferential and consistent use of the same hand during the performance of skilled unimanual tasks[90] is complicated by the fact that with some individuals it is not necessarily consistent in the performance of an assortment of tasks. Richardson[91] and others[92] have found that of seven tasks employing the hands, i.e., writing, throwing, cutting with scissors, playing with a racquet or bat, brushing one's teeth, striking a match, hammering a nail (males) or threading a needle (females), handwriting proved to be the most reliable index of handedness. For the purpose of this dissertation, let us agree that sinistrality refers only to the use of the left-hand in the act of writing or lettering.

For reasons that many writers of numerous papers, articles, and books have tried to explain, society has for centuries condemned rather than condoned the individual so unfortunate as to be born with the inclination to left-handedness. In English and other languages, we have associated left-handedness with awkwardness, stuttering, weakness, uncleanliness, and numerous other equally disparaging characteristics. Some writers have noted that ninety percent of chimpanzees are left-handed.[93]

Somewhat remarkably, history recounts for us that many of our highly-regarded world figures, such as Alexander the Great, Charles Chaplin, Rex Harrison, Harpo Marx (who rested the harp on his left shoulder), the British monarch George VI (who stammered, probably because his father George V insisted that he be broken of his left-handedness[94]), Leonardo da Vinci (who drew with his left hand and painted with his right), President Harry Truman (U.S.A.), Babe Ruth (of baseball fame), Kim Novak and Danny Kaye (both of film stardom), Paul McCartney (of the Beatles), and some Caesars, were southpaws, lefties, or sinistrals.[95]

The Phoenicians, a Semitic tribe who inhabited the Mediterranean coast currently recognized as Israel and Lebanon, are credited with the origin of writing. Studies have proven that the direction of their writing was from right to left, as is still the practise with Hebrew and Arabic. This was followed by boustrophedon writing in which the direction of writing alternated with every line. Finally, as students of history contend, the Greeks settled on writing from the left to right that became the convention of Roman writing and styles that developed in societies to the north and west of Rome. Under these circumstances, it has been argued that Arabs and Hebrews were primarily left-handed writers, but there seems to be little substance to the argument. Nevertheless, we are without an acceptable explanation for our alphabet being written from left to right, although it is obvious that when it is executed by the right hand the product can be more conveniently observed.

In elementary schools of our time, left-handed pupils seldom receive standardized instructions delineating a proper writing posture. Consequently, there is remarkable between-subject variability. There are, however, two principal positions adopted by sinistral writers that are generally referred to as the inverted hand posture or position (IHP) and the noninverted hand posture or normal handwriting position (NHP). The common criteria defines the first as one in which the hand is placed above the line of writing and the writing instrument grasped so that it points generally towards the bottom of the page. This position seems to be correlated, though not invariably, to the tendency to slant the page to the left of vertical, as is done by dextrals. The second is described as one in which the hand is placed below the line of writing and the instrument is grasped to point generally towards the top of the page. This position seems to be correlated to the tendency to slant the page to the right of vertical. Guiard and Millerat[96] have suggested a more reliable criteria for identifying the IHP: the slant of the page relative to the vertical (inverters to the left and noninverters to the right), the slant of the writing forearm relative to the vertical edge of the sheet (inverters perpendicular and noninverters parallel), and the position of the nonwriting hand on the page (inverters below and to the left of the writing point and noninverters to the right and often above the writing point). The latter tendency is comparable to the position of the left hand with a noninverted right-handed writer.

McKeever and VanDeventer[97] chose to subdivide the inverted hand position (IHP) into two classes: normally inverted (in which the point of the pen or writing instrument is directed towards the writer and the bottom of the page), and markedly inverted (in which the point of the pen is directed to the left of the writer). In their study, however, only 3 of 65 left-handed writers fell into this category.

A third, but much less frequently employed, position of the hand has been observed in young sinistral writers that is described as parallel, in which the hand is neither clearly above nor below the line of writing.[98] These findings report that most young sinistrals with this propensity eventually change to a fully inverted hand position. Furthermore, studies of young female sinistrals show an early preference for the noninverted writing position, in contradistinction to their opposite sex. It should also be noted that Allen and Wellman[99] reported finding, quite remarkably, a number of dextral writers employing the parallel position, but the tendency apparently declines with age and maturity in writing.

This discussion would not be comprehensive if mention was not made of the fact that the inverted-hand posture (IHP) is not peculiar to left-handed writers exclusively. It was observed by astute investigators, such as Gould[100] in larger studies nearly a century ago that there were a number of dextrals using the inverted-hand posture for writing. More recent studies, by Porac, Coren, and Searleman[101] of 450 triads of father/mother/offspring revealed that 4.7 percent of the parents and 9.1 percent of the offspring that wrote with the right-hand employed an inverted-hand posture. One may speculate that the rise in the frequency of IHP in the younger generation is a consequence of the lack of attention that penmanship now receives in the school systems, but the authors suggest that a complex, multicausal mechanism may be involved.

The incidence of inversion in right-handers varies between 1 and 10 percent, whereas the estimates of inversion within left-handers ranges from 30 to 75 percent, as is mentioned in more detail below. The point to note is that inversion does occur with both dextral and sinistral writers that studies and discussion should not overlook (Figure 18).

Nor should one overlook the rare, but nonetheless, real occurrence of sinistral writers that invert the paper position (IPP), but not the pen (Figure 19). This interesting orientation of paper, pen, and person results in the reversal of stroke directions, as in IHP writing, but also alters the relationship of the writing to a ruled or imaginery line. It doesn't sit on a baseline, but hangs from a clothesline so to speak, and, insofar as the writer is concerned, is executed upside down from right to left rather than left to right (Figure 20). Despite this highly unorthodox approach to the writing act, reasonable writing skill is still achievable.

Despite numerous efforts made in the 1970s to find relationships between writing posture of the left-handers and neurological causes, none has yet to be confirmed. The most parsimonious working hypothesis seems to be that the phenomenon of IHP, at one time thought to be an abnormal phenomenon, is definitely normal and represents an adaptation by sinistrals born of necessity: the need to see what has been written. Studies of the 1980s have shown that the IHP produces more consistency in letter slants than the NHP (noninverted hand position) does, which supports the theory that the IHP is more a matter of adaptation to technical demands than anything else. Even this approach has been challenged on the grounds that right-handers executing Hebrew or Arabic from right to left do not generally develop an IHP while a proportion of Hebrew and Arabic left-handers do. Perhaps of even greater import is the fact that the incidence of IHP in left-handers, regardless of the sex of the writer, is definitely lower among Israelis than Americans.[102]

The incidence of IHP, a writing position that has never been taught anywhere, but is a recognizable pattern of writing conduct across many countries and several generations, has increased in recent years in parallel with social permissiveness respecting this writing behaviour. It develops with maturation and writing practise and this observation is clearly consistent with the hypothesis that the IHP is an adaptive kind of behaviour.[103]

More than fifty years ago Clark[104] asserted that in our western civilization "...All systems of writing have been based on the assumption that the writer will use the right hand. The left-hander is forced into a system not in the least adapted to his needs.... Pupils are not taught to write with the left hand, only permitted" (Figure 21). In recent years, society has been more tolerant and accommodating toward left-handedness. This more permissive attitude toward left-handers in the early school grades, or the decline of interest in and need for quality penmanship may, in part, account for the seeming increase in sinistral tendencies in recent generations. The earlier constraints upon unorthodox writing

Figure 18 Two sinistral writers employing IHP (inverted hand position), although the first employs a more moderate turn of the hand.

practises may explain the report by Beukelaar and Kroonenberg[105] that in a sample of 331 left-handed Dutch persons none born prior to 1940 used the left hand for writing.

Much has been studied and recorded in endeavours to explain left-handedness and to identify its causes. The subject is of interest to writing examination, however, primarily because of its effects upon the writing of the individual and the potential for distinguishing sinistrality from dextrality in the written product. In the course of these studies, a number of long standing notions have been challenged and dispelled. For example, Trankell[106] and others have provided substantial evidence that writing with the left hand is not necessarily poorer or slower than writing with the right. In the days of steel-nibbed pens and slower drying inks, however, there was a greater chance of young writers smudging their work,[107] and undoubtedly this condition influenced a reader's judgment. Peters and McGrory[108] have settled any dispute with their findings that "The writing performance of right-handers

Figure 19 This sinistral writer employs an inverted paper position (IPP) that results in her writing upside down and backwards (from right to left) as she views the writing. The writing hangs from the ruled lines. She is copying from a document that is rightside up (used with permission).

The quick brown fox jumps, over the lazy dog.

Mary had a little lamb. Its fleece was white as snow.

And every where that Mary went the lamb was

1, 2, 3, 4, 5, 6, 7, 8, 9, 10, 1, 2, 3, 4, 5, 6, 7, 8, 9, 0

20, 40, 80, 90, 20, 40, 70, 90, 20, 30, 40, 50, 60, 70, 80, 90.

From the first of November, to the last

Figure 20 The inverted paper position (IPP) does not inhibit writing with reasonable skill (used with permission).

Figure 21 The writing of an individual, born a sinistral writer, and coerced to convert to a dextral writer at an early age (she wore a blue ribbon around her right wrist to remind her which hand she should use to write). She continues to be sinistral in other activities, e.g., playing tennis, throwing a ball, using household tools, in kitchen activities (stirring, cutting bread), ironing, and sewing (the backhand slope was a voluntary change adopted during adolescence to imitate a sibling).

and left-handers, when writing with the preferred posture, was well matched" and that the performance of inverted writers was by no means inferior to that of noninverted writers (Figure 22).

To put sinistrality into perspective for the purpose of handwriting identification we need to reflect upon two matters of statistics: the frequency of occurrence of left-handedness in our populations, and the frequencies of the different hand positions that are employed. The reason for this is simply that handwriting characteristics may change depending on whether the writing instrument is being pushed or pulled across the paper surface.

Beacom[109] reported that the incidence of sinistrality may be as much as 30 percent at infancy, and 11 percent in adulthood. The latter is double the percentages for adults reported in 1945. Furthermore, the numbers are larger for males than for females. Clark[110] reported that a survey of 72,238 Scottish children in 1953 disclosed that 6.7 percent of the males and 4.4 percent of the females (i.e., 5.5 percent overall) were left-handed writers. Then, in a second survey of 5,790 Scottish children in 1956, she reported 8 percent of boys and 6 percent of girls (i.e., 7 percent overall) to be sinistral. A 1964 to 1965 survey of English children indicated 11.3 percent of males and 8.8 percent of females to be left-handed. Peters and Petersen[111] in a sample of 5,910 Canadian school children found 11 percent to be sinistral, provided by 11.9 percent of the males and 10 percent of the females. Spiegler and Yeni-Komshian[112] in a study of 1,816 American university students, their siblings, and their parents, found a 13.8 percent incidence of left-handedness provided by 15.2 percent of the males and 12.6 percent of the females. Furthermore, the incidence of familial sinistrality, that is brothers, sisters, and other relatives (not parents) being left-handed, had no significant effect upon the subjects of the study. However, the incidence of left-handedness was effected by parental handedness in that maternal left-handedness could be significantly associated with increased sinistrality in both sons and daughters, whereas paternal left-handedness could be significantly associated with increased sinistrality in sons, but not in daughters. While parental sinistrality produced left-handedness in the offspring to levels as high as 22 percent this study did not support the findings in other reports that ran as high as 87.5 percent. McKeever and VanEys[113] are now suggesting that grandparents may have a significantly greater effect than parents do upon the occurrence of IHP left-handedness in children. A further study by Peters[114] of 2,194 German school

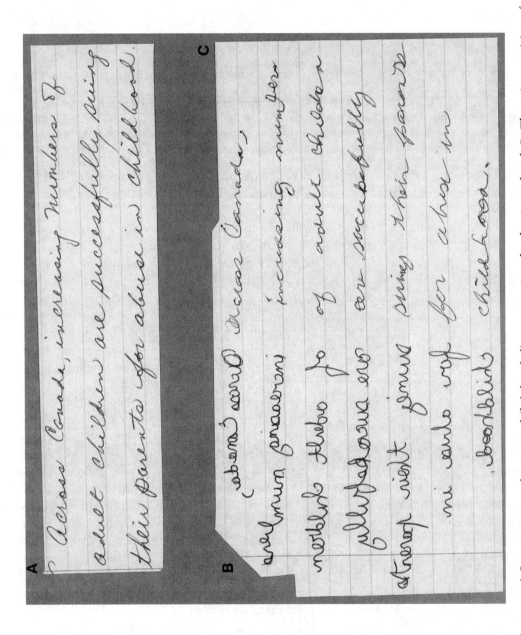

Figure 22 A. The normal fluent writing of a sinistral (left-handed) person, using the dominant hand. B. The mirror writing of the same person, using the dominant hand. C. The writing of the same person, using the nondominant (right) hand. Hold the page in front of a mirror and compare the qualities of the two executions B and C.

children revealed that 9.5 percent of the males and 6.9 percent of the females wrote with the left hand. The difference between the German and Canadian figures was ascribed to the significantly lower incidence of left-handedness among females, but the lower levels of left-handedness among German children suggest that pressures against the use of the left hand may be more operative within the German sample.

These studies suggest some growth in numbers over half a century and a persistent difference in the incidence of sinistrality between the sexes. Other studies that have attempted to correlate the condition with such matters as academic discipline and immune disorders have met with little success.[115] Levy's graph[116] of percentages of left-handed writers that displayed a sharp increase from 1932 (2.2 percent) through 1947 (8.2 percent) plateaued at around 11 percent from 1960 to 1972. In a study of 580 subjects of various ages, Horton[117] reported that 64 (11 percent) were sinistral. Berthold[118] found that in a small sample of 25 subjects, mainly twenty-year-olds, 3 (12 percent) wrote with the left hand. These figures provide us with as reliable an approximation to the actual value within the present generation as we are likely to get.

Having established an acceptable national average (11 percent) for sinistrality recent studies of the subject have directed their attention at other aspects of the phenomenon. For example, no correlation was found between left-handedness and irrational thinking, but some correlation has been noted between left-handedness and the season of births; a greater number of sinistral men being born in the period March/July than in the period August/February.[119] The reader is left to speculate as to the use this information may be in the study of handwriting.

Other studies[120] have suggested that the percentage of sinistrals in many populations tends to drop continuously with the age of individuals over 30 years. The persistent conversion of left-handed writers to right-handedness in earlier generations is suggested as one of several causes. Some evidence has also been found that the proportion of nonright-handers is higher in children with specific reading problems (e.g., dyslexic).[121]

We mentioned earlier that the observation has been made that sinistrality is more common among the hearing-impaired population than among others. Studies of deafness due to external causes at or near the time of birth, the prenatal and postnatal exogenous groups, disclosed that 16.7 percent were left-handed in writing as opposed to 11 percent of the population generally. Among the hereditary deaf group, that is the endogenous group, 30 percent were sinistral.

The incidence of IHP among left-handed writers is another matter that has been given much attention. While Peters and Petersen (1978) had found in Canadian children approximately 40 percent of sinistral males used the IHP and 29.75 percent of sinistral females (many writers were not classified by their procedure), McKeever[122] reported on the results of two studies that found the incidence of inversion in American university students to be 75.8 percent in males and 44.2 percent in females. In his later (1986) study, Peters reported that in his sample of German school children, 65.25 percent of sinistral males used the IHP and 58.75 percent of sinistral females did the same, but the difference between the sexes may not be significant for the sample size involved. Levander and Schalling's[123] study of Swedish college students found 60.4 percent of males and 38.9 percent of females utilized IHP.

As these studies point out there is clearly a preference in males for the inverted hand position that is not found among females. This may be at least partly due to a higher sensitivity in females to social pressures against the use of the IHP. Also worthy of note is that Peters and Petersen (1978) as well as Bryson and MacDonald[124] observed a significant increase in the incidence of IHP over Grades 1 to 5 or to 6 in school children of both sexes which may be related to an increase in proficiency in rapid cursive writing, or due in part to the growing permissive attitude toward left-handers in recent years. Also worthy of note is that Levander and Schalling observed that self-assessment of the IHP produced a notably lower frequency of inversion, perhaps due to a reluctance of left-handers to identify themselves with the awkward hand posture. Also of significance to handwriting examiners is the findings of this latter study that 76 percent of noninverters and 48 percent of inverters chose handprinting or lettering as their normal style of writing. The suggestion we are left with through this and other studies is that for left-handers, the inverted hand posture is more often the posture of choice for cursive writing.

The evidence of sinistrality in handwriting has received little attention until recently. Lester, Werling, and Heinle,[125] in a study of 2,168 people, sought evidence in some 40 aspects of writing by which left-handed writers could be differentiated from right-handers, and failed. Totty, Hardcastle, and Dempsey[126] endeavoured to find a dependence of slope in handwriting upon the sex and handedness of the writer, and while results suggested that right-handers and males tended to write with a greater forward slope than left-handers and females, the figures did not achieve statistical significance. Wing[127] in a study of the neurological controls affecting the amplitude (height) of handwriting found that there was no difference between the handedness or the sex of writers in the height of the writing produced. In this respect, he supported the findings of Reed and Smith[128] that there was no difference in the writing performance of left and right-handed people. In general, prior to this decade, little was known of the differences between right and left-handed writings and there was no completely reliable technique for determining the hand used.

Authors[129-131] whose material was published before 1975 suggested that indications of left-handed writing might be as follows:

1. Smudging or messiness (due to IHP?)
2. Terminal strokes upwards and to the left (due to IHP?)
3. Inconsistent slopes to letters
4. Heavier pressure on upstrokes than downstrokes (due to IHP?)
5. Right to left horizontal strokes, tapering and curving upwards at left end (due to IHP?)
6. Tendency to vertical slope or backhand
7. Right to left "t" crossings (due to IHP?)
8. Right to left "i" dots and punctuation marks (due to IHP?)

As we have suggested by the question in parenthesis, it may be that this evidence was reported without considering the hand position as a likely cause.

The tendency to write more vertically, contended earlier, is supported by studies by Goodnow and Levine,[132] Goodnow,[133] and by Nihei.[134]

Somewhat contrary to others, Zitzelsberger[135] cautioned that the elements of skill and speed, slant, size, proportions, and alignment were not always reliable indicators of sinistrality. This has now been supported by more recent studies that we have previously discussed. Stroke direction was, in the past, more readily determined by the graphite deposits in pencil writings, or the tracks of split nibs in ink writings. More recent research argues that, although the evidence is sometimes subtle, whether it be determined by: (1) the location of graphite deposits from pencils on the edges of paper fibres as seen under the microscope, (2) the spread of the tracks of split nib pens that are now less frequently encountered, or (3) the burr striations of ball-point pens, the study of stroke direction in particular letters seems to offer the greatest promise for distinguishing the sinistral writer from the dextral at the present time.

The potentials of stroke direction in sinistrality determination was suggested by a number of individuals. Fryd[136] dealt with the cross stroke to the block letter "T." Shanon[137] studied cross strokes in the lowercase cursive "t" and the upper case "H," the crossbar to the "7" and the Hebrew letter Daleth, in the writing of dextral and sinistral Americans and Israelis, as well as in the drawing of a horizontal straight line. All right-handers with only one or two exceptions, whether English or Hebrew, executed these strokes from left to right. Among left-handers, higher percentages of Hebrew writers than English writers executed the strokes from right to left, the direction Hebrew writing normally takes. Brandt,[138] while not pursuing this topic particularly, sagaciously observed that right to left horizontal (RLH) strokes never or very rarely occurred in the writing of right-handers. Although these strokes did not occur in all writing of left-handers, he concluded, and many will now concur, that when they did occur they were a reliable indication of the product of a sinistral. Nicholson and Hartley are reported by Franks to have noted the tendency of some left-handers to execute the figure "0" in a clockwise manner. Although statistics are not provided, Thomassen and Teulings[139-140] commented on the fact that they found a larger proportion of left-handers than of right-handers tended to write the digit "0" in a clockwise fashion. Coincidentally, Connolly and Elliott,[141] in a study of the painting strokes of children, found that left-handers frequently drew horizontal strokes from right to left and tended to make clockwise curves.

The burr striations found in ball-point pen writing,[142-145] are described as the linear voids that occur with most ball-point pens when curves in the stroke tend to change the rotation of the ball and expose a part of its surface lacking in ink. These voids invariably move from the inner to the outer radius of the curve in the direction of the stroke. Franks, Davis, and Totty[146] and Franks, Davis, Totty, Hardcastle, and Grove[147] attempted to determine more precisely the potential that stroke direction may have for discriminating left-handed writing from right-handed writing. These were broader studies of curved and almost straight horizontal strokes in lettering, numerals and the bowls of cursive letters, such as "g" and "d," that suggested some significant differences in writing performance. For many left-handers' circular forms were executed clockwise (39 percent), whereas right-handers almost invariably (99 percent) moved the pen in a counterclockwise direction. Furthermore, horizontal strokes were executed from right to left (RLH) by 69 percent of the left-handers but never by the right-handers. Thus, in their sample of 347 left-handed writers, stroke direction in one or more of the target letters "O," "A," "E," "J," "T," "H," "G," "Q," "F," "t," "o," "g," "q," and the numerals "5," "9," and "0," indicated sinistrality in some 276 (80 percent) of the writers. A problem encountered in these studies was that stroke direction was determinable by burr striations in only a percentage of the writing samples that varied (22 percent to 97 percent) with the target letter or numeral. Clearly the tendency to produce striations varies with the ink and/or writing instrument.

Unfortunately, perhaps, we do not have any information from these studies as to whether RLH and clockwise-executed zeros are characteristics peculiar to inverted-hand writers only or are shared to some extent by all kinds of left-handed writers. It seems obvious to some that these unusual grips (e.g., IHP) will result in some difference in letter forms, even within the sinistral sector of the population. Further studies are necessary, however, to establish what these differences may be and how they correlate with the IHP.

59. What Are the Symptoms of Sex?

M. Alfred Binet, a French psychologist, in his book *Les Révélations de L'Ecriture* (Paris 1906), claimed that, in French writing of that era, sex could be determined accurately in 75 percent of the cases. In the ensuing three decades, a number of investigators attempted to duplicate Binet's work with American writers, but the accuracy achieved was notably lower. Two of these investigators were Downey[148] and Newhall.[149] Young[150] summarizes the results by saying simply "There appears to be good evidence for the view that the sex of the writer can be determined from handwriting in a manner superior to chance." His results led him to state that untrained judges are able to determine the sex of the writer from handwriting with an average performance 11 percent better than chance... 50 percent. We emphasize the words *untrained judges* as none of these studies were conducted with the assistance of competent handwriting examiners. There were few of them in existence at that time. Only one of the early studies involved a graphologist.

Since there was a success rate slightly better than chance in identifying the sex of the writer some investigators sought to determine what aspects of the writings constituted the sex signs that judges were using to indicate gender. Young reported several adjectives and phrases offered by his 50 (25 male) judges in making their assessments, that are of little value owing to the conflicts and inconsistencies the list contains.

Middleton's study[151] involving 200 judges (100 male) provided 10 reasons influencing judgments:

1. A woman's writing is neater.
2. Women write more slowly and achieve greater finish.
3. A woman's writing is prettier.
4. Men tend to dot the "i" with a dash instead of a dot.
5. When a man does write well, his writing is likely to be almost perfect.
6. Men write larger than women.
7. Any backward writing or printing is likely to be the writing of a woman.
8. The use of an epsilon "ϵ" is likely to indicate a woman's writing.
9. A woman's writing is likely to be more readable than a man's.
10. Men press harder on their pens than women.

Reasons 1, 2, 3, and 9 seem to relate to or stem from quality of writing or penmanship. This is consistent with the findings of Starch[152] that females are superior to males in quality and slightly superior in speed, but the differences found were small. Broom, Thompson, and Bouton,[153] in a study of 40 randomly selected sample writings (18 male), had similar findings that regularity, curves, conventional form, and uniformity of slant were characteristic of samples most frequently judged to be feminine handwriting. Conversely, irregularity, unconventional form, angles, and nonuniformity of slant were characteristic of samples most frequently judged to be masculine handwriting. Tenwolde[154] simply stated that: "The advantage discovered in average penmanship quality favoured the girls."

Newhall declined to report the criteria that his judges reported as he felt unable to determine which criteria were actually used and which were rationalizations. He does go so far as to say that:

"The handwriting most frequently judged to have been written by men appears characteristically different from that most frequently judged to have been written by women."

Of particular interest to us is the fact that, notwithstanding the consistency in these sex guides, the success rates in distinguishing the sex of the writer seldom exceeded 66 percent of the judgments made on average. Evidently, substantial numbers of males and females don't fit their respective patterns.

In the U.K. and Canada, at the beginning of this century, the angular system of writing was taught exclusively to women in ladies' schools, and served to be indicative of sex. The angular system was not taught in the U.S.A. but, because it became a fashionable style, it appealed to women anywhere, and so was imitated.

Osborn[155] wrote that:

"…The distinctive, angular, woman's hand is usually coarse and heavy and often of a sprawling awkward character with abnormally wide spacing between words and between lines and with horizontal concluding strokes to words."

Handwriting has changed significantly in more recent years and the sex indicators of a century ago are no longer available. What indicators today's writings provide are not numerous and, just as sex guide indicators were 75 years ago, they may be misleading.

Sex is often indicated by the choice of words, cumbersome use of expressions or idioms characteristic of one of the sexes. Threats of violence tend to be masculine, however threats using words such as *horrid* and *awful* are invariably feminine. Remarkably enough, in anonymous letters, the excessive and awkward use of profanity or lewdness is also a feminine characteristic.

Osborn maintained that the writing of women is, as a rule, more delicate containing more superfluous peculiarities and mannerisms. It is generally more finished. Shading, if present in older writings, is likely to be in bunches, particularly at ends of words. Heavy shading of every stroke, and jabs of the pen, is more often masculine. Studies of more recent times have generally confirmed Osborn's statements. Hodgins[156] determined that good quality, small size, neatness, and fluency with carefulness were the bases for judging a writing to be that of a female.

Evidently, there is no historical basis for quality, neatness, and fluency being more characteristic of female than male writing. This seems the more remarkable when we recall that education, including penmanship, was, generally, the prerogative of males until the latter part of the nineteenth century. Bookkeeping, accounting, record keeping, and correspondence were male domains, almost until the advent of the typewriter in the late 1880s, when "type writer" was a title accorded the female who mastered the mechanical keyboard.

What there is in the mental or neuromuscular composition of the female that predisposes her, on average, to a better quality or skill in writing is a question that graphologists have attempted to exploit, but remains unanswered.

Notwithstanding the apparent correlation between quality, neatness and fluency, and the sex of the writer, Hodgins found, as did Goodenough[157] before him, that accurate determinations as to sex could only be made in about 66 percent of the writings examined. Furthermore, Hodgins' panel of 25 judges consisting of 11 document examiners, 11 lay persons and 3 master penmen, were not successful in making a correct sex determination of any one of 40 writing specimens 100 percent of the time. Totty, Hardcastle, and Dempsey[158] sought to correlate sex and handedness with writing slope, but found that the overlapping nature of the distributions would not permit it. Although their results suggest that males and right-handers tend to write with a greater forward slope than females and left-handers, the results did not achieve statistical significance.

Fluckiger, Tripp, and Weinberg,[159] in their review of the literature published between 1933 and 1959, stated that pressure seems to be the most important clue to sex, among all the clues considered. Along these lines Cambridge[160] propounded that an evenness of and somewhat greater "pressure emphasis" in vertical strokes was indicative of masculinity, whereas an evenness of and somewhat greater "pressure emphasis" in horizontal strokes was indicative of femininity. Nevertheless, as Hodgins suggested, despite the fact that determinations of sex may be made with accuracy better than chance, the proportion of errors is high. The level of accuracy was not sufficient to warrant the use of handwriting to infer the sex of the writer. Graphologists argue, of course, that handwriting need not be congruent with physical sex, but may simply reveal psychological masculinity and/or femininity of the writer. It must be allowed that there may be some credibility to this point.

Numerous studies have been conducted in recent years in search of psycho-sexual symbolism. Lester, Werling, and Heinle[161] claimed that 11 of 40 aspects of writing significantly differentiated males and females in all age groups from 20 to 49. Anderson and Wolowitz,[162] attempting to test the claims of Freud,[163] found evidence in the proportions of the capital letter "I," when used as the personal pronoun, that seemed to confirm the male's preference for elongating constructions in contrast to women's better balance of proportions in the letter's construction. In a subsequent study, Anderson[164] found that the letter "I," when executed by homosexuals, tended to reflect the proportions of the female rather than the elongations of the male.

Hecker[165] reviewed and listed the success rates of 30 studies, conducted between 1906 and 1991, that endeavoured to determine the sex differences in writing with reasonable accuracy. The results ranged from 57 percent accuracy to 94 percent (Vniise Institute in Russia) with a mean of 71.7 percent. With these results, arguments have arisen as to how sex is being defined: whether biologically or physiologically, whether psychologically in terms of femininity/masculinity, or in terms of dominance. Furthermore, there seems to be at least two methods of judging writing for sexual indicators. One group takes a wholistic approach and seeks evidence in the general character of the writing, or the appearance of the writing as a whole. Other researchers have sought to measure specific features (e.g., slant or size) in search of a correlation with gender. Another criticism of the methodology has been directed at the variability of the populations from which the samples were drawn. Goodenough (1945) and Hodgins (1971) suggested that the rater's sex had a bearing on the results, females being superior to males in judging the sex of writers, whereas earlier investigators did not seem to agree.

Hecker ran two studies of the digitized writing images in the FISH data pool. One employed pattern recognition and image processing techniques for feature extraction and classification. The second was a more traditional view of the digitized handwriting image in the FISH system in terms of conventional features such as slant, shape of loops, etc.

Hecker's sample consisted of 96 males and 96 females between the ages of 16 and 40 years selected from writings in the FISH data base.

For comparison, the same samples were examined by 21 handwriting experts (4 females) of one of the German State Crime Labs, and 50 lay persons (22 females). The lab examiners and lay persons correctly judged the sex of the writer in 63 percent of the cases, the experts performing only slightly better than the nonexperts (64.7 percent vs. 62.3 percent). The writings of males were judged correctly by the experts in 76.5 percent of the cases and of females in 61.8 percent of the cases. There was considerable variation in the results of the raters.

Insofar as the computer data was concerned, discriminant analysis found higher coefficients for measured features such as the length of ascenders, the shape of upper loops and the size of lower loops. Factor analysis suggested three factors having some bearing on this type of study: the size of writing, the slant of writing and the shape (?) of writing. The best rate of correct matches with sex was 72.4 percent, and the mean success rate resulting from computer-assisted feature processing was 71.5 percent, that can only be said to be superior to the 63 percent success rate of examiners and the 62.3 percent of nonexperts, but hardly acceptable.

It is Hecker's view that there are no group-specific handwriting features that can be attributed to the sex of writers. Females and males do exhibit different mean values for their various writing features, but there is invariably a large area of overlap. The only general statements that Hecker ventures to make are that females tend to write larger (contrary to the findings of others), more rounded, and more upright than males. As a diagnostic tool that fails in 1 out of 4 cases, however, it cannot be considered to be acceptable and is, therefore, of use to only a very limited extent.

Some psychologists are inclined to the view that until sex can be determined reliably from handwriting, other attempts to correlate writing with personality traits might as well be put on hold.

60. Is Writing with the Subdominant Hand (i.e., the Nonpreferred, Unpractised, Unaccustomed, Weak or Opposite Hand) Recognizable?

In the discussions of dextrality and sinistrality in handwriting many terms have come into use to refer to the writing produced by the *other* hand. Some call it the *nonpreferred* hand, others the *unpractised* or *unaccustomed* hand. Still others refer to it as the *awkward* or *unskilled* or *weak* hand and there are those who elect to call it simply the *off-hand* or *opposite* hand writing. Some of these designations are not as correct or descriptive as one would like to use. For dextral-sinistral writers (who were originally left-handed writers, but were trained to use the right), the left hand is hardly the nonpreferred hand. Moreover, the writing of these individuals with their left hands is often quite skilled, though it may or may not be as skillful as that produced by the hand enjoying greater or more frequent use. To say it is unskilled, however, would be an underestimation. It is equally incorrect to call it the weak hand, for it may well be the stronger of the two.

Except for the rare individual who is fully ambidextrous insofar as writing is concerned, the many studies of writing with the other hand are consistent in their findings. Regardless of the nature of the material under study, be it lettering, signatures, or extended cursive writing, when one changes to the "other" hand to hold the writing instrument, there is some loss, however great or small, in writing quality, fluency, or skill.

To induce some consistency in the language of writing examination, it appears much more appropriate to refer to the products of the other hand as writing or lettering of the subdominant hand, as opposed to that of the dominant or regnant hand. The terms selected must be equally applicable to both dextral and sinistral writers, yet indicative of the preference held by the individual. For consistency and clarity, we have adopted these terms in our dissertations on handedness.

From the viewpoint of forensic handwriting examination, any discussion of sinistrality or left-handedness must address the matter of subdominant hand writing regardless of the term chosen to indicate writing hand preference, be it *nonpreferred, awkward, unskilled, opposite, unaccustomed* or *weak* hand. For the most part, such writings appear in matters in which the writer has a reason to conceal his/her identity, such as in anonymous or threatening letters, or in hold-up notes presented with a demand for money. In these cases, writing with the subdominant hand is a chosen method of disguise, though the effectiveness of it is a matter that the writer seldom considers. There are also other instances, of course, in which the writing hand must be changed due to disease, injury or amputation.

Studies of the effectiveness of a change of hands to accomplish disguise have shown that, insofar as a sinistral using the right hand, in as many as 80 percent of the cases competent examiners have been able to accurately associate subdominant hand writing with that of the regnant or normal hand, and 87 percent of the time insofar as a dextral using the left hand (Comeau[166]). Comeau offered these results as support for Harrison's contention that it is very difficult for most people to disguise their writing merely by using their unaccustomed hand. Comeau's samples consisting of 34 dextral and 6 sinistral were small, however, and thus, reliability of the study is somewhat in doubt.

In an earlier study, Stevens[167] found, rather by good fortune, 200 files of prison inmates in Wisconsin correction institutions containing sample signatures apparently executed with both hands. While some success appears to have been achieved in distinguishing subdominant handwritten signatures from normal regnant executions, the task was exacerbated by the fact that standards were limited to single samples from each hand.

A point that Stevens makes is that subdominant hand or awkward hand written signatures, because of the loss of skill that they almost invariably exhibit, may be mistaken for traced signatures, writings of the aged or infirm, or simply ordinarily unskilled handwriting. Consequently, more specific characteristics are needed to discriminate between subdominant hand written signatures and others that are executed under unusual circumstances.

While the use of the subdominant hand is addressed in most of the more recently published books on document examination, principally as a method of disguise, the formal studies that have been conducted and reported in the last 25 years are relatively few. Harrison,[168] Conway,[169] Stangohr,[170] Anthony,[171] Sperry,[172] Zimmerman,[173] and Dawson[174] have each claimed success in the identification of subdominant hand writings. These have been referred to variously as awkward hand, weak hand, or unaccustomed hand writings or letterings. The authors have described observations that these cases have proffered. Empirical data based on large samples, however, is limited. Nevertheless, what is available supports a number of general statements respecting writings of the subdominant hand.

Mature and practised handwriting is substantially the product of the mind, implemented through a level of manual dexterity or muscular coordination peculiar to the individual. The mental picture of writing and of its characteristics does not change for the writer with a change of the hand chosen to operate the writing instrument.

Some have maintained that the difference between the writings of the dominant and the subdominant hands is due to a difference in manual dexterity and also to a difference in the neurophysiological processes that are involved.[175] While this may be so we are without any information as to precisely which changes are due to a difference in writing skill and which are attributable to a different mental process at work.

Whatever the reason for it, the writings, letterings, and signatures executed with the subdominant hand, as compared to those of the dominant hand, invariably display a loss of skill and fluency that is manifest in a number of fashions:

1. A reduction in writing speed that may result in a poorer line quality displaying tremour, abrupt changes in pen pressure and/or disconnections between letters of cursive writing,
2. A noticeable loss of pen or muscular control that is evident in the execution of curves, loops, eyelets, the retracing of staffs or stems between arches, and the quality of straight lines, such as "t" crossings. In lieu of smooth turns, there may be abrupt directional changes.
3. An inability to maintain consistency and quality in letter forms, letter sizes, letter alignments, terminations, and the finer movements with which some letters are constructed and others are connected.
4. An inability to maintain consistency in the slope of the writing or in particular letters, and perhaps a tendency to write more vertically.
5. A more deliberate inscription of diacritics and punctuation marks, although the pattern of use by the individual is not likely to change.
6. The omission or abbreviation of initial and terminal strokes, however, terminal strokes are known to be somewhat variable in length and direction.
7. Some simplification of complex letter forms.
8. Hesitation and/or pen stops that may indicate some uncertainty as to succeeding movements.

Consistency between the written issues of the two hands can be expected in the following:

1. The relative sizes of internal letters in words, according to Hotimsky.[176] Relative sizes, however, may be subject to considerable modification. The control of the pen by the subdominant hand is, understandably, more difficult, and attention has to be concentrated on the creation of recognizable letter forms, regardless of normal writing habits. Relative sizes of letters tend to approach copybook. Indeed, as a general rule, any handwriting written under difficulty tends to lose its individuality and approach the copybook standard.
2. The basic designs of less complex letter forms, according to Newman.[177]
3. General lateral expansion. It has been suggested that writings of the subdominant hand will exhibit some increase in size, but studies of larger samples of writings, such as Newman's 120 subjects, did not prove this to be the case. One can expect an enlargement of the finer elements of writing, however, if only because the subdominant hand is not likely to function with the same dexterity as the other.

Greater consistency is to be found between the subdominant and dominant hand writings of sinistral rather than dextral writers. Generally speaking, left-handers produce a better quality of writing using their right hand than right-handers do with their left. The reason for this is uncertain. It may be that most sinistrals have had some experience earlier on in an endeavour to convert or be converted to right-handers.

At this point, the caution expressed by Stevens and others bears repeating. Without adequate standards in number and kind, the writings of the subdominant hand can be easily confused with that of the aged or infirm, or mistaken for a spurious execution of one kind or another.

References

1. Cole, Alwyn, *Autoforgery.* Presented at the meeting of the American Society of Questioned Document Examiners (Silver Spring, MD, 1973).

2. McCarthy, J., *Excellence in Forgeries. A Case Study.* Presented at the meeting of the American Society of Questioned Document Examiners (Houston, TX, 1970).

3. Buglio, James and Gidion, Hans M., *Another Adept Penman.* Presented at the meeting of the American Society of Questioned Document Examiners (San Francisco, 1977).

4. McCarthy, John F., *Two Penmen's Abilities in Simulating Signatures.* Presented at the meeting of the International Association of Forensic Sciences (Oxford, 1984).

5. Totty, R. N., *Skilled Copies of Signatures.* Presented at the meeting of the American Society of Questioned Document Examiners (Chicago, 1995).

6. Foley, Bobby G. and Kelly, James H., Guided Hand Signature Research. *Journal of Police Science and Administration,* 1977; 5: 2: pp 227-231.

7. Locard, Dr. Edmond, The Inert Hand. *International Criminal Police Review,* 1951 February; 45: pp 45-47.

8. Mayther, Jacques, *Handwriting and Signatures Made by "Guided Hand."* Presented at the First International Meeting of Document Examiners, April 1963. (rewritten and presented at the meeting of the American Society of Questioned Document Examiners, Colorado Springs, CO, 1975).

9. Hilton, Ordway, Consideration of the Writer's Health in Identifying Signatures and Detecting Forgery. *Journal of Forensic Sciences,* 1969 April; 14: 2: pp 157-166.

10. Osborn, Albert S., *Questioned Documents.* 2nd ed. (Albany: Boyd Printing Co., 1929) p 309.

11. Frazer, Persifor, *Bibliotics or the Study of Documents* (Philadelphia: Lippincott, 1901), pp 152-170.

12. Sellers, Clark, Assisted and Guided Signatures. *Journal of Criminal Law, Criminology and Police Science,* 1962; 53: pp 245-248.

13. Mayther, Jacques, *Writing and Signatures Made by the "Guided Hand."* Presented at the First International meeting in Questioned Documents (London, April 1963).

14. Skelly, James D., Guided Deathbed Signatures. *Canadian Society of Forensic Science Journal,* 1967 December; 20: 4: pp 147-149.

15. McNally, Joseph P., *The Guider is the Writer.* Presented at the meeting of the American Academy of Forensic Sciences (Washington, February 1976).

16. Harrison, Wilson R., *Suspect Documents* (New York: Frederick A Praeger, 1958), p 409.

17. Ruenes, Rafael Fernandez, *Guided Hand Signature and Forgery.* Presented at the meeting of the American Society of Questioned Document Examiners (Colorado Springs, CO, 1975).

18. Jones, D. G., Guided Hand or Forgery? *Journal of the Forensic Science Society,* 1986; 26: pp 169-173.

19. Gähwiler, H.-J., Unauthorized Assistance by a Third Person at the Signing of a Testament. *Journal of the Forensic Science Society,* 1984; 24: p 607.

20. Mayther, Jacques, op. cit.

21. Sellers, Clark, op. cit.

22. Osborn, Albert S., *Questioned Documents* (Albany: Boyd Printing Co., 1929), p 407.

23. Saudek, R., *Experiments with Handwriting* (New York: William Morrow & Co.), 1929.

24. Mansfield, W. W., Disguise in Handwriting. *Medico-legal and Criminology Review,* 1943 Jan/Mar; 11: pp 23-29.

25. Harris, J. J., Disguised Handwriting. *Journal of Criminal Law, Criminology and Police Science,* 1953; 43: pp 685-689.

26. Harrison, Wilson R., *Suspect Documents* (New York: Frederick A. Praeger, 1958), p 349 et seq.

27. Alford, Edwin F., Disguised Handwriting. A Statistical Survey of How Handwriting is Most Frequently Disguised. *Journal of Forensic Sciences,* 1970 October; 15: 4: pp 476-488.

28. Herkt, A., Signature Disguise or Signature Forgery. *Journal of the Forensic Science Society,* 1986; 26: pp 257-266.

29. Konstantimidis, Siv., Disguised Handwriting. *Journal of the Forensic Science Society,* 1987; 27: pp 383-392.

30. Alford, Edwin F. Jr. and Bertocchi, Michael P., *Punctuation as an Aid in Examining Disguised Writing.* Presented at the meeting of the American Academy of Forensic Sciences (Dallas, TX, 1974).

31. Keckler, Jon A., *Felonious Disguise.* Presented at the meeting of the American Society of Questioned Document Examiners (Aurora, CO, September 1988).

32. Regent, James, Changing Slant: Is It the Only Change? *Journal of Forensic Sciences,* 1979; 22: pp 216-224.

33. Jamieson, John Allen, Effects of Slope Change on Handwriting. *Canadian Society of Forensic Science Journal,* 1983; 16: 3: pp 117-122.

34. Halder-Sinn, Petra and Wegener, Kerstin, Controllability of the Slant in Simple and Multiple Strategies for Disguised Handwriting. *Perceptual and Motor Skills,* 1992; 74: pp 905-906.

35. Kropinak, Robert, *Disguised Writing — Effective or Noneffective.* (Study conducted at the RCMP Crime Detection Laboratory, Regina, unpublished, circa 1965).

36. Parker, Joseph L., *Repeated Disguise Beats the Clone Defence.* Presented at the meeting of the American Society of Questioned Document Examiners (Crystal City, VA, 1989).

37. Galbraith, Nanette G., *Another Look at Disguised Writing.* Presented at the meeting of the American Society of Questioned Document Examiners (Rochester, 1979).

38. Crane, Adrian, *An Examination of the Influences of Sex and Education on Disguised Writing.* Reported by John H. Hodgins at the meeting of the American Society of Questioned Document Examiners (Washington, 1973).

39. Hull, J. Michael, *The Relationship Between Disguised Handwriting and Years of Formal Education: Final Results.* Presented at the meeting of the Southwestern Association of Forensic Document Examiners (San Francisco, April 1993).

40. Behnen, Adam P., *Disguise and Alternate Writing Styles.* Presented at the meeting of the American Society of Questioned Document Examiners (Ottawa, 1993).

41. Hart, Linda, *Illusions of Disguise.* Presented at the meeting of the American Society of Questioned Document Examiners (Montreal, September 1985).

42. McCarthy, J. F. and Winchester, Janis, The Autopen. *Journal of Forensic Sciences,* 1973 October; 18: 4: pp 441-447.

43. Radley, R. W., *Stencil Forgery? Considerations of a Case History.* Presented at the meeting of the American Society of Questioned Document Examiners (Lake Tahoe, 1983).

44. Harris, J. J., The Document Evidence and Some Other Observations About the Howard R. Hughes "Mormon Will" Contest. *Journal of Forensic Sciences,* 1986; 31: pp 365-375.

45. Cabanne, R. A., The Clifford Irving Hoax of the Howard Hughes Autobiography. *Journal of Forensic Sciences,* 1975; 20: pp 5-17.

46. Michel, I. and Baier, P. E., The Diaries of Adolph Hitler. Implication for Document Examination. *Journal of the Forensic Science Society,* 1985; 25: 3: pp 167-178.

47. Grant, J., The Diaries of Adolph Hitler. *Journal of the Forensic Science Society,* 1985; 25: 3: p 189.

48. Cabanne, Robert A., *The Clifford Irving Hoax of the Howard Hughes Autobiography.* Presented at the meeting of the American Academy of Forensic Sciences (Las Vegas, NV, 1973).

49. Grant, Julius, Mussolini Diaries Forgeries. *Journal of the Forensic Science Society,* 1969; 9: pp 43-44.

50. Osborn, Albert S., *Questioned Documents* (New York: Boyd Printing Co., 1929), pp 264, 267, 364, 367.

51. Harrison, Wilson R., *Suspect Documents* (New York: Frederick A Praeger, 1958), p 352.

52. Masson, Janet Fenner, *An Evaluation of Simulated and Traced Signatures and Consideration of the Potential for Determination of the Writer's Identity.* Presented at the meeting of the American Academy of Forensic Sciences (Nashville, 1996).

53. Conway, James V. P., *Authenticity v. Simulation.* Presented at the meeting of the American Society of Questioned Document Examiners (Boston, 1982).

54. Leung, S. C., Cheng, Y. S., Fung, H. T., and Poon, N. I., Forgery 1— Simulation. *Journal of Forensic Sciences,* 1993 March; 38: 2: pp 402-412.

55. Herkt, A., Signature Disguise or Signature Forgery. *Journal of the Forensic Science Society,* 1986; 26: 4: pp 257-266.

56. Horan, James J., *The Size of Forged Signatures.* Presented at the meeting of the American Society of Questioned Document Examiners (Chicago, 1985).

57. Hilton, Ordway, *Scientific Examination of Questioned Documents.* Revised edition (New York, Elsevier/North-Holland, Inc., 1982), p 185.

58. Muehlberger, Robert J., Identifying Simulations: Practical Considerations. *Journal of Forensic Sciences,* 1990 March; 35: 2: pp 368-374.

59. Osborn, John Paul, *Writing Instruments' Effects on Traced Signatures.* Presented at the meeting of the American Society of Questioned Document Examiners (Nashville, TN, 1984).

60. Harrison, W. R., *Forgery Detection: A Practical Guide* (New York: Frederick A. Praeger Inc., 1964).

61. Muehlberger, Robert J. and Vastrick, Thomas W., *A Traced Forgery: Is There a Need for Handwriting Comparisons?* Presented at the meeting of the American Society of Questioned Document Examiners (Milwaukee, WI, 1992).

62. Harrison, Wilson R., *Suspect Documents* (New York: Frederick A. Praeger, 1958), p 390.

63. Harrison, Wilson R., *Suspect Documents* (New York: Frederick A Praeger, 1958), p 383.

64. Herkt, A., Signature Disguise or Signature Forgery? *Journal of the Forensic Science Society,* 1986; 26: 4: pp 257-266.

65. de la Pena, Julia Elena, *Can an Apparently False Signature Turn Out to be Genuine?* Presented at the meeting of the American Society of Questioned Document Examiners (Orlando, FL, 1991).

66. Walters, A. and Flynn, W., Illusion of Traced Forgery on Zinc-Oxide-Coated Photocopy Paper. *Journal of Police Science and Administration,* 1974 December; 2: 4: pp 376-380.

67. Vastrick, T. W., Illusions of Tracing. *Journal of Forensic Sciences,* 1982 January; 27: 1: pp 186-191.

68. Gamble, D. J., *Dry Transfer Printing* (unpublished paper, circa 1970).

69. Kraemer, J. I., A New Development in Graphic Transfer Material and an Illustration of Its Illegal Use. *Journal of Forensic Sciences,* 1979 October; 24: 1: pp 875-879.

70. Welch, J. R., The Linking of a Counterfeit Document to Individual Sheets of Dry Transfer Lettering Through the Transfer of Fluorescent Glue. *Journal of the Forensic Science Society,* 1986; 26: pp 253-256.

71. Ellen, David, *The Scientific Examination of Documents, Methods and Techniques* (Chichester, Eng.: Ellis Horwood Ltd., 1989), pp 136-137.

72. Hodgins, John H., *A Resume of Some Recent Research.* Presented at the meeting of the American Society of Questioned Document Examiners (Washington, 1973).

73. Carney, B. B., Transfer of Pencil Writing by Cellophane Tape. *Journal of Forensic Sciences,* 1980; 25: 2: pp 423-427.

74. Carney, B. B., *Transfer of Pencil Writing by Cellophane Tape — an Update.* Presented at the meeting of the American Academy of Forensic Sciences (Cincinnati, 1983).

75. Tappolet, J. A. and Ottinger, E., Transfer of Signatures with Transparent Pressure Tape: Some Experiments. *Forensic Science International,* 1982; 20: pp 61-69.

76. Gencavage, John S., *Facsimile Signatures Produced by Gelatin Transfer Duplicators: Recognition and Identification.* Presented at the meeting of the American Society of Questioned Document Examiners (Nashville, May 1984).

77. Osborn, Albert S., *Questioned Documents.* 2nd Ed. (Albany: Boyd Printing Co., 1929), p 689.

78. Muehlberger, Robert J., *Variation, a Measure of Genuineness.* Presented at the meeting of the American Society of Questioned Document Examiners (Boston, MA, 1982).

79. Frazer, Persifor, *Bibliotics or the Study of Documents.* 3rd Ed. (Philadelphia: J. B. Lippincott Co., 1901).

80. Osborn, A. S., *Questioned Documents.* 2nd Ed. (Albany: Boyd Printing Co., 1929), p 150.

81. Kapoor, T. S., Kapoor, M., and Sharma, G. P., Study of the Form and Extent of Natural Variation in Genuine Writings with Age. *Journal of the Forensic Science Society,* 1985; 25: pp 371-375.

82. Lester, David, Werling, Norma, and Heinle, Norma H., Differences in Handwriting as a Function of Age. *Perceptual and Motor Skills,* 1983; 57: p 738.

83. Hilton, Ordway, op. cit., p 21.

84. Harrison, Wilson R., op. cit., p 339.

85. Boisseau, M., Chamberland, G., and Gautier, S., Handwriting Analysis of Several Extrapyramidal Disorders. *Journal of the Forensic Science Society,* 1987; 20: 4: pp 139-146.

86. Carney, Brian B., *A New Tremour in Handwriting.* A book review presented at the meeting of the American Society of Questioned Document Examiners (Ottawa, Ont, 1993).

87. Elbe, R. J. and Koller, W. C., *Tremour* (Baltimore: The John Hopkins University Press, 1990).

88. Behrendt, J. E., *Problems Associated With the Writing of Senile Dementia Patients*. Presented at the meeting of the American Society of Questioned Document Examiners (Boston, 1982).

89. Hilton, Ordway, *Influence of Age and Illness on Handwriting Identification Problems*. Presented at the meeting of the American Society of Questioned Document Examiners (Colorado Springs, CO, 1975).

90. Porac, Clare, Coren, Stanley, and Searleman, Alan, Inverted vs. Straight Handwriting Posture: a Family Study. *Behaviour Genetics,* 1983; 13: 3: pp 311-320.

91. Richardson, John T., A Factor Analysis of Self-Reported Handedness. *Neuropsychologia,* 1978; 16; pp 747-748

92. Annett, M. A., A Classification of Hand Preference by Association Analysis. *British Journal of Psychology,* 1970; 61: pp 303-320.

93. Beacom, Mary, Was This Document Written With the Left Hand? *Journal of Forensic Sciences,* 1961; 6: 3.

94. Thorton, Michael, *Royal Feud* (New York: Simon & Schuster, 1985), p 69.

95. Barsley, Michael, *The Left-Handed Book* (Toronto: Ryerson, 1966).

96. Guiard, Yves and Millerat, Francoise, Writing Postures in Left-Handers: Inverters are Hand Crossers. *Neuropsychologia,* 1984; 22: 4: pp 535-538.

97. McKeever, Walter F. and Van Deventer, Allen D., Inverted Handwriting Position, Language, Laterality and The Levi-Nagylaki Genetic Model of Handedness and Cerebral Organization *Neuropsychologia,* 1980; 18: 99-102.

98. Bryson, Susan E. and MacDonald, Valerie, The Development of Writing Posture in Left-Handed Children and Its Relation to Sex and Reading Skills. *Neuropsychologia,* 1984; 22: 1: pp 91-94.

99. Allen, M. and Wellman, M. M., Hand Position During Writing. Cerebral Laterality and Reading: Age and Sex Difference. *Neuropsychologia,* 1980; 18: pp 33-40.

100. Gould, G. M., *Right Handedness and Left Handedness with Chapters Treating of the Writing Posture. The Rules of the Road, etc.* (Philadelphia: J. P. Lippincott, 1908).

101. Porac, Clare, Coren, Stanley, and Searleman, Alan, Inverted vs. Straight Handwriting Posture: A Family Study. *Behaviour Genetics,* 1983; 13: 3: pp 311-320.

102. Shanon, B., Writing Positions in Americans and Israelis. *Neuropsychologia,* 1978; 16: pp 587-591.

103. Guiard, Yves and Millerat, Francoise, Writing Postures in Left Handers: Inverters Are Hand-Crossers. *Neuropsychologia,* 1984; 22: 4: pp 535-538.

104. Clark, Margaret, *Psychology of the Elementary School Subjects* (New York: Farrer and Rinehart, 1934).

105. Beukelaar, Leen and Kroonenberg, Pieter M., Changes Over Time in the Relationship Between Hand Preference and Writing Hand Among Left-Handers. *Neuropsychologia,* 1986; 24: 2: pp 301-303.

106. Trankell, Arne, The Influence of the Choice of Writing Hand on the Handwriting. *British Journal of Educational Psychology,* 1956; 26: pp 94-103.

107. Barsley, Michael, *The Left-Handed Book* (Toronto: Ryerson Press), p 179.

108. Peters, Michael and McGrory, Jay, The Writing Performance of Inverted and Noninverted Right- and Left-Handers. *Canadian Journal of Psychology,* 1987; 41: 1: pp 20-32.

109. Beacom, Mary, Was this Document Written with the Left Hand? *Journal of Forensic Sciences,* 1961; 4: 3.

110. Clark, M. M., *Left-Handedness: Laterality Characteristics and their Educational Implications* (London: University of London Press, 1957).

111. Peters, Michael and Petersen, Kris, Incidence of Left-Handers with Inverted Writing Position in a Population of 5910 Elementary School Children. *Neurophychologia*, 1978; 16: pp 743-746.

112. Spiegler, Brenda J. and Yeni-Komshian, Grace H., Incidence of Left-Handed Writing in a College Population with Reference to Family Patterns of Hand Preference. *Neuropsychologia*, 1983; 21: 6: pp 651-659.

113. McKeever, Walter F. and VanEys, Patricia P., Inverted Handwriting Posture in Left Handers is Related to Familial Sinistrality Incidence. *Cortex*, 1989; 25: pp 581-589.

114. Peters, Michael, Incidence of Left-Handed Writers and the Inverted Writing Position in a Sample of 2194 German Elementary School Children. *Neuropsychologia*, 1986; 24: 3: pp 429-433.

115. Temple, C. M., Academic Discipline, Handedness, and Immune Disorders. *Neuropsychologia*, 1990; 28: 3: pp 303-308.

116. Levy, J., Psychobiological Implications of Lateral Bisymmetry, eds. Dimond S. J. and Beaumont, J. G., *Hemisphere Function in the Human Brain* (London: Elek Science, 1974).

117. Horton, Richard A., *A Study of the Occurrence of Certain Handwriting Characteristics in a Random Population*. Presented at the meeting of the American Society of Questioned Document Examiners (Milwaukee, 1992).

118. Berthold, Nancy, *Principle Number One, Uno, Eins*. Presented at the meeting of the American Society of Questioned Document Examiners (Chicago, 1995).

119. Rogerson, Peter A., On the Relationship Between Handedness and Season of Birth for Men. *Perceptual and Motor Skills*, 1994; 79: pp 499-506.

120. Iwasaki Syoichi, Kaiho, Takehito, and Iseki, Ken, Handedness Trends Across Age Groups in a Japanese Sample of 2316. *Perceptual and Motor Skills*, 1995; 80: pp 979-994.

121. Eglinton, Elizabeth and Annett, Marian, Handedness and Dyslexia: a Meta Analysis. *Perceptual and Motor Skills*, 1994. 79: pp 1611-1616.

122. McKeever, Walter F., Handwriting Posture in Left-Handers: Sex, Familial Sinistrality and Language Laterality Correlates. *Neuropsychologia*, 1979; 17: 429-444.

123. Levander, Maria and Schalling, Daisy, Self-Assessed and Examiner-Assessed Writing Hand Posture in Swedish Left-Handers. *Neuropsychologia*, 1988; 26: 5: pp 777-781.

124. Bryson, Susan E. and MacDonald, Valerie, The Development of Writing Posture in Left-Handed Children and Its Relation to Sex and Reading Skills. *Neuropsychologia*, 1984; 22: 1: pp 91-94.

125. Lester, David, Werling, Norman, and Heinle, Norman H., Graphoanalytic Differences by Sex and Handedness. *Perceptual and Motor Skills*, 1982; 55: p 1190.

126. Totty, R. N., Hardcastle, R. A., and Dempsey, Jane, The Dependence of Slope of Handwriting Upon the Sex and Handedness of the Writer. *Journal of the Forensic Science Society*, 1983; 23: pp 237-240.

127. Wing, Alan M., The Height of Handwriting. *Acta Psychologica*, 1980; 46: pp 141-151.

128. Reed, G. F. and Smith, A. C., A Further Experimental Investigation of Relative Speeds of Left- and Right-Handed Writers. *Journal of Genetic Psychology*, 1962; 100: pp 275-288.

129. Harrison, Wilson R., *Suspect Documents* (New York: Frederick A. Praeger, 1958).

130. Conway, James V. P., *Evidential Documents* (Springfield, Charles C Thomas, 1959), pp 201-202.

131. Beacom, Mary S., Was This Document Written With the Left Hand? *Journal of the Forensic Sciences*, 1961 July; 6: 3: pp 321-330.

132. Goodnow, J. J. and Levine, R. A., The Grammar of Action: Sequence and Syntax in Children's Copying. *Cognitive Psychology,* 1973; 4: pp 82-98.

133. Goodnow, J., *Children Drawing* (Cambridge, Mass: Harvard University Press, 1977).

134. Nihei, Y., Developmental Change in Motor Organization: Covert Principles for the Organization of Strokes in Children's Drawing. *Tohoku Psychologica Folia,* 1980; 39: pp 17-23.

135. Zitzelsberger, A., The Left-Handed Writer. *Proceedings of Seminar No. 5 "Questioned Documents in Crime Detection"* (Ottawa, Royal Canadian Mounted Police, Crime Detection Laboratories, 1958).

136. Fryd, C. S. M., The Direction of Pen Motion and Its Effects Upon the Written Line. *Medicine, Science, and the Law,* 1975; 15: pp 167-171.

137. Shanon, G., Graphological Patterns as a Function of Handedness and Culture. *Neuropsychologia,* 1979; 17: pp 457-465.

138. Brandt, V., Changes in Graphic Characteristics in Writing Executed with the Abnormal Writing Hand. *Zeitschrift für Menschenkunde,* 1976; 40: pp 344-410.

139. Thomassen, A. J. W. M. and Teulings, Hans-Leo H. M., The Development of Directional Preferences in Writing Movements. *Visible Language,* 1979; 13: pp 299-313.

140. Thomassen, A. J. W. M. and Teulings, Hans-Leo H. M., The Development of Handwriting, ed. M. Matthew, *The Psychology of Written Language* (New York: John Wiley & Sons, 1983).

141. Connolly, K. and Elliott, J., The Evolution and Ontogeny of Hand Function ed. N Blurton Jones, *Ethological Studies in Child Behaviour* (Cambridge: Cambridge University Press, 1972).

142. Mally, R., The Ball-Point Pen. *Kriminalistik,* 1956; 10: pp 56-60.

143. Hilton, Ordway, Characteristics of the Ball-Point Pen and Its Influence on Handwriting Identification. *Journal of Criminal Law, Criminology and Police Science,* 1957; 47: 5: pp 606-613.

144. Snape, K. W., Determination of Ball-Point Pen Motion From the Orientation of Burr Striations in Curved Penstrokes. *Journal of Forensic Sciences,* 1980; 25: pp 386-389.

145. Franks, J. E., The Direction of Ballpoint Penstrokes in Left and Right-Handed Writers as Indicated by the Orientation of Burr Striations. *Journal of the Forensic Science Society,* 1982; 22: pp 271-274.

146. Franks, J. E., Davis, T. R., and Totty, R. N., *The Discrimination of Left and Right-Handed Writing.* Presented at the meeting of the American Society of Questioned Document Examiners (Lake Tahoe, NV, 1983).

147. Franks, J. E., Davis, T. R., Totty, R. N., Hardcastle, R. A., and Grove, D. M., Variability of Stroke Direction Between Left and Right-Handed Writers. *Journal of the Forensic Science Society,* 1985; 25: pp 353-370.

148. Downey, June E., Judgments on the Sex of Handwriting. *Psychological Review,* 1910; 45: pp 205-216.

149. Newhall, S. M., Sex Differences in Handwriting. *Journal of Applied Psychology,* 1926; 10 S: pp 151-161.

150. Young, Paul Thomas, Sex Differences in Handwriting. *Journal of Applied Psychology,* 1931; 15: pp 486-498.

151. Middleton, Warren C., The Ability to Judge Sex from Handwriting. *The Scientific Monthly,* 1938; 46 S: pp 170-172.

152. Starch, Daniel, The Measurement of Handwriting. *Journal of Educational Psychology,* 1913; 4: pp 445-464.

153. Broom, M. Eustace, Thompson, Blanche, and Bouton, M. Thelma, Sex Differences in Handwriting. *Journal of Applied Psychology,* 1929; 13: pp 159-166.

154. Tenwolde, Harry, More on Sex Differences in Handwriting. *Journal of Applied Psychology,* 1934; 18 S: pp 705-710.

155. Osborn, Albert S., *Questioned Documents.* 2nd Ed. (Albany: Boyd Printing Co., 1929), p 140.

156. Hodgins, John H., Determination of Sex from Handwriting. *Canadian Society of Forensic Science Journal,* 1971 December; 4: 4: pp 124-132.

157. Goodenough, Florence I., Sex Differences in Judging the Sex of Handwriting. *Journal of Social Psychology,* 1945; 22: pp 61-63.

158. Totty, R. N., Hardcastle, R. A., and Dempsey, Jane, The Dependence of Slope of Handwriting Upon the Sex and Handedness of the Writer. *Journal of the Forensic Science Society,* 1983; 23: pp 237-240.

159. Fluckiger, Fritz A., Tripp, Clarence A., and Weinberg, George H., A Review of Experimental Research in Graphology. *Perceptual and Motor Skills,* 1961; 12: pp 67-90.

160. Cambridge, Joan, *Factors Relating to the Identification of Masculinity and Femininity in Questioned Handwriting.* Presented at the meeting of the International Association of Forensic Sciences (Edinburgh, 1972).

161. Lester, David, Werling, Norman, and Heinle, Norman H., Graphoanalytic Differences by Sex and Handedness. *Journal of Perceptual and Motor Skills,* 1982; 55: p 1190.

162. Anderson, Timothy and Wolowitz, Howard, Psychosexual Symbolism in the Handwriting of Men and Women. *Journal of Perceptual and Motor Skills,* 1984; 59: pp 233-234.

163. Freud, S., *Interpretation of Dreams* (London: Hogarth, 1900).

164. Anderson, Timothy, Psychosexual Symbolism in the Handwriting of Male Homosexuals. *Psychological Reports,* 1986; 58: pp 75-81.

165. Hecker, Manfred R., *The Scientific Examination of Sex Differences in Handwriting.* Presented at the meeting of the American Society of Questioned Document Examiners (Washington, 1996).

166. Comeau, G. W., *Left-hand Writing vs. Right-Hand Writing of the Same Person.* (Ottawa: unpublished paper prepared for the RCMP Crime Detection Laboratories, September 1973).

167. Stevens, Viola, Characteristics of 200 Awkward-Hand Signatures. *ICPO Review,* 1970 April; pp 130-137.

168. Harrison, Wilson R., op. cit., p 367.

169. Conway, James V. P., *Evidential Documents* (Springfield: Charles C Thomas, 1959), p 204.

170. Stangohr, Gordon R., Opposite-Hand Writings. *Journal of Forensic Sciences,* 1968 July; 13: 3: pp 376-389.

171. Anthony, Arthur T., *Examination of Unaccustomed-Hand Signatures.* Presented at the meeting of the American Academy of Forensic Sciences (Philadelphia, 1988).

172. Sperry, Grant R., *Off-Handed Identification, in Aggravation.* Presented at the meeting of the American Society of Questioned Document Examiners (San Jose, CA, 1990).

173. Zimmerman, Jeannine, *Handwriting Identification Based on an Unaccustomed-Hand Standard.* Presented at the meeting of the American Society of Questioned Document Examiners (Orlando, 1991).

174. Dawson, G. A., An Identification of Handprinting Produced with the Unaccustomed Left-Hand. *Canadian Society of Forensic Science Journal,* 1993; 26: 2: pp 61-67.

175. Dawson, Greg A., Brain Function and Writing with the Unaccustomed Left Hand. *Journal of Forensic Sciences,* 1985 January; 30: 1: pp 167-171.

176. Hotimsky, Suzanne, *Anonymous Letters Written by Left-Hand.* Presented at the meeting of the International Association of Forensic Sciences (1972).

177. Newman, Kenneth W., *A Study of Unaccustomed-Hand Writing.* Washington, D.C.: unpublished paper prepared at Georgetown University Forensic Science Laboratory, June 30, 1975).

The Scope of Document Examination

12

61. Can an Examiner Whose Native Alphabet is Roman Conduct Examinations of Writing in Other Alphabets or Manners of Communication?

This question presupposes that the examiner is not skilled in any manner of writing other than one using the English (i.e., Roman or Latin) alphabet and Arabic (actually Brahminic) numerals. But English is not the only language that uses the Roman alphabet. French, Dutch, Belgian, Danish, Swedish, Norwegians, Spanish, Italians, Germans, Swiss, and others utilize it. This gives rise to another closely-related question as to how important it is for the examiner to know the language in order to properly conduct an examination within it. Whether knowledge of the language is necessary or not, examinations of writing in foreign languages have been and are conducted with reasonable success.

The task of conducting examinations of writing in other alphabets or methods of communication and the success achieved in doing so is well reported. There are many examples of studies and examinations that have been made in a wide variety of subjects including shorthand,[1-2] Chinese pictograms,[3] Eskimo symbolism,[4] hand-produced musical scores,[5] Arabic writings,[6] historical writing scripts in long discarded writing systems,[7-8] signatures to works of art,[9-11] and others.[12] Miller[13] has reported on the successful identification of the artist/originator of human figure drawings, following standard writing examination techniques. Whether these examinations should or should not be conducted, the fact remains that they have, and the techniques employed have been presented and/or published in a number of public forums.

Attempts have been made to provoke a controversy of sorts in the conduct of examinations in such cases, but the response to solicitations for comment from document examiners has apparently not been of the kind or quantity to warrant pursuit of the topic.[14]

There is no doubt that the case records of most document examiners of reasonable experience will encompass at least one matter whose study and investigation lay outside the scope of orthodox handwriting or document examination, that challenged the mind and enticed the ingenuity of the investigator. Undoubtedly, if the study was reasonably successful, the matter was or will be reported, if only to describe the uniqueness of the case and to credit the examiner with some merit in the approach to the examination.

Hensel, Khan, and Dizon,[15] an American, a Pakistani, and a Filipino, working in Saudi Arabia, none of whom were document examiners, found themselves in the somewhat bizarre situation. They were compelled to look at document examination for analytical approaches to the study of writings in foreign alphabets, principally Arabic, that were entirely independent of literacy or understanding of the language or the writing system. It was their experience that "Forgery can be detected, handwriting identified, and typewriting compared by an intelligent illiterate who uses the criminalistics techniques commonly employed with toolmarks, firearms, and footmarks."

Hanna[16] in describing her approach to the examination of Chinese characters maintains that, if the principles of identification and the appropriate preparatory steps are taken, an unfamiliar script may be intelligently studied. She draws a valid analogy to the examination of writings in the English language, produced during certain illnesses, under the influence of certain medications, comprised of chemical or physical formulae, or mathematical equations etc. (e.g., scholastic examination papers) not within the normal purview of the document examiner. As long as the language is English, the examiner's competence is seldom questioned.

Other studies of a more physical nature may also become a part of an examiner's repertoire, which are comparable to unusual writings in that the subject material is widely diversified and there are no prescribed methods of approach to the study. The situation seems to beg the question: Is there a common approach to be taken to such cases that will ensure the legitimacy of whatever results ensue?

Epstein[17] offers his approach to the examination of the Josef Mengele handwritings as a guide to any examination of foreign handwriting.

> "Some familiarity with the language...is necessary. It would be preferable to be able to read and write the language, thereby, being familiar with the basics of...alphabet, accentuation, diacritical marks, punctuation, word order, syllabication, capitalization, compounding, and orthography. This is, of course, the ideal, and we know that the ideal seldom occurs."

Epstein recommends that time be taken to learn something about the language. Time is necessary as well to seek information in books, speak to language teachers and/or to contact national or local organizations that support the language. Time is also required to obtain and to study samples randomly obtained from writers of the language of a similar age or contemporary times. Time is obviously considered to be an essential part of this kind of an examination.

We are persuaded that the identification process, that was described earlier and that applies to the examination of any kind of physical evidence, holds the key. As was stated, the process is one having three distinct stages: analysis, comparison and evaluation.

The analytical stage should address the elements of the material under examination that are subject to variation or change with each member of the population to which it belongs. These will be its discriminating elements. If this is not known at the outset, it will be necessary to collect sufficient samples of the same kind of material from different sources to clearly establish what it is that may vary from source to source, and to what extent. Ideally, this will consist of writing samples in the same language and alphabet as the questioned material and preferably containing the same letter or character combinations. The assistance of a translator may be necessary to ensure that writing characters are being properly identified, as some alphabets such as Cyrillic employ characters so similar to one another that only an understanding of the language can reliably distinguish between them.[18] Furthermore, knowledge and understanding of the method of production of the subject material (e.g., the number of independent strokes and the order in which they are or should be executed) leads the examiner in the direction that makes the search for useable evidence more efficient. Hanna[19] has illustrated the process commendably with respect to Chinese writing.

When the analyses of both the known and questioned materials is complete they have, thereby, each been reduced to an aggregate of elements that vary from source to source. The combination of these elements may serve to distinguish one member or group of members of the population from another, and the second stage of comparison may be initiated. If the analysis has revealed and isolated the variables of the matter, their comparison should not be overly complex. To ensure, however, that comparisons are being made between like elements it is wise to engage the services of someone competent to speak and write the language.

The third stage of the mechanism, that of evaluation of the significance of similarities or differences perceived through comparison, is the part of the process that is not normally a component of the examiner's experience. It is the most subjective aspect of the process, that, in the majority of cases, is dependent upon the examiner's experience in other languages and alphabets, or in other types of examination. It is also the most important, for, what analysis has identified and comparison has disclosed only proper evaluation can render material (i.e., "Of such significance as to be likely to influence the determination of a cause" — Oxford). Exposure to large numbers of writings or other samples of the kind that is the subject of the current study, may provide a crash course in evaluation, if it is used judiciously. This seems to be the current practise.

In a given case, it may be that the discriminating elements, that is, the varying elements, that the analysis has divulged are not fully independent of one another, but share with other variables some common heritage, as class or system characteristics would do. It may also be that comparison has disclosed similarity between these elements in the known and unknown materials under study. In such circumstances, because of their common heritage, the evaluation of such elements must be appropriately modified. Herein the assistance of someone knowledgeable in the conditions or circumstances that might be common to groups of this foreign population, whether it be human or material, writings, printings, paintings, or whatever, is frequently necessary.

The writing examiner is normally quite cognizant of the limitations of his/her experience and knowledge insofar as the particular material undergoing study. Usually the reports reveal that appropriate assistance was obtained before conclusions were drawn. Usually he/she errs on the side of conservatism, if experience in other examinations has been a fitting teacher.

The accumulation of information from various sources on various items responsible for or related to methods of communication, and its consolidation in a manner facilitating the examination of questioned documents is a process common to many scientific and quasi-scientific practises. The identification of inks, typewriters, printing devices, papers, and other products is dependent upon the assembly of knowledge from different manufacturers as to the characteristics and behaviour of their products and the respects in which various products and their behaviour are similar or different.

Similarly, the identification of writings in foreign languages using different alphabets is achieved by the assembly of information from various sources familiar with the alphabet and the language. The laws and principles discovered by research are utilized by other scientists in further studies of the same subject without having to repeat the original research, personally, to justify such use. Science is not expected to continuously reinvent the wheel. Erudition is built on such premises.

The function of the forensic scientist (in this case the forensic document examiner) lies in his or her use of the information obtained. That information must be evaluated in terms of its reliability and its significance for identification purposes, or its support of other conclusions that may be drawn from it.

Once this process is understood, some progress may be made in identifying matters not within an examiner's normal purview. As we reported earlier, problems respecting Chinese or Eskimo writing may be addressed with a measure of success. Typewritings may be identified with typewriters, by persons never employed in typewriter factories. Printing methods may be distinguished from each other, by persons never engaged as printers. Counterfeit currency may be recognized reliably as such, by persons who never made a dollar.

For an example of some of the problems foreign writings present, see Figure 23.

62. What Are the Various Kinds of Examinations That Might be Conducted by Document Examiners?

There are nine fields of endeavour that frequently fall within the scope of study of the document examiner. To cover the work completely, then, we can think of the discipline as including:

1. *Handwriting examinations* — including handlettering and signatures.
2. *Imprint examinations* — including those produced by manual devices (rubber stamps, dater stamps, and some postal cancellation stamps), mechanical devices (typewriters and cheque writers), electronic printing devices (typewriters, computer printers, time clocks, and cash registers), and including the manufacture of counterfeits (currency, negotiable instruments, travel documents, licences and various personal credentials and identification documents).
3. *Reprographic examinations* — including photocopies, facsimile reproductions, machine generated writings and photographs.
4. *Writing media examinations* — including instruments, inks, and papers.
5. *Dating examinations* — including absolute determinations (i.e., dates of introduction or DOI's of products) and relative determinations (i.e., the sequence of ink strokes with other ink strokes, printings, typewritings, perforations, and folds).
6. *Examination of falsifications and alterations* — including removals, (i.e., erasures), changes, insertions and substitutions.
7. *Examination of invisible, faded, obscured writings and impressions of writings* — including those on charred documents.
8. *Examination of preternatural paper characteristics* — including tears, fasteners (i.e., paper clips and staples), cuts, and perforations.
9. *Miscellaneous examinations* — including envelope tampering, adhesives, laminations, typist's characteristics, and linguistics.

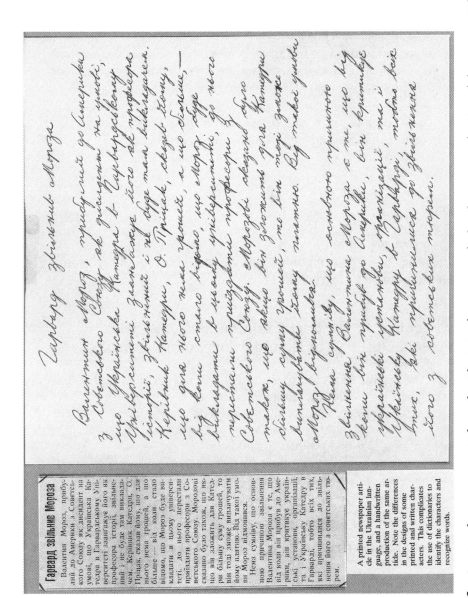

Figure 23 A printed newspaper article in the Ukrainian language, and a handwritten production of the same article. Note the differences in the designs of some printed and written characters. This complicates the use of dictionaries to identify the characters and recognize words.

Thus, in addition to identifying or eliminating particular persons with a questioned writing, some of these various examinations might be rephrased as endeavours to determine:

1. Whether and what alterations have occurred to the document.
2. Whether writing media (i.e., instrument, ink or paper) is related or similar to that of known sources.
3. Whether writing abnormalities occurred, e.g., age, infirmity, alcohol, or drugs.
4. What can be said about the typewriting or electronic printing, if present, and its relationship to particular machines?
5. What was the sequence in which two or more inscriptions were executed?
6. What was the sequence in which inscriptions, folds, or perforations occurred?
7. What were the absolute dates of origin of inscriptions?
8. What can be said about the nature or source of the materials involved?
9. What can be said about a document's preternatural characteristics?
10. What can be said about the indentations a document may bear?
11. What can be said about the original text of a faded, erased, obliterated, or charred document?
12. What can be said about the process and/or the equipment involved in producing the document.
13. What can be said about the integrity of the printed document (i.e., genuine or counterfeit or perhaps valid or forged)?
14. What is the generation of the reproduction (e.g., a [2] copy produced from a [1] copy produced from an [0] original)?

63. What is Required to Conduct Examinations of Aspects of Documents Other Than Handwriting Examinations?

Almost invariably, these examinations must be made of original documents, that have not been folded, marked, or altered since becoming questioned.

Other requirements are of the examiner him or herself:

1. A knowledge of products and product manufacture
2. Some experience with materials and their performances
3. An understanding of appropriate technologies
4. An appreciation for scientific method

64. How Are Nonhandwriting Examinations Conducted?

Generally speaking, nonhandwriting examinations are conducted:

1. by a study of the consistencies and inconsistencies of various aspects or elements of the questioned document;
2. by a comparison of the particular characteristics, features or properties of a document or of the inscription thereon, that may be either physical or chemical, with the known or recorded characteristics emanating from formulations or particular processes of production, and;

3. with the assistance of the following:
    a. the stereomicroscope,
    b. low power magnification, using episcopic (reflected) and diascopic (transmitted) light facilities,
    c. photographic facilities,
    d. electrostatic facilities,
    e. sources of ultraviolet and infrared radiation and a means of observing the fluorescence they promote.
    f. appropriate physical or chemical analytical facilities,
    g. collections of standard products, including type styles, writing instruments, writing inks, writing papers, and watermarks.

65. What Results can be Expected from Nonhandwriting Examinations?

Some examinations in the practise of document examination deal with factual matters (e.g., a feature or condition is present or absent), and are, therefore, more objective in nature. In such cases, definitive statements can frequently be made.

In other instances involving documents with printed inscriptions investigative leads and other information respecting the source of the document can be obtained through a study of the typestyle of the lettering. Typestyles employed on typewriters, printers, and facsimile machines may be searched against collections of typestyles that are constantly being produced and upgraded. These collections will permit a style to be identified by name or design, and in some cases can provide information as to the equipment on which it might have been installed. The association of a questioned document with a particular piece of equipment is a more complex task depending usually upon a fault in the equipment that makes itself evident in the printed product in some atypical fashion.

The level of certainty in a conclusion of identity respecting a given machine will vary with the uniqueness of the fault or circumstance of the machine. Suffice it to say, with today's constantly changing technology, an examiner is constantly challenged as to the adequacy of his/her knowledge.

The identification of inks, the differentiation of inks, and the relative age of ink inscriptions are questions that are frequently put to the document examiner. The proof of difference or the proof of sameness are fields usually calling for an ink specialist, of which there are only too few. The document examiner is, invariably, unable to do much more than illustrate the effects of differences in the physical/chemical properties of inks, if such differences are present. That is not always the case, however, and chemical techniques such as chromatography must be employed. The proof of sameness in the inks of two inscriptions is another matter and, although chromatography can help, it may not provide all the answers.

66. What Should One Expect to Find in a Technical Report Prepared by a Handwriting or Document Examiner?

It is generally agreed that there are four basic modes of discourse from which all technical reports stem: *narration, description, argumentation and exposition*. For the most part the reports of forensic science are expository, although in some instances, such as lists of items, they may be quite descriptive, while insofar as continuity details respecting how, when, and from whom material, substances, or standards were received, they may be quite narrative. These are incidental aspects of the technical report, however, whose purpose is unquestionably a matter of exposition. Reports respecting research conducted are indisputably matters of exposition.

Exposition is derived from the Latin *Ex-ponere* meaning to put on display, where a matter can be seen and understood. World Fairs and other international expositions have been just that — displays of objects of significance to provide illustration and foster understanding.

Description and narration are two modes of discourse that can enlist the imagination and even play upon the emotions; through argumentation we endeavour to convince a reader or to move him or her to action or to a modification in thinking. But exposition is concerned primarily with the communication of ideas or facts in a manner that the reader can understand and use.[20]

> "Exposition may be defined, loosely, as the systematic, orderly setting forth of ideas, made always with some underlying shaping purpose, and with such interpretive comment as the reader needs."

Exposition is the strategy by which we pursue certain objectives, those of informing, clarifying, explaining, and instructing. It is the language of textbooks written for scientific disciplines. There are various rhetorical devices used in an exposition to organize and deal with material, such as topical arrangement, exemplification, definition, classification, division, comparison, and causal analysis, but these are simply the means by which the goals of informing the reader and/or explaining a process are achieved.

As Houpe and Pearsall[21] describe them, these modes, meaning narration, description, argumentation and exposition, are the different strategies that enable the writer of the report to present his or her material in a persuasive way. And "All writing," they say, that is, "All purposeful communication, has a persuasive element. You must, at least, persuade your audience that you have mastered your material." Weiss[22] was more emphatic.

> "This I do know. The structure of a scientific paper is inherently persuasive. It starts with a thought-provoking problem and ends with a conclusion (even though it is usually called a "discussion")...a scientific paper is a communication structured to persuade."

Most authorities on the subject of technical report writing place emphasis on audience analysis, a term intended to direct attention to the questions: who might read the report, and, what might they expect to learn from it? Here, the forensic scientist finds himself or herself in something of a dilemma, for he or she has, in point of fact, two audiences: one comprised largely of lawyers, law enforcement people and lay persons (few of whom may be technically oriented), and the other consisting of scientists or technically competent personnel interested in reviewing the procedure followed and the evidence found. The first audience is primarily concerned with the final results, that is, the conclusions drawn. The second audience is only interested in the conclusions if the premises for them have been properly established.

Feeling perhaps that it is not possible to serve two masters, some forensic science laboratories and their personnel have opted to address only the nontechnical audience and, in so doing, to omit the material that only the technically competent reader might fully comprehend. Certainly, this simplifies the task of report writing, for it reduces it to a matter of expressing conclusions or listing findings without having to provide justification or accountability. The end is offered without revealing the means. There is a danger, however, that short cuts of this kind in the exposition may induce an abbreviation of the examination since details of it don't have to be described. Science, however, has seldom been able to afford the luxury of short cuts, or been inclined to take the risks.

Furthermore, the practise tends to violate the rules for proper technical reports that numerous authorities have been advocating for many years. Certainly, it eliminates all elements of persuasion that, as mentioned, Houpe and Pearsall consider to be essential.

Daniel Marder[23] provides a thoughtful approach to the subject:

"The human mind recognizes a problem and devises means for solving it. The means for organizing the work so that it carries a problem toward a solution — from a beginning, through a middle, and to an ending — is systematic thought. For purposes of exposition, this systematic thought is called rhetoric; for purposes of science, it is called (*scientific*) method."

In the United States, a new Rule 26 of the Federal Rules of Evidence is being implemented that prescribes the manner in which forensic science reports must be prepared to be acceptable as evidence. These requirements[24] include:

1. A complete statement of all opinions and the basis for each opinion offered.
2. All data relied upon to support the opinion.
3. A curriculum vitae that includes a listing of all papers written and published in the last 10 years.
4. Copies of all documents to be used at trial.
5. A list of all depositions and court testimonies rendered in the last four years.
6. A statement of the compensation expected to be received by the examiner.

The first four of these requirements are little more than we would, and are, recommending in this dissertation. The last two are requirements that are open to dispute as to their value. The number of depositions and court attendances that a document examiner may make are not necessarily a reliable measure of the quantity or quality of the work that the examiner has performed. Certainly, insofar as civil litigation is concerned, work that is well performed and equally well reported is likely to persuade court officials or disputants to accept the report without further argument and without the attendance of the examiner. Incomplete or poorly written reports may induce the opposition to insist on the attendance of the examiner.

The argument has been made that the Codes of Ethics, that most professions espouse, assert certain principles governing the conduct of the professional without providing many specifics respecting performance standards. Furthermore, handwriting experts, or document examiners, do not communicate well insofar as the intimate details of their work, feeling perhaps that this information is proprietary and that this part of their conduct is a matter of some privacy.

There is, however, too much variety in the approach to handwriting problems in some areas and perhaps even more in the manner in which reports are written. Many discussions have been held and papers published regarding the language to be employed and the meanings intended by expressions used in reporting findings.

For more than 20 years, some examiners have appealed for the development of a battery of performance standards (see Section 79: If Full Scientific Status Has Yet to Be Acquired, Is Handwriting Identification A Profession At Least or Simply A Craft?) that might describe, in part at least, the manner of doing things within the framework of a given code of ethics.

Some years of experience, perhaps more than any other practitioner in Canada in this discipline, have convinced the present authors that there are a number of self-evident standards regarding the writing of reports that should be universally acceptable to all examiners. In some respects, but not all, the proposals we would make are similar to the outline of Purdy.[25] There may be some examiners who will argue that they are required to comply with the administrative policy of an employer at the expense of such standards, but such convention verges on the questionable practise of subjecting scientific reports to the critique and control of nonscientific personnel.

Much has been written within recent years to standardize and to provide guidance "In the forms of expression in scholarly writing, and the general technical requirements of journals, such as details for typing manuscripts, standard abbreviations, and citation of references." In the latest (6th) edition, 1994, of *Scientific Style and Format: the CBE Manual for Authors, Editors, and Publishers*, the scope of the manual has been broadened to cover all sciences, and affords authoritative recommendations respecting scientific style and format for scientific papers, journal articles, books, and other forms of publication.

A variety of formats are needed for formal reports, and no single format will be a panacea. Nevertheless, the manual provides some general principles to follow.

Most scientific articles (and reports) must have the structure of critical argument suggested by Huth,[26] which consists of the following:

1. A question or hypothesis that is posed.
2. The presentation of the evidence pro and con bearing on the question.
3. The assessment of the evidence.
4. The conclusion that is reached.

Reports of scientific research or investigation generally follow this structure, but include one or two additional elements.

5. The means by which the investigator gathered the evidence bearing on the question or hypothesis, must be described in detail sufficient to enable another investigator to replicate the research or study.
6. The evidence gathered by the investigator must be separated from that available in the scientific literature.

The format widely used in many scientific fields divides and sequences the content of the report to fall under the general captions of: Introduction, Methods, Results, Discussion, and if necessary, References, whether or not these five captions are used. These captions are readily applicable to reports respecting traditional research projects, but their appropriateness to the daily bench work of the document examiner is less obvious. Indeed, the components of Huth's critical arguments (1 to 4) with their additional two elements (5 and 6) appear to be more pertinent to the daily tasks of the forensic scientist, rather than the research scientist. This is not surprising. The *Scientific Style and Format Manual* states clearly that "No single format can serve all possible needs."

We hold that a proper report should have in its composition five elements:

1. A section to describe the material studied and to satisfy the legal requirements respecting *continuity* (Item "5").
2. A section to set down the objective or purpose of the study (Item "1").
3. A section to report the data found that the study has taken into consideration, (Items "2" and "3").
4. A section to report the findings or conclusions drawn from the evidence found (Item "4").
5. A section to accommodate miscellaneous matters that are not essential ingredients of the work that was performed or the results achieved.

The first (Item "5") may be captioned Continuity and Description. We call it "The Call of the Four W's:" *What* was received, *When* it was received, *Where* it was received, and from *Whom* it was received. It should be sufficient to account for the possession of all items examined and to leave no doubt as to the identity of each one of them.

It is our practise to insert the purpose of the study as the second section under the caption Examination(s) Requested. All technical or scientific work must have a purpose, of course, even if it is simply the study of an unknown, without any particular goal in mind. Forensic science examinations have theirs, and these should be stated at the beginning of a report to set the stage, so to speak, for the work to follow. They are, in fact, the hypotheses (Item "1") that are being pursued: e.g., that subject K.1 wrote item Q or that item Q was not written by subject K.1.

The third section may be captioned Data or sometimes Observations and serves to describe the nature of the material, its adequacy or otherwise, the observations that have been made that will serve as the basis for any conclusions that might be drawn from the facts found (Items "2" and "3"). This is the factual evidence provided by the physical objects that have been studied. Without it in the technical report, there are no grounds for drawing inferences.

The fourth section may be captioned Conclusions or sometimes Findings and is confined to statements that can be made and supported on the strength of the evidence that the study revealed. Conclusions are the inferences that may be drawn from the factual evidence within the report (Item "4"), but it must be borne in mind that not all findings are conclusions. Some are observations made with the assistance of particular technical devices.

The fifth may be captioned Remarks and provides a haven for comments or advice that are not necessarily an integral part of the study conducted.

The organization of a technical report in a manner such as this ensures that it has a proper beginning, an informative body, and a logical and understandable ending. It starts with premises that lead to conclusions, and so the syllogism is complete, as it should be.

As we have stated elsewhere in this dissertation, handwriting identification or document examination is only worthy of the label *science* when its endeavours and principles achieve a measure of universal agreement. A second examination by another competent investigator should produce the same results. Furthermore, to demonstrate the scientific nature of the discipline the first examiner should welcome re-examination by a peer. It behooves him or her, therefore, to produce a document that clearly charts the course of his examination in a manner that others may follow. This is the essence of Item "5," following the structure of Huth's critical argument. Work must be reported in a fashion that allows for it to be replicated by a second or a third investigator. Agreement between investigators, and the more the better, is the road to universality, one of the two criteria of science.

References

1. Bradley, Julio H., *Shorthand Identification*. Presented at the meeting of the American Society of Questioned Document Examiners (Aurora, CO, 1988).

2. Brown, Donald N., *Shorthand Individuality*. Presented at the meeting of the American Academy of Forensic Sciences (Honolulu, Hawaii, 1967).

3. Brown, Donald Neil, *The Identification of Oriental Handwriting* (unpublished paper, 1965).

4. Huber, Roy A., *The Identification of Eskimo Writing* (Ivugivik, Quebec: unpublished report in the case of Eskimo SEEGOALOOK, Writing Threatening Letters, 1955).

5. Calvert, Jack R., *The Identification of Handprinted Musical Scores*. Presented at the meeting of the American Society of Questioned Document Examiners (Rochester, 1979).

6. Jacquin-Keller, A. M., *Is It Possible to Verify a Manuscript Document Written in Foreign Characters?* Presented at the meeting of the American Society of Questioned Document Examiners (Montreal, 1985).

7. Kroon-van der, Kooij, *A Master Unmasked or the Pergolesi-Ricciotti Puzzle Solved* (The Hague, Netherlands: an unpublished paper of the Criminal Investigation Department, 1985).

8. Huber, R. A., On Looking Over Shakespeare's "Secretarie." *Stratford Papers on Shakespeare*, ed. B. A. W. Jackson (Toronto: W. J. Gage Ltd., 1960).

9. Hanna, Georgia A., Art Forgery: The Role of the Document Examiner. *Journal of Forensic Sciences*, 1992 July; 37: 4: pp 1096-1114.

10. Goetschel, Corinne, *Problems of Identifying Disputed Signatures on Works of Art*. Presented at the meeting of the American Society of Questioned Document Examiners (Arlington, VA, 1989).

11. Mayther, Jacques, *A New Dimension in Document Examination: The Scientific Study of Oil Artist Paintings and of Pencil Artist Drawings. A Recent Case*. Presented at the meeting of the American Society of Questioned Document Examiners (Milwaukee, WI, 1974).

12. Ellen, D. M., *Handwriting Examination of Unfamiliar Scripts* (London: unpublished paper of the Metropolitan Police Forensic Science Laboratory, 1977).

13. Miller, Larry S., Identification of Human Figure Drawings through Questioned Document Examination Techniques. *Forensic Science International*, 1995; 72: pp 91-105.

14. Anon., Twice Told Signatures, an English Script and a Chinese Language Forgery. *Scientific Sleuthing Review*, 1991 winter; 15: 1: p 14.

15. Hensel, E. R., Khan, I. A., and Dizon, J. F., Forensic Examination of Peculiar Writing Systems. *Journal of the Forensic Science Society*, 1973; 13: pp 143-152.

16. Hanna, Georgia A., A Preliminary Classification of the Writing Elements of Chinese Characters. *Journal of Forensic Sciences*, 1989 March; 34: 2: pp 439-448

17. Epstein, Gideon, Examination of the Joseph Mengele Handwriting. *Journal of Forensic Sciences*, 1987 January; 32: 1: pp 100-109.

18. Muehlberger, Robert J., *The Bulgarian Connection: An Examination of Cyrillic Handwriting.* Presented at the meeting of the American Society of Questioned Document Examiners (Nashville, TN, 1984).

19. Hanna, Georgia A., A Preliminary Classification of the Writing Elements of Chinese Characters. *Journal of Forensic Sciences,* 1989 March; 34: 2: pp 439-448.

20. Nelson, J. Raleigh, *Writing the Technical Report* (New York: McGraw-Hill, 1940), p 3.

21. Houpe, Kenneth W. and Pearsdall, Thomas C., *Reporting Technical Information* (New York: McMillan Publishing Co., 1984), p 99.

22. Weiss, Edmond H., *The Writing System for Engineers and Scientists* (Englewood Cliffs, New Jersey: Prentice Hall Inc., 1982), pp 116-117.

23. Marder, Daniel, *The Craft of Technical Writing* (New York: The MacMillan Co., 1960), p 7.

24. Anon., Federal Rule 26 Brings Changes to Expert's Report Preparation. Part IV — In the Courts. *Journal of Forensic Document Examination,* 1994 Fall; 7: p 110.

25. Purdy, Dan C., The Requirements of Effective Report Writing for Document Examiners. *Canadian Society of Forensic Science Journal,* 1982; 15: 3/4: pp 146-151.

26. Huth, Edward Janavel, *How to Write and Publish Papers in the Medical Sciences* (Philadelphia: ISI Press, 1982).

The Sources of
Document Examiners

13

67. Where Might a Capable Document Examiner Be Found?

There is no single source for information respecting the qualifications and competence of practising document examiners.

The American Board of Forensic Document Examiners (ABFDE) publishes, annually, a list of practitioners whom they have tested and certified and who are, thereby, entitled to the designation *Diplomate*. Application for certification is voluntary, however, and not all competent practitioners have applied.

The American Society of Questioned Document Examiners (ASQDE) established by Albert S. Osborn who wrote some of the most highly-regarded books on the subject, has been functioning for some 55 years, and has attracted some of the most reputable practitioners on this continent and in other parts of the world.

The Association of Forensic Document Examiners (AFDE), formed in 1986, was a splinter group from the International Association of Questioned Document Examiners (IAQDE), whose interests and work scope included graphology. The AFDE has disassociated itself with graphology. Like the ABFDE, it conducts a certification program open to all practitioners, with prerequisites that are slightly different from those of the ABFDE. In particular, the AFDE prides itself in not having included a grandfather clause in the inauguration of its certification program. The principal difference now prevailing, however, is in the examination panel set up by the AFDE for the testing of candidates. This panel reportedly includes members of the judiciary and lay persons. Whether the inclusion of lay persons avoids bias at the expense of the good judgment of scientific or technical qualities is a moot point.

The certification programs of both the ABFDE and the AFDE have requirements to demonstrate continuing currency or proficiency in specified intervals of time.

The Natinoal Association of Document Examiners (NADE), an organization founded in 1980 that is sympathetic to the interests of graphologists, and the American Board of Forensic Examiners, founded in 1992 by Robert L. O'Block, are also known to offer certification programs, but there is no information available as to how these various programs compare with one another.

The National Forensic Centre in Princeton, NJ publishes a Forensic Services Directory, annually, listing experts in various fields. Listing is open to any person paying the appropriate fees. No attempt is made to judge proficiency or qualification and graphologists are listed with document examiners. Those who have been certified by the American Board of Forensic Document Examiners, however, are indicated by the letters D-ABFDE.

Other agencies which endeavour or have endeavoured to list persons offering services as handwriting experts or examiners of questioned documents, but without comment as to qualification, include the following:

The National Academy of Forensic Scientists, Reston, VA

R & W Computer Research Inc., Vero Beach, FL

The Technical Advisory Service for Attorneys (TASA), Blue Bell, PA

The National Directory of Expert Consultants and Advisors, Nova Law Publications, Inc., Pensacola, FL

Seak, Inc., Legal & Medical Publishers, Falmouth, MA, in *The Expert Witness Journal*

The Expert Services Section of *Best's Directory of Recommended Insurance Attorneys*, A. & M. Best Co., Ambest Rd., Oldwick, NJ

Directory of Scientific and Technical Consultants and Expert Witnesses, ASTM Accounting Control Group, Philadelphia, PA

Expert Witnesses, published by Law Times, Aurora, Ontario, Canada

The Expert Pages, available on the Internet: http://www.expertpages.com

All provide similar services. TASA and R & W Computer Research Inc. are accessible through WESTLAW. A few of these organizations endeavour to screen applicants to some extent before listing.

68.   How Does One Judge Proficiency and Competence?

By academic qualification.   Within the profession it is generally agreed that a Bachelors degree from a recognized university is a first requirement, preferably in a field of science, but psychology, mathematics, and other fields might also be considered appropriate. Some American universities offer degrees in forensic science that devote a very limited time to the subject of questioned documents.

While none of the present university programs are directly related to the examination of questioned documents beyond the bounds of introductory courses, it is generally held that university education reflects a level of intelligence and understanding that document examination requires. The ASQDE, AAFS, and the ABFDE all require university graduation in some appropriate field as a minimum level of academic achievement.

By training.   On this continent, no formal instruction in the examination of questioned documents or handwriting identification is available to the general public. The training of those in private practise in Canada is usually obtained through earlier employment with the R.C.M.P. Forensic Science Labs in many provinces or the Centre of Forensic Sciences in Toronto or the Direction des Expertises Judiciaires in Montreal. Similarly, in the United States many private practitioners were formerly trained in municipal, state, and federal forensic laboratories in such cities as Chicago, New York, Washington, and Atlanta.

It must be emphasized, however, that while government labs are the institutions in which training is received by the multitude of examiners, there is little standardization to the training programs provided, largely due to the fact that they are all based on home-grown versions of the apprenticeship system.

Some government questioned document laboratories consist of one or two individuals who endeavour to train their own replacements. Similarly, many private practitioners employ understudies that assist in the preparation of charts for court purposes, the maintenance of collections of writing media and typewriting samples. From this, the understudy's interests are expanded to develop into an apprentice.

Although we are sometimes inclined to do so, it is difficult to judge the quality of the training or the competence attained by the trainee by the size of the laboratory in which the training was obtained. Appropriate standards are lacking, and it is for this reason that certification boards have been created.

Instruction by correspondence of questionable quality is offered by the International Graphoanalysis Society of Chicago to persons who have taken their course in graphology. None of the instructors in or designers of this program are widely-recognized document examiners, or indeed are recognized at all, and none have contributed significantly to the published literature, in recognized scientific journals.

At one time, the Institute of Applied Science in Chicago advertised and sold a correspondence course in handwriting examination through the pulp magazines, but this institute was more interested in selling the books than it was in monitoring the progress of the customer.

Among recognized practitioners, it is generally agreed that training requires two years to complete and must be acquired under the direct supervision of a qualified tutor. The reason for this is that proficiency depends upon the proper selection of appropriate evidence, the assessment of its significance, and some familiarity with scientific method. The first two of these are matters that vary with the material under examination, and therefore, cannot be found in books. Assistance can only be obtained from teachers and by experience, and tutorage couples the experience of the tutor with that acquired by the student, which is particularly important for novices in the field.

Similarly it might be argued that examiners who work alone are without the benefit of the variations in the experience of others and the consequent modifications to evaluations. Obviously self-taught individuals are at a distinct disadvantage and run the risk of repeating undetected errors.

By professional affiliations.   A reasonable indication of proficiency in document examination, i.e., the level of skill acquired, may be obtained from a review of the professional associations in which membership is held. These organizations are interested in attracting the most qualified practitioners in their field and are, therefore, sufficiently concerned about the qualifications of their present members to weed out or avoid those who would reflect adversely on the reputation of the group. Unfortunately, however, the standards for some groups or associations are not equal to those of others, and the affiliation with such groups will not speak to the same level of qualification.

Another indication of proficiency may be obtained from the elected offices and appointments held in professional organizations. This kind of acceptance by one's peers is a reliable measure of the respect enjoyed by the individual among those who should be in the best position to judge competence.

By the quality and quantity of material published.   Many fields of science consider published material to be a measure of an individual's qualification for two reasons. To begin with, it is material that is publicly available for review and assessment. Secondly, but not necessarily, it is frequently subject to peer review prior to publication. Standards of peer review, however, vary widely and one needs to know something of the review board and journal policy to properly judge the quality of the publication's material.

Summary.   Qualification must, therefore, be judged on the basis of the following:

1. The level of achievement in a recognized academic institution.
2. The type and duration of training received.
3. The qualification of the instructor(s).
4. The professional memberships held and the affiliations enjoyed.
5. The offices held in professional associations.
6. The number of contributions to the literature on the subject and the nature of the journals in which they have been published.
7. The program of self-improvement followed.
8. The scope of the service offered.
9. The dimensions of the experience acquired.
10. The answers given to questions such as are dealt with herein.

Furthermore, competence to conduct the work will be found in the sufficiency of many of these elements of the examiner's curriculum vitae, and in the capacity of his or her facilities to handle the task, as indicated by (1) the equipment utilized, and (2) the resources available (e.g., library, consultants, etc.).

The question that must be addressed, however, is, how does one judge the adequacy of an examiner's facilities and resources to properly conduct an examination, or, indeed, to commence a practise?

Initially by the sufficiency of his/her facilities. There seems little justification in offering services as a writing examiner or purporting to conduct an examination unless that examination and study is going to be complete. If I suspect I have a mechanical problem in my car, I have not been properly served or, in fact, served at all by a mechanic who tells me simply that my tires and battery are fine.

It was said in Section 2: What is Document Examination? that document examination (of which writing identification is a principal component) is a study to determine the history of the events that have occurred to a document. Although in this discourse we are addressing the topic of handwriting identification, handwriting identification cannot be divorced from the media with which and on which the writing has been executed.

It is not uncommon for signatures to be identified as genuine, but other evidence to reveal that the signature was not inscribed to the document when in its present form. An examination of the writing of the signature without any consideration of the other evidence is hardly complete and is a disservice to the client.

The examiner must therefore possess:

1. facilities for the examination of writing strokes microscopically and stereoscopically, under a variety of lighting conditions;
2. facilities for the study of writings while superimposed upon one another, with transmitted light;

3. facilities for the precise measurement of the physical dimensions of the document and of the writing, lettering or printing thereon;
4. facilities for the study and record of the reaction of inks, papers, and other materials to radiations beyond the visible range of the electromagnetic spectrum, i.e., in the ultraviolet and infrared regions.
5. facilities for the examination and study of indentations in the document produced by writings on other documents executed while superimposed upon the document under examination; and,
6. facilities to record photographically or otherwise what these other facilities have revealed.

The growth in the number of government and law enforcement laboratories in the last 25 years has produced many examiners that are now (1998) considering retirement from these services and establishing private practises as "cottage" type businesses. The expense of equipment to establish the facilities we have listed above is often avoided or deferred, if possible, which raises some questions as to whether a client can be provided with a complete and proper service. We caution that the examiner without the facilities to examine completely all aspects of the document on which a questioned writing resides may never know what segments of significant evidence has escaped his/her study.

69. How Does One Maintain Proficiency in Document Examination?

The most efficacious means document examiners have for maintaining skills, gaining and testing new knowledge, and improving performance is through professional affiliations and participation in professional organizations and their meetings. Some of these conduct workshops in particular areas of the work.

Certification by the ABFDE requires the diplomate to demonstrate every five years, by courses taken, meetings attended, and papers presented and/or published, that one is current in one's knowledge of the subject. This may be one of the greater virtues in the program, for there are a number of one-time document examiners who, for one reason or another, have left the field for a number of years and who, upon retirement or termination of their present employment, re-enter the field and offer their services to the public as though inactivity over a period of time has no effect whatsoever upon the state of their knowledge or their skills.

In the absence of a professional licensing system or some appropriate form of control by courts or the profession itself, the risks of this practise to clients, to courts, and to the examiners themselves are not likely to be avoided.

70. How Competent Does a Person Need to be to Testify as an Expert Witness in a Court of Law?

It seems generally agreed that, by definition, an expert witness is a person who possesses special skills or knowledge, acquired by way of training or experience, not normally possessed by the layman, and is, thereby, permitted to draw conclusions or to express opinions that are otherwise inadmissible in testimony.

One school of thought has held the view that a level of competence is implied by the definition, notwithstanding the fact that it may be difficult to stipulate a level to satisfy all disciplines. Furthermore, the level of competence so implied is greater than that which can be achieved by simple exposure to the questioned document laboratory. Were that not so, every secretary of every document examiner (or indeed of any other forensic specialist) would be qualified to testify as an expert witness. In fact, some secretaries have professed, after a period of time, to be competent examiners, but their level of competence has not been widely recognized within the discipline. It hardly warranted stating that legal authorities did not have this broad a coverage in mind when the qualifications of the expert witness were being considered and defined, but this line of thinking may be in error.

At the turn of this century, Thayer, in his *Preliminary Treatise On Evidence at Common Law* wrote:

> "There is ground for saying that, in the main, any rule excluding opinion evidence is limited to cases where, in the judgment of the court, it will not be helpful to the jury. Whether accepted in terms or not, this view largely governs the administration of the rule."

As recently as 1961, the Supreme Court of Canada endorsed the comments of Justice Aylesworth J. A. who made reference to Thayer in his reasons for decision.[1] Legal thinking, it would seem, has not changed significantly.

Similarly, Wigmore[2] said:

> "But the only true criterion is: On this subject can a jury from this person receive appreciable help?"

Thus, the bottom line for qualification as an expert witness is legally defined as "that which can provide appreciable help to the court" and no more. There is no other formula for ascertaining whether a witness is indeed an expert or should be considered to be an expert in a particular field. Practical experience is important, but is rarely a sole criterion. The same may also be said of academic achievement. The law prefers to deal with levels of competence primarily as a guide to the weight to be given to the testimony. This situation has prompted Imwinkelried to comment:

> "At least in federal practise, it is almost inconceivable that an expert will be kept off the witness stand altogether for lack of competency."[3]

As early as 1905, courts in Canada recognized that a clear distinction must be made between admissibility and value of expert testimony.[4] Courts have stated repeatedly that "the weight and value of opinion evidence are questions for the jury...."[5] Few cases, however, suggest how the assessment is to be made other than to say that "Testimony of experts must be appreciated and weighed in the same manner as that of any other witness."[6]

Undoubtedly, then, the weight assigned to the testimony of the expert will derive from two aspects of it: (1) whether it can be believed, and if believed, (2) what contribution it makes to the determination of innocence or guilt, or to the facts at issue in civil litigation.

Obviously the believability of the testimony will be directly related to the competence of the witness. That being the case, competence is a matter that is left to the triers of fact to determine during or after the presentation of the expert testimony. The weakness in the system begins to show when one enquires as to the basis on which the judge or jury will make the assessment. How will they know whether the principles on which the expert has predicated his opinion are valid? How will they judge whether they are the recipients of help or the victim of deception?

The argument may be made that shortcomings in the testimony of incompetent experts can be brought out in the testimony of opposing experts. Circumstances, however, do not always make this possible, and opposing testimony from two expert witnesses often diminishes the credibility of the discipline as much as it may affect the believability of either witness.

It is reassuring that in recent years some courts have adopted a more critical attitude toward the admissibility of expert testimony. They have held that such witnesses are unqualified when they have minimal practical experience,[7] when they have gained their knowledge merely from self-study and/or a correspondence course,[8] and when they use their expertise as a hobby and not as a profession.[9] One court has held that training as a graphologist or a graphoanalyst is irrelevant for testimony as a document examiner.[10]

71. Is an Individual Trained in Another Area of Forensic Science Capable of Conducting Questioned Document Examinations?

Notwithstanding the fact that the identification process of analysis, comparison, and evaluation underlies all disciplines of forensic science, the steps of analysis and evaluation are different for each discipline and must be learned separately and independently. The greater the disparity in the materials to be examined in different disciplines, or in the natural laws governing their creation, their composition or their behaviour, the more irrefutably this question would be answered in the negative.

We attempted to enunciate the respects in which handwriting examination differs from the examination of other materials in forensic science in Section 26: What Makes Handwriting Identification Different? As we said there, writing is the conscious and deliberate issue of an animate body, whereas the material other disciplines examine is an involuntary issue of an animate body or a property of an inanimate one. Consequently, this difference in the voluntary control of the issue makes substantial changes in the approach to evidence.

Other fields of forensic science examine and study properties, reactions, and attributes of material substances that are the consequences of constitution or composition. In these respects, there is consistency between different samples of the same material.

Writing identification is an examination and study of a particular facet of human behaviour or performance that is depicted by personal habits — habits of behaviour. There is less, perhaps much less, consistency between samples. We call it natural variation. The consistent material substances involved in writing examinations are simply the substrates on which the behaviour is recorded.

Accordingly, the education, training, and perspectives of a person practising in other disciplines differs significantly from that of a person practising in the field of handwriting examination.

It has been assumed by some courts that there is a fundamental knowledge that is common to all forensic science disciplines, just as the many rules of evidence and procedure prevail throughout the various divisions of law. Or it has been assumed that there is a basic education in forensic science after which specialization or field selection occurs, as in law or medicine. Other than an understanding of scientific method and a fundamental sense of evidence, however, the many fields of forensic science have little in common.

72. What do Different Fields of Forensic Science Have in Common?

To begin with, and as aforementioned, the identification process of analysis, comparison, and evaluation underlies all disciplines of forensic science. Furthermore, all disciplines share an understanding of the scientific method for it provides the guidelines within which the work is conducted. Lastly, they share the same sense of evidence.

An appreciation for evidential standards, however, emanates not from common training, but from common sense, that science has made more efficient by using it more systematically.

> "The scientist begins with the primitive sense of evidence which he possessed as a layman, and uses it carefully and systematically. He still does not reduce it to rule, though he elaborates and uses sundry statistical methods in an effort to prevent it from getting out of hand in complex cases." [11]

Thus, the "sense of evidence" is a product of intelligence that training will simply equip the student to use more efficiently. The factors to which it is applied differs distinctly from discipline to discipline, and so the commonness stops there.

The focus of a handwriting examination, that is: the physical evidence, is the conscious and deliberate issue of an animate body, a human being. In this respect, it is not unlike two other kinds of study of recent inception, primarily for their forensic application, i.e., voice identification and linguistics. Despite the gross differences in the parts of the body involved in the issue of what may become physical evidence, all three appertain to the conscious and controllable issues of humans, the animate bodies. The matter other sciences examine, e.g., explosive residues, glass, blood, or urine samples, is inanimate or is an unconscious or uncontrollable issue of the animal.

Findings in other scientific studies have a bottom line below which results are not determinable, i.e., certain steps in a process must be completed. The findings in writing examinations may vary to a substantial degree, with the quantity and quality of the evidence submitted for examination.

References

1. *Fisher v. The Queen,* 130 C. C. C. 1, 19 (1961).

2. Wigmore, J. H., *Wigmore On Evidence.* 3rd ed. (Boston: Little, Brown, 1940), p 1923.

3. Imwinkelried, Edward J., *The Methods of Attacking Scientific Evidence* (Charlottesville: Michie, 1982), p 37.

4. *R. v. Young,* 38 N. S. R. 427, 10 C. C. C. 466, 18 (Can. Abr. 851 1905).

5. *R. v. Buckingham & Vickers,* 86 C. C. C. 76 (1946).

6. *Shawinigan Engineering Company v. Naud,* S. C. R. 341 (1929).

7. *Micciche v. Forest Hill Cemetery Association,* 55 D and C 621 (Lock. Jus 261).

8. *United States v. King,* 532 F. 2d 505 Cert. Denied, 429 US 960 (5th Cir.) 1976.

9. *Keys v. Keys,* 23 Tenn. App. 188, 120 S.W. 2d 1103 (1939).

10. *Carroll v. State,* 165, 634 S.W. 2d 99, 102 276 Ark. 160, (1982).

11. Quine, W. V., The Scope and Language of Science. *British Journal for the Philosophy of Science,* 1957; Bol. 8: 29: pp 1-6. With permission.

Science, Scientific Method, and Writing Identifications

14

73. Science and Scientific Method

Little is more often encountered, but less often understood than science, scientists, and scientific method. Numerous attempts have been made to provide precise definitions and while each has merit none has, as yet, been universally accepted, or has adapted readily to the ages of space and technology. To some extent, the reason is that the proliferation of new fields of scientific study and the sophistication of study methods in all fields are constantly subjecting established definitions to modification.

It is not intended to consume numerous pages and much of the reader's time in a further endeavour to explain what other more competent authors have devoted entire books to resolve. Something, however, might be said on this subject to assist legal minds in understanding where forensic scientists in general, and document examiners in particular, should be coming from.

Certainly, any dissertation on document examination risks raising the question as to whether handwriting identification, as it is presently conducted, qualifies as a scientific pursuit. Thus, we will be obliged, sooner or later, to provide a definition of science against which the discipline may be judged.

Osborn is reported by Swett[1] to have written years ago (but not in his books) in an obvious attempt to marry document examination to science:

> "The scientific spirit need not develop an attitude of timidity, but it will develop an attitude of caution. Extended knowledge and experience will develop the ability to draw correct inferences from what may seem slight evidence, but the inference will still be drawn from actual evidence."

Some years later, Sellers[2] argued, in a similar vein, that the document examiner needed a scientific approach:

> "The scientific approach to a questioned document problem is the unbiased systematic application of all of one's knowledge acquired through experience, research and study, the search for facts. It is adequate observation to which is applied correct reasoning."

Sellers went on to say that the scientific approach might, in fact, lessen the complexity of any questioned document problem.

Cole[3] was one of the first to tackle the direct question, "Is handwriting identification a science?" and provided the response that many others have adopted when required:

"In the sense that it is classified, formulated, and verifiable knowledge gathered by observation, research, and experiment, it is *scientific knowledge*."

Others have responded to the question in manners that are more of an embarrassment than a help. If they do nothing else, however, they serve to illustrate the discipline's craving over many years to be classified as a science, a craving that has readily enlisted the support of the definitions proffered by such publications as the encyclopaedias, that say that science is "…Knowledge in any field of study investigated by the scientific method…."[4]

Others, without employing a strict definition of the term, have argued, perhaps too loosely, that handwriting identification is a science because "…It employs the concepts of the method of science in its general research and a scientific approach to its practical problems…."[5] Thus, the discipline offers its public esteem for and adoption of the scientific method as its key to admission into the scientific community.

In less sombre moments, when asked whether handwriting identification is a science, Brohier[6] confided that he has been tempted to respond that it is, if one is prepared to accept Einstein's definition of science that he apparently described as "The posterior reconstruction of the external world by the process of conceptualization." Jurors, however, are likely to prefer something more comprehensible. Let us begin by generalizing that valid science follows proven procedures in seeking answers. These procedures are called, collectively, the scientific method.

74. What Is Scientific Method?

Scientific method is a misnomer. It is not a method in the sense of being a formal procedure. It furnishes no map for exploring the unknown. It is an attitude and a philosophy for the collection and study of data. Consequently, it makes no contribution to the fundamental determination of what is and what is not science.

Scientific method is the offspring of a branch of philosophy called epistemology (from the Greek episteme, *knowledge*, and logos, *theory*). It began when, in the seventeenth century, Francis Bacon offered the scientist a fourfold rule of thumb for their work:[7]

1. Observe
2. Measure
3. Explain
4. Verify

Random House[8] defines scientific method as "A method of research in which a problem is identified, relevant data are gathered, a hypothesis is formulated from these data, and the hypothesis is empirically tested." Oxford[9] describes it as "A method of procedure consisting in systematic observation, measurement and experiment, and the formulation, modification, and testing of hypotheses."

In even more appropriate terms for its application to handwriting identification or to document examination generally, Webster[10] defines scientific method as the following:

"Principles and procedures for the systematic pursuit of knowledge involving the recognition and formulation of a problem, the collection of data through observation and experiment, and the formulation and testing of hypotheses."

In somewhat more specific language, students of the subject have modified Bacon's rule to read:

1. Pose a question
2. Collect evidence
3. Hypothesize
4. Deduce its implications
5. Test them experimentally
6. Accept, reject, or modify the hypothesis

When these terms are applied to (1) handwriting examinations, or to (2) other questioned document problems, the process might become:

1. Pose a question
   a. Who wrote the particular document "Q"?
   b. Is this writing in ink or toner?
2. Collect evidence
   a. Assemble writing standards of person "K."
   b. Set the document on a microscope stage.
3. Hypothesize
   a. That this person "K" did/did not write "Q."
   b. That the ink is toner and not an original document.
4. Deduce its implications
   a. That the writing standards of "K" and "Q" will contain similarities or differences in writing habits.
   b. That toner will be accompanied by trash marks and have a vertical dimension, or that a pen will display evidence of pressure, or that ink deposits may sometimes be seen on fibres.
5. Test them experimentally
   a. Examine the writing habits of "K" in duplications of "Q."
   b. Examine by stereo microscopy.
6. Accept, reject, or modify the hypothesis
   a. That he/she did/did not write document "Q."
   b. That the document is a photocopy.

As many will be quick to point out to us, Step 5 experimental testing is an aspect of the process that the forensic nature of most handwriting examinations will not permit. If it did the task of identification would be made simpler, for the standards obtained would be reasonable duplications of the several circumstances of the questioned writing, and the variables which oftentimes influence the writing act would be astutely controlled. Instead of the more ideal experimental situation, we are compelled for the most part to work with only that which is available, and draw conclusions from observations, as astronomers have done for centuries and will continue to do, undoubtedly, for many years to come.

In summary then, it may be said that scientific method has four corners to its character:

1. The recognition and formulation of the problem
2. The systematic pursuit of knowledge
3. The collection of data through observation and/or experimentation
4. The formulation and testing of an hypothesis

It has a consequence that is the acceptance, rejection, or revision of the hypothesis. It has a condition that it employs the principles of logic (that is, the science of reason) to draw conclusions from the information the study produces.

In the particular application of the criteria of science and scientific method to the examination and study of handwriting, there are certain hallmarks to a scientific undertaking:

1. Based on accepted principles of science
   a. Habitualness and heterogeneity
2. Follows the process called *scientific method*
   a. Recognizes and formulates the problem
      Did writer of "K" execute writing "Q"?
   b. Systematically pursues knowledge
      Studies writing habits of writer of "K."
   c.. Collects data by observation and experimentation
      Compares writing habits present in "K" and "Q."
   d. Formulates and tests one or more hypotheses
      That writer of "K" wrote "Q."
      That, if so, there will be a significant combination of similar writing habits in "K" and "Q," and no inexplicable disparities.
   e. Accepts, rejects, or revises hypotheses
      That writer of "K" wrote "Q."
      That writer of "K" did not write "Q."
      That writer of "K" wrote "Q" under some unusual circumstances.
3. Employs the science of reason, i.e., the principles of logic, to draw conclusions from the information the study produces
   a. There are a number of significant similarities in writing habits in "K" and "Q"
   b. That number is greater than that which would be expected to occur by pure coincidence in any two writings
   c. They exist as a combination of similarities
   d. There are no inexplicable disparities
   e. There is no evidence present of spuriousness
   f. There is no other reasonable explanation for this measure of similarity in two writings, but that they were written by the same individual
   g. Therefore, it must be concluded that writer "K" wrote "Q"

Other writers on this subject have characterized scientific method from a slightly different viewpoint. In their description, it is said that the philosophy of the scientific method is to strive constantly for objectivity. It orders knowledge so that it may be considered in proper and logical sequence. It classifies knowledge as the only systematic means to its organization and retrieval. It advances verification as the most reliable form of proof. It utilizes observation and/or experimentation designed expressly to control variables. It is constantly critical of itself. It entertains no dogmas, maintains no absolutes or infallibility, and is both cautious and sceptical. It is the epitome of "The man from Missouri."

These two approaches to scientific method are not in conflict, but tend to supplement one another. The first is simply a procedural outline for the task, whereas the second is a policy of conduct for carrying out the procedure.

It has been written that what distinguishes scientific knowledge from other knowledge is (1) the method by which it is created or collected, (2) a systematic extension of common sense, and (3) sound scepticism, that, when combined, is referred to as *scientific method*. District Judge D. J. McKenna, in his recent decision in *United States v. Roberta and Eileen Starzecpyzel*, 880 Fed. Sup. 1027, (April 4, 1995), quotes the words of Green in *Expert Witnesses and Sufficiency of Evidence in Toxic Substances Litigation*, 86 N. W. U. L. Rev. 643, 645 (1992), who states:

> "Scientific methodology today is based on generating hypotheses and testing them to see if they can be falsified; indeed, this methodology is what distinguishes science from other fields of human inquiry."

The practise of the method requires several different types of mentality: keen observers, ingenious experimenters, painstaking classifiers, imaginative theorists, and hair splitting logicians coupled with practical pragmatists. By these criteria, everyone who employs the scientific method scrupulously, including examiners of handwriting, would seem then to qualify for the title *scientist* and the same umbrella of respectability.[11]

Scientific method constantly probes by asking *why* and constantly provokes by challenging *so what*. Indeed, these are the hallmarks that distinguish scientific method from mere technical routine, and scientific method is the hallmark that distinguishes valid and reliable writing identification from graphology. One obtains a reasonable indication of the scientific quality of his or her bench work by the frequency with which these two questions, *why* and *so what* rise in one's mind during the course of one's examinations.

So, if science is some systematized body of knowledge, scientific method is the framework for or method of acquiring and using it, and a spirit imbued in those who pursue it, regardless of the nature of the matter under study. There are many bodies of knowledge besides science, but the scientific method provides a kind of garment by which the scientist may be distinguished. The scientist's pursuit, which differs from all others, is built entirely out of the brass tacks of fact and logic, not depending on historical report, not governed by majority opinion, and not influenced by fashion or taste.

75. What Is Science?

Science began as a branch of pure learning that aimed at intellectual satisfaction. Science is not the only branch of pure learning, however, and we must determine, if we can, what distinguishes science from other academic-pursuit branches such as economics, history, mathematics, or philosophy.

At one time, science was considered to have but a handful of rather unrelated divisions, e.g., chemistry, physics, or astronomy. Today, science is a veritable supermarket of specialties. The National Science Foundation recognized 620 fields of scientific study in 1964, but that number may be astronomical today. Even the Foundation is not prepared to suggest.

Norman Campbell, in his book[12] *What is Science*, has succeeded where many others have failed. In a sage dissertation, Campbell concludes that science is a single whole. He asserts that the divisions between its branches are largely products of our own thinking without ulterior significance. His definition of science is as profound as we are likely to encounter:

"The study of those judgments concerning which universal agreement can be obtained."

It is not our intention to develop Campbell's basis for his definition. It is sufficient for readers to note that Campbell's definition serves as the nucleus for the description of science provided by the Encyclopaedia Britannica. Understanding of it is assisted if one thinks of judgments as being observations or experiences that may be acquired from empirical studies or experimentation.

In applying this definition expressly to handwriting identification, recall that we have made the observation that there are 21 discriminating elements of writing, no more no less, that may serve to differentiate the products of any one person from another. Should this proposition acquire universal agreement, it might constitute the initial step in the growth of writing examination as a science. Other observations that examiners have made, e.g., the heterogeneity of writing, need to be duly investigated and tested. Once done and accorded as universal agreement, we will have climbed a second essential step up the stairway of qualification.

As the number of observations grows on which agreement is reached, the disputed observations or judgments will be shed from our thinking. This is the stuff of which laws are made, that, in turn, can obtain universal agreement.

In a strikingly similar vein Sullivan[13] wrote:

"…The essential distinction between science and art consists in the fact that science makes appeal to universal assent, whereas art does not. A scientific statement is open to verification by anybody, whereas a work of art appeals only to people with certain sensibilities…music means nothing to a man who is tone deaf. Science deals with a public world, whereas art is concerned with a private world."

What is important in Campbell's and Sullivan's definitions is the requirement for *universal agreement* that distinguishes science from other branches of pure learning. It follows that scientific method is simply the framework within which universal agreement in the theories, laws, and principles of a field of science may be sought and realized.

Universal agreement, however, is only one of the two distinguishing characteristics of science. What then is the other?

A hallmark of science is that it endeavours to define data as precisely as possible through measurement.[14] The kinds of measures employed vary a great deal, but by this means, a numerical value can be assigned to a fact, that heretofore had only sensory or aesthetic value.

There are those who insist that the assignment of numbers to represent properties, data, or facts is a necessary ingredient of all disciplines of science. They maintain that the purely verbal definitions couched in somewhat ambiguous qualitative terms, that still remain in science, are temporary expedients.   •

Such was the case respecting colour, that early in our lifetime was considered to be immeasurable because "colours cannot be arranged in a single order." We have now learned, however, how to classify colour on multiple scales in terms of brightness, hue, and saturation, by measuring photometric quantity, dominant wavelength, and purity.

Nonetheless, there are properties of some substances that we may never define by numbers, e.g., hardness of solids. Commonly, this refers to the resistance of a substance to surface abrasion, and although scales of relative hardness have been created, they indicate simply the order in which substances may be placed. We are, as yet, without a means of determining precisely how much harder any one substance may be relative to its neighbour on the scale.

The process of measurement is vital to science for a number of reasons:

1. Measurement is the most convenient means of establishing a meaningful rank/order for information. Order is needed to file/retrieve information and to establish relationships between their parts.
2. Measurement enables us to distinguish between minutely different yet similar properties.
3. Measurement enables us to confirm constancy in a property, without which it is no longer a property.
4. Measurement is necessary for the purpose of communication and verification. Science is science only where there can be universal agreement, and verification is essential to achieve such agreement.
5. Measurement is essential to the discovery of laws in which properties are involved. When we are unable to measure a property, we are unable to articulate a law governing it.

Indeed, measurement is the only process available to us to convert observations, properties, and evaluations that are qualitative, subjective, and private to forms that are quantitative, objective, and public, and that are, therefore, communicable.[15]

This statement is of great significance to writing identification and of equally great significance to science for it is the second characteristic of science that distinguishes it from the arts and other branches of pure learning. Hence, we have answered the question, What sets science apart? It is simply *universal agreement* and *measurement*.

The great British physicist, William Thomson, Lord Kelvin, is reported to have said in 1883:

> "When you can measure what you are speaking about, and express it in numbers, you know something about it; but when you cannot measure it, when you cannot express it in numbers, your knowledge is of a meagre and unsatisfactory kind: it may be the beginning of knowledge, but you have scarcely, in your thoughts, advanced to the stage of science."

To communicate information to all persons regardless of their understanding of the language involved, science has learned that numbers are the least ambiguous, most specific means available. So, measurement became the integral requirement of science, by way of which universal agreement can be obtained.

Some years ago we expressed the conviction that if we have any hope of achieving accuracy and precision in examination results, and any aspiration to acquire the mantle of science for the discipline, we must embark on the pursuit of measurement in writing identification. We now read:

> "If the field of forensic handwriting examination is to be considered a scientific endeavour, then the move toward the inclusion of objective measurement as part of the overall comparison methodology must be made."[16]

In the minds of some persons, there is an aura placed about science and scientists that suggests that what is done in their laboratories is complex and beyond the lay person's comprehension. On occasion, it has been employed as a defence mechanism by some handwriting experts to avoid having to answer direct questions about their expertise. But, as Quine has so profoundly expounded, science should be comprehensible to the lay person, for science is not a substitute for common sense but an extension of it.[17]

> "We imbibe an archaic natural philosophy with our mother's milk. In the fullness of time, what with catching up on current literature and making some supplementary observations of our own, we (i.e., scientists) become clearer on things. But the process is one of growth and gradual change: we do not break with the past, nor do we attain to standards of evidence different in kind from the vague standards of children and laymen.
>
> "The scientist is indistinguishable from the common man in his sense of evidence, except that the scientist is more careful. The increased care is not a revision of evidential standards, but only the more patient and systematic collection and use of what anyone would deem to be evidence. If the scientist sometimes overrules something which a superstitious layman might have called evidence, this may simply be because the scientist has other contrary evidence which, if patiently presented to the layman, bit by bit, would be conceded superior. Or it may be that the layman suffers from some careless chain of reasoning of his own whereby, long since, he came wrongly to reckon certain types of connection as evidential; wrongly in that a careful survey of his own ill-observed and long forgotten steps would suffice to disabuse him."

An example is the gambler's fallacy that argues that the more often black pays on a roulette wheel the more likely red becomes. We would reiterate, however, that science's fundamental distinction from common sense rests in a single word: system. As Quine said, "The scientist introduces system into his quest and scrutiny of evidence. System, moreover, dictates the scientist's hypotheses themselves."

76. Where Does this Leave Handwriting Identification — Science or Art?

The studies of writing for identification purposes have always considered some measurable elements, such as size, relative heights, and spacing, although the recording of the measurements has not been a standard practise for some. We are, however, compelled to recognize the assignment of numbers to represent facts as a necessary ingredient of most, if not all, disciplines of science. It must be pursued in handwriting identification if it is hoped to achieve universal agreement.

During the first half of this century, a number of attempts were made (we are aware of eight) to measure different aspects of writing using specially constructed devices. These efforts seemed to culminate with the work of Tripp, Fluckiger, and Weinberg[18] who endeavoured to measure handwriting variables such as pressure and speed. For this, a specially designed writing instrument was used to record pressure in terms of the *perpendicular vector* (i.e., force applied perpendicular to the axis of the pen), the *parallel vector* (i.e., force applied parallel to the axis of the pen), and the *table vector*, that we now refer to as *point load*. And point load, we know, is in fact the product of the vertical components of the other two vectors (Figure 5).

Since then, with the advent of the International Graphonomics Society (IGS) and other groups with related interests virtually hundreds of studies[19-20] have been conducted to better understand the writing process, to determine what of it might be measurable, and to offer formula for diagnosing the results. In these studies, the computer has played and is playing a major role.

To a large extent, the focus has been on the potential of an automated system of signature verification, the merits of which are now widely recognized. The handwritten signature is considered to be one of the best means of personal identification. It is a kind of identification that must be produced or created anywhere and at any time, unlike passwords or identity cards, that must only be possessed. The security of passwords has its weaknesses and ID cards have the inherent risk of loss or theft. The computer must be engineered to recognize a touchstone that will discriminate between the genuine product and the spurious or the "coincidentally similar" writing of another person.

The touchstone may prove to be the major problem to resolve, and currently is receiving much of the scientists' attention. Much research has been directed at dynamic techniques in which computer input is acquired during the writing process, as in signature verification for access control purposes. But progress has also been made in static techniques in which input is acquired from the completed writing as it appears on a document or a sheet of paper. The computer analysis of writing features has been reported by several authors.

Software has now been designed to assist in the measurement of line lengths, distances between points, areas within loops, and angles of intersecting strokes. Organizations of scientists have been formed whose interests embrace the writing process. We are aware of five, four of whom are worth mentioning:

1. The International Graphonomics Society (1984)
2. The International Association for Pattern Recognition (1982)
3. The Pattern Recognition Society (1968)
4. The Institute of Electrical & Electronics Engineers (Systems, Man, and Cybernetics Group) (1971)

A number of new scientific publications have been spawned. We are aware of five that are printed in the English language:

1. *The IEEE Transactions on Pattern Analysis and Machine Intelligence*
2. *Pattern Recognition*
3. *Pattern Recognition Letters*
4. *The IEEE Transactions on Systems, Man and Cybernetics*
5. *The International Journal of Pattern Recognition and Artificial Intelligence*

An excellent review of the literature and a state of the art survey, with a list of some 180 published references, has been provided by Plamondon and Lorette[21] that should be a reading must for serious students and practitioners of handwriting identification. Almost as many published papers have surfaced in the eight years since. Nevertheless, much work has yet to be done to develop and consolidate the findings of these studies, and to convert them to usable forms.

As was said above, this work has focused principally on the two applications of the knowledge likely to become its foremost beneficiaries: identification and verification. Identification is the system for selecting a writer, if present, from a reference database, on the basis of some specific attributes of extended writing. A verification system, on the other hand, endeavours to accept or reject a particular writing, usually a signature, by a one-to-one comparison of the elements of the writing with one or more reference standards in an electronic storage. The identification system is the electronic development of the manually conducted classification systems introduced by Livingston and others some 50 years ago. The verification system is an attempt to computerize the standard bench work of the document examiner, but in a small fraction of the time required.

One of the instruments developed and marketed in the last 15 years by Rediffusion Computers Ltd., is the SIGNCHECK Signature Verification System designed to verify static signatures on cheques. A study by Totty and Hardcastle[22] found the system unsuitable at that time for forensic applications and of questionable value to banks and like institutions. Systems of this kind require a quality of resolution or sensitivity to do much more than assess a pictorial effect, as some do. They need to have a capacity to appraise letter design, line quality, stroke sequence, pressure variance, line continuity, and other factors, properties that have so far eluded them.

Another study by Brocklehurst[23] employed a computer to digitize signatures and data reduction techniques to obtain coded descriptions of signatures. In tests of "simply spurious" signatures, rejection rates of 97 percent were obtained at thresholds that accepted 90 percent of genuine signatures. Although the process did not function as well as required to be considered practical, the author did feel that, with modification, the system had some potential as a verification technique.

Other studies are being conducted of writings in other languages and other alphabets. El-Wakil and Shoukry[24] had some success in the recognition of isolated Arabic characters in Egyptian writing. The isolated Arabic characters seems to offer similar advantages in the recognition process that others have experienced with hand lettering.

The methods being employed in these efforts to harness the efficacy of the computer do evince clearly that the basic has been accepted, that writing identification must strive to meet the measurement criteria for science. Indeed, it is the measurement of motion, direction, distance, and pressure on which these systems of verification and identification depend. Notwithstanding the fact that the discipline, in some respects at present, does not meet this criteria, there is no reason to doubt that at some time in the not too distant future it will.

77. What Must be Done to Transform Handwriting Identification Into A Science?

Difficult as the pill may be to swallow, the ruling of District Court Judge Lawrence L. McKenna of New York on April 4, 1995,[25] that forensic document examiners are not scientists, but are more in the nature of skilled craftsmen; that their opinions may be less precise, and do not have the demonstrable certainty that some sciences have, should prompt many document examiners to rethink the state and nature of their profession, as currently practised, if indeed, it is a profession. The analogy to "harbour pilots" that the court made will undoubtedly be challenged by the vast majority of practitioners, but it may be exceedingly difficult to dispute the analogy or to find another that is more representative of the work and, at the same time, more closely related to the accepted fields of science.

The points made in the decision of Judge McKenna correspond in many respects to the criticisms expressed somewhat unprofessionally by Risinger, Denbeaux, and Saks in their paper published in the *University of Pensylvania Law Review*.[26] Indeed, Saks was a witness in the *Starzecpyzel* case. Volumes have been written in response to this article including papers by Buglio and Wiersma,[27] Scott,[28] Crown,[29] Wenderoth,[30] Galbraith et al.,[31] and others. Obviously, these authors have been distressed by the Risinger et al. article, but much of that distress may stem from the sarcasm of its title or of its initial remarks, and its obvious agenda to indict the discipline of writing identification. Similarly, the McKenna decision is generating many comments by many examiners.

With perhaps two exceptions, all of the responses that have sprung from the Risinger et al. paper and the McKenna decision have been reactionary in nature; attempts to rationalize, to justify, and to criticize the criticisms. Only Found and Rogers[32] and Huber[33] have been proactionary; prepared to concede that a problem exists and offering some direction to rectify the situation.

Nevertheless, handwriting identification, as it is presently practised on this continent, fails to meet the criteria for a science; i.e., (1) universal agreement on its fundamentals and (2) measurement of its facts (see Section 75: What is Science). There are, of course, many elements of writing that are measurable to some extent, and yet, are subjectively judged in the course of a handwriting study: size, slope, spacing, relative heights, and proportions, to name a few. Few examiners make a practise of recording with reasonable accuracy the measurement of these features, but then only the marginally different writing elements warrant measurement.

It has been argued that many aspects of the handwriting study cannot be conveniently reduced to numbers, such as matters of shape, and that natural variation complicates any endeavour to conduct measurements. Furthermore, it is claimed that measurement would greatly extend the process of examination to an intolerable degree considering most examiners' case loads. Then too, similarity or difference in measurable elements of writing is usually obvious, and the need to record the fact numerically may be debatable.

As a criterion for science, however, measurement is not an instrument to be employed in every examination or in all elements of it. Measurement's place is primarily in the proof and development of the principles and precepts on which the discipline is established. Measurement can assist in casework just as frequency of occurrence statistics, if properly compiled, can be expected to contribute to evaluations of significance. Measurements can confirm subtle differences in size, slopes, and spacing that subjective assessments may not accurately determine. Nevertheless, they will never serve alone to identify a writer, any more so than the reading of a temperature will serve alone to diagnose an illness in medical science.

There is no doubt that the constraints under which most document examiners normally work have mitigated against extending examination times by recording many measurements. Case loads, costs, and legal counsels have coerced handwriting examiners into standards of practise within their laboratories that a true science may find unacceptable. There are, however, many areas of the work perhaps as basic as measurement that need attention about which much can be done.

Klimoski and Rafaeli provided a criteria (see Section 80: What Is Graphology All About?), for the admission of a discipline respecting the study of handwriting into the scientific community. To render it more germane to handwriting identification, we have revised this model to six points. The criteria had its origin in the field of psychology, we believe, where it was developed as the basis for the scientific study of any aspect of human behaviour. When thoughtfully considered by handwriting examiners, this criteria, as revised, now constitutes a most appropriate basis from which a new science of handwriting examination might emerge. Briefly, the discipline must demonstrate at an acceptable level:

1. Reliability of the behaviour that will be the subject of study: i.e., writing.
2. Reliability of interpretation:
   a. conspectus reliability — the agreement between examiners as to what constitutes evidence in a given sample, and how significant it is (inter-rater reliability).
   b. inference reliability — the consistency of judgments across different samples from the same writer (Test-retest reliability).
3. Discriminative reliability of the process — the consistency of judgments across samples from different writers, including simulations.
4. Validity of premises: habituation and heterogeneity of the population (i.e., the uniqueness of writing to the individual).
5. Validity of process: the level of correctness of assessments or analyses, across samples from different writers, or from the same writer.
6. Skill in analysis: the level of education and special training required vs. intuition.

Unfortunately, handwriting identification, as conducted within the field of document examination, has suffered from the same ailments as graphology. As Klimoski and Rafaeli have outlined with respect to graphology, many reports have been presented or published over the years, but too large a percentage of these have been anecdotal in nature, i.e., case histories or descriptions, lacking empirical data of any sort. Among those that might be considered systematic investigations or true research studies that have been pursued, few have been rigorously performed.

Research hypotheses, if stated at all, have been vague or imprecise. Subjects have been selected in nonrandom ways and writing sample collection has been haphazard. Finally, conclusions are often based on samples too small to be reliable.

These circumstances notwithstanding (and hopefully to be avoided in the future), in the absence of any proposed alternative, let us assume that this proposed six-point criteria is a reasonable goal to be sought. How much has been achieved and what needs to be done?

A.   Reliability of the Behaviour

It is an almost universal belief that handwriting is stable, at least over short periods of time. The ability of most if not all of us to recognize familiar writing is testimony to the fact. If writing was not stable, recognition would not occur. Yet, although each of us may have experienced writing recognition, not all of us are in a position to explain why.

Stability and consistency in writing features, however, has been established in and demonstrated by several objective published studies. Harvey[34] obtained samples from 50 subjects two months apart and measured 16 handwriting variables. He found a correlation between samples of each subject of 0.77. Birge[35] had two raters measure five writing variables in 50 samples from the same subject, and obtained an average correlation of 0.97. Lockowandt[36] quotes studies by Timm, Fischer, Prystav, and others that have yielded high correlation coefficients for measured handwriting characteristics (most beyond 0.90) indicative of great consistency between samples from the same writer. Squire[37] focused particularly on the stability of handwriting and obtained specimens of writing from 26 subjects at a two-week interval. The nine characteristics studied and measured (looping of the letter "t," closing of the letters "a" and "o," degree of slope, etc.) revealed consistency for all the characteristics studied, with the exception of slope. In our view, this may be an indication that slope is subject to a wider range of natural variation.

Furthermore, whether or not we accept handwriting examination as a scientific procedure, we cannot ignore the fact that, over a hundred years, many thousands of identifications or eliminations (nonidentifications) of handwritings have occurred. We cannot deny that some of these were made at the hands of charlatans or examiners who lacked the necessary competence for the task. In the last half century, the vast majority of cases have involved questioned writings of various kinds and of various ages that have been correctly and properly associated with standards of writing from an equal number of persons, in the course of civil and criminal litigation. Valid identifications and valid eliminations could not and would not have been possible if the discriminating elements of handwriting on which the examinations depended were not stable over periods of time of various lengths. Practical experience, then, contributes substantially to the evidence we are seeking.

In summary, research evidence and practical experience seems more than sufficient to affirm the stability of the behaviour of writing and its reliability as a subject of study.

B. Reliability of Interpretation

1. Conspectus Reliability

Conspectus reliability in handwriting identification is universal agreement as to what is evidence in a set of standards and its significance. It seems to be a subject that has been glossed over. The anecdotal descriptions of cases that are presented or published highlight particular elements of evidence that are unusual in some respect, but seldom are all elements described or dealt with. The argument is given that all aspects of writing that might serve as evidence of identification are mentioned in the books of Osborn, Hilton, Harrison, or Conway. Nonetheless, no attempt has been made by any of these authors, to organize and itemize, classify and consolidate these various aspects, as a science is wont to do. Though the substance may be there, the system, that demarcates science from lay thinking, is missing.

In its absence, agreement between examiners as to what should be considered evidence is difficult to demonstrate. Even more difficult is the task of finding some agreement in the evaluation of the evidence that each examiner might consider. Some progress is achievable, however, and appeals have been made for greater interest in its pursuit.

It should be noted that in the sense in which *conspectus reliability* is being used here it can be defined, as The Oxford English Dictionary, 2nd Ed. Vol III, 1989 and other dictionaries do, as "A comprehensive survey or digest of those elements of writing that are or may be taken into consideration in a study for the purpose of a writing's identification."

Obviously, there must be universal agreement within the discipline (see Section 75: What Is Science?) as to the evidence that will be considered. This is not to suggest that all examiners evaluate that evidence the same way — although this should be the ideal — but only to clarify and to achieve agreement as to what it is that will constitute evidence and the language employed to refer to it.

2. *Inference Reliability*

Inference reliability, in handwriting identification is the consistency of judgments made on the basis of different standards from the same writer (technically termed *test-retest reliability*) and introduces a number of conditions upon which proof of reliability will depend. Two situations seem to present themselves.

The several sets of standards from the subject will have to provide the same or very similar textual material to ensure that, qualitatively and quantitatively, the same evidence will be present. We are then in the position of simply proving the stability of writing generally, the criterion referred to as *the reliability of the behaviour*, that we concluded was adequately demonstrated by the research already conducted and the practical experience already gained.

If, however, we propose to work from standards of different textual material, then we must recognize that each set of standards may contain different assortments of evidence, having different levels of identification value. Within different sets of standards, evidence may differ in both kind and quantity. As long as the standards are adequate in number and we allow consistency of judgment, that which we wish to achieve, to include differing levels of certainty within the same upper or lower quadrants of the scale of probability, we expect that we should experience little difficulty. By this approach, we are making due allowance for some difference in evidential values.

If the judgments of different sets of standards are to be made by the same examiner, and consistency in results is the principle object of the study, it may be difficult to conduct. Exposure to one set of standards may influence the outcome of a second examination of a second set of standards by the same examiner.

On the other hand, judgments of different standards by different examiners is a common occurrence in contested cases. Consistency in results between examiners working with different standards would appear to provide substantial support for the reliability of inferences that may be drawn from writing, if, and only if, it can be assumed that both examiners are considering the same universal standard for kinds of evidence. In other words, after conspectus (inter-rater) reliability has been achieved.

In our experience, we have had a number of cases in which other examiners have been employed first by the "other side," and we have been asked to conduct a second examination (we have no way of knowing the number of cases in which the situation has been reversed). In the vast majority of these cases, the standards submitted to the two examiners are quite different in kind and number. It has also been our experience that only in rare cases do the two examiners fundamentally disagree. When disagreement does occur, qualifications, competence, and/or experience of the examiners are equally dissimilar, and we are without reliable information as to the extent that these disparities contributed to the disagreements. Thus, for the purpose of our present discussion such exceptional cases of disagreement can be disregarded. In so far as the vast majority of cases, what we are lacking is a record of those in which agreement occurs, in order that a compilation can be made that allows this information to serve as evidence of inference reliability.

C. Discriminative Reliability of the Process

This pertains to the accuracy of judgments made across samples of writing from different persons, including those that are simulations of another person's writing, despite the process of imitation employed. In fact, it is an exceedingly important corollary to one of the two premises underlying writing identification: the heterogeneity of writing. If the process employed is not capable of discriminating between the writings of any two individuals, we are without the means of proving that writing is, without exception, heterogeneous. Furthermore, we are without a facility for knowing when and if, in our examination and study of the heterogeneity of writings, we are being deceived.

Although we have suggested a compilation of 21 discriminating elements of writing that are or may be involved in the writing identification process, we require some more or less universal agreement that these, and perhaps only these, are the elements of writing that would be involved. Following that we must provide some reasons for believing that these aspects of writing will serve to discriminate between any two writers of a given population, and to differentiate between the genuine and spurious executions respecting any single writer.

The ability of the process to discriminate will hinge largely on a proper and thorough study of the heterogeneity of writing, which is the next constituent of the criteria to be established. If the process does not discriminate in all cases some revision of our 21 discriminating elements, or of an examiner's capabilities and facilities, may be required. The study of the heterogeneity of writing will likely provide an answer to the question of the discriminatory reliability of the process, as a corollary to the fundamental question respecting the uniqueness of writing. If the heterogeneity of writing can be proven by the process being used, then the process has been vindicated and must be reliable.

As difficult as it may be to accept, if a study of heterogeneity is to be conducted in accordance with scientific method, we must be prepared to acknowledge that a null hypothesis could be the result; that is, that we will find that the process is not capable of discriminating between the writings of all persons. We may learn, however, what the margin of error of the process may be, and what must be done to reduce that margin.

Harris[38] has alerted us to the similarity he found in signatures of the same names, particularly those consisting of six letters or less. His study also disclosed that some letters provide less variation in form or design from one writer to the next, and that other somewhat peculiar letter forms can become popular and appear more frequently than might be expected.

Accordingly, the discriminative ability of the writing examination process must be considered with regard to the kind and quantity of writing to be involved in the study, if valid results are to be obtained.

Our practise of saving handwritten addressed envelopes that we have received over many years has provided us with examples of essentially the same textual material from upwards of a thousand different writers. It is our belief that these writings, that now number 2,000 or more in total, can provide some empirical support for the hypotheses that: (1) handwriting is sufficiently unique to the individual to permit discrimination between writers, and that (2) competent examiners, employing the documented 21-point criteria (or a better one), are sufficiently capable of discriminating between writers with acceptable low levels of error — to sanction the acceptance of both hypotheses.

D. Validity of the Premises

As we have propounded in Section 25: What Makes Handwriting Identification Possible?, handwriting identification is based on two underlying premises, that may, when both have been proven, constitute the scientific principles, perhaps the only scientific principles, on which the work can be based:

Habituation.   People are primarily creatures of habit and writing is a collection of them that have habit hierarchies of at least three levels: the letter habit, the word habit, and the phrase habit, that are employed according to the degree to which the action process is subjugated to the thought process.

Writing habits are neither instinctive nor hereditary, but are complex processes that are developed gradually. Handwriting, or indeed footwriting, mouthwriting or typewriting, is a neuromuscular behaviour that develops as an acquired perceptual-motor skill. It involves successively higher stages of integration as learning proceeds.

Thus, in handwriting comparisons, letters, combinations of letters, words, or phrases must be considered according to the degree to which they constitute a collective habit. It is a classic example of synergism in which the whole constitutes more than the sum of its parts. Accordingly, the influence of adjoining letters upon one another will vary according to the role these letters play in words or phrases that have become writing habits as units, rather than as individual letters. Variation in shape and movement can be expected to occur in relation to this factor.

The Heterogeneity of Writing.   The uniqueness of writing to the individual is a subject that we have discussed at length elsewhere (see Section 25: What Makes Handwriting Identification Possible?). In the context in which we are now addressing the topic, some of our statements bear repeating.

Writing identification is predicated on the heterogeneity of the writing of the population; that is, on the principle that handwriting is unique to the individual. The argument in support of this contention, however, stems largely but simply from the truism that "Nature never offers her handiwork to us in facsimile." Thus, people are likened to leaves or to stones, no two of which have been found to be precisely the same. Isaac D'Israeli is quoted as saying, more than a century and a half ago, "To every individual, nature has given a distinct sort of handwriting, as she has given him a peculiar countenance, voice, and manners."

Any two items of nature may be distinguished from each other if the scale of judgment that is used is appropriate and sufficiently precise. Whether or not the method employed in handwriting examination is fitting and sufficiently precise to discriminate between the writings of any two individuals is the initial challenge that has to be addressed.

There is a constantly growing volume of casework that demonstrates the ability of the process and the people using it to discriminate between handwritings correctly, despite the absence of the kind and quality of empirical data that critics claim is necessary. Notwithstanding this data shortcoming, one has to allow that the risk of deceptive duplicity that may escape the discriminating process employed is extremely low, low enough to deserve the confidence and credibility the discipline has enjoyed.

Questions worthy of investigation are whether a sample of the population can provide sufficient information respecting the differences between writers to indicate: (1) what the probability of deceptive duplicity might be, and (2) to what extent deception may be an inverse function of the size or quantity of the writing specimen.

A somewhat academic question that we have posed and pondered is whether heterogeneity can be proven by a discriminatory process whose capability to do so has not been proven, except on relatively small samples. This is the corollary to the premises, that was identified earlier.

E. Validity of the Processes

This is related to, but not an alternative for "the discriminative reliability of the process" previously discussed. There we were interested in the process's ability to discriminate between (i.e., to differentiate), the writings of different persons. Here we are concerned with the process's ability to recognize (i.e., to identify), with reasonable certainty, two writings as being products of the same person.

Admittedly, the two problems utilize the same discriminating elements in their determinations. The task of discrimination, however, relies on the evaluation of differences, whereas the task of identification procures its support from the evaluation of similarities.

The level of correctness of the assessments made by examiners from the day-to-day casework is not likely to prove to be a credible source for the data needed. On the other hand, this should not be a difficult situation to simulate in test material. Nevertheless, the degree of certainty or level of probability that the test situation is hoping to exceed may complicate the process.

Test material in the candidate files of the American Society of Questioned Document Examiners and the American Board of Forensic Document Examiners and other organizations might be mustered and published (without identification) as data in support the validity of the handwriting identification process. Whether the numbers would be sufficient to constitute an adequate sample from which to generalize to the population of examiners at large or to any strata of it is the only uncertainty that might exist. Publication is needed, however, to render the information useable. Even then, its useability may be questioned until conspectus reliability has been established, providing grounds that all assessments are being made by examiners that agree as to the evidence to be considered, and its significance.

F. Skill in Analysis

The roles of skill, training, intuition, and education in the performance of an examiner is a matter that many have spoken about, but not in a fashion that delineates their relative merits. Few studies have been conducted and reported, and there are those who maintain that intuition plays a most significant role. Graphologists have cited some studies as evidence of their capabilities over lay persons. Frederick[39] is one such study that investigated the identification of a suicidal personality by analyzing faked and genuine handwritten notes purportedly left by persons before suicide was committed. Trained graphologists were able to distinguish the spurious notes from the genuine at a level exceeding chance, whereas a control group of persons comprised of detectives and secretaries were not. The study by Kam, Wetstein, and Conn[40] provided some evidence that trained document examiners were significantly more successful at identifying writings than lay persons. Neither of these studies, however, provide any indication of the reasons for the success of the graphologists or of the document examiners; whether it was skill, training, education, or intuition. In comments made informally at the 1995 meeting of the ASQDE, Dr. Kam stated that post-test interviews with the subjects suggested that a fifth factor may have been involved: attitude. The trained document examiners approached the test situation far more seriously.

Other studies of graphology, particularly that of Rafaeli and Klimoski,[41] were unable to demonstrate the presumed importance of professional training. We are unsure whether the negative results obtained in these studies are due to the limited benefit that graphologists receive from professional training or to the failure of graphology to perform as is claimed for it.

In recent years, some organizations, namely the American Society of Questioned Document Examiners, the American Board of Forensic Document Examiners, the American Academy of Forensic Sciences and the Canadian Society of Forensic Science, have insisted upon academic qualifications, at a bachelor level at least, for admission or certification, without any particular stipulation as to the program of institutional learning. The result has been that the academic backgrounds of document examiners are widely diversified, and few contain a great deal of science. Understandably, such wide diversification makes it difficult to demonstrate and prove the worth of nonspecific academic qualifications.

Details of the training programs offered to neophyte examiners are seldom divulged and the books on which these programs depend, from which a measure of the intellectual level of the course might be inferred, are not identified. Those by Osborn, Hilton, Conway, and Harrison, that may not be true textbooks, are the works generally used. "Training Manuals" are now surfacing, that outline course contents, best described as "what to -" rather than "how to -" programs of learning.

In the absence of any stipulation or proposal respecting the course content, the question that must be addressed, sooner or later, is why a university education is necessary at all to perform document examination. Knowing as we do that there are few courses that appear to be directly related, what reasons can be offered?

1. University education, even that which is not directly related, ensures the possession of the minimum level of intelligence necessary.
2. University education can provide some direction in abstract and analytical thinking, vital aspects of the occupation of any document examiner.
3. Handwriting is a human behaviour, an understanding of which is practicably obtained through the psychology courses offered by universities.
4. The basics of ink chemistry and an understanding of the electromagnetic spectrum is knowledge needed and practicably obtained through university courses.
5. An understanding of statistical analysis is essential to the application of measurements to the examination of writing, if it is to rate as a branch of science. This is practicably and perhaps only obtained through university courses.
6. To justify being accepted as bedfellows of other disciplines within forensic science, practitioners must offer reasonably corresponding backgrounds.

7. Professional competence in forensic science, like justice itself, must not only be done, but must seem to be done. It is essential to secure the client's and the court's confidence. A university education is germane to this acquisition.
8. Growth and development in the discipline of writing identification or document examination will occur only in conjunction with growth in intellectual stature and the gain of broader and more profound understanding of various branches of science. University education is the practical route to this end.
9. Self instruction cannot meet these needs.

These arguments supporting the need of university education are, admittedly, somewhat arbitrary. The reader may have other arguments to add to these. Acceptable research to study this component of the handwriting examiner may be extremely difficult to conduct. We recognize, however, the need for some particular professional training and an education in the sciences as the basis for the development of skills in this unique discipline. If this cannot be articulated and demonstrated, the esteem of science may be beyond our reach.

O'Block's[42] national survey of the number and content of academic courses in forensic document examination being taught in the U.S.A. revealed to him that only six institutions offered any instruction, and all programs were not more than an introduction to the field. Of greater import is that he found neither push nor funding "For the development of a major in forensic document examination."

Papers and publications (see Section 11: How Is Handwriting Identification Taught?) suggested curricula for the post-secondary education of document examiners. What reasoning underlies course selection is seldom stated. Our selection of courses that would be appropriate for the practising document examiner because of their direct application to the day-to-day tasks would include the following as essential or highly desirable, to which other courses would be added. The titles are those of one university, which may differ in other institutions.

1. *English* to prepare reports properly, without grammatical and spelling errors, and with the use of appropriate words.
   a. Writing and Language
2. *Philosopy* (at least 2 courses) to comprehend logic, semantics, and the elements of reasoning.
   a. Knowledge and Reality
   b. Science and the Human
   c. Informal Reasoning
   d. Philosophy of Law — in Logics
   e. Issues in the Philosophy of Science
   f. Language and Communication
3. *Chemistry* (at least three courses) to understand the composition of inks, eradicators, and the process of their analysis.
   a. General Chemistry
   b. Inorganic Chemistry
   c. Organic Chemistry
   d. Analytical Chemistry

4. *Physics* (at least two courses) to understand light reflection and refraction, optics, the electromagnetic spectrum, particularly the ultraviolet and infrared regions, measurements, and weights.
    a. Introductory or General Physics
    b. Wave Motion and Optics
    c. Electricity and Magnetism
5. *Mathematics and Statistics* (at least two courses) to understand the application of statistics to empirical data, the matter of probabilities, sampling techniques, and the testing of hypotheses.
    a. Calculus
    b. Introduction to Statistical Analysis
    c. Probability Models
    d. Probability and Statistics
    f. Sampling Methodology
6. *Psychology* (at least two courses) to understand human behaviour, the sociology of the human being, and the experimental study of human performance.
    a. Introductory or General Psychology
    b. Introduction to Psychological Research and Statistics
    c. Introduction to Cognitive Psychology
    d. Experimental Psychology
7. *Computer Science* (one or two courses) to understand computer use.
    a. Introduction to Computers for the Sciences
8. *Foreign Languages* (at least two courses) to study those languages in which he/she expects to have to operate occasionally. Languages are also important in comprehending foreign technical information, particularly German, and perhaps Spanish and French.
    a. German (accents and central European writing systems)
    b. French or Spanish (accents)
    c. Russian, Ukrainian, or Yugoslavian (Cyrillic alphabets)

This program was compiled from the experience of persons who entered the field of questioned documents first, and later undertook a program of university courses selected as appropriate for application within the field.

There are several reasons for suggesting the foregoing course content. To begin with, practising examiners who lack the courses we have suggested might be persuaded to enroll in such courses when and where available, simply for the purpose of better equipping themselves to perform the work in which they are engaged. Secondly, it should be of some guidance to students that may be contemplating a future in the questioned document field. Third, the adoption of such a program of courses by professional organizations as a preferred standard academic background might change the capabilities and qualifications of the next generation of examiners. The advantages of education to the conduct of the work might then be articulated and indisputably demonstrated. Furthermore, it might so consolidate the thinking of competent examiners that fewer disparities would be found in the testimony and reports of practitioners.

To return to the question posed in this section, we would contend that the transformation of writing identification into a science must begin with the establishment of conspectus reliability and the heterogeneity of writing. The ability of the process employed to discriminate between writers, and the nature and quantity of writing necessary to do so reliably, follow as two further aspects of the work that will have to be addressed. Finally, at some point in time, a general agreement should be reached as to the program of higher learning to be followed by students in preparation for work in the discipline, if only to more appropriately equip the next generation.

It brings the discussion back to the recent *Starzecpyzel* ruling that identified handwriting identification as "purely practical in nature," stating that handwriting examiners are "nonscientific expert witnesses," and that handwriting examination is "closer to a practical skill, such as piloting a vessel, than to a scientific skill." The court was even critical of the use of terms such as *scientific* and *laboratory* by document examiners, alleging that it is an attempt to gird themselves in the trappings of science to garner some of the respect science traditionally enjoys.

This criticism may be unfair if not invalid. There are a number of kinds of investigations conducted as part of a document's study that are clearly within the parameters of science. The chromatographic analysis of the composition of inks, the chemical analysis of paper additives, the botanical analysis of paper fibres, the optical examinations of the responses of writing media in the ultraviolet and near infrared regions of the electromagnetic spectrum are but a few.

In these areas, however, document examination is not performing as a science in its own right. Rather it is employing the precepts and principles of various branches of science to pursue its studies. It relies on the principles of chemistry in its study of inks. It uses the precepts of botany in its study of papers. It employs the laws of physics in its studies of UV (ultraviolet) and IR (infrared) radiations. Even Risinger, Denbeaux, and Saks, in their attack on document examination cited earlier, allowed that many kinds of document examination employ techniques based on principles of applied science.

Document examination is a conglomerate of many kinds of study. The greater segment of its service, that which involves writing examination, has no acknowledged branch of science upon which to draw. Consequently, if writing examination is to achieve the status of a scientific calling it will have to do it on its own. As it stands, handwriting examination, ergo, document examination, may have a distance to go to put itself on an acceptable footing.

In summary then, the pursuit of these six criteria is necessary to achieve the station of a science. Several are interdependent, however. There must be some agreement on the evidence to be considered (conspectus reliability) before the discriminative reliability of the process can be tested. Furthermore, establishing the heterogeneity of writing will depend on the reliability of the process being employed to make discriminations. If the process is too fallible, it may require revision. On the face of it, however, it appears to us that conspectus reliability is deserving of priority treatment.

In their discussion of the issues in the wake of the *Starzecpyzel* case, Found and Rogers[43] comment that:

"…there is a lack of an accepted theoretical basis on which we conduct our work and an absence of proof of our reliability. If we are to be recognized as adhering to the process of science, this theoretical basis must be supported by appropriately designed research, and the application of the resulting theory must then be validated. In the scientific environment, validation studies do not refer to case examples or even the features associated with known forgeries, for example, but rather to extensive and realistic tests of examiners to produce the correct result when the true answer is not known to them. There is no question that there has been a significant lack of these classically-designed validation trials. As a profession, we are responsible for this shortfall and should heed the criticism, regardless of its source, in a professional manner."

In conclusion they write:

"It is unlikely… that forensic handwriting examination will ever be considered as a science similar to… traditional scientific paradigms. The results of the Daubert hearing, given the type of information that they were provided with, appears reasonable almost to the point of generosity. The future for our profession is based on learning from the types of criticisms that have been raised and recognizing that some of the traditional beliefs in the field must be abandoned."

78. So Handwriting Identification as Presently Practised Is Not a Science. So What?

The generation of document examiners from which the present authors emerged devoted much time and thought to the arguments that supported the contention that document examination and handwriting identification, when properly conducted, had many of the attributes of science. Our efforts have been directed for many years at the action necessary to develop the discipline further in pursuit of a sound scientific base. The foregoing section is one such endeavour.

Consequently, it is disappointing, to say the least, to encounter a court ruling that publicly rejects the discipline as having any scientific merit. What is perhaps more disappointing is to learn that there are many practising document examiners that are not overly disturbed by the McKenna decision; who, perhaps for want of a scientific background, are content to be classified simply as skilled workers.

There are some examiners that have long held the view that they are forensic scientists and have sought recognition as such. Whether their self-esteem will be effected by the McKenna decision one can only guess. Undoubtedly, document examiners will continue to be admitted to the American Academy of Forensic Sciences, the Canadian Society of Forensic Science, the Forensic Science Society of the United Kingdom, and the International Association of Forensic Science, despite this court ruling. Organizations of forensic science have usually recognized disciplines that are marginal in their qualifications as sciences. Perhaps all of this is reason enough to accept the present term coined by the media to refer to those disciplines supporting law enforcement as simply *forensics* without mention of the noun *science* that it once modified.

Contentment with the category of "skilled workers" and the analogy to harbour pilots will allow the field to continue as it is and has been. Furthermore, it excuses document examination from the Daubert ruling of the U.S. Supreme Court. It is not likely to stimulate research and study to develop the discipline further into a full science. Indeed, it may discourage it. To a significant degree, it puts handwriting identification back in bed with graphology, where it lay a century ago. If, as a consequence, the discipline loses ground and is less respected, one wonders if it will survive.

Found and Rogers, cited earlier, state the matter profoundly:

"It could be argued that the severity of criticism that we have been subjected to is probably related to the power that this branch of forensic science has claimed. The claim is simply not supported in theory, nor have we supplied the evidence in practise. We, as a group, are responsible for this reality. We are, however, like those before us, only transient in this process. We have (an opportunity) to participate in reconstructing and validating the discipline such that its value, if we find it to have value, is maintained for those who follow us."

And later:

"The future of our profession is based on learning from the types of criticisms that have been raised and recognizing that some of the traditional beliefs in the field must be abandoned.

79. If Full Scientific Status Has Yet to Be Acquired, Is Handwriting Identification a Profession at Least? Or Simply a Craft?

An editorial in the Journal of the Forensic Science Society[44] states quite unequivocally that:

"The cornerstone of any legal system of criminal justice must be the professionalism of its professionals, and society needs to be reassured that the professionals are up to the standards it has grown to expect, and that such standards will be maintained once they are reached."

In his introduction to *Professional Ideals*, Albert Flores[45] explains that professionalism is commonly described as a complex set of role characteristics involving:

1. specialized knowledge and training,
2. autonomous decision-making authority in matters of importance to society,
3. dedication to public service, and
4. that aspect of professionalism, usually implied, that marks the standard of responsible behaviour.

Some years earlier, Huber,[46] in an endeavour to differentiate professions from nonprofessions, claimed in slightly different terms that, "There are differences, not only in amount and kind of training, but in commitment, status and working conditions." From another perspective, Godown,[47] himself a highly-respected document examiner, expressed the view that a professional organization was based on unification with regard to the following:

1. Certification procedures
2. Educational and training standards
3. Promotion of research
4. Standards of practise, ethical and practical

Professionals are expected to be persons of integrity whom you can trust, more dedicated to assisting a cause than exacting a fee. They are experts who, by the use of their skills, contribute to the good of society, in a variety of contexts, for a multitude of purposes, and they are respected for the myriad of ways they contribute to our fund of knowledge and advance our quality of life. Then too, there are aspects of professionalism that define, perhaps ideally, the standard of good conduct, virtuous character, and commitment to excellence that go beyond the norms ordinarily governing relationships between persons.

Ravets[48] offered four criteria that distinguish a true learned profession from a craft, a trade, or an occupation that provides a particular service.

1. The client needs a service, is unable to satisfy the need for his/herself, and, thereby, is dependent upon and vulnerable to the professional's services.
2. The client is not competent to assess the adequacy or quality of the service.
3. Recognized competence in the set of tasks is legally restricted to those certified to have completed a training of a scientific character.
4. In exchange for the monopoly of practise, the group accepts responsibility for the achievement of the aims of clients.

In these criteria, there is an essential fiduciary element, a vesting of trust, at least to a reasonable degree, and professionals are expected to honour this trust. Abuse of professional authority, incompetence, or malfeasance is a betrayal of the client's trust. Whatever legally rendered monopoly (e.g., licensing or certification) that the profession enjoys may be put at risk. Thus, the profession must maintain standards of work to protect the interests of clients, and a code of behaviour is necessary to prevent the relaxing of standards and the neglect of client's interests.

Every major profession has established a professional code of ethics for its members, defining the duties and moral responsibilities that members are expected to follow. It is based on the primacy of the purpose of the task: serving the client's interests. As a guiding principle, the professional ethic is necessary if the fiduciary relationship is to be justified and preserved, indeed, reinforced, and the client's fear of being exploited or poorly served is to be rationally assuaged.

Additionally, given the claim of autonomy that most professions make, and assuming a posture of self-regulation, the professions have historically established these rules of conduct to assure the quality of services and to promote a sense of responsibility for the moral consequences that ensue. Moreover, self-regulation and adherence to professional codes enhances the profession's public image and, thereby, aids in sustaining its integrity in the mind of the public.

In recent years, increasing public criticism of the routine activities of professionals has precipitated a new interest in the normative aspects of professionalism. Consequently, major professions have undertaken the task of revising their codes of ethics as an expression of their commitment to ethical behaviour. Furthermore, the education of professionals has increasingly focused on ethical issues. Academic curriculums are including courses on ethics and professionalism. There has been increased discussion of and a growth in the literature on professional ethics illustrating the serious thought currently being given to the moral dimensions of professionalism.

Flores claims this interest focuses almost exclusively on examining the issues and responsibilities of professionals as defined by the rules promulgated in codes of ethics. The rules and principles that these codes incorporate provide a framework for evaluating professional activities and advocating condemnation when they are breached. Unfortunately, this exclusive emphasis on rules can create the mistaken impression that being professionally proper means no more than observing a variety of rules governing the conduct of one's routine activities. Professionalism so conceived is reduced to rule-governed behaviour involving simply the application of formal codes. While this approach has its value in giving professionals general guidance as to how they ought to act, it can distort our understanding of some fundamental aspects of professionalism.

Rules provide little perspective as to the virtues and ideals essential to professionalism, or to the kind of person one should be in addition to how one should act, in order to be considered a true professional.

What is missing in our picture of professionalism as rule-governed conduct is reference to the virtues and ideals that make the duties and responsibilities incorporated in codes intelligible as moral rules. Without this foundation, codes may be seen as an ideology involving rules of behaviour that simply promote the self-interests of the profession. On the other hand, reference to virtues such as honesty and integrity and to ideals such as truth and justice deepens our understanding of what it means to be a professional, and of how professionalism must imply something more than mere rule-governed behaviour.

The standard concept of professionalism focuses attention on how we should act, and particularly whether each act conforms to the rules. Flores maintains, however, that professionalism conceived as a virtue regards action to be of secondary importance to the question of what kind of person the professional is — the moral quality of one's character. Professionalism, thus conceived, is a way of living that is bound to certain habits of character and mind, such as honesty, impartiality, integrity, and public service. Because of such traits, one is disposed to act in ways consistent with the rules, not as an obligation defined by the rules, but rather as a consequence of the kind of person one is. This difference in focus rests on adopting a set of ideals involving a commitment to excellence and a dedication to serve the common good that defines the kind of person one should be or become. In pursuing these ideals, one develops certain habits, attitudes, and dispositions that fashion the quality of one's mind and character. Hence, how one acts will depend not on one's will to follow rules, but rather on the moral goodness underlying one's character.

Hilton[49] spoke along these lines when he said:

> "Ethics is far deeper than a set of rules. It has to be an inborn or developed basic honesty which precludes the worker from undertaking anything which is not completely and fully honorable. It is not a matter which can be legislated."

Thus, the concept of professionalism is a commitment to the ideal of excellence in the exercise of professional skills. Indeed, because professional practise generates goods of value to both society and the profession, the professional who is committed to ideals of excellence will normally uphold standards of conduct that go beyond those an ordinary individual accepts, in fact, is expected to. In addition, dedication to the ideals of integrity, justice, wisdom, and truth will convey honour to the profession and command respect from others. Thus, the definition of a professional should, morally speaking, include recognition of a variety of ideals that underpin the virtues central to professionalism.

The definition of a profession is itself a matter of some controversy. As *profession* became, more and more, an honorific title, it was thought to be to the advantage of every occupational group to be so gowned and to advance definitions that included the favoured group and excluded rivals. The exclusion of graphologists from any self-respecting family of document examiners is a case in point. As Watts[50] put it, "The aim of the game is status."

For Newton,[51] a profession is an aggregate whose members:

1. possess a specialized art, skill, or capacity, requiring long and difficult education, and extended practise,
2. individually and/or collectively render a service to individual clients and to society in that practise, and,
3. are employed full-time and for pay in the practise of the art or skill.

This definition differs from that of Flores in its distinction of a profession on the basis of remuneration (Newton) and dedication (Flores). Indeed, the remunerative aspect that Newton includes has provided the particular criteria that commonly distinguishes the professional from the amateur in the arts and athletics. The dedication to public service that Flores embraces keeps our discussion within the realm applicable to science. Furthermore, somewhat as a by-product, the professional, by possession of specialized skill, is one who retains his/her professional identity regardless of employment status.

Thus, for professional status to be correctly conferred there must be an extensive educational basis, there must be full-time practise, and a special relationship between practitioner and client centered upon service. Elements will be differently emphasized in different professions, but invariably all will be present.

Like Flores, Newton also distinguishes between the internal and the external aspect of any group of rules or guidelines for a field of practise. The internal is the larger, more serious aspect with which the professional begins — one's ideals and virtues. The external is the more visible, logically coherent, enforceable aspect — the code of ethics, to which the professional subscribes. The internal aspect, one's ideals and virtues, has its roots in each individual; the external is always linked to a professional organization, as a code of ethics, and is the product of its political process.

Neither aspect alone is satisfactory as an ethic. The internal ethic is apt to be ill-formed, and more a personal expression of feelings or a conscience, rather than a set of examinable rules. As for the external aspect, as a set of rules to be applied more or less mechanically, it can hardly be adequate to the infinite variety of situations that present us with ethical dilemmas. Then too, practises that the ethic is supposed to guide may change to meet changing conditions putting a strain to adapt on practitioners and organizations alike, and the maintenance of a rational ethic may be an all but impossible task.

Concern has been expressed by Hilton[52] and others that codes of ethics are unenforceable in any practical fashion and that the threat of condemnation or of expulsion from a professional body may not be adequate to affect the control of conduct. There are few cases within the discipline of document examination by which we can judge, however, and it seems unwise to abandon the intended function of the code, at least until greater evidence is available.

Just a few decades ago, science was portrayed and widely, though not universally, accepted as an activity good and ennobling in itself, and productive of enormous benefits for mankind in general. In recent years, the image has been tarnished; not only is science blamed for the horrors of war and threats to our environment, but there is a new genre of literature and media manifestations exposing the human foibles of scientists. We are tempted to believe that science as a whole has declined from its state of pristine purity, although we tend to condemn it on extremely limited and unreliable evidence.

Forensic scientists have been especially targeted, perhaps because every finding becomes public, subject to challenge, and the population of available forensic scientists has grown substantially. Only the limit of resources to pursue the challenge limit the number of disputes. Nevertheless, findings and qualifications of alleged forensic scientists have been found to be false, and these few individuals have discredited the disciplines in the minds of many.[53]

The special nature of scientific enquiry demands the adoption of an ethical code if work is to be done fittingly. Social mechanisms, individual actions, and commitments must then be engaged if this code is to be enforced and maintained.

The health and vitality of scientific inquiry are not guaranteed, either by the objects of inquiry or by the social aspects of the work. Unless there is an effective scientific ethic, even more refined than a professional ethic, the delicate and sensitive work of science will not continue to be well-governed or well-performed.

The importance of a professional ethic should be obvious, then, to any aspiring scientific pursuit and its practitioners, including the examination of writings.[54] Whether we are aware of it or not, each of us has, already, his/her own ethical code, good or bad as it is. It may be little more than a moral code, but it is there. What is required is an awareness of their existence and a collective agreement as to the components of our codes that should be common to all.

Insofar as the question that prompted this discussion, it is, suffice to say, that professionalism is not determined by the kind of work that one does; rather, it embodies the attitude and behaviour with which one approaches and performs it.[55]

When given appropriate thought, the following eight provisions warrant a place in the personal or collective codes of ethics endorsed by writing examiners:

1. To apply appropriate principles of science and of logic, in accordance with scientific method, to the examination and study of written or lettered inscriptions on any material substrate.
2. To ensure that the scope of the examination and study is objective and appropriate to the task(s) presented by the document(s).
3. To ensure that the conclusions drawn and/or findings discovered are in accordance with, and not misrepresentative of the physical evidence present, and its proper interpretation; and to report them clearly, concisely and impartially.
4. To acknowledge one's personal limitations and those of the discipline in the resolution of questions posed.
5. To respect the confidentiality due a matter under examination as long as it is under investigation or sub judice, and as long as that confidentiality is sustained by the client and his/her counsel.
6. To maintain technical competence, intellectual currency, and professional skills.
7. To exhibit and to maintain a commitment to excellence in the exercise of professional skills, and to the ideals of integrity, wisdom, and truth.
8. To endorse and to adopt for personal use, such standards of practise as may be or become preferred practises for the conduct of handwriting examination.

It will be obvious from the wording of this proposed code of ethics that the work of the handwriting examiner is being represented as two-phased: (1) examination, and (2) study. The term *examination,* as used in the expression *document examination,* has been employed, almost since the inception of the discipline, as an all-inclusive term covering the various aspects of the work, from writer identification, writing machine discriminations, to sobriety determinations.

The examination, that we have identified elsewhere as the analysis and comparison stages of the three-stage identification process, is the search for and scrutiny of certain facts. It must be followed, however, by a study, that we have identified as the evaluation stage of the identification process, that considers the evidence of similarity or difference, of variation or of change, in the light of extenuating circumstances. The finding of the unusual "black W," in questioned and known writings, or the finding of certain tremours in a writing, will vary as to their significance in different locales or situations. This becomes a matter of "The application of the mind to the acquisition of knowledge," in the words Webster uses to define *study.* It is, in reality, a review and deliberation of the facts, quite apart from the examination and the comparison that disclosed them.

It will also be obvious that we use the term *discipline* rather than *vocation, occupation, field,* or any other term in reference to writing identification or document examination. In this, we have been influenced by the definition of *discipline* provided by Roget's Thesaurus,[56] which is: "An area of academic study that is part of a larger body of learning." In this sense, the term seems more appropriate than any other.

To improve the precision of the language that we are using in matters of some importance we say that the discipline involves the examination and study of documents. For simplicity and the economy of words, we may speak of the discipline, in a somewhat vernacular sense, as *document examination.*

In some respects it can be said that the first clause of this proposed code is, by far, the most important. It prescribes that document examination be conducted on the basis of the three fundamental elements that are characteristic of any scientific pursuit:

1. Building on the universally accepted principles of a science
2. Following the process ordained as *scientific method*
3. Employing the science of reason, i.e., the principles of logic, to draw conclusions from the information any study provides

These three fundamental elements are what distinguish document examination (as it should be practised) from graphology, phrenology, astrology, and the like. Graphology and the others aren't based on scientific principles, they don't follow scientific method and they don't employ logic.

Furthermore, to be a science you cannot have one without the others. You must (1) employ the laws of science as the foundation from which work will proceed. You must (2) systematically pursue knowledge, recognize and formulate the problem, collect data through observation or experimentation, and formulate and test one or more hypotheses. In brief, you must follow the accepted course of scientific method. Finally, (3) the conclusions reached must be only those that reason and/or logic can support. All three are essential ingredients.

Having said all this there remains a number of ethical questions that arise in fields of forensic science and particularly questioned document examination that codes, such as that proposed here, do not seem to address.

These questions probably arise more often in handwriting identification because the field does not and cannot yet control the admission of persons having questionable qualifications and competence. For years, graphologists have moved into the forensic arena of handwriting identification on the premises that: (rightly) graphology deals with the same aspect of human behaviour — handwriting — and that: (wrongly) evaluation for a different purpose does not involve a different competence or sense of evidence. Others, that have had limited instruction or that are essentially self-taught, have also made themselves available to the legal profession and to private individuals, neither of whom were in a position to judge their competence.

The ethical questions that arise might be assembled as one. In the absence of a legally established licensing system, mandatory standards of competence, or broadly accepted appropriate academic qualification, should a competent examiner become involved in a matter in which, in the conduct of another examiner:

1. improper techniques are advocated for the study of the material,
2. improper practises are followed in the examination or report, or
3. improper assertions are made or rhetoric used in oral testimony, such that the reputation of the discipline is put at risk or the pursuits of justice may be jeopardized?

The answer to this question is obvious in extreme cases of incompetence, but there are other cases when the degree of incompetence is less pronounced and less apparent. Moreover, there is no anthology of acceptable books, of recent issue, on writing identification or examination procedures to which courts may refer.

Much has been written on this topic. The American Society of Questioned Document Examiners solicited the views of its most distinguished members (Cole, Conway, Harris, and Purtell) and distributed their comments to members and guests of their 1974 meeting under the title of *Ethics of the Document Examiner.* McNally[57] opposed involvement by a second examiner when the intent was to confuse or distract the judicial process. Lindblom[58] raises several questions on these issues, but provides no answers, other than to suggest that involvement implies partisanship and codes of ethics prescribe impartiality, thereby, prohibiting involvement. This, however, is not a viable argument for it cannot be applied to a second examiner without being applied to the first. We are prompted to ask What became of the old fashioned "Quest for Truth"? Alford[59] spoke on the matter of one examiner reviewing a report of another examiner and suggests that such action may be justified on the principle of an accused's entitlement to the best defence possible. Alford also speaks of providing questions for cross-examination as being generally to discredit the witness, or to attack weaknesses in his/her evidence. None of these authors appear to entertain the thought that the involvement of the second examiner could emanate purely from a quest for truth or the pursuit of the best evidence.

Much that has been written, and certainly the papers cited earlier, tend to oppose involvement by a second examiner, but principally on the basis of motivation; that is, involvement for the purpose of distracting the court, confusing the evidence or impeaching a witness. Such motivation, however, would be unacceptable insofar as any individual acting as a consultant, whether a document examiner or not. An answer must be sought, then, on grounds where motivation is legitimate and honourable, where truth and the interests of the discipline are the principal concerns.

In a more sagacious approach to the question, Knight[60] stated:

"...we possess — or perhaps suffer — the most stringent form of quality control in the form of cross-examination in the courts, where any malpractice, omissions, or fudging is very likely to be revealed both by opposing Counsel and through him by the expert on the "other side."

Obviously, Knight has no doubts that forensic scientists will counsel lawyers regarding the work and testimony of other forensic scientists. Such involvement provides a kind of quality control, and quality control is good for the profession.

The strength of the argument against involvement varies with the kind and qualifications of the individual giving the principal testimony. Many reputable examiners would willingly participate and have done so, when the witness is a graphoanalyst, or someone of questionable integrity. Some have prepared lists of questions for the cross-examination of "graphos" and others, for which the only conceivable purpose would be submission to counsel for their use in court. The renowned Clark Sellers[61] wrote, "If graphologists and graphoanalysts are not so (properly) qualified, should not these shortcomings be made known?" Clearly this is counselling Counsel whether or not it is done in the courtroom.

The American Dental Association Principles of Ethics and Code of Professional Conduct[62] points out that, "A dentist's duty to the public imposes a responsibility to report instances of gross or continued faulty treatment." The American Medical Association Code of Ethics states similarly that "A physician should expose, without fear or favour, incompetent or corrupt, dishonest or unethical conduct on the part of members of the profession." While the analogy to document examination is not true in every sense, there is a degree of correspondence.

There are agonizing situations that document examiners encounter involving the testimony of other expert witnesses, some in which the findings of the other witness are right, but for the wrong reasons. There are other situations in which testimony respecting the identification of a signature is only part of the examination the circumstances demand. Further work would show the document to have been signed in blank, or that material has been added to the document above the signature that alters the intent of the document that it had when the signature was applied.

Thus, the question to be addressed is, when does one counsel a lawyer in cross-examining another handwriting witness? The answer is suggested in the final wording of the ethical question posed earlier: (1) when the pursuits of justice may be jeopardized, and/or (2) when the reputation of the discipline is put at risk.

Other dilemmas arise out of a difference in the evaluation of the evidence within the writing — one examiner considers it sufficient to identify a writer while another considers it only adequate to support a qualified conclusion, e.g., a strong probability. If the second examiner testifies does he/she defeat justice?

We think not. Assuming that the second examiner is correct in his evaluation or honestly feels so, if handwriting evidence is being over evaluated, or under evaluated, the testimony of the first examiner may influence the court to place too much, or too little, reliance upon the handwriting in reaching a decision. This, in fact, may be action that defeats justice. Putting a proper evaluation on physical evidence cannot be defeating justice, but only promoting it.

The issue must not be confused by a consideration of whether the testimony tends to incriminate or to exonerate an individual, whether it supports or weakens a particular side of a case. Physical evidence should be allowed to speak, but only as loudly as it deserves.

The present authors hold that it behooves the competent to do what is necessary to reflect a level of skill, professionalism, and scientific sagacity that will preserve or enhance the reputation of the discipline when it may be at risk, and to ensure that evidence is properly interpreted. If that involves counselling Counsel or court testimony, then so be it. The provisions of the proposed Code of Ethics would allow for involvement in such a matter by a concerned and competent examiner subscribing to such codes.

The issue, however, cannot always be so simply resolved. What are the proper techniques, proper assertions, and proper practises? Are these not matters of opinion on which many practitioners will find that they differ? And if this is so, are judicial forums the proper arena for the resolution of these differences?

Handwriting experts are not alone in contending with such disputes. Many cases can be cited in which medical experts have testified in opposition to one another as to proper standards of practise.[63] If judicial forums are to be avoided, however, what alternatives are available to practitioners to police their own discipline and resolve the arguments? Clearly there are none, and handwriting examiners who are concerned about matters of ethics should be pursuing measures that will settle the issues raised by the questions that we have posed. In the meantime, handwriting examiners will continue to oppose other handwriting examiners, and the courts will continue to wrestle with the question Who do we believe? It might be hoped that in these exchanges the incompetent will learn from the competent, but experience tells us that this is too much to expect.

In a plea for greater professionalism in the American Society of Questioned Document Examiners, Godown[64] asserted, as previously noted, that a professional organization is based, in part, on "unification with regard to ... standards of practise, ethical and practical." In a paper entitled Standards For The Document Examiner, Alwyn Cole ($\geq$1978) appealed for a set of Standards of Practise falling within the document examiner's Code of Ethics dealing more specifically with the description of documents and the writing of reports, among other things. Purdy[65] advocated a quality control system based on the development of a methods manual prescribing axioms governing the handling of documents, the examination of documents, and the writing of reports, among other things.

Notwithstanding what is obviously a reasonable consensus, little has been done to develop Standards of Practise and attention seems long overdue. Standards of practise are simply the answers sought by the questions we raised a moment ago. They should prescribe the proper techniques, proper assertions, and proper practises for work done "at the bench" rather than "before the bench."

Before we proceed too far, let us put the matter of standards into proper perspective. Standards of practise in document examination is not a revolutionary concept. Each practising examiner has his/her own set, whether aware of them or not. They are the rules and procedures that we develop for ourselves, or that are imposed upon us by superiors, regarding the ways that we handle documents, the ways that we examine documents, the ways that we express ourselves with respect to our conclusions, and the ways in which we compose reports and record our facts and our findings.

Osborn[66] prescribed them under different headings, several respecting the care of questioned documents, a number respecting the examination process, a 76-point check list covering all aspects of a document where significant facts may be found, and others respecting the issuance of reports in writing. Little can be read in the writings of other authors regarding examination procedures and the manner of reporting findings. This is understandable if one allows that these publications were not issued as true textbooks.

The Standards of Practise that Cole and Godown were seeking, and that we would like to initiate, are a consolidation of the best of our respective standards, that examiners can agree are the practises that each of us should follow. They will be practises that have been extensively discussed, reviewed, and revised. They will be practises that wisdom and intelligence advance as worthy of universal adoption. Presumably those practises on which agreement is reached will be considered and become, for good reasons, the preferred practises for the conduct of the work, and will assume the role of standards for the discipline.

Standards of practise are not laws or regulations. They carry no punitive consequence when violated. Nevertheless, while compliance is not compulsory, noncompliance places an onus upon the examiner to defend his decision not to follow the practise of his/her peers, but this is only reasonable and to be expected. What should be of even greater importance to document examiners, however, is the message of reassurance that standards convey to the public and to the courts that the discipline is sincere in its endeavours to unify procedures to ensure competence, consistency, and reliability in results. Standards of practise are essential to science. Without them, variables cannot be controlled. Without controls, results cannot be validated. Although seldom recognized for what it is, scientific method is the foremost standard of practise for scientific study.

We offer the following as initial suggestions for standards that should be acceptable to knowledgeable practitioners.

Standards of Practise for the Examination of Handwriting

The Recording of Material

1. A document* on which a writing or lettering is or may be present, that is the subject of an examination and described in a report, shall be identified as an *item* and given an alphabetic or numeric designation. It shall be designated an *exhibit* only if it has been so designated by a judicial forum to which it has been submitted.
2. An item that is the subject of an examination, to which reference is made in a report, shall be described in sufficient detail to discriminate it from any other item of a like nature that may be involved in the same matter.

The Protection of Material

3. Items that are the subject of an examination shall be kept, whenever possible, in clear plastic or cellophane covers and direct contact with them by the hands, writing instruments, and other devices shall be minimized or avoided completely.
4. While documents are in an examiner's custody nothing shall be done to them that will alter their physical state or condition, without the consent of the party for whom they are being examined or his/her counsel.

* For the purpose of these standards, "a document" is considered to include any portion of paper, or of like material or any other substrate on which writing or lettering is or may be present.

The Approach to Examination and Study

5. Whenever possible, an examination of handwriting shall proceed from a study of the known to the unknown. In the process, notation shall be made of the following:
   a. The discriminating elements and their range of variation exhibited by the known
   b. The degree of correspondence that is found in the discriminating elements of the unknown
6. The examination of textual writing in a language in which the examiner is not fluent shall not be conducted without a print-out of the text that identifies each allograph, or the assistance of a person competent to do so.

The Basis and Reporting of Results

7. A definitive conclusion respecting the identification of a questioned writing or signature with provable standards shall be based on (1) the presence of a number of similarities in writing habits, in combination, sufficient in significance to preclude their occurrence by coincidence, and on (2) the absence of inexplicable disparities.
8. In the writing of reports, statements reflecting the consequence of a finding, e.g., that a signature is genuine or spurious, or is a forgery are not to be expressed.
9. Reports respecting a writing/signature appearing in a photograph or photocopy must be phrased to ensure that the findings are understood to relate to a writing or signature on another document, as yet unseen, of which the photograph and/or photocopy examined purports only to be an honest, reliable reproduction.
10. The findings of a handwriting examination are reasoned conclusions drawn from observed and evaluated physical evidence. They should be expressed as *conclusions* in the lexical sense, despite the fact that when stated orally in a civil or criminal litigation they may sometimes constitute opinion testimony in a legal sense.

The Certainty of Conclusions

11. A definitive statement respecting the identification of a signature and/or of a writing is a moral certitude based on a matter of probability at a level that implies that the probability of any other occurrence, while not impossible, is too remote to be considered practical. Accordingly, a conclusion drawn from a writing study is not and cannot be expressed as an absolute certainty.
12. When a questioned signature or writing is examined in isolation from known standards of particular writers, and if appropriate evidence is present, it may be described as "exhibiting classic symptoms of genuineness or spuriousness," but such symptoms are insufficient to support a definitive statement.

The Assertion of Qualifications

13. It is not to be assumed that practise as a graphologist or graphoanalyst is a creditable element of a writing identification examiner's qualifications owing to the risk of conflict between the vocations in studying and evaluating writing habits.

Undoubtedly there are other standards of practise worthy of inclusion. Moreover, there may be good reason for modifying or reconsidering some that are offered here. Unquestionably, standards of practise such as these will run into conflict with old habits that are well ingrained in both practitioners and laboratories. These standards, however, are proposed simply as a beginning to solve a need that has been recognized by leading examiners for 25 years. Although standards of practise have been a stated objective of professional bodies of document examiners, as yet, none has attempted to prescribe a set for consideration and adoption.

We would reiterate that insofar as the terms of a code of ethics and the provisions of a set of standards of practise, we are not revolutionizing the approach of the examiner to his/her discipline. We are merely formalizing in more understandable terms what has underlay the "bench work" of the examiner for many years, perhaps since its inception, but which has escaped much needed attention. Consequently, codes and standards vary with the individual examiner and/or with the organization in which he/she is employed. As we said earlier, however, in order for writing examination to qualify as science, the pursuit of universal agreement is required in most, if not all, things. In this pursuit, the guise of science is the same for all intellectual excercises.

There may be opposition in many sectors to the adoption of some sections of our proposed standards. If these standards or the proposed code of ethics above stimulate thinking and discussion, however, perchance they may provoke action.

References

1. Swett, George C., *Science and Document Examination.* Presented at the meeting of the American Society of Questioned Document Examiners (1959).

2. Sellers, Clark, *The Scientific Approach.* Presented at the meeting of the American Society of Questioned Document Examiners (1941).

3. Cole, Alwyn, Cross Examination. *RCMP Gazette,* 1946 January 23; 8: 4.

4. The Universal Standard Encyclopaedia. *Science,* 1954; 21: p 7564.

5. Casey, Maureen A., *Is Handwriting Identification a Science?* Presented at the meeting of the American Society of Questioned Document Examiners (1968).

6. Brohier, G., *Towards a Mature Profession.* Presented at the joint meeting of the American Society of Questioned Document Examiners and RCMP Labs (Ottawa, 1965).

7. Margenau, Henry and Bergamini, David, *The Scientist* (New York: Time Inc. Life Science Library, 1964).

8. *Random House Dictionary of the English Language.* 2nd ed. (New York: Random House, 1987).

9. *Oxford English Dictionary.* 2nd ed. (Oxford: Clarendon Press, 1989).

10. *Webster's New Encyclopedic Dictionary* (New York: B.D. & L., 1994), p 912.

11. Margenau, Henry and Bergamini, David, *The Scientist* (New York: Time Inc. Life Science Library, 1964), p 30.

12. Campbell, Norman, *What Is Science?* (New York: Dover Publications Inc, 1952), p 27.

13. Sullivan, J. W. N., *The Limitations of Science* (New York: New American Library, 1949), p 169.

14. Margenau, Henry and Bergamini, David, *The Scientist* (New York: Time Inc. Life Science Library, 1964), p 54.

15. Huber, Roy A. and Headrick, A. M. (Tom), Let's Do It by Numbers. *Forensic Science International,* 1990; 46: 209-218.

16. Found, Bryan, Rogers, Doug, and Schmittat, Robert, A Computer Program Designed to Compare the Spatial Elements of Handwriting. *Forensic Science International*, 1994; 68: pp 195-203.

17. Quine, W. V., The Scope and Language of Science. *British Journal for the Philosophy of Science*, 1957; 8: 29: pp 2 and 5. With permission.

18. Tripp, Clarence A., Fluckiger, Fritz A., and Weinberg, George H., Measurement in Handwriting Variables. *Perceptual and Motor Skills*, 1957; 7: pp 279-294. (27 references)

19. van der Plaats, Rudolph E. and van Galen, Gerard P., Effects of Spatial and Motor Demands in Handwriting. *Journal of Motor Behaviour*, 1990; 22: 3: pp 361-385. (39 references)

20. Brault, Jean-Jules and Plamondon, Réjean, A Complexity Measure of Handwritten Curves: Modelling of Dynamic Signature Forgery. *IEEE Transactions on System, Man and Cybernetics*, 1993 March/April; 23: 2: (64 references)

21. Plamondon, R. and Lorette, G., Automatic Signature Verification and Writer Identification — the State of the Art. *Pattern Recognition*, 1989; 22: pp 107-131.

22. Totty, R. N. and Hardcastle, R. A., A Preliminary Assessment of the SIGNCHECK System for Signature Authentication. *Journal of the Forensic Science Society*, 1986; 26: pp 181-195.

23. Brocklehurst, E. R., Computer Methods of Signature Verification. *Journal of the Forensic Science Society*, 1985; 25: pp 445-457.

24. El-Wakil, Mohamed S. and Shoukry, Amin A., On-Line Recognition of Handwritten Isolated Arabic Characters. *Pattern Recognition*, 1989; 22: 2: pp 97-105.

25. *U.S. v. Starzcepyzel*, (880 Fed. Sup. 1027, April 4, 1995).

26. Risinger, D. M., Denbeaux, M. P., and Saks, M. J., Exorcism of Ignorance as a Proxy for Rational Knowledge: the Lessons of Handwriting Identification "Expertise." *University of Pensylvania Law Review*, 1989; 137: pp 731-792.

27. Buglio, James and Wiersema, Sandra J., *An Examination of Assertions Concerning the Validity or Reliability of Handwriting Identification Expertise.* Presented at the meeting of the American Society of Questioned Document Examiners (Arlington, VA, 1989).

28. Scott, Charles C., Errata. *American Society of Questioned Document Examiners Newsletter*, 1989 Fall.

29. Crown, David A., Statistical Articles. *American Society of Questioned Document Examiners Newsletter*, 1989 Fall.

30. Wenderoth, Mary, Frye Test and Competency. *American Society of Questioned Document Examiners Newsletter*, 1989 Fall.

31. Galbraith III, Oliver, Galbraith, Craig, and Galbraith, Nanette G., *The "Principle of the Drunkard's Search" as a Proxy for Scientific Analysis: the Misuse of Handwriting Test Data in a Law Journal Article.* Presented at the meeting of the American Society of Questioned Document Examiners (Crystal City, VA, August 1989).

32. Found, Bryan and Rogers, Doug, Contemporary Issues in Forensic Handwriting Examination. A Discussion of Key Issues in the Wake of the Starzecpyzal Decision. *Journal of Forensic Document Examination*, 1995 Fall; 8: pp 1-31.

33. Huber, Roy A., *Handwriting Examination as a Scientific Discipline.* Presented at the meeting of the American Society of Questioned Document Examiners (Chicago, 1995).

34. Harvey, O. L., The Measurement of Handwriting Considered as a Form of Expressive Movement. *Character and Personality*, 1934; 2: pp 310-321.

35. Birge, W. R., An Experimental Enquiry into the Measurable Handwriting Correlates of Five Personality Traits. *Journal of Personality*, 1954; 23: pp 215-223.

36. Lockowandt, O., *Present Status of the Investigation of Handwriting Psychology as a Diagnostic Method*. Journal Supplement Abstract Service, American Psychological Association, 1976.

37. Squire, H. W., *Graphology as a Method of Selecting Employees* (The Ohio State University: unpublished Master's thesis, Department of Business Administration, 1967).

38. Harris, John J., How Much do People Write Alike? *Journal of Criminal Law, Criminology and Police Science,* 1958; 48: 6.

39. Frederick, C. J., An Investigation of Handwriting and Suicide Persons through Suicide Notes. *Journal of Abnormal Psychology,* 1968; 73: pp 263-267.

40. Kam, Moshe, Wetstein, Joseph, and Conn, Robert, Proficiency of Document Examiners in Writer Identification. *Journal of Forensic Sciences,* 1994; 39: 4.

41. Rafaeli, A. and Klimoski, R. J., Predicting Sales Success through Handwriting Analysis. An Evaluation of the Effects of Training and Handwritten Sample Content. *Journal of Applied Psychology,* 1983; 68: pp 212-217.

42. O'Block, Robert L., The Status of Academic Education in Forensic Document Examination. *Journal of Questioned Document Examination,* 1992; 1: 2: pp 4-14.

43. Found, Bryan and Rogers, Doug, Contemporary Issues in Forensic Handwriting Examination. A Discussion of Key Issues in the Wake of the Starzecpyzel Decision. *Journal of Forensic Document Examination,* 1995 fall; 8: pp 1-31. With permission.

44. Editorial, But is This Being Professional? *Journal of the Forensic Science Society,* 1992; 32(2): pp 99-100.

45. Flores, Albert W., What Kind of Person Should a Professional Be? *Professional Ideals,* ed. Albert Flores (Belmont CA: Wadsworth Publishing Co., 1988).

46. Huber, Roy A., Police Work — Profession or Trade? *International Review of Criminal Policy* (New York: United Nations, 1977), 33. (A reprint of a paper written in 1971)

47. Godown, Linton, *Marks of the Professional.* Presented at the meeting of the American Society of Questioned Document Examiners (Houston, TX, 1970).

48. Ravetz, Jerome R., *Scientific Knowledge and its Social Problems* (London: Oxford University Press, 1971).

49. Hilton, Ordway, *Ethics and the Document Examiner.* Presented at the meeting of the American Society of Questioned Document Examiners (Milwaukee, WI, 1974).

50. Watts, Geoff, Seeing through Professionalism. *New Scientist,* 1979 March: p 881.

51. Newton, Lisa H., Lawgiving for Professional Life: Reflections on the Place of the Professional Code. *Business and Professional Ethics Journal,* 1981 fall; pp 41-53.

52. Hilton, Ordway, Ethics and the Document Examiner under the Adversary System. *Journal of Forensic Sciences,* 1976; 21: 4: pp 779-783.

53. Anon., The State of the Profession. The Caducity of Truth in the Forensic Sciences. *Scientific Sleuthing Review,* 1994; 18: 2.

54. Hilton, Ordway, *Document Examination and the ASQDE Code of Ethics.* Presented at the meeting of the American Society of Questioned Document Examiners (Aurora, CO, 1988).

55. Anon., *Code of Professional Conduct.* Published by the office of the Auditor General of Canada, 1983.

56. American Heritage Dictionary Editors. *Roget's II The New Thesaurus* (Boston: Haughton Miffin Co., 1980).

57. McNally, Gregory A., *Professional Ethics in the Court Room — Assisting in Cross Examination.* Presented at the meeting of the American Academy of Forensic Sciences (Philadelphia, 1988).

58. Lindblom, Brian, *The Examiner as Forensic Consultant and Expert Witness — Professional and Ethical Considerations.* Presented at the meeting of the American Society of Questioned Document Examiners (Orlando, 1991).

59. Alford, E. F., *Responsibilities and the Document Examiner.* Presented at the meeting of the American Society of Questioned Document Examiners (Colorado Springs, CO, 1975).

60. Knight, Bernard, Ethics and Discipline in Forensic Science. *Journal of the Forensic Science Society,* 1988; 29: 1: pp 53-59.

61. Sellers, Clark, *Rights and Responsibilities of a Questioned Document Examiner.* Presented at the meeting of the American Society of Questioned Document Examiners (Lexington, 1968).

62. Gorlin, Rena A., ed. *Codes of Professional Responsibility.* 2nd ed. (Washington: BNA Books, 1990).

63. Harris, John J. and Mills, Don Harper, Medical Records and the Questioned Document Examiner. *Journal of Forensic Sciences,* 1963; 8: 3: p 456.

64. Godown, Linton, Op. cit.

65. Purdy, Dan C., *Basic Elements of a Quality Assurance System for Forensic Document Examiners.* Presented at the meeting of the International Association of Forensic Sciences (Oxford, 1984).

66. Osborn, Albert S., *Questioned Documents.* 2nd ed. (Albany: Boyd Printing Co., 1929), pp 20-22, 286-293.

Graphology

15

80. What Is Graphology All About?

Graphology is an endeavour to correlate handwriting features with personality traits. It is not handwriting identification per se.

For different reasons, interest in handwriting as a purveyor of information respecting the writer has probably existed as long as writing has been common to society. Camilo Baldi, an Italian scholar and physician, in 1622, published *Treatise on a Method to Recognize the Nature and Quality of a Writer from his Letters*, a book that is credited with being one of the first to make public an intellectual interest in the subject. Johann Kasper Lavater at the University of Zurich is reported to have written and published on similar subjects in the late years of the eighteenth century, but not until the publication of the works of Abbe Jean Hippolyte Michon of France, in 1871, on *The Practical System of Graphology* was the generic term coined for handwriting analysis.

Around 1900, a disciple of Michon, Crepieux-Jamin, because of his interest in the French psychologist Alfred Binet, originator of the first intelligence tests, pursued Michon's studies in handwriting analysis as a technique for testing personality.

Since then, interest has been expressed by many writers in many countries, to the point where libraries now offer a wide selection of books on graphology, of an equally wide range of quality. Notwithstanding their range, these books generally represent variants of three major schools of graphology — the trait school, the Gestalt school, and the grapho-analysis system.

The trait school, of which Michon was an early proponent, claims graphic signs (e.g., length, width, or slant of a certain stroke) reflect specific personal traits.

The Gestalt school, that evolved later and largely in Germany under the influence of Ludwig Klages, advocated (1910) that graphological interpretations must be based on the examination of writing as a whole entity, and not from individual configurations. Klages dealt with "expressive movements" rather than particular graphological elements. The Gestalt approach deviates significantly from the trait school in relying on judgment and intuition of the graphologist. Following Klages, other authors, e.g., Dr. Bernard Wittlich and Dr. Klara Roman, attempted to integrate individual graphological traits into the Gestalt picture of the writer.

In 1929, M. N. Bunker founded *graphoanalysis* as a middle-of-the-road compromise between the one-to-one sign graphology that typified the French trait school and the broad intuitive Gestalt graphology of the German school. Bunker's contention that related traits produce an overall effect different from that of any single trait is referred to as the *holistic* or *global* personality pattern, whereas the approach of the trait school of France is labelled *atomistic*.

So, contrary to the manner in which many have used the term as synonymous with graphology, graphoanalysis is, in fact, merely one of three principle approaches to handwriting analysis, that fall under the umbrella of graphology.

Graphology is presently proffered in a variety of applications:

1. In personnel selection
2. In aptitude determinations
3. In studies of the effects of certain mental health conditions
4. In forensic identifications
5. As a psycho diagnostic tool

Many persons have been critical of the research performed in this area and have publicly condemned graphology as a fraudulent pursuit. Many document examiners on this continent share these sentiments. Unfortunately, the arguments proffered against graphology have been, too often, as flawed as the research in support of it.

Writing is a self-recorded behaviour and any specific domain of behaviour can be considered a legitimate object of research in differential psychology:

1. If people differ from one another in respect of this behaviour (heterogeneity)
2. If the behaviour is reasonably stable and can be recorded and measured reliably (reliability)
3. If the behaviour is significant on its own merits or is related to some other interesting psychological trait or behaviour (validity)[1]

While prominent psychologists expressed an interest in the behavioral domain of handwriting 75 years ago, scientific handwriting psychology today is a more neglected area. Undoubtedly, the negative findings regarding the validity of handwriting interpretations, the lack of ethics, the low professional standards, and the pretensions of hundreds of graphologists who lacked formal education in psychology have contributed to the suspicious attitude of professional people towards graphology. Solicitations for the empirical data on which graphology is presumed to be based, made through the officers or offices of eight organizations of persons engaged in graphology that were listed in the Yearbook of International Organizations (1983), met with completely negative results.[2]

However, as Nevo[3] has stated:

"There is no sense in fighting phoney graphologists by ignoring the whole domain of handwriting behaviour. Relinquishing graphology into the hands of nonprofessionals has already caused great damage."

Notwithstanding Nevo's appeal, the literature is still populated with controversial dissertations[4-7] by persons employed under the authorities of reputable institutions endeavouring to establish the validity of graphology as a predictor of academic achievement,[8] as a predictor of occupational success,[9-10] as a personnel selector,[11] as a predictor of success in women,[12] or as a reliable instrument for other purposes. Even the training, certification, and experience of graphologists[13] has been the subject of scrutiny. Despite the copious quantities of studies conducted on the discipline, its usefulness is still in serious doubt. Even if one was to accept the idea that some personal information is sometimes conveyed through a person's handwriting, the question remains, How strong is the phenomenon? In a recent statement, Nevo[14] has conceded that, "On the basis of these (current) findings, the practical application of graphology as a single psychodiagnostic tool cannot, in fact, be recommended."

Few persons have been as comprehensive in their review of graphological research as Klimoski and Rafaeli.[15] These authors methodically set out the ground rules for acceptable scientific research in handwriting. They critically and objectively review the important writings on the subject of recent years, and then cautiously and conservatively conclude that:

> "...graphology should not be ruled out as a possible additional source of information in a diagnostic or selection context.... But script (handwriting) analysis used in this manner has yet to be (properly) evaluated. Thus, given the evidence we do have, great reliance on inferences based on script must be considered unwarranted."

For anyone uncertain as to its usefulness, Klimoski and Rafaeli have provided a criteria for examination in evaluating graphological studies as follows:

1. Reliability of the behaviour tested (handwriting)
2. Reliability of handwriting interpretation:
   a. conspect reliability (agreement between analysts on inferences from the same writing sample)
   b. reliability of inferences (consistency of judgments across different samples)
3. Representativeness of the writing samples
4. Validity (correctness of a graphological assessment)
5. Professional skill in analysis (knowledge and training vs. intuition)

It is in one or more of these respects that graphology has failed, to date, to render itself acceptable to the scientific community. Indeed, it constitutes a large part of the criteria that we have suggested (see Section 77: What Must Be Done to Make Handwriting Identification A Science?) that handwriting identification itself must meet to be included under the umbrella of science.

However, Klimoski and Rafaeli, Nevo, and other authors of the last two decades have offered more than a critical review of graphological research and an evaluation of graphological principles in which much has been found wanting. They have recommended specific objectives for proper research into handwriting and presented a challenge to those who will pursue new studies in handwriting behaviour according to new standards.

References

1. Nevo, Baruch, ed. *Scientific Aspects of Graphology* (Springfield Ill: Charles C Thomas, 1986), p vii.

2. Moore, Michael, About the Sad State of Scientific Graphology. *Psychological Documents,* 1985; 15: 1.

3. Nevo, Baruch, Op. cit., p viii.

4. Vestewig, R. E., Santee, A. H., and Moss, M. K., Validity and Student Acceptance of a Graphoanalytic Approach to Personality. *Journal of Personality Assessment,* 1976; 40: pp 592-598.

5. Crumbaugh, J. C., A Reply to "Validity and Student Acceptance of a Graphoanalytic Approach to Personality" by Vestewig, Santee, and Moss. *Journal of Personality Assessment,* 1977; 41: pp 351-352.

6. Vestewig, R. E. and Moss, M. K., On the Validity of Graphoanalysis: A Rejoinder to Crumbaugh's Reply. *Journal of Personality Assessment,* 1977; 41: pp 589-590.

7. Crumbaugh, James C., On the Validity of Graphoanalysis: A Rebuttal of Vestewig and Moss' Rejoinder to Crumbaugh's Reply to "Validity and Student Acceptance of a Graphoanalytic Approach to Personality" *Perceptual and Motor Skills,* 1988; 67: pp 461-462.

8. Oosthuizen, Stanley, Graphology as a Predictor of Academic Achievement. *Perceptual and Motor Skills,* 1990; 71: pp 715-721.

9. Nevo, Baruch, Yes. Graphology can Predict Occupational Success: Rejoinder to Ben Shakhar et al. *Perceptual and Motor Skills,* 1988; 66: pp 92-94.

10. Ben-Shakhar, Gershon, Bar-Hillel, Maya, Bilu, Yoram, Ben-Abba, Edor, and Flug Anat, Can Graphology Predict Occupational Success? Two Empirical Studies and Some Methodological Ruminations. *Journal of Applied Psychology,* 1986; 71: 4: pp 645-653.

11. Rafaeli, Anat and Drory, Amos, Graphological Assessments for Personnel Selection: Concerns and Suggestions for Research. *Perceptual and Motor Skills,* 1988; 66: pp 743-759.

12. Wellingham-Jones, Patricia, Evaluation of the Handwriting of Successful Women through the Roman-Staempfli Psychogram. *Perceptual and Motor Skills,* 1989; 69: pp 999-1010.

13. Peeples, E. Edward, Training, Certification, and Experience of Handwriting Analysts. *Perceptual and Motor Skills,* 1990; 70: pp 1219-1226.

14. Nevo, Baruch, Validation of Graphology Through Use of a Matching Method Based on Ranking. *Perceptual and Motor Skills,* 1989; 69: pp 1331-1336.

15. Klimoski, Richard J. and Rafaeli, Anat, Inferring Personal Qualities Through Handwriting Analysis. *Journal of Occupational Psychology,* 1983; 56: pp 191-202.

Understanding the Terms

16

81. How Might One Best Identify, Describe, or Refer to the Various Elements of the Graphemes of Writing and/or Lettering, their Designs, their Constructions, and their Correlation?

There seems to be considerable diversity in the manner in which examiners identify, describe, or refer to the various elements of the graphemes of writing and/or lettering? Some of the expressions employed are quite homegrown, others are quite descriptive and readily identified with the circumstances in which they are used. Our concern is with the variety of terms that are employed, that we feel are not characteristic of a profession. In the interests of lucidity, some terms or expressions should be discouraged.

Every discipline, whether scientific or not, has a language of its own. There are terms that the practitioners of the discipline have found or coined to more precisely describe their work or the materials with which they deal. Indeed, it has been suggested that a discipline without a language of its own has made little progress. Document examiners have theirs, although, as was stated at the beginning of this dissertation, a certain consistency in language and other things is lacking. The same terminology should describe the same subject, but our experience has been that it doesn't.

The relatively new field of graphonomics may have some influence on the situation for the level of research being conducted is demanding greater precision in the nomenclature used and their meanings. The following are terms that are being and have been utilized, respecting the examination of writing with the meanings that they should convey. A few terms have been added that respect other examinations within the purview of the document examiner, that may serve only to broaden, in a small way, the reader's understanding of the scope of the work.

82. Glossary

Abbreviation　A shortened form of a word or title.

Accent　A mark indicating an emphasis on a syllable or word or quality of a vowel sound, sometimes called diacritics or diacritical accents. It may be positioned above, below, or through the alphabetic character.

Accent	Name	Example	Accent	Name	Example
´	acute	á	‾	macron	Ā
\	grave	à	˘	breve	ă
^	circumflex	ê	¨	diaeresis	ä
~	tilde	Ã	,	cedilla	ç

Acronyms　Abbreviations of private and governmental agencies or organizations in which the initial letters of the words in the name are written and spoken as a single word, e.g., NATO.

Affix　A morpheme attached to a word root, a prefix, or a suffix.

Alignment　The spatial organization of the writing pattern, its linear arrangement of words and intervening spaces and their accommodation on the page.

Allograph　A writing or signature made by one person for another; or a style (block capital, print script, or cursive form) of one of the 26 graphemes of the English alphabet or of the ligatures and other symbols that accompany it (Ellis 1979).

Allolog　Different forms of a word created by adding an affix, e.g., hope to hoped.

Alphabet　A system of writing in which a set of allographs represent the graphemes of a language.

Ambidexterity　Equal skill and facility with both hands.

Ampersand (ampassy)　The sign, "&," used as a symbol for "and" in several hundred languages.

Ample letter　That which encompasses more than the standard inner space in a given letter. Characterized by fulsomeness and expanded ovals and loops.

Angular　See connective forms.

Apex　Up-pointing or down-pointing free-ending juncture of two stems, e.g., "A," "M," "V," or "W."

Aphasia　The loss of a previous ability to speak, or impairment of the power to use and understand words.

Apostrophe　The superscript sign, " ' ," used to indicate the omission of a letter from a word, the possessive case, and certain plurals.

Appendage or paraph　A final pen-flourish of a free sweeping line made over or under a name written as a signature; sometimes a simple terminal stroke or dot.

Arc　Part of a circle; a bow-like curved line.

Arcade The rounded style used to form the arches of the cursive letters "n," "m," and "h."

Arch The rounded hump or top curve of such letters as "n," "m," and "h."

Arm A horizontal or upward-sloping short stroke starting from the stem of a character, ending free, e.g., "K," "E," or "F."

Arrangement The order or organization of a written inscription on a sheet.

Ascender Part of the lowercase letters extending above the body or x-height, e.g., "b," "d," "h," or "k," usually a loop, but including the stem of the "t."

Assisted writing The result of a guided hand, produced by the cooperation of the two minds and two hands of two persons.

Asterisk A star-shaped symbol or figure, "*," used to indicate a reference to a footnote or an omission.

Autograph A person's signature, his handwriting; a manuscript in an author's own handwriting.

Axial direction In the direction of the axis.

Balloon Printing that resembles speed ball-pen lettering.

Ball-point pen A writing instrument having as its distinguishing feature or characteristic a writing tip containing a rotatable ball that contacts the writing surface for the purpose of depositing the writing fluid.

Ball terminal Small round globe, found at the end of some printing strokes, e.g., "r" and "g."

Bar Horizontal or oblique short final stroke of some cursive letters, not to be confused with terminal strokes.

Bar, connecting Intermediate stroke, connecting strokes of a letter to other strokes, usually a dual-staffed letter.

Bar, cross A stroke intersecting the stem or main portion of the letter; a cross-stroke.

Baroque Certain stylistic tendencies of the seventeenth and eighteenth century arts, characterized by exuberance and extravagance — grotesque, whimsical — used in reference to older designs of currency.

Base line The horizontal real or assumed line upon which letters reside.

Beard A slight hook preceding the body of a letter, not to be confused with that frequently forming a part of the initial stroke.

Beginning strokes See strokes, initial.

Bitmap A mosaic of dots or pixels defining an image, including dot matrix imprints. The smoothness of the image contour depends upon the fineness of resolution and the number of dots or pixels per inch.

Blind eyelet An eyelet formation of such small size or narrow width that it has been filled in.

Blind loop   A loop formation that has been completely filled in with ink.

Block formation   Letters set so closely together within a word as to make the word stand out as a compact unit or block.

Blobbing   The accumulation of ink on the exterior of the point assembly of a ball-point pen, that drops intermittently to the surface being written upon.

Blotter image   A natural, involuntary record on a blotter or similar substrate of script, figures, etc.

Blunt ending   The effect produced on commencement and terminal strokes of letters, both upper and lowercase, by the application of the writing instrument to the paper prior to the beginning of any horizontal movement; an action that usually omits any beard, hitch, knob, or tick.

Boat   A dish-shaped figure consisting of a concave stroke and a straight line, sometimes forming the base of letters.

Body   That portion of a letter, the central part, that remains when the upper and lower projections, the terminal and initial strokes, and the diacritics are omitted.

Body-height   See x-height.

Bold face   A heavier version of a regular typeface; used for emphasis or visual effect.

Boustrophedon   Writing in which alternate lines are written in opposite directions and even have the posture as well as the direction of reversed letters.

Bow   A vertical curved stroke, as in capitals "D" and "C."

Bowl   The line fully enclosing a counter; a complete bowl, formed by a curved stroke only; a modified bowl, in which the stem forms a side of the bowl.

Braces   Two symbols ( ), used to connect or segregate written material.

Bracket or fellet   A wedge-shaped structure joining a serif to a stem.

Braille   A system of representing letters, numerals, etc., by raised dots that a visually-impaired person can read by touch.

Brush   Balloon-style printing extended to a script.

Buckle knot   The loop followed by a horizontal stroke that is sometimes used to complete letters such as the "A," "f," and "t."

Buckles   The means by which an element of a letter ties itself to the staff, as in the letters "K" and "R."

Burring   A division of a written line into two or more, more or less equal portions, by a noninked area generally running parallel to the direction of line generation, but moving away from the radius of a curving stroke, sometimes referred to as "splitting."

Cane   See "strokes, walking cane."

Caret   A mark, "∧" used to show where something is to be inserted in written or printed matter.

Capital letter or capital   Uppercase or majuscule (see also "uncial").

Character   Any typed or handwritten mark, sign or insignia, abbreviation, punctuation mark, letter, or numeral, whether legible, blurred, or indistinct.

Check mark   A mark usually consisting of a short downward stroke, made with considerable pressure, followed by a lighter upward stroke at an angle toward the right (or to the left, as constructed by most, if not many, left-handed writers).

Chevrons   Horizontal (see "guillemets").

Cicero   A typographic unit of measurement used predominantly in Europe. It consists of 12 Didot points, each measuring .01483 inch. Thus, a cicero is .1776 or 4.511 mm.

Cipher   The arithmetic symbol "0," representing naught or zero.

Clockwise   The direction in which the hands of the clock move.

Coadjutant   One who works together with another; the individual providing enabling aid to a signer or signatory of a document, when required.

Codicil   A supplement to a will, the purpose of which is to alter or augment the provisions of the already executed will.

Collected standards   A sample of writing made during the normal course of business or social activity, not necessarily related to the matter in dispute.

Colophon   A short note at the end of a book, usually handwritten, giving details of its author and the making of the book. Also, the emblem or device of a publishing house, carried on the spine, title page or back of a book.

Concave   A curved stroke that projects to the left or downward.

Condensed face   A typeface that has narrow letter widths.

Conjoined letters   Two letters that have been written in the common manner, such that the terminal stroke of the first is the initial stroke of the second.

Connectedness, degree of   The extent to which letters within a word are joined without lifting the writing instrument from the paper.

Connecting stroke   An expression commonly used to refer to the fusion of the terminal stroke of one lowercase cursive letter and the initial stroke of another, having no identifiable or describable entity of its own (see "conjoined letters").

Connection subtypes

> Unsupported — the body of the letter does not follow or retrace the stem.
> Supported — the body of the letter rests against or retraces the stem.
> Looped — the initial stroke forms a loop with the stem of the letter.

Contraction   A form of word abbreviation wherein one or more letters are omitted.

Convex   A curved stroke that projects to the right or upward.

Copybook   A manual of writing instruction that places models before the learner, to be copied.

Counter   A printer's term for the fully or partially-enclosed interior white space within a character, as in the "a," "b," "c," "d," "e," "g," "j," "o," "p," "q," "s," and many capitals.

Counterclockwise   The direction opposite to the movement of a clock's hands.

Counterstroke   A stroke that originates from a movement that stresses a direction opposite to the expected one.

Crossbar   The connecting horizontal stroke between two stems of a letter, as in "A" or "H," or the projecting horizontal stroke necessary for the formation of a letter, as in the cursive "t," or the printed "f."

Cross mark   A crude "X" used historically by those who could not write. Still used by illiterates and, if properly witnessed, can be legally accepted as a signature.

Crotch   Space where an arm or an arc meets a stem at an acute or obtuse angle.

Crown (cap)   The horizontal (sometimes undulating) stroke forming the top of some letters; found only in majuscules, "T," "F."

Cursive   A form of continuous writing in which letters are connected to one another, and designed according to some commercial system; the most common allograph of a grapheme.

Curtailment   An abbreviation wherein the last letter(s) of a word are omitted.

Curvilinear   Consisting of or contained by a curved line or lines; opposite of rectilinear.

Cusp   The point at which two curved lines meet.

Dash   Short, usually horizontal, hastily written stroke.

Delta   Fourth letter of the Greek alphabet, "δ," the Greek d.

Dent   Slight hollow formation.

Descender   A part of a letter extending below the base line, as in "g," "j," "p," "q," "y."

Dextrality   Right-hand preference, as opposed to sinistrality or left-hand preference.

Diacritical mark or point   A sign added to a letter or symbol to give it a particular phonetic value. An accent. Sometimes used to refer to the dots over the "i" and "j."

Diagonal stroke   See "virgule."

Didot system   A typographic measuring system, used in Europe and based on the Didot point, similar to the U.S.-English pica system (see cicero).

Digraph   A group of two successive letters representing a single sound or a complex sound that is not a combination of the sounds ordinarily represented by each in other occurrences, e.g., "ph" in digraph, "ch" in chin.

Diphthong   The combination of two vowels in succession, the sound of which begins with one and ends with the other, e.g., "oil," "boy," or "out."

Directional skipping   A skip that may occur after an abrupt (≥90 degree) change in the direction of line generation.

Disguise   The consequence of any deliberate attempt to alter the elements of one's own writing.

Disguised writing   The writing of a person who is deliberately attempting to alter his/her usual writing habits in the hope of concealing his/her identity.

Dismembered letter   A letter that lacks a structural part, is separated into parts, or has a part cut off.

Displacement   A stroke or letter written in one zone when it normally belongs in another.

Document   Any material that carries a communication, explicit or implied.

Dominating stroke   An extended horizontal stroke above a word; it may be an extended t-bar.

Dot   A minute, roundish, solid mark. Also called a point or period. It signifies interruption, stop, or silence.

Dotting   The deposit of small amounts of extraneous ink on the paper, occurring with predictable regularity under given conditions.

Double-length letters   Small or lowercase letters that have components that extend both above and below the x-height of the letter, e.g., "f."

Downstroke   That part of a letter that is made when the writing instrument is moving from the top to the bottom of the letter, or a stroke directed toward the bottom of the paper.

Drag line   A very thin or light stroke of a writing instrument in areas where its movement is not normally recorded.

Duct   A stroke drawn or traced.

Ductus, link or junction-connected   The continuous line that joins two letters.

Ductus-broken or junction-broken   The disconnected or noncontinuous stroke between two letters.

Dys-   Destroying the good sense of a word, e.g., "dysfunction."

Dysgraphics   Inability to write or draw with any skill (Beacom).

Dyslexia   A disturbance of the ability to read.

Ear   the small stroke projecting from the top of the lowercase "g" in the printed letter. Sometimes given to a similar element of the printed letter "r."

Elision   An abbreviation usually made for metrical and linguistic reasons that frequently affects the pronunciation of the word.

Ellipsis   A mark "…", used to indicate the omission of a part of quoted material or of words needed to complete a sentence.

Em space   A typographic unit of horizontal space, equal to the point size of any font.

En space   A typographic unit of horizontal space, equal to one half of the point size of any font.

Ending stroke   Finishing stroke of a letter.

Endstroke   The terminal stroke of a written form, word, or letter.

Endstroke obliteration   An endstroke that thrusts abruptly to the left, bisecting a word or signature crosswise.

Epistle   A letter or communication, especially a formal one.

Epsilon   The fifth letter of the Greek alphabet, "ε," representing the letter "e."

Escapement   The spacing of the letters or characters along the line of typewriting; the pitch.

Essential tremour   A common neurological condition causing tremour of the arms, and/or hands.

Exclamation mark   A punctuation mark "!," used after an exclamation.

Exemplar   An example of a person's writing, a standard for use in comparisons, a "collected" or a "request" specimen.

Expanded typeface   A typeface that has wide letter widths.

Expansion   The spread of writing, usually horizontally, upon the writing space.

Extended writing   Writing, usually cursive, of a textual nature, of any amount, but other than a signature.

Extensions   Ascending and descending stems and loops of bizonal and trizonal letters.

Eyelet, blind   An eyelet formation of such size or width that it is "filled in."

Eyelet   A small, round or oval formation beginning or closing a curve or spiral, or completing the inside shape of a round letter, e.g., "e," "D," or "w."

Facsimile   An image of printed matter that has been transmitted electronically.

Feathering   The condition in which the writing/printing fluid spreads laterally in a pattern that usually follows the direction of the surface fibres away from the written or printed line. Characteristic of intaglio printing involving extreme pressures of the plate on the paper; thus, also called *gushing*.

Fixed spacing   Uniform horizontal spacing of the characters of a type font, as opposed to proportional spacing that varies with the design of the character.

Flourish   A decorative pen stroke that serves only as an ornament.

Flow-back   An increase in the density of an ink line caused by the run of excess ink along the finish of a stroke, occurring when the pen is lifted from the paper.

Fluctuation   Alternating changes of direction, position or conditions, i.e., alternating acceleration and deceleration of writing speed, or alternating expansion and contraction of the writing pattern.

Fluency Freedom, and other like terms, referring to a generally higher grade of line quality that is smooth, consistent, and without any evidence of tremour or erratic changes in direction or pen pressure.

Fluorescence The phenomena in which some substances absorb light and re-emit part of it as light of a longer wave length. Fluorescence ceases when incident or exciting illumination ceases.

Flying finish The diminishing taper of a terminal stroke when the motion of the instrument does not stop at the completion of a word, or the minute barb sometimes growing out of it.

Flying start The growing taper of an initial stroke, or the delicate initial hook, that appears where the motion of the instrument precedes actual writing.

Folio Originally, four pages of text on a single sheet of paper.

Font (= fount) A complete set or collection of letters, figures, symbols, punctuation marks, and special characters that are of the same design and size, for a particular typeface.

Foot That portion of the downstroke of a letter, written or printed, touching the base line.

Forced hand A person's signature or writing executed while the hand was under the physical compulsion or control of another person.

Forward oval An oval made by a clockwise circular motion.

Fount See "font."

Fraudulent handwriting The forgery of a signature, a word, a figure, a number of lines of writing, or of an entire document.

Freehand simulation A fraudulent signature that is produced by copying or imitating the style and size of a genuine signature, without the use of physical aids or involving a tracing process.

Garlanded A writing style in which rounded trough-like strokes and movements dominate.

Gooping The accumulation of excessive amounts of ink on the exterior of the point assembly of a ball-point pen as a result of the rotation of the ball, that is usually transferred to the paper surface immediately after the direction of rotation is substantially changed.

Graph The pattern of ink on the paper representing, for that writer, a particular allograph.

Grapheme The smallest identifiable unit of writing; not divisible; the abstract concept of a letter of the alphabet.

Graphics Of, or pertaining to writing or drawing.

Graphometry A method of characterizing a handwriting by measurement of the proportionate values of the angles and ratios of the heights and widths of letters.

Graphoanalysis A registered trade name that identifies the system of handwriting analysis taught by the International Graphoanalysis Society, Inc.

Graphonomics   The study of the science and technology of handwriting and other graphic skills (coined in 1982), or the scientific study concerned with the systematic relationships involved in the generation and analysis of writing and drawing movements, and the resulting traces of writing and drawing instruments, either on conventional media, such as paper and blackboard, or on electronic equipment.

Graphonym   Two different words or letter combinations that, when written cursively, appear nearly identical. Rare in English, but includes "win/urn," "bi/lr," "d/cl," etc.

Greek "e"   See epsilon.

Guided-hand signature   A signature that is executed while the writer's hand or arm is steadied or assisted by another person.

Guillemets   Horizontal chevrons, « … », used in French to mark quotations.

Guilloche   Free swinging, asymmetrical curves; a succession of smooth convoluting lines that intersect themselves, characteristic of intaglio security printing.

Gutter   The space between printed columns of text.

Habit   Any persistently repeated element or detail of writing that occurs when the opportunity allows.

Hairline   A very thin stroke.

Handlettering   A disconnected style of writing in which letter design usually follows that of the uppercase printed character. Handprinting.

Haplography   The unintentional omission in writing or copying of one or more adjacent and similar letters, syllables, words, or lines.

Harpoon   The snapped-back ending of a written stroke; shaped like a harpoon.

Hiatus   A gap in a writing stroke of a letter formed when the instrument leaves the paper; an opening; an interruption in the continuity of a line.

Hind link   The stroke by means of which a letter links with a preceding letter.

Hitch   The introductory backward stroke added to the beginning of many capital letters and some lowercase letters.

Holograph   A document written entirely in the handwriting of the person whose signature it bears.

Homographs   The writing of "homonyms."

Homonyms   Words that are both pronounced and spelled the same, but have different meanings, e.g., lead (verb) and lead (noun).

Homophones   Words that sound alike, but have different spelling and meaning, e.g., stair and stare. In ancient writings they were different symbols with the same phonetic value or sound.

Hook   A small curved stroke.

Horizontal chevrons   See "guillemets."

Horizontal dash   A punctuation mark "-" used to indicate a break or omission.

Horizontal line   The base line of writing or printing or a line parallel to it.

Horizontal malalignment   A typewriter alignment defect in which the character prints to the right or left of its proper position.

Hyphen   A punctuation mark "-" used to connect the parts of a compound word or the syllables of a divided word.

Iconographs   The first attempts by neolithic man to depict objects and ideas.

Ideographs   Picture symbols and stick figures employed by neolithic man to graphically represent objects and ideas in drawings on cave walls.

Imprimature   A licence to print.

Inert hand   An execution of writing in which the person holding the writing instrument exercises no motor activity whatever, conscious or unconscious. The guide leads the writing instrument through the medium of the hand of the first person. The writer may be feeble or a complete illiterate.

Infralinear letters   Small or lowercase letters that have components that extend below the baseline of writing, e.g., "g," "j," "p," "q," "y," and "z."

Initial stroke   The first stroke of a letter or a word.

Initial spur   The long initial rising stroke of a letter.

Interline   The insertion of additional words between the lines of a written document.

Interlinear spacing   The distance between the baselines of two successively occurring lines of writing.

Interstice   An intervening space between things, e.g., between fibres in paper or between lines of writing.

Inverted posture   That in which the point of the writing instrument is directed toward the body of the writer.

Italic   Type that slants forward.

Joint or juncture   The point or position at which two or more strokes meet within a letter.

Justified   Vertically-aligned side margins; line lengths of equal measure.

Kerning   The spacing of two letters closer together than customary when their designs leave too much intercharacter white space.

Knob   A round lump or bulge, as in the copybook design of the lowercase cursive "k."

Lacunae   See "hiatus."

Lateral expansion   The horizontal dimension of writing produced by the width of letters, the space between letters and words, and the width of margins.

Lateral writing   Writing characterized by wide letters and spacing.

Left-handed curve   A stroke that is made in a counterclockwise direction.

Leg   An appendage; usually a lower extension from the body, as in "R" and "K."

Legibility   The ease with which a reader recognizes individual letter and character shapes.

Letter   Any drawn, written, printed, or typed character, lowercase or uppercase, that can be recognized as an allograph of the alphabet of any language.

Lexical   Pertaining or related to the words of a language (hence *dyslexia* meaning a disturbance of the ability to read).

Ligature   A group of connected characters treated typographically as a single character; sometimes a stroke or bar connecting two letters.

Limb   See "leg."

Line measure   The length of a line of printing expressed in picas, points, or ciceros.

Line quality   A term characterizing the visible record of the stroke of writing. It is the product of a combination of factors including speed, rhythm, shading, pen pressure, and pen position.

   The degree of regularity (i.e., smoothness or gradation) in the written stroke as may be judged from the consistency of its path in a prescribed direction. It varies from smooth and controlled to tremulous and erratic.

Linear letters   Small or lowercase letters having no components that extend above or below the x-height, e.g., "a," "c," "e," "i," "m," "n," "o," "r," "s," "u," "v," "w," and "x."

Link   The stroke connecting the top and bottom segments of a lower case printed "g."

Lithographic printing   See "lithography."

Lithography   Printing from a smooth surface plate that has been treated so that the printing areas are ink attracting and the nonprinting areas are ink repelling.

Look-through   The appearance of paper when viewed by transmitted light, thus, disclosing the texture or formation of the sheet.

Loop   The circular figure formed when a line crosses itself, as in the cursive letters "e" and "l."

Lowercase letters   Small letters of the alphabet as opposed to capital letters; minuscules.

Lower loop   A loop extending below the baseline; a descender.

Luminescence   The visible glow of certain substances (e.g., components of some inks) when subjected to stimulation by electromagnetic radiation, electric fields, or heat. Luminescence embraces fluorescence and phosphorescence.

Main script   The most important stroke of a letter (see "stem").

Majuscule   The capital or upper case forms of letters. Uncials.

Manuscript writing   A disconnected form of writing using many printed letter forms, frequently taught to children in elementary schools as the first step in learning to write.

Margins   The space at the top, bottom, and sides of the page that frames the body of written, typed, or printed matter.

Microphotography   The term used in Europe for the making of large photographs of small objects, usually through a microscope. In the U.K. and the U.S.A. this is called photomicrography, and microphotography is used to refer to the technique of making microscopically small photographs by the process of optical reduction.

Mid-arm   The cross stroke in letters such as "H" and "A."

Midline   The line halfway between the baseline and headline of writing or printing, either real or imaginary.

Minim   A short, vertical stroke on the baseline, e.g., the legs on an "m."

Minuscule   The small or lower case forms of letters, as opposed to capitals.

Mirror writing   Writing that runs in the opposite direction to the normal pattern; starts on the right side of the pages and proceeds from right to left, with reversed order in spelling and turning of the letter images.

Model signature   A genuine signature used to prepare a simulated or traced forgery.

Moiré   A pattern that is the mathematical solution to the interface of two periodic functions. Most moiré patterns are generated by figures that consist of lines, but lines are not strictly necessary. They may be interacting figures having some sort of solid and open regions of any geometric form. In simplest form, a moiré pattern arises from the imperfect superimposition of two sets of equidistant parallel lines.

Money bag   A vernacular term sometimes used to describe an inflated, oversized lower loop.

Monogram   A character composed of two or more letters interwoven together, the letters being usually the initials of a formal name.

Morpheme   The meaningful constituent of a word; the "root."

Natural variation   The imprecision with which the habits of the writer are executed on repeated occasions (Huber), or the divergence of one execution from another in an element of an individual's writing that occurs invariably in the graph but may also occur in the choice of the allograph (Huber), or normal or usual deviations found between repeated specimens of any individual's handwriting or in the product of any typewriter or other record making machine (Hilton).

Neck   See "link."

Nodule   A small, rounded mass or lump of ink caused by an excessive deposit; the result of "gooping" in some ball-point pens.

Nonce word   A word coined to fit a special situation.

Normal posture   That in which the writing instrument is pointed away from the body of the writer.

Numeral   Any drawn, written, printed, or typed character representing a quantity, of which numbers are formed; a digit.

Oblique   See "virgule."

Obliteration   The blotting out or smearing over of writing, lettering, or printing to make the original invisible or undecipherable.

Obverse   The side that bears the principal design; the front or principal surface of anything.

Octothorpe   The symbol, "#," used to represent the word *number*, when it precedes one or more digits, or the word *pound* when it succeeds one or more digits.

Off-its-feet   The condition of a typeface, that prints heavier on one side or corner than the remainder of the character.

Offset printing   See "lithography."

Orthography   The principles by which the alphabet is set into correspondence with the speech sounds; the art of spelling.

Oval forms   Bowls of letters that have an oval shape, e.g., "a," "d," "g," "o," "q."

Paradigm   A pattern, an exemplar, an example, or model.

Paraph   A flourish or sweeping line, stroke or dot, above, through or below a signature; an appendage; a rubric; the figure formed by the flourish of a pen at the conclusion of a signature.

Parenthesis   Either or both of the upright curved lines used to mark off explanatory or qualifying remarks, e.g., "()".

Patching   Retouching or going back over a defective portion of the writing stroke; retracing.

Pen emphasis   The act of intermittently forcing the pen against the paper surface with increased pressure.

Pen lift   An interruption in a stroke due to the removal of the writing instrument from the paper.

Pen position   The angle relationship between the axis of the pen and the paper.

Pen hold   The manner in which the writing instrument is held in the hand; includes the pen position relative to the paper surface, the direction of the instrument relative to the writing line and to the writer.

Perfins   Pinhole designs, initials, or numerals, made through stamps (after 1860 in Great Britain, and 1908 in the U.S.A.), coined from "Perforated Insignia."

Period   A punctuation mark " . " indicating a full stop and placed especially at the end of sentences.

Phoneme   A symbol representing a phone (i.e., a distinctive sound), abstracted from spoken words.

Phosphorescence   A kind of fluorescence that continues for a time after the stimulating light source ceases.

Photomicrography   The making of large photographs of small objects often via a microscope (on this continent and in the U.K.). See also "microphotography."

Pica   A unit of measure of printer's type, approximately $^1\!/_6$ inches or 12 points typically used for vertical measurement. Also a term used to denote conventional monotone typewriter typeface that has a fixed character width of 10 to the inch.

Pilcrow   A proofreader's mark to indicate a paragraph's beginning, "¶."

Pitch   See "escapement."

Point   The basic typographic unit of measurement of fonts, line spacing, rules and borders; there are 12 points to a pica and 72 points to the inch; typically used for vertical dimensions.

Point load   The vertical component of the force applied to the tip of a writing instrument during line generation.

Polyphones   Symbols having more than one phonetic value.

Pressure   The amount of force exerted on the point of the writing instrument, technically termed *point load*. Pressure may manifest itself in line quality, i.e., thickness and shading of the stroke; also noted in the amount of indentation in the paper surface.

Proportional spacing   Spacing that varies with the design of the character of the font.

Proportions   The comparative relations between letters and parts of letters.

Pseudo expansion   The result of wide interspaces between narrow letters.

Pump handle   A term some give to the projecting element of the printed "r."

Question or query mark   A punctuation symbol, "?," written at the end of an interrogatory sentence. (See also "inverted question mark.")

Rebound   A typewriter defect in which a character prints a double impression with the lighter one slightly offset to the right or left.

Recto   In printing, the right hand page of an open book, hence, the front of the leaf, as opposed to the back or verso.

Reference collections   Collections of typewriting, cheque writer specimens, inks, pens, pencils, papers, etc. compiled and organized by the document examiner as standards of the products.

Request standards   Writing samples written at the request of another person.

Retouching   Touching up to correct or perfect a graphic execution.

Retracing   That portion of a letter in which a downstroke is superimposed upon an upstroke, or vice versa.

Reverse curve   A section of curve where its radius changes to an opposite direction; an undulation.

Reverse   That side of a page or document that does not bear the main device or inscription.

Rhythm   A harmonious recurrence of stress, impulse, or motion; sometimes used to classify writing quality, e.g., smooth, intermittent, or jerky.

Ribbon impression   A sample of typewriter text made directly through a fabric or carbon film ribbon.

Right-handed curve   One that is made in a clockwise direction.

River   Gaps in the writing or printing pattern that form a straggling white stream down the page.

Rubric   A flourish after or under a name written as a signature, an underscore or underline. In ancient times it was a red ornamental letter at the beginning of a chapter or a division of a manuscript.

Sans serif   A class of typefaces without serifs.

Sawtooth   See "serrations."

Script   Handwriting as distinguished from printing or lettering; cursive writing.

Semicolon   A mark of punctuation, ";", indicating a degree of separation, intermediate between the comma and the period.

Serif   A broadening of the ends of the main strokes of a character; may be of many designs and sizes.

Serrations   Roughness along the edges of an ink line seen under a microscope.

Set   The width of an individual typewritten letter.

Set-off   The unwanted transfer of ink from one sheet of paper to the back of the sheet above.

Shading   Stressed contrast between thin upstrokes and thick downstrokes. A widening of the ink stroke due to the added pressure on the writing instrument.

Shaft   See "stem."

Shoulder   A joint, bridge, or hump on top of the small cursive letter "r" between the up and downstrokes; the curved arches of the "h," "m," and "n."

Signatory   A signer, with another or others; a person whose name is being inscribed on a document who requires assistance in doing so.

Signature   The name of a person, or mark representing it, as written by himself or herself.

Sinistrality   Left-hand preference, as opposed to dextrality or right-hand preference, particularly in writing.

Skeletal stem   Letter extensions made without the required loop formation.

Skip   The self-recoverable, temporary interruption (without deposition of ink) in an otherwise continuous writing line.

Slant   The angle or inclination of the axis of letters relative to the baseline of writing.

Slash   "/", see "virgule."

Soldered break   A corrective retracing by which the writer attempts to fit together the two ends of a broken stroke so that no hiatus remains.

Solidus   The diagonal line used to separate; amounts in English currency, e.g., 12/6 for 12 shillings, 6 pence, or the numerator and denominator in fractions, e.g., 1/2 (see virgule).

Spacing   The distance between letters or words (see also "interlinear spacing").

Speed "r"   The Roundhand, Palmer, or Mills "r"; the "v" type "r."

Spine   The main slightly curved stroke of a lower case or capital "S."

Spiral   That portion of a letter executing a spiral formation, popular designs of commencement and termination in older styles of writing.

Splicing   A term used to denote the slight overlapping of two strokes after an interruption in the writing action.

Splitting   The division of an ink line into two or more, more or less equal portions, by a noninked area running generally parallel to the direction of the stroke, sometimes called *burring*.

Springboard   An initial stroke commencing far below the baseline and to the left of the stem.

Spur   A small projection off the main stroke seen on some printed uppercase "G"s; or the short lateral finishing stroke found in the lowercase "b," "v," and "w."

Spurious signature   A fraudulent signature in which there was no apparent attempt at simulation or imitation.

Staff   That portion of the letter forming the backbone.

Starving   A condition in which there is an inadequate flow of writing fluid to the writing surface.

Stem   The main or heavy stroke of a letter to which the other parts are attached.

Stress   See "pressure."

Strike-through   The condition in which the writing fluid has traversed vertically through the paper so as to appear on the underside of the sheet opposite the written line.

Stroke   A single written line, either ascending, descending, or lateral in the formation of a letter or any of its parts.

Subscript   A character or symbol written next to and slightly below a letter or number.

Superscript   A character or symbol written next to and slightly above a letter or number.

Supralinear letters   Small or lowercase letters that have components that extend above the x height, e.g., "b," "d," "h," "k," "l," "t."

Swash   A fancy flourish replacing a terminal stroke or serif.

Symbol   In writing, a character that is used to represent something that might be expressed in one or more words, e.g., "$," "@," "#," "%," "£," "¢," and is considered part of a typing or printing font.

System   See "writing system."

Tail   A terminal or ending stroke; sometimes used to refer to the leg of an "R" or "K," or to the final element of the "Q."

Tenting   A term used to describe a letter that contains a tent-shaped form.

Terminal stroke   The last stroke of a word; endstroke.

Textual writing   That pertaining to a text, extended writing, usually cursive, but not inclusive of a signature.

Tick   Any superfluous small stroke preceding or succeeding the body of a letter.

Tilde   A small stroke or mark used in writing or printing placed above certain letters in some languages to denote a change in sound; a diacritical mark.

Trace   The mark, track, rail, or imprint of a stroke.

Traced forgery   Any fraudulent signature executed by a manual, mechanical or electronic endeavour to follow the outline of a genuine signature.

Tremour   A lack of smoothness, due to lack of skill, consciousness of the writing act or to the deliberate control of the instrument in copying or tracing, or an involuntary, roughly rhythmic, and sinusoidal movement.

Tremulous   An unsteady, wavering stroke produced by an involuntary vibratory motion of the writing hand.

Trough   The bend, crook or inner side of a curve opening upwards, or, the valleys of letters such as "u," "v," "w," and "y."

Typeface   The name of a particular design of printed characters and symbols.

Typeface family   A range of typeface designs that are variations of one basic style of alphabet.

Uncial   A script writing style of the fourth to ninth centuries that introduced what became minuscule or lowercase forms to the alphabet.

Undercurve   A forward oval movement in an upstroke.

Undercut   A connection that falls below the base of the succeeding letter.

Uppercase letters   A printing term for capital letters; majuscules.

Upper loop   A loop extending above the baseline or the height of linear letters; an ascender.

Upstroke   A stroke directed toward the top of the paper.

Versal letters   Those that mark important parts of the text, used for headings and words written at the beginning of books or chapters; often distinguished by size, colour, and ornamentation which tends towards curves and flourishes.

Verso   The left-hand page of a book or the reverse side of a leaf; opposite of recto.

Vertex   The apex, top, or crown; the highest point of a letter.

Vertical expansion   Product of the height of letters and distance between lines.

Vertical misalignment   A typewriter alignment defect in which the character prints above or below its proper position.

Vertical writing   Perpendicular to the baseline, upright writing.

Vertical stroke   An upright stroke perpendicular to the baseline of the writing.

Virgule   A short oblique stroke "/", between two words indicating that whichever is appropriate may be chosen to complete the sense of the text in which they occur; a dividing line as in dates, fractions, etc. Also called a diagonal, solidus (in English currency and in fractions), oblique, slant, and slash mark. Used to mean "or" (as in and/or), or "per" (as in miles/hour). Separates figures of a date (e.g., 2/10/97).

Visible light   Rays that can be seen by the human eye, but are only a part of the complete spectrum of so-called electromagnetic radiation. Rays of other parts of the spectrum cannot be seen but can be detected.

Walking cane   A term sometimes given to the initial loop and stem of some capital letters when the curvature and design suggests the resemblance.

Whirl   The curving upstroke, usually on letters that have long loops, but also on some styles of the capital "W."

Whorl   A form composed of spiralling strokes, produced by a loose, circling writing movement.

Writing   The act of generating a line.

Writing angle   The included angle measured from the plane of the writing surface to the longitudinal axis of the pen when in writing position.

Writing movement   A three-dimensional pattern of the action of a writing instrument; variants in the predominating action of the writing instrument.

Writing offset   The transfer of fresh ink upon contact with another document producing a mirror image of part of the writing.

Writing speed   The rate of line generation, sometimes wrongly regarded to be the rate of word generation, that varies with the size of the writing.

Writing system   The combination of basic letter design and writing movement prescribed by a publication or taught in a school.

Wrong-handed writing   Any writing executed with the opposite hand from that normally used; writing of the nondominant or nonpreferred hand.

X-height   The height of the linear letters (no ascenders or descenders).

Epilogue  17

This book was begun with two particular objectives, insofar as its content:

Our first objective was to present a concise catalogue of the discriminating elements of handwriting that the discipline uses, that serve to identify writings and differentiate between them, that will, therefore, direct and facilitate a proper analysis.

In the course of its compilation, it was hoped that this book might offer some guidance respecting the measures to be taken for the discipline to advance toward scientific stature. A six-point criteria has been provided that includes "conspectus reliability," defined as (1) universal agreement as to what constitutes evidence in a given writing sample (i.e., its discriminating elements), and (2) a reckoning of its significance.

Unusual facets of the catalogue of discriminating elements became evident in the course of its compilation. It consists of 21 elements of writing that are employed, when possible, in the examination and study of written products. To explore the comprehensiveness of this list one may ask: What elements of writing are there that this catalogue does not include? The answer, it seems, is none.

Quite unexpectedly, it has become obvious to us that the 21 discriminating elements are, in fact, all of the physical attributes of writing. As aspects that are sought in analysis, they involve no interpretation or evaluation at this point. They may require some understanding of causes and effects. They are physical, however, and may, with appropriate facilities, be measured or categorized.

To add to the list one would have to identify and describe another physical attribute, and there are none of which we can presently conceive. On the other hand, to deny any of these attributes their place in the process of writing examination would be to deny the contribution of an element of physical evidence in the determination of a matter. This, too, cannot be done.

In the study of the physical attributes of writings, evaluations are made of the significance of similarities or differences that are observed, but this does not alter the composition of the catalogue of attributes to be considered.

If, then, the catalogue cannot be justifiably enlarged or reduced, it warrants reception by all examiners as complete and comprehensive. In so doing, we are conceding "universal agreement" to it, and have, thereby, established one of the two principal components of "conspectus realiability" that the examination of writing must demonstrate. We have spoken of this frequently on these pages and consider it to be a first step in the discipline's rise to science. The assignment of values to each of the discriminating elements, i.e., the physical attributes, that may be present in a writing comparison will require much further study.

Our second objective was to consolidate much of the work that has been done by others and by us, related or applicable to writing identification. We have reviewed publications in the English language principally, and the more that we read the more we found to read. We have cited approximately 800 different articles or papers, books, and commentaries and would emphasize that this is just a beginning. We have record of another 150 papers, many of which deal with the application of computer technology to the recognition of signatures, both static and dynamic. Our point is that there is much material available to be studied and woven into the fabric of writing identification. Would that we could find the funds to finance the task. Unfortunately, the potential for profit or reward is insufficient to attract academic or fiscal interests.

The recently made assessments of the shortcomings of forensic document examination (FDE) as a science or as an applied science have not been made by scientists or by persons having any significant scientific background; that is, they have not been made by persons possessing sufficient knowledge of science to make a fair and valid judgment. Furthermore, the assessments do not reflect any attempt to assemble and digest even some of this mountain of knowledge more recently produced and now available for review.

Writing identification will not become a science by decree, or by simple reference to it as such. The status of a science lies in the mind of the knowledgeable beholder. It is a quality that must be earned, acquired by valid and persuasive argument emanating largely from work performed, methods followed, and public discussion, over periods of time. It is a growth like most natural growth, that cannot be compressed or accelerated, and suffers, as natural growth often does, from neglect or want of stimulation.

The attacks on writing identification plus the manner in which these attacks are being pursued gives rise to questions respecting the motives of its critics. If it is in the interests of justice, one might have expected that examples of injustices due to erroneous findings would be proffered. In their absence, we suggest that it may be an antagonism stemming, perhaps, from adverse court decisions in which writing examiners played a part; or simply from a distrust of the writing examiner and of his/her profession, a profession that the critics feel offers insufficient safeguards against errors.

Errors are possible in any determination based on the assembly of evidence, particularly when the evidence may change from study to study. Errors are possible in writing identification just as they are in the determination of innocence or guilt in a court of law. We noted earlier that the court's own criterion for establishing guilt "beyond a reasonable doubt" discretely avoids stipulating "with certainty" or "beyond any doubt." It would be absurd to dispense with the system for determining culpability because of a possible fallibility of the procedure. It is equally ill-advised to discard handwriting identification as an instrument of technical assistance to the court or jury, for want of absolute certainty in its findings. What is desired is to decrease any risk of error to the point where its consideration may be unwarranted.

We cannot overemphasize the words of Elton Trueblood, whom we quoted earlier as saying:

"The fact that we do not have absolute certainty in regard to any human conclusions does not mean that the task of enquiry is fruitless. We must, it is true, always proceed on the basis of probability, but to have probability is to have something. What we must seek in any realm of human thought is not absolute certainty, for that is denied us as men, but rather the more modest path of those who find dependable ways of discerning different degrees of probability."

But the parallel between writing identification and our judicial system goes beyond this. Writing identification has been condemned by some for not being able to provide the statistical data to support the conclusions reached, that is, the data that allows the significance of writing elements to be evaluated statistically. Much material is available, but it has not yet been converted into formulae to advance identifications.

Neither do we have formulae for evaluating the significance of evidence of various kinds in the court's resolution of innocence or guilt. Indeed, it seems inconceivable that we ever will. We do, however, continue to review and assess the reliability of these different kinds of evidence (e.g., voice identification and hair analysis) and keep open minds respecting the contributions they may make to the court's determinations.

To eradicate the risk or to decrease the frequency of error, and to establish levels of certainty based on probabilities, will be a task difficult to achieve. Science seldom enjoys the luxury of instant solutions, immediate corrections, and new discoveries waiting in the wings to be revealed. This needn't alter the fervour with which the task is pursued, although it may tax our patience.

Writing examination has been criticized for not adequately articulating its principles and processes in order to persuade the users of its services that it is valid and reliable, and, thereby, worthy of confidence in its endeavours. The books commonly cited of A. S. Osborn and others written as long ago as 90 years, embraced a world of documents quite different from that of the present era. Handwriting examiners have been castigated for being unable to cite an authoritative source of recent origin wherein the knowledge that has been acquired respecting handwriting has been assembled and organized in some learned fashion. As we said above, however, the market for books of this kind may not justify the effort required, except as a labour of love.

Nevertheless, by definition, analysis, exposition, extraction, consolidation, and organization we have striven to furnish some of the needs of these deficiencies. What has been achieved we leave to others to judge. These efforts notwithstanding, what the discipline requires now from all concerned is stimulation, not condemnation.

DNA analysis has set a standard for statistical determinations in blood identifications that has induced it to become a model for all of the applied sciences. At the same time, we are reminded that serologists conducted analyses and identifications of blood on which our judicial and social systems relied heavily, for nearly 100 years using much less precise techniques, but we thought none the less of them as serologists or of serology as a science.

We have tried to make the point that handwriting is different from the numerous other materials that are usually subject to examination by scientific process. The circumstances of any two cases entailing writing are never exactly the same. The evidence that becomes available to resolve identification questions varies to some degree both quantitatively and qualitatively with every identification problem. Consistency is not a characteristic of the cases or circumstances involved, at least to the extent that it may be in other disciplines.

This is because we are not dealing with the composition that an inanimate substance may have, but with what an animate creature does or how it acts, over which that creature has certain limited voluntary control. Other disciplines within forensic science seek to identify an unknown's properties, physical, biological and/or chemical attributes or mechanisms. In writing identification, we are not analyzing properties, attributes, or mechanisms. We are studying behaviour or performance. There is no analogy to be considered. Any search for correspondence would be a commission of the classic error of comparing apples to oranges.

Studies of performance and judgments of the level and complexity of the skill involved are exceedingly difficult matters to classify numerically unless there is a measure or means of scoring that can be applied, as in many athletic endeavours. Other skilled undertakings such as figure skating, art or dramatics are often judged differently by different judges. To minimize this variance dedicated persons are constantly attempting to introduce and develop more and better systems for the assessment of performances, in the pursuit of greater objectivity and consistency. To the aspiring profession of handwriting identification, systems of assessment are especially important, for, as has been said, the fundamental difference between the thinking of the scientist and the lay person in the comprehension of evidence is system.

Although we support and approve of the greater use of measurements and statistical analysis in writing identification, we recognize that there are some aspects of handwriting examination that don't appear, as yet, to lend themselves readily to a numerical assessment. Probability theories cannot be lucidly applied to measurements of performance. Evaluations are not equally judged universally. This is not to suggest, however, that findings of any two examiners are diametrically opposed in many cases, for this is not so. Indeed, it is rare.

For reasons that we have spelled out in our dissertation, we cannot claim that we have done all that is necessary to qualify handwriting identification as a science. It was one of our goals, however, to give it some quality of a system, the particular quality that differentiates the thinking of the scientist from that of the lay person. If then, our thinking is correct or reasonably so, the path to the scientific community, despite its length, will be at least more direct. The future, then, will be encouraging.

The recent criticisms of the profession are disturbing to some, but they need not be. As Professor William Montevecchi of Memorial University in Newfoundland recently wrote, "Science is based on criticism…healthy criticism…it's really what makes the world come up with better answers…this is a very positive constructive action very important for all of us." This was our second goal: to provide better answers to some of the more rigorous questions.

We little know the nature of the human mental powers;
We only think each other's functions much the same as ours.
But if our thoughts are different; we disagree somehow;
*I'm sure such disagreements prove that we're **both** thinking now.*

Author Unknown

Authors and Sources Cited

(Chapter/Reference No.)

Adams, J. A. – 2/14

Aiken, Lewis R. and Zweigenshaft, Richard L. – 6/38

Aitken, C. G. G. – 4/20

Alford, Edwin A. – 7/10

Alford, Edwin F. – 11/27, 14/59

Alford, Edwin F. Jr. and Bertocchi, Michael P. – 11/30

Allan, A. R. and Pearson, E. F. – 7/32

Allan, A. R., Pearson, E.F., and Brown, C. – 7/31

Allen, M. and Wellman, M. M. – 11/99

Allport, G. W. and Vernon, P. E. – 2/2

American Heritage Dictionary Editors — 14/56

Ames, D. T. – 7/16

Andersen, Dan W. – 6/47

Anderson, Diane J. – 8/20

Anderson, Timothy – 11/164

Anderson, Timothy and Wolowitz, Howard – 11/162

Anderson, Gilbert J. – 9/27

Angst, E. and Erismann, K. – 7/28

Annett, M. A. – 11/92

Anonymous – 6/42, 12/14, 12/24, 14/53, 14/55

Ansell, Michael – 7/34

Ansell, M. – 7/62

Ansell, M. and Strach, S. J. – 7/7, 7/30

Anthony, Arthur T. – 6/16, 11/171

Askov, Eunice, Otto, Wayne, and Askov, Warren – 2/7

Baier, Peter E., Hussong, Jürgen, Hoffman, Elisabeth, and Klein, Michaela – 2/10

Baig, Mizra S. A., Shen, Winston, W., Caminal, Edouardo, and Huang, Tsung-Dow – 8/99

Baird, J. B. – 9/17

Barsley, Michael – 11/95, 11/107

Baxendale, D. and Renshaw, I. D. – 5/15

Baxter, P. G. – 3/13, 7/27

Beacom, Mary S. – 2/71, 8/6, 8/43, 8/50, 8/59, 8/70, 11/93, 11/109, 11/131

Beardsley, Monroe C. – 4/28, 4/29

Beck, Frederick A. G. – 2/57

Beck, Jan – 7/90, 9/29, 10/30

Behnen, Adam P. – 11/40

Behrendt, James E. – 3/11, 3/23, 8/24, 8/63, 8/66, 11/88

Bein, W. – 7/70

Bellomy, David A. – 8/16, 8/53

Ben-Shakhar, Gershon, Bar-Hillel, Maya, Bilu, Yoram, Ben-Abba, Edor, and Flug, Anat – 15/10

Bergamini, David – 4/5

Berthold, Nancy – 11/118

Berthold, Nancy N. and Wooton, Elaine X. – 3/29

Bertillon, Alphonse – 4/15, 7/55

Beukelaar, Leen and Kroonenberg, Pieter M. – 11/105

Bey, Robert F. and Ryan, Dennis J. – 9/10

Birge, W. R. – 14/35

Blackburn, D. and Caddell, W. – 7/18

Blake, Martha – 6/4, 7/45, 7/65, 7/66

Blueschke, Arnold – 8/44, 9/52

Bogan, E. – 9/18

Laws and Legal Decisions Cited
(Chapter/Reference No.)

Canada Evidence Act, 1868 SC, Chap. 76 – 1/8

Carroll v. State – 13/10

Common Law Procedure Act – 1/5

Fisher v. The Queen – 13/1

Folkes v. Chadd, 3 Doug, 157, 99 Eng. Rep. 589, (K. B. 1782) – 1/3

Goodtitle d. Revett v. Braham – 1/2

Keys v. Keys – 13/9

Micciche v. Forest Hill Cemetery Association – 13/7

Mutual Benefit Life Ins. Co. v. Brown, 30 N.J. Eq. 193, 201 (1878) – 1/15

Moody v. Rowell, 34 Mass., 17 Pick. (1836) – 1/4, 1/14

R. v. Young – 13/4

R. v. Buckingham and Vickers – 13/5

Reid v. Warner – 1/7

Shawinigan Engineering Company v. Naud – 13/6

United States v. Roberta and Eileen Starzecpyzel – 5/18

United States v. King – 13/8

United States v. Starzecpyzel – 10/24, 14/25

INDEX

A

Absolute size 104
Accidental occurrences 46, 51
Adept penmen - See professional forgers, under
    Forgery
Allograph 48, 87, 95, 98-101
Alphabet, the
    Arabic 87, 327
    examination of various 327
    origins of 14, 16
    Roman or Latin alphabet 17, 327
    various modern 87
Ancient writing
    alphabetic system 16
    Anglo-Iris hands 19
    Anglo-Saxon hands 19
    Beneventan 18
    boustrophedon 17, 303
    calligraphy 9, 17
    Carstairs system (England) 20
    Chinese 15
    Caroline Minuscules 18
    cuneiform 15
    cursive minuscles 18
    demotic 15
    Egyptian writing 15
    Germanic Caroline scripts 19
    Gothic letter styles 19
    hieratic 15
    hieroglyphics 15
    iconographs 14
    ideographs 14
    Ionic Greek 17
    Italics 20
    Japanese writing 16
    Lombardic Minuscule 18
    libelli 18, 25
    Merovigian script 19
    origins of writing 18
    pictographs 14
    Roman or Latin alphabet 17
    Roman cursive capitals 18
    Secretarie hand (England) 20
    syllabic 15
    tackygraphy 17
    Uncials and Semi-uncials 18
    Visigothic script 19
Anonymous letters and writings 149-152, 283, 316

    envelopes 151
    obscenities 151
    of illiterates 283
    profanities 151
Association Index (AI) 74
Attributes, physical - See Physical attributes
Autoforgery - See Forgery

B

Bubble writing 74, 217, 218

C

Certainty of conclusions 69, 144, 261-264
    point counts 61-63
    probabilities 265
    qualified opinions 56, 57, 64-66, 258-261
    sources of error 266-268
Certification programs 341
Charlemagne of France 19
Classification systems for handwriting 152
    Allan and Pearson 156
    Allan, Pearson, and Brown 156
    Angst and Erismann 155
    Ansel and Strach 155
    completion method 154
    computerized image processing 157, 159
    feature catalogue 160, 163
    FISH 157
    Hardcastle and Kemmenoe 158
    Hardcastle, Thornton, and Totty 158
    Harvey and Mitchell 155
    inherent writing characteristics 155
    Livingston 153, 154
    Nicholson 157
    pattern recognition 157
    Schroeder 154
    Smith T. L. 153
    Taylor and Chandler 158
Codes of ethics 377
collected writings - See Standards for comparison
Conclusions vs. opinions 257
Consistency in writing 73, 89, 117, 133, 285
    See also Handwriting, habituation
Copybook 24, 102, 176, 182

D

F

I

L

Note:

Readers are directed to the Glossary beginning on page 394 for the definition of words, not all of which will be found in this index.

The Thinker, Rodin, Auguste (1840-1917)
The Metropolitan Museum of Art, Gift of Thomas F. Ryan, 1910. (11.173.9)